Teacher's Book
with digital resources and assessment package

Kate Fuscoe, Clementine Annabell

CONTENTS

Introduction

Students' Book contents	4–7
Welcome to Roadmap	8–9
Course components	10–11
Students' Book	12–15
Support components	16–19
Workbook	16
Mobile app	16
Online practice	17
Teacher's Book	18
Teacher's digital resources	18
Presentation tool	19
Course methodology	20–23

Teacher's notes

Units 1–10	24–163

Resource bank

Photocopiable activities index	165–166
Photocopiable activities	167–256
Photocopiable activities notes and answer key	257–279

STUDENTS' BOOK CONTENTS

Contents

MAIN LESSON	GRAMMAR/LANGUAGE	VOCABULARY	PRONUNCIATION	SPEAKING GOAL
UNIT 1 page 6				
1A Talking to strangers page 6	question forms	verbs with dependent prepositions	intonation in formal and informal questions	start a conversation and keep it going
1B Life lessons page 8	past simple, past continuous, *used to, would, keep* + *-ing*	phrases to describe emotions	*n't* in natural speech	describe an experience and a life lesson
1C Personalities page 10	verb + noun collocations	adjectives of character	weak *your, the, a*	interview someone about their personality
1D English in action page 12	FUNCTION: contribute effectively to a conversation or discussion	verbs to describe a healthy lifestyle	word linking	contribute effectively to a conversation or discussion
Go online for the Roadmap video.				
UNIT 2 page 14				
2A What's the truth? page 14	present perfect simple and continuous	phrases with *get*	weak *been*	outline problems with your work
2B Running wild? page 16	the passive	social action	weak forms of *be*	make recommendations
2C It's so annoying! page 18	*-ed* and *-ing* adjectives	common complaints	intonation in phrases with *so* + adjective	respond to complaints
Check and reflect: Units 1 and 2 page 20 Go online for the Roadmap video.				
UNIT 3 page 22				
3A I remember … page 22	past perfect simple and continuous	memory	weak forms: *had*	narrate a childhood memory
3B Great rivals page 24	comparatives and superlatives	character adjectives	emphasising a big difference	express an opinion about rivals
3C Life's too short page 26	forming adjectives	arguments	word stress in adjectives	summarise an argument
3D English in action page 28	FUNCTION: complain and give and respond to feedback	adjectives to describe food	using intonation to sound polite	complain and give and respond to feedback
Go online for the Roadmap video.				
UNIT 4 page 30				
4A Possessions page 30	relative clauses	adjectives to describe things	pauses with non-defining relative clauses	describe a precious possession in detail
4B Job skills page 32	obligation and prohibition	job requirements	*have* and *'ve*	talk about the requirements of a job
4C Unwritten rules page 34	forming verbs with *en*	21st-century words	word stress in verbs with *en*	give advice through an informal presentation
Check and reflect: Units 3 and 4 page 36 Go online for the Roadmap video.				
UNIT 5 page 38				
5A Splashing out page 38	mistakes in the past	money phrases	*should have* and *could have*	have a conversation about spending money
5B Crime scene page 40	quantifiers	crime (robbery)	*(a) little* and *(a) few*	talk about quantities
5C Bubble trouble page 42	adverb + adjective collocations	money	word stress in adverb + adjective collocations	summarise a text
5D English in action page 44	FUNCTION: deal with and resolve conflicts	phrases with *leave*	stress and meaning	deal with and resolve conflicts
Go online for the Roadmap video.				

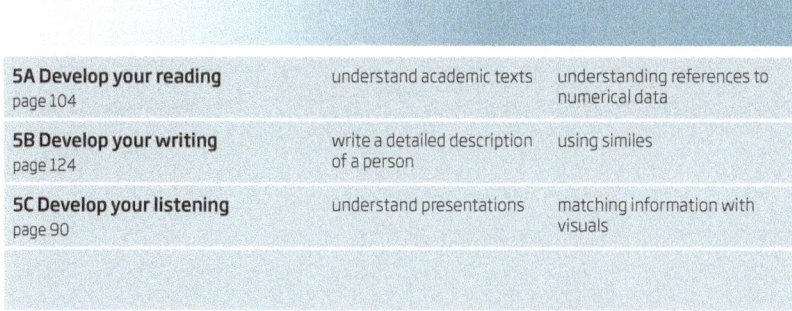

EXTENDED ROUTE

DEVELOP YOUR SKILLS LESSON	GOAL	FOCUS
1A Develop your listening page 86	understand common informal conversations	recognising exaggeration
1B Develop your writing page 116	write a detailed description of a place	adding interest to a description
1C Develop your reading page 96	understand an article with survey results	understanding cause and effect relationships
2A Develop your writing page 118	write an informal email to a friend	asking for and giving personal news
2B Develop your reading page 98	understand what makes a text formal	identifying formal and informal texts
2C Develop your listening page 87	understand detailed guidance	recognising positive and negative instructions
3A Develop your writing page 120	write a personal anecdote	showing the time and sequence of events
3B Develop your listening page 88	understand most of a TV/radio programme	ignoring filler phrases
3C Develop your reading page 100	understand a magazine article	using a monolingual dictionary
4A Develop your reading page 102	understand a magazine article	understanding the writer's purpose
4B Develop your writing page 122	write a covering email	matching a covering email with a job advert
4C Develop your listening page 89	understand phone messages	understanding understatement
5A Develop your reading page 104	understand academic texts	understanding references to numerical data
5B Develop your writing page 124	write a detailed description of a person	using similes
5C Develop your listening page 90	understand presentations	matching information with visuals

STUDENTS' BOOK CONTENTS

Contents — FAST-TRACK ROUTE

MAIN LESSON	GRAMMAR/LANGUAGE	VOCABULARY	PRONUNCIATION	SPEAKING GOAL
UNIT 6 page 46				
6A Love it or loathe it? page 46	verb + -ing and infinitive with to	common idioms	sentence stress	talk about things you love and loathe
6B We can work it out page 48	reported speech	negotiating	s and ss	summarise a negotiation
6C Tricky conversations page 50	verb patterns after reporting verbs	reporting verbs	word stress in verbs	paraphrase what someone has said
Check and reflect: Units 5 and 6 page 52 — Go online for the Roadmap video.				
UNIT 7 page 54				
7A Possible futures page 54	real conditionals	social issues	schwa sound	talk about possible consequences of situations
7B Business plans page 56	future forms and degrees of probability	collocations with make, take, do and give	sentence stress	describe future plans with degrees of probability
7C Cultural awareness page 58	introductory It	personal and professional relationships	sentence stress	summarise a situation and give opinions and advice
7D English in action page 60	FUNCTION: lead a discussion and come to a decision	meetings and discussions	linking w and y sounds	lead a discussion and come to a decision
Go online for the Roadmap video.				
UNIT 8 page 62				
8A It's so predictable … page 62	second conditional	events in films	linking w sound	talk about your favourite film/TV series
8B On the run page 64	conditionals in the past	searching and hiding	would have and wouldn't have	talk about other options and outcomes in the past
8C Great art? page 66	linkers of concession	visual art	linkers of concession	develop an argument for a class debate
Check and reflect: Units 7 and 8 page 68 — Go online for the Roadmap video.				
UNIT 9 page 70				
9A Mysteries page 70	past modals of deduction	mystery	sentence stress	speculate about unsolved mysteries
9B Strange theories page 72	verb patterns	knowledge	vowel sounds in verb/noun pairs	plan and give a convincing argument
9C Celebrity page 74	phrasal verbs	common phrasal verbs	word linking	describe a personal experience
9D English in action page 76	FUNCTION: explain a problem and ask for action	describing problems with products and services	elision	explain a problem and ask for action
Go online for the Roadmap video.				
UNIT 10 page 78				
10A Will I be happy? page 78	future perfect and future continuous	personal fulfilment	Will you have? and Will you be?	talk about future events
10B Believe it or not! page 80	articles	fame	the	maintain a discussion on interesting facts
10C New solutions page 82	compound adjectives	persuasion and enforcement	word stress in compound adjectives	give detailed opinions
Check and reflect: Units 9 and 10 page 84 — Go online for the Roadmap video.				

Language bank page 136 Vocabulary bank page 156 Communication bank page 166 Irregular verbs page 176

EXTENDED ROUTE

DEVELOP YOUR SKILLS LESSON	GOAL	FOCUS
6A Develop your listening page 91	understand informal discussions	recognising signpost expressions
6B Develop your reading page 106	understand a website	recognising irony
6C Develop your writing page 126	write an email of complaint requesting action	using comment adverbs
7A Develop your reading page 108	understand websites and longer texts	recognising cohesive devices
7B Develop your writing page 128	write notes during a conversation	using abbreviations in notes
7C Develop your listening page 92	understand a radio programme	recognising examples
8A Develop your listening page 93	understand fast, unscripted speech	recognising when words are missed out
8B Develop your reading page 110	understand the plot of a narrative	distinguishing background detail from main events
8C Develop your writing page 130	write a review of a film or book	including relevant information
9A Develop your listening page 94	understand fast, scripted speech	understanding pauses in speech
9B Develop your writing page 132	write a simple discursive essay	structuring a simple discursive essay
9C Develop your reading page 112	predict content from headlines	understanding newspaper headlines
10A Develop your writing page 134	write a magazine article	attracting and keeping the reader's attention
10B Develop your listening page 95	extract the main points from a news programme	distinguishing fact from opinion
10C Develop your reading page 114	understand an article	inferring the meaning of words from context

WELCOME TO *ROADMAP*

Roadmap is a new, flexible eight-level general English course for adults. Recognising that every class is different and every learner is unique, *Roadmap* provides a dual track approach that allows all learners to develop confidence in speaking while taking a more tailored approach to skills development. It does this by providing smooth syllabus progression based on the *Global Scale of English*, by putting clear and achievable speaking goals at the heart of every lesson, and by providing in-depth skills development lessons for teachers to choose from at the back of the Students' Book. Multiple opportunities are provided for learners to practise outside the classroom in print, online and using the mobile app.

Map your own route through the course

It can be challenging for institutions and teachers to deal with the different needs, interests and abilities of each student, especially if they have a wide mix of learners in the same class. The unique dual track approach of *Roadmap* helps you solve this problem.

- The **fast track route** concentrates on developing learners' speaking skills as well as giving them the grammar, vocabulary and functional language they need to achieve their goals.

- The **extended route** gives learners valuable practice in reading, writing and listening as well as specific training and strategies for developing these skills.

Fast track route:
10 core units featuring grammar, vocabulary and pronunciation with each lesson leading to a final GSE-related speaking activity.

Extended route:
10 core units plus additional skills-based lessons (reading, writing and listening) linked to the content of each lesson.

This unique approach also allows you to adapt material to suit different course lengths. Whatever the number of hours in your course and whatever the interests of your learners, the flexible organisation of *Roadmap* makes it easy for you to choose the best route for your students' success.

Build your students' confidence

Learners need to know what they are aiming for and why. This is key to building confidence, increasing motivation and helping learners make rapid, tangible progress.

- *Global Scale of English* learning objectives provide students with clear goals for every lesson (the goals have been selected to be useful and relevant to students in real-life situations).

- Grammar and vocabulary has been specifically selected according to how useful it is in terms of helping learners reach specific goals.

- Carefully structured tasks with 'models' and opportunities to review performance, *Check and reflect* activities and regular progress tests allow learners to see how well they are doing and highlight the areas they need to improve.

Make the most of your skills as a teacher

Roadmap is designed to be as supportive and easy to use as possible, whatever your level of experience, with:

- 'pick-up-and-go' lessons with clear aims and outcomes that are guaranteed to work.
- clear instructions on how to exploit each lesson, including help with tricky language points, ideas for warmers, fillers, extension and homework activities.
- a huge range of additional support materials, including video, photocopiable games and activities, online and mobile app practice activities, are provided to add variety to your lessons.

The front of class presentation tool makes it easy to access all the support material in one place and enhances your performance as a teacher.

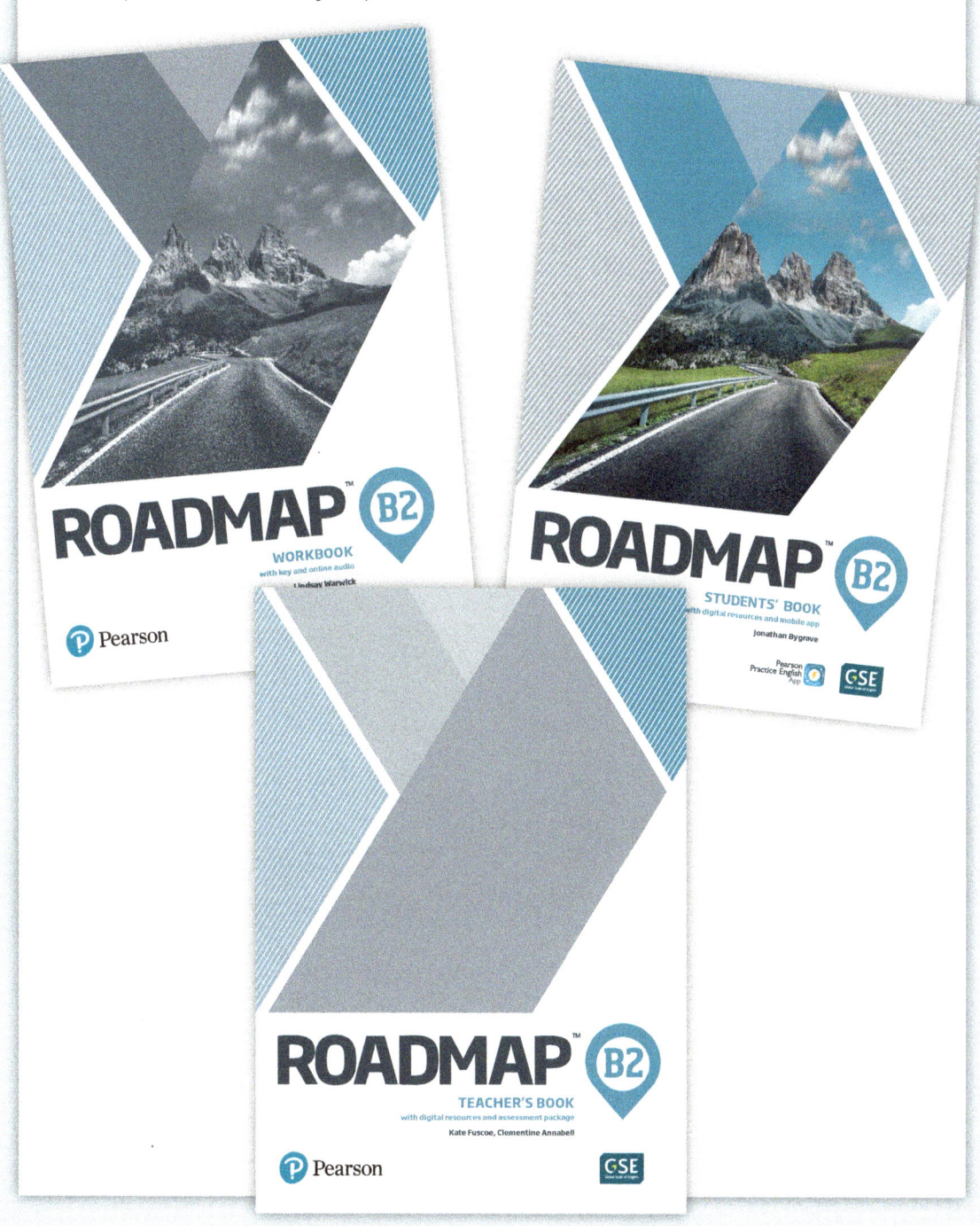

COURSE COMPONENTS

FOR LEARNERS

STUDENTS' BOOK WITH DIGITAL RESOURCES AND MOBILE APP

- Ten units with three main input lessons linked to three *Develop your skills* lessons at the back of the book.
- Each lesson includes grammar/language focus, vocabulary and pronunciation and leads to a final speaking task based on *Global Scale of English* learning objectives.
- Key language presented and cross-referenced to a *Language bank* at the back of the book.
- A *Vocabulary bank* extends some of the key lexical sets in each unit and focuses on important areas such as word-building and collocation.
- An *English in action* lesson in each odd unit covers key functional language.
- *Check and reflect* pages at the end of each even unit show learners how their confidence and mastery of spoken language has improved.
- Light-hearted video clips and worksheets (available online) extend and consolidate key language covered in the unit.
- Extra grammar/language focus and vocabulary exercises, available on the mobile app (the *Pearson Practice English* app), consolidate language points covered in the Students' Book.
- *Develop your skills* lessons at the back of the book expose learners to different genres and give them strategies for developing skills.
- Audio/video scripts and word lists available online.

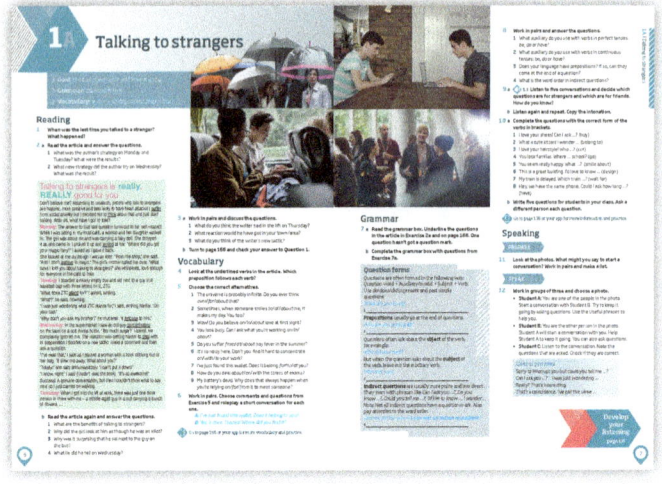

STUDENTS' BOOK WITH ONLINE PRACTICE, DIGITAL RESOURCES AND MOBILE APP

- Provides online practice for students, class management for teachers and a gradebook to review performance.
- Includes all the Students' Book material plus a digital version of the exercises and activities from the Workbook and Tests.
- Includes tools for managing and assigning self-study and practice activities to students, with automatic marking to save time.
- Includes a gradebook for reviewing performance of individual students and classes.

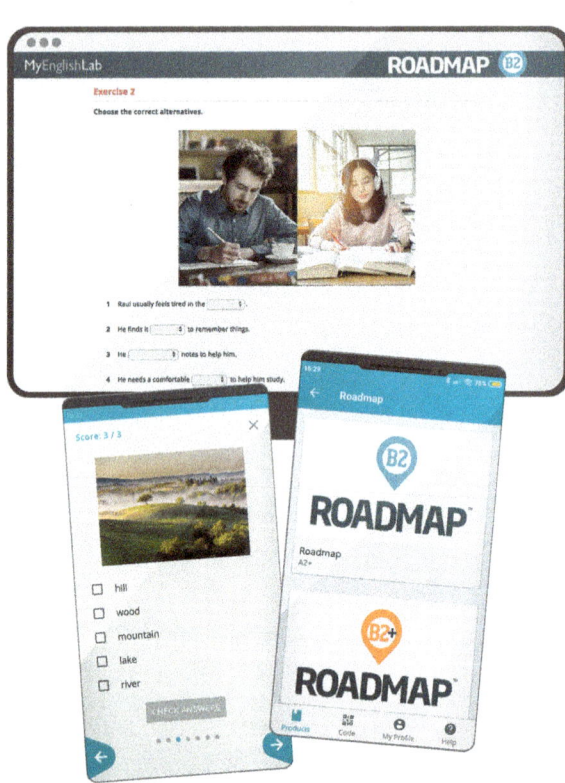

WORKBOOK WITH KEY AND ONLINE AUDIO

- Ten units provide additional practice of material covered in the Students' Book.
- Additional grammar/language focus, vocabulary and functional language practice activities.
- Additional reading, writing and listening practice activities.
- Answer key at the back of the book allows learners to check their answers.
- Audio available online.

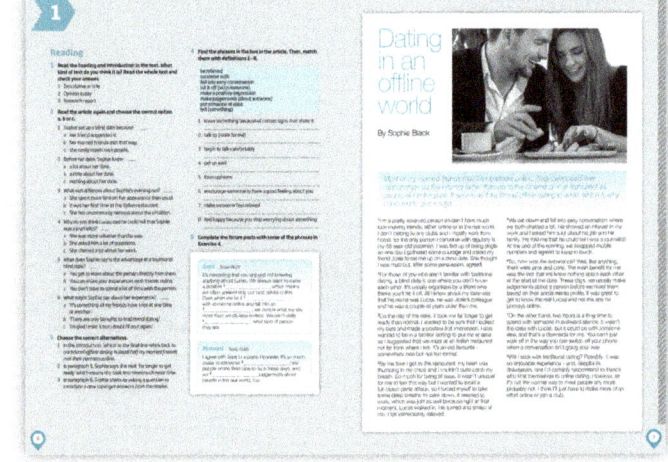

FOR TEACHERS

TEACHER'S BOOK

The Teacher's Book features a host of support materials to help teachers get the most out of the course.
- Teacher's notes for every unit with warmers, fillers, alternative suggestions, advice on dealing with tricky language items, culture notes etc.
- Teaching tips on useful areas such as dealing with mixed abilities, teaching grammar, vocabulary and pronunciation.
- Grammar, vocabulary and language focus photocopiable worksheets for every unit, including accompanying teacher's notes and answer keys.
- Class audio scripts and answer keys.
- Photocopiable worksheets for each Students' Book unit accompanied by teaching notes and answer key.

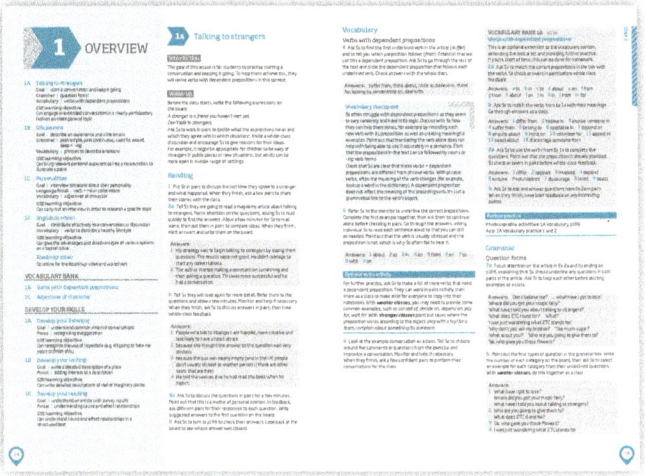

TEACHER'S DIGITAL RESOURCES

Additional resources can be accessed on the *Pearson English Portal* using the access code in the Teacher's Book.
- Class audio.
- Video and video worksheets.
- Audio and video scripts.
- Word lists.
- Students' Book answer key.
- Assessment package with a range of tests including unit tests (grammar, vocabulary and functional language), achievement and mid and end of course tests (grammar, vocabulary, functional language and skills), with accompanying audio.
- Workbook audio.

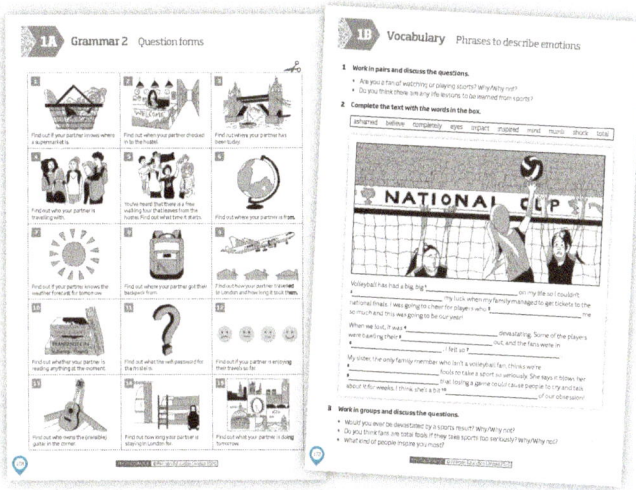

VIDEO

- Ten videos – one for each unit – designed to consolidate key language and illustrate some of the quirkier aspects of real life.
- Each video features a roving reporter who goes out on location to visit interesting places, meet interesting people and/or try new experiences.
- Video clips are 2–3 minutes in length and are designed to entertain learners and provide a bit of light relief.
- Video worksheets (to exploit the language in the videos) are available online.

PRESENTATION TOOL

- Interactive version of the Students' Book with integrated audio and video is available on the *Pearson English Portal*.
- Planning mode (includes teacher's notes) and teaching mode.
- Easy navigation via book page and lesson flow.
- Answers to exercises at the touch of a button.
- Integrated audio.
- Integrated video, with timed-coded video scripts.
- A host of useful classroom tools.

STUDENTS' BOOK

The **Students' Book** has ten units featuring three double-page main lessons containing approximately 90 minutes of teaching material. Each lesson features grammar/language focus, vocabulary and pronunciation activities which lead up to a final speaking task. Each lesson links to a *Develop your skills* lesson and other material at the back of the book including a *Language bank*, *Vocabulary bank* and *Communication bank*.

1. Clearly defined *Global Scale of English* objectives at the start of each lesson.
2. Different topics for each lesson to maintain interest and motivation.
3. Striking images provoke interest in the topic and provide a vehicle for teaching vocabulary.
4. Short reading and/or listening texts featuring real-life information are used to present grammar and/or vocabulary.
5. Key vocabulary is presented in context and practised through personalised activities.
6. Grammar rules are clearly highlighted and target language practised through form-based and communicative practice activities.
7. Pronunciation is highlighted and practised in each lesson.
8. Additional practice is provided on the mobile app and in the *Language bank* at the back of the book.
9. Carefully staged speaking tasks with 'models' and time to prepare build learners' confidence.
10. Relevant, meaningful tasks engage learners and prepare them for real life.
11. Each odd unit ends with *English in action* pages that focus on functional language.
12. Each even unit ends with a *Check and reflect* pages that consolidates key grammar and vocabulary.

1C Personalities

> **Goal:** interview someone about their personality
> **Language focus:** verb + noun collocations
> **Vocabulary:** adjectives of character

Vocabulary and listening

1 **Look at the photos and answer the questions.**
1 What adjectives would you use to describe the people's appearance?
2 What sort of people do you think they are? Use two or three adjectives for each photo.
3 Do you think the way people look always reflects their personality? Why/Why not?
4 What personality traits do you think are important:
- in a good friend?
- in a boss?
- in a partner?

5 Do you think people can change the main characteristics of their personality? Why/Why not?

2 a **Read the beginning of an article. Can you think of adjectives to describe personality traits which begin with *C, E, A* and *N*?**

Psychologists often talk about the big five personality traits. These are five basic ways that we can describe people. Together these are referred to as OCEAN; each letter stands for one of the personality traits.
The 'O' of the first character trait is 'open to experiences'. People who are more open to experiences tend to be adventurous, while people who are less open to experiences tend to be more cautious.

b 1.7 **Listen and check your answers.**

3 a **Listen again and complete the scales for each character trait with the words in the box.**

~~adventurous~~ careless ~~cautious~~ confident nervous organised outgoing reserved suspicious trusting

1 How **open** are you?
adventurous + ←——→ - *cautious*
2 How **conscientious** are you?
______ + ←——→ - ______
3 How **extrovert** are you?
______ + ←——→ - ______
4 How **agreeable** are you?
______ + ←——→ - ______
5 How **neurotic** are you?
______ + ←——→ - ______

b **Work in pairs and choose a scale from Exercise 3a. Then decide where you sit on that scale. Explain your answers.**

Go to page 156 or your app for more vocabulary and practice.

Language focus

4 a **Read the quiz on page 11. Work in pairs and check any words or phrases that you don't understand.**
b **Take turns asking and answering the quiz questions.**
c **Do you agree with your results? Explain why/why not.**

10

What kind of person are you?

1 Do you speak your mind, no matter what?
☐ ALWAYS ☐ SOMETIMES ☐ NEVER
2 Do you meet your deadlines?
☐ ALWAYS ☐ SOMETIMES ☐ NEVER
3 Do you get angry when you have to wait in line?
☐ ALWAYS ☐ SOMETIMES ☐ NEVER
4 Would you say you lose your temper easily?
☐ ALWAYS ☐ SOMETIMES ☐ NEVER
5 Do you find it extremely important to keep your promises?
☐ ALWAYS ☐ SOMETIMES ☐ NEVER
6 Do you make your bed every morning?
☐ ALWAYS ☐ SOMETIMES ☐ NEVER
7 Do you break the rules to get what you want?
☐ ALWAYS ☐ SOMETIMES ☐ NEVER
8 Do you voice your opinion during meetings or discussions?
☐ ALWAYS ☐ SOMETIMES ☐ NEVER
9 When no one knows what to do, do you take charge?
☐ ALWAYS ☐ SOMETIMES ☐ NEVER
10 If there's an argument, do you try to resolve the dispute?
☐ ALWAYS ☐ SOMETIMES ☐ NEVER
11 During presentations, do you take notes?
☐ ALWAYS ☐ SOMETIMES ☐ NEVER
12 Do you find it hard to remain calm?
☐ ALWAYS ☐ SOMETIMES ☐ NEVER
13 Do you take an interest in the opinions of others?
☐ ALWAYS ☐ SOMETIMES ☐ NEVER
14 Do you make time for tasks like ironing?
☐ ALWAYS ☐ SOMETIMES ☐ NEVER
15 If someone helps you out, do you try to return the favour?
☐ ALWAYS ☐ SOMETIMES ☐ NEVER
16 When you were a child, did all the rules make sense to you?
☐ ALWAYS ☐ SOMETIMES ☐ NEVER

Which did you mainly answer, *Always, Sometimes* or *Never*? Turn to page 166.

5 **Complete the language focus box with verbs from the quiz.**

Verb + noun collocations

Collocations are two or more words that are often used together. They are 'preferred combinations' of words. For example, it is possible to say *change your ideas* about something, but it is more usual to say *change your mind*. Keep a list of collocations that you meet in a notebook or in a flashcard app.
Here are some common collocations from the quiz.

1 *speak* your mind	9 ______ charge
2 *meet* your deadlines	10 ______ a dispute
3 *wait* in line	11 ______ notes
4 ______ your temper	12 ______ calm
5 ______ your promises	13 ______ an interest
6 ______ your bed	14 ______ time for (tasks)
7 ______ the rules	15 ______ a favour
8 ______ your opinion	16 ______ sense

6 a **Complete the sayings with collocations from the Language focus box. You may need to change the form of the verb.**
1 If you can ______ your mind, you can change your life.
2 ______ your deadlines is good, but beating your deadlines is better.
3 Don't ______ your temper, use your temper. If you ______ your temper, you lose the fight.
4 Everyone has the right to ______ their opinions. That doesn't mean that everyone's opinions are right.
5 Try to ______ your promises to others. And make sure you ______ your promises to yourself.
6 Your ability to ______ calm is a measure of your intelligence.
7 A true leader will ______ disputes rather than create them.

b 1.8 **Underline *your, the* and *a* in Exercise 6a. Then listen. How are those words pronounced?**
c **Listen again and repeat.**

7 **Work in pairs. Which sayings in Exercise 6a do you agree with? Why?**

Go to page 136 or your app for more information and practice.

Speaking

PREPARE

8 a 1.9 **Listen to the end of an interview between Emily and Rudi. Emily is reading from a questionnaire that she wrote. Look at the title of the questionnaire below and choose the correct alternative.**
How *open/conscientious/extrovert/agreeable/neurotic* are you?

b **Listen again and answer the questions.**
1 How many questions in total are there in the questionnaire?
2 What does the questionnaire suggest about Rudi?
3 Does Rudi think that the answers to the questionnaire give an accurate picture of him?

9 **You're going to write a questionnaire and interview other students. Choose one of the personality traits from Exercise 3a and write ten questions.**
- Use *Yes/No* questions. Make sure that the answers always point to one end of the scale or the other.
- Use appropriate verb + noun collocations.
- Always ask a follow-up question such as *Why/Why not?*

SPEAK

10 a **Work in pairs. Take turns asking the questions in your questionnaire. Then tell your partner what kind of person he/she is.**
b **Repeat your questionnaire with other students.**

Develop your reading page 96

1C | Personalities

11

11

1D English in action

> **Goal:** contribute effectively to a conversation or discussion
> **Vocabulary:** verbs to describe a healthy lifestyle

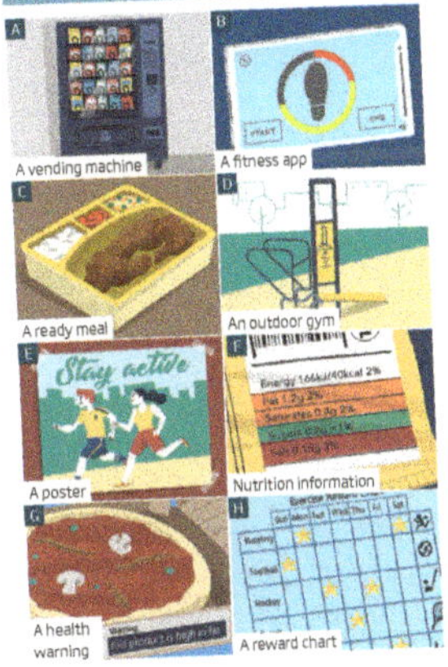

Vocabulary

1 **Look at pictures A–H. Does each one make a healthier lifestyle easier or more difficult? How?**

2 a **Work in pairs and read the sentences. Which picture could each sentence apply to?**
The fitness app encourages you to exercise.
1 It **encourages** you to exercise.
2 It **tracks** your daily activity.
3 It **promotes** a healthy lifestyle.
4 It **provides** useful information.
5 It **offers an alternative to** cooking.
6 It **makes it possible to** exercise for free.
7 It **warns** you **about** the dangers to your health.
8 It **discourages** you from eating unhealthy food.

b **Ask and answer *What else …?* questions. Use the vocabulary in Exercise 2a.**
A: What else encourages you to exercise?

Listening 1

3 a 1.10 **Listen to a discussion about diet and exercise. Which of the things in pictures A–H do they mention?**

b **Listen again and answer the questions.**
1 Why is one of the men trying to get healthy again?
2 How does the woman feel about the changes to her vending machine at work?
3 How have times changed, according to one of the men?
4 How is the bank encouraging its customers to be more healthy?
5 Why does the woman think the bank's plan wouldn't work for her?
6 How does one of the men suggest she should see the bank's plan?

4 **Complete the Useful phrases with the words in the box.**

look conclusion with experience point bet

Useful phrases 1

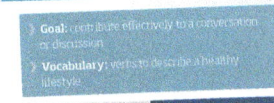

Agreeing or disagreeing with someone
You've got a [1]______.
That's a good point.
You're absolutely right.
You might be right, I guess.
I'm not really [2]______ you on that one.

Asking a question about what someone has said
How did you come to that [3]______?
What makes you say that?
Can you explain that a bit more?

Commenting on what someone has said
I [4]______ that's (difficult to measure).
That's an interesting thought.
You're not serious!

Giving your own experience or thoughts
In my [5]______ (that kind of thing never works).
That reminds me of (a story I read).
That happened to me once.
You could [6]______ at it another way. You could see it as (a reward).

5 **Complete the conversations with phrases from the Useful phrases box.**
1 A: I think ready meals are unhealthy.
B: Really? You might ______, I guess.
2 A: Outdoor gyms are a waste of money.
B: How did you come to ______?
3 A: They should put warning labels on unhealthy food.
B: That's ______ thought.
4 A: I missed my flight this morning.
B: That happened ______

12

12

Check and reflect: Units 1 and 2

1 a **Put the prepositions in the box in the correct place in the questions.**

with on (x 2) to from for in about

1 Do you belong any clubs or organisations?
2 In what situations do you suffer nerves?
3 If a movie has a PG rating, what do the letters stand?
4 Do you ever think what you'll do when you retire?
5 Do you rely any of your friends more than others?
6 How do you deal people who take advantage of you?
7 Do you believe ghosts?
8 Is it usually easy to concentrate what you're doing?

b **Work in pairs and ask and answer the questions in Exercise 1a.**

2 **Put the words in the correct order to make questions.**
1 did / that / Where / jacket / buy / you
2 thinking / you / What / about / are
3 delays / constant / causes / these / What
4 you / where / are / the / Do / rooms / changing / know
5 tower / Who / build / decided / that / to / strange
6 why / to / I'd / off / know / get / many / here / so / people / love
7 you / are / text / sending / to / Who / that / message
8 to / another / bar / they / Why / open / here / want / did / coffee

3 **Match 1–8 with a–h to make sentences.**
1 When the test results came back, I felt totally
2 My first experience of travelling abroad had a big
3 When I got the job, I simply couldn't believe
4 When I saw the effects of the flood, I was literally in
5 It was my chemistry teacher who inspired
6 Losing all the money I'd invested was completely
7 For days after the accident, I just sat and bawled
8 Going to Nepal a few years ago completely blew

a my eyes out.
b my mind.
c impact on me.
d devastating.
e numb.
f me.
g shock.
h my luck.

4 **Find five of the underlined phrases with a mistake and correct them.**

My parents didn't have much money when we were kids, so we [1] didn't used to go abroad much – we [2] used to go on day trips around the local area. Then, when I was around 14, my uncle [3] was getting a job in Paris and things [4] would change. He [5] didn't have a big apartment, so [6] we'd all sleep in the same room, but it was fun. Once we went to a really nice restaurant. While we [7] waited for our food, there was suddenly huge excitement. I [8] looked round and saw that Jennifer Lawrence was there. I couldn't believe my eyes. I [9] kept looking at her and I was too nervous to eat my food. Then I went to the toilet, which [10] was meaning I had to walk past her table. I told her how much I liked her.

5 **Complete the sentences with the adjective form of the words in brackets.**
1 I grow more cautious as I get older, but I used to be quite ______. (adventure)
2 I wouldn't say I'm really an extrovert, but I guess I'm fairly ______. (outgo)
3 Jenny's very ______. She hardly said a word all evening. (reserve)
4 You can trust Jake to do the job well. He's very ______. (conscience)
5 It was ______ of you to leave the back door unlocked. (care)
6 John's a real worrier. He gets ______ about every little thing. (nerve)
7 Julie will be good company on the trip. She seems very ______. (agree)
8 I don't know why Greg wants the money. I'm a bit ______. (suspect)

6 a **Complete the questions with the correct form of the verbs in the box.**

break speak return make take meet remain keep lose

1 Do you often ______ your temper or do you tend to ______ calm?
2 Can you remember the last time you ______ a rule?
3 In what situations would you not ______ your mind?
4 When did you last fail to ______ a promise you'd made?
5 Is it important to ______ favours?
6 Are you good at ______ deadlines when you work?
7 Do you ______ an interest in world politics?
8 Do most things in life ______ sense to you?

b **Work in pairs. Discuss three of the questions in Exercise 6a.**

7 a **Complete the sentences with one word.**
1 Do you ever **get the** ______ **that** something has happened before?
2 Does it **get on your** ______ when people talk loudly on their mobile phones?
3 Is it difficult to **get** ______ **of** old computer equipment where you live?
4 Should you ever snap your fingers to **get** a waiter's ______?
5 Do you ever use social media sites to **get in** ______ **with** old friends?
6 Have you got a friend who talks and talks but never **gets to the** ______?
7 Do most people you know **get** ______ at the end of the month?
8 Are you a football fan? Do you **get** ______ **away** when your team scores a goal?
9 Does your family usually **get** ______ to celebrate birthdays?

b **Work in pairs. Ask and answer five of the questions in Exercise 7a.**

20

STUDENTS' BOOK

The **Students' Book** also features *Develop your skills* lessons at the back of the book. These lessons are based on GSE learning objectives and are thematically linked to the main lessons. They focus on developing specific strategies for improving reading, writing and listening and expose learners to a wide variety of different text types/genres. The *Develop your skills* lessons can either be done in class following the main lessons they are linked to, or they can be used for homework.

1. *Develop your listening* lessons provide practice in different types of listening such as short talks and monologues, conversations, radio interviews and discussions.

2. *Develop your writing* lessons provide practice of specific genres such as stories, formal and informal emails, blog posts, descriptions, invitations and reviews.

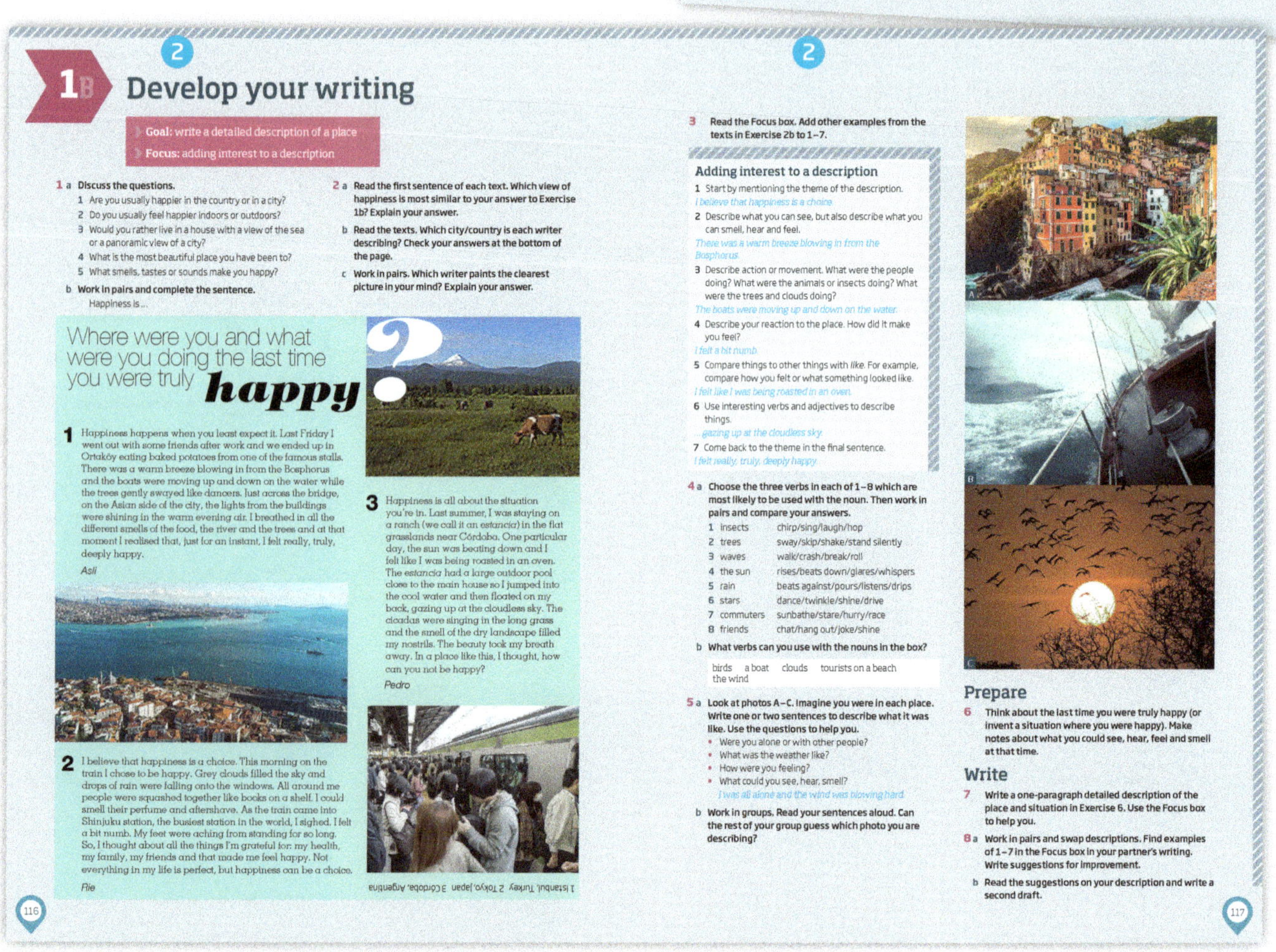

3. *Develop your reading* lessons provide practice of specific genres such as stories, articles, reviews, factual texts, reports, social media and blog posts.

4. Each *Develop your skills* lesson has a clearly defined genre-related goal and a focus which teaches a sub-skill related to the genre.

5. Special *Focus boxes* highlight reading, listening and writing sub-skills such as identifying the main ideas in a text, guessing the meaning of words from context, identifying positive and negative attitudes, organising ideas, using paragraphs, explaining reasons and results, using time expressions and linkers etc.

6. Practice exercises are provided to ensure learners can recognise and use the sub-skills in focus.

7. Follow-up questions round up the lesson and provide opportunities for further discussion.

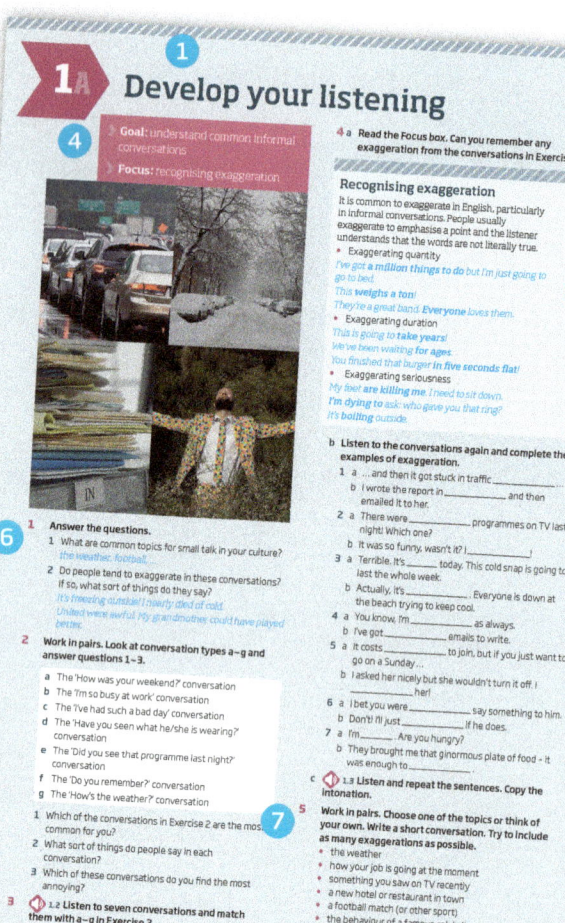

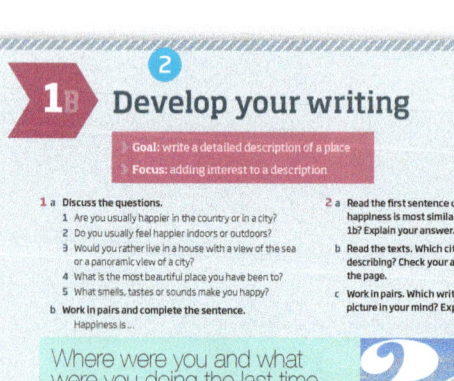

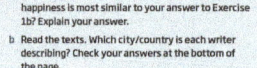

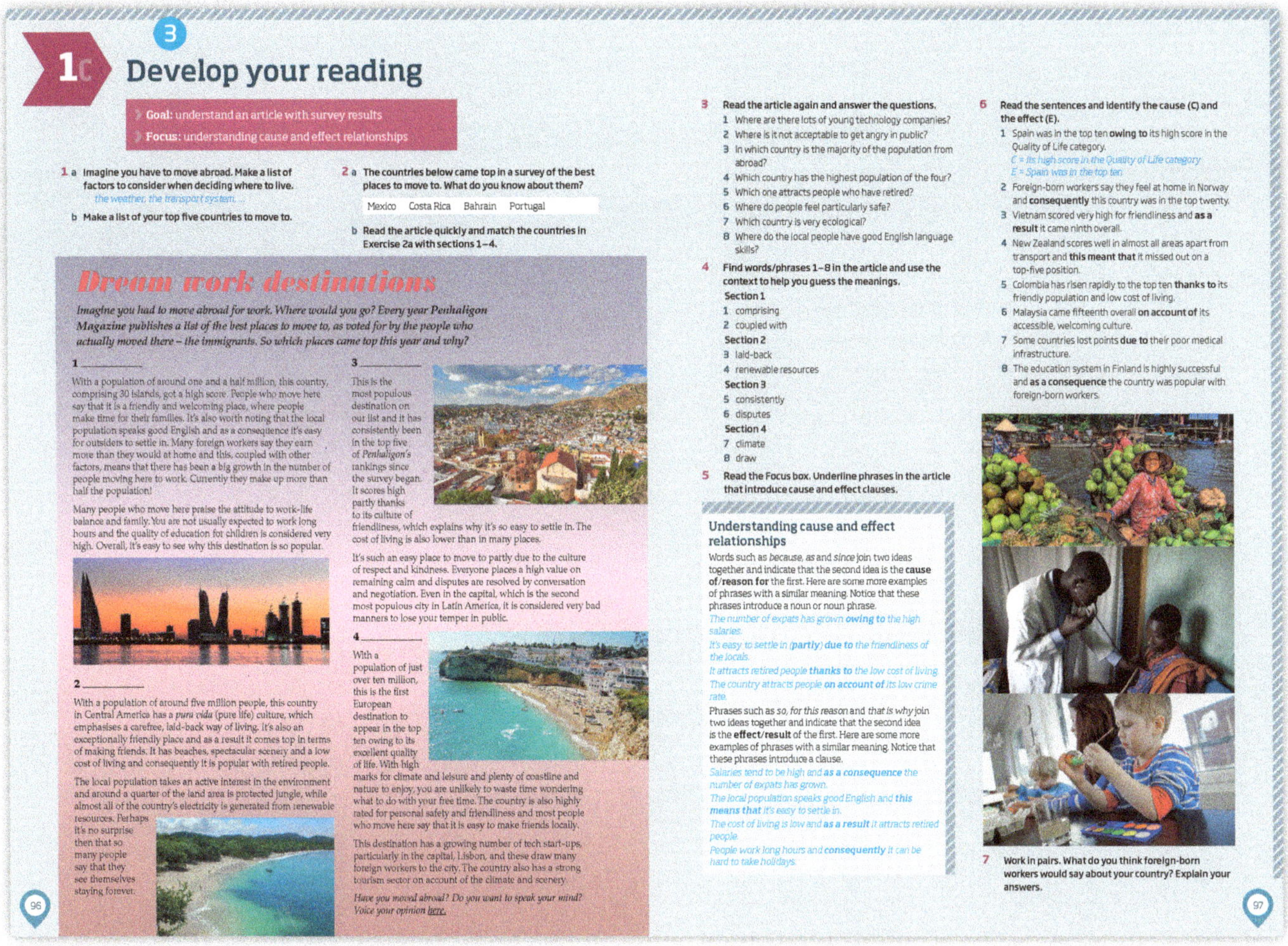

1C Develop your reading

3

Goal: understand an article with survey results

Focus: understanding cause and effect relationships

1 a Imagine you have to move abroad. Make a list of factors to consider when deciding where to live.

the weather, the transport system, …

b Make a list of your top five countries to move to.

2 a The countries below came top in a survey of the best places to move to. What do you know about them?

Mexico Costa Rica Bahrain Portugal

b Read the article quickly and match the countries in Exercise 2a with sections 1–4.

Dream work destinations

Imagine you had to move abroad for work. Where would you go? Every year Penhaligon Magazine publishes a list of the best places to move to, as voted for by the people who actually moved there – the immigrants. So which places came top this year and why?

1 ________

With a population of around one and a half million, this country, comprising 30 islands, got a high score. People who move here say that it is a friendly and welcoming place, where people make time for their families. It's also worth noting that the local population speaks good English and as a consequence it's easy for outsiders to settle in. Many foreign workers say they earn more than they would at home and this, coupled with other factors, means that there has been a big growth in the number of people moving here to work. Currently they make up more than half the population!

Many people who move here praise the attitude to work-life balance and family. You are not usually expected to work long hours and the quality of education for children is considered very high. Overall, it's easy to see why this destination is so popular.

2 ________

With a population of around five million people, this country in Central America has a *pura vida* (pure life) culture, which emphasises a carefree, laid-back way of living. It's also an exceptionally friendly place and as a result it comes top in terms of making friends. It has beaches, spectacular scenery and a low cost of living and consequently it is popular with retired people.

The local population takes an active interest in the environment and around a quarter of the land area is protected jungle, while almost all of the country's electricity is generated from renewable resources. Perhaps it's no surprise then that so many people say that they see themselves staying forever.

3 ________

This is the most populous destination on our list and it has consistently been in the top five of *Penhaligon's* rankings since the survey began. It scores high partly thanks to its culture of friendliness, which explains why it's so easy to settle in. The cost of living is also lower than in many places.

It's such an easy place to move to partly due to the culture of respect and kindness. Everyone places a high value on remaining calm and disputes are resolved by conversation and negotiation. Even in the capital, which is the second most populous city in Latin America, it is considered very bad manners to lose your temper in public.

4 ________

With a population of just over ten million, this is the first European destination to appear in the top ten owing to its excellent quality of life. With high marks for climate and leisure and plenty of coastline and nature to enjoy, you are unlikely to waste time wondering what to do with your free time. The country is also highly rated for personal safety and friendliness and most people who move here say that it is easy to make friends locally.

This destination has a growing number of tech start-ups, particularly in the capital, Lisbon, and these draw many foreign workers to the city. The country also has a strong tourism sector on account of the climate and scenery.

Have you moved abroad? Do you want to speak your mind? Voice your opinion here.

96

3 Read the article again and answer the questions.
1 Where are there lots of young technology companies?
2 Where is it not acceptable to get angry in public?
3 In which country is the majority of the population from abroad?
4 Which country has the highest population of the four?
5 Which one attracts people who have retired?
6 Where do people feel particularly safe?
7 Which country is very ecological?
8 Where do the local people have good English language skills?

4 Find words/phrases 1–8 in the article and use the context to help you guess the meanings.

Section 1
1 comprising
2 coupled with

Section 2
3 laid-back
4 renewable resources

Section 3
5 consistently
6 disputes

Section 4
7 climate
8 draw

5 Read the Focus box. Underline phrases in the article that introduce cause and effect clauses.

Understanding cause and effect relationships

Words such as *because*, *as* and *since* join two ideas together and indicate that the second idea is the **cause of/reason for** the first. Here are some more examples of phrases with a similar meaning. Notice that these phrases introduce a noun or noun phrase.

*The number of expats has grown **owing to** the high salaries.*
*It's easy to settle in (**partly**) **due to** the friendliness of the locals.*
*It attracts retired people **thanks to** the low cost of living.*
*The country attracts people **on account of** its low crime rate.*

Phrases such as *so*, *for this reason* and *that is why* join two ideas together and indicate that the second idea is the **effect/result** of the first. Here are some more examples of phrases with a similar meaning. Notice that these phrases introduce a clause.

*Salaries tend to be high and **as a consequence** the number of expats has grown.*
*The local population speaks good English and **this means that** it's easy to settle in.*
*The cost of living is low and **as a result** it attracts retired people.*
*People work long hours and **consequently** it can be hard to take holidays.*

6 Read the sentences and identify the cause (C) and the effect (E).
1 Spain was in the top ten **owing to** its high score in the Quality of Life category.
C = its high score in the Quality of Life category
E = Spain was in the top ten
2 Foreign-born workers say they feel at home in Norway and **consequently** this country was in the top twenty.
3 Vietnam scored very high for friendliness and **as a result** it came ninth overall.
4 New Zealand scores well in almost all areas apart from transport and **this meant that** it missed out on a top-five position.
5 Colombia has risen rapidly to the top ten **thanks to** its friendly population and low cost of living.
6 Malaysia came fifteenth overall **on account of** its accessible, welcoming culture.
7 Some countries lost points **due to** their poor medical infrastructure.
8 The education system in Finland is highly successful and **as a consequence** the country was popular with foreign-born workers.

7 Work in pairs. What do you think foreign-born workers would say about your country? Explain your answers.

97

The **Students' Book** also has extensive back of book material including a *Language bank*, a *Vocabulary bank* and a *Communication bank*.

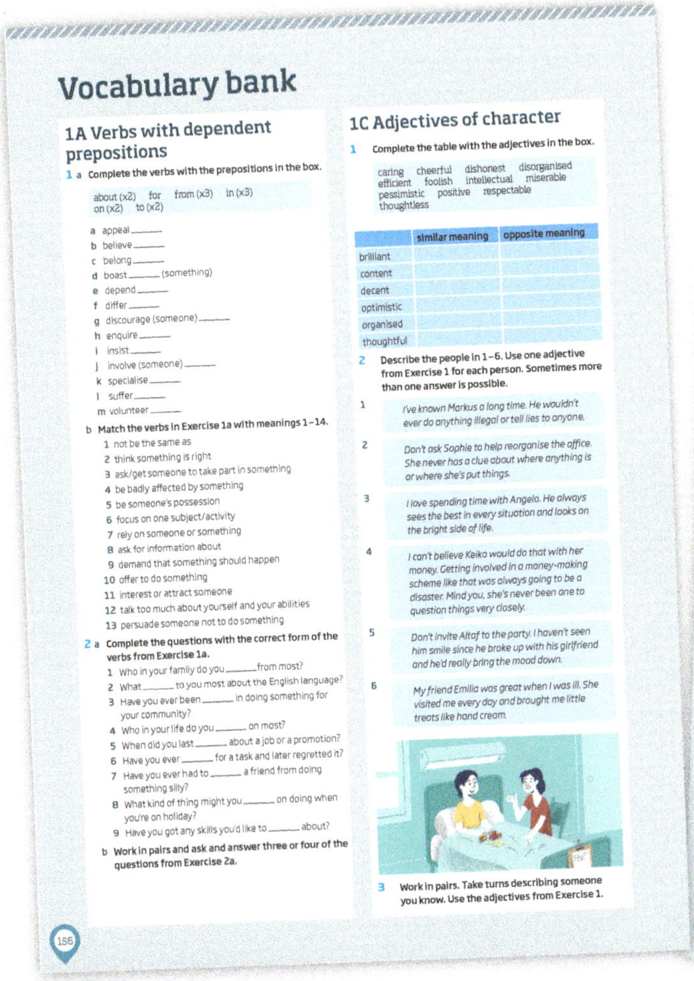

Vocabulary bank

1A Verbs with dependent prepositions

1 a Complete the verbs with the prepositions in the box.

about (x2) for from (x3) in (x3) on (x2) to (x2)

a appeal ____
b believe ____
c belong ____
d boast ____ (something)
e depend ____
f differ ____
g discourage (someone) ____
h enquire ____
i insist ____
j involve (someone) ____
k specialise ____
l suffer ____
m volunteer ____

b Match the verbs in Exercise 1a with meanings 1–14.
1 not be the same as
2 think something is right
3 ask/get someone to take part in something
4 be badly affected by something
5 be someone's possession
6 focus on one subject/activity
7 rely on someone or something
8 ask for information about
9 demand that something should happen
10 offer to do something
11 interest or attract someone
12 talk too much about yourself and your abilities
13 persuade someone not to do something

2 a Complete the questions with the correct form of the verbs from Exercise 1a.
1 Who in your family do you ____ from most?
2 What ____ to you most about the English language?
3 Have you ever been ____ in doing something for your community?
4 Who in your life do you ____ on most?
5 When did you last ____ about a job or a promotion?
6 Have you ever ____ for a task and later regretted it?
7 Have you ever had to ____ a friend from doing something silly?
8 What kind of thing might you ____ on doing when you're on holiday?
9 Have you got any skills you'd like to ____ about?

b Work in pairs and ask and answer three or four of the questions from Exercise 2a.

1C Adjectives of character

1 Complete the table with the adjectives in the box.

caring cheerful dishonest disorganised efficient foolish intellectual miserable pessimistic positive respectable thoughtless

	similar meaning	opposite meaning
brilliant		
content		
decent		
optimistic		
organised		
thoughtful		

2 Describe the people in 1–6. Use one adjective from Exercise 1 for each person. Sometimes more than one answer is possible.

1 *I've known Markus a long time. He wouldn't ever do anything illegal or tell lies to anyone.*
2 *Don't ask Sophie to help reorganise the office. She never has a clue about where anything is or where she's put things.*
3 *I love spending time with Angelo. He always sees the best in every situation and looks on the bright side of life.*
4 *I can't believe Keiko would do that with her money. Getting involved in a money-making scheme like that was always going to be a disaster. Mind you, she's never been one to question things very closely.*
5 *Don't invite Altaf to the party. I haven't seen him smile since he broke up with his girlfriend and he'd really bring the mood down.*
6 *My friend Emilia was great when I was ill. She visited me every day and brought me little treats like hand cream.*

3 Work in pairs. Take turns describing someone you know. Use the adjectives from Exercise 1.

156

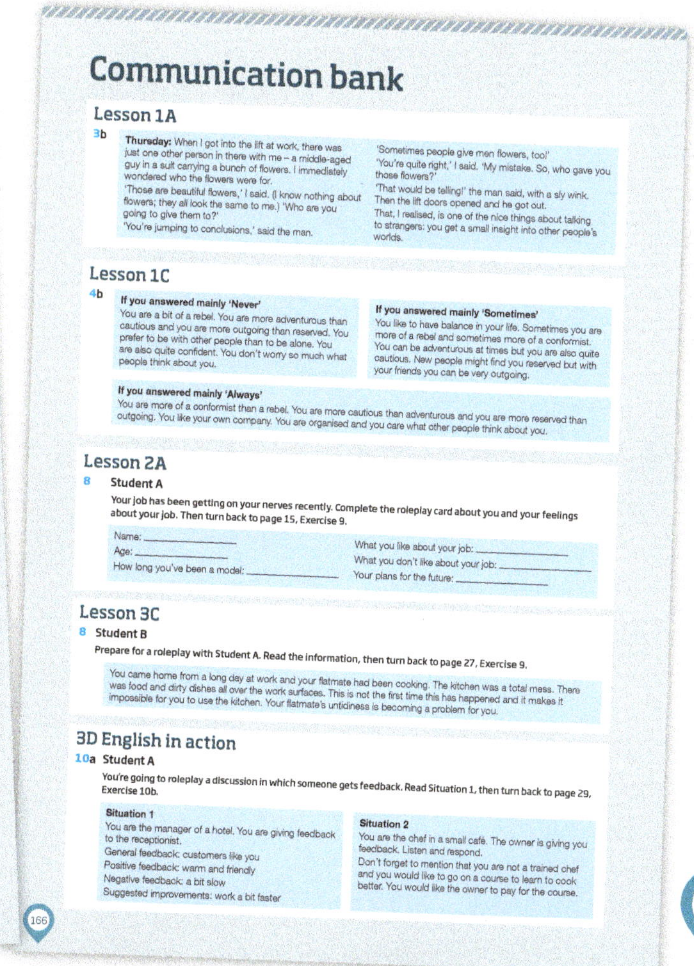

Communication bank

Lesson 1A

3b **Thursday:** When I got into the lift at work, there was just one other person in there with me – a middle-aged guy in a suit carrying a bunch of flowers. I immediately wondered who the flowers were for.
'Those are beautiful flowers,' I said. (I know nothing about flowers; they all look the same to me.) 'Who are you going to give them to?'
'You're jumping to conclusions,' said the man. 'Sometimes people give men flowers, too!'
'You're quite right,' I said. 'My mistake. So, who gave you those flowers?'
'That would be telling!' the man said, with a sly wink. Then the lift doors opened and he got out.
That, I realised, is one of the nice things about talking to strangers: you get a small insight into other people's worlds.

Lesson 1C

4b **If you answered mainly 'Never'**
You are a bit of a rebel. You are more adventurous than cautious and you are more outgoing than reserved. You prefer to be with other people than to be alone. You are also quite confident. You don't worry so much what people think about you.

If you answered mainly 'Sometimes'
You like to have balance in your life. Sometimes you are more of a rebel and sometimes more of a conformist. You can be adventurous at times but you are also quite cautious. New people might find you reserved but with your friends you can be very outgoing.

If you answered mainly 'Always'
You are more of a conformist than a rebel. You are more cautious than adventurous and you are more reserved than outgoing. You like your own company. You are organised and you care what other people think about you.

Lesson 2A

8 Student A

Your job has been getting on your nerves recently. Complete the roleplay card about you and your feelings about your job. Then turn back to page 15, Exercise 9.

Name: ________
Age: ________
How long you've been a model: ________
What you like about your job: ________
What you don't like about your job: ________
Your plans for the future: ________

Lesson 3C

8 Student B

Prepare for a roleplay with Student A. Read the information, then turn back to page 27, Exercise 9.

You came home from a long day at work and your flatmate had been cooking. The kitchen was a total mess. There was food and dirty dishes all over the work surfaces. This is not the first time this has happened and it makes it impossible for you to use the kitchen. Your flatmate's untidiness is becoming a problem for you.

3D English in action

10a Student A

You're going to roleplay a discussion in which someone gets feedback. Read Situation 1, then turn back to page 29, Exercise 10b.

Situation 1
You are the manager of a hotel. You are giving feedback to the receptionist.
General feedback: customers like you
Positive feedback: warm and friendly
Negative feedback: a bit slow
Suggested improvements: work a bit faster

Situation 2
You are the chef in a small café. The owner is giving you feedback. Listen and respond.
Don't forget to mention that you are not a trained chef and you would like to go on a course to learn to cook better. You would like the owner to pay for the course.

166

SUPPORT COMPONENTS

WORKBOOK WITH ONLINE AUDIO

The *Roadmap* **Workbook** contains a wide variety of grammar, vocabulary and functional language exercises that review all the areas covered in the Students' Book. It also features additional listening, reading and writing practice.

- Extensive practice of grammar, vocabulary and functional language covered in the Students' Book.
- Additional listening, reading and writing practice to further develop learners' knowledge and mastery of skills.
- Full answer keys and audio scripts are provided at the back of the book.

Roadmap Workbook audio is available online for students and teachers in the *Pearson English Portal*.

MOBILE APP

Extra grammar and vocabulary exercises, available on the mobile app (the *Pearson Practice English* app), consolidate language points covered in the Students' Book.

- On-the-go, bite-sized practice which can be done anywhere, any time.
- Instant feedback provided to students.
- Progressive levels of challenge.

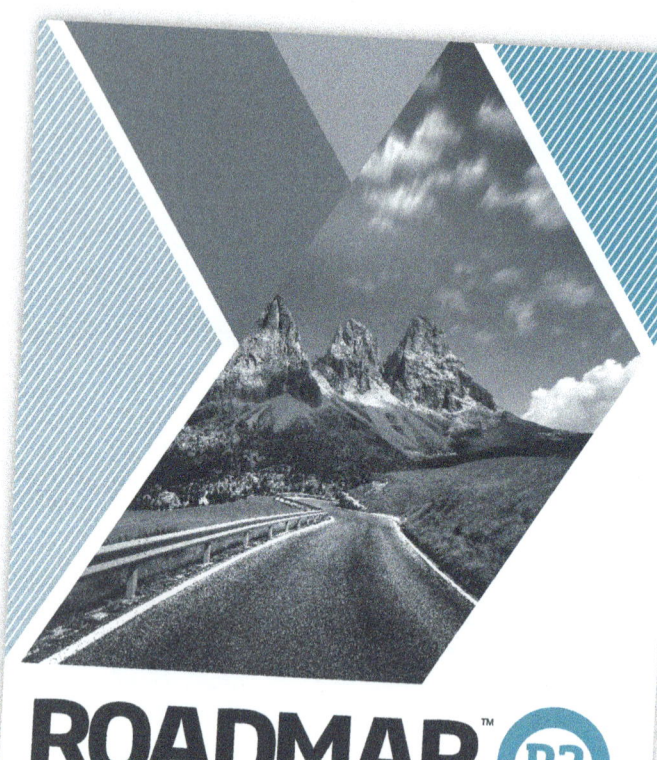

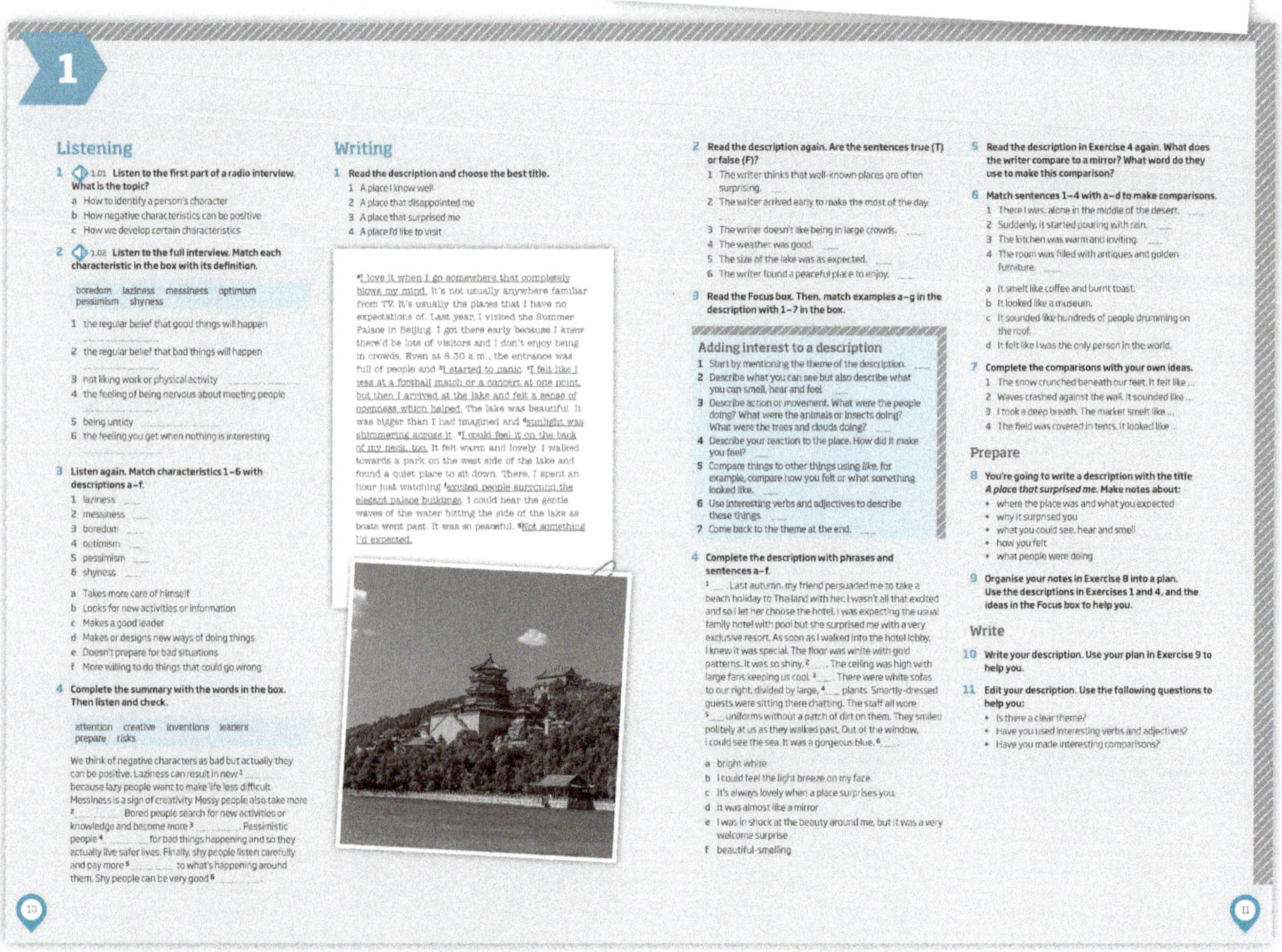

1

Listening

1 1.01 **Listen to the first part of a radio interview. What is the topic?**
a How to identify a person's character
b How negative characteristics can be positive
c How we develop certain characteristics

2 1.02 **Listen to the full interview. Match each characteristic in the box with its definition.**

boredom laziness messiness optimism pessimism shyness

1 the regular belief that good things will happen ______
2 the regular belief that bad things will happen ______
3 not liking work or physical activity ______
4 the feeling of being nervous about meeting people ______
5 being untidy ______
6 the feeling you get when nothing is interesting ______

3 **Listen again. Match characteristics 1–6 with descriptions a–f.**
1 laziness ___
2 messiness ___
3 boredom ___
4 optimism ___
5 pessimism ___
6 shyness ___

a Takes more care of himself
b Looks for new activities or information
c Makes a good leader
d Makes or designs new ways of doing things
e Doesn't prepare for bad situations
f More willing to do things that could go wrong

4 **Complete the summary with the words in the box. Then listen and check.**

attention creative inventions leaders prepare risks

We think of negative characters as bad but actually they can be positive. Laziness can result in new [1] ______ because lazy people want to make life less difficult. Messiness is a sign of creativity. Messy people also take more [2] ______. Bored people search for new activities or knowledge and become more [3] ______. Pessimistic people [4] ______ for bad things happening and so they actually live safer lives. Finally, shy people listen carefully and pay more [5] ______ to what's happening around them. Shy people can be very good [6] ______.

Writing

1 **Read the description and choose the best title.**
1 A place I know well
2 A place that disappointed me
3 A place that surprised me
4 A place I'd like to visit

[a] I love it when I go somewhere that completely blows my mind. It's not usually anywhere familiar from TV. It's usually the places that I have no expectations of. Last year, I visited the Summer Palace in Beijing. I got there early because I knew there'd be lots of visitors and I don't enjoy being in crowds. Even at 8.30 a.m., the entrance was full of people and [b] I started to panic. [c] I felt like I was at a football match or a concert at one point, but then I arrived at the lake and felt a sense of openness which helped. The lake was beautiful. It was bigger than I had imagined and [d] sunlight was shimmering across it. [e] I could feel it on the back of my neck, too. It felt warm and lovely. I walked towards a park on the west side of the lake and found a quiet place to sit down. There, I spent an hour just watching [f] excited people surround the elegant palace buildings. I could hear the gentle waves of the water hitting the side of the lake as boats went past. It was so peaceful. [g] Not something I'd expected.

2 **Read the description again. Are the sentences true (T) or false (F)?**
1 The writer thinks that well-known places are often surprising. ___
2 The writer arrived early to make the most of the day. ___
3 The writer doesn't like being in large crowds. ___
4 The weather was good. ___
5 The size of the lake was as expected. ___
6 The writer found a peaceful place to enjoy. ___

3 **Read the Focus box. Then, match examples a–g in the description with 1–7 in the box.**

Adding interest to a description
1 Start by mentioning the theme of the description. ___
2 Describe what you can see but also describe what you can smell, hear and feel. ___
3 Describe action or movement. What were the people doing? What were the animals or insects doing? What were the trees and clouds doing? ___
4 Describe your reaction to the place. How did it make you feel? ___
5 Compare things to other things using *like*, for example, compare how you felt or what something looked like. ___
6 Use interesting verbs and adjectives to describe these things. ___
7 Come back to the theme at the end. ___

4 **Complete the description with phrases and sentences a–f.**

[1] ___. Last autumn, my friend persuaded me to take a beach holiday to Thailand with her. I wasn't all that excited and so I let her choose the hotel. I was expecting the usual family hotel with pool but she surprised me with a very exclusive resort. As soon as I walked into the hotel lobby, I knew it was special. The floor was white with gold patterns. It was so shiny, [2] ___. The ceiling was high with large fans keeping us cool. [3] ___. There were white sofas to our right, divided by large, [4] ___ plants. Smartly-dressed guests were sitting there chatting. The staff all wore [5] ___ uniforms without a patch of dirt on them. They smiled politely at us as they walked past. Out of the window, I could see the sea. It was a gorgeous blue. [6] ___.

a bright white
b I could feel the light breeze on my face.
c It's always lovely when a place surprises you.
d it was almost like a mirror
e I was in shock at the beauty around me, but it was a very welcome surprise
f beautiful-smelling

5 **Read the description in Exercise 4 again. What does the writer compare to a mirror? What word do they use to make this comparison?**

6 **Match sentences 1–4 with a–d to make comparisons.**
1 There I was, alone in the middle of the desert. ___
2 Suddenly, it started pouring with rain. ___
3 The kitchen was warm and inviting. ___
4 The room was filled with antiques and golden furniture. ___

a It smelt like coffee and burnt toast.
b It looked like a museum.
c It sounded like hundreds of people drumming on the roof.
d It felt like I was the only person in the world.

7 **Complete the comparisons with your own ideas.**
1 The snow crunched beneath our feet. It felt like ...
2 Waves crashed against the wall. It sounded like ...
3 I took a deep breath. The market smelt like ...
4 The field was covered in tents. It looked like ...

Prepare

8 **You're going to write a description with the title *A place that surprised me*. Make notes about:**
- where the place was and what you expected
- why it surprised you
- what you could see, hear and smell
- how you felt
- what people were doing

9 **Organise your notes in Exercise 8 into a plan. Use the descriptions in Exercises 1 and 4, and the ideas in the Focus box to help you.**

Write

10 **Write your description. Use your plan in Exercise 9 to help you.**

11 **Edit your description. Use the following questions to help you:**
- Is there a clear theme?
- Have you used interesting verbs and adjectives?
- Have you made interesting comparisons?

10

11

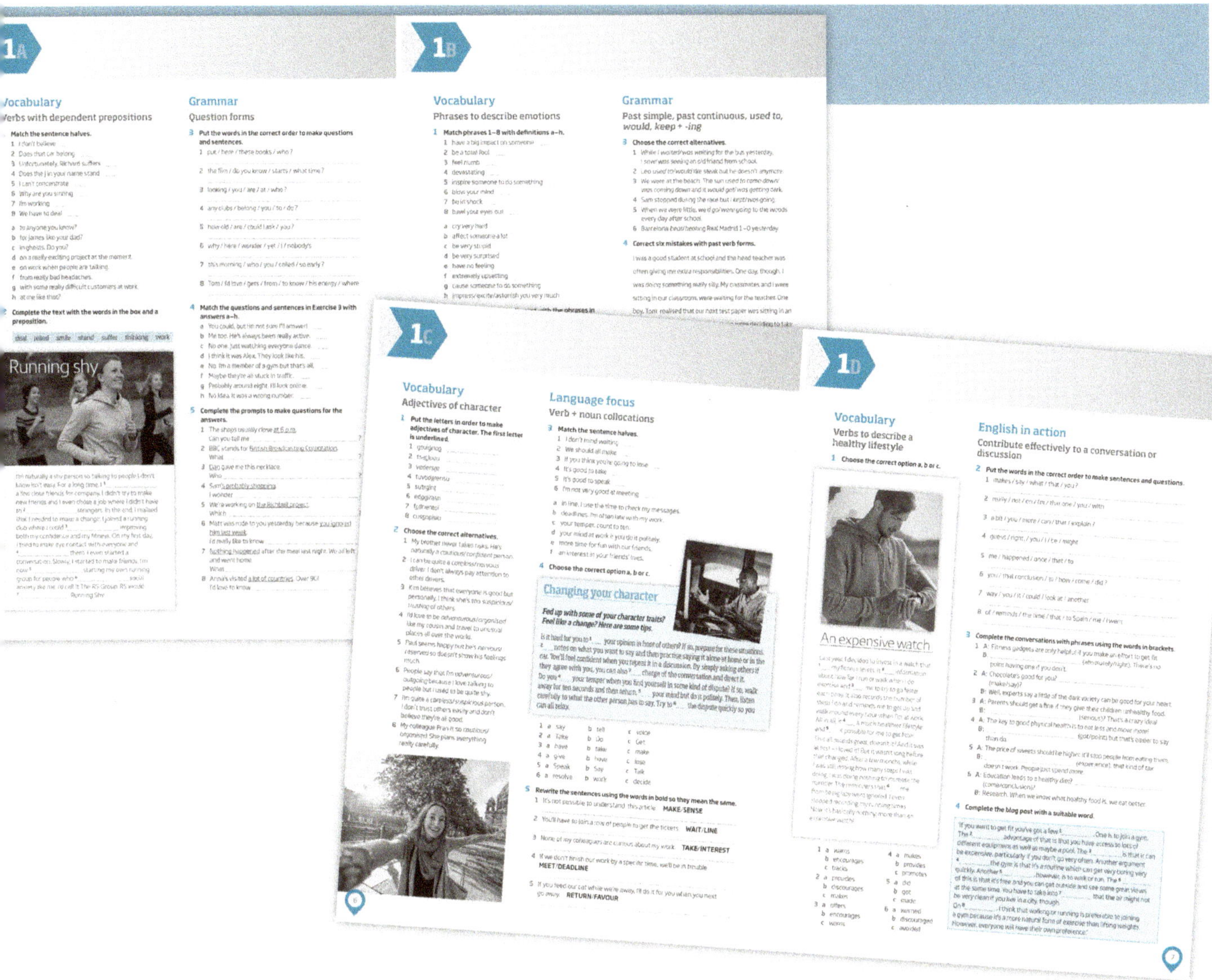

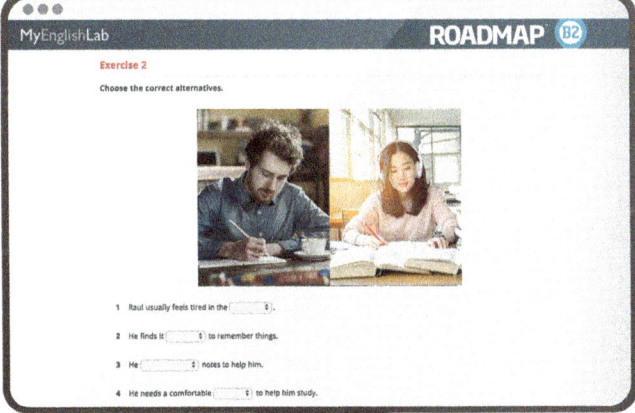

ONLINE PRACTICE

Roadmap **Online practice** provides a blended and personalised learning environment with materials that can be assigned at the touch of a button.

- Interactive Workbook exercises with instant feedback and automatic grade book.
- Common errors report that highlights mistakes learners are making.
- Tips and feedback that direct learners to reference materials and encourage them to work out answers themselves.
- Unit, achievement, mid and end of course tests.

SUPPORT COMPONENTS

TEACHER'S BOOK

The *Roadmap* **Teacher's Book** provides step-by-step instructions on how to exploit the material.

- Teacher's notes for every unit with warmers, fillers, alternative suggestions, culture notes and answer keys.
- Generic teaching tips on useful areas such as grammar, lexis, pronunciation, etc.
- Photocopiable grammar and vocabulary worksheets for every unit.
- Class audio scripts.

TEACHER'S DIGITAL RESOURCES

The *Roadmap* digital resources area (accessed via the *Pearson English Portal*) provides a host of support materials to help teachers get the most out of the course.

- Photocopiable grammar and vocabulary worksheets for every unit, with teacher's notes and answer keys.
- Class audio and scripts.
- Workbook audio and scripts.
- Word lists.
- Students' Book answer key.
- Video, video scripts and video worksheets.
- Unit, achievement, mid and end of course tests.
- Tests audio, audio scripts and answer keys.

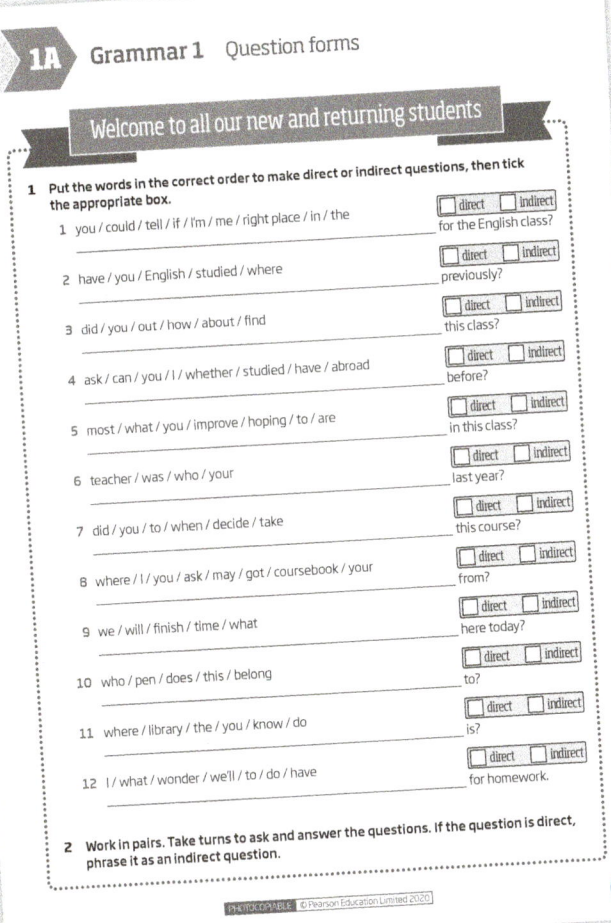

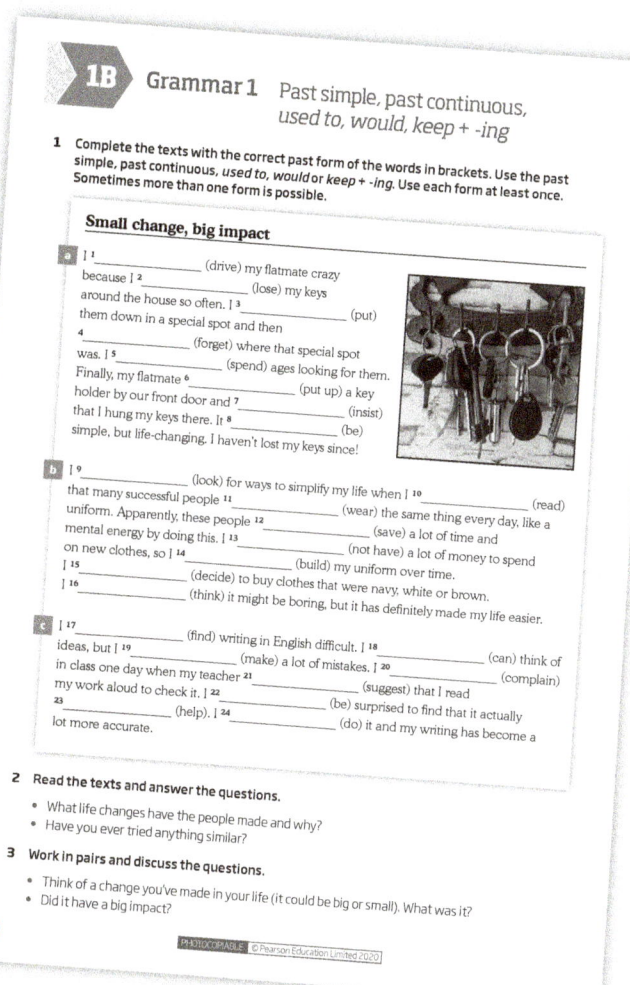

1A Grammar 1 Question forms

Welcome to all our new and returning students

1 Put the words in the correct order to make direct or indirect questions, then tick the appropriate box.

1 you / could / tell / if / I'm / me / right place / in / the ______ for the English class? ☐ direct ☐ indirect

2 have / you / English / studied / where ______ previously? ☐ direct ☐ indirect

3 did / you / out / how / about / find ______ this class? ☐ direct ☐ indirect

4 ask / can / you / I / whether / studied / have / abroad ______ before? ☐ direct ☐ indirect

5 most / what / you / improve / hoping / to / are ______ in this class? ☐ direct ☐ indirect

6 teacher / was / who / your ______ last year? ☐ direct ☐ indirect

7 did / you / to / when / decide / take ______ this course? ☐ direct ☐ indirect

8 where / I / you / ask / may / got / coursebook / your ______ from? ☐ direct ☐ indirect

9 we / will / finish / time / what ______ here today? ☐ direct ☐ indirect

10 who / pen / does / this / belong ______ to? ☐ direct ☐ indirect

11 where / library / the / you / know / do ______ is? ☐ direct ☐ indirect

12 I / what / wonder / we'll / to / do / have ______ for homework. ☐ direct ☐ indirect

2 Work in pairs. Take turns to ask and answer the questions. If the question is direct, phrase it as an indirect question.

PHOTOCOPIABLE © Pearson Education Limited 2020

167

1B Grammar 1 Past simple, past continuous, *used to, would, keep + -ing*

1 Complete the texts with the correct past form of the words in brackets. Use the past simple, past continuous, *used to, would* or *keep + -ing*. Use each form at least once. Sometimes more than one form is possible.

Small change, big impact

a I [1] ______ (drive) my flatmate crazy because I [2] ______ (lose) my keys around the house so often. I [3] ______ (put) them down in a special spot and then [4] ______ (forget) where that special spot was. I [5] ______ (spend) ages looking for them. Finally, my flatmate [6] ______ (put up) a key holder by our front door and [7] ______ (insist) that I hung my keys there. It [8] ______ (be) simple, but life-changing. I haven't lost my keys since!

b I [9] ______ (look) for ways to simplify my life when I [10] ______ (read) that many successful people [11] ______ (wear) the same thing every day, like a uniform. Apparently, these people [12] ______ (save) a lot of time and mental energy by doing this. I [13] ______ (not have) a lot of money to spend on new clothes, so I [14] ______ (build) my uniform over time. I [15] ______ (decide) to buy clothes that were navy, white or brown. I [16] ______ (think) it might be boring, but it has definitely made my life easier.

c I [17] ______ (find) writing in English difficult. I [18] ______ (can) think of ideas, but I [19] ______ (make) a lot of mistakes. I [20] ______ (complain) in class one day when my teacher [21] ______ (suggest) that I read my work aloud to check it. I [22] ______ (be) surprised to find that it actually [23] ______ (help). I [24] ______ (do) it and my writing has become a lot more accurate.

2 Read the texts and answer the questions.

- What life changes have the people made and why?
- Have you ever tried anything similar?

3 Work in pairs and discuss the questions.

- Think of a change you've made in your life (it could be big or small). What was it?
- Did it have a big impact?

PHOTOCOPIABLE © Pearson Education Limited 2020

170

PRESENTATION TOOL

The *Roadmap* **Presentation tool** contains everything you need to make the course come alive. It includes integrated whiteboard software that allows you to add notes, embed files, save your work and reduce preparation time.

Presentation tool:

- Fully interactive version of the Students' Book.
- Planning mode (includes teacher's notes) and teaching mode.
- Easy navigation via book page and lesson flow.
- Answers to exercises at the touch of a button.
- Integrated audio.
- Integrated video, with time-coded video scripts.
- A host of useful classroom tools.

Resources area:

- PDFs of the *Language bank* materials.
- Video worksheets.
- Photocopiable activities with teacher's notes.
- Audioscripts.
- Assessment package containing all the course tests.

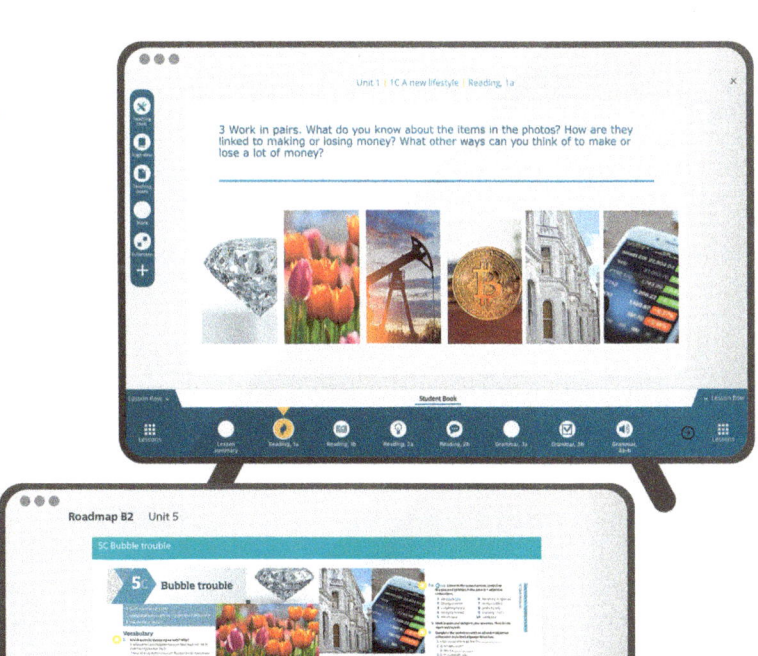

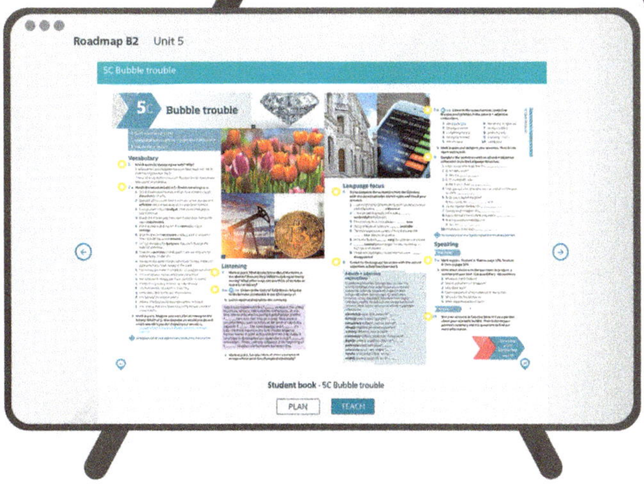

COURSE METHODOLOGY

Syllabus

The *Roadmap* syllabus is built on *Global Scale of English* language learning objectives (see below) but there is a strong focus on the key grammar, functional language, vocabulary and pronunciation needed to perform those objectives in each of the main lessons. Language items have been selected according to their level of difficulty and how useful they are in helping learners to achieve the communicative goal which is at the heart of each lesson. As a result, learners never feel that they are studying grammar, functional language, vocabulary or pronunciation for its own sake and can immediately see the relevance of what they are learning.

- Syllabus built on *Global Scale of English* learning objectives so learners can immediately see the relevance of what they are learning.
- Strong focus on the grammar, vocabulary, functional language and pronunciation needed to achieve the speaking objective at the heart of every lesson.

The Global Scale of English

The **Global Scale of English** (**GSE**) is a standardised, granular scale that measures English language proficiency. Using the GSE, students and teachers can now answer three questions accurately: Exactly how good is my English? What progress have I made towards my learning goal? What do I need to do next if I want to improve?

The GSE identifies what a learner can do at each point on a scale from 10 to 90, across all four skills (listening, reading, speaking, and writing), as well as the enabling skills of grammar and vocabulary. This allows learners and teachers to understand a learner's exact level of proficiency, what progress they have made and what they need to learn next.

The GSE is designed to motivate learners by making it easier to demonstrate granular progress in their language ability. Teachers can use their knowledge of their students' GSE levels to choose course materials that are precisely matched to ability and learning goals. The GSE serves as a standard against which English language courses and assessments can be benchmarked, offering a truly global and shared understanding of language proficiency levels.

Teacher Mapping Booklet and GSE Toolkit

You will find the GSE Teacher Mapping Booklet for *Roadmap* online on english.com/roadmap. This booklet provides an overview of all the learning objectives covered in each unit of *Roadmap*, lesson by lesson.

These GSE learning objectives are only a selection from the larger collection contained within the GSE. To explore additional resources to support students, there is an online GSE Teacher Toolkit. This searchable online database gives you quick and easy access to the learning objectives and grammar and vocabulary resources. It also gives you access to GSE job profiles: 250 job skills mapped to GSE learning objectives, enabling you to pinpoint the specific language skills required for professional learners.

For more information please go to english.com/gse.

Topics

Maintaining learners' interest is a vital part of the teacher's role. Research suggests that learners get bored if they stay on the same topic for too long so each lesson in *Roadmap* introduces a fresh theme, although there is always a coherent link in terms of language items covered from one lesson to the next. There is also a topic link with the *Develop your skills* lessons which are an extension of the main lesson. Fresh angles on familiar topics have been used wherever possible and reading and listening texts have been designed to be as authentic as possible. The texts are based on real-world sources and although they have been graded, especially at the lower levels, to make them accessible for students, the 'tone' of the texts is as realistic as possible. Every unit contains a variety of rich and authentic input material including specially filmed video clips.

- New topics are introduced in every lesson so learners never get bored.
- Fresh angles on familiar topics have been introduced wherever possible.
- Reading and listening texts are designed to be as authentic as possible and are based on real-world sources.

Grammar/Language focus

Successful communication is dependent on an ability to recognise and use grammatical structures. Learners can often manage to make themselves understood with a limited repertoire of words and phrases but, as their level progresses, they increasingly need grammar together with a larger vocabulary bank in order to navigate more complex situations and communicate more sophisticated ideas and opinions. Grammar and enrichment of vocabulary are a core feature of learning a language and *Roadmap* recognises this by giving them a central role in each of the main lessons:

- Grammar is introduced in context through short listening/reading texts and are then presented and practised using a 'guided-discovery' approach. Learners study the patterns of a grammar point and are often asked to identify aspects of meaning or form by completing simple exercises and/or rules and tables.
- Language items are presented in a concise form in a Grammar box in the main lesson with fuller explanations in the *Language bank* at the back of the book.
- Each grammar point has one or two controlled practice exercises plus a freer personalised activity designed to offer students the opportunity to say something about themselves or the topic.
- The *Language focus* carries more of a lexico-grammar approach. This is designed to introduce a vocabulary system, rather than include a long, exhaustive list of vocabulary.
- The *Language bank* in the Students' Book, the Workbook and mobile app have additional grammar/language focus practice exercises. There are also further photocopiable activities in the Teacher's Book.

Vocabulary

Developing a wide range of vocabulary is also key to developing communicative competence. A good knowledge of vocabulary helps learners to improve their reading and listening skills and is also important for writing. A knowledge of high-frequency collocations and fixed and semi-fixed phrases is also an effective way to increase spoken fluency. Vocabulary is an important feature of every lesson in *Roadmap*. Vocabulary items have been selected a) according to the topic of the lesson and b) according to how useful they are for the final speaking task. Vocabulary is always presented in context through photos or texts and practised through controlled and freer practice activities. Vocabulary is also constantly recycled throughout the course and learners are actively encouraged to use the new vocabulary they have learned to give their personal opinions on the topics in focus and to talk about their own lives and experiences.

- Vocabulary is an important feature of every lesson. It is usually presented in context through quotes and/or short reading texts or illustrated with photos and/or cartoons so that learners can understand how and when an item is used.
- The emphasis throughout is on high-frequency, useful vocabulary. At lower levels, the focus is on presenting lexical sets and at higher levels there is an increased focus on word-building, collocation and useful fixed phrases.
- Vocabulary is practised in a variety of ways with one or two controlled practice activities for each vocabulary section. Learners are often asked to relate the vocabulary they have learned to their own lives making it more memorable.
- Vocabulary is constantly recycled throughout the course and further practice is provided in the *Check and reflect* pages, on the mobile app, in the Workbook and photocopiable activities in the Teacher's Book.
- The *Vocabulary bank* at the back of the Students' Book further extends some of the key vocabulary areas covered in the main lessons.

Functional Language

Learners need to manage communication in a wide variety of different situations and they need to be able to recognise and use phrases and expressions that are appropriate for each situation. These include transactional exchanges, where the focus is on getting something done or interactional exchanges where the focus is on socialising with others.

Roadmap recognises the importance of functional language and each unit has an *English in action* page which focus on useful areas such as giving directions, asking for information, clarifying information etc. Each *English in action* lesson has a communicative outcome based on a GSE learning objective and key functional language items are highlighted in a *Useful phrases* box.

- *English in action* lessons focus on useful functional areas such as giving directions, clarifying information etc.
- Each *English in action* lesson has a communicative outcome based on a GSE learning objective.
- Key functional language items are highlighted in a *Useful phrases* box.

Pronunciation

Teachers often have mixed attitudes towards teaching pronunciation in their lessons. Some consider that it is relatively unimportant, especially if their learners can generally make themselves understood, but others place great importance on developing pronunciation that is more than just intelligible. They consider that a systematic focus on pronunciation in a lesson, however brief, can have a significant impact on developing learners' communicative competence.

In *Roadmap*, we have taken a practical, integrated approach to developing students' pronunciation by highlighting features that often cause problems in conjunction with the areas of grammar, vocabulary or functional language in focus. Where relevant to the level, a grammatical or functional language focus is followed by practice of a feature of pronunciation, for example, the weak forms of auxiliary verbs or connected speech in certain functional exponents. Students are given the opportunity to listen to models of the pronunciation, notice the key features and then practise it.

- Pronunciation is a prominent feature of the syllabus, and practice is generally linked to the main grammar, vocabulary and functional language in focus.
- *Listen and repeat* activities reinforce pronunciation of new language. As and when appropriate, there is an emphasis on areas of pronunciation that affect communication, for example, sentence stress/intonation.

Skills development

Roadmap recognises that effective communication involves receptive as well as productive skills. Although speaking is the main skills focus in each of the main lessons, short reading and listening texts are used to present and practise new language and introduce topics for discussion. These cover a variety of different genres – blogs, articles, fact files, etc. – but are never very long as research indicates that teachers want to maximise speaking practice during class time. *Roadmap* also recognises the importance of writing and suggestions for writing extension activities are suggested in the teacher's notes for each of the main lessons.

In addition to the reading, writing and listening material in the main lessons, there is a *Develop your skills* section at the back of the book for learners who want to improve their reading, writing or listening skills. There are three *Develop your skills* lessons for each unit. Each lesson is built around a GSE learning objective and concentrates on a specific skill – reading, listening or writing. They are linked thematically to one of the main lessons and can be done at home or in class. The *Develop your skills* lessons expose learners to different text genres of reading (articles, blogs etc.), writing (emails, reports, essays, etc.) and listening (radio broadcasts, conversations, etc.) and focus on different strategies or sub-skills to improve general competence in each skill. These strategies are particularly useful for exam training.

Speaking

Most learners, whatever their age and whatever specific goals or reasons they might have for learning English, want to improve their speaking skills. Many learners lack opportunities to practise in the real world so they need to make the most of opportunities to speak English in the classroom. *Roadmap* recognises the importance of speaking and there are many opportunities throughout the course for learners to participate in a wide variety of different speaking activities. For example, learners might be asked to discuss a series of questions, respond to photos or cartoons, give their opinions about the content of a reading or listening text or take part in conversations, discussions and role-plays. Speaking is a fundamental part of each lesson and learners are frequently asked to work together in pairs or groups to maximise opportunities to speak in class.

Many learners are reluctant or unable to speak because they have nothing to say or lack the language they need to say what they want to say. *Roadmap* helps learners to overcome these problems and one of the key aims of the course is to increase learners' confidence and fluency. Each of the four core lessons in each unit are built around a *Global Scale of English* speaking objective and all the grammar, functional language, vocabulary and pronunciation is geared towards helping learners achieve that objective. Learners develop fluency when they are motivated to speak and for this to happen, engaging topics and relevant, carefully-staged speaking tasks are essential. In each lesson of *Roadmap* there is a logical sequence of linked activities that have been carefully constructed and staged to help learners perform the final speaking task to the best of their ability. Learners are given time to prepare their ideas and think about the language they need for the final speaking task in a structured way. Giving learners time to rehearse is crucial in terms of building their confidence and this in turn leads to better motivation and greater accuracy and fluency. As learners' confidence increases, their willingness to experiment with the language also increases. Speaking is systematically developed in *Roadmap* through the following activities:

- Lead-in questions and/or striking images engage learners' interest and activate passive knowledge of vocabulary related to the topic.
- Grammar and vocabulary relevant for the final speaking activities are presented and practised.
- Personalised practice activities encourage learners to give their own opinions on the topic and talk about their own lives and experiences
- Learners are given 'models' and time to prepare their ideas for the final speaking task.
- Useful phrases give learners ideas and provide prompts to help them get started.
- Learners perform the speaking task in pairs or groups and are invited to reflect on their performance through a whole class round up activity.

Listening

Listening is an important skill for all users of English and one which learners often find quite challenging. Many learners complain that they can understand their teacher but find it difficult to understand people speaking English outside the classroom, especially if speakers do not make any concessions to their audience in terms of their speed of delivery. Learners with poor listening skills are unlikely to be competent communicators or users of the language, so listening features almost as prominently as speaking in the main lessons in *Roadmap*. It is important to expose learners to real language in use as well as different varieties of English. Listening material, particularly at lower levels, is scripted but aims to reflect the patterns of natural speech and is designed to be as authentic-sounding as possible whilst bearing in mind the need to make it accessible for the level. Listening texts are often used to present new grammar or vocabulary and can act as a springboard to stimulate discussion in class. In addition, there is a listening 'model' for each of the speaking tasks in which one or more speakers perform whole or part of the task. Learners listen to this and try to replicate what they have heard when they come to perform the task themselves.

Listening is a prominent feature in the main lessons but more in-depth practice of different genres, for example, short talks and monologues, conversations, radio interviews and discussions, etc. is provided in the *Develop your listening* lessons at the back of the book. The *Develop your listening* lessons also provide invaluable training in listening sub-skills, for example, predicting information, recognising discourse markers and weak forms, identifying examples and sequencing words. Each *Develop your listening* lesson provides an example of the genre as well as highlighting a sub-skill which is outlined in a special *Focus box* and practised in the lesson. As mentioned in the introduction to the Teacher's Book, the *Develop your listening* lessons are optional and can be selected according to the needs of individual learners or classes. They can be used in conjunction with the main lessons to form the extended route through the course or they can be used individually and/or given to learners to do for homework.

- Listening is a prominent feature of the main lessons and is often used to present new grammar or vocabulary or act as a springboard to stimulate discussion.
- Listening 'models' are provided to build learners' confidence.
- Listening material is designed to be as authentic-sounding as possible whilst bearing in mind the need to make it accessible for the level.
- More in-depth practice of different listening genres – short talks and monologues, conversations, radio interviews and discussions – is provided in the *Develop your listening* lessons at the back of the book.
- *Develop your listening* lessons provide an example of the genre as well as highlighting different sub-skills needed to develop mastery of the skill.
- Listening sub-skills are outlined in a special *Focus box* and practised in the lesson.
- *Develop your listening* lessons are optional and can be selected according to the needs of individual learners or classes. They can be used individually and/or given for homework.

Reading

Reading is important for many students, particularly if they need it for their work or studies. The learner who develops confidence in reading both in and outside the classroom will undoubtedly make faster progress. We now have access to a very wide range of English language reading material and it is a good idea to encourage learners to read as much as possible outside the classroom. *Roadmap* provides ample opportunities for learners to practise their reading skills, both in the main lessons and in the *Develop your reading* sections at the back of the book.

Short reading texts are included in the main lessons to contextualise new grammar or vocabulary and they also often serve as a springboard for discussion. As with the listening material, there is an emphasis on authenticity, and although reading texts have been adapted or graded for the level, there is an attempt to maintain authenticity by remaining faithful to the text type in terms of content and style. Texts are relevant and up-to-date, and are designed to stimulate interest and motivate learners to read. The texts represent a variety of genres and mirror the text types that learners will probably encounter in their everyday lives. Texts are generally not exploited in any great depth in the main lessons (as in-depth work on reading is provided in the *Develop your reading* section) but learners are always given a reason to read along with basic comprehension exercises.

More in-depth practice of different genres is provided in the *Develop your reading* lessons at the back of the book. The *Develop your reading* lessons also provide invaluable training in reading sub-skills such as identifying the main ideas in a text, guessing the meaning of words from context, identifying positive and negative attitudes, understanding pronouns, missing words, etc.

Each *Develop your reading* lesson provides an example of the genre as well as highlighting a sub-skill which is outlined in a special *Focus box* and practised in the lesson. As mentioned in the introduction to the Teacher's Book, the *Develop your reading* lessons are optional and can be selected according to the needs of individual learners or classes. They can be used in conjunction with the main lessons to form the extended route through the course or they can be used individually and/or given to learners to do for homework.

- Reading is a prominent feature of the main lessons and is often used to present new grammar or vocabulary or act as a springboard to stimulate discussion.

- Reading material is designed to be as authentic as possible whilst bearing in mind the need to make it accessible for the level. Text types mirror those learners will encounter in their everyday lives, for example, blogs, social media posts, etc.

- More in-depth practice of different reading genres – stories, articles, reviews, factual texts, reports, social media and blog posts, etc. – is provided in the *Develop your reading* lessons at the back of the book.

- *Develop your reading* lessons provide an example of the genre as well as highlighting different sub-skills needed to develop mastery of the skill.

- Reading sub-skills are outlined in a special *Focus box* and practised in the lesson.

- *Develop your reading* lessons are optional and can be selected according to the needs of individual learners or classes. They can be used individually and/or given for homework.

Writing

In recent years the growth of email and the internet means that people worldwide are writing more than ever before – for business, for their studies and for personal communication. Learners need effective writing skills for professional and academic purposes but people also use writing – email, text messages, social media posts, etc. – as an informal means of communication far more than they used to. The latter isn't simply speech written down and there are all sorts of conventions for both informal and formal writing. It is therefore important to focus on a range of genres, from formal text types such as essays, letters and reports to informal genres such as blog entries and personal messages. *Roadmap* provides extensive training in all these types of writing.

Writing is not a prominent feature of the main lessons in *Roadmap* although learners are frequently asked to make notes as preparation for the speaking task. There are also suggestions in the teacher's notes on ways to extend the tasks with follow-up written work. However, in-depth practice of different genres of writing is provided in the *Develop your writing* lessons at the back of the book. The *Develop your writing* lessons also provide invaluable training in writing sub-skills such as organising ideas, using paragraphs, explaining reasons and results, using time expressions and linkers, constructing narratives, etc.

Each *Develop your writing* lesson provides an example of the genre as well as highlighting a sub-skill which is outlined in a special *Focus box* and practised in the lesson. As mentioned in the introduction to the Teacher's Book, the *Develop your writing* lessons are optional and can be selected according to the needs of individual learners or classes. They can be used in conjunction with the main lessons to form the extended route through the course or they can be used individually and/or given to learners to do for homework. Each *Develop your writing* lesson follows a similar format:

- Some writing practice is provided in the main lessons and in-depth work on different genres of writing as well as writing sub-skills is provided in the *Develop your writing* section at the back of the book.

- Each *Develop your writing* lesson starts with a few discussion questions designed to activate learners' vocabulary and get them thinking about ideas related to the topic.

- Each *Develop your writing* lesson provides a model of the genre in focus. These are designed to be as authentic as possible whilst bearing in mind the need to make them accessible for the level. Types of writing mirror those that learners will encounter in their everyday lives, for example, stories, formal and informal emails, blog posts, descriptions, invitations, reviews, etc.

- *Develop your writing* lessons provide examples of the genre as well as highlighting different sub-skills needed to develop mastery of it, for example, organising ideas, using paragraphs, explaining reasons and results, using time expressions and linkers, constructing narratives, etc.

- Writing sub-skills are outlined in a special *Focus box* and practised in the lesson.

- Learners prepare and then write their own example of the genre in focus and are encouraged to use the sub-skills they have practised in the lesson.

- *Develop your writing* lessons are optional and can be selected according to the needs of individual learners or classes. They can be used individually and/or given for homework.

Review and consolidation

Language items are regularly recycled in each lesson of *Roadmap*. At end of each unit, there is a *Check and reflect* page which is designed to review all the language points covered and give learners an opportunity to reflect on how their confidence and mastery of the language has improved. In addition, each unit is accompanied by a short video – the *Roadmap report* – that can be used to provide a break from the routine of the Students' Book as well as revise and consolidate language in a fun, light-hearted way. Each *Roadmap report* features a 'roving reporter' who goes out on location to visit interesting people and places and has a variety of new experiences. The videos are designed to illustrate some of the quirkier aspects of real life as well as show language items covered in the unit in realistic contexts.

- Video clips and extension activities consolidate key language covered in each unit and illustrate some of the quirkier aspects of real life.

- Video clips are 2–3 minutes in length and are designed to entertain learners and provide a bit of light relief.

- Video worksheets (to exploit the language in the videos) are available online.

1 OVERVIEW

1A Talking to strangers
Goal | start a conversation and keep it going
Grammar | question forms
Vocabulary | verbs with dependent prepositions
GSE learning objective
Can engage in extended conversation in a clearly participatory fashion on most general topics

1B Life lessons
Goal | describe an experience and a life lesson
Grammar | past simple, past continuous, used to, would, keep + -ing
Vocabulary | phrases to describe emotions
GSE learning objective
Can bring relevant personal experiences into a conversation to illustrate a point

1C Personalities
Goal | interview someone about their personality
Language focus | verb + noun collocations
Vocabulary | adjectives of character
GSE learning objective
Can carry out an interview in order to research a specific topic

1D English in action
Goal | contribute effectively to a conversation or discussion
Vocabulary | verbs to describe a healthy lifestyle
GSE learning objective
Can give the advantages and disadvantages of various options on a topical issue

Roadmap video
Go online for the Roadmap video and worksheet.

VOCABULARY BANK

1A Verbs with dependent prepositions
1C Adjectives of character

DEVELOP YOUR SKILLS

1A Develop your listening
Goal | understand common informal conversations
Focus | recognising exaggeration
GSE learning objective
Can recognise the use of hyperbole (e.g. *It's going to take me years to finish this.*)

1B Develop your writing
Goal | write a detailed description of a place
Focus | adding interest to a description
GSE learning objective
Can write detailed descriptions of real or imaginary places

1C Develop your reading
Goal | understand an article with survey results
Focus | understanding cause and effect relationships
GSE learning objective
Can understand cause and effect relationships in a structured text

1A Talking to strangers

Introduction
The goal of this lesson is for students to practise starting a conversation and keeping it going. To help them achieve this, they will revise verbs with dependent prepositions in this context.

Warm-up
Before the class starts, write the following expressions on the board:
A stranger is a friend you haven't met yet.
Don't talk to strangers.
Ask Ss to work in pairs to decide what the expressions mean and which they agree with in which situations. Invite a whole-class discussion and encourage Ss to give reasons for their ideas. For example, it might be appropriate for children to be wary of strangers in public places or new situations, but adults can be more open in a wider range of settings.

Reading

1 Put Ss in pairs to discuss the last time they spoke to a stranger and what happened. When they finish, ask a few pairs to share their stories with the class.

2a Tell Ss they are going to read a magazine article about talking to strangers. Focus attention on the questions, asking Ss to read quickly to find the answers. Allow a few minutes for Ss to read alone, then put them in pairs to compare ideas. When they finish, elicit answers and write them on the board.

Answers:
1 His strategy was to begin talking to strangers by asking them questions. The results were not good. He didn't manage to start any conversations.
2 The author started making a comment on something and then asking a question. This was more successful and he had a conversation.

b Tell Ss they will read again for more detail. Refer them to the questions and allow a few minutes. Monitor and help if necessary. When they finish, ask Ss to discuss answers in pairs, then have whole-class feedback.

Answers:
1 People who talk to strangers are happier, more creative and less likely to have a heart attack.
2 because she thought the answer to the question was very obvious
3 because the bus was nearly empty (and in the UK people don't usually sit next to another person if there are other seats that are free)
4 He told the woman that he had read the book when he hadn't.

3a Ask Ss to discuss the questions in pairs for a few minutes. Point out that this is a matter of personal opinion. In feedback, ask different pairs for their responses to each question. Write suggested answers to the first question on the board.

b Ask Ss to turn to p166 to check their answers. Look back at the board to see whose answer was closest.

Vocabulary

Verbs with dependent prepositions

4 Ask Ss to find the first underlined verb in the article (*suffer*) and to tell you which preposition follows (*from*). Establish that we call this a dependent preposition. Ask Ss to go through the rest of the text and circle the dependent preposition that follows each underlined verb. Check answers with the whole class.

Answers: suffer from, think about, smile at, believe in, stand for, belong to, concentrate on, deal with

Vocabulary checkpoint

Ss often struggle with dependent prepositions as they seem to vary randomly and have little logic. Discuss with Ss how they can help themselves, for example by recording each new verb with its preposition as well as creating meaningful examples. Point out that translating the verb alone does not help with being able to use it accurately in a sentence. Elicit that the prepositions in the text can be followed by nouns or *-ing* verb forms.

Check that Ss are clear that these verbs + dependent prepositions are different from phrasal verbs. With phrasal verbs, often the meaning of the verb changes (for example, *look up* a word in the dictionary). A dependent preposition does not affect the meaning of the preceding verb. It's just a grammatical link to the verb's object.

5 Refer Ss to the exercise to underline the correct prepositions. Complete the first example together, then ask them to continue alone before checking in pairs. Go through the answers, asking individual Ss to read each sentence aloud so that you can drill as needed. Point out that the verb is usually stressed and the preposition is not, which is why Ss often fail to hear it.

Answers: 1 about 2 at 3 in 4 on 5 from 6 on 7 to 8 with 9 on

Optional extra activity

For further practice, ask Ss to make a list of more verbs that need a dependent preposition. They can work in pairs initially, then share as a class to make a list for everyone to copy into their notebooks. With **weaker classes**, you may need to provide some common examples, such as *consist of, decide on, depend on, pay for, wait for*. With **stronger classes** point out cases where the preposition varies according to the object: *play with a toy/for a team, complain about something/to someone*.

6 Look at the example conversation as a class. Tell Ss to choose around five comments or questions from the exercise and improvise a conversation. Monitor and help if necessary. When they finish, ask a few confident pairs to perform their conversations for the class.

VOCABULARY BANK 1A p156
Verbs with dependent prepositions

This is an optional extension to the vocabulary section, extending the lexical set and providing further practice. If you're short of time, this can be done for homework.

1a Ask Ss to match the correct prepositions in the box with the verbs. Ss check answers in pairs before whole class feedback.

Answers: a to b in c to d about e on f from g from h about i on j in k in l from m for

b Ask Ss to match the verbs from Ex 1a with their meanings. Go through answers as a class.

Answers: 1 differ from 2 believe in 3 involve someone in 4 suffer from 5 belong to 6 specialise in 7 depend on 8 enquire about 9 insist on 10 volunteer for 11 appeal to 12 boast about 13 discourage someone from

2a Ask Ss to use the verbs from Ex 1a to complete the questions. Point out that the preposition is already provided. Ss check answers in pairs before whole-class feedback.

Answers: 1 differ 2 appeals 3 involved 4 depend 5 enquire 6 volunteered 7 discourage 8 insist 9 boast

b Ask Ss to ask and answer questions from Ex 2a in pairs. When they finish, have brief feedback on any interesting points.

Further practice

Photocopiable activities: 1A Vocabulary, p169
App: 1A Vocabulary practice 1 and 2

Grammar

Question forms

7a Focus attention on the article in Ex 2a and its ending on p166, explaining that Ss should underline any questions in both parts of the article. Ask Ss to help each other before eliciting examples as a class.

Answers: Don't believe me? … what have I got to lose?
'Where did you get your magic fairy?'
'What have I told you about talking to strangers?'
'What does ZTC stand for?' 'What?'
'I was just wondering what ZTC stands for.'
'Why don't you ask my brother?' 'Too much sugar?'
'What about you?' 'Who are you going to give them to?'
'So, who gave you those flowers?'

b Point out the four types of question in the grammar box. Write the number of each category on the board, then ask Ss to select an example for each category from their underlined questions. With **weaker classes**, do this together as a class.

Answers:
1 What have I got to lose?
  Where did you get your magic fairy?
  What have I told you about talking to strangers?
2 Who are you going to give them to?
  What does ZTC stand for?
3 So, who gave you those flowers?
4 I was just wondering what ZTC stands for.

8 Ask Ss to work in pairs to ask and answer the grammar questions. Check answers with the whole class and be prepared to give further explanations or examples where necessary.

> Answers: **1** have **2** be **3** Ss' own answers
> **4** subject + verb + object (as in normal affirmative statements)

9a 🔊 1.1 Tell Ss they are going to listen to some conversations and they should decide whether the questions are for a friend or a stranger, and to think about the factors that led them to each decision. Once you have played the recording, elicit answers, discussing whether the questions are for friends or strangers and how we know.

> Answers:
> 1 Could you tell me what the time is?
> 2 What are you reading?
> 3 I was just wondering where you bought that.
> 4 Why did you buy that?
> 5 Do you know where the entrance is?

Questions for strangers (1, 3 and 5):
tend to use indirect question phrases
tend to start at a higher pitch
tend to use more exaggerated intonation
Questions for people you know (2 and 4):
tend to use direct questions
tend to start at a lower pitch (unless expressing surprise or other strong emotions) and use less exaggerated intonation.

Audioscript 1.1

1
A: Could you tell me what the time is?
B: Yes, it's half past one.
A: Great. Thanks.

2
A: What are you reading?
B: An article about how to make friends.
A: Sounds interesting!

3
A: Excuse me. I was just wondering where you bought that.
B: This sandwich? Just down the road at the café.
A: OK. Thanks.

4
A: Why did you buy that?
B: This hat? I thought it looked good.
A: Oh. It's … different.

5
A: Do you know where the entrance is?
B: Yes, it's just over there.
A: Thanks a lot.

b Ask Ss to listen again and repeat each question. Share the information in the Pronunciation checkpoint if you think it's useful.

Pronunciation checkpoint
When we are being polite, we tend to use a wider pitch range and start and end at a higher pitch. This attracts and engages the person we are speaking to and is also a feature of speech when we talk to young children. When we are with friends or family, we don't need to make so much effort and our pitch can be flatter. Knowing this helps Ss with their listening and exaggerating their range by copying a recording or their teacher is a useful awareness-raising exercise.

10a This exercise assesses how accurately Ss can make the question types seen in the grammar box. Write the first sentence starter on the board with the word in brackets and elicit the completion (*you where you bought them*). Discuss why this answer is correct (it follows the word order of an indirect question). Ask Ss to continue completing the sentences alone then check in pairs, referring to the grammar box. Check answers with the whole class and accept reasonable variations. Remind Ss to stress the key words and drill a few examples to consolidate if necessary.

> Answers:
> 1 Can I ask (you) where you bought them? (indirect question)
> 2 I wonder who it belongs to? (indirect question)
> 3 Who cut it (for you)? (subject question)
> 4 Where did you go to school? (QASV)
> 5 What are you smiling about? (preposition question)
> 6 I'd love to know who designed it. (indirect question)
> 7 Which train are you waiting for? (preposition question)
> 8 Could I ask how long you've had yours / your phone? (indirect question)

b This is an opportunity to personalise the language. Ask Ss to try and include all four question types from the grammar box in their set of questions. With **weaker classes**, complete one example of each question type as a class. As they work, monitor and correct. There is no need for whole-class feedback as all their questions will be different, but you can elicit some good examples and deal with queries. When they finish, ask Ss to move around the class asking each other their questions.

LANGUAGE BANK 1A   pp.136–137
Stronger classes could read the notes at home. Otherwise, go over the notes with Ss. In each exercise, elicit the first answer as an example. Ss work alone to complete the exercises, then check their answers in pairs. In feedback, check answers with the whole class. Ss can refer to the notes to help them.

> Answers:
> 1 a Have you known the Swanns for a long time?
>   b Can I ask you what you think about the sports centre?
>   c What kind of after-school activities does it offer?
>   d What made you decide to join it?
>   e Which school does your daughter go to?
>   f Could you tell me if the Black Horse restaurant is near here?
> 2 1f 2a 3b 4d 5e 6c

Further practice
Photocopiable activities: 1A Grammar 1, p167; 1A Grammar 2, p168
App: 1A Grammar practice 1 and 2

Speaking

Prepare

11 Ask a student to read the instruction to the class or read it yourself. Tell Ss to work in pairs to write the conversation starters. Monitor and help. Allow a few minutes for this. There is no need for feedback, but stop when all Ss have written at least two conversation starters.

Speak

12 Point out the Useful phrases. Put Ss in groups of three and allocate role A, B or C to each. With **weaker classes**, get a stronger group to demonstrate the activity, then ask all groups to start. Monitor and make notes on good language or language for correction. When they finish, write some examples of good language and errors for Ss to correct on the board, focusing particularly on question formation.

Optional extra activity

If you have time, repeat the activity twice more, changing roles each time so that each student gets the chance to do each role.

Reflection on learning

Write the following questions on the board:
How confident did you feel forming all the question types?
In what situations do you think you'll use these questions in the future?
Put Ss in pairs to discuss the questions. When they have finished, ask if anyone wants to share their ideas with the class, but don't force them to if they'd rather not.

Homework ideas

If you are in an English-speaking country and you feel it's appropriate, give Ss a speaking homework: to start a conversation with a stranger in a public place.
Language bank: 1A Ex 1–2, pp.136–137
Workbook: Ex 1–5, p4
App: grammar, vocabulary and pronunciation practice

Fast route: continue to Lesson 1B
Extended route: go to p86 for Develop your listening

1B Life lessons

Introduction

The goal of this lesson is for students to describe an experience and a life lesson. To help them achieve this, they will learn phrases to describe emotions and revise a range of past verb forms in the context of experiences.

Warm-up

Before the class starts, ask Ss in pairs to discuss where they go for advice: family, friends, social media, teachers, etc. Ask Ss to consider whether they go to different people/places for different kinds of advice (for example, for work, relationships, health or money). While they are working, monitor and help with vocabulary. When they finish, elicit feedback and see which people or places are the most popular for advice. Write useful vocabulary on the board.

Listening and vocabulary

Emotions

1 Put Ss in pairs and give them a few minutes to discuss the question. When they finish, elicit answers.

Teaching tip

Ss are not always ready to discuss their personal feelings. At the start of a lesson, they can also feel a bit rusty and uncomfortable speaking in English and may find it difficult to get started. To help them, give a simple example yourself, which is not too personal. This gives them an idea of what to expect and a model of how to express it. Most Ss also like to hear what their teacher has to say.

2 Focus attention on the quotes, asking Ss in pairs to discuss the questions. Complete the first together as an example. When they finish, elicit answers and discuss as a class, clarifying any vocabulary as necessary.

Possible answer:
3 b and **e** possibly contradict **d** because **b** and **e** don't appear to allow for anything but the best outcome, whereas **d** allows – if not encourages – failure along the way.

3 ◆ 1.4 Tell Ss they're going to listen to four people talking about an experience where they learnt something. They should listen and match each person to a life lesson from Ex 2. **Stronger classes** can make notes while listening, then discuss in pairs and decide which life lesson links to each speaker. **Weaker classes** can look at the life lessons and mark them 1–4 as they listen. Check answers with the whole class.

Answers: 1 c 2 d 3 a 4 f

Audioscript 1.4

1
A few years ago, I was going out with this guy and he was like ... perfect, you know, or so I thought at the time. Cute, funny, clever. We used to hang out together all the time. I was like totally in love, I mean head-over-heels. We'd spend every moment together, you know, we were inseparable. So anyway, one day, I was eating a sandwich at work, having my lunch break, and I got this text from him and he said he was breaking up with me. Just like that! Totally out of the blue, you know. It was completely devastating, and like, what was worse, I didn't have anyone

to turn to. I'd completely lost touch with all my friends just to be with this guy. For a couple of days I felt totally numb but then I went and found my old friends. They were still hanging out in the same place, and I cried, like, I just bawled my eyes out and they were great, I mean really great. I learnt my lesson, you know? I'm not doing that again.

2
A couple of years ago I was preparing for this engineering exam – The Undergraduate Aptitude Test in Engineering. I was studying hard, you know, I'd get up, have breakfast, go to the library, then I wouldn't come home till eight or nine at night. I really needed to pass. There was a lot of expectation, a lot of pressure on me and I needed a good mark to get a place at university. … So, I took the exam and I felt reasonably confident and on the day of the results I checked the website, you know, my hands were shaking, and guess what? I'd failed. Completely failed. No place at university, no future in engineering. I felt so ashamed. … For days, I didn't know what to do. I didn't tell my parents. I didn't eat, I didn't sleep, I was quite literally in shock. I just kept crying. … Three or four days I carried on like that and then finally, my friend asked me a question. She said, 'Do you really want to be an engineer?' I was so surprised because no one had ever asked me that, but I realised that yes, I really did want to be an engineer. So I took a year out, got a job and studied really hard for the exam all over again. And when I took the exam a second time, … I passed! I think I was really determined not to fail again.

3
This sounds really unimpressive as a story but for some reason it changed my life. So, … one day in secondary school, it was raining and we were sitting in the classroom waiting for our English lesson to start. And, you know, I wasn't a great student. I mean, I wouldn't really misbehave or anything but I used to spend most of my time daydreaming. Anyway, the teacher walked in and switched off the lights, which was odd, and he said, 'Today I just want you to listen to the rain. So, at first we were playing around, making jokes, but after a while we all kind of calmed down and the only noise was the sound of rain. Just the rain. 'Don't think,' he said, 'just listen'. And the rain kept falling and we kept listening … and after 40 minutes or so, by the end of the lesson, I felt completely calm – just completely … present … in the moment, and I just wanted to express myself, you know, to write. It had a big, big impact on me and ever since then, I've written every day in my journal. Before that, I never used to have any ambitions but, since then, … yeah, that lesson, you know, it really inspired me to become a writer.

4
I always felt that I never measured up to my older brother. I used to think that he was better than me. He was the high achiever while I was just average. He would get the high marks at school while I would just get the average marks. He was always studying while I was just hanging out with friends. This thought followed me all through my 20s. … Then one day, I got a new job, a good job and I was so happy, I simply couldn't believe my luck, and my brother said, 'It's not luck. You've always been the smart one.' And I said, 'What? What are you talking about?' And he said, 'You've always known how to be happy and get what you want. I've always had to work hard, but you sail through life!' And this completely blew my mind, you know, I realised what a total fool I'd been to always think that I was inferior to my brother.

4a Ask Ss to look at the words in the box and discuss any they are not sure of. Ask Ss to complete each sentence with a word in the box, working alone, then in pairs and discussing what caused the feelings.

b Ask Ss to listen again and check their answers. In feedback, confirm answers with the whole class. Ss may or may not remember what caused the feelings. Drill phrases chorally.

Answers: 1 devastating 2 felt 3 out 4 ashamed 5 in 6 big 7 me 8 luck 9 blew 10 fool

Vocabulary checkpoint
At this level, Ss should have awareness of lexical 'chunks', where a fixed or semi-fixed phrase is made up of a group of two or more words and should be memorised as a single unit of language. In feedback, help learners to notice chunks by underlining the key unchangeable elements and noticing which parts can change. For example:
3 *bawl my/your eyes out*: The verb *bawl* is rarely seen outside this phrase.
5 *I was in shock* is fixed, but *quite literally* can be added for emphasis.
9 *blew my mind* is unchangeable, but *completely* can be replaced with *totally, just, absolutely*, etc.

Optional extra activity
For further practice, ask Ss to work in pairs. Student A says a key word from each phrase and Student B should then try and say the whole phrase, for example:
A: bawl   **B:** I bawled my eyes out.
A: luck   **B:** I couldn't believe my luck.

5 This activity asks Ss to comment on and respond to the content they have listened to in Ex 3. Ask Ss to discuss in pairs, then share ideas as a class. There are no fixed answers.

Optional extra activity
Ask Ss to sit in small groups and retell one of the four experiences, aiming to include the phrases focused on. **Weaker classes** can look at the vocabulary when retelling, to act as prompts. **Stronger classes** can try without. **Fast finishers** can retell more than one experience.

Further practice
Photocopiable activities: 1B Vocabulary, p172
App: 1B Vocabulary practice 1 and 2

Grammar

Past simple, past continuous, *used to*, *would*, *keep* + *-ing*

6 Ask Ss to tell you when the experiences in the recordings happened, present or past. Elicit 'past' and tell Ss you're now going to look at the verb forms used. Focus attention on the words in the box, then ask Ss to use them to complete the grammar box. Check answers with the whole class, giving further explanations or examples where necessary. With **weaker classes**, do this activity as a class. Go over the question and negative forms, especially with *used to* where the spelling changes to *use to*.

Answers: 1 complete 2 main 3 background 4 continuous 5 many times 6 longer

7 This exercise checks if Ss have absorbed the rules covered in the grammar box. Write the first pair of sentences on the board, asking Ss to decide individually which is correct and then discuss in pairs. If Ss show any doubt, refer them to the grammar box before moving on. Ss choose the correct sentences alone, then check in pairs. Monitor to see how they are doing. Check answers with the whole class by asking individuals to read the correct sentence aloud, then discussing the reason for their decision.

Answers:
1a *Hate* is a state verb and they are not generally used in the continuous. The second sentence is possible, but the first is more likely.
2a Both are completed actions, so they need the past simple. Past continuous implies she didn't finish making the sandwich which is illogical because she ate it!
3b The subject and auxiliary are unnecessarily repeated. This is a stylistic issue.
4a *Would* is not used for state verbs like *adore*. *Would* is used for repeated actions.
5b The thinking was repeated while the speaker was awake, so *kept + -ing* is more appropriate.

Grammar checkpoint
Discuss with Ss why we need to have a range of past forms. Up to now, Ss have probably managed with using mainly the past simple. Point out that to fully express themselves and to clarify the timing and frequency of events they need to use a range of past forms. Let Ss know that you will give extra credit to them if they try to use a range of past forms in their written work.

8a 1.5 Ask Ss to look at the sentences and the underlined verbs, which are negative. Ask them to listen and notice how *n't* is pronounced. When they finish listening, discuss as a class.

Answers:
When the verb/word immediately after starts with a consonant sound, we tend not to pronounce the *t* of the *n't*:
I wasn't working, I didn't really …
When the verb/word immediately after starts with a vowel sound, we may or may not pronounce the *t* of the *n't*. If we do pronounce it, we link it to the first syllable of the next word:
*I wasn' tin*terested

b 1.6 Ask Ss to listen to the recording again and repeat.

9 This exercise checks if Ss have absorbed the rules when seen in context. Complete the first example as a class, then ask Ss to decide individually which alternatives are correct and then discuss in pairs. Go through the answers as a class, writing them on the board to ensure that Ss record the correct ones.

Answers: 1 didn't use to worry 2 was playing
3 started 4 wanted 5 would never ask
6 really thought 7 was sitting 8 chatting 9 came
10 wondered 11 decided 12 said 13 realised

Optional extra activity
Ss work in pairs and take turns to read the complete, corrected text to each other, focusing on pronunciation. Some Ss enjoy this form of self-drilling. Monitor and give feedback on, for example, their pronunciation of regular past tense endings such as *realised* or *started*, or weak forms of *was* and *were* in past continuous.

10 Tell Ss they now have a chance to personalise their practice. Give them a few minutes to think and make a few notes, then put them in pairs to discuss. Monitor and help if necessary. When they finish, ask a few pairs to share interesting stories they heard, then pick up on any errors during feedback.

LANGUAGE BANK 1B pp.136–137
Stronger classes could read the notes at home. Otherwise, go over the notes with Ss. In each exercise, elicit the first answer as an example. Ss work alone to complete the exercises, then check their answers in pairs. In feedback, check answers with the whole class. Ss can refer to the notes to help them.

Answers:
1 1 joined 2 was studying 3 had/used to have
4 knew 5 kept interrupting 6 used to/would discuss
7 came across 8 was sitting 9 looking 10 didn't tell
2 1 When my brother and I were younger, we didn't use̶d̶ to go anywhere without each other.
2 We were horrified to see that the ferry le̶ft̶ *was leaving* the port as we arrived.
3 When I was little I w̶a̶s̶ ̶u̶s̶e̶d̶ ̶t̶o̶ ̶h̶a̶v̶i̶n̶g̶ *used to have/had* almost golden hair, but it turned to a mousey brown before I was ten.
4 There was a man in the dentist's waiting room who kept tap*ping* his foot. It was so annoying!
5 I shared a bedroom with my older sister until she w̶a̶s̶ l̶e̶a̶v̶i̶n̶g̶ *left* home.
6 Where we live, we don't usually have snow, but one winter I u̶s̶e̶d̶ ̶t̶o̶ ̶s̶t̶a̶y̶ *stayed* with my cousins in Canada, where we had snow all the time.
7 ✓
8 The actor was just standing silently on the stage, wait*ing* for the people in the audience to stop talking.

Further practice
Photocopiable activities: 1B Grammar 1, p170; 1B Grammar 2, p171
App: 1B Grammar practice 1 and 2

Speaking
Prepare
11a Remind Ss of the topic of life lessons and read the example together. Give Ss time to think of their life lesson before writing it down and sharing it with a partner.

Optional alternative activity
If your class is very young and they lack life experience, they may struggle to come up with life lessons. Discuss this when setting up the activity. Point out that the example given could be a young person and that they could think about everyday situations, such as their study habits or relationships with siblings or friends. If they really can't think of anything, they can use the experiences that they heard earlier or talk about a famous person who has made a public mistake and learnt from it.

b Read the instruction as a class. Give Ss plenty of time to think and make notes about their experience, using the bullet points to organise their thoughts. Point out that this is a chance to practise some of the language studied in this lesson. Monitor and help with ideas and language.

Speak
12a Ask Ss to read through the Useful phrases, then put them in small groups to tell each other. Encourage them to ask follow-up questions. Monitor and listen to their control of the verb forms and phrases studied.

b Ask Ss to reflect and comment on what they have learnt from each other.

Unit 1

Teaching tip
Observe Ss during fluency activities and make notes on their language use. Look for common problem areas in vocabulary or grammar. When Ss finish, decide which errors to focus on and add them to the board one by one for Ss to try and correct. If there is a pronunciation problem, write the phrase/word and ask Ss to say it, then model it yourself so they can hear the difference. Try and include examples of positive language use in your feedback as well, so Ss don't feel disheartened.

Reflection on learning
Write the following questions on the board:
How confident do you feel about describing experiences and emotions?
How do you plan to remember the vocabulary from this lesson?
Put Ss in pairs to discuss the questions. When they have finished, ask if anyone wants to share their ideas with the class, but don't force them to if they'd rather not.

Homework ideas
Ss write a paragraph about the life lesson they talked about in Ex 12a.
Language bank: 1B Ex 1–2, pp.136–137
Workbook: Ex 1–5, p5
App: grammar, vocabulary and pronunciation practice

Fast route: continue to Lesson 1C
Extended route: go to p116 for Develop your writing

1C Personalities

Introduction
The goal of this lesson is for students to interview someone about their personality. To help them achieve this, they will revise verb + noun collocations and adjectives in the context of describing character.

Warm-up
Ask Ss to work in pairs to make two lists of character adjectives, positive and negative. In feedback, see how many they have and elicit some ideas. Tell them that this is the topic of today's lesson. With **weaker classes**, leave the suggestions on the board so Ss can use them during the lesson. Put Ss in pairs and ask them to describe themselves and explain their reasons. Give an example yourself to show what they need to do, for example: *I'm quite anxious. When I'm travelling I have to leave very early in case there's a problem getting to the airport. Then I spend ages waiting around!* When they finish, ask Ss if they are similar to their partner or if they learnt anything surprising.

Vocabulary and listening

Adjectives of character

1 Refer to the photos and discuss the first question as a class. Then ask Ss to write two or three personality adjectives for each person in the photos. Put Ss in pairs to compare ideas and discuss the other questions, then have a whole-class discussion to see if Ss agree.

Suggested answers:
2 A adventurous, brave, confident, excited, exhilarated
B confident, successful
C suspicious, threatening
D hard-working, calm, organised, confident, successful
E nervous, excited

2a Focus attention on the beginning of the article. Ask Ss to suggest personality adjectives starting with the letters C, E, A and N and write the words on the board.

b 🔊 1.7 Ask Ss to listen and note the adjectives. Ss then compare in pairs before whole-class feedback. See if any of their predictions were correct.

Answers: C = conscientious   E = extrovert   A = agreeable
N = neurotic

Audioscript 1.7

The 'O' of the first character trait is being 'open to experiences'. People who are open to experiences like trying new things and tend to be adventurous, while people who are less open prefer familiar people and events and tend to be more cautious.

The second character trait is conscientiousness. People who are conscientious take a lot of care when they do things and like to do them very well. For example, when a conscientious person writes an essay, they make sure they don't have any spelling mistakes. Conscientious people tend to be very organised, but sometimes it can be difficult to change their minds. Less conscientious people are more flexible but can also be careless sometimes.

The third character trait is extroversion. Extrovert people like meeting new people. They enjoy going out and socialising. People who are extrovert tend to be outgoing, while people who are less extrovert tend to be more reserved and don't like socialising so much.

The fourth character trait is agreeableness. People who are more agreeable tend to like helping others. They are more trusting and think that other people are basically good. Less agreeable people are more suspicious. They tend to care less about what other people think and often believe that other people are selfish.

The 'N' of the final character trait is for neurotic. Neurotic people have strong and difficult emotions. They tend to be nervous and can get depressed easily. Less neurotic people are more emotionally stable and confident.

Everyone can be placed somewhere on these five scales and once you know where each person is, you get an idea of their personality. For example, you will know if someone is a bit of a rebel who likes to take risks and break the rules, or more of a conformist who prefers to stick to the rules and minimise risks. So, what kind of person are you?

3a Refer Ss to the adjectives in the box. Ask them to listen again and note down the adjectives at the correct points on the scales. Ss compare in pairs before whole-class feedback. Discuss the meaning of words they are unsure of and work on pronunciation, including word stress, drilling chorally and individually.

Answers:
1 adventurous, cautious
2 organised, careless
3 outgoing, reserved
4 trusting, suspicious
5 nervous, confident

Teaching tip
The scale task in Ex 3a helps with meaning. If Ss like this, introduce them to other visual ways of linking up vocabulary such as vocabulary spidergrams or mindmaps. Drawing and using graphs or grids are all visual ways of showing vocabulary. Encourage Ss to look through their books and organise vocabulary in different ways.

Pronunciation checkpoint
In order to be confident using new vocabulary, Ss need to be able to pronounce new words with the correct stress. Go over longer words in particular, eliciting the stressed syllable and marking the stress on the board. Point out unusual sounds that do not reflect the spelling. For example: *conscientious* /kɒnʃiˈenʃəs/, *cautious* /ˈkɔːʃəs/.

b Put Ss in pairs to discuss. Monitor and help if necessary. When they finish, give feedback on pronunciation of new words.

Optional extra activity
Ss write down three people who know them well, such as a parent, sibling, friend or employer. They then write three character adjectives beside each person. The adjectives should describe what each person is likely to think of the student who writes them down. For example, an employer might think you are conscientious, but a parent might think you are lazy! Ss read each set of adjectives to their partner who must guess who thinks their partner is like this. This could be a good option for **stronger classes** or classes that need extra speaking practice.

VOCABULARY BANK 1C p156
Adjectives of character
This is an optional extension to the vocabulary section, extending the lexical set and providing further practice. If you're short of time, this can be done for homework.
1 Ask Ss to complete the table with the adjectives in the box. They can use guesswork, or their devices or dictionaries, depending how much time you have. Ss check answers in pairs before whole-class feedback. Drill the vocabulary.

Answers:

	similar meaning	opposite meaning
brilliant	*intellectual*	*foolish*
content	*cheerful*	*miserable*
decent	*respectable*	*dishonest*
optimistic	*positive*	*pessimistic*
organised	*efficient*	*disorganised*
thoughtful	*caring*	*thoughtless*

2 Ask Ss to use vocabulary from Ex 1 to describe the people. Remind them that there is sometimes more than one possible answer. Ss check answers in pairs before whole-class feedback.

Answers: **1** decent, respectable **2** disorganised
3 optimistic, positive **4** foolish **5** miserable
6 thoughtful, caring

3 Ss work in pairs to describe people they know. If you have plenty of time, they can write a paragraph about someone they know.

Further practice
Photocopiable activities: 1C Vocabulary, p175
App: 1C Vocabulary practice 1 and 2

Language focus
Verb + noun collocations
4a Refer Ss to the quiz. Ask them to work in pairs to discuss any words and phrases they are unsure of. After a few minutes, have a whole-class discussion to clarify any vocabulary.
b Ask Ss to take turns asking and answering the quiz questions. At the end of the quiz, Ss should turn to p166 to read their results.
c When they finish the quiz, ask Ss to discuss in their pairs if they agree with the quiz results, then discuss as a class.
5 Ss will probably have noticed numerous collocations in the quiz. Refer them to the explanation of collocations in the Language focus box, then ask them to complete the collocations using the quiz. Go through the answers as a class. With **stronger classes**, ask Ss to suggest other verbs that can collocate with the nouns, for example: *change* your mind, *make up* your mind.

Answers: **1** speak **2** meet **3** wait **4** lose **5** keep
6 make **7** break **8** voice **9** take **10** resolve **11** take
12 remain **13** take **14** make **15** return **16** make

Optional extra activity
Ss work in pairs. One says the noun or noun phrase and their partner tries to remember the collocating verb without looking at their book. They change roles after a few turns.

6a Ask Ss to complete the sayings with an appropriate form of a collocation from Ex 5. Ss work alone, then discuss answers together. In feedback, check answers with the whole class and discuss the meaning of the sayings.

Answers: **1** speak **2** Meeting **3** lose, lose **4** voice
5 keep, keep **6** remain **7** resolve

b 🔊 1.8 Ask Ss to underline the words given, then listen to the sayings. Ask Ss to discuss how the words are pronounced and see if they can tell you why. Share the information in the Pronunciation checkpoint if you think the Ss will find it useful.

Answers: *Your*, *the* and *a* are unstressed so the vowel sound becomes /ə/.

Pronunciation checkpoint
Ss should be aware of sentence stress, where the key information-carrying words are louder and longer. The unstressed words are shorter and often reduced to a weak form including the schwa sound /ə/. Articles are most often pronounced in this way, so point out that this is why some Ss sometimes miss them out – they can't hear them easily.

c Play the recording again sentence by sentence, asking Ss to repeat chorally and individually.
7 Ask Ss to work in pairs to discuss which sayings they agree with and why. When they finish, have whole-class feedback to see which are the most popular.

LANGUAGE BANK 1C pp.136–137

Stronger classes could read the notes at home. Otherwise, go over the notes with Ss. In each exercise, elicit the first answer as an example. Ss work alone to complete the exercises, then check their answers in pairs. In feedback, check answers with the whole class. Ss can refer to the notes to help them.

Answers:
1 1 make time   2 take notes (also: make notes)
   3 take part in   4 remain calm   5 make sense
   6 making mistakes   7 follow the rules
   8 taking the exams   9 meet deadlines   10 take charge
   11 make the most of   12 great success

Further practice

Photocopiable activities: 1C Language focus 1, p173; 1C Language focus 2, p174
App: 1C Language focus practice 1 and 2

Speaking

Prepare

8a 1.9 Tell Ss they are going to listen to part of a student interview using a questionnaire and they should underline the correct word to complete the title. When they have listened, elicit the answer.

Answer: extrovert

Audioscript 1.9

Emily: OK, Rudi, question nine. Do you make time to see your friends most days of the week?
Rudi: Um, no, not really.
Emily: Why not?
Rudi: Well … I like my own company. I don't want to meet up with friends every day, that's too tiring.
Emily: OK, good answer, Rudi. And question ten …
Rudi: Is that the final question, Emily?
Emily: Yes, final question, here it is – and I think I know the answer already: do you find it difficult to remain calm during a discussion?
Rudi: Um, no, not at all. I find it quite easy.
Emily: OK. Why?
Rudi: Well, I prefer listening to talking. If everyone is talking, then no one is listening and that's a bit stressful.
Emily: All right, that's your ten questions, Rudi, and eight of your answers were 'no', so I think that makes you more reserved than outgoing. Do you think that's right?
Rudi: Yes, I think so, although I'm not always reserved.
Emily: No, not always, I understand that, but in general you're more reserved than outgoing.
Rudi: Yes, I think that's right. OK, now my questions for you, Emily. Question one, how …

b Ask Ss to read the questions before they listen again and tell them to note the answers as they listen. With **weaker classes**, you may want to listen a third time. After they listen, put Ss in pairs to compare, then elicit the answers from the class.

Answers:
1 ten
2 that he's more reserved than outgoing
3 yes, fairly accurate

9 Tell Ss they are now going to write their own questionnaire. Ask them to choose one of the personality traits from Ex 3a and write ten questions. Read through the guidance points together. Give them a few minutes to decide what to focus on and start to make notes. It's important that they write yes/no questions. Monitor and help where necessary.

Optional alternative activity

Some Ss may benefit from preparing in pairs, particularly **weaker classes** or groups that need more speaking practice. They can share ideas and discuss. Both Ss need to write down all the questions, however, for the speaking stage that follows. Re-pair Ss for the speaking stage so that they can answer new questions. **Weaker pairs** can write fewer questions.

Speak

10a Put Ss in pairs to ask their questions, taking turns to speak. Monitor and encourage pairs to give a follow-up assessment of their partner, according to their answers.

b Ask Ss to pair with another student and repeat the questionnaire. **Fast finishers** can repeat more than once with different partners.

Reflection on learning

Write the following questions on the board:
How easy did you find it to write and ask the questionnaire?
In what situations do you think you could use this language in the future?
Put Ss in pairs to discuss the questions. When they have finished, ask if anyone wants to share their ideas with the class, but don't force them to if they'd rather not.

Homework ideas

Ex 10a: Ask Ss to practise their questionnaire on an English speaker outside the class.
Language bank: 1C Ex 1, pp.136–137
Workbook: Ex 1–5, p6
App: grammar, vocabulary and pronunciation practice

Fast route: continue to Lesson 1D
Extended route: go to p96 for Develop your reading

1D English in action

Introduction

The goal of this lesson is for students to contribute effectively to a conversation or discussion. To help them achieve this, they will revise verbs to describe a healthy lifestyle.

Warm-up

Ask Ss to pair up and discuss what they consider to be the main factors in a healthy lifestyle, for example: diet, exercise, sleep, socialising. After a few minutes, lead whole-class feedback to see if Ss agree and add relevant vocabulary to the board.

Vocabulary

Verbs to describe a healthy lifestyle

1 Refer to the pictures and ensure Ss know what they are. Ask pairs to discuss the questions. When they finish, have a whole-class discussion, talking about each item in turn. There are no fixed answers.

> **Optional extra activity**
>
> Describing the purpose of each item previews the language that is focused on in the next task. With **weaker classes**, use feedback time during Ex 1 to feed in some of the language from Ex 2a and write it on the board, so that when they come to it, they are prepared.

2a Read the example together. Point out that some of the sentences could apply to more than one picture. Put them in pairs to discuss, labelling each sentence with letters A–H. Monitor and help with any vocabulary where necessary. When they finish, ask pairs to share their ideas with the class. Drill new vocabulary that they struggle with.

Suggested answers:
1 B, D, E, H   2 B   3 E   4 F, G   5 A, C   6 D   7 G   8 F, G

b Look at the example question together. Drill the question, then ask Ss to suggest another one in the same format. Demonstrate the exchange with a **stronger student**, then put Ss in pairs to continue. Monitor and help if necessary. When Ss finish, ask a few pairs to ask and answer in front of the class.

Listening 1

3a 🔊 1.10 Explain that Ss are going to listen to a discussion about diet and exercise. Tell them to look at the pictures and tick the ones that are mentioned. Check answers as a class.

Answers: vending machine, fitness app

Audioscript 1.10

A: … so a friend of mine at work is training to do a marathon, so she's kind of inspired me, you know, to get healthy again.
B: Sounds like a good idea.
A: I know, right? None of us are getting any younger, are we? We can't keep eating chocolate every day and expect to stay healthy!
C: You've got a point. But you'll never guess what they've done at my work.
A: What?
C: They've replaced all the chocolate and sugary snacks in the vending machines with fruit and water.
A: What, all of it?
C: Yep, the whole lot. You can't get a sugary snack anywhere now. It's ridiculous. They're treating us like children.
B: I'm not really with you on that one. They're not saying you can't have sweet snacks. They're just saying that they're not going to sell them to you.
C: Yeah, but come on. We've had chocolate in the vending machines for years.
B: Times change, I guess. It's not the same as it was in the past.
A: How did you come to that conclusion?
B: Well, I think now companies have a duty to look after their staff …
A: That's a good point. Maybe they have a duty to look after their clients, too, when they visit your workplace.
C: Yeah …
B: That reminds me of a story I read in the paper last week. A bank somewhere has started giving its customers a higher interest rate if they do more exercise.
A: You're not serious!
B: I *am* serious. The more exercise you do, the more interest you earn. I think you have to walk three kilometres a day to earn their highest interest rate.
C: I bet that's difficult to measure.
B: I don't think so. When you open an account, you get a free fitness app and the app counts your steps every day. You don't have to do more exercise, but it definitely encourages you to.
C: In my experience that kind of thing never works.
B: What makes you say that?
C: Well it just feels like they're punishing you for not doing enough exercise. I mean, I have a busy life, you know. I don't have time to walk three kilometres a day.
B: You might be right I guess. But then again, you could look at it another way. You could see it as a reward for doing exercise rather than a punishment for not doing it.
C: Well, it certainly doesn't seem like that to me …
A: Yeah, that's an interesting thought actually. I like the idea. The advantage is that you …

b Tell Ss they are going to listen again for more detail. Give them time to read the questions before listening and making notes. Ask Ss to compare in pairs after they listen, then go through the answers as a class.

Answers:
1 He's been inspired by a friend at work who's training to do a marathon.
2 She's not happy. She thinks it's ridiculous.
3 Companies have a duty to look after their staff.
4 by giving them a higher rate of interest if they exercise more
5 She's too busy to walk three km a day.
6 as a reward rather than a punishment

4 Ask Ss to complete the Useful phrases alone, using the words in the box. They should be able to do this without listening again. Go through the answers as a class. With **weaker classes**, drill the sentences.

Answers: 1 point   2 with   3 conclusion   4 bet
5 experience   6 look

5 Ask Ss to complete the conversations with phrases from the Useful phrases box. Ss can compare in pairs, then go through the answers.

Answers: 1 be right   2 that conclusion   3 an interesting
4 to me once

> **Optional extra activity**
>
> Nominate Ss to read the conversations across the class. Drill as needed.

Listening 2

6a 🔊 1.11 Tell Ss they will now listen to more of the discussion. Ask them to read through the sentences and mark them T or F as they listen. Put them in pairs to check answers and correct the false sentences. Go through the answers as a class.

Answers:
1 T
2 F Norway introduced a sugar tax in the 1920s.
3 T
4 F He thinks they weren't effective because everyone ignored them.
5 F In the end they agree that you shouldn't do this.

Audioscript 1.11

B: ... but if you really want to improve people's health, I mean, you know, improve everyone's health, then you've got to start with children. You've got to do something about *their* health first.
A: Yeah, but what? That's the question.
B: Well, you've got a few options. One is to make unhealthy food more expensive, you know, kind of punish people for eating unhealthy food.
A: Like the sugar tax?
B: Yeah, exactly, Mike.
C: What's the sugar tax?
B: Well, it's a tax or extra cost on anything containing sugar. There are a number of pros and cons to the idea and some countries have tried it.
C: Really?
B: Yep, Norway has had a sugar tax since the 1920s. The main advantage is that it's simple. The disadvantage, however, is that people don't agree how much it should be.
A: What are the other options?
C: Well, you could also promote healthy food in schools, Mike. You know, posters and lessons on sensible eating and things like that to encourage children to eat well.
B: Exactly. The benefit of that is that you aren't punishing people.
C: Yep, as you say, it's better to provide information than to punish.
A: Yeah, the drawback is that it's not very effective. I remember my school had posters about healthy eating and that kind of stuff and we didn't pay any attention at all!
C: I suppose ...
B: Yeah, but you have to take into account the fact that all those posters and advice might actually have had an effect. It's just that you didn't realise it.
A: True ... I think there are a number of other possibilities as well. For instance, you could reward people for eating well.
B: That's a bit like the bank that pays you a higher interest rate if you do more exercise!
A: Exactly.
C: I still don't believe that story.
B: It's true! I read it in the paper.
C: But how would that work for children in schools?
B: Well, for schools you could provide healthy snacks or lunches and give children higher marks if they eat that sort of food.
C: That's ridiculous!
B: Is it? On the plus side, it's very easy to understand. If you eat salad instead of sweets, you get a better grade.
A: On balance, I think it's best to avoid that kind of thing.
B: You mean rewarding children with better grades?
A: Yes, it just seems a bit extreme.
B: OK, you might be right, I guess.
C: Absolutely. Overall, I think it's best to leave it up to the parents what they feed their children. I mean think of the problems if someone ...

Vocabulary checkpoint
The term *pros and cons* may be new to Ss. The words are almost always seen together and come from the Latin words for 'for' and 'against'. Despite its Latin origin, the phrase is used in everyday speech. Point out that the phrase is a binomial, where two words are closely associated in a fixed order. Other examples are *fish and chips, black and white, bits and pieces, more or less, peace and quiet* and *neat and tidy*.

b Refer Ss to the gapped sentences and ask them to listen again and complete them. Put Ss in pairs to compare answers, then go through them as a class. Write the answers on the board to ensure Ss have the correct spelling.

Answers: 1 options 2 advantage 3 drawback
4 possibilities 5 balance 6 Overall

7 Point out the phrases in bold and ask Ss to add them to the correct section of the Useful phrases box. Complete the first one together, then ask Ss to continue in pairs. If time is short, ask Ss to write the phrase number or draw a line to the Useful phrases box. Go through the answers as a class.

Answers:
1 Well, you've got a few options. One is to (make unhealthy food more expensive).
2 I think there are a number of other possibilities (as well). For instance, (you could reward people for eating well).
3 The main advantage is that (it's simple).
4 The drawback is that (it's not very effective).
5 On balance, I think (it's best to avoid that kind of thing).
6 Overall, I think (it's best to leave it up to the parents).

8a Refer Ss to the conversations and ask them to write the responses in full in their notebooks, using the words in brackets. Explain that this is to practise getting the whole sentence correct. Monitor and prompt self-correction as they do this.

Teaching tip
When Ss are completing a written exercise, it's important to monitor and help them correct themselves early in the process. Ways to prompt self-correction of written tasks include: pointing with a pencil at the section with the error; or reminding Ss with a specific clue – *you need a verb here/there's a word missing*, etc. When Ss have finished, telling them how many are correct, or which they have made a mistake with, requires them to look back over their work and try and correct it.

b Ask Ss to check their answers with the Useful phrases box in pairs, then go through the answers as a class.

Answers:
1 ... the (main) disadvantage is that it's expensive.
2 I think there are a number of (other) possibilities.
3 On balance, I think it's a bad idea.
4 Don't forget we could ...
5 ... there are a number of pros and cons.
6 The drawback is that it isn't easy to understand.

9a 1.12 Read the instruction as a class. Ask Ss to listen and note how the consonant sounds and vowel sounds link.
b Play the recording again for Ss to listen and repeat the word linking, or model the sentences yourself.

10 1.13 Explain to Ss that they will need to choose which of the two underlined options in each sentence has the two linking words. You may need to play the recording more than once. Check the answers as a class.

Answers:
1 Another argument against it is that it's complicated.
2 You have to take into account the fact that it's expensive.
3 All in all, I think that it's a lot of money.
4 I think there are a number of possibilities.

Speaking

11a Put Ss in groups of three and name them A, B and C. Ask a strong trio to demonstrate how the activity works, with A choosing and saying a statement, B agreeing and C disagreeing. Point out that this activity is for Ss to practise the language of the lesson, so groups can refer to the two Useful phrases boxes if necessary. Then ask the threes to continue. Monitor and see how they manage.
b Ask Ss to switch roles so they get the chance to discuss a new statement and use different language. If you have time, change a further time so that all Ss try all roles. **Stronger classes** can try to discuss all six statements.

Teaching tip
Where activities have roles, it's worth setting up the task carefully. If your class doesn't split easily into groups of three, make one group of four. Or if you have a very large class, do the activity in groups of five. The roles B and C can be doubled up without impacting on the task. If you have **weaker Ss**, allocate role A to them first as it is the simplest.

Reflection on learning
Write the following questions on the board:
In what situations do you think you can use this language in the future?
Which of today's activities was most challenging for you? Why?
Put Ss in pairs to discuss the questions. When they have finished, ask if anyone wants to share their ideas with the class, but don't force them to if they'd rather not.

Homework ideas
Reflection on learning: Write your answers.
Workbook: Ex 1–4, p7
App: grammar, vocabulary and pronunciation practice

Roadmap video
Go online for the Roadmap video and worksheet.

1A Develop your listening

Introduction
The goal of this lesson is for students to understand common informal conversations. To help them achieve this, they will focus on recognising exaggeration.

Warm-up
Ask Ss to discuss what they usually talk about when they arrive at work or school, when they get home at the end of the day and when they go to a party. Introduce the term *small talk* (= polite conversation about unimportant or uncontroversial matters, especially between people who don't know each other well).

Culture notes
In the UK it's usual and polite to have small talk whilst mingling at a social event or sometimes in a public place like a waiting room or queue. Common topics are the weather, what people do for a living, what they did at the weekend, family/children, sports results and transport problems. Topics usually avoided are politics, religion and how much people earn.

1 Put Ss in pairs and ask them to discuss the questions. In feedback, make a list of topics and discuss any cultural or social variations they notice. There are no fixed answers.

Teaching tip
Some Ss may come up with phrases commonly used in their own language. Work as a class to translate these into natural English by using your own skills or an online translation tool. Point out that expressions can sometimes be translated directly but on other occasions the phrase does not sound natural, so the English equivalent needs to be found and learnt.

2 Put Ss in pairs to discuss the questions for a few minutes. You can then ask Ss what their partners had told them.

3 🔊 1.2 Ask Ss to listen to seven conversations and match each one with a conversation type from Ex 2a. Complete the first one together to ensure all Ss know what to do, then play the rest of the conversations, pausing after each one for Ss to compare answers. Go through the answers as a class.

Answers: 1 c   2 e   3 g   4 b   5 a   6 d   7 f

Audioscript 1.2

Conversation 1
A: Oh, I've had such a bad day!
B: Oh! Why?
A: First off, I was late for work. My train was cancelled and I had to wait for a bus and then it got stuck in traffic for hours … .
B: That's a bad start.
A: I know, right? So, I finally got to work and my boss called me into her office and asked why I was late, so I explained, and then she asked for the sales report. I'd completely forgotten about it! I was supposed to work on it yesterday but, you know, it just slipped my mind. So I said I'd get it for her and I dashed back to my desk, got hold of the figures and then I wrote the report in five seconds flat and then emailed it to her.
B: Did she realise you'd forgotten about it?
A: I think she must have guessed.

Conversation 2
C: Did you see that programme on TV last night?
D: There were millions of programmes on TV last night! Which one?
C: The comedy, you know, about the family …
D: Oh the family with five children?
C: Yes, that's the one.
D: Oh that! Yes, it was brilliant.
C: It was so funny, wasn't it? I nearly died laughing!
D: Me too. The main character is great.
C: Yeah, she's hilarious. The way she deals with her children …
D: I know. It cracked me up.

Conversation 3
E: Hi Mum! How's it going?
F: Oh, fine dear, thank you. How are you?
E: We're all fine. How's the weather there?
F: Terrible. It's freezing today. This cold snap is going to last the whole week.
E: Oh, poor you.
F: Yes. We're all suffering from winter blues. I guess it's lovely there in Sydney as always?
E: Actually, it's absolutely boiling. Everyone is down at the beach trying to keep cool.
F: Oh dear, sounds awful.
E: I know!

Conversation 4
G: Things all right?
H: Yeah, not bad. You know, I'm snowed under as always.
G: I know how you feel.
H: It's relentless, isn't it?
G: I've got a ton of emails to write.
H: Me too.
G: It's best not to think about it. Just get on with the job in hand.
H: That's right. Well, can't stand around chatting all day. Better get back to it!
G: Yep – catch you later.

35

Conversation 5
I: So, how was your weekend?
J: Oh, yeah, it was quite good, thanks.
I: Did you do anything special?
J: We went to that new sports centre near the university. Have you been? It's amazing.
I: No, I haven't.
J: It's got tennis courts and an indoor pool and everything.
I: Sounds very posh.
J: It costs a fortune to join, but if you just want to go on a Sunday, you can pay a one-off fee and use it for that day. Then it's quite reasonable.
I: I'll have to give it a go.
J: What about you. How was your weekend?
I: Oh, nothing special, really. I went to see a film on Saturday but I could barely concentrate on it. The girl next to me, her phone kept buzzing and pinging. I asked her nicely, but she wouldn't turn it off. I could have killed her!
J: That's so annoying!

Conversation 6
K: Have you seen what he's got on today?
L: Who?
K: You know who – my boss! The head of design.
L: No – what's he wearing?
K: Skinny jeans and trainers!
L: No! At his age? I bet you were dying to say something to him.
K: I just smiled at him and told him he looked very smart!
L: He thinks he's still a teenager.
K: He'll get an earring and a tattoo soon.
L: Don't! I'll just die of embarrassment if he does.
K: I just think you should dress sensibly for work, you know.
L: Exactly! What's wrong with a shirt and tie and a decent pair of shoes?

Conversation 7
M: I'm starving. Are you hungry?
O: Not yet.
M: I could really do with something to eat.
O: Hey, do you remember that time you were starving in Texas and you ordered the Chef's Special?
M: Oh yeah! They brought me that ginormous plate of food – it was enough to feed an army.
O: The look on your face!
M: I ate most of it though, didn't I?
O: Yeah, you did, but you didn't enjoy it!

4a Refer Ss to the Focus box. Ask individual Ss to read sections aloud to the class or read it yourself. Ask Ss for any exaggerations they can recall from the conversations they just heard.

Optional alternative activity
If transcripts are available, ask Ss to read the transcript of one or more of the conversations, listen and underline the exaggerations. They should compare answers in groups, then move on to Ex 4b.

b Ask Ss to listen again and complete the examples. When they finish, ask them to compare answers, then go over them as a class. Ask Ss to identify the type of exaggeration as shown in the Focus box.

Answers:
1 a for hours   b five seconds flat
2 a millions of   b nearly died laughing
3 a freezing   b absolutely boiling
4 a snowed under   b a ton of
5 a a fortune   b could have killed
6 a dying to   b die of embarrassment
7 a starving   b feed an army

c  1.3 Ask Ss to listen and repeat. Encourage them to exaggerate their pronunciation like the recording.

Audioscript 1.3
1 It got stuck in traffic for hours.
2 There were millions of programmes on TV last night!
3 Actually, it's absolutely boiling.
4 I've got a ton of emails to write.
5 It costs a fortune to join.
6 I bet you were dying to say something to him.
7 I'm starving.

5 Put Ss in pairs, then ask them to choose a topic and improvise a conversation. Ss can change pairs to improvise another conversation if you have time. Give Ss a target of five exaggerations to include in each conversation. They can use the same ones more than once in different conversations.

Optional extra activity
Decide on a context and characters for each improvised conversation, for example: neighbours in the building hallway; colleagues at the water cooler; colleagues in the lift; strangers at a bus stop. Tell Ss the first context and ask them to begin the first conversation. Allow exactly two minutes, then quickly move on to the next context/conversation. If possible, ask Ss to conduct the conversations standing up and move to a new partner each time.

Homework ideas
Workbook: Ex 1–4, p10

1B Develop your writing

Introduction
The goal of this lesson is for students to write a detailed description of a place. To help them achieve this, they will focus on adding interest to a description.

Warm-up
Put Ss in pairs and ask them to talk about a time they felt happy or unhappy and what made them feel that way. After a few minutes, ask for feedback on their ideas. Discuss if Ss found it easier to recall a happy time or an unhappy time.

1a Ask Ss to discuss the questions in pairs. After a few minutes, ask for feedback and have a show of hands to see which choices are more popular in the class.

b Ask Ss to work in pairs and agree on a completion for the sentence. In feedback, ask pairs for their ideas and decide as a class which endings are best.

2a Refer Ss to the first lines of the three texts. Ask Ss to tick the view of happiness that is most similar to their own, then to explain why to a partner.

Culture notes

Ortaköy is a neighbourhood in Istanbul, Turkey. It is on the banks of the Bosphorus which runs through Istanbul. The Bosphorus has Asia on one side and Europe on the other.

Shinjuku is an area in Tokyo. There is a very busy station there, as well as lots of shopping malls, bars and high buildings.

Córdoba is a city in Argentina, capital of the province with the same name. Named after Córdoba, Spain, it is in the geographic centre of the country in the foothills of the Sierras Chicas. (The text is about Córdoba in Argentina rather than Spain because an *estancia* is South American, not Spanish.)

b Ask Ss to read the three texts and try to identify the city/country in each. Allow a few minutes, then ask Ss to check at the bottom of the page.

Answers: 1 Istanbul, Turkey 2 Tokyo, Japan
3 Córdoba, Argentina

c Ask Ss to talk about the question in pairs. After a few minutes, elicit ideas. There are no fixed answers, but you could have a show of hands to see which description is the most popular and why.

3 Refer Ss to the Focus box. Ask them to read it, then find other examples in the texts in Ex 2. Ss can underline examples or write the relevant number from the Focus box beside each one. Go through the answers as a class. If you have access to a projector, project the texts and highlight the answers there.

Possible answers:
1 Happiness happens when you least expect it.; Happiness is all about the situation you're in.
2 The smell of the dry landscape filled my nostrils.
3 Drops of rain were falling onto the windows.
4 The beauty took my breath away.
5 The trees gently swayed like dancers.
6 All around me people were squashed together.
7 Not everything in my life is perfect, but happiness can be a choice.; In a place like this, I thought, how can you not be happy?

4a This exercise develops Ss' vocabulary. Ask Ss to choose three options that collocate well with each noun. Go through the answers as a class, calling on individuals to read the options aloud and discussing meaning and pronunciation as needed.

Answers:
1 chirp/sing/hop
2 sway/shake/stand silently
3 crash/break/roll
4 rises/beats down/glares
5 beats against/pours/drips
6 dance/twinkle/shine
7 stare/hurry/race
8 chat/hang out/joke

Optional alternative activity

If you think your Ss won't know many of the words, make it a research activity. Divide the exercise among pairs, with each pair looking up the words in the dictionary or on their device, then peer teaching. This approach is suited to **weaker classes** or groups that enjoy speaking practice.

b Discuss what verbs can be used for the first example, then put Ss in pairs to continue. Elicit ideas and build up vocabulary on the board. There are no fixed answers.

Possible answers:
birds: chirp, sing, swoop
a boat: drift, rock, glide
clouds: gather, darken, roll
tourists on a beach: stroll, relax, doze
the wind: howl, blow, whistle

5a Refer Ss to the photos and read out the instruction. Give an example yourself and ask Ss to identify which picture you are 'in', then ask them to write their own sentences. Monitor and help/correct as they write.

b Put Ss in small groups, asking them to take turns to read their sentence(s) aloud while the others listen and identify the photo(s). When they finish, ask a few groups to share a sentence for the whole class to listen and guess.

Teaching tip

Working in pairs and small groups helps Ss develop confidence in their speaking skills. Speaking in front of the whole class is time consuming and can be a bit stressful, so has to be limited, but it's an important next step for Ss to be heard in the larger group. Avoid directly correcting Ss who are reading their work out to the whole group – unless there's a breakdown in understanding – as it can be demoralising. It's better to give overall general feedback at the end of the speaking stage.

Prepare

6 This exercise links back to the warm-up at the start of the class and is a chance to revisit that with new language skills. Ask Ss to think about a happy time and make notes, but not complete sentences yet. Point out that Ss are welcome to use their imagination and it doesn't have to be true. Monitor and help with vocabulary.

Teaching tip

Ss sometimes don't see their progress, especially at this level where they can 'plateau'. It can be helpful to record Ss when they first talk about a topic, then record them again after they have had some language input. If recording is not practical, Ss could write about a happy time at the start of the lesson, then do so again at the end, then compare the two pieces. They should see a greater depth of expression and richer vocabulary.

Write

7 Ss work alone to write their description, using the Focus box and their notes from Ex 6. As another student will read their work, remind Ss to write neatly. Allow plenty of time for this, monitoring and helping where needed.

Optional extra activity

Provide some phrases for Ss to use. Write the examples on the board and get pairs to suggest other continuations or alternative adjectives. Leave the phrases on the board for Ss to draw on as they write. This may help **weaker classes**.

All around me people were …
There was a cool/warm breeze.
A long queue of people were waiting for the bus.
The sky was cloudless/filled with grey clouds.
The city was bustling/cosmopolitan/deserted.

8a Ask Ss to exchange descriptions with a partner and then check each other's writing for the points in the Focus box. Suggest that they tick a point when they see it being used. Ss should also add a few feedback comments, including two or three suggestions for improvement. Finally, ask Ss to add an encouraging note to the end of their partner's work and then return it.

b Ask Ss to read their feedback and try and incorporate any suggestions into a final draft.

Optional extra activity
Collect final drafts of Ss' descriptions for a wall display. Make this into a bigger project by getting Ss to research and print images to go with their texts and to enhance their visual appeal with different fonts, colours and presentation features.

Optional extra activity
Write the following reflective questions on the board after Ss assess each other's work:
Did you use language from this lesson?
Was it easier to include some descriptive features than others?
Were you able to improve your description when you wrote the final draft?

Homework ideas
Workbook: Ex 1–11, pp.10–11

1C Develop your reading

Introduction
The goal of this lesson is for students to understand an article with survey results. To help them achieve this, they will focus on understanding cause and effect relationships.

Warm-up
Display a map of the world and give Ss the following place names to locate on the map: Portugal, Mexico, Bahrain, Costa Rica. Add a few others of your choice. You could give each pair a place name to stick on the map or just write the names for them to discuss and locate. After checking answers, tell Ss the lesson is going to be about living in other countries.

1a Read the instruction aloud or ask a student to read it out. Ask Ss to discuss and make a list in pairs. After a few minutes, ask pairs for their ideas and build up a list on the board. Ask Ss what might affect the factors (age, lifestyle, language knowledge, etc.) and check if anyone has already lived abroad.

Possible answers: work options, schools, accommodation, culture, cost of living, safety, language

b Ask Ss to make their own lists. Discuss the fact that they should be in five different regions of the world. Go over the continents if possible, referring to your map.

2a Ask Ss to look at the country names and discuss what they know. Give them a few minutes for this.

Optional extra activity
Bring/download some images of the named countries to show the class. Project them on the board or display/circulate them for Ss to talk about. This may be helpful for classes with less world knowledge.

b Ask Ss to read the article quickly and match each country in Ex 2a with a section of text. Tell them to mark the text where they find the clues. Give them a few minutes to read, then discuss answers in small groups. Go through as a class.

Answers: 1 Bahrain 2 Costa Rica 3 Mexico 4 Portugal

3 Tell Ss they will now read the article again more carefully. Refer them to the questions, asking them to read and choose a country for each. Ss can write the country's initial letter beside the question. Ask pairs to compare answers before going over them as a class.

Answers: 1 Portugal 2 Mexico 3 Bahrain 4 Mexico
5 Costa Rica 6 Portugal 7 Costa Rica 8 Bahrain

4 Ask Ss to look back at the article and underline the words/phrases there. Ask pairs to discuss the meaning before going through the answers as a class. Tell Ss not to look up the words on their devices but to try and use the context to help them. In feedback, discuss the word class in each case and how context helped them understand the meaning.

Answers:
1 this country, comprising 30 islands – made up of 30 islands
2 this, coupled with other factors – combined with other factors
3 laid-back way of living – relaxed, not trying too hard
4 renewable resources – forms of renewable energy, e.g. solar power, wind power
5 it has consistently been in the top five – time and time again
6 disputes are resolved – arguments
7 high marks for climate, on account of the climate – the typical weather conditions
8 draw many foreign workers – attract or bring many foreign workers

Teaching tip
When reading, Ss need to read 'past' unknown vocabulary, while still being able to understand the overall meaning of a text, so it's wise to set time limits and discourage the use of dictionaries. Additionally, being able to use context to work out what unknown vocabulary means is an important skill to develop. Ways to develop this skill include: working out the word class of the unknown item by its position in a sentence; looking for the root of the word and analysing any affixes; using existing knowledge of related words.

5 Refer Ss to the Focus box and read it through, pointing out that a noun phrase must contain a noun and a clause must contain a subject + verb. Ask Ss to work alone to underline examples of the cause/effect phrases in the article. Let them compare in pairs before going through the answers as a class.

Answers:
Section 1: as a consequence; this … means that
Section 2: as a result; consequently
Section 3: thanks to; partly due to
Section 4: owing to; on account of

6 Write the first sentence on the board and get Ss to identify the cause (C), and effect (E). If Ss struggle with this, complete another example as a class before asking them to continue alone. Go over the answers as a class.

> **Answers:**
> 1 C = its high score in the Quality of Life category;
>   E = Spain was in the top ten
> 2 C = Foreign-born workers say they feel at home in Norway;
>   E = this country was in the top twenty
> 3 C = Vietnam scored very highly for friendliness;
>   E = it came ninth overall
> 4 C = New Zealand scores well in almost all areas apart from transport;
>   E = it missed out on a top-five position
> 5 C = its friendly population and low cost of living;
>   E = Colombia has risen rapidly to the top ten
> 6 C = its accessible, welcoming culture;
>   E = Malaysia came fifteenth overall
> 7 C = their poor medical infrastructure;
>   E = some countries lost points
> 8 C = The education system in Finland is highly successful;
>   E = the country was popular with foreign-born workers

7 Put Ss in pairs to share their ideas. **Weaker classes** may benefit from writing a few sentences first. When they finish, ask pairs of Ss to report back on something interesting their partner told them.

Homework ideas

Workbook: Ex 1–5, pp.8–9

2 OVERVIEW

2A What's the truth?
Goal | outline problems with your work
Grammar | present perfect simple and continuous
Vocabulary | phrases with *get*
GSE learning objective
Can outline an issue or problem clearly

2B Running wild?
Goal | make recommendations
Grammar | the passive
Vocabulary | social action
GSE learning objective
Can recommend a course of action, giving reasons

2C It's so annoying!
Goal | respond to complaints
Language focus | *-ed* and *-ing* adjectives
Vocabulary | common complaints
GSE learning objective
Can answer complaints from dissatisfied employees and customers politely

Check and reflect
Review exercises and communicative activities to practise the grammar, vocabulary and functional language from Units 1 and 2.

Roadmap video
Go online for the Roadmap video and worksheet.

VOCABULARY BANK

2A Phrases with *come, go* and *look*

2B Collocations with *problem*

DEVELOP YOUR SKILLS

2A Develop your writing
Goal | write an informal email to a friend
Focus | asking for and giving personal news
GSE learning objective
Can write personal emails/letters giving and commenting on news in detail

2B Develop your reading
Goal | understand what makes a text formal
Focus | identifying formal and informal texts
GSE learning objective
Can identify the key structural characteristics of a range of text types

2C Develop your listening
Goal | understand detailed guidance
Focus | recognising positive and negative instructions
GSE learning objective
Can understand detailed instructions well enough to be able to follow them without making mistakes

2A What's the truth?

Introduction
The goal of this lesson is for students to outline problems with their work. To help them achieve this, they will revise present perfect simple and continuous and phrases with *get*.

Warm-up
Display a selection of social media icons, including Instagram. Ask Ss to work in pairs to identify them. To make this more challenging, display the icons in black and white and ask Ss to recall the colour (without looking at electronic devices). When they finish, ask a few pairs to share which social media apps they use and tell Ss this is today's lesson focus.

Listening and vocabulary
Phrases with *get*
1 Ask Ss to work in pairs and give them a few minutes to talk about the questions. Monitor and help with new vocabulary where necessary. With **weaker classes**, pre-teach *post* (= to put information online). When they finish, survey the class to see whether most people feel positively or negatively about social media.

Culture notes
An **influencer** is an individual who has a high social media profile and can use this to have an impact on their followers' purchasing decisions. Influencers spend a lot of time on their social media presence, often on Instagram, and use their posts and pictures to display an attractive lifestyle. This attracts brands which then give them goods or pay them when people click through and make a purchase.

2a Look at the text and pictures as a class, asking Ss to work in pairs and guess the answers to the questions. When they finish, elicit answers onto the board but don't confirm or reject any.

Teaching tip
Before Ss listen or read, bring their attention to the topic by having them predict or guess about it. This activates Ss' 'schemata', i.e. their existing knowledge and experience of the topic. It allows Ss to anticipate potentially useful vocabulary and is also likely to make them more interested in what they are about to read or listen to. A prediction/guessing task also provides Ss with a clear reason to listen as they will be keen to find out whether their predictions were accurate.

b 🔊 2.1 Tell Ss they'll now listen and check their ideas. Play the recording for Ss to make notes, then have Ss compare in pairs before going through the answers.

Answers:
1 They have a lot of freedom. No two days are the same. They are their own boss. They get to do amazing stuff.
2 They are paid by companies to promote their products in their social media posts.
3 Around €500 for a post. Last month they earnt around €4,000.
4 It's exhausting. It's not easy to make money. They have to work hard to find companies who will pay them. Competition is getting harder. They don't get to enjoy the time on the beach. It's expensive to travel. They get on each other's nerves. They always have to look perfect. They feel like they have lost their home. Corinna feels she has lost herself – she doesn't know what's real and what's fake.
5 They're going to take a break from travelling and go back to the UK for a rest.

Audioscript 2.1

Interviewer: My guests today are the popular social media stars Corinna Wells and Victor Galan. You've probably read their posts or seen updates. So, let's get straight to the point. Corinna and Victor, what's it like to travel the world for a living?
Corinna: … Well, … that's a good question. Overall, it's great …
Victor: It's a great job … Well, … You get lots of freedom and, you know, no two days are alike. Plus of course, you're your own boss.
Corinna: And we get to do a lot of amazing stuff.
Victor: … like scuba-diving and bungee-jumping and stuff like that …
Corinna: And we've just got back from Thailand, which was amazing.
Victor: But there are some downsides …
Corinna: Yeah. … We've been travelling nonstop for two years now …
Victor: Yeah, that's quite exhausting.
Corinna: It's not easy to make enough money to live.
Interviewer: So, how do you make money?
Corinna: Well, basically companies pay us to promote their products in our social media posts. Usually we just include the product in the photo but sometimes we mention it, too.
Victor: Yeah.
Corinna: It's mostly stuff like sun cream, drinks, clothes or sometimes it's actual holiday resorts.
Interviewer: Really? And how do you find those companies?
Victor: You have to hustle.
Interviewer: Hustle?
Victor: Yeah, you know, you've got to find work. Work doesn't find you. Advertisers don't get in touch with you, you have to get in touch with them.
Corinna: You have to get their attention.
Interviewer: Oh, so you actually pitch for work?
Corinna: Oh, yeah, yeah. Absolutely. We send a lot of emails to companies but we're lucky if we hear back from one in ten.
Victor: Yeah.
Interviewer: So, when we see a photo of you on the beach looking all relaxed, it's not really the truth?
Corinna: Not really. You have to remember that we were only there to take that photo. We didn't have time to enjoy it.
Interviewer: So, can I ask a really rude question? How much do you get paid?
Corinna: Oh well, it really depends.
Victor: Yeah, on average we get about 500 euros for a post.
Corinna: Which sounds like a lot of money, but you've got to remember it takes a lot of work to organise that deal. And we've just lowered our prices. There's a lot of competition.
Interviewer: You've lowered your prices? So, how much do you earn a month?
Victor: Well, in the last month, we've probably earnt about 4,000 euros.
Corinna: But again, you've got to remember that most of the money goes back into the business.
Victor: Yeah, we've probably spent 5,000!
Corinna: Yeah, I mean travel isn't cheap and we have to pay for everything: like hotels, flights, meals …
Victor: Other social media influencers earn much more, but then you need literally millions of followers.
Interviewer: But you've seen some great places, right?
Corinna: Oh yeah, yeah, sure, sure. I was a graphic designer before I started this. I liked my work but I didn't love it. You know, I used to get home late most days. It wasn't a very exciting lifestyle. Then I met Victor on holiday and we just decided …
Victor: … we decided to keep travelling!
Interviewer: Do you still enjoy travelling together?
Corinna: For the most part – yeah.
Victor: Sometimes we get on each other's nerves.
Corinna: But you still have to look like you're having the time of your life in the photos. We've learnt to fake it. We have to look perfect!
Victor: Yeah, but you get a bit carried away with the whole perfection thing …
Corinna: *I do not!* It's what our followers expect! If we start posting photos where we look like we're not having fun …
Interviewer: OK, OK, so … what's the plan now?
Corinna: Well, we've been talking about what to do recently and …
Victor: I haven't seen my family for a long time.
Corinna: We've been to hundreds of different places – and they're all beautiful but they start to blend into one.
Victor: So, we're, like, thinking of taking a break. Going back to the UK for a while.
Corinna: After two years of holidaying we need to get some rest.
Interviewer: Ah, so, stopping travelling for a while?
Victor: Yeah. Our friends don't get it. They think we're mad.
Interviewer: It seems to me that your life on social media looks perfect but you sound a bit disillusioned. Is it all fake?
Corinna: Yes and no. Like, when we first got together, going on holiday was fun. But now it's all we do and it's become a bit … unreal.
Victor: And I guess we've been getting on each other's nerves even more recently.
Corinna: I always wanted to travel, but what I've realised is that if you want to travel, you need a home to travel from. I sometimes get the feeling that I've lost my home, and I've lost myself. I'm not sure what's real and what's for show.

3a Ask Ss to look at the phrases in the box and underline any they think they heard. Listen again to confirm.

Answer: all are in the listening

b Ask Ss to work alone, ticking the phrases they understand and circling those they use. Then put them in pairs to discuss those they are unsure of. Monitor, prompt and listen. Follow with a whole-class discussion and give feedback on any pronunciation or other problems with the new vocabulary.

Vocabulary checkpoint

Ss may sometimes think they understand vocabulary but in fact, they misunderstand it or don't fully understand it. It is useful to ask some concept-checking questions to make sure Ss have the correct meaning. Simple questions with yes-no answers can be used after Ss discuss. For example: *When you get on someone's nerves, are they happy with you?* (No) *When you get straight to the point, do you waste time on small talk?* (No)

4a Ask Ss to complete each sentence with a phrase from Ex 3a. Point out that they may need to change the verb form. Ss can work alone before comparing answers in pairs. When they finish, ask individuals to read out complete sentences and further clarify as needed.

Answers: 1 get carried away 2 get the feeling
3 get straight to the point 4 get some rest 5 get it
6 get … attention 7 getting on my nerves 8 got together
9 get in touch 10 get to do

b Ask Ss to tick the sentences that are true for them and change those that are not to make them true. This is an opportunity to personalise the vocabulary. Monitor, correct and support.

c Put Ss in pairs. Ask them to read any sentences they changed to a partner, who should ask follow-up questions to find out more. When they finish, ask a few pairs to tell you something interesting they learnt from their partner.

> **Teaching tip**
> Research shows that new language is more memorable when Ss make a personal connection with it. It is important to enable several opportunities to practise new items so Ss can shift them from short-term to long-term memory. Ss need to meet a new vocabulary item an average of eight times before it is committed to memory! Share this information with Ss if you think it may help them.

VOCABULARY BANK 2A p157
Phrases with come, go and look
This is an optional extension to the vocabulary section, extending the lexical set and providing further practice. If you're short of time, this can be done for homework.

1a Read the instructions as a class. Ss work in pairs, then go through the answers as a class.

Answers: 1 in the eye 2 to mention it 3 to pieces 4 too far 5 your age 6 and go

b Ss work alone to choose the correct alternatives. Check answers as a class.

Answers: 1 come 2 go 3 look 4 go

2 Ss work alone to match the phrases and meanings, then check in pairs. Go through the answers as a class.

Answers: 1 look on the bright side 2 come and go 3 go to great lengths 4 look your age 5 go too far 6 come to the point 7 go without saying 8 look someone in the eye 9 go to pieces 10 (now you) come to mention it

> **Further practice**
> Photocopiable activities: 2A Vocabulary, p178
> App: 2A Vocabulary practice 1 and 2

Grammar

Present perfect simple and continuous

5a 2.2 Ask Ss to listen and complete the sentences with the verb forms they hear. Point out that the verb is given in brackets at the end of the sentence. Elicit the answers.

Answers: a 've been travelling b 've just lowered c 've probably earnt d 've been talking e haven't seen f 've just got back

> **Vocabulary checkpoint**
> Ss may spell *earnt* as *earned*. Tell them that there are some geographical differences: in American English only *earned* is used; in British English and most other varieties of English, both forms are used. Other past simple/past participle forms which share this double spelling are *spelt/spelled, dreamt/dreamed, smelt/smelled* and *learnt/learned*.

b Tell Ss to read the grammar box, then match the sentences in Ex 5a with their use. Point out examples 1 and 2. Check answers as a class.

Answers: 1 b 2 c 3 e 4 f 5 a 6 d

> **Optional extra activity**
> Ss will probably have studied present perfect simple and continuous before. Ask them to identify examples of the two verb tenses in Ex 5a, then elicit the form (*have* + past participle for present perfect simple, *have* + *been* + *-ing* for present perfect continuous). Ask Ss to discuss the difference in meaning between the two tenses, using the examples. Elicit ideas. Then ask Ss to look at the grammar box and match each sentence to its use.

6a 2.3 Ask Ss to listen to the pronunciation of *been*. Ask Ss why it is pronounced this way (because it's a weak form/unstressed).

Answer: *been* is pronounced /bɪn/

b Ask Ss to listen again and repeat the sentences after the recording. Encourage them to use the weak form of *been* and to copy the intonation.

> **Pronunciation checkpoint**
> Weak forms such as /həv/ and /bɪn/ occur due to 'stress timing' in English: a spoken sentence has a certain rhythm in which key information-carrying words are usually stressed and other less important words are unstressed or in a weak form. Ss may have come across this before but if their first language is syllable timed, they may naturally tend to stress each word equally. Remind them to reproduce the stresses naturally by marking which words are stressed or weak and drilling thoroughly.

c Put Ss in pairs to ask and answer. When they finish, ask a few pairs to share an interesting answer with the class.

7a Ask Ss to complete the questions using either present perfect simple or continuous. Where both are possible, they should choose the continuous. Complete the first one together, then ask Ss to continue alone before checking in pairs. Go through the answers and discuss any doubts.

Answers:
1 have you been doing, 've only just started
2 Have you lowered, 've been thinking (*have thought* is also possible here with a change in emphasis – it suggests that we are not going to raise prices. The opposite is implied with the continuous form.)
3 's been getting
4 have you been to, 've been travelling, 've been to (You may need to remind Ss that *go* has two participles, *been* and *gone* – see Grammar checkpoint below)
5 have you earnt, haven't worked / haven't been working, 've only earnt
6 have started

> **Grammar checkpoint**
> The verbs *go* and *be* share a past participle – *been*. *Go* also has the past participle *gone*. The difference in meaning is whether somebody returned or not. When we say *He's gone to India*, it means he is not here, he's now in India. When we say, *She's been to India*, she's not in India now, she's come back and is here.

b Ask Ss to complete the sentences about themselves, then compare with a partner. Pairs should say each sentence to practise their pronunciation. They can add additional information if they want to, for example: *My brother's been getting on my nerves a bit lately. He's been borrowing all my clothes!*

LANGUAGE BANK 2A pp.138–139

Stronger classes could read the notes at home. Otherwise, go over the notes with Ss. In each exercise, elicit the first answer as an example. Ss work alone to complete the exercises, then check their answers in pairs. In feedback, check answers with the whole class. Ss can refer to the notes to help them.

Answers:
1 1 I've *never* been to a fancy dress party.
   2 My brother has *just* returned from a gap year in Thailand.
   3 We've been saving up for this trip *since* last February.
   4 Has your family been to a traditional wedding here *before*?
   5 The price of travelling abroad has been rising a lot *recently*.
   6 We've been waiting for this opportunity *for* over a year.
   7 They have *already* been to more than ten shops to try to find it.
   8 They *still* haven't finished building the new rail link.
2 1 have just managed   2 have been waiting
   3 have been living   4 has been   5 have built
   6 have been painting 7 has been doing/has done
   8 haven't had

Further practice

Photocopiable activities: 2A Grammar 1, p176; 2A Grammar 2, p177
App: 2A Grammar practice 1 and 2

Speaking

Prepare
8 Tell Ss they are going to interview someone for a podcast. Put Ss in pairs and name Ss in each pair A or B. Ask them to turn to the relevant pages to read their roles. Allow a few minutes for Ss to think about the lifestyle of their person.

Speak
9 Ask pairs to use the Useful phrases to interview their partner and make some notes about the areas given. Student A can interview Student B first, before changing roles.

Teaching tip

Ss sometimes enjoy pretending to have a more exciting lifestyle than their own. For this to work well, **weaker classes** may need to prepare in groups before starting the roleplay. All roleplays should be taking place at the same time, to maximise student talk time. When they finish, one or two more confident pairs could perform their roleplays for the class if they would like to.

Optional alternative activity

Instead of using the roles provided, Ss could research a real famous person and use this information in their roleplay interview.

Optional extra activity

Interviewers use the notes they make to write a profile of their interviewee. This will provide good practice of the positive/negative forms of the verbs as until now they have mainly been practising the question form.

Reflection on learning

Write the following questions on the board:
How did you feel doing the interviews?
What do you need to spend more time on: today's grammar or vocabulary? How will you do that?
Put Ss in pairs to discuss the questions. When they have finished, ask if anyone wants to share their ideas with the class, but don't force them to if they'd rather not.

Homework ideas

Ex 9: Ask Ss to write about the person they interviewed or another famous person they admire.
Language bank: 2A Ex 1–2, pp.138–139
Workbook: Ex 1–4, p12
App: grammar, vocabulary and pronunciation practice

Fast route: continue to Lesson 2B
Extended route: go to p118 for Develop your writing

2B Running wild?

Introduction

The goal of this lesson is for students to make recommendations. To help them achieve this, they will revise the passive and learn vocabulary relating to social action.

Warm-up

Write these life stages on the board: *baby, toddler, primary school child, teenager, young adult, adult, older person*. Ask Ss to discuss which stages are the easiest/hardest and why. Have a whole-class discussion to see which ages most Ss consider the easiest/hardest and tell them this lesson will be about the teenage years.

Vocabulary

Social action
1 Focus attention on the questions and put Ss in pairs to discuss. Conduct brief feedback (there are no fixed answers). Work as a class to brainstorm the problems teenagers have. Accept any reasonable suggestions and write useful vocabulary on the board.

2a Refer Ss to the phrases in the boxes and check the meaning. Ask Ss where they might see them (in news reports/articles). Explain that they must read carefully to insert each phrase in the correct place. They don't need to change the form. Give them a few minutes for this.

b Tell Ss to compare in pairs before going through the answers as a class. Discuss which problem is the biggest.

Answers: 1 carry out research   2 tackle the problem
3 increase funding   4 warn about the dangers
5 take action   6 ban the use of   7 do more to   8 enforce a law
9 offer alternatives   10 crack down on

43

3a Tell Ss they should think about their own country to complete the sentences with phrases from Ex 2a. Point out that it's a matter of personal opinion. Some Ss may lack opinion on this matter, so put them in small groups to complete the sentences.

b Ask Ss to compare in pairs, saying if they agree or disagree. In feedback, ask a few Ss to report on what their partner told them or any ideas that they thought were good.

> **Teaching tip**
> If you have a class of teenagers, they should have plenty to say. In mixed-age groups, you might find some interesting variation in opinions. Think how to maximise discussion by pairing different ages or genders to gather ideas, then re-pairing with different ages to create discussion. If Ss become heated, they may end up lapsing into their first language. Remind them that the objective is to practise English and revise a few appropriate agreeing and disagreeing phrases to help.

VOCABULARY BANK 2B p157
Collocations with *problem*
This is an optional extension to the vocabulary section, extending the lexical set and providing further practice. If you're short of time, this can be done for homework.

1 Read the instructions as a class. Ss work in pairs, then go through the answers as a class.

Answers:
verb + noun: cause a problem, overcome a problem, pose a problem, resolve a problem, tackle a problem
noun + verb: a problem arises, a problem exists, the problem lies in
noun + *of* + noun: the heart of the problem, the root of the problem
noun + noun: a problem area, a problem child

2 Ss work alone to choose the correct phrases, then check in pairs. Explain that sometimes more than one option may be possible. Go through the answers as a class.

Answers: 1 has existed   2 causing   3 lies in
4 heart/root of   5 causes/poses
6 tackling/overcoming/resolving   7 areas
8 tackle/resolve/overcome

3 Ss work in pairs to identify a problem in their own town or area and discuss solutions to it. Pairs should then compare ideas.

Further practice
Photocopiable activities: 2B Vocabulary, p181
App: 2B Vocabulary practice 1 and 2

Listening

Culture notes
Iceland is a Nordic island in the North Atlantic. It is Europe's most sparsely populated country with a population of around 360,000 people on 103,000km². Two thirds of the population live in and around the capital, Reykjavík. The country is volcanically active and famous for its hot springs.

4a Ask Ss to look at the introduction and write a one-line summary of the problem. Elicit their ideas and work together to create a class summary.

Suggested answer:
In the 80s and 90s, Icelandic teens were so badly behaved that the government had to come up with a new plan to tackle the problem.

b Put Ss in pairs to discuss. Elicit ideas to the board and have a brief whole-class discussion. Don't confirm or reject any suggestions at this point.

5a 2.4 Tell Ss they are going to listen and check their ideas. Play the recording, let Ss discuss in pairs, then go through the answers as a class, ticking off any correct predictions on the board.

Answers:
The government carried out research to identify the problems. Then they devised a plan with four main points: they banned all tobacco and alcohol advertising; they introduced a teen curfew for 13–16 year-olds; they introduced contracts between parents and children; they spent lots of money on providing leisure activities for teenagers.

Audioscript 2.4
You're back with Leona McKenzie and this is my *Talking Teens* podcast. Today we're looking at the problem of misbehaving teens in Iceland and what the government has done to tackle this problem.

As we said earlier in the programme, the first thing Iceland did was carry out research to find out exactly what the problems were. Then they created a plan to tackle the problems and the plan that Iceland came up with was called *Youth in Iceland*. It had four main points. Firstly, the law was changed and all tobacco and alcohol advertising was banned. Now, you can really understand why the government did this. On the one hand, teenagers were being told not to do something, but on the other they were being shown advertisements on every street corner encouraging them to do it.

Secondly, Iceland started to crack down on misbehaviour. A 'teen curfew' was introduced. Children between 13 and 16 years old weren't allowed to be outside after 10 o'clock at night in winter and midnight in summer. If you got caught outside after this time, you got taken home and you *and* your parents got told off! Today this law is still enforced by groups of parents who patrol the streets, looking for teenagers who shouldn't be out.

Thirdly, groups of parents in each area wrote parent-child contracts and local parents were then asked to sign them. The contracts contained the rules that parents should enforce, for example, teenagers should not be allowed to have a party without an adult present. Parents were also told to spend more time at home with their children and some parents were encouraged to go to classes that taught them parenting skills.

Fourthly, the government realised that funding for teens needed to be increased. Hundreds of clubs were set up around the country offering a wide range of leisure activities, for example sports clubs, music clubs, art clubs and so on. These clubs offered teenagers an alternative to bad behaviour. At the same time, parents were given a 'leisure card', worth €300 per child per year to spend on leisure activities for their children. These days, almost half the teenage population goes to a sports club four times a week or more.

Indeed, since the project began, the lives of hundreds of thousands of teens have been changed for the better. Using Iceland as a model, many cities across the world have started to tackle the problem of teenage behaviour – or perhaps it's more accurate to say that they have begun to tackle the problem of how society treats teenagers.

b Tell Ss they are going to listen again more carefully. Ask them to read the sentences, then listen and fill the gaps. After listening once, ask Ss to compare in pairs and play the recording again if needed before going through the answers.

Answers: 1 was changed   2 were being told
3 got caught, got taken   4 is, enforced
5 should not be allowed   6 have been changed

Grammar

The passive

6 Ask Ss to read the grammar box carefully, then identify whether the verbs are active or passive in Ex 5b. They should also identify the tenses used. Ss work alone then check in pairs. Go through the answers and deal with any questions.

Answers: They are all passive.
1 past simple   2 past continuous   3 past simple
4 present simple   5 present simple (with modal)
6 present perfect simple

Grammar checkpoint

Ss will have studied passives before but may be unfamiliar with the use of *get* instead of *be*. The *get* passive is common in informal speaking and is often used to emphasise accidental or unexpected actions: *Jenny got sacked after just three weeks in the job! Our car got stolen last night.* We can use the *get* passive with action verbs but not state verbs: *Nothing is known about the thief. Nothing gets known about the thief.* The *get* passive appears in many common expressions: *get dressed/engaged/married/divorced/lost/started.*

7a ◆ 2.5 Tell Ss they will listen to a short speech and should count how many passive constructions they hear by keeping a tally in their notebook. Check the answer.

Answer: four

Audioscript 2.5

It is a great honour for me, as the mayor, to open this new sports club for teenagers. It was requested by local parents. It has been paid for by local taxes. It has been constructed by local builders and it will be enjoyed by local teenagers for years to come. I declare this sports club ... open!

b Tell Ss to number some lines in their notebook 1–4, then listen again and write the passive constructions. Ask them to focus on the pronunciation of the verb *be* in the passive. Go through the answers.

Answers: 1 It was requested   2 It has been paid
3 It has been constructed   4 it will be enjoyed
The different forms of *be* are not stressed (they are weak forms). With weak forms you often hear a schwa /ə/ (or other weak vowel sound) rather than the strong vowel sound. However, in the final example, the word after *be* begins with a vowel sound, so *be* remains long and is followed by an intruded /j/ sound: /biːjɪnˈdʒɔɪd/.

> **Teaching tip**
>
> If your Ss enjoy dictation such as this, use it regularly. You could dictate homework tasks rather than write them on the board or dictate an instruction. It can be a useful way to calm a lively class or change focus. It is also an effective way to draw attention to word order, spelling or features of pronunciation.

c ◆ 2.6 Ask Ss to listen to the speech again and repeat it, line by line. Clarify that this is the same speech as before, but with pauses added to allow for repetition. The aim is to focus on stressing the key words and not stressing the weak auxiliaries.

8 Ask Ss to work alone to complete the paragraph using the verbs provided. Point out that they must choose active or passive and then the correct tense. More than one tense may be possible. Ask Ss to compare in pairs, then go through the answers, with individual Ss reading out sentences so you can hear their pronunciation of the weak auxiliary.

Answers: 1 were given   2 had been offered   3 began
4 is loved   5 can be enjoyed
6 need to be registered/need to register   7 can travel
8 is now being spent / is now spent   9 has also helped
10 will be started

Optional alternative activity

Place several copies of the complete text around the room, pinning them to the wall, and arrange Ss in small groups – one per copy of the text. One group member goes up to their copy of the text, reads and memorises a short section, returns to their group and dictates it. They then go back to the text again to read and memorise the next section. Group members can change roles after every couple of sections. This 'running dictation' provides pronunciation, listening and speaking practice. It is good for all levels and can be a very lively activity, particularly when conducted as a race between groups. To ensure the activity is successful, make sure groups are not sitting too close to the texts and that group members speak quietly when dictating so that other groups can't hear!

LANGUAGE BANK 2B   pp.138–139

Stronger classes could read the notes at home. Otherwise, go over the notes with Ss. In each exercise, elicit the first answer as an example. Ss work alone to complete the exercises, then check their answers in pairs. In feedback, check answers with the whole class. Ss can refer to the notes to help them.

Answers:
1 1 behave   2 labelled   3 being   4 being influenced
    5 dealing   6 are given   7 are praised   8 be controlled
2 1 three teenagers have been banned from this shop
    2 can/may be taken into the examination room
    3 need to be exposed to sunlight every day
    4 it is being reseeded
    5 shorts or trainers will not be admitted into the club
    6 offenders will be sent to the police

Further practice

Photocopiable activities: 2B Grammar 1, p179;
2B Grammar 2, p180
App: 2B Grammar practice 1 and 2

Speaking

Prepare

9a Ask a ***stronger student*** to read the instruction to the class or read it yourself. Have a discussion about the problems and which are the most serious or common.

> **Culture notes**
>
> All state schools in the UK are inspected by a body called **OFSTED** (Office for Standards in Education) and their reports are published on the schools' websites alongside exam results, performance tables and information on accessibility. In the UK, parents have the option to select their children's state school and many may choose one school over another because of these reports. In other countries such as the Netherlands, pupils simply attend the state school that is nearest their home and there is no possibility of selecting a different one.

b Read the instruction as a class. Tell Ss they are now going to make some recommendations, using vocabulary from Ex 2a. Put Ss in pairs to get some ideas on paper.

Speak

10 Re-group Ss in fours, ideally not with their original partners. Refer them to the Useful phrases box and give them a few minutes to think how to present their points. Tell group members to take turns giving their recommendations. Remind them to use the passive where possible, as well as the vocabulary from Ex 2a. After the first group member speaks, encourage questions, then move to the next speaker. In feedback, ask groups to vote on which plans they prefer.

> **Optional alternative activity**
>
> Set up a roleplay with these roles: head teacher, teacher, parent, student representative. Split the class into four groups, one for each role. Groups can first prepare their recommendations from their perspective, then re-group with all the roles to have a formal meeting.

> **Reflection on learning**
>
> Write the following questions on the board:
> *How did you feel making recommendations?*
> *What can help you next time?*
>
> Put Ss in pairs to discuss the questions. When they have finished, ask if anyone wants to share their ideas with the class, but don't force them to if they'd rather not.

> **Homework ideas**
>
> Ask Ss to write a paragraph about their country's school system.
> **Language bank:** 2B Ex 1–2, pp.138–139
> **Workbook:** Ex 1–5, p13
> **App:** grammar, vocabulary and pronunciation practice

Fast route: continue to Lesson 2C
Extended route: go to p98 for Develop your reading

2c It's so annoying!

Introduction

The goal of this lesson is for students to respond to complaints. To help them achieve this, they will study vocabulary for common complaints as well as *-ed* and *-ing* adjectives.

Warm-up

Tell Ss about an invented or real scenario where you didn't get good service and you complained. Ask Ss what their experience is of making or dealing with complaints. Put Ss in groups of three or four to tell each other about a time they complained about something. When they finish, ask groups to report on any similarities.

Reading and vocabulary

Common complaints

1 Ask Ss to discuss the questions in pairs and make a few notes on their ideas. When they finish, elicit answers and add them to the board. Find out which things your Ss complain about the most.

> **Culture notes**
>
> **#firstworldproblems** (first world problems) is a hashtag used when people complain online about something trivial which is not really a true problem. It suggests that the complainer's life is privileged. *First world* is an old term for the developed world as opposed to *third world*, meaning less developed or developing countries. Examples of first world problems might be: your coffee was served with the wrong kind of milk; your wifi only supports four devices at a time; your flight ran out of gluten-free meals; you ate too much and now you're too sleepy to work.

2a Ask Ss to read the list quickly and decide if they agree with the order of the complaints. Give them a few minutes for this, then have a whole-class discussion.

b Ask Ss to make their lists alone, then put them in pairs to discuss. If you have a multilingual class, mix up the nationalities. After a few minutes, ask groups to report back and share interesting examples.

3 Ask Ss to match each social media complaint with an item in Ex 2a. Give them a few minutes for this, then go through the answers.

> **Answers:** a 6 b 3 c 4 d 8

4a Explain that Ss should match the complaints in Ex 3 with the problems in the box. With **weaker classes**, tell Ss that a and b match three problems each and c and d match two problems each. Discuss the meaning of any they are unsure of.

> **Answers:**
> a rude staff, billing disputes, false advertising
> b faulty product, poor customer service, lack of communication
> c slow delivery, broken promises
> d aggressive salespeople, cold callers

> **Culture notes**
>
> **Cold calling** is when salespeople call in person or by phone without having made an appointment. They attempt to convince potential customers to purchase a product or service or to make a donation. It is a practice which is sometimes associated with pushy sales techniques and is illegal in some countries.

b This is a chance to practise talking about the problems. Give an example yourself if possible. Then give Ss time to make notes. Ss take turns to describe scenarios and guess problems.

c Ask Ss to discuss their experiences in pairs. When they finish, ask pairs to share the most interesting or shocking complaints.

> **Teaching tip**
> Some Ss may complain that they already did this activity at the start of the lesson! Point out that they are now doing it after some language input, so should be able to describe their problems more easily and accurately. Ask Ss if they noticed any improvement in their performance after Ex 4c. This is an example of consciousness-raising learning.

Further practice

Photocopiable activities: 2C Vocabulary, p184
App: 2C Vocabulary practice 1 and 2

Language focus

-ed and -ing adjectives

5 Refer Ss to the text. Ask them to read it quickly and decide if this strategy would work or not. Elicit answers and reasons.

6a ▶ 2.7 Tell Ss they are going to listen to four complaints. Tell them to draw a table in their notebooks. They should note the complaint in the first column and the alternative more positive view in the second column. Make sure they make notes only. Ss can compare ideas after they listen, then go through the answers as a class. Check that Ss understand a *rip-off* = poor value.

Answers:

	Complaint	More positive view
1	the lift is taking too long to come	it's better to have a lift than not
2	the news is always bad/depressing	it's good to know what's going on in the world
3	waiting on hold to speak to the bank	it's a chance to play a mobile phone game
4	charging for plastic bags is a rip-off	it's good for the environment

Audioscript 2.7

Conversation 1
A: Oh come on! What is this lift doing?
B: Oh. Have you been waiting a while?
A: Yeah. I feel like I've been waiting ages.
B: I know what you mean. This lift is so infuriating. But it's an old building and I guess it's better to have a lift than not to have a lift.
A: That's true!

Conversation 2
C: Oh no! Not the news.
D: You don't like the news?
C: It's always so bad. It makes me depressed.
D: Yeah, I feel the same sometimes. It's overwhelming.
C: Yeah, completely.
D: I guess the good thing is that we know what's going on in the world. A hundred years ago we had no way of knowing what was happening.
C: Yeah … that's one way of looking at it, I guess.

Conversation 3
E: This is ridiculous! I've been on hold for ten minutes. I've got better things to do!
F: You must be feeling so irritated.

E: Completely! It's insulting! Why do I have to wait for ten minutes to speak to someone at my bank?
F: Yeah, you're right. But you do get to play that horribly entertaining new game on your phone while you're waiting.
E: Hey – good point!
F: Don't forget to keep checking whether they've answered your call … Can I have a go?

Conversation 4
G: That's 29.90, please.
H: Can I have a bag, please?
G: Of course. That's an extra five pence so that's 29.95.
H: Five pence for a plastic bag? That's a rip-off!
G: You're right, it's expensive and some of our customers feel really infuriated, but it's part of our drive to cut down on the use of plastic and improve the environment for future generations.
H: Oh, I see. Well … that's a fairly convincing argument. Perhaps there should be a sign that says that.
G: I'll suggest that to my manager.

b Tell Ss to complete the gaps with the adjective form of the word in brackets, listening to the audio again if necessary. There's no need for feedback as they will check their answers with the Language focus box.

c Refer to the Language focus box and ask Ss to use the information to check Ex 6b. They should establish whether each adjective focuses on the person's feelings or on the thing that caused the feelings. Ss work alone, then compare with a partner. With **weaker classes**, go through the Language focus box as a class and elicit further examples. Check answers with the whole class.

Answers: 1 infuriating 2 depressed 3 overwhelming
4 irritated 5 insulting 6 convincing

> **Optional extra activity**
> If Ss can access the transcripts, put them in pairs to read and practise the conversations. Many Ss enjoy this as they have a chance to practise speaking without worrying about making mistakes. When they finish, they can try again without looking at the scripts.

7 ▶ 2.8 Focus attention on the sentences. Ask Ss to listen for and copy the intonation. If you think it's useful, share the information in the Pronunciation checkpoint below.

> **Pronunciation checkpoint**
> A wide range of intonation is associated with high emotion. That could be a positive feeling such as happiness, or a negative one such as anger and frustration. Encourage Ss to really exaggerate their range when copying the recording and point out that meaning is carried by more than words alone.

8a Ask Ss to underline the correct alternative in each sentence. They should compare in pairs, then go through the answers as a class. As you elicit each answer, encourage individuals to say the sentence with exaggerated intonation as practised in Ex 7.

Answers: 1 frustrating 2 embarrassing 3 astonished
4 disgusting 5 exhausted 6 insulted 7 overwhelmed
8 stressful

b Ask Ss to work alone and write a cause for each feeling. They will need a few minutes for this. Monitor and prompt with ideas as needed.

c Model an example exchange with a **stronger student** to show how the activity works:
A: *Superhero films*
B: *Do you feel entertained when you watch them?*
A: *No, I hate them. They make me feel depressed.*
Put Ss in pairs to practise. Monitor and listen to how they are pronouncing the key adjectives and give feedback when they finish.

Optional extra activity

Ss write short conversations of their own. They underline the stressed words, then practise the conversations aloud in pairs, emphasising the intonation. Alternatively, they record the conversations on their phones. More confident Ss can perform one or two conversations for the class if they like.

LANGUAGE BANK 2C pp.138–139

Stronger classes could read the notes at home. Otherwise, go over the notes with Ss. In each exercise, elicit the first answer as an example. Ss work alone to complete the exercises, then check their answers in pairs. In feedback, check answers with the whole class. Ss can refer to the notes to help them.

Answers:
1 1 frustrating/irritating   2 concerned   3 disgusting
   4 stressful/irritating/frustrating   5 cooked   6 alarming
   7 astonishing   8 irritated/frustrated

Further practice

Photocopiable activities: 2C Language focus 1, p182; 2C Language focus 2, p183
App: 2C Language focus practice 1 and 2

Speaking

Prepare

9 Tell Ss they are going to make complaints and use *-ing* and *-ed* adjectives to express their feelings. Refer Ss to the list they made in Ex 2b and ask them to work alone to write their complaints and feelings. Monitor and help with accuracy.

Speak

10a Ask Ss to work in pairs to share their complaints and feelings. Refer them to the Useful phrases. Listening Ss should try and use the strategy from Ex 5 to respond to each complaint. Monitor, listening to Ss' control of *-ing* and *-ed* adjectives as well as their use of intonation.
b When they finish, invite Ss to repeat with another partner. Conduct whole-class feedback on their use of language in the activity.

Teaching tip

Ss get better with more turns of practice because they gain confidence. Encourage Ss to notice this by giving feedback between each stage of a roleplay or speaking activity and by asking Ss to reflect on whether they noticed an improvement. Ss need to monitor their own language in order to keep improving, so getting them to correct language at the board is another good technique to use after speaking activities.

Reflection on learning

Write the following questions on the board:
What will you do to remember the language from this lesson?
How will you use this language outside the classroom?
Put Ss in threes to discuss the questions. When they have finished, ask if anyone wants to share their ideas with the class, but don't force them to if they'd rather not.

Homework ideas

Ss write a paragraph about a time they felt delighted, frustrated or stressed.
Language bank: 2C Ex 1, pp.138–139
Workbook: Ex 1–5, p14
App: grammar, vocabulary and pronunciation practice

Fast route: continue to Check and reflect
Extended route: go to p87 for Develop your listening

2 Check and reflect: Units 1–2

Introduction

Students revise and practise the language of Units 1 and 2. The notes below provide some ideas for exploiting the activities in class, but you may want to set the exercises for homework or use them as a diagnostic or progress test.

1a Ss complete the sentences alone, using the prepositions in the box, then check in pairs. In feedback, ask Ss to say the whole sentence so you can check for correct pronunciation.

Answers:
1 Do you belong to any clubs or organisations?
2 In what situations do you suffer from nerves?
3 If a movie has a PG rating, what do the letters stand for?
4 Do you ever think about what you'll do when you retire?
5 Do you rely on any of your friends more than others?
6 How do you deal with people who try to take advantage of you?
7 Do you believe in ghosts?
8 Is it usually easy to concentrate on what you're doing?

b Ask Ss to ask and answer in pairs. Conduct brief feedback to hear a few Ss' answers.

2 Ss work alone to put the words in the correct order, then check in pairs. Go through the answers with the class. Ask Ss to read the questions aloud so that you can check their pronunciation and drill if necessary.

Answers:
1 Where did you buy that jacket?
2 What are you thinking about?
3 What causes these constant delays?
4 Do you know where the changing rooms are?
5 Who decided to build that strange tower?
6 I'd love to know why so many people get off here.
7 Who are you sending that text message to?
8 Why did they want to open another coffee bar here?

3 With **weaker classes**, do the first one together as an example. Ss match the sentence halves alone, then check in pairs. Go through the answers with the whole class.

Answers: 1 e 2 c 3 h 4 g 5 f 6 d 7 a 8 b

4 Ss work alone to find the incorrect underlined phrases in the text, then compare answers in pairs before going through them as a class.

Answers: 1 didn't use to go 2 ✓ 3 got 4 changed 5 ✓ 6 ✓ 7 were waiting 8 ✓ 9 ✓ 10 meant

5 Ss work alone to complete the sentences with the correct adjective forms. With **weaker classes**, brainstorm the possible adjective forms of each before Ss start. Go through the answers.

Answers: 1 adventurous 2 outgoing 3 reserved 4 conscientious 5 careless 6 nervous 7 agreeable 8 suspicious

6a Ss work alone to complete the questions with the correct form of the verbs provided. Ask pairs to compare answers, then go through them as a class.

Answers: 1 lose, remain 2 broke 3 speak 4 keep 5 return 6 meeting 7 take 8 make

b Ss discuss three questions of their choice. There are no fixed answers. **Fast finishing** or **stronger Ss** can discuss more questions.

7a Ss complete the sentences with a word that connects with the words provided to make a phrase with *get*. When they finish, they can check in pairs and refer back to their notes before going through the answers as a class.

Answers: 1 feeling 2 nerves 3 rid 4 attention 5 touch 6 point 7 paid 8 carried 9 together

b Ss choose questions to ask each other. There are no fixed answers. **Fast finishing** or **stronger Ss** can discuss more questions.

8 Ss choose a verb in the box to complete the sentence pairs, once with present perfect simple and once with continuous. Ask them to compare answers, then go through them as a class.

Answers:
1 a been cutting b 've cut
2 a 've been playing b 've played
3 a been doing b done
4 a 've worked b 've been working
5 a 've seen b 's been seeing

9 Ss work alone to complete the questions with the correct form of one of the verbs in brackets. Ask them to check in pairs, then go through the answers.

Answers: 1 cracking 2 warned 3 tackling 4 banned 5 enforce 6 increased

10 Ss complete each sentence with the verb provided in either its active or passive form. Go through the answers.

Answers: 1 has been banned 2 are being set up 3 gained 4 be chosen 5 have caused

11 Ss complete the phrases alone or in pairs. **Weaker classes** can look at their notes as they do this. Go through the answers.

Answers: 1 faulty product 2 rude staff 3 cold callers 4 slow delivery 5 billing disputes 6 false advertising

12 Ss complete the sentences with the *-ing* or *-ed* adjective form of the words in the box. Ask them to compare answers, then go through them as a class.

Answers: 1 exhausted 2 convincing 3 infuriating 4 overwhelmed 5 entertaining 6 worried

13a Ask Ss to read the opinion and complete the responses with the appropriate words in the box. Go through the answers as a class.

Answers: 1 say 2 explain 3 experience 4 come 5 serious 6 balance 7 with 8 cons

b Ss work in pairs to discuss if each response agrees (A) or disagrees (D) with the opinion.

Answers:
1 D (We often use questions like these to ask for an explanation for something we disagree with.)
2 D (mild disagreement, requesting clarification before the speaker will agree)
3 A
4 D
5 D
6 A
7 D
8 A (mild agreement or at least sympathy with the opinion)

c Ss work in pairs to read out the opinions and respond. There are no fixed answers.

Reflect

Ask Ss to rate each statement alone, then compare in pairs. Encourage them to ask any questions they still have about any of the areas covered in Units 1 and 2.

Roadmap video

Go online for the Roadmap video and worksheet.

2A Develop your writing

Introduction
The goal of this lesson is for students to write an informal email to a friend. To help them achieve this, they will focus on asking for and giving personal news.

Warm-up
Write the following questions on the board, asking Ss to talk about them in pairs: *When do you use email? What for? How many emails do you receive/send a day? Do you answer right away?* Ask for a brief report back to see how much this medium is used and for what purposes.

1 Put Ss in pairs to discuss the questions. After a few minutes, conduct brief feedback and ask Ss to justify their ideas. If appropriate, consider how different age groups view digital communication.

2a Ask Ss to read the post and emails and make notes on points 1–4. Ss should work alone, highlighting relevant parts of the texts, then discuss in pairs before checking as a class. Go over the answers.

> **Answers:**
> 1 Ji is going to leave Italy and go home.
> 2 The performance review didn't go well. Alex is looking for a new job.
> 3 Alex has split up with Adrianna, so he's single again.
> 4 Ji has spent all the money that he saved for the trip.

b Ask for a show of hands to see which situation Ss prefer and why.

Culture notes
It is quite common in the UK to take a **year off** (or gap year) between significant study periods, at age 18 or 21, to travel and then return to work or study.
A **performance review** is a workplace procedure where employees and their line manager have a discussion to assess how their job is going and decide whether they need to make any changes.

3 Refer to the Focus box. Ask Ss to match phrases a–d with the appropriate headings in the box, then discuss in pairs. Confirm answers with the whole class and spend some time on any expressions that may be new. Ask Ss to identify tenses (present and present perfect) and point out how these tenses are associated with new information.

> **Answers:** a 4 b 3 c 1 d 2

4 Ask Ss to read the email and find five errors. Point out that they relate to the phrases in the Focus box. Give them a few minutes to encourage focused reading. Ask Ss to compare in pairs, then go through the answers as a class.

> **Answers:**
> Hi Bobbi,
> How are you? What have you been up to recently? It seems so long since we've seen each other. I saw online that you've been busy at home. **How's** it going with the decorating? Is it all finished?
> Have you heard the **latest** about my law studies? I passed the bar exam! That means I need to find a law firm that will take me on as a trainee.
> As **for** my social life, I basically don't have one! I've been so busy studying that it hasn't been possible. But I'm going to put that right this summer. I'm going away for a week with a few friends. We haven't decided where yet, but I'm excited already!
> Say hi to Tony from me! What's he been doing **recently**? Hope we can all meet up soon.
> Love,
> Padme

Culture notes
The **bar exam** is a written exam that every UK law graduate must pass if they want to become a barrister (= a lawyer who specialises in courtroom litigation). Following the exam, they need to complete a further period of training to get practical experience in a law firm before being fully qualified.

5 Discuss as a class what's wrong with the underlined phrases (they are blunt and sound unfriendly). Refer Ss to Ex 3 and the Focus box, discussing which phrase they could use to replace the first underlined section. Clarify that more than one answer may be possible. Ss continue alone before comparing answers in pairs. Go through the answers as a class.

> **Suggested answers:**
> 1 Congratulations on passing your bar exam! / Great news about the bar exam! / I'm really pleased to hear about the bar exam.
> 2 I'm sorry to hear that your social life is so boring. / I'm so sorry about your social life!
> 3 What's the latest on your holiday?
> 4 I don't know if you've heard, but Tony and I have decided to adopt a child.

Prepare
6a Refer Ss to the post, telling Ss to read it and find out where Dylan is living (Buenos Aires). Tell them they are going to write to Dylan, incorporating the ideas and language studied in this lesson.
b Explain that Ss should think about the points before they start writing. With **weaker classes**, Ss should make notes of their ideas. **Stronger classes** may not need to. Monitor and help with ideas and vocabulary. There is no need for whole-class feedback because all Ss will be working on different ideas.

Write
7 Ask Ss to write, following the suggested structure and using their notes if they made any. When they finish, Ss could swap with a partner, read each other's emails and suggest improvements and changes.

Optional extra activity
Ask Ss to read their email aloud, but quietly, and ask themselves these focus questions:
- Is it clear and friendly?
- Did I use some phrases from the Focus box?
- Did I start and end my email in a suitable way?
- Does it sound natural?

Optional extra activity

When they finish, ask Ss to exchange emails and reply to each other in role (as Dylan). If there is anything they don't understand in the email they received, they can ask about it in the reply.

Homework ideas

Workbook: Ex 1–10, pp.18–19

2B Develop your reading

Introduction

The goal of this lesson is for students to understand what makes a text formal. To help them achieve this, they will focus on identifying formal and informal texts.

Warm-up

Bring in or display digitally a range of texts and ask Ss to identify them. Choose a mixture of formal and informal text types such as leaflets, letters, emails, contracts or magazine articles. They don't need to be in English. Discuss how texts can vary in presentation (colour/font/headings/images) as well as language. Tell Ss today's lesson is about recognising different text types.

1 Put Ss in pairs and ask them to discuss the questions. In feedback, ask Ss if there are any interesting strategies they can share.

2 Ask Ss to read the three texts quickly to answer the questions. Give them a few minutes to read alone, then a further minute to compare in pairs. Go through the answers as a class and deal with any new vocabulary.

Answers:
1 **Text 1:** late payment of road tax
Text 2: people throwing rubbish on the ground
Text 3: trying to improve students' exam results
2 **Text 1:** writing a personalised letter warning people about the possible loss of their car and including in the letter a photo of their car
Text 2: a pair of bins with a customised question and two possible answers, to allow people to express their opinion at the same time as disposing of their rubbish appropriately
Text 3: giving teachers their bonus at the start of the year, which they would have to repay at the end of the year if their students failed their exams

3a Refer Ss to the three sentences, clarifying that they are final sentences for the texts they just read. Ask Ss to read the three texts again and match each with its final sentence. Tell them they should not use phones or dictionaries. Let Ss compare in pairs before going through the answers as a class.

Answers: 1 c 2 b 3 a

b Tell Ss they will now answer the questions, reading the texts again. Ask them to underline or highlight where they find the information, then compare in pairs before going through the answers as a class. If you are able to, project the text and highlight where the answers were found.

Answers:
1 It's too heavy-handed and over-the-top.
2 a fine
3 the letter with the new wording and the photo
4 It has one opening for each possible answer.
5 because the target group was young men, who were mainly responsible for dropping the most rubbish
6 They want to put the new bins in other parts of Britain.
7 They wanted to improve students' exam results.
8 nothing
9 fear of losing money that they have already received

Teaching tip

Ss benefit from marking a text, underlining or highlighting sections where answers are found. In this way, they can retrieve the answers when checking (and re-read later if they need to). This is good for reading skills development and an excellent exam technique, but Ss don't tend to do it unless you encourage them, as they often don't like to (or may not have previously been allowed to) 'spoil' their book!

4a Ask Ss to look again at the texts, circling the personal pronouns and underlining the passives. If you have access to a projector, complete the first example as a class, then ask Ss to continue. Go through the answers as a class.

b Discuss as a class which text is the most formal or informal, using Ss' feedback to annotate the texts on the board if possible. Clarify that personal pronouns *I* and *you* are more common in less formal texts (as in text 1), while the passive is often used in more formal texts (as in texts 2 and 3).

Answers:
Most formal = text 2 (most passive forms)
Least formal = text 1 (fewest passive forms; most personal pronouns (*you*))

c Discuss what else makes a text formal and informal. Add Ss' ideas to the board, then ask Ss to read the Focus box to check their ideas. Conduct whole-class feedback.

5a Ask Ss to read the text and identify three phrases that are too informal. Ask Ss to work alone to underline the phrases, then go through the text as a class and discuss their suggestions.

Culture notes

Petrified wood is when a tree or other vegetation has turned to stone due to fossilisation.

Answers:
the top bosses (placed a sign)
stop being so naughty
Me and a few others reckon

b Ask Ss to work alone to rewrite the informal phrases. After a few minutes, ask them to help each other in pairs, then conduct feedback. Ask Ss to comment on the visitors' reaction to the sign.

Suggested answers:
the top bosses (placed a sign) → a sign was placed by management/the authorities
stop being so naughty → avoid this/such behaviour
Me and a few others reckon → It is thought/believed that

6a This task enables Ss to engage personally with the topic. Ask them to work in pairs to make suggestions for each point. **Weaker classes** can choose and discuss just one of the points.

> **Possible answers:**
> 1 on their bill, compare their usage to the average person; tell people how much money they could save by using less energy
> 2 put signs up saying, 'Silence is golden'; play messages over the loud speakers reminding people not to use phones in the quiet carriages
> 3 use pictures of people eating healthy food; ensure that the healthy choices are displayed prominently in supermarkets

b Ask pairs to take turns to present to the class, then conduct a class vote on the best ideas.

Optional alternative activity

If time is short, put Ss in groups to present their ideas. If they spend longer on one topic than another, it's fine, but give them an idea of the total time available so they can be conscious of this. When they finish, ask each group to feed back to the class on one of the points they discussed.

Optional extra activity

Ss can make a poster presenting their persuasion ideas or write an article about them for a class magazine.

Homework ideas

Workbook: Ex 1–6, pp. 16–17

2c Develop your listening

Introduction

The goal of this lesson is for students to understand detailed guidance. To help them achieve this, they will focus on recognising positive and negative instructions.

Warm-up

Write a selection of jobs on the board, for example: *banker, nurse, lawyer, teacher, cleaner, politician, farmer*. Ask Ss to work in pairs and rank them according to social importance. Then ask them to rank them again according to whether they'd like to do them. Finally, they should rank them according to salary. Take feedback. Discuss with Ss whether pay always reflects the importance of a job and whether it should do so.

1a Ask Ss to discuss the questions in pairs. After a few minutes, ask a few pairs for their answers.

b Refer Ss to the four suggested approaches to asking for a pay rise. Ask Ss to tick those they think are a good idea and cross those they don't like. Discuss as a class and write the predictions on the board but don't confirm answers yet.

2a 2.9 Tell Ss they are going to listen to a programme on how to ask for a pay rise. Ask them to listen and check their answers to Ex 1b. Go through the answers as a class, checking against their predictions on the board.

Answers: 1 should do 2 shouldn't do 3 shouldn't do 4 shouldn't do

Audioscript 2.9

Presenter: And so to our final piece today: asking for a pay rise. It can be frightening to ask your boss for a pay rise, but as the saying goes, 'If you don't ask, you don't get'. So, if you think you're worth more than you're getting, don't feel embarrassed: just ask. But what *is* the right way to ask for a pay rise?

According to Madison Bligh, a careers adviser from Wyoming, there are two things you must do and one thing you mustn't.

Madison: First and foremost, it's vital that you prepare before you ask. Take the time to make a list of your achievements, those things that you have done successfully, so that you can show your boss how valuable you are. Be confident and convincing. Explain how you've helped the company achieve its goals. It's sometimes tempting to explain why you need the pay rise. Perhaps your rent has gone up or you're saving to buy a car – but you need to resist that temptation. It's a bad idea. What you do with the money is your business – don't mix your personal life with your professional life.

Also what you must do, and this is crucial, is arrange a face-to-face meeting and let your boss know in advance that you want to talk about pay. Your boss won't thank you for asking out of the blue and you're more likely to be disappointed if you do.

Presenter: Requesting a pay rise, even when you've prepared, can still be worrying. But one way to help yourself is to choose the right moment. Professor Roger Hillman of the Bergmont Institute of Management Studies explains more.

Professor: The day of the week and the time of year are always important. Don't make the mistake of asking first thing Monday morning or last thing on a Friday. Everyone has their mind on other things at those times and the last thing they want to hear is someone asking for more money. Equally, if the company has just announced job cuts, it might be better to wait. Sometimes you have to ask yourself: is it better that I have this job or no job at all?

On that topic, if your boss says no, it's important to know what to do, and I'm assuming here, by the way, that you've made a reasonable request. I wouldn't advise asking for a very big increase. It's hard to take someone seriously if they don't understand their worth and their value to the company. So, if your boss says no, it's obviously going to be annoying and a bit depressing, but keep smiling anyway and ask what you need to do to get a raise. Alternatively, you might want to request more training or a travel allowance or something else that you want. If your boss says no to these requests, you might feel insulted or frustrated, but try not to show it. If you threaten to resign or mention another job with a different firm, you are showing that you are not committed to the company, and that won't help you in the future.

Presenter: And Madison has one other piece of advice.

Madison: Somebody I know once asked for a pay rise and offered to work harder if he got it. This is a big no-no. Firstly, it suggests you're not working hard enough now and secondly, you should be asking for a pay rise on the basis of the work you have done, not on the work you promise to do in the future. I have a feeling this person was made redundant a few months after his request, which just goes to show!

Presenter: So, feeling a bit overwhelmed by all that advice? No need to be. You can visit the show's website and access all the information in a handy document. Till next week!

b Tell Ss they are now going to listen again more carefully. Give them a minute or two to read through the questions, then play the recording. Ask Ss to compare in pairs, then go through the answers as a class.

Answers: 1 a 2 a 3 a 4 c 5 b 6 a

| Optional extra activity |

Ss ask and answer the questions in pairs before they listen again. This approach may help **weaker classes** or classes that need or enjoy more speaking practice.

3 Go through the Focus box as a class, reading each section and discussing the examples. When you finish, ask Ss to work alone and choose a category for phrases 1–3. Check the answers as a class.

Answers: 1 positive   2 negative   3 positive

4a ◆)) 2.10 Tell Ss to read through actions 1–4, then listen and mark them P for positive or N for negative. Ask Ss to compare in pairs then go through the answers.

Answers: 1 negative   2 positive   3 positive   4 negative

| Audioscript 2.10 |

1
Most people appreciate face-to-face communication. They like the human touch. For this reason alone, your boss won't thank you for asking for a pay rise by email.
2
What to pack on a business trip – that is the question. It's important that you pack light so that you're mobile, but at the same time it's always advisable to take an extra suit in case something happens to the one you're wearing.
3
Imagine this situation: you walk into the lift and find that the only other person in there is the CEO. She doesn't say anything, so what do you do? Well, remember that good managers like to know what their staff are thinking so it's always better to talk than not, unless of course the CEO is on the phone.
4
Office politics is a fraught game. It's sometimes tempting to ignore it altogether but that might not be the best course of action. You could find yourself the victim of other people's games. Instead, it's good to stay aware of the politics so that you know what is happening and can play the game if you really have to.

b Ask Ss to look at the Focus box while they listen again and tick the phrases that they hear. Check the answers as a class.

Answers:
It's important that you …
It's always advisable to …
It's always better to … than not.
It's sometimes tempting to … but
Your boss won't thank you for …

5 Put Ss in pairs to discuss the questions. When they finish, ask a few pairs to share their best ideas.

| Optional extra activity |

Ss list their ideas for questions 1 and 2, then conduct the conversation as a roleplay. Ss could take turns asking for the pay rise and responding. If Ss like this topic, video or audio recording with a tablet or phone can extend the roleplay into areas such as body language and intonation.

| Homework ideas |

Workbook: Ex 1–5, p15

3 OVERVIEW

3A I remember …
Goal | narrate a childhood memory
Grammar | past perfect simple and continuous
Vocabulary | memory
GSE learning objective
Can narrate a story in detail, giving relevant information about feelings and reactions

3B Great rivals
Goal | express an opinion about rivals
Grammar | comparatives and superlatives
Vocabulary | character adjectives
GSE learning objective
Can justify and sustain views clearly by providing relevant explanations and arguments

3C Life's too short
Goal | summarise an argument
Grammar | forming adjectives
Vocabulary | arguments
GSE learning objective
Can summarise the position at the end of a negotiation in some detail

3D English in action
Goal | complain and give and respond to feedback
Vocabulary | adjectives to describe food
GSE learning objective
Can give feedback to an employee about what they are doing well and what they need to improve on

Roadmap video
Go online for the Roadmap video and worksheet.

VOCABULARY BANK

3A 'Memory' idioms

3B Adjective suffixes *-(ic)al, -ic, -ive, -ous* and *-y*

DEVELOP YOUR SKILLS

3A Develop your writing
Goal | write a personal anecdote
Focus | showing the time and sequence of events
GSE learning objective
Can signal time sequence in a longer narrative text about a real or imagined event, using a range of language

3B Develop your listening
Goal | understand most of a TV/radio programme
Focus | ignoring filler phrases
GSE learning objective
Can understand a large part of many TV programmes on familiar topics

3C Develop your reading
Goal | understand a magazine article
Focus | using a monolingual dictionary
GSE learning objective
Can use a monolingual dictionary to check the meaning of words without needing to refer to a bilingual dictionary

3A I remember …

Introduction
The goal of this lesson is for students to narrate a childhood memory. To help them achieve this, they will revise past perfect simple and continuous in the context of memories.

Warm-up
Before the class starts, show Ss 8–10 different items on a tray, or display a picture of them. Choose everyday items that Ss will definitely know (keys, phone, pencil, etc). Show the items for 30 seconds to one minute. Cover or remove them and ask Ss to work alone, then in pairs, to make a list of the items. Find out who can remember the most. Ask Ss what they are testing (memory) and tell them that this is today's topic.

Reading

1 Ask Ss to complete the memory quiz alone, then compare scores in pairs. Find out who got the highest score.

Optional extra activity
Ask Ss if they think having a good memory is something that is natural or whether you can work on it. Ss may be aware of memory games or techniques. Discuss what strategies they have for remembering English and any aids such as vocabulary apps that can help them.

2a Tell Ss they are going to read about someone's memory. Allow a few minutes for Ss to look at the picture and read the text. When they finish, check the answer, pointing out that *superior* means very good or above average.

> **Answer:**
> She has HSAM (Highly Superior Autobiographical Memory) and can recall childhood events from very early in life.

b Ask Ss to discuss the question in pairs. When they finish, have whole-class feedback.

> **Possible answers:**
> **Advantages:** you will have no problem with exams, you can perform well in card games or other activities requiring memory
> **Disadvantages:** your mind is always busy, you are different from other people, it can be overwhelming and confusing

Optional extra activity
Ss roleplay Rebecca and a journalist. This is a fun way to quickly refresh past tenses while enabling speaking practice. **Stronger classes** can do this without looking at the text, while **weaker classes** may need to have a list of key words to help them recall the events. If Ss struggle with past simple, you may need to revise this before moving on to past perfect.

54

Grammar

Past perfect simple and continuous

3a Ask Ss to decide what the main events of the birthday story were (the family visit, Rebecca being put in her cot, etc). Look at the list of events and decide which happened before the main events. Ask Ss to work alone and then in pairs. When they finish, elicit feedback.

Answers: 2, 5

Optional alternative activity

Enlarge and photocopy the events in Ex 3a and cut them into strips. Give each small group of Ss a set of sentences and ask them to put them in the order they happened. After this, discuss what the main events of the story were and what went before them. Discuss the tenses used and why they are used. This approach may suit a class who like to explore grammar.

b Ask Ss to work alone to identify the tenses in all the events in Ex 3a. Allow a few minutes, then ask Ss to check together. Don't confirm answers yet.

c Refer Ss to the grammar box to check their answers, then have whole-class feedback discussing any questions and giving further clarification as needed. It could be helpful to build up a timeline showing the interaction of the tenses.

Answers: 1 past simple 2 past perfect continuous
3 past simple 4 past continuous 5 past perfect simple
6 past simple

Grammar checkpoint

The past perfect is not usually used alone – it is most often used alongside the past simple. Both tenses are used to talk about past actions or events but the past perfect usually indicates which happened first. Point out that *by the time* is often used with two clauses, one with past simple and the other with past perfect. It is also possible to use *by the time* with both clauses in the past perfect. Use of the past perfect is sometimes essential for accurate meaning – as in Ex 4, items 2 and 4. The use of adverbials such as *already* and *just* can further specify how two events are related.

4 Ask Ss to look at each pair of sentences and discuss the difference in meaning, if any. Emphasise that both sentences are correct and there will be two pairs where there is no difference. Allow plenty of time for this discussion, monitoring to see how well Ss understand the differences. When they finish, call on pairs to answer and explain the differences where relevant. Use timelines to further check understanding.

Answers:
1 no difference
2 a = I wasn't running anymore. b = I was still running.
3 no difference
4 a = she started when/after I got home
  b = she finished before I got home

5a 🔊 3.1 Explain that Ss should listen and complete the text, using the verbs in brackets in either the past simple or past perfect simple. Give Ss a minute to read through first, then play the recording. Pairs can compare answers and listen again as needed before going through as a class.

Answers: 1 'd had 2 'd practised 3 'd even saved
4 bumped 5 failed 6 waited 7 tried 8 failed

Pronunciation checkpoint

Point out that the contracted 'd can be hard to hear. It's easier to hear when the following word starts with a vowel sound, since the two sounds link together, as in example 3: *I'd even saved*. Remind Ss that they can choose not to use contracted forms if they prefer when speaking but they still need to be able to recognise them when listening.

b 🔊 3.2 Tell Ss they'll now listen again and repeat each sentence after the recording. Play the recording and drill chorally and individually as needed.

6a Ask Ss to read the text and complete with the correct form of the verbs provided. Point out that sometimes more than one option is possible. With **weaker classes**, you may prefer to go through the first few as a class. Then ask Ss to work alone, discuss in pairs, then check with the whole class. Refer Ss to the grammar box as needed.

Answers: 1 hadn't planned/hadn't been planning 2 opened
3 found 4 had organised 5 had tidied 6 (had) decorated
7 had been cooking 8 started 9 gave 10 had bought
11 had been learning 12 felt

Optional alternative activity

When Ss are giving the answers, ask them concept-checking questions to help them confirm their understanding. For example: *Did they put up the balloons before she came into the room?* (Yes) – so we need past perfect. *Is learning the guitar a single event?* (No) – so we need a continuous form.

b This exercise enables Ss to use the forms studied. Look at the first sentence starter as a class and discuss continuations. Point out that it does not need to be a real occasion – Ss can invent one. Ss continue alone. Finally, put Ss in pairs to tell their partner.

LANGUAGE BANK 3A pp.140–141

Stronger classes could read the notes at home. Otherwise, go over the notes with Ss. In each exercise, elicit the first answer as an example. Ss work alone to complete the exercises, then check their answers in pairs. In feedback, check answers with the whole class. Ss can refer to the notes to help them.

Answers:
1 1 [2] [1] 2 [2] [1] 3 [1] [2] 4 [2] [1]
  5 [1] [2] 6 [1] [2]
2 1 held
  2 had never had
  3 had never been
  4 involved
  5 had been working (*had worked* also possible but less likely because of the focus on duration)
  6 had won
  7 gave
  8 had read
  9 realised (*had realised* also possible, but we would probably drop *had* here)
  10 had been trying

Further practice

Photocopiable activities: 3A Grammar 1, p185;
3A Grammar 2, p186
App: 3A Grammar practice 1 and 2

Vocabulary

Memory

7a Ask Ss to work in pairs and match the phrases in bold with their meanings, writing the letters a–h beside the sentences. Ss should ignore the underlined words for the moment. Go through the answers as a class and drill the phrases.

Answers: 1 c 2 e 3 h 4 b 5 f 6 d 7 a 8 g

Vocabulary checkpoint

Ss should be encouraged to notice all parts of lexical chunks, including dependent prepositions and verb patterns, so that they can use them with accuracy. Point these out as you go through the answers, for example: *have a good memory for*, *have no memory of*, *remind someone of* + noun/ -ing, *bear in mind the fact that*.

b Ss practise using the vocabulary alone by replacing the underlined parts with their own ideas. Monitor to check they are making correct sentences. When they finish, ask them to tell each other in pairs and try to extend the conversation by asking follow-up questions. There's no need for feedback, but when they finish, ask a few individuals to share something they learnt from their partner.

VOCABULARY BANK 3A p158
'Memory' idioms

This is an optional extension to the vocabulary section, extending the lexical set and providing further practice. If you're short of time, this can be done for homework.
1 Put Ss in pairs to match the phrases in bold with the meanings, using dictionaries, guesswork or their devices. Go through the answers.

Answers: 1 b 2 g 3 a 4 h 5 f 6 c 7 e 8 d

2a Ask Ss to complete the sentences using a form of the expressions from Ex 1. Allow plenty of time for this. Go through the answers.

Answers: 1 have a bad memory for   2 childhood memory
3 refresh your memory   4 slip your mind
5 serve as a reminder   6 in living memory

b Ask pairs to discuss their opinions about the statements in Ex 2a. There are no fixed answers. At the end, have a show of hands to see which opinions are most popular.

Further practice

Photocopiable activities: 3A Vocabulary, p187
App: 3A Vocabulary practice 1 and 2

Speaking

Prepare

8a 🔊 **3.3** Tell Ss they are going to talk about a childhood memory but first they will hear two people doing the same. Refer them to the instruction to make notes, then play the recording.

b Ask Ss to compare notes in pairs, then play the recording again before dealing with any questions. You may need to explain the term *to help yourself* = to take without asking or needing to ask. Ask Ss which of the memories they found most interesting or familiar.

Audioscript 3.3

1
Anyway, I'll never forget the time my brother tricked me. I was about 12 and I'd been studying for a science exam and my brother said to me, 'Do you want to know the secret of doing well in an exam? You have to sleep with the book under your pillow!'.
Now for some reason, I believed him. I thought this would help me recall the information during the exam. So, that night, I put the science book under my pillow. But then I thought, 'Why not put all my school books under my pillow and then I'll learn everything in one night?'. So, I did. And when my mum woke me up the next morning, she found this big pile of books under my pillow and I hadn't slept much because it was so uncomfortable. So of course, I did worse than usual in the exam because I was so tired. Anyway, my brother thought this was all hilarious, but my mum didn't and he got punished for it!

2
My first train journey was very memorable because it was also the first time I got told off by my father. I was about seven and I was travelling by train with my whole family in India. I don't know if you've seen Indian trains, but they're huge and some of them have bunk beds for sleeping in – three beds stacked on top of each other. So, I'd been sleeping on the top bunk and, when I woke up, I felt rather hungry and I saw a boy passing through the carriage with a basket on his head. He was selling chocolate. So, I thought, 'I can just take one bar!' because I was above him, on the bunk bed. So as he walked past, I did. I helped myself to a chocolate bar from the basket on his head.
A bit later, I got down from the bed and the chocolate wrapper fell to the floor. My father said, 'Where did you get this?' I didn't say anything – he understood and suddenly I felt totally ashamed. I realised then what I'd done. So, my father took me by the hand to find the boy and he made me explain what I'd done and apologise and then he paid the boy for the chocolate that I'd stolen. Now, whenever I eat chocolate, it reminds me of that incident.

Optional alternative activity

Before Ss listen, ask them to predict the stories using these prompts: 1) *science exam, pillow, book, tired*; 2) *chocolate, train, bunk bed, chocolate wrapper, apologise*. Ss then listen and compare their predictions with the stories they hear. This is a nice additional listening task for groups that would benefit from an extra exposure to the recording.

Optional extra activity

Ss work in pairs and retell the stories they heard on the recording, using their notes to help them. If they have access to the audioscript, **weaker classes** can retell using it first, then try without it.

9 Ask Ss to choose a childhood memory and make notes. Emphasise that they should not write sentences, just key words. Allow time for this. If they can't think of one, they can make up a memory or retell the ones from the recording.

Optional extra activity

Add prompts to the board to help Ss structure their notes. This may help **weaker classes**.
When did it happen?
Where were you?
Who else was there?
What were the key events?
Were there any memorable details?

Speak

10 Put Ss in pairs to narrate and compare their memories. Refer them to the Useful phrases and encourage them to develop the conversation. When they finish, ask Ss to share any fun or interesting stories they heard.

> **Reflection on learning**
> Write the following questions on the board:
> *What did you do well in this lesson?*
> *How will you memorise some of the words and phrases from this lesson?*
> Put Ss in pairs to discuss the questions. When they have finished, ask if anyone wants to share their ideas with the class, but don't force them to if they'd rather not.

Homework ideas
Ex 10: Ss write a paragraph about a childhood memory.
Language bank: 3A Ex 1–2, pp.140–141
Workbook: Ex 1–4, p20
App: vocabulary and pronunciation practice

Fast route: continue to Lesson 3B
Extended route: go to p120 for Develop your writing

3B Great rivals

Introduction

The goal of this lesson is for students to express an opinion about rivals. To help them achieve this, they will revise character adjectives and study comparatives and superlatives.

Warm-up

Provide pictures or names of some great contemporary rivals and ask Ss to say what is the same about them and what is different. Examples: Pepsi and Coca Cola, Microsoft and Apple, Rafael Nadal and Roger Federer, cats and dogs. Ask Ss to discuss in pairs and monitor and listen to see if they are using comparative adjectives correctly but don't correct them. When they finish, have a whole-class discussion about which of the two in each pair they consider better.

Reading and vocabulary

Character adjectives

1 Ask Ss to look at the photos and discuss the questions in pairs. When they finish, work as a class to identify the people and their rivals and ask a few Ss to report back on one interesting point from their discussion.

> **Answers:**
> 1 Serena Williams: tennis player
>   Bobby Fischer: chess player
>   Bill Gates: businessman (main founder of Microsoft Corporation)
>   1972 American Olympic basketball team: famous for losing a very close match to their rivals, the Soviet team

2 Ask Ss to read about two sets of rivals. They should ignore the words in bold for the moment. When they finish, put Ss in pairs to tell each other who won and how, without looking at their books. Go through the answers as a class.

> **Answers:**
> **Chess rivals:** Fischer won. He lost his temper, which upset Spassky and allowed Fischer to fight back and win.
> **Basketball rivals:** the Soviet Union won. They scored in the final three seconds by throwing the ball from one end of the court to the other.

Optional alternative approach
Allocate texts to Ss, with Student A reading one text and Student B the other. AB pairs then tell each other about the texts they read.

3a Ask Ss to work in pairs to guess the meaning of the words in bold, using the context to help them. They should not use dictionaries or devices. If time is short, you can do this as a whole class.

> **Vocabulary checkpoint**
> Encourage Ss to notice the root words and use their understanding of affixes to help them guess meaning. For example, the root word *experience* and the prefix *in* can be unpacked to help understand the word *inexperienced*. Similarly: *un* (not), *predict* (say what will happen), *able* (can) means that *unpredictable* = cannot say what will happen. In other cases, the context is all that Ss have to work with, so discuss how they can identify a word's grammar and meaning by its position in the sentence.

b Ask Ss to now match the words in bold with their meanings, writing each word beside its definition. Emphasise that you do not expect them to know all the words and they should still not use dictionaries. When they finish, go through the answers as a class and discuss any items they are uncertain about. Drill the words as you check them. Point out the unusual pronunciation of *tough* /tʌf/.

> **Answers:** 1 competitive 2 stubborn 3 confident
> 4 unpredictable 5 inexperienced 6 arrogant 7 reasonable
> 8 determined 9 tough 10 thoughtful 11 bold
> 12 remarkable

4 3.4 Ask Ss to read the example and explain that they should use one of the adjectives in Ex 3b to rephrase what they hear in the recording. **Weaker classes** may need to pause after each and discuss answers.

> **Answers:**
> 1 She sounds quite reasonable.
> 2 He sounds quite arrogant.
> 3 He sounds quite tough.
> 4 She sounds quite stubborn.
> 5 She sounds quite inexperienced.
> 6 He sounds quite determined.
> 7 He sounds quite confident.
> 8 She sounds quite remarkable.
> 9 He sounds quite unpredictable.
> 10 She sounds quite competitive.
> 11 She sounds quite thoughtful.
> 12 He sounds quite bold.

Unit 3

Audioscript 3.4

1. She's usually very fair and sensible.
2. I hate him. He thinks he's better than everyone else.
3. You won't win. He's strong and not afraid.
4. She never changes her mind. It's really frustrating.
5. She doesn't know what she's doing. She hasn't done this kind of work before.
6. You won't be able to stop him once he's made up his mind.
7. He believes that he's good enough to win.
8. You'll be surprised – amazed even – when you meet her.
9. You never know what he'll do next.
10. She always tries hard to win.
11. She's quite serious and quiet.
12. He's not usually afraid of taking risks.

VOCABULARY BANK 3B p158
Adjective suffixes -(ic)al, -ic, -ive, -ous and -y

This is an optional extension to the vocabulary section, extending the lexical set and providing further practice. If you're short of time, this can be done for homework.

1 Put Ss in pairs to complete the table using dictionaries, guesswork or their devices. Go through the answers.

Answers: 1 ambitious 2 competitive 3 creative
4 curious 5 energetic 6 enthusiastic 7 generous
8 greedy 9 historical* 10 imaginative 11 musical
12 romantic 13 trendy 14 wealthy

(*If Ss put *historic* rather than *historical*, explain that *historical* = concerning history, but *historic* = important moment in history; this will be covered in Lesson 3C.)

2 Ask Ss to underline the correct options in the sentences, then compare in pairs. Go through the answers.

Answers:
A 1 curious 2 enthusiastic 3 creative
B 1 wealthy 2 romantic 3 generous
C 1 energetic 2 imaginative 3 competitive 4 ambitious

3 Ask Ss to choose three adjectives from Ex 1 that describe them, then tell a partner. There are no fixed answers.

Further practice

Photocopiable activities: 3B Vocabulary, p190
App: 3B Vocabulary practice 1 and 2

Grammar
Comparatives and superlatives

Optional alternative activity

Ask Ss to recall how Spassky and Fischer were different and to provide examples. Prompt them with adjectives if necessary (*stubborn, arrogant, reasonable, young*). Write their ideas on the board and if there are any problems with the basic rules for comparatives, for example with short and longer adjectives, go over them. Elicit the form, then move on to Ex 5a. This approach may be suitable for **weaker classes**.

5a Ask Ss to identify which person or team from Ex 2 is referred to in each opinion. Tell Ss to compare in pairs, then elicit the answers.

Answers: a Spassky b Fischer c Soviet team
d American team e Spassky f Fischer g American team

b Ask Ss what is similar about the sentences in Ex 5a (they all make comparisons). Tell Ss they are going to use these examples to study some grammar. Give Ss plenty of time to read the grammar box and match an example to each rule, before checking in pairs. Check answers with the class and be prepared to give further explanations/examples where necessary.

Answers: 1 d 2 e 3 a 4 g 5 b 6 f 7 c

6a 🔊 3.5 Focus attention on the sentences. Ask Ss to listen to the recording to notice how they're pronounced. If you think it's useful, explain the information in the Pronunciation checkpoint below, using the examples given.

Pronunciation checkpoint
We emphasise the extra information when we describe a big difference, stressing words such as *near* or *so*, to help the listener understand the emphasis. The greater the difference, the greater the stress. We tend to use much more exaggerated intonation when we express bigger or more surprising differences, and narrower or more hesitant intonation when we talk about smaller differences.

b Ss discuss which word gets emphasised in describing a big difference.

Answers: 1 b near 2 b so 3 b nearly

c Ask Ss to listen again and repeat, paying attention to the intonation. Drill chorally and individually if necessary.

7 This exercise practises the forms studied. Go through the first example with the class, eliciting the correct form of the adjective. Ss complete the sentences alone, then check in pairs. Check answers with the whole class. You may need to ask Ss questions to help them come up with the correct form such as: *Is it a short adjective? Is it a regular adjective? Is it positive or negative?*

Answers: 1 the best 2 as competitive as 3 much harder
4 far less stable 5 by far the tougher
6 older she got … tougher she became
7 a bit more thoughtful 8 more of a family person
9 far more stable 10 more elegant 11 a lot more popular

Culture notes

The story of what happened between Tonya Harding and Nancy Kerrigan, as described in this short text, is explored in the award-winning 2017 film *I, Tonya*. If your Ss are interested in this story, you could watch it as a class.

8 Write the example prompt on the board and provide a possible continuation yourself, using a friend or family member. Ask Ss to work alone to think of statements. Point out that they will share these, so they need to be sensitive to other people in the class. There is no need for feedback as Ss will all have different answers but when they finish, ask Ss to tell a partner and give reasons where they can.

LANGUAGE BANK 3B pp.140–141

Stronger classes could read the notes at home. Otherwise, check the notes with Ss. In each exercise, elicit the first answer as an example. Ss work alone to complete the exercises, then check their answers in pairs. In feedback, check answers with the whole class. Ss can refer to the notes to help them.

Answers:
1   1 My twin sister was always *a lot more confident than me*.
    2 At school, she was *by far the most popular girl in the class* or *the most popular girl in the class by far*.
    3 It seemed that *the more popular* she got, *the less confident I became*.
    4 In class, she always worked *a lot more quickly than me*.
    5 But she was never *as hardworking as me*, and my results were always *far better than hers*.
    6 It was *less of a rivalry* and *more of a constant battle*.
2   1 among 2 slightly 3 hungrier/more hungry
    4 as competitive as 5 better and better 6 greater

Further practice

Photocopiable activities: 3B Grammar 1, p188; 3B Grammar 2, p189
App: 3B Grammar practice 1 and 2

Speaking

Prepare

9a Explain that Ss are going to read about two different inventors. Put Ss in pairs and name them A and B, then ask them to turn to the relevant pages and read.
b Ask AB pairs to tell each other about their inventor and say why the one they read about was better. **Fast finishers** can read each other's information and then decide which one was the best.
10a Work as a class to name famous rivals. You can prompt with the ones from the warm-up stage and elicit others that Ss are aware of in the categories mentioned. Make a list on the board.
b Ask Ss to choose one set of rivals and make notes about them in the areas given.

Teaching tip

For an activity to be successful, Ss benefit from having plenty of information to work with, especially **weaker classes**. Ss also benefit from discussing and preparing with others before speaking in pairs. This kind of preparation is particularly useful as it's a speaking task in itself. If you have time, it is worth extending this task to a research one, where a pair research one of the rivals each and practise what they are going to say before they share the information. The 'prepare and rehearse' stage helps them gain confidence.

Speak

11 Put Ss in pairs to tell each other. Encourage them to ask follow-up questions. When Ss finish, ask them to discuss and decide which pair of rivals was the most interesting and why.

Optional extra activity

Ss write a biographical text or magazine article describing the rivals they talked about. Encourage them to add pictures. These can be used for a wall display or online class magazine.

Reflection on learning

Write the following questions on the board:
What can you do better after this lesson?
What part of the lesson was most fun for you? Why?
Put Ss in pairs to discuss the questions. When they have finished, ask if anyone wants to share their ideas with the class, but don't force them to if they'd rather not.

Homework ideas

Language bank: 3B Ex 1–2, pp.140–141
Workbook: Ex 1–5, p21
App: grammar, vocabulary and pronunciation practice

Fast route: continue to Lesson 3C
Extended route: go to p88 for Develop your listening

3c Life's too short

Introduction

The goal of this lesson is for students to summarise an argument. To help them achieve this, they will revise forming adjectives and the vocabulary of arguments.

Warm-up

Write on the board: *argument, disagreement, war, debate, fight*. Ask Ss to discuss the difference in meaning between the words in groups and write them in order of strength (*debate, disagreement, argument, fight, war*). When they finish, nominate a student from each group to share their ideas with the class. Tell them this is today's topic.

Reading and vocabulary

Arguments

1 Put Ss in pairs to discuss the questions for a few minutes. Monitor and help if necessary. When they finish, have a show of hands to see who Ss argue with the most (sibling, parent, other relative, partner, boss, teacher, strangers) to see if there is a pattern.
2a Tell Ss they are going to read about three disagreements. They should choose one word in the box that caused each. Point out that two are not needed. Give Ss a few minutes, then ask them to check in pairs before going through the answers as a class.

Answers:
1 food (Ss may say age and respect – these are features, but food is the main cause.)
2 work
3 housework

b Ask Ss to read a second time for more detail and decide who is in the right in each case. Ask pairs to discuss before you check answers with the class. There are no fixed answers.

3 Ask Ss to choose phrases in bold from Ex 2a to replace the underlined phrases with similar meaning. Pairs can discuss ideas before whole-class feedback. Go over pronunciation and level of formality. *Pick a fight, gang up on* and *back down* are all informal.

Answers: 1 clashed with 2 backed down
3 find a compromise 4 contradict 5 intervened
6 didn't see eye to eye 7 picks a fight 8 underlying issue
9 had an issue with 10 ganged up on

4 Ask Ss to work in pairs and retell each story, using the words in bold. **Stronger classes** may be able to do this without looking. **Weaker classes** can have prompts to help them. Write a few of the phrases for each story on the board in the correct order for them to look at.

Optional extra activity

Put Ss in pairs to roleplay (one of) the three disagreements. If your Ss enjoy this kind of activity, elicit and input a few agreeing and disagreeing phrases first to help them and discuss how the situations require different levels of formality. For example: *That's just not right. I'm not very happy about that. I can't agree, I'm afraid. Let's try and find a compromise. No way! I see what you mean, but …*

Further practice

Photocopiable activities: 3C Vocabulary, p193
App: 3C Vocabulary practice 1 and 2

Language focus
Forming adjectives

5a Tell Ss they are going to look at adjective formation. Ask Ss to read the Language focus box and complete each adjective by adding the correct suffix. Complete the first answer as a class, then Ss continue in pairs.
b Tell Ss to check answers by finding the adjectives in the texts in Ex 2a. They should also decide if the meaning of each adjective is negative, positive or neutral. They can mark each word with (+), (−) or (n). Ask Ss to compare in pairs before going through the answers and discussing as a class.

Answers: 1 childish (−) 2 ridiculous (−) 3 sensible (+)
4 ethical (+) 5 tricky (−) 6 disrespectful (−)
7 apologetic (n) 8 hopeless (−)

Vocabulary checkpoint

The shades of meaning between adjectives with similar forms can be explored through examples in context:
economical = cheap – A large box of washing powder is more economical than two small ones.
economic = connected with finance – We can study economics at university.
childish = immature – It was childish to throw the cup on the floor.
childlike = innocent – She's like a child in a positive way.
Ask Ss to give examples to demonstrate the differences between other adjectives with similar forms (*sensible/sensitive, historic/historical, classic/classical*, etc.).

6a Ask Ss to say the words to themselves and decide which one is different in each group. Point out that you are looking at pronunciation, not meaning. For **weaker classes**, tell Ss to focus on word stress. Don't go through the answers as they will listen to the recording.

b 3.8 Ss listen to the words. Ask them to underline the stressed syllable in each word and then identify the odd one out in each group. Check answers with the whole class. Remind Ss that weak forms are common in unstressed syllables and highlight these if Ss are interested. Ss listen again and repeat the examples chorally and individually.

Answers: 1 out<u>ra</u>geous 2 <u>com</u>fortable 3 <u>co</u>lourful
4 tra<u>di</u>tional

7 Go through the first example with the class and write the answer on the board. Ss then work alone to complete the text before comparing in pairs. In feedback, nominate Ss to read the sentences aloud focusing on correct stress and weak forms. Write the answers on the board so Ss can confirm the spelling.

Answers: 1 likeable 2 sensible 3 hopeless 4 acceptable
5 disrespectful 6 apologetic 7 pointless 8 ridiculous
9 reasonable 10 outrageous

Optional alternative activity

Create two versions of the text in Ex 7 and make copies, with half the correct answers filled in for Ss A and the other half for Ss B. Ss then complete their five missing words. Organise Ss in AB pairs and get them to check each other's answers against the ones given. Monitor and listen to their pronunciation. This is a good approach for **weaker classes** and classes that need more speaking practice.

LANGUAGE BANK 3C pp.140–141

Stronger classes could read the notes at home. Otherwise, check the notes with Ss. Elicit the first answer as an example. Ss work alone to complete the exercise, then check their answers in pairs. In feedback, check answers with the whole class. Ss can refer to the notes to help them.

Answers:
1 1 sensible 2 foolish 3 pointless 4 respectful
   5 curious 6 Historical 7 logical 8 scary

Further practice

Photocopiable activities: 3C Language focus 1, p191;
3C Language focus 2, p192
App: 3C Language focus practice 1 and 2

Speaking
Prepare

8 Explain that Ss are going to do a roleplay about a disagreement. Name Ss A or B and refer them to the relevant pages to read their information and instructions. Ask them to prepare phrases and vocabulary they could use. Monitor and help as needed.

Speak

9 Put Ss in pairs to roleplay their disagreement. Remind them that they should try and find a compromise as well as express their feelings. Monitor and listen, taking note of good language and errors.

10 Ask Ss to sit with a new partner to report on the discussion they had, what they and their partner said and the final compromise (if any). When Ss finish, discuss their compromises as a class and give feedback on their language.

> **Optional extra activity**
>
> Put Ss A together in small groups and Ss B the same. Ss work together to read, plan and make notes. Regroup them in AB pairs to roleplay their disagreement. At the end of this, give feedback, then re-pair to repeat the roleplay. This is good for **weaker classes** who need more support and practice.

> **Reflection on learning**
>
> Write the following questions on the board:
> *How important was the language you learnt in today's lesson? In what situations will today's vocabulary be useful outside the class?*
> Put Ss in pairs to discuss the questions. When they have finished, ask if anyone wants to share their ideas with the class, but don't force them if they'd rather not.

> **Homework ideas**
>
> Language bank: 3C Ex 1, pp.140–141
> Workbook: Ex 1–5, p22
> App: grammar, vocabulary and pronunciation practice

Fast route: continue to Lesson 3D
Extended route: go to p100 for Develop your reading

3D English in action

Introduction

The goal of this lesson is for students to be able to complain and give and respond to feedback. To help them achieve this, they will revise some useful phrases for such situations and adjectives to describe food.

Warm-up

Ask Ss to discuss how often they eat out and what kind of places they visit. Elicit the kinds of problems that can occur when eating out (no tables available, food not good, service slow, etc). Tell Ss that today's lesson is about how to express complaints in such situations.

Vocabulary

Adjectives to describe food

1 Ask Ss to discuss the questions in pairs. When they finish, discuss answers as a class and write useful vocabulary on the board. There are no fixed answers.

2a Refer Ss to the sentences and words in bold. Ask them what kind of words are in bold (adjectives) and what they refer to (food). Point out that some are negative but not all. Ask Ss to match sentences 1–9 with letters a–i. Ss can compare in pairs before you go through the answers, drilling as needed.

Answers: 1 c 2 i 3 b 4 g 5 a 6 e 7 f 8 d 9 h

b Ask Ss to identify the adjectives that are negative. Check as a class.

Answers: tough, bland, greasy

c Ask Ss to decide which adjectives could describe the foods shown. Check as a class. Ss can make more suggestions of which foods can be described with the adjectives.

Suggested answers:
A creamy B crunchy, salty C filling D greasy, filling E spicy
F spicy, crunchy G creamy, bland H raw, crunchy, bland

3 Look at the first sentence as a class. Ask Ss to suggest completions, then ask pairs to continue with the remaining sentences. Check answers as a class.

Possible answers: (accept reasonable alternatives)
1 salty, greasy 2 crunchy, bland, raw 3 creamy, greasy
4 spicy, salty

Listening 1

4 3.9 Explain that Ss are going to listen to seven short conversations about a problem in a restaurant and match them to the reasons a–c, writing the letter beside the numbers 1–7 as they listen. Go through the answers.

Answers: 1 c 2 c 3 a 4 c 5 b 6 a 7 b

> **Audioscript 3.9**
>
> **Conversation 1**
> **W1:** How's your dish, madam?
> **A:** The vegetables are a bit raw, actually.
> **W1:** Oh, I'm sorry to hear that. I can ask the kitchen to cook them a bit longer.
> **A:** Yes, OK. If you would.
> **W1:** Of course, madam. Just bear with me a few minutes …
> **A:** Sure.
>
> **Conversation 2**
> **B:** Excuse me.
> **W2:** Yes, sir.
> **B:** Is this dish supposed to be so spicy?
> **W2:** Well, yes, it is one of our more spicy dishes.
> **B:** It's just too spicy for me.
> **W2:** Oh, I'm sorry to hear that, sir.
> **B:** Could I choose something else?
> **W2:** Yes, of course. If you'd like to take a look at the menu, …
> **B:** Yes, OK. … Sorry, I just wasn't expecting something quite so hot.
> **W2:** That's absolutely fine. I'll mention it to the chef.
> **B:** Thanks.
> **W2:** Do you know what you'd like instead?
> **B:** Not yet. Could you give me a couple of minutes to take a look?
> **W2:** Of course. I'll come back.
>
> **Conversation 3**
> **W1:** How's your food, guys?
> **C:** It's nice, but the side dishes haven't come yet.
> **W1:** Oh, I'm really sorry about that. Something must have gone wrong. I'll go and check where they are.
> **C:** Thanks. *[The waiter goes to the kitchen.]*
> **D:** He's very friendly, isn't he?
> **C:** Yeah, they're always very friendly in here.
> **D:** Oh, he's coming back.
> **W1:** I'm really sorry, but they forgot to do them. They'll be with you in a couple of minutes.
> **C:** Oh, OK.
> **W1:** I'm sorry again. I'll deduct them from your bill.
> **C:** Oh, that's nice of you, thanks.
> **W1:** And can I offer you another drink, compliments of the house?
> **C:** Oh, that sounds good.
> **D:** Great, I'll have a fresh orange juice, please.

Unit 3

Conversation 4
- **E:** Excuse me.
- **W2:** How can I help?
- **E:** Could you warm this up for me?
- **W2:** Oh, I'm sorry. Is it not warm enough?
- **E:** No, it's completely cold in the middle.
- **W2:** Oh, of course. I'm sorry about that. I'll do that for you right now.
- **E:** Thank you.

Conversation 5
- **F:** Excuse me! This isn't what I ordered.
- **W1:** No?
- **F:** No. I ordered the vegetarian pie, not the meat one.
- **W1:** Oh, that's odd. Are you sure it's meat?
- **F:** Totally sure.
- **W1:** I'll check it out for you. Hold on a minute.
- **F:** He could have been a bit more apologetic.
- **G:** I know. I don't think he believes you!
- **F:** He's coming back!
- **W1:** Yeah, er, the chef says it *is* vegetarian.
- **F:** Right. Well, it's not because I'm looking at pieces of meat right now. Could I speak to the manager?
- **W1:** Er, yeah, I'll see if I can find her. I won't be a minute …

Conversation 6
- **H:** Excuse me.
- **W2:** Yes, sir?
- **H:** We need to be somewhere in half an hour and the food still hasn't come yet.
- **W2:** Oh, that's no good.
- **H:** Could you check on the order for me?
- **W2:** Yes, of course. What did you order?
- **H:** I ordered the lasagne and my friend ordered the pancakes.
- **W2:** OK, let me check for you. Just give me a moment.

Conversation 7
- **W1:** How is everything?
- **I:** Well, the sauce is very creamy, which is nice …
- **W1:** That's good to hear.
- **I:** … but I asked for no tomatoes and this dish has got tomatoes in it.
- **W1:** I'm sorry about that. I'll change it for you right away.
- **I:** OK, thanks.

5a Tell Ss they will listen again more carefully to complete the sentences. Clarify that Ss should put three words in each gap and that a contraction counts as one word. Play the recording and pause as needed to allow Ss time to write. Ask Ss to compare answers in pairs.

b Ask Ss to check their answers with the Useful phrases box. When they finish, clarify any words or phrases Ss are unsure of.

Answers:
1. a bit raw
2. **a** spicy for me   **b** quite so hot
3. haven't come yet
4. **a** warm this up   **b** in the middle
5. **a** what I ordered   **b** the meat one
6. **a** be somewhere in   **b** you check on
7. no tomatoes and …

Optional alternative activity
If Ss have access to the audioscript, they can check the answers there. They can then listen again and read the script at the same time. This approach can support **weaker classes** or those who struggle with hearing small words such as articles and prepositions.

6a 3.10 Tell Ss they are going to listen carefully to notice the pitch of some speakers' voices when they want to sound more polite. You may need to pause the recording after each section.

b Play the recording again for Ss to repeat, focusing on their intonation.

Pronunciation checkpoint
Point out that rising intonation will help Ss to sound polite. Flat intonation suggests the opposite. Encourage Ss to repeat the phrases after you (or after the recording) with animated intonation and a wide pitch range. It doesn't matter if the intonation seems too exaggerated to begin with – this will help raise Ss' awareness of how intonation can reflect attitude.

7 Ask Ss to decide what they could say, using the Useful phrases box to help them. Ss can compare ideas, then go through the answers as a class.

Suggested answers:
(accept reasonable alternatives)
1. Excuse me. This isn't what I ordered.
2. The meat is a bit tough.
3. We need to be somewhere soon. Could you check on the order for me?
4. Could you warm it up?
5. I wasn't expecting something quite so spicy. Could I choose something else?
6. The side dish hasn't come yet.
7. Is this dish supposed to be so salty?

Listening 2

8 3.11 Tell Ss they are going to listen to conversations between a restaurant manager, David, and his staff. They should listen and match each conversation with one job, one piece of positive feedback and one piece of negative feedback. Ask Ss to compare answers, then check as a class. Ask Ss if they think the owner is good at giving feedback.

Answers:
Conversation 1: head chef, the food arrives quickly, some dishes a bit greasy
Conversation 2: waiter, never late for work, not polite enough
Conversation 3: owner, easy to work with, not friendly enough

Culture notes
It is a convention to give some good feedback as well as not so good. The theory is that we are more open to negative feedback if we have some praise first and then, after the negative feedback, we need to be built up again with more praise. This is called **the sandwich model**. Ask Ss if they have similar methods in their country and if they agree with this approach.

Audioscript 3.11

Conversation 1
- **A:** Sylvia, is now a good time to talk about the survey?
- **B:** Yeah, it's as good a time as any.
- **A:** Good, well, as you know we've been carrying out a customer satisfaction survey over the last couple of weeks and we've had about a hundred responses now …
- **B:** A hundred?
- **A:** Yep.
- **B:** That's good.
- **A:** Yes, it is, and we've looked at the results, so now I want to give you, as the head chef, feedback on what customers think about the food.
- **B:** OK. Go ahead.
- **A:** The first thing to say is that customers are very positive about most of the food here.
- **B:** Good …
- **A:** In particular, the delicious desserts get a big thumbs up.
- **B:** Ah, everyone loves my desserts!

A: Absolutely, me included!
B: [laughs]
A: And they also said that they like the fact that they don't have to wait long for the food to arrive.
B: Yeah, well, we try to be quick.
A: Now, there was the occasional comment about some of the dishes being too spicy but, to be honest, some people hate spicy food and some people love it and it's impossible to satisfy everyone.
B: And we do clearly label those dishes as spicy on the menu.
A: That's right. Also, quite a few customers did comment that the meat dishes are a bit greasy and a bit tough, that was the biggest complaint.
B: Oh, really?
A: Yeah. I think people like their food to be healthy these days and our customers are no exception.
B: I think that's true, but at the same time I want to explain my side. We have a new supplier for our meat and fish and, to be honest, the quality is not as good as the previous supplier.
A: OK, that's a good point and it's one I'll bring up at the next meeting with the owner.
B: OK.
A: But for now, perhaps you could bear that feedback in mind when you're preparing the dishes.
B: If the ingredients are poor quality, there's not much I can do …
A: I understand and I know you're doing your best but like I say, please bear it in mind.
B: All right. I'll do that.
A: Great. I think that's it. And you've got to get back to work.
B: Yep. … Darren, how are you getting on with those chocolate mousses?

Conversation 2
A: Lex, have you got a moment to talk about the survey results?
C: Survey results?
A: Yeah, you know, the customer satisfaction survey.
C: Yeah, OK, sure.
A: Great. Now, as you know, we've asked a lot of customers to fill out a short questionnaire about what they like and what they don't like about the restaurant …
C: Well, I'm sure I was very popular! I always get on with the customers …
A: Well, that's what I want to talk about. But first, I want to say that your punctuality is very good.
C: Thank you very much!
A: You're always on time and that is one of your strong points.
C: 'Course! Never late, me.
A: However, as one of our waiting staff, it's important that you know exactly what people think about the service.
C: Yeah, understood.
A: The general feeling was that the service is a bit too … informal at times.
C: Informal?
A: Yes. Unfortunately, many people felt that they were being treated like a friend rather than a customer.
C: Really?
A: Really. Basically, they'd like to be treated with a little more … politeness.
C: Don't they like having a chat and a laugh with me?
A: Some customers like it but a lot of them don't.
C: Oh … I see.
A: You might like to try being a bit more … professional. Still friendly, still warm, but also professional.
C: Right, yeah. I'll take that on board.
A: Thanks, Lex. I knew I could rely on you to understand.
C: Yeah, OK.
A: You'd better get back to work, I guess. The doors are opening in half an hour.
C: All right, yeah, thanks, boss.

Conversation 3
D: Come in, David.
A: Thank you.
D: So, how has it been going with the feedback from the survey? Have the staff taken it on board?
A: By and large, yes. Some of them found it quite hard to accept that not everything is perfect, but overall, they've responded very well.
D: Good, OK, well, that means that as the owner I also need to give you feedback on your performance here as the manager.
A: OK.
D: Because you've been with us for about 18 months now?
A: That's right.
D: Well, I've spoken to some of the staff to get their opinions and also some of our regular customers.
A: OK.
D: And of course, I have my own opinions.
A: Of course.
D: So, overall people felt that you do your job very well.
A: That's good.
D: They appreciate your honesty and your directness …
A: OK …
D: And they find you easy to work with and reliable.
A: All right. Any criticisms?
D: Just one really. Some people felt you could be a bit more … friendly.
A: Friendly?
D: Yes, that was something that one or two customers mentioned and also a couple of the staff.
A: Right.
D: They said that you're very professional and reliable, but sometimes they also wanted someone who could give them a smile and make them feel … appreciated.
A: I see.
D: I don't think this is a big deal at all, but perhaps it's something that could be improved?
A: I'd like to respond to that if I may.
D: Sure.
A: From my point of view, I think it's my job to make sure that everyone is working well and that customers are happy, but I don't think it's my job to make the *staff* happy.
D: Yes, I see what you mean. But perhaps it's something as simple as a smile and a, 'How are you?' People like to feel that the manager notices them.
A: OK. I'll try to be a bit more … positive to staff …
D: And customers?
A: And the customers, of course. I'll try to be a bit more friendly.
D: Great. Now let's talk about the new restaurant that we're going to open up in Whiteside Bay next year. As you know, …

9a Refer Ss to the Useful phrases and tell them you will play the three conversations again. As they listen, they should mark the phrases in the box 1, 2 or 3, depending on which conversation they heard them in. Pause after each conversation so they can compare answers. Go through the answers as a class.

> **Answers:**
> **Conversation 1**
> The first thing to say is that (customers are very positive).
> (The delicious desserts) get a big thumbs up.
> That was the biggest complaint.
> Perhaps you could (bear that feedback in mind).
> I want to explain my side.
> **Conversation 2**
> The general feeling was that (the service is a bit too informal).
> (Punctuality/That) is one of your strong points.
> Unfortunately, many people felt that (they were being treated like a friend).
> You might like to try being a bit more (professional).
> I'll take that on board.
> **Conversation 3**
> Overall people felt that (you do your job very well).
> They appreciate (your honesty).
> Some people felt you could be a bit more (friendly).
> (It's something that) could be improved.
> From my point of view, (I think it's my job to …).

b Ask Ss to write feedback notes for the six situations, using the words in brackets and the Useful phrases. Monitor and help.

> **Possible answers:**
> 1 Perhaps you could be a bit more punctual.
> 2 Customers appreciate your positive attitude.
> 3 The first thing to say is that you're hard-working.
> 4 Customers have to wait a long time for their food. That was the biggest complaint.
> 5 The cleanliness of the kitchen is one of your strong points.
> 6 People felt you could be more polite.

Speaking

10a Put Ss in pairs and name them A and B. Ask them to turn to the relevant page and read their roles.

b Ask Ss to have their discussion for Situation 1, referring to the Useful phrases to help them. Monitor and listen. Give Ss feedback on what they did well and not so well.

11 Ask Ss to repeat the activity with Situation 2. **Fast finishers** can improvise more conversations with other members of staff.

Optional extra activity
If Ss have access to the audioscript, put them in pairs to practise reading the conversations in Ex 8 before preparing their own. This is a good stepping stone for **weaker classes** who need to gain confidence.

Reflection on learning
Write the following questions on the board:
How will the language of today's lesson be useful in your daily life?
How will it be useful for you on holiday or when at work?
Put Ss in pairs to discuss the questions. When they have finished, ask a few Ss to share their ideas with the class, but don't force them to if they'd rather not.

Homework ideas
Reflection on learning: Write your answers.
Workbook: Ex 1–5, p23
App: grammar, vocabulary and pronunciation practice

Roadmap video
Go online for the Roadmap video and worksheet.

3A Develop your writing

Introduction
The goal of this lesson is for students to write a personal anecdote. To help them achieve this, they will focus on showing the time and sequence of events.

Warm-up
Ask Ss to discuss whether they read personal stories and where (in print, on the computer, on their phone). Find out if they have been inspired to take action after reading a personal story. If time allows, describe a personal story currently in the news where someone is standing up for themselves (or show a short video) and ask for comments.

1 Put Ss in pairs to discuss the quotes and say which they agree with. After a few minutes, conduct brief feedback.

2 Refer Ss to the two personal stories. Ask them to read and decide if each question applies to Story 1, Story 2, both stories or neither. Check that Ss understand the difference between *humiliated* (= publicly made to feel foolish) and *ashamed* (= personally sorry about something you did). Give them a few minutes to read and mark the questions. Then ask Ss to check in pairs before going over the answers.

> **Answers:** 1 neither 2 2 3 both 4 neither 5 1 6 2
> 7 both 8 2

3 Look at the example, then ask Ss to match the phrases in bold to the meanings. Then put Ss in pairs to compare answers. After a few minutes, elicit answers.

> **Answers:**
> **Story 1**
> 1 As soon as 2 One day 3 in the late 90s 4 immediately
> 5 Nowadays 6 The following day 7 in the meantime
> **Story 2**
> 8 Eventually 9 Over time 10 Not so long ago
> 11 A fortnight later 12 After years of 13 Meanwhile
> 14 In the end 15 all of a sudden

4 Tell Ss to read the Focus box, then deal with any questions. Ask Ss to find one more expression for each category in the stories in Ex 2. Go through the answers.

> **Answers:**
> 1 **One day**, we had to do a science project …
> 2 **A fortnight later**, I quit my job.
> 3 **Meanwhile**, I just calmly did my make-up.
> 4 I **immediately** realised what a fool I'd been.

5a Ask Ss to work alone to select the best option to complete the sentences. They will need to think about punctuation, sentence position, tense and meaning. Clarify that more than one option may be possible.

b Put Ss in pairs to compare answers, then go through them as a class. Where more than one option is possible, discuss any difference in meaning.

Answers:
1 in the early 00s
2 Over time (= gradually)/In the meantime (= while something else was happening)
3 All of a sudden (= suddenly)/In the end (= after some time)
4 meanwhile
5 immediately
6 After years of
7 Eventually/In the end (little difference in meaning)
8 Nowadays

6 Ask Ss if they can recall an occasion when they stood up for themselves. Tell a relevant anecdote of your own, if possible.

Optional alternative activity

Ask Ss if they know any stories about standing up for yourself in films, books, TV series, etc. You could suggest examples such as *Mean Girls*, *Matilda*, *Billy Elliot* or *The Karate Kid*. Ask them to summarise the story.

Prepare

7a Ask Ss what they are going to do now. They will know that they are going to write a personal anecdote. Tell them they can choose the experience they talked about in Ex 6 or they can invent one.

b Ask Ss to use the questions to prepare their story, noting down key words but not writing full sentences. Monitor and help with ideas and vocabulary. There is no need for whole-class feedback because all Ss will be working on different ideas.

c Ask Ss to select some time phrases from this lesson that they will include in their story. Suggest that they include at least three of the phrases.

Write

8a Ask Ss to write their anecdote, using the notes they have made. They should write alone, then work with a partner using the checklist provided to give each other feedback.

b Ask Ss to write a second draft, using the feedback they have received. Monitor and help as needed.

Homework ideas

Workbook: Ex 1–8, pp.26–27

3B Develop your listening

Introduction

The goal of this lesson is for students to understand most of a TV/radio programme. To help them achieve this, they will focus on ignoring filler phrases.

Warm-up

Ask Ss what kind of street entertainers are common in their country (singers, musicians, living statues, acrobats, magicians, etc.). Ask Ss whether they enjoy street performances and why the performers do this.

1 Ask Ss to look at the photo and discuss the questions in pairs. After a few minutes, elicit answers.

2a Tell Ss they are going to hear an interview with a world champion living statue. Before they listen, they should predict his answers to the questions. Ask Ss to discuss in pairs, then ask for feedback, writing some predictions on the board.

b 3.6 Play the recording and ask Ss to listen and check their predictions. They can discuss in pairs before you check answers as a class.

Answers:
1 19 years
2 several hours
3 detail-oriented, competitive, determined, a bit tough, a bit stubborn
4 one hour
5 connection or interaction with your audience
6 never perform on an empty stomach, good stomach muscles,
7 because he's well-known, so he's invited to perform at company parties and conferences

c Ask Ss to work in pairs and discuss what they found surprising.

Audioscript 3.6

Evan:	… So, being a living statue is not actually something I planned to do, it was kind of just a fun job I took on while I was at university, you know, to earn a bit of extra money and when I did it actually, it turned out that I was quite good at it.
Interviewer:	So, how long have you been doing it now?
Evan:	About 19 years.
Interviewer:	Wow! And what was your degree in?
Evan:	Actually, it was in economics!
Interviewer:	Oh, right, so your degree had absolutely nothing to do with performance or anything.
Evan:	No, nothing at all!
Interviewer:	But has it helped you in any way?
Evan:	I would say no, it hasn't really helped me much. Studying economics and working as a living statue have nothing in common with each other. Plus I've pretty much forgotten almost everything I learnt at university.
Interviewer:	And you're actually a world champion living statue, aren't you?
Evan:	Yep, that's right. I, um, yeah, I actually won the World Living Statue Championships in the Netherlands a couple of years ago and that was, well, that was a great honour for me. It's like an invitation-only event and they're, well, you could say they're the Academy Awards of our profession so, yeah, yeah I was really pleased to win.
Interviewer:	And what do you actually have to do as a living statue? I mean, the short answer I'm sure is nothing, you just keep very still for as long as possible, but there's more to it than that, isn't there?

Evan:	Yes, absolutely. The first thing really is coming up with a kind of new and creative idea for a performance and then you have to, you know, you have to practise and find the right clothes and the props and stuff and do the full body make-up.	
Interviewer:	Full body make-up?	
Evan:	Yeah, for example, if I'm a gold statue then, you know, I'll, like, paint my whole body gold, or if I'm a marble statue obviously, I'll paint my whole body white, and then I'll paint in the faint blue lines, and that kind of thing, to make it look realistic, and that can take several hours.	
Interviewer:	What did you do for the World Championships?	
Evan:	Um, for the World Championships I was a stone statue and I painted in these tiny cracks so that I looked like a kind of old, almost falling apart statue, and I think the judges really appreciated that, so to speak, they liked the attention to detail and that's the difference between people like me who do it for a living and … students who are just doing it for a bit of money over the summer, you know. We're much more experienced, much more convincing and really just a lot better at the job, you know, we have a lot more inner peace, so to speak.	
Interviewer:	So you need to be quite detail-oriented to be a living statue. What else?	
Evan:	Well, I think you need to be quite competitive and determined, you know, because you're like battling against yourself and your natural desire to move. So yeah, I would say you've got to be a bit tough and a bit stubborn to stand there for that amount of time.	
Interviewer:	What's the maximum amount of time you can stand still without moving?	
Evan:	Well, if I really have to, I can stand completely still for an hour, but a whole session might last six hours …	
Interviewer:	Six hours?	
Evan:	Yes, but, you know, you need to take breaks in that time and change position and stuff like that. But, you know, standing still is not actually the point of being a living statue because otherwise, they might as well get a real statue if you see what I mean.	
Interviewer:	Yep, I get it. So, what is the point, I mean why do you do this job?	
Evan:	The point really is the connection you make with your audience and that connection comes from the small, surprising movements that you make when people are looking at you. Those tiny movements that are, how can I put it, part of the character.	
Interviewer:	So you mean the winks and the small smiles …	
Evan:	Yes, that's right. Some people really believe you are a statue and even if they don't, they're waiting for you to, you know, to do something, so when you do make a tiny movement, they tend to kind of explode with laughter, so to speak. And it's that interaction between the audience and the performer, that's really what it's all about.	
Interviewer:	What is the secret then of being a good living statue?	
Evan:	Well, yes, firstly never try and perform on an empty stomach. If you get hungry you can, like, start to feel light-headed or dizzy so you know, you always need to eat something first. And what else? Well, good stomach muscles are key. You need to have good stomach muscles to hold those positions.	
Interviewer:	And the million-dollar question – how much do you earn as a living statue?	
Evan:	Ah, well, that's a bit of a secret really but I earn more, now that I'm kind of, well-known, so to speak, because I get paid by companies to perform at their parties and conferences and things like that.	
Interviewer:	Oh, I see.	
Evan:	But if you're starting out, then you have to perform on the streets and the money you earn is what people throw into your hat, if you know what I mean, and that, that's not really enough to live on, particularly if it's winter and you're standing in the wrong place, if you see what I mean …	

3 Tell Ss they are going to listen again more carefully. Play the recording for them to complete the sentences, pausing as needed. Go through the answers. Ask Ss what the phrases have in common (they are fillers that don't add meaning).

Answers: 1 Actually 2 I would say 3 well 4 you know 5 and that kind of thing 6 kind of 7 so to speak 8 if you see what I mean 9 how can I put it 10 like

4 Read the Focus box as a class, with different individuals reading sections aloud. Then ask pairs to discuss the question, adding more fillers to the box.

Answers: Phrases 3, 5, 7, 8, 9

5 🔊 3.7 Tell Ss they will hear six more extracts from the interview and they should write the answer, not including the fillers. Ask them to read through the questions first to prepare, then listen. Before feedback, put Ss in pairs to check their answers are grammatically correct, then go through the answers.

Suggested answers:
1 About ten euros each time I get dressed up.
2 No, because you need to be very patient and determined.
3 I set an alarm on my phone to vibrate after an hour, then I hide my phone in my costume.
4 You don't scratch it and eventually it goes away.
5 When people come really close and breathe all over you.
6 I don't have one. I do the job because I enjoy it.

Audioscript 3.7

1
Interviewer: How much do you spend on make-up?
Evan: Oh, um, good question. Well, let me think, I guess it, um … it probably costs a bit less than, let's say, ten euros each time I get dressed up.

2
Interviewer: Can anyone learn to be a living statue?
Evan: Well, I would say not, because, you know, you need to be, like, very, very patient and determined.

3
Interviewer: If you're paid to perform for an hour, how do you know when your hour is finished?
Evan: Hah! That's a good one! Yes, well, it's like this you see, I set the alarm, you know, on my phone to, like, vibrate after an hour or so, and then I kind of hide the phone somewhere in my costume and, you see, when it vibrates I know it's, like, time to stop.

4
Interviewer: What do you do when you need to scratch an itch?
Evan: Um, that's kind of a simple one really, you kind of, just, don't do it and, like, eventually it just kind of goes away.

5
Interviewer: What do you hate about the work you do?
Evan: Well, I'm glad you asked that because it's kind of like this: what I really can't stand, and this is no offence to my audience, but I really can't stand it when people come really close and kind of breathe all over you. Yuk!

6
Interviewer: What is your goal now that you're a world champion living statue?
Evan: Actually, I would say that, you know, I don't really have a goal any more. I just do the job because, strangely, I really enjoy it.

Optional extra activity

If Ss have access to Audioscript 3.7, they can underline the filler phrases in it. Play the audio at the same time so that Ss can notice the way the fillers are spoken. Ask them to read the extracts with and without the fillers to see what is added. Point out that the fillers make speech sound more natural, even if they are not essential to meaning. They also allow the speaker to 'buy time' while they think about how they want to respond.

Teaching tip

Ss often enjoy listening again while reading the audioscript, as they can catch details that they may have missed. While it does not help with developing listening skills, it can be enjoyable when analysing a text for features or looking for specific language.

6 Ask Ss to discuss the questions in pairs, then discuss their answers as a class and see which type of street entertainer is the most popular and why. Elicit a list of problems faced by street performers (people being rude, the weather, needing the bathroom, not enough people passing by, etc.).

Homework ideas

Workbook: Ex 1–3, p26

3c Develop your reading

Introduction

The goal of this lesson is for students to understand a magazine article. To help them achieve this, they will focus on using a monolingual dictionary.

Warm-up

Tell Ss that today you'll be looking at using dictionaries. Ask them to discuss the following questions: *Do you use a paper dictionary or your phone/device to translate? When and why? What are the advantages of using a monolingual/bilingual dictionary? Are dictionaries still valid?*

1 Put Ss in pairs to talk about the questions. After a few minutes, conduct brief feedback. Ask a few groups what they answered and see if there are any common choices in the class.

2 Ask Ss to read quickly and find out the answer to the question. Give them a few minutes, then check the answer.

Answers:
Three:
1 the invention of the sandwich
2 the arrival of pre-prepared sandwiches
3 machines taking over the production of sandwiches from humans.

Teaching tip

Reading a text quickly for the first time is called reading for gist. This is a strategy for Ss to get an overview of a text as well as being better prepared for its content when looking at it in detail later. A time limit helps Ss develop their gist-reading skills, so it's a good idea to give a specific time frame. Simply asking Ss to 'read quickly' may make them feel stressed!

Culture notes

Marks & Spencer is a British clothing and homeware store which also has a high-quality food department. It is a popular lunch stop for workers as, like many British supermarkets, it sells ready-made sandwiches and salads. It is quite unusual for workers to eat lunch in a restaurant on a working day and the majority will eat a sandwich at their desk – the most popular filling being cheese. The average 'lunch hour' is about 30 minutes, with more than half the population having no lunch hour at all. Ss may like to compare this with their own countries.

3 Tell Ss they will now read the article more carefully and choose the correct answers to the questions. Allow a few minutes, then ask Ss to compare choices in pairs before going through the answers as a class. In each case, ask Ss to locate the answers in the article.

Answers: 1 b 2 c 3 c 4 b 5 a 6 c 7 a 8 b

4a Ask Ss to look at the context for the word *momentous* and suggest meanings. This can be a brief stage as Ss will check their ideas in the next exercise.

b Ask Ss to look at the Focus box and find the answer. Discuss how close Ss were in their guesses.

5a Ask Ss to guess the meaning of the other words in bold. Tell them they have a few minutes and they should refer to the context to help them, but they should not use any phones, devices or dictionaries yet. Then ask them to check in a monolingual dictionary.

b Point out that Ss should use dictionary entries to find out the number of syllables and common collocations for each word in bold. Discuss how syllables are usually shown in a dictionary (with a short vertical line or dot between each syllable; the vertical line comes before the stressed syllable). Ss make notes and then compare in pairs.

Optional alternative activity

Ask half the class to use a device, bilingual dictionary or online translation tool, and the other half to use a monolingual dictionary. When they finish, pair up Ss from different halves of the class to discuss their experience and which method is better, quicker, more accurate, etc.

6 This is an opportunity for Ss to comment on what they have read. Ask them to work in pairs. When they finish, open up a whole-class discussion.

Homework ideas

Workbook: Ex 1–7, pp.24–25

4 OVERVIEW

4A Possessions
Goal | describe a precious possession in detail
Grammar | relative clauses
Vocabulary | adjectives to describe things
GSE learning objective
Can describe objects, possessions and products in detail, including their characteristics and special features

4B Job skills
Goal | talk about the requirements of a job
Grammar | obligation and prohibition
Vocabulary | job requirements
GSE learning objective
Can clearly describe their professional aspirations

4C Unwritten rules
Goal | give advice through an informal presentation
Language focus | forming verbs with *en*
Vocabulary | 21st-century words
GSE learning objective
Can give advice on a wide range of subjects

Check and reflect
Review exercises and communicative activities to practise the grammar, vocabulary and functional language from Units 3 and 4.

Roadmap video
Go online for the Roadmap video and worksheet.

VOCABULARY BANK
- **4A** Adjectives to describe things
- **4C** Words from other languages

DEVELOP YOUR SKILLS

4A Develop your reading
Goal | understand a magazine article
Focus | understanding the writer's purpose
GSE learning objective(s)
Can understand the author's purpose and intended audience

4B Develop your writing
Goal | write a covering email
Focus | matching a covering email with a job advert
GSE learning objective
Can write a covering letter addressing specific information mentioned in a job posting

4C Develop your listening
Goal | understand phone messages
Focus | understanding understatement
GSE learning objective
Can understand in detail work-related phone messages

4A Possessions

Introduction
The goal of this lesson is for students to describe a precious possession in detail. To help them achieve this, they will revise relative clauses and adjectives for describing things.

Warm-up
Before the class starts, ask Ss to think about an important possession and imagine they are holding it in their hands. Give an example yourself, cupping your hands as if you are holding the object: *This is a pearl necklace my mum gave me. I wear it on special occasions. It's important because it reminds me of her.* Then ask Ss to 'hold' their object (it can be anything they like) and walk around the class explaining what the possession is and why it's important. When they have spoken to several people, ask them to sit down again and tell Ss this lesson is about describing things.

Vocabulary

Adjectives to describe things

1a Ask Ss to make a list of five possessions. Point out that they can be valuable emotionally even if they are not really worth a lot of money.

b Put Ss in pairs to compare their lists and explain why they have chosen those objects. Have whole-class feedback to see what kind of items are most popular.

2 Ask Ss to look at the photos and complete the descriptions using the adjectives provided. Check they understand *flimsy* = not strong. Give them a few minutes to work alone and then compare answers in pairs. Monitor and help with new vocabulary where necessary. When they finish, go through the answers and correct the word order as needed.

Answers: 1 identical, oval 2 elegant, designer
3 cheap, flimsy 4 priceless, decorative 5 chunky, rectangular 6 sparkly, vivid pink

3 Ask Ss to read through the six types of adjective. Then put Ss in pairs to add more adjectives to each category. They can think of their own adjectives and/or use some from Ex 2. Conduct a brief whole-class discussion and write new adjectives on the board.

Possible answers: 1 lovely, uninteresting 2 tiny, large
3 rough, sturdy 4 square, round 5 purple, gold
6 glass, rubber

Vocabulary checkpoint
Remind Ss that adjectives typically go before the noun they modify: *a wooden door*. These are attributive adjectives. Most adjectives can also appear after the noun they modify: *the door is wooden*. These are predicative adjectives. However, a few adjectives can only be in the attributive position: *my elder sister* (not *my sister is elder*), *a mere scratch* (not *a scratch is mere*). And some adjectives can only be in the predicative position: *the woman was alone* (not *an alone woman*), *the man felt afraid* (not *an afraid man*). Note that most adjectives which can only be in the predicative position begin with *a*: *asleep, awake, aware, alert, alike, ashamed, alive*.

4 Ask Ss to look at their list of possessions in Ex 1a and add adjectives to them. They can then check with a partner.

VOCABULARY BANK 4A p159
Adjectives to describe things
This is an optional extension to the vocabulary section, extending the lexical set and providing further practice. If you're short of time, this can be done for homework.

1 Ss read the sentences, then add the words to the correct column of the table. They can work alone, then check in pairs. Check answers with the whole class, then drill and mark stress.

Answers:

Opinion	Size	Quality	Shape	Material
bizarre	massive	artificial	circular	cotton
stunning		delicate	oval	wooden
exclusive		hi-tech	rectangular	

2a Ss complete the sentences using adjectives from Ex 1 to describe the pictures. More than one answer may be possible. Go through the answers.

Possible answers:
1 stunning, exclusive, delicate
2 massive, circular, bizarre/stunning
3 exclusive, rectangular, hi-tech

b Ss work in pairs to compare answers and then use adjectives from Ex 1 to describe an object of their own.

Further practice
Photocopiable activities: 4A Vocabulary, p196
App: 4A Vocabulary practice 1 and 2

Listening

Culture notes
Michael Landy (born 1963) is a member of a group of Young British Artists (YBAs) who emerged in the late 1980s from the art school at Goldsmith's College. *Break Down* is his most famous work and is considered to be about Western consumerism. It plays on the words *breakdown* = emotional collapse and *break down* = physically take apart.
The Turner Prize is an annual art award named after the English painter J. M. W. Turner. Until 2016 it was limited to artists under the age of 50.
Chris Ofili is a YBA best known for using elephant dung in his art.

5a Ask Ss to read and answer the questions.
b When they finish, ask pairs to compare, then discuss their answers.
6 4.1 Tell Ss they'll now listen to a description of the artwork and answer some true/false questions. Allow a minute for Ss to read through the questions first, then play the recording. Ask Ss to compare answers in pairs, then go through them.

Answers: 1 T 2 F 3 T 4 T 5 F 6 F

Audioscript 4.1
Each day this week we're looking at a different artist who has challenged what we think art is. Yesterday we looked at Japanese artist Yayoi Kusama. Today it's the turn of British artist Michael Landy.

Landy has always been a controversial artist. Once he created a work of art for an art gallery in London. The gallery's cleaners mistook it for rubbish and threw most of it away.

But his best-known work is *Break Down*, an event where Landy and 12 helpers systematically destroyed everything that Landy owned. The event took place in an old department store on London's Oxford Street, and lasted for two weeks. Absolutely everything that Landy owned was taken apart and ground down into dust. That included love letters, his car, his own art, his clothes and so on. At the end, all that was left were the clothes Landy was wearing that day.

Visitors to the exhibition were often confused. Some thought that the old department store was still there and they tried to return things that they had bought. Landy's mother also turned up and started crying and Landy had to ask her to leave because she was so emotional.

Landy's helpers sometimes seemed to take a special joy in their work. One helper took a coin and scratched out all the heads on Landy's photographs before shredding them. Another read all his love letters before shredding those.

Controversially, Landy also destroyed works by other artists during the event. For example, he destroyed a valuable print, which he'd won in a competition. The print, which was worth thousands of pounds, was by Chris Ofili who had won the Turner Prize for art a few years previously. For Landy, however, the most difficult thing for him to destroy was a chunky sheepskin coat which had belonged to his father. It had a lot of sentimental value to him and it was so expensive that Landy's father had had to pay for it in instalments. One visitor wanted to swap it for her coat, but Landy couldn't accept new possessions. He suggested instead that she steal it. He actually wanted someone to take it away but no one did and so in the end, the coat was destroyed.

Break Down was a hugely successful art project. It had 45,000 visitors and got many people talking about art. It also asked important questions about who we are and how our possessions define us. Landy himself compared it to watching his own funeral. *Break Down*, however, didn't win any prizes. Many people suspect that this was because Landy destroyed the work of other artists during the show.

And what was the first thing that Landy did after it was all over? He went out and got a new set of keys, a shaver and a credit card.

Grammar
Relative clauses
7 Ask Ss to read the grammar box and answer the questions in pairs, referring back to the text in Ex 5a. Allow plenty of time for this. Monitor and listen to how Ss are doing, then lead feedback and deal with any questions.

Answers:
1 6, 7
2 2 The relative pronoun is the object so it can be left out: an essay (which/that) he had paid ...
3 7
4 in non-defining relative clauses: 3, 4, 5, 8

8a 4.2 Ask Ss to listen to the pairs of sentences and decide which clause is defining and which is non-defining. Go through the answers.

Answers: 1 a non-defining b defining
2 a defining b non-defining 3 a defining b non-defining

Audioscript 4.2
1a My friends, who always remember my birthday, are very special to me.
1b The friends who always remember my birthday are the most special to me.

2a I'd really like a satisfying and challenging job which didn't stress me out too much.
2b I'd really like a satisfying and challenging job, which isn't too much to ask for.

3a I'm an introvert, so I hate going to parties where I don't know anyone.
3b I'm an extrovert, so I love having parties, which doesn't please my neighbours!

b Ask Ss to listen again and chorally repeat the sentences after they hear them. You may want to pause the audio after each sentence and drill individuals to check. If you think it's useful, explain the information in the Pronunciation checkpoint below, using the examples given. Ask Ss which sentences are true for them.

> **Pronunciation checkpoint**
> A non-defining clause usually has a noticeable pause before it, reflecting the comma separating it from the preceding clause. For example: *I found £10 in the street, which was lucky!* There may also be another pause after a non-defining clause if more information comes after it. For example: *My sister, who's a doctor, is married.*

9a Ask Ss to work alone and tick the correct completions. Clarify that more than one option may be correct. Ask Ss to compare in pairs before going through the answers as a class.

> **Answers:** 1 a, c   2 a, b   3 c
> 4 a, b, d (while grammatically correct, b is quite an old-fashioned/ formal way of speaking)
> 5 a, b, c   6 d   7 d

b Ask Ss to work in pairs to ask and answer the questions. Remind them to include brief pauses before and after non-defining relative clauses (see Pronunciation checkpoint). When they have finished, conduct brief feedback, asking them if they disagreed on any questions.

> **Optional alternative activity**
> Ss ask the questions across the class in open pairs, choosing who should answer each question. This can be a change from the usual classroom dynamic and raise Ss' awareness of others in their class.

> **LANGUAGE BANK 4A**   pp.142–143
> **Stronger classes** could read the notes at home. Otherwise, go over the notes with Ss. In each exercise, elicit the first answer as an example. Ss work alone to complete the exercises, then check their answers in pairs. In feedback, check answers with the whole class. Ss can refer to the notes to help them.
>
> **Answers:**
> 1   1 which/that (can be omitted)
>   2 which/that (can be omitted)   3 in   4 to   5 who
>   6 whose   7 where
> 2   1 Have you seen the designer watch that my grandfather gave me ~~it~~?
>   2 The police wanted a photo of the painting *which/that* was stolen last week.
>   3 Can you tell me the year in ~~when~~ *which* the vase was made?
>   4 ✓
>   5 I bought a little marble statue of a cat, ~~that~~ *which* I put in the garden.
>   6 They've demolished the part of town where I used to live ~~in~~. (or: They've demolished the part of town ~~where~~ I used to live in.)

> **Further practice**
> **Photocopiable activities:** 4A Grammar 1, p194; 4A Grammar 2, p195
> **App:** 4A Grammar practice 1 and 2

Speaking

Prepare
10 Tell Ss they are going to do a roleplay. Name half the class Student A and the other half Student B and ask them to turn to the relevant pages. Tell all Ss to follow the instructions and begin preparing. Allow plenty of preparation time, helping with vocabulary where necessary.

> **Teaching tip**
> Think about who you put together for roleplay. It can be a good idea to put Ss of similar ability together. While **weaker pairs** carry out a simple roleplay without pressure and perhaps with more support from you, **stronger pairs** can have a more detailed exchange. This is different from pairwork, where Ss are completing an exercise together. In this case, a **stronger student** can help and support a weaker partner.

Speak
11 Put Ss in AB pairs to roleplay the interview. When they finish, ask them to swap roles and repeat. Monitor and listen for examples of good language or mistakes for correction. At the end, put some examples on the board and ask pairs to decide if they are correct or not, then have whole-class feedback.

> **Reflection on learning**
> Write the following questions on the board:
> *What can you do better after this lesson?*
> *What do you want to spend more time on? Why is it important for you?*
> Put Ss in pairs to discuss the questions. When they have finished, ask if anyone wants to share their ideas with the class, but don't force them to if they'd rather not.

> **Homework ideas**
> **Ex11:** Ss write a detailed description of something that is very precious to them.
> **Language bank:** 4A Ex 1–2, pp.142–143
> **Workbook:** Ex 1–6, p28
> **App:** grammar, vocabulary and pronunciation practice

Fast route: continue to Lesson 4B
Extended route: go to p102 for Develop your reading

4B Job skills

Introduction
The goal of this lesson is for students to talk about the requirements of a job. To help them achieve this, they will revise vocabulary for job requirements in the context of obligation and prohibition.

Warm-up
Ask Ss to write down what career they wanted when they were younger and what they do now (if working) or what they'd like to do in the future. Ask them to discuss how suited they were to their childhood and adult job aspirations. Conduct brief feedback as a class, taking the opportunity to feed in work-related vocabulary relevant to the lesson.

> **Teaching tip**
> For lessons to be relevant, they should have meaning in Ss' own lives. Relating the lesson content to their own careers and ambitions should make it accessible for all. If appropriate, give your own examples and share sentence starters to prompt Ss: *When I was a child, I wanted to be … I always dreamt of being … I always imagined I'd be … I used to think I'd be …*

Vocabulary and listening
Job requirements
1 Ask Ss to look at the photos and work in pairs to discuss the question. After a few minutes, elicit ideas. Add useful vocabulary to the board in two columns under *have* and *be*.

2a Ask Ss to look at the job requirements and decide which of the three jobs in Ex 1 they go with, marking each A (astronaut), J (journalist) or V (video games designer). Look at the example, then ask Ss to continue alone before comparing in pairs. Don't check answers yet, as Ss will hear them.

b 🔊 4.3 Ask Ss to listen and check their predicted answers. Clarify that some requirements may go with more than one job in real life, but that the answers match the audio.

> **Answers:** 1 astronaut 2 video game designer 3 journalist
> 4 journalist 5 astronaut 6 journalist 7 video game designer
> 8 astronaut 9 astronaut 10 video game designer

> **Audioscript 4.3**
>
> **Astronaut**
> Back in the 1960s, you weren't allowed to become an astronaut without a pilot's licence and a background in engineering. You also had to be shorter than 1 metre 80 centimetres in order to fit in the Mercury space capsule. These days you don't have to have a pilot's licence – although it's handy if you do – but you must have a degree in science, engineering or mathematics and three years' post-graduate experience. That means a strong background in one of those disciplines. In terms of character, you mustn't be a loner or a wannabe-hero. It's all about being a team-player who doesn't take risks. And of course, you have to be able to cope with zero gravity. It takes three or four days to get used to that when you first go into space.
>
> **Journalist**
> In the past, you typed your stories up on paper and faxed them in or even dropped them on someone's desk. Back then, you didn't need to know how to live-tweet a story and there was no internet to check your facts. You had to get up off your chair and knock on doors. These days it's all different. You're expected to be social-media savvy but you're not normally required to have a university degree, unless it's a specialist subject you want to report on. Some things are still the same. It helps to have a driving licence and it helps to be fluent in at least one foreign language. But in terms of character, you need to be willing to question everything. And you can't be too bothered about having free time. If a story breaks, you drop everything to be there, evenings, weekends, even nights if necessary.
>
> **Video game designer**
> This job, you know, it's a relatively new profession, but the older game designers in the business, I mean the ones who've been doing it for a while, they didn't have to have any qualifications, they just had to be able to code, you know. And they had to have a passion for gaming, which is still the case today. But the job is evolving really fast. These days a really big game costs more to make than a Hollywood movie, so there are definitely job opportunities, but you have to have qualifications and strong problem-solving skills. Designing games is really about solving problems. Plenty of universities offer a degree in game design and it helps if you have that. And you've got to be able to use the software packages, of course. But the really successful game designers, they just have something else. I guess you could call it a flair for visual storytelling.

3 Discuss the phrases in bold and how they could be varied, or if they are limited. For example: *be fluent in* only applies to languages; *degree* could be substituted with *diploma*. Ask Ss to apply the phrases to themselves or someone they know.

> **Optional alternative activity**
> Put Ss in pairs and give them a few minutes to make notes on someone well-known. You could show some photos of famous faces to prompt ideas. The people can be of any background or profession, as Ss are just being prompted to apply the phrases. Ss then tell each other about the people. This is an opportunity to practise the vocabulary in Ex 2 in a less personal way.

> **Further practice**
> Photocopiable activities: 4B Vocabulary, p199
> App: 4B Vocabulary practice 1 and 2

Grammar
Obligation and prohibition
4a Tell Ss you're going to use the listening text to study some grammar. Ask them to read through the sentences and choose the correct verb. Point out that all are grammatically correct, but they are trying to recall what was said on the recording. Don't check answers yet as Ss will hear them.

b 🔊 4.4 Play the recording for Ss to check their answers. Check the answers with the class.

> **Answers:** 1 weren't allowed 2 mustn't 3 must
> 4 didn't need 5 not normally required 6 didn't have to
> 7 have to 8 've got to

5 Ask Ss to read the grammar box and answer the questions about Ex 4a. **Stronger classes** can do this before looking at the grammar box. Check as a class.

> **Answers:** 1 P: Past 2 P 3 O 4 NO: Past 5 NO
> 6 NO: Past 7 O 8 O

Grammar checkpoint

Ss may query the form *have got to* and its negative *haven't got to*. These forms are more common in British English spoken in the UK. In other countries, Ss are more likely to hear *have to* and *don't have to*. Assure Ss that both forms are perfectly valid. However, *haven't to* is not valid as a negative form, so be alert to this common error and point it out if Ss make it. Point out also that *got* is only used with the present form so *had got to* is wrong. Some Ss wrongly use *don't have to* for prohibition as they think it has an opposite meaning to *have to*. They may also use *don't have to* when they want to say *shouldn't*. Look out for and correct these common errors.

6 🔊 **4.5** Ask Ss to read the sentences and listen to the recording. If you think it's useful, explain the information in the Pronunciation checkpoint below, using the examples given.

Answers: 1 /f/ 2 /v/ 3 /f/ 4 /f/, /v/

Pronunciation checkpoint

/v/ is a voiced consonant and /f/ is unvoiced. The difficulty for Ss is that both are articulated in the same place, using the teeth and lips. The difference is that with /v/ the vocal folds vibrate and with /f/ there is no such voicing. If Ss put their hand on their throat and make each sound alternately, they should hear and feel the voicing. Ask Ss to chorally repeat the sentences after they hear them.

7 This activity checks if Ss have understood and can apply the various forms studied. Ask Ss to work alone to complete the sentences using the verbs provided, referring to the grammar box. Ask Ss to check in pairs, then go through the answers with the whole class. Ask Ss for individual answers. Drill as needed.

Answers: 1 you didn't have to 2 You only needed to
3 You're required to 4 (you) have to 5 you can't
6 You've got to 7 You need to 8 you didn't need to
9 You just had to 10 You still don't have to
11 you still don't need to 12 You've got to 13 you mustn't
14 You must

8 Ask Ss to work in pairs to discuss the changing obligations of the different jobs shown. **Weaker classes** may benefit from writing their sentences first. When they finish, ask pairs to say or read out sentences to the group and discuss which was the most surprising, interesting or unusual.

Possible answers:
Farmer then: They had to do a lot of physical labour. They weren't allowed to have many days off.
Farmer now: They have to know how to use hi-tech equipment.
Architect then: They had to draw everything by hand.
Architect now: They have to know how to use design software.

Optional extra activity

Ss talk or write about changes in obligations in their own jobs or other jobs that are of interest to them.

LANGUAGE BANK 4B pp.142–143

Stronger classes could read the notes at home. Otherwise, go over the notes with Ss. In each exercise, elicit the first answer as an example. Ss work alone to complete the exercises, then check their answers in pairs. In feedback, check answers with the whole class. Ss can refer to the notes to help them.

Answers:
1 1 don't have to 2 you're required to 3 have had to
  4 need to 5 you'll have to 6 couldn't 7 mustn't
  8 needn't have brought
Possible answers:
2 1 don't have to / don't need to 2 weren't allowed to
  3 you really must 4 You have to 5 are required to

Further practice

Photocopiable activities: 4B Grammar 1, p197;
4B Grammar 2, p198
App: 4B Grammar practice 1 and 2

Speaking

Prepare

9a Tell Ss they are going to talk about job requirements. Remind them of the jobs discussed at the start of the lesson. Ask Ss to choose a job they would like to do and make notes. Monitor and help with vocabulary and ideas as needed. **Weaker classes** may benefit from preparing in pairs or small groups.

Optional alternative activity

If you have a more mature class that are already working, the job they 'would like to do' may not feel relevant. Point out that they can think about jobs they are interested in, even if their career path is settled. If they prefer, they can choose a job for a family member or friend.

b Ask Ss to prepare what they are going to say, working from the notes they have made and reflecting on the language of the lesson. If they like, they can record themselves rehearsing using their phones.

Speak

10 Put Ss in pairs and go through the Useful phrases with the class. With **weaker classes**, you may want to ask Ss to underline the stressed words and pronounce the expressions. Point out that they should try and use these while they are talking. Ss talk about their job requirements and respond to questions. Monitor and help if necessary.

11 Put Ss in new pairs to repeat their discussion. In whole-class feedback, find out who has the most interesting-sounding future job.

Optional extra activity

Pairs could talk about transferable skills between the two jobs they have discussed – what training/skills/qualities are important in both roles?

Reflection on learning

Write the following questions on the board:
What was important for you in this lesson? Why?
How could you use this language again outside class?
Put Ss in pairs to discuss the questions. When they have finished, ask if anyone wants to share their ideas with the class, but don't force them to if they'd rather not.

Homework ideas

Language bank: 4B Ex 1–2, pp.142–143
Workbook: Ex 1–5, p29
App: grammar, vocabulary and pronunciation practice

Fast route: continue to Lesson 4C
Extended route: go to p122 for Develop your writing

4C Unwritten rules

Introduction

The goal of this lesson is for students to give advice through an informal presentation. To help them achieve this, they will study forming verbs with *en* as well as vocabulary relating to the 21st century.

Warm-up

Write various different centuries on the board, for example: *14th, 19th, 20th* and *21st,* and ask Ss to note one or two key words or events for each and tell each other. When they finish, have brief feedback on each of the chosen centuries, then tell them that the focus of this lesson is the 21st.

Vocabulary

21st-century words

1 Ask Ss to discuss any behaviours they feel belong to the 21st century. If Ss can't think of any, suggest areas such as transport, food, learning and media. Give a few examples such as working remotely, online learning or increased use of food delivery. When they finish, have a whole-class discussion to see if Ss agree.

2a Focus attention on the bullet points. Ask Ss to look at them in pairs and match the words in the box to the best category. Point out that some may belong in more than one. When they finish, compare ideas as a class and discuss the meaning of words Ss are unsure of. Ask Ss if they use any of these words in their language.

Suggested answers:
social media/internet: animated gif, crowdsource, emoji, google, hashtag, meme, selfie, tech-savvy, unfriend, virtual assistant, virtual tour
entertainment: binge-watch
money/finance/work: contactless, paywall, time-poor
messaging/texting: animated gif, emoji, hashtag

Culture notes

Each year, dictionaries are updated to reflect language changes. In 2018, several new words added to the OED (Oxford English Dictionary) started with *e-* or *self-*. For example: *e-publishing, e-shopping, self-build* and *self-assemble*. You can find details of OED's regular updates here: https://public.oed.com/updates/.

Optional extra activity

Ask Ss if there are new words they have become aware of recently in their first language. If necessary, prompt with examples of your own or see the Culture notes above.

b Ask Ss to read and complete the quiz with words in the box, changing the verb forms as necessary. Complete the first example together, then ask Ss to continue alone. After a few minutes, ask pairs to help each other, then go through the answers as a class. In feedback, choose individuals to read out questions so you can check pronunciation.

Answers: 1 selfie 2 crowdsourced 3 emoji 4 hashtag
5 animated gif 6 unfriended 7 virtual tour
8 binge-watched 9 virtual assistant 10 paywall
11 contactless 12 tech-savvy 13 time-poor 14 googled
15 meme

3 Ask Ss to do the quiz for themselves, then ask and answer in small groups. When they finish, discuss as a class to find out who is the most '21st century' and which questions got the most positive answers.

4 Ask Ss to work in pairs to explain how to do 1–6 in the quiz. If necessary, put some simple prompts on the board: *Try (not) to …; Make sure you …; I'd recommend …; Click on …; Type …*. When they finish, ask different pairs to say which items were the easiest to explain and which were the hardest.

VOCABULARY BANK 4C p159
Words from other languages

This is an optional extension to the vocabulary section, extending the lexical set and providing further practice. If you're short of time, this can be done for homework.

1 Ss match the words in the box with the correct pictures, then check in pairs. Check answers with the whole class.

Answers: 1 chocolate 2 mosquito 3 carafe 4 judo
5 yoghurt 6 piano 7 shampoo 8 barbecue

2 Ss match each word from Ex 1 with a part of the world. When they finish, ask them to turn the page upside down and check their answers. See how many they got right.

Answers:
1 h 2 d 3 c 4 a 5 g 6 f 7 b 8 e

3a Ask Ss to choose three words from Ex 1 and write three facts about themselves, two true (but not obvious) and one false.

b Ss read their sentences to each other and guess the false one.

Further practice

Photocopiable activities: 4C Vocabulary, p202
App: 4C Vocabulary practice 1 and 2

Reading

Culture notes
The story of Frank Thomas Brinkley appears to be fictional. However, there have been many cases of long-term prisoners leaving jail and finding society has changed during their incarceration. Re-offending can be high in these groups as they struggle to integrate back into a society which has changed dramatically.

5 Tell Ss they are going to read about someone who spent over 13 years in jail and what happened when they came out. Give Ss a minute to read, then ask them to check in pairs before going through as a class. Ask Ss if they believe this could happen.

Answers:
– the things people said because those words hadn't existed before he went to prison
– why everyone stared at their phones and tapped on the screen, when previously they used their phones for talking

6a Ask Ss to read alone, then work in groups of three or four to discuss. In feedback, find out which piece of advice is the most popular in each group and why.

b Ask Ss to read again more carefully to answer the questions. They can compare in pairs before going through the answers as a class.

Answers:
1 It will make his group of friends wider and give him a broader view of life.
2 Will they make him and his life more joyful or will they make life more dangerous for him?
3 It can make your life richer and allow you to do a lot more than was possible before.
4 It will make the shock of the new technology less and because we all need face-to-face communication.

Optional extra activity
Ask Ss to think about what other advice they would give Frank. Pairs can try to come up with three pieces of advice, then share these with other pairs. You can also lead a class discussion to find out whether Ss think prisoners have (or should have) access to all current forms of communication in prison.

Language focus

Forming verbs with *en*

7 Write *shorten* on the board and ask Ss to identify what kind of word it is (a verb) and what the root is (*short* – an adjective). Ask Ss if they can think of other verbs made by adding *en* at the end or beginning of a word. Refer them to the Language focus box to read through, then ask them to find eight similar verbs in Ex 6a. Go through the answers as a class, discussing whether each verb is formed from an adjective or a noun and underlining the root word in each case.

Answers: widen, broaden, brighten, endanger, enrich, enable, soften, enforce
Point out or elicit that *en* comes at the end of four of the verbs and the beginning of four.

8a 4.6 Tell Ss to listen to the recording and to underline where they hear the stress in each word. Check answers with the whole class.

Answers: 1 en<u>force</u> 2 en<u>dan</u>ger 3 <u>weak</u>en 4 en<u>rage</u>
5 <u>sad</u>den 6 <u>wors</u>en 7 en<u>rich</u> 8 <u>short</u>en

b Ask Ss to listen and repeat.

9a Tell Ss they are going to practise the verbs. Ask them to choose the correct word in brackets to complete each sentence. They also need to change it to the correct verb form, checking with the Language focus box if necessary. Allow plenty of time for this. When Ss finish, check answers with the whole class.

Answers: 1 sure: ensure 2 rich: enrich 3 soft: soften
4 short: shorten 5 worse: worsens 6 danger: endanger
7 able: enables 8 bright: brightens

b Ask Ss to work in pairs and discuss the rules in Ex 9a, saying if they agree or disagree with them. When they finish, ask a few pairs to share an example where they didn't agree and say why.

LANGUAGE BANK 4C pp.142–143
Stronger classes could read the notes at home. Otherwise, check the notes with Ss. Elicit the first answer as an example. Ss work alone to complete the exercise, then check their answers in pairs. In feedback, check answers with the whole class. Ss can refer to the notes to help them.

Answers:
1 1 broaden 2 lessens 3 shorten 4 enrages 5 enrich
   6 enable 7 brighten

Further practice
Photocopiable activities: 4C Language focus 1, p200; 4C Language focus 2, p201
App: Language focus practice 1 and 2

Speaking

Prepare

10a Explain that Ss are going to prepare to make a short, informal presentation. Put them in pairs and ask them to choose a topic from the list.

b Ask pairs to brainstorm ideas and make notes, then decide on a logical order to use them in a presentation. Discourage them from writing full sentences. Monitor and help with vocabulary as necessary. Encourage them to include some verbs from the lesson in their notes. Pairs also need to decide who will present which part of their presentation.

Teaching tip
Some Ss may benefit from support with making notes. Rather than making linear notes, Ss can be encouraged to make a mind map or spidergram. Another good method is to write each separate point on a self-adhesive note. These can then be discussed and physically put in order later when planning the presentation.

Speak

11a Refer Ss to the Useful phrases to read through. Then ask pairs to take turns to make their presentation.

b After each presentation, ask the class to give some brief feedback on clarity and use of language.

Optional extra activity

Separate pairs who have prepared together and ask them to take turns to give their presentations in small groups. This takes less time and is less stressful than presenting to the whole class. It also allows each student to speak more, as they need to give the whole presentation. Groups can use a checklist and give each presenter feedback. If time allows, they can then follow this 'rehearsal' stage with whole-class presentations.

Reflection on learning

Write the following questions on the board:
How useful was the language you learnt in today's lesson?
How might today's activities be helpful outside the class?
Put Ss in pairs to discuss the questions. When they have finished, ask if anyone wants to share their ideas with the class, but don't force them to if they'd rather not.

Homework ideas

Language bank: 4C Ex 1, pp.142–143
Workbook: Ex 1–5, p30
App: grammar, vocabulary and pronunciation practice

Fast route: continue to Check and reflect
Extended route: go to p89 for Develop your listening

4 Check and reflect: Units 3–4

Introduction

Students revise and practise the language of Units 3 and 4. The notes below provide some ideas for exploiting the activities in class, but you may want to set the exercises for homework or use them as a diagnostic or progress test.

1 Ss complete the text alone with the correct form of the verbs provided, then check in pairs. In feedback, ask Ss to read the whole sentences so you can check pronunciation.

Answers: 1 had managed 2 had recommended
3 had been travelling 4 had trusted 5 had been dancing
6 had fallen 7 remembered 8 discovered

2a Ss choose the correct alternatives alone, then check in pairs. Check answers with the whole class.

Answers: 1 reminded 2 memory 3 memorised 4 recall
5 bear 6 memorable

b Ss work in pairs to ask and answer the questions.
3 Ss complete the adjectives alone, then check in pairs. Check the answers with the whole class.

Answers: 1 inexperienced 2 competitive 3 stubborn
4 confident 5 unpredictable 6 reasonable 7 determined
8 thoughtful

4a Ss write the sentences in order alone, then check in pairs. Check answers with the whole class.

Answers:
1 Darts is the most unexciting sport imaginable.
2 Cycling isn't nearly as exciting as motor racing.
3 Men and women are just as competitive as each other.
4 The Brazilian football team is nowhere near as good as it was.
5 The more I watch boxing, the more I think it should be banned.
6 Tennis umpires treat some players more fairly than others.

b Put Ss in small groups to discuss three of the opinions. **Stronger classes** can discuss more. When they finish, ask a few groups to share a point from their discussion.
5 Ss match the sentence halves alone or in pairs. Go through the answers as a class.

Answers: 1 d 2 h 3 f 4 b 5 a 6 e 7 c 8 g

6 Ss complete the sentences with adjectives formed from the word provided. Go through the answers as a class.

Answers: 1 pointless 2 dangerous, scary 3 tricky, doable
4 allergic 5 childish, colourful 6 acceptable, disrespectful

7 Ss add the adjectives in the box to the sentences, thinking about the best position for each adjective, then check in pairs. Go through the answers.

Answers:
1 Those flimsy, plastic garden chairs …
2 … my beautiful, identical twin nieces.
3 … a huge, black, hairy spider …
4 … a pair of priceless, gold statues.
5 … some elegant, designer shoes …
6 … a pair of chunky, leather boots …

8 Ss identify and correct the four sentences with grammar or punctuation mistakes, then check in pairs. Go through the answers as a class.

Answers:
1 ✓
2 My father, who now has a studio in New York, is a well-known painter. (commas necessary around non-defining relative clause)
3 ✓ (relative pronoun not essential)
4 The main character dies at the end of the film, which made me cry. (comma necessary before non-defining relative clause)
5 My workshop is in London, **which** means travelling up by train every day. (*which* and not *that* in non-defining relative clauses)
6 The customer who Jim made the sculpture **for** didn't like it. (position of preposition)
The customer for **whom** Jim made the sculpture didn't like it. (use of the formal pronoun *whom*)

9a Ss complete the sentences with words from boxes A and B, then check in pairs. Go through the answers as a class.

Answers: 1 fluent in 2 cope with 3 background in
4 bothered about 5 flair for 6 degree in

b Ss talk in pairs about their work or studies, using three of the phrases from Ex 9a. **Stronger classes** can use more. When they finish, ask a few pairs for examples.

10 Ss complete the second sentence so that it means the same as the first, using the word in brackets, then check in pairs. Tell *weaker classes* they should put two or three words in each gap, with contractions counting as one word. Go through the answers as a class.

Answers: 1 are required to   2 don't need to   3 had to
4 got to   5 weren't allowed to

11 Ss complete each definition with a 21st-century word or phrase, then check in pairs. Go through the answers as a class.

Answers: 1 selfie   2 emoji   3 meme   4 binge
5 time-poor   6 crowdsource   7 hashtag

12a Ss complete the sentences with words in the box, adding *en* as a prefix or suffix, then check in pairs. Go through the answers as a class.

Answers: 1 ensure   2 enforce   3 shorten   4 brightens
5 weakens   6 endanger   7 widens   8 enables

b Put Ss in small groups to discuss three of the statements. *Stronger classes* can discuss more. When they finish, ask a few groups to share a point from their discussion.

13a Ss put the words in the conversations in the correct order, then check in pairs. Go through the answers as a class.

Answers:
1 A: I wasn't expecting it to be quite so spicy.
   B: We'll take your comments on board, sir.
2 A: What was the general feeling about the film?
   B: It got a huge thumbs up from everyone.
3 A: My biggest complaint was the 45-minute wait.
   B: Yes, I don't think punctuality is one of their strong points.
4 A: Perhaps you could try getting up earlier.
   B: OK, but I want to explain my side.

b Ss read the conversations in pairs, then practise again with books closed.

Reflect

Ask Ss to rate each statement alone, then compare in pairs. Encourage them to ask any questions they still have about any of the areas covered in Units 3 and 4.

Roadmap video
Go online for the Roadmap video and worksheet.

4A Develop your reading

Introduction
The goal of this lesson is for students to understand a magazine article. To help them achieve this, they will focus on understanding the writer's purpose.

Warm-up
Display a map of the world if possible. Ask Ss to name the continents and the major seas/oceans. Ask Ss which continents they have visited or would most like to visit and why.

Culture notes
Research stations are operated in the Arctic and Antarctic. Antarctica is a place of worldwide co-operation with dozens of research stations representing around 30 countries. They conduct scientific research all year round, studying the weather, ice, wildlife and so on.

1a Ask Ss to work in pairs to try and answer the questions. Conduct brief feedback but do not confirm answers yet – they will find this out by reading.

b Ask Ss to read the paragraph and check their answers. When they finish, invite feedback and see how many predictions were correct.

Answers:
1 It's the southernmost continent of Earth.
2 It's twice the size of Australia.
3 It has no indigenous people but 4,000 scientists live there.

2 Tell Ss they are going to have a reading race to find the answers to the questions. Make sure everyone begins at the same time and tell the class that the first person to finish should raise their hand (you could set a stopwatch to time the race). Encourage Ss to mark where they find the answers. When around half the Ss have raised their hands, stop the race and tell Ss to compare answers in pairs. Check answers as a class.

Answers: 1 35,000   2 1975   3 20
4 They got lost in bad weather.   5 up to five times a day
6 in the 1820s   7 below –60°C   8 in order to go home
9 31   10 She ran Halley station in Antarctica.

Teaching tip
Reading fast for specific information is called scanning. It's an important skill for Ss to develop and one that we use when looking for specific data such as dates, times, numbers, etc. Having the occasional reading race is a fun way to encourage Ss to scan texts efficiently. Set a timer for five minutes, which is generous, and ask Ss to raise their hands when they have got all the answers. Point out that they should read the questions first, underlining the question words or key words, then underline in the text where they find the answers.

3 Ask Ss to read the article again more carefully to answer the questions. Give a time limit of no more than five minutes to encourage fast but careful reading, then have Ss compare in pairs before you elicit the answers.

Answers:
1 The population of the Arctic is permanent while the population of Antarctica is temporary.
2 about 100
3 A plaque is placed at the highest point of Rothera.
4 because it's important that everyone is accounted for (to check that no one has gone missing)
5 We can read their memoirs.
6 to collect penguins' eggs (he was a zoologist)
7 the darkness and isolation

4 Tell Ss you are going to discuss the purposes of texts and ask for a few example purposes (to inform, to entertain, to advertise, etc.). Then ask Ss to read the Focus box and answer the questions in pairs. Conduct feedback and ask for examples where possible to support their choices.

Answers: 1 facts 2 more serious
3 more advanced vocabulary 4 objective 5 a range of views

Optional extra activity

Bring in some different text types for Ss to look at. You could include leaflets, academic journals, flyers, magazine articles, signs, etc. They don't need to be in English. Discuss as a class what other elements help us to identify a text type, apart from language. For example, the use of pictures, punctuation, headlines, headings, fonts and columns can all be indicators of certain text types.

5 Ask Ss to read the two text extracts and decide on the writer's purpose, using the Focus box to help them. Pairs should compare answers before going through them as a class.

Answers:
Text 1: The purpose is to entertain: the text includes humour, it is subjective, it gives just the views of the writer.
Text 2: The purpose is to inform: the text contains facts, it is serious, it uses advanced vocabulary, it is objective.

6 Ask Ss to discuss in pairs what they like to read in different situations. Give them a few minutes, then discuss their answers as a class.

7 Tell Ss they should decide if they'd like to spend a year in Rothera and think about reasons. Ask Ss to compare answers, then have a show of hands to see if any would like the experience.

Homework ideas

Workbook: Ex 1–6, pp.32–33

4B Develop your writing

Introduction

The goal of this lesson is for students to write a covering email. To help them achieve this, they will focus on matching a covering email with a job advert.

Warm-up

Ask Ss to discuss in pairs how they last applied for a job and what the process was. If Ss have not done this yet, they can talk about the typical process as they understand it. Have a whole-class discussion about their answers.

1 Put Ss in pairs to discuss the questions. After a few minutes, conduct brief feedback.

Culture notes

Job applications have changed a lot. A covering letter would traditionally be sent in the post with a CV (Curriculum Vitae – a document listing qualifications and work experience) or application form. A covering email fulfils this purpose in online applications. A CV now often also includes a personal statement summarising transferable and soft skills like leadership and adaptability. Some companies prefer not to look at CVs at all, preferring to hire directly through recruitment websites like LinkedIn. Increasingly, job applications involve several stages, with online tests, video interviews, written tasks and assessment days involving team exercises.

2a Ask Ss to read the advice of a professional interviewer and decide if they agree with it. Conduct whole-class feedback to see how many Ss think it's good advice.

b Ask Ss to match the job advert extracts with the personal descriptions. Give them a few minutes, then put them in pairs to discuss and compare. After a few minutes, elicit answers and in feedback identify any phrases that helped them decide.

Answers: 1 c 2 a 3 d 4 b

c Give Ss a few minutes to brainstorm words and phrases. Refer them to pp.32–33 where they described characteristics and skills. Share answers as a class and write useful vocabulary on the board.

3a Ask Ss to read the job advert and email and write paragraph numbers 1–3 beside the information they match. Clarify that one paragraph matches two pieces of information. Go through the answers.

Answers: a 1 b 2 c 1 d 3

b This exercise is to see if Ss can evaluate and check the points made in the email against the advert. Ask Ss to work alone, then compare in pairs before going through the answers and discussing how the person meets the brief. Allow plenty of time for this.

Answers:
Must be able to provide exceptional service to our clients – *friendly individual*
take control of all aspects of the hotel's reception – *extremely organised*
English essential but other languages are an advantage – *fluent in English and Polish and has conversational Spanish*
Experience preferred – *I have relevant experience in the hotel industry*
checking guests in and out with our IT systems – *I am IT literate*
providing advice and assistance to guests – *friendly individual*
being aware of who enters and exits the building – *security-conscious*
The right candidate must be able to work different shifts at short notice. – *flexible*
She's responded to the advert well. She's covered all the main things that the hotel is looking for.

4 Ask Ss to read the Focus box and the three job adverts (A–C), then choose which job they'd like to respond to.

Optional extra activity

Work as a class to add completions or substitutions to each phrase in the Focus box. Discuss what changes need to be made to the phrases when substituting, for example: *I am extremely* (+ positive adjective), *I am fluent in* (+ language), *I feel I would be a great asset to* (+ the team/company), *I became expert at* (+ skill), *I gained valuable experience in* (+ skill). This task is particularly suitable for **stronger classes**.

Prepare

5a Ask Ss to note useful adjectives and phrases for the job they have chosen. Ss can work in pairs to help each other. Monitor and help as needed.

b Refer Ss to the email in Ex 3 and ask them to underline phrases they could use, as well as write down others that they may find useful. When they finish, discuss the phrases they have chosen.

Write

6a Ask Ss to work alone to write their covering email. If it's practical, have Ss use computers or other devices to write the email.

Unit 4

b Refer Ss to the checklist and ask them to look back at their emails and make sure they have addressed every point.

c Ask pairs to exchange emails and add suggestions for improvement to each other's work. If they are working on computers, they can send them to each other and add comments.

Optional extra activity

When Ss finish, ask them to decide whether to invite their applicant to interview or not and write the invitation email.

Homework ideas

Ss write a covering email for a real job they are interested in.
Workbook: Ex 1–8, pp.34–35

4c Develop your listening

Introduction

The goal of this lesson is for students to understand phone messages. To help them achieve this, they will focus on understanding understatement.

Warm-up

Ask Ss if they prefer speaking English face to face or on the phone and ask them to discuss why. Ask if they feel the same in their first language. Tell them the lesson is about understanding phone messages.

1 Ask Ss to work in pairs and discuss the questions. Conduct brief whole-class feedback to see if there are common patterns in the class.

2a Tell Ss they are going to talk about work-related voicemail messages. Ask pairs to decide on the best order for the actions in the list and number them. In feedback, ask Ss to share their answers. Don't check answers yet as Ss will hear them.

b 4.7 Tell Ss they are going to listen to check the correct order according to an expert. Play the recording, then go through the answers, comparing with Ss' predictions. Ask Ss if this order is different from their experience.

Answers: 1 f   2 e   3 d   4 a   5 g   6 b   7 c

Audioscript 4.7

Because of email and instant messaging, voicemail is undoubtedly used less than it used to be. However, in a work context, voicemail is still relatively common, mostly because people call each other much more in business. And when you call, you often find the other person is not there. In fact, a recent survey by AT&T found that five out of every six calls goes to voicemail. So, what's the right way to leave a voicemail message?

Assuming the other person doesn't know you or doesn't know you well, first say who the message is for, then say your name and your company's name, then say your phone number, and it's probably best to repeat the number. The reason for saying your phone number at the beginning of the call is that the person often has to listen to the message again to write the number down and it's annoying to sit through the whole message because the number is at the end.

When you've repeated your number, you can give the reason for the call and say what action you want, for example: you want the other person to call you back. Be simple, be concise and be friendly – that is the key to leaving voicemail messages at work.

3a 4.8 Ask Ss to look at Isabella in the picture and explain that people a–g have left her voicemails. Play the recording, asking Ss to listen and match each speaker with their voicemail summary. Ss can compare in pairs before going through the answers as a class.

Answers: 1 e   2 g   3 f   4 d   5 a   6 c   7 b

Audioscript 4.8

V: You have seven new messages. Press one to listen to your messages.
V: Message one.
D: Hi, this is a message for Isabella. My name's Daniel and I'm calling from Nixon Property Management on 09474 632334. That's 09474 632334. I'm calling about the new café you wish to open. I have a property that you might be interested in taking a look at. It's in the Beachwood area. It's a bit on the small side. But give me a call back if you'd like to take a look at it. Look forward to speaking to you.
V: Message two.
N: Hi Isabella, this is Naomi from Rockport Café Furniture. I'm calling about a very special offer we have at the moment and I wanted you to be one of the first to know about it. We have some incredible deals on café chairs and tables and I'd really like the chance to tell you more about them. You can reach me by calling 0933 446783. That number again is 0933 446783. Just ask for Naomi. I look forward to speaking to you and thanks in advance for returning my call.
V: Message three.
VK: Hello, er, is this Ms Isabella Almeida, or, er, a voicemail? Ms Almeida, this is Vincent Karlsson from Karlsson Coffee Beans. Umm, we had an appointment for next week, but I'm afraid something has come up, so I need to cancel the appointment. I'll get back in touch with you to rearrange as soon as I get out of hospital. OK, er … thanks. Goodbye.
V: Message four.
S: Hi, I was just wondering if it's possible to hire out your café for a party for 200 guests this Friday evening. We have a small problem with the current venue – it burnt down. Um … my name's Sigrid, that's S-I-G-R-I-D and my number is 0932 4778302. That's 0932 4778302. Please get back to me as soon as you can. Thanks!
V: Message five.
B: Hi Isabella, it's Beatriz. There's a small issue with my shift this afternoon. I'm afraid I can't make it. I'm just feeling really lousy. I'm sorry. Hopefully I can come in tomorrow … if I'm feeling better. I'll let you know.
V: Message six.
H: Isabella. This is Harper at Best Move. Um, I've got a new flat that you could rent. It's just come on the market. I know you've got to move out of your flat soon. This one is a little bit over budget, but it's got a lovely view of the park. And it's available at the end of the month. Give me a call if you'd like to see it. Thanks!
V: Message seven.
T: Hey, Isabella, it's Tarik. Err … where are you? We've got a bit of a problem. The contactless machine isn't working and it's slowing everything down. It's madness in here today, so call me back when you get this because we need to get the machine fixed.

b Tell Ss they will listen again and they should note who is speaking and what their relationship is with Isabella. Pause between each message if necessary. Pairs can compare ideas and help each other to complete the information. Go through the answers as a class.

Answers:
1 Daniel: her property manager
2 Naomi: salesperson
3 Vincent: supplier/business contact
4 Sigrid: potential customer
5 Beatriz: staff
6 Harper: estate agent
7 Tarik: staff

Daniel follows the advice about leaving a voicemail message.

78

4 Tell Ss they will listen again for more detail. Refer them to the information and then ask them to make notes in the same format in their notebooks for each voicemail. Pause between each message to allow time to write, then ask Ss to compare before conducting feedback.

Answers:

Name	Number	Message	Action
Daniel	09474 632334	new café property available	call back to look at it
Naomi	0933 446783	special offers on café furniture	call her back
Vincent Karlsson	n/a	needs to cancel their appointment	none
Sigrid	0932 4778302	is the café available for hire on Friday evening	call back as soon as possible
Beatriz	n/a	can't work this afternoon	none
Harper	n/a	new flat for rent	call her back to look at it
Tarik	n/a	contactless machine has broken	call him back

5 Ask Ss to read through the Focus box. **Stronger classes** can try to remember which speaker didn't use understatement and then check their answers in the audioscript, if they have access to it. **Weaker classes** can listen again if necessary.

Answer: Naomi

Culture notes

Understatement is a common feature of British communication – consider the expression *Not bad* when paying a compliment. Overstatement is also a feature – consider the expression *I'm dying of thirst*. Both forms of expression can cause cultural misunderstandings. Ask Ss if their language uses understatement or overstatement and if they can share any expressions.

6 4.9 Ask Ss to listen to two more voicemail messages and note the understatements. You may want to pause the recording after each one. Ask pairs to discuss what each understatement is and what they think it means, then check as a class.

Answers:
1 **Understatement:** I'll be a bit late.
   Truth: She'll be between 45 minutes and one hour 45 minutes late.
2 **Understatement:** There's been a bit of a hold-up with the delivery of the laptops.
   Truth: Delivery will be delayed by between two weeks and a month.

Audioscript 4.9

V: Message 1
Woman: Oh, hi, umm, this is a message for Mustafa. My name is Benazir and I'm calling about my appointment today. Um, I'm afraid I'll be a bit late because I sort of overslept, so, let me see, it's 10.30 now and the appointment is in 15 minutes, but I should be able to get there in about an hour or two, so ... I hope that's OK! Thanks!
V: End of message. Message 2
Man: Mustafa, hi, it's Kerem Yildiz. Listen, Mustafa, there's been a bit of a hold-up with the delivery of the laptops. Um, they're stuck in customs at the moment and they're asking for paperwork. Don't worry, it'll all get sorted, but it might delay things by a couple of weeks or possibly a month. Anyway, give me a call when you get this message. Thanks
V: End of message.

7 This is an opportunity to practise the target language. Put Ss in pairs to read through the situations and come up with some sentences which include understatement. Conduct brief feedback by asking a few pairs for ideas.

Optional extra activity

Ask Ss to read the example about the stolen car. Put them in pairs to look back at the Focus box and choose two or three more understatement phrases to include in a short, written conversation. Monitor as they do this to help with ideas and vocabulary. When they finish, ask a few pairs to read their conversation aloud. Praise and encourage appropriate intonation.

Homework ideas

Workbook: Ex 1–5, p31

5 OVERVIEW

5A **Splashing out**
Goal | have a conversation about spending money
Grammar | mistakes in the past
Vocabulary | money phrases
GSE learning objective
Can justify the reasons for a particular decision or course of action

5B **Crime scene**
Goal | talk about quantities
Grammar | quantifiers
Vocabulary | crime (robbery)
GSE learning objective
Can and comment on a short story or article and answer questions in detail

5C **Bubble trouble**
Goal | summarise a text
Grammar | adverb + adjective collocations
Vocabulary | money
GSE learning objective
Can summarise and comment on a short story or article and answer questions in detail

5D **English in action**
Goal | deal with and resolve conflicts
Vocabulary | phrases with *leave*
GSE learning objective
Can suggest solutions to problems and explain why they would work

Roadmap video
Go online for the Roadmap video and worksheet.

VOCABULARY BANK

5B Nouns and verbs with the same form

5C Noun suffixes

DEVELOP YOUR SKILLS

5A **Develop your reading**
Goal | understand academic texts
Focus | understanding references to numerical data
GSE learning objective
Can understand the use of numerical data in graphs and charts in a linguistically complex academic text, if guided by questions

5B **Develop your writing**
Goal | write a detailed description of a person
Focus | using similes
GSE learning objective
Can write detailed descriptions of real or imaginary people

5C **Develop your listening**
Goal | understand presentations
Focus | matching information with visuals
GSE learning objective
Can relate information in a presentation to the same information given in graphs, charts and tables

5A Splashing out

Introduction
The goal of this lesson is for students to be able to have a conversation about spending money. To help them achieve this, they will revise grammar for mistakes in the past and phrases connected with money.

Warm-up
Write the following words and phrases on the board: *reckless, economical, overdrawn, good credit history, in the red, budget-conscious*. Ask Ss which ones relate to someone who is good with money and which relate to someone who is not so good with money. If it is not too sensitive, you could ask Ss to discuss whether they are good with money or not. Tell them to give some examples where they have been good with money or not so good. Give an example yourself if you can. If you think your class might like it, share this quotation from the character Mr Micawber in Charles Dickens' novel *David Copperfield*:
'Annual income twenty pounds, annual expenditure nineteen [pounds] nineteen [shillings] and six [pence], result happiness. Annual income twenty pounds, annual expenditure twenty pounds ought and six, result misery.'

Vocabulary

Money phrases

1 Ask Ss to work in pairs and discuss the questions. When they finish, have a brief whole-class discussion about the things people buy that are not needed and why we might do this.

2a Focus attention on the three experiences. Ask Ss to read them and decide who is the most/least sensible. Elicit ideas in a brief class discussion. There are no fixed answers. When they finish, ask Ss to say who they are most similar to.

b Ask Ss to look at the phrasal verbs in bold, discuss what they think they mean and then check in a dictionary or device. You could go over the meanings as a class as an additional check or if your Ss have dictionaries, they can use them.

Suggested answers:
live on = spend to survive
go on = be spent on
stock up on = buy lots of
splash out on = spend extravagantly on
get into debt = spend more than you have
cut back on = reduce
take out = get cash from the bank
pay back = give money back
set aside = save (for later)

Vocabulary checkpoint
Phrasal verbs should be a familiar concept at this level: verbs that consist of a main verb plus one or two particles. Point out that *go on* has more than one meaning, so Ss must locate the correct meaning in the dictionary. Here it means *be spent* and the subject is money rather than a person, but it can also mean continue or complain. Point out that Ss should note down whether phrasal verbs are separable or not: *live on, go on, stock up on, splash out on, get into* and *cut back on* are all inseparable. *Take out, pay back* and *set aside* are separable. Point out useful common collocations, for example: *take money/cash/time/someone out*.

3 Ask Ss to underline the correct verb in each question. Ss should work alone, then compare in pairs. Go through the answers and discuss which verbs can be separated (see Vocabulary checkpoint above – 3 and 7 can be separated). Put Ss in pairs to ask each other the questions. Conduct brief feedback to see what Ss think and find out whether there are any common ideas.

Answers: 1 cut back on   2 live on   3 set aside
4 splash out on   5 getting into   6 go on   7 take out
8 stock up on

Optional alternative activity

If space allows, divide the questions among the class. Ask Ss to take two or three questions each and survey the group, moving around the class. When they finish, ask a few Ss to summarise the responses and report back to the class.

Teaching tip

Many Ss enjoy getting out of their seats and mingling to talk to different people, if space allows. Asking the same question several times in a mingling activity offers good practice – and for the listening student it's more challenging as they are not working through the questions in a predictable order. The reporting-back stage should be of interest to everybody as the questions were asked to the whole group, not just the usual one or two neighbours. While Ss mingle, move around in the group yourself and help them find new partners as needed. Tell Ss not to ask you their questions so that you can focus on monitoring.

Further practice

Photocopiable activities: 5A Vocabulary, p205
App: 5A Vocabulary practice 1 and 2

Listening

Culture notes

An **economy** is the wealth of a country. An economy is also a saving, so *making economies = saving money*. A *false economy* appears to save money at the beginning but over a longer period of time, it wastes more money than is saved. This leads to the saying, 'Buy cheap, buy twice'. Ss might like to discuss whether in their culture people generally buy pricier, better-quality items for long-term investment, or cheaper, lower-quality ones for short-term use.

4a Ask Ss to read about false economies, then express the meaning of the phrase in their own words. Ask pairs to briefly tell each other an example of something they bought that was a false economy. Discuss ideas as a class but don't spend too long on this as Ss will revisit the question in Ex 9.

b Refer Ss to the pictures and discuss as a class why they might be considered as false economies.

Possible answers:
A You might not eat all the bread.
B They might wear out quickly.
C You probably won't use it.
D You probably won't need all of them.

5a ◁ 5.2 Ask Ss to listen and write the letter of each picture A–D next to the relevant conversation. Ss can compare and discuss why the items are false economies before whole-class feedback.

Answers:
1 D He's already got a set of spanners (which he doesn't use very often).
2 A They won't eat all that bread and it's almost past its sell-by date. They can't freeze it because the freezer is full.
3 B The soles are coming away so it would have been better to spend more money on a better-quality pair of shoes.
4 C He'll never use it.

Audioscript 5.1

Conversation 1
A: Why did you buy those?
B: Well, I thought they might come in handy one day.
A: But you were supposed to buy a packet of screws.
B: Yeah, I got those, but I bought these spanners, too.
A: You thought they might come in handy?
B: Yeah. And they were half price!
A: But you've already got a set of spanners. It's in the cupboard.
B: Yeah, but it's only a small set.
A: And when was the last time you used them?
B: Well, let's see now. Not for a while, that's true.
A: I wish you hadn't wasted your money on those spanners. Why didn't you just buy the things you actually needed?
B: Hmm, maybe I shouldn't have bought them.
A: Yeah, maybe you shouldn't.

Conversation 2
C: Why did you buy three loaves?
D: Oh, they were on special offer. Three for two. Why not, eh?
C: But the shopping list I gave you said *one* loaf of bread.
D: Yeah, but the third loaf is free. Gratis!
C: But we'll never get through that much bread. And it's almost past its sell-by date.
D: We can freeze it …
C: The freezer's full. Oh, Dan! You were only supposed to buy one loaf.
D: Yeah, I suppose I didn't really think. Sorry.
C: Now I have to throw two loaves of bread away! Oh, if only you'd stuck to the things on the list, Dan!

Conversation 3
E: Look at this.
F: What?
E: The soles are coming away.
F: Already? That's really bad. How long have you had them?
E: A couple of weeks. Terrible, isn't it?
F: Yeah. How much did you pay for them?
E: Um, I can't remember, but they were cheap … really cheap.
F: You know, it's important to buy good quality. You ought to have chosen better shoes.
E: I suppose you're right. … Yeah, I wish I'd paid more for better ones now. I wasted my money on these.
F: Let that be a lesson to you!

Conversation 4
G: What's this?
H: It's a present for you.
G: Oh! What on earth is it?
H: It's a coffee cup holder. Cool, huh?
G: Why on earth did you buy that?
H: Because it's a useful present.
G: You really could have saved your money. I'm never going to use it.
H: Oh …
G: It clips on to the side of the table?
H: Yeah.
G: Well, why wouldn't I just put my cup on the table?
H: Umm …
G: Huh?
H: I guess I should have thought a bit more before I bought it.

b Ask Ss to listen again to complete the sentences, comparing answers in pairs before you go through them as a class. Write the answers on the board to ensure Ss have written the correct words. NB *have* not *of*.

Answers:
1 hadn't wasted, shouldn't have bought
2 supposed to, you'd stuck
3 ought to, wish I'd paid
4 could have saved, should have thought

Grammar
Mistakes in the past

6 Ask Ss to look back at the sentences in Ex 5b. Tell Ss you are going to look at how these forms differ in meaning. Focus attention on the first rule in the grammar box and ask Ss to use this and the examples to choose the correct alternative. Ss continue reading the grammar box and choosing the alternatives alone, using the examples to help them, then check in pairs. Check answers with the whole class and be prepared to give further explanations/examples where necessary.

Answers: 1 regret 2 didn't work 3 didn't ask
4 didn't listen 5 didn't buy 6 spent 7 didn't happen
8 happened

Grammar checkpoint
Ss may struggle with the differences in meaning between *should have* and *could have*. Point out that *could have* expresses possibility but not necessarily regret. Give further linked examples, such as:
Miles studied maths and physics. He could have become a doctor.
Ask: *Did he want to become a doctor?* (We don't know.) *Did he become a doctor?* (No)
Miles studied maths and physics. His mum said he should have become a doctor.
Ask: *Did she want him to become a doctor?* (Yes) *Did he become a doctor?* (No)

7a 5.2 Focus attention on the conversation. Play the recording for Ss to listen to how *should have* and *could have* are pronounced. If you think it's useful, explain the information in the Pronunciation checkpoint below, using the examples given.

Answers: /ˈʃʊdəv/ /ˈkʊdəv/

Pronunciation checkpoint
The auxiliary *have* is unstressed in these forms. This means it is pronounced as a weak form with /əv/. Sometimes it is so reduced that /v/ disappears and it is simply pronounced /ə/. The modal auxiliary *could* or *should* is stressed because it carries meaning.

b Ask Ss to roleplay the conversation in pairs, listening again if necessary. Remind them to pronounce reduced forms of *have*.

8 Look at the example with the class, clarifying that the word in brackets indicates which form to use. Ask Ss to complete the sentences alone, then check in pairs using the grammar box. Check answers with the whole class. Drill the complete sentences with attention to the reduced forms.

Answers:
1 I shouldn't have bought this gadget.
2 I could've bought a cheaper one.
3 If only you'd taken enough/more time to choose.
4 You ought to have asked (me) for my opinion.
5 I wish I hadn't wasted my money.
6 You were supposed to fix it, not break it.

9 Ask Ss to work alone to think, then tell a partner. With **weaker classes**, you may want to complete this as a written exercise, where Ss write sentences before they tell each other.

LANGUAGE BANK 5A   pp.144–145
Stronger classes could read the notes at home. Otherwise, check the notes with Ss. In each exercise, elicit the first answer as an example. Ss work alone to complete the exercises, then check their answers in pairs. In feedback, check answers with the whole class. Ss can refer to the notes to help them.

Answers:
1 1 b 2 b 3 a 4 a 5 b 6 a
2 1 shouldn't have done 2 ought to have taken
   3 could have stayed 4 hadn't spent 5 could have studied
   6 might have been 7 was supposed to start
   8 hadn't been

Further practice
Photocopiable activities: 5A Grammar 1, p203; 5B Grammar 2, p204
App: 5A Grammar practice 1 and 2

Speaking
Prepare

10a Tell Ss they are going to look at what Hamid, a student, spent. Refer them to the list and ask for first impressions – was he good with money last week? Ask pairs to discuss what was a false economy and why, then discuss as a class.

Possible answers:
takeaway meal and coffees (They're much more expensive than making your own.)
bulk buy box of biscuits (They might go stale before he eats them all.)
apple-peeling machine (He might not use it much.)

b Ask Ss to prepare and practise what they could say to Hamid, using the language from the lesson. Encourage them to include some money-related phrasal verbs and language for describing mistakes in the past. **Weaker classes** can write.

Speak

11a Ask Ss to read the Useful phrases, drilling pronunciation if needed. Put Ss in pairs and tell them to follow the instructions, with Student A starting as Hamid's friend. Monitor and listen to the roleplay. When they finish, give feedback on the language used.

Optional alternative activity
Put Ss in pairs of Hamid, and pairs of the friend to prepare. This means they can discuss and help each other with ideas. It is a good approach for **weaker classes** and also gives increased speaking practice. While they prepare, monitor and help. When they finish, re-pair them as Hamid and friend to start the roleplay.

b Ask Ss to change roles and repeat the roleplay. When they finish, give feedback and discuss whether they would ever talk to a friend or family member about their spending.

> **Reflection on learning**
> Write the following questions on the board:
> *What did you learn today?*
> *In what situations do you think you'll use this language in the future?*
> Put Ss in pairs to discuss the questions. When they have finished, ask if anyone wants to share their ideas with the class, but don't force them to if they'd rather not.

> **Homework ideas**
> Language bank: 5A Ex 1–2, pp.144–145
> Workbook: Ex 1–5, p36
> App: grammar, vocabulary and pronunciation practice

Fast route: continue to Lesson 5B
Extended route: go to p104 for Develop your reading

5B Crime scene

Introduction
The goal of this lesson is for students to talk about quantities. To help them achieve this, they will revise quantifiers and vocabulary about crimes, in particular robbery.

Warm-up
List some crime types on the board, for example: *murder, robbery, drug smuggling, fraud*. Ask Ss to suggest a few more, then ask them to rank the crimes in order of seriousness. Ss can discuss in pairs. Ask Ss if crime is ever justifiable.

Vocabulary and listening
Crime (robbery)
1 Refer to pictures 1–10 and ask Ss to match them with the list of stages. Give them a few minutes to do this alone. When they finish, ask pairs to compare ideas, then check answers with the whole class.

> **Answers:** 1 i 2 a 3 g 4 e 5 b 6 c 7 f 8 h 9 d 10 j

> **Optional alternative activity**
> Ask Ss to discuss a famous bank robbery that they can recall. When they finish, ask a few Ss to report back. Have a brief whole-class discussion if they are interested. If necessary, prompt Ss to recall a certain crime by providing a headline or photo that will trigger their memories. Alternatively, show a brief clip or still from a robbery film. Clips could be from a classic film such as *The Italian Job* (1969) or a later one such as *American Heist* (2015), *Ocean's 8* (2018) or *Widows* (2018). The objective is to recall some vocabulary related to robbery, so it doesn't matter if Ss don't remember very well or don't agree on what happened.

> **Culture notes**
> The UK legal process often uses the **jury** system. A jury usually consists of 12 members of the public aged 18–75 who are called to serve and decide if someone is guilty or innocent, based on the evidence presented. They are not paid. Their judgement is guided by the judge, who decides the sentence if a defendant is guilty. If Ss are interested in the process, they may enjoy classic courtroom dramas like *12 Angry Men* and *To Kill a Mockingbird*. Ss may want to comment on what they think of this system if they don't have it in their country. You could ask them if they'd like to be on a jury.

2 🔊 5.3 Tell Ss they are going to listen to a radio programme about bank robberies. Ask Ss to read the questions, then listen and answer them. When they finish, ask pairs to compare ideas, then go through the answers as a class.

> **Answers:**
> 1 to check that he understood the building
> 2 They drove through tunnels that they had dug.
> 3 within 24 hours
> 4 He wanted to get free healthcare in prison.

> **Audioscript 5.3**
> More than 60 percent of bank robberies are quickly solved by police and typically the robberies follow these stages.
>
> **Stage 1:**
> The leaders of a gang of bank robbers, usually called the ringleaders, research and plan the raid. They visit the bank and work out the best way in. George Leonidas Leslie, an American bank robber from the late 19th century, sometimes broke into the banks he planned to rob first, without taking anything, just to check that he understood the building.
>
> **Stages 2 and 3:**
> The gang break into the bank and steal the money. Then they try to leave the scene of the crime without attracting attention. This is often more difficult than breaking in itself. In 1986 the so-called Hole-in-the-ground Gang in Los Angeles removed almost 100 cubic metres of earth below Hollywood to create tunnels, which they then drove through in order to escape after a bank robbery.
>
> **Stages 4, 5 and 6:**
> The gang must then try to evade arrest. Usually this doesn't last long as most banks are in urban areas and there are lots of witnesses and CCTV cameras. The police usually catch the robbers within 24 hours and charge them with robbery. If the gang have used guns, it becomes armed robbery, which is much more serious.
>
> **Stages 7 and 8:**
> When the police and the prosecution service have gathered enough evidence and built a case, the gang go on trial in front of a judge and jury. If the robbers plead guilty, they usually get a more lenient sentence. If they plead not guilty, the sentence can be more severe.
>
> **Stages 9 and 10:**
> Ultimately, it's the jury who decides if the gang are guilty or not guilty. If the jury finds the robbers guilty, it's the judge's job to sentence them. He or she must decide how long the robbers must spend in prison. In one strange case, the robber found the sentence too lenient. James Verone of North Carolina was suffering from various health-related problems, but he had no insurance and couldn't afford the treatment. So instead, he walked into a bank and politely demanded one dollar. He then sat down to await arrest. His reasoning was that the only place he could get free health treatment was in prison. Unfortunately, his crime was not thought serious enough and he didn't get the length of sentence he needed to get the health treatment!

3 Refer Ss to the photo and headline. Ask them to use the phrases in bold in Ex 1 to guess what happened. They don't need to know or to get it right – this is just a chance to practise the vocabulary.

Unit 5

Culture notes

Hatton Garden is London's jewellery quarter. An area in central London that is famous for independent jewellers, it is home to the largest group of such businesses in the UK. In a relatively small area, there are about 300 jewellery businesses and 55 jewellery shops.

Some people use a **safety deposit box** to keep their jewellery, documents or other precious items secure. The boxes are located in secure institutions like banks. They often don't have to show what they put in there to the institution.

VOCABULARY BANK 5B p160
Nouns and verbs with the same form

This is an optional extension to the vocabulary section, extending the lexical set and providing further practice. If you're short of time, this can be done for homework.

1 Ss find the answers alone, using their mobile device or guesswork, then check in pairs. Check answers with the whole class.

Answers:
1 convict, judge, suspect, witness
2 appeal, convict, fine, judge, release, sentence
3 arrest, charge, suspect, witness
4 convict, permit, suspect (The stress is on the first syllable in the noun form, and the second syllable in the verb form.)

2 Ss work alone to complete the sentences with a form of words from Ex 1, using each word once. Ask them to check in pairs, then go through the answers.

Answers: 1 fine, permit 2 appealed, witnesses
3 arrested, suspects, charged, released
4 convicted, judge, sentence

3 Ss work in pairs to order the words in Ex 1, describing what happens after a crime. When they finish, ask a few pairs to give examples.

Answers: witness, suspect, arrest, charge, judge, convict, sentence, fine, appeal, release

Further practice

Photocopiable activities: 5B Vocabulary, p208
App: 5B Vocabulary practice 1 and 2

Grammar
Quantifiers

4 Ask Ss to read the text and answer the questions. Check the answers as a class.

Answers: Nobody knows how much was stolen because the contents of a safety deposit box are a secret. The case was unusual because of the age of the gang members.

5 Give Ss plenty of time to work in pairs to read the grammar box and look at the underlined phrases in Ex 4. Explain that they need to replace each underlined phrase with one of the alternatives provided. Point out that only one option in each pair is grammatically correct. Check answers with the class and be prepared to give further explanations/examples where necessary.

Answers: 1 b 2 a 3 a 4 b 5 a 6 a 7 b 8 b

Grammar checkpoint

Ss sometimes find it puzzling that what appears to be a plural subject takes a singular verb, for example: *Everybody speaks English* but *All the people speak English*. Go over some examples and get Ss to underline the subject and verb agreement in their notebooks. If they find it helpful, they can write a translation alongside.

6a 5.4 Play the recording for Ss to listen for *little/few* or *a little/a few*. Suggest that they write down the correct words as they listen (but not the whole sentences). Go through the answers.

Answers: 1 little 2 few 3 a few 4 a little 5 a little
6 Few 7 little 8 a few

Audioscript 5.4

1 The police have little time between arresting someone and charging them.
2 It was early, so there were few people on the streets.
3 The gang left a few clues behind at the scene of the crime.
4 The burglar took my TV and a little bit of money.
5 They need a little more time to interview the ringleaders.
6 Few people know anything about the robbery.
7 There's little reason to think that they will go on trial.
8 They opened a few safety deposit boxes but not many.

Pronunciation checkpoint

Articles in English are generally unstressed, so *a* can be hard to hear as it's often pronounced as a schwa /ə/. However, if the word before *a* ends in a consonant sound, it can be easier to notice because the two sounds link together, as in the examples in Ex 6a: *left‿a few …; and‿a little bit …; need‿a little …; opened‿a few …*.

b Ask Ss to listen again and repeat the sentences. They can focus on using linking to make the article *a* more noticeable in sentences 3, 4, 5 and 8 (see Pronunciation checkpoint above).

7 Go through the first example with the class, eliciting the correct alternative and discussing why it's correct, then ask Ss to continue alone before checking in pairs. Check answers with the whole class. Discuss why each option is correct.

Answers: 1 some 2 all 3 a couple of 4 most 5 None
6 no 7 several 8 none 9 some 10 all 11 a lot of

8 Now Ss have a chance to personalise. Give them a few minutes to work alone and change the sentences, then put them in small groups to discuss. Monitor and help where necessary, paying attention to the use of quantifiers. When they finish, ask a few groups to share an interesting point they talked about.

Optional alternative activity

With multilingual classes, put Ss in small groups with people from other countries. If in the UK, Ss could talk about the UK rather than their own countries.

LANGUAGE BANK 5B pp.144–145

Stronger classes could read the notes at home. Otherwise, check the notes with Ss. In each exercise, elicit the first answer as an example. Ss work alone to complete the exercises, then check their answers in pairs. In feedback, check answers with the whole class. Ss can refer to the notes to help them.

Answers:
1 1 some evidence is necessary to prove guilt.
   2 a few witnesses saw the robbery.
   3 no fingerprints were left at the scene of the crime.
   4 every defendant intends to plead guilty.
   5 neither burglar was / neither of the burglars were found guilty.
2 1 Both of the runners ~~was~~ *were* exhausted after the race finished.
   2 Take *a* little money with you tonight …
   3 Every member of the winning team ~~were~~ *was* given a medal.
   4 ✓
   5 She was wearing a lot of jewellery, several bracelets on ~~every~~ *each* wrist. (or *on both wrists*)
   6 ✓
   7 None of the witnesses to the crime ~~didn't report~~ *reported* anything.
   8 Few people bother to report this type of crime because it is rarely solved. (or *Very few people*)

Further practice

Photocopiable activities: 5B Grammar 1, p206; 5B Grammar 2, p207
App: 5B Grammar practice 1 and 2

Speaking

Prepare

9 Tell Ss they are going to describe a robbery. Name half the class Student A and the other half Student B, then ask Ss to turn to the relevant pages and read their information. Monitor and be available for questions.

Speak

10a Put Ss in AB pairs and ask them to take turns to describe their robbery. Refer listening Ss to the questions and encourage them to use these and other follow-up questions. Monitor and make notes on good use of language or errors with target language. When they finish, write the errors on the board and ask pairs to try and correct them before clarifying as a class.

> **Teaching tip**
> With extended speaking activities, try playing background music at a low volume. It can make Ss feel less self-conscious and more relaxed. Instrumental music is best. For this particular activity, you could choose something a bit more dramatic and suspenseful since Ss are talking about robberies! The switching on and off of the music can act as a cue for the speaking activity to begin and end.

b Once Ss have both described their robbery, ask them to find general similarities and differences. Look at the example as a guide. **Weaker classes** may benefit from writing and then speaking. When they finish, elicit some examples of similarities and differences.

c Discuss which robbery Ss think is real and why, then tell them the answer.

> **Answer:** The Securitas robbery is real, but the BoxSafe Robbery is invented.

Optional alternative activity

If Ss are interested, they can retell the robbery they talked about in the warm-up stage, either speaking or in writing. They should try to include the lesson's target language and should therefore notice they have improved over the lesson.

> **Reflection on learning**
> Write the following questions on the board:
> *How well do you think you managed to use quantifiers in this lesson?*
> *What learning goal would you like to set for yourself in this area?*
> Put Ss in pairs to discuss the questions. When they have finished, ask if anyone wants to share their ideas with the class, but don't force them to if they'd rather not.

Homework ideas

Language bank: 5B Ex 1–2, pp.144–145
Workbook: Ex 1–5, p37
App: grammar, vocabulary and pronunciation practice

Fast route: continue to Lesson 5C
Extended route: go to p124 for Develop your writing

5c Bubble trouble

Introduction

The goal of this lesson is for students to summarise a text. To help them achieve this, they will look at adverb + adjective collocations and money-related vocabulary.

Warm-up

Ask Ss to think of something that was worth a lot in the past and now is not worth much, or the reverse, for example: things which gained value – an artwork, property, stocks/shares; things which lost value: an old smartphone, a used car. Give them a few minutes to think of and write their ideas. Ask Ss to share their ideas, then discuss generally why things lose or gain value.

Vocabulary

Money

1 Ask Ss to discuss the quotes in pairs. If you have a multilingual class, try and mix the nationalities. If not, try and mix ages and/or genders to generate more discussion. If your class is monolingual and of similar ages, you could also ask Ss why money is important or necessary. Conduct brief whole-class feedback and ask if Ss can suggest other money-related quotes from their language.

2a Focus attention on meanings a–j and ask Ss to work in pairs to match them with the phrases in bold (1–8). Go through the answers and clarify meaning as needed.

Answers: 1 i 2 h 3 d 4 e 5 interest a, savings b
6 recession f, income j 7 g 8 c

Optional alternative activity

With **weaker classes**, divide up the words in bold and allocate them to different pairs. Ask Ss to check in a dictionary and match, then peer-teach the meanings. This can be quite time-consuming and you need to monitor closely to ensure Ss are teaching the correct meanings. It does, however, involve a lot of useful speaking practice and fosters learner independence.

b This is an opportunity to practise and personalise the vocabulary. Ask Ss to work in pairs and discuss. With **weaker classes**, quickly revise the second conditional form as needed. Conduct brief feedback and encourage different pairs to listen to each other's ideas.

Teaching tip

Ss don't always fully take opportunities to practise because they may not realise the purpose of an exercise. It can be helpful to point out to Ss that this is an opportunity to practise the vocabulary just seen in a personal way. Reinforce this by monitoring for that language in particular and focusing on its pronunciation and use in feedback after the activity.

VOCABULARY BANK 5C p160
Noun suffixes

This is an optional extension to the vocabulary section, extending the lexical set and providing further practice. If you're short of time, this can be done for homework.

1 Elicit the first answer as an example. Ss choose the correct box for each verb alone, then check in pairs. Check answers with the whole class and drill, pointing out the stress patterns.

Answers:
1 inflation, regulation, taxation
2 demonstrator, director, investor
3 employment, investment, management
4 citizenship, partnership, sponsorship
5 banking, funding
6 availability, stability

2 Ss choose the correct noun for each sentence, first working alone, then comparing in pairs. Go through the answers.

Answers: 1 taxation 2 availability 3 partnership
4 demonstrators 5 regulation 6 stability 7 inflation
8 management 9 funding/investment 10 citizenship

3 Put Ss in pairs to ask and answer the questions. When they finish, ask a few pairs to share an interesting answer.

Further practice

Photocopiable activities: 5C Vocabulary, p211
App: 5C Vocabulary practice 1 and 2

Listening

3 Look at the pictures as a class and identify what is shown. Ask Ss to discuss the questions in pairs, then have a whole-class discussion about how the images could be linked to money. Don't confirm any ideas yet as Ss will listen to information about this.

4a 🔊 5.5 Tell Ss they are going to hear a talk about tulips and they should make notes on why and how they became valuable as they listen. Allow Ss to compare answers, but there is no need to go over them in detail as Ss will complete a summary.

Answers:
Demand for tulip bulbs grew dramatically – they started to be seen as something in which people could invest their money, so their prices rose in the same way because the supply couldn't match the demand.

Optional alternative activity

Ss first discuss how the pictures could be connected, making up a story, then listen and check to see whether any of their ideas are mentioned.

Audioscript 5.5

Tulips. One of the brightest, most colourful plant varieties that Mother Nature has to offer. Who doesn't love the sight of a field of tulips or a vase full of them on the dining table? But did you also know that tulips were the cause of one of the first financial bubbles? By bubble, I don't mean the kind that children play with. I mean the kind of bubble where the price of something goes up and up and up until it becomes absolutely ridiculous, and then crashes and a lot of people lose all their savings.

Back in the seventeenth century, the Netherlands was known as the United Provinces and it was a highly successful global power. The new middle classes found that they had more than enough money to live on and they wanted to spend some of that extra money on beautiful things, like tulips. But rather than buy the flower, which would quickly wither and die, people wanted the tulip bulbs, because from each bulb you could grow a flower and get several more bulbs.

This demand for tulip bulbs was completely new and the prices began to rise because people started to see them as an investment. The more beautiful and rare the tulip, the more expensive the bulb. Today all kinds of tulips are widely available, but at that time it was difficult to grow the really exotic varieties with stripes and spots and so they remained rare. This is crucial for bubbles. It's only when demand is high and supply is low that a financial bubble starts to grow.

The most expensive variety of tulip bulb was the extremely rare *Semper Augustus*. Rich people began to offer their life savings for just one, partly because from one bulb it's relatively easy to cultivate many more. Perfectly normal people began borrowing money at high rates of interest in order to buy and then sell tulip bulbs and the prices continued to rise. It is said that a single *Semper Augustus* bulb became more expensive than a house on the most fashionable street in Amsterdam.

Looking back, it seems obvious what was going to happen – nothing can keep growing forever. Suddenly, at the beginning of 1637, the prices of tulip bulbs stopped rising and started falling. In fact, the prices crashed and demand for the bulbs collapsed. Panic set in. Those who had hoped to become rich were bitterly disappointed and those who had spent their life savings lost everything. Legend has it that some people threw themselves into the canals to escape their debts. Tulip bulbs went from being worth the same as an expensive house to being worth no more than an onion. In some ways, the world would never be the same again. It had experienced its first, but certainly not its last, financial bubble.

b Tell Ss they will now listen again for more detail. Give them a few minutes to read through the summary, then play the recording for them to complete it. Go through the answers as a class.

Answers: 1 17th 2 (new) middle classes 3 rise 4 rare
5 house 6 1637

c Put Ss in pairs to discuss. Conduct feedback to share ideas as a class. Ss might mention ideas such as company stocks and shares, digital currencies like Bitcoin, etc.

Language focus

Adverb + adjective collocations

5 Tell Ss they are going to look at sentences from the listening to study a language point. Ask Ss to try to complete the sentences from memory (without writing yet). Then play the recording for Ss to check, pausing as necessary to allow writing time. Ask pairs to compare answers, then check them with the whole class. Write the adverbs on the board so Ss can check their spelling. Mark the stress and drill pronunciation.

> **Answers:** **1** absolutely **2** highly **3** completely **4** widely **5** extremely **6** relatively **7** Perfectly **8** bitterly

6 Ss should now match each adjective in bold in Ex 5 with its collocating adverb in the Language focus box. This is simple, as they already have the answers, but explain that they need to read and understand the meaning of the other collocates as well. Go through the answers, asking Ss to pronounce any new adjectives. Discuss any that Ss have difficulty with.

> **Answers:** **1** ridiculous **2** disappointed **3** new **4** rare **5** successful **6** normal **7** easy **8** available

Grammar checkpoint

Many of the adverb + adjective collocations in this lesson are quite limited. For example, we can say *highly qualified* or *bitterly cold* but not *highly opposed* or *bitterly lost*. These collocations, therefore, have to be learnt as chunks. Remind Ss that many people use *really* as a general modifier. However, it does tend to be overused. *Absolutely* and *totally* can also be used with a wider range of adjectives than most adverbs.

7a 🔊 5.6 Ask Ss to listen for the pronunciation of the adverb + adjective collocations. Ask Ss why the adverbs are stressed (to add emphasis).

Audioscript 5.6

1
A: So it's true, is it?
B: It's absolutely true.

2
A: They're opposed to the idea.
B: They're bitterly opposed.

3
A: I think she's honest.
B: She's completely honest.

4
A: Are you concerned?
B: I'm deeply concerned.

5
A: That's new.
B: It's entirely new.

6
A: It looks dangerous.
B: It's extremely dangerous.

7
A: Is he qualified?
B: Yes, he's highly qualified.

8
A: So, it's safe.
B: It's perfectly safe.

9
A: Is it simple?
B: It's relatively simple.

10
A: We're lost.
B: We're totally lost.

b Ss should compare answers, then go through them as a class. Ask them to listen to the sentences again and repeat, paying attention to the rhythm and stress of the adverbs and adjectives.

> **Answers:** **1** absolutely true **2** bitterly opposed **3** completely honest **4** deeply concerned **5** entirely new **6** extremely dangerous **7** highly qualified **8** perfectly safe **9** relatively simple **10** totally lost

8 Go through an example with the class, then ask Ss to work alone to complete the sentences before comparing ideas in pairs. In feedback, nominate Ss to say each sentence in full so they can demonstrate the pronunciation.

> **Answers:** **1** totally lost **2** relatively simple/easy **3** absolutely true **4** highly qualified **5** bitterly opposed **6** perfectly legal **7** entirely possible **8** extremely dangerous **9** deeply concerned **10** completely honest

Optional extra activity

Ss work in pairs to write their own mini conversations including adverb + adjective collocations. They read them out to another pair or to the class, pausing before each collocation for their peers to try and guess it.

LANGUAGE BANK 5C pp.144–145

Stronger classes could read the notes at home. Otherwise, check the notes with Ss. In each exercise, elicit the first answer as an example. Ss work alone to complete the exercises, then check their answers in pairs. In feedback, check answers with the whole class. Ss can refer to the notes to help them.

Answers:
1 highly **2** perfectly **3** seriously **4** bitterly/completely **5** totally/completely **6** deeply **7** utterly/totally **8** completely

Further practice

Photocopiable activities: 5C Language focus 1, p209; 5C Language focus 2, p210
App: 5C Language focus practice 1 and 2

Speaking

Prepare

9a Explain that Ss are going to read about two more economic bubbles. Name half the class Student A and the other half Student B, then ask them to turn to the relevant pages to read their texts.

b Refer Ss to the questions to make notes. Point out that they should use quantifiers rather than specific numbers. AA and BB pairs can help each other with this. Monitor and make sure Ss are completing the task correctly. There's no need for whole-class feedback.

> **Teaching tip**
> Information gap activities rely on Ss having separate information and maintaining this gap is important for the activity to remain communicatively purposeful. In practical terms, this means finding a way to support each group and check their answers separately. Making AA and BB pairings is a useful way of allowing initial student peer support. If you plan to do this, make sure you get neighbouring Ss to read the same information, to avoid them having to move more than once.

Speak

10 Put Ss in AB pairs. Read through the instructions together, then ask Ss to take turns telling their partners about what they read. The listening Ss should ask follow-up questions. When they finish, ask pairs to tell the class which story they found the most interesting and which outcome was the most predictable.

> **Teaching tip**
> In activities like this one, it can be hard to keep all pairs working at the same pace. To try and keep things on track, tell the class that Student A will start and set a time limit of around three minutes. When time is up, or when most Ss appear to be ready, call the class to attention again and ask Student B to speak. If a pair finish early, ask them to read each other's texts and discuss the two stories together before whole-class feedback.

> **Reflection on learning**
> Write the following questions on the board:
> *How could the activities you did in today's lesson help you in your everyday life?*
> *What ideas can you suggest for remembering the vocabulary we studied?*
> Put Ss in pairs to discuss the questions. When they have finished, ask if anyone wants to share their ideas with the class, but don't force them to if they'd rather not.

Homework ideas

Language bank: 5C Ex 1, pp.144–145
Workbook: Ex 1–5, p38
App: grammar, vocabulary and pronunciation practice

Fast route: continue to Lesson 5D
Extended route: go to p90 for Develop your listening

5D English in action

Introduction

The goal of this lesson is for students to deal with and resolve conflicts. To help them achieve this, they will learn some language used to apologise, accept responsibility and negotiate resolutions, plus vocabulary of phrases with *leave*.

Warm-up

Write the following expressions on the board:
Let's agree to disagree.
Never go to sleep on an argument.
Ask Ss to tell each other in pairs what they mean and which they agree with. Conduct brief class feedback to compare opinions.

1a Ask Ss to discuss the questions in pairs. After a few minutes, invite a few pairs to give their answers and have a brief whole-class discussion about who Ss disagree with the most (sibling/colleague/partner, etc.) and why.

b Refer Ss to the photos and ask them to discuss what they would say. With **weaker classes**, talk about the first picture together, then ask them to continue in pairs. When they finish, have a whole-class discussion and add useful expressions to the board.

2a Explain that Ss should complete the conversations using sentences a–h. They don't need to change the form of any words. Ask Ss to compare answers in pairs before conducting feedback.

> **Answers:** 1 h 2 g 3 e 4 d 5 f 6 c 7 b 8 a

b Ask Ss to match the phrases in bold in Ex 2a with the correct meanings. Complete the first one together, then ask Ss to continue alone. Ask Ss to compare answers in pairs, then go through the answers and further explain as needed.

> **Answers:** 1 Leave it to me! 2 left on 3 left a mark
> 4 left a message 5 leave lying around 6 left in a mess
> 7 left at home 8 leave alone

> **Teaching tip**
> When words have multiple collocations, as with the word *leave* in this exercise, Ss need to use careful dictionary work and context to help them grasp the correct meaning. In this case, translation can be a useful tool. Remind them to record the full phrase in their notebook and add a translation. It doesn't matter if you don't speak your Ss' first language(s), but if you have several Ss that speak the same language they could compare answers.

Listening 1

3a ◯ 5.9 Tell Ss they will listen to five conversations about a problem. They should listen and choose the correct alternatives. Give them a minute to read through, then play the recording. Go through the answers.

> **Answers:** 1 open 2 off 3 on 4 used all the
> 5 has been stolen

Audioscript 5.9

Conversation 1
A: Who left the front door open this morning?
B: I have to own up. It was me! Sorry!
A: OK, but try not to do it again.
B: I'll try.

Conversation 2
C: Hey, who left the oven on? Ruth? Was it you?
D: Me? Why me? It's got nothing to do with me!
C: OK, I'm only asking.
D: Yeah, but you always blame me for everything.

Conversation 3
E: Who left the central heating on all night?
F: It was my fault. I apologise. I forgot to turn it off when I went to bed.
E: Heating costs money, you know.
F: I know, I'm really sorry.
E: All right. It was cold last night anyway, so it's no big deal. But try to remember next time.
F: I will.

Conversation 4
G: Who left this big mess in the kitchen?
H: Dunno.
G: And who finished all the eggs? Gretchen?
H: Don't blame me. I don't even like eggs.
G: Well, who did then?
H: Dunno. Ask Felix.
G: Felix?
I: Ah, the great disappearing egg mystery. I had nothing to do with it, I'm afraid! I'd ask Helen if I were you.
G: Helen, did you eat all the eggs?
J: No ... but I might have dropped them.
G: Dropped them?
J: But it wasn't my fault. You shouldn't have left them lying around.

Conversation 5
K: Hey, my bicycle is gone. Has anyone seen it?
L: Oh, I borrowed it to go to the shops, but I brought it back. I left it outside.
K: Did you lock it again?
L: Um, maybe not. Oh, no!
K: So it's been stolen!
L: I'm so sorry. It's entirely my fault.
K: You're telling me!
L: I'll sort it out, I promise ... Nina, I'm sorry ...
K: Oh, just leave me alone.

b Refer Ss to the Useful phrases box. Tell Ss that they will listen again and should tick the sentences they hear. Tell **weaker classes** they will hear all of them apart from three. Play the recording, pausing between conversations if needed, then ask Ss to compare before going through the answers.

Answers:
Tick all except:
I'm so sorry, did I (tread on your toe)?
I should have been more careful.
Don't worry. It's nothing

4 Ask Ss to read the questions and choose the most suitable responses. Ask Ss to compare in pairs, then go through the answers and deal with any questions.

Answers: 1 a 2 b 3 a 4 b

Vocabulary checkpoint

Ask Ss to identify which of the phrases means 'it's not important' (= *it's no big deal*) and which means 'I'll organise it' (= *I'll sort it out*).

Point out that these phrases are rather informal and discuss when they might not be suitable (for example, in a job interview or formal writing). Point out that *it's got nothing to do with me* and *I had nothing to do with it* are the same phrase but used with different subjects and tenses.

5a 5.10 Write *I'm not angry* on the board and ask Ss which word is stressed (Ss will probably suggest *not*). Ask them how the meaning changes if we place the stress on *I'm* or *angry*. Say these aloud so Ss can hear the difference. Then ask them to read the information box to check. Ask Ss to listen and choose the appropriate answer according to the meaning implied by the stress. With **weaker classes**, do the first one together as an example.

b Ask Ss to compare answers in pairs. Go through the answers as a class. Discuss what the speaker might say to get the other response in each case.

Answers: 1 a 2 a 3 b

Listening 2

6 5.11 Tell Ss they are going to listen to two conversations where people disagree about something. Give Ss a minute to read the sentence beginnings, then play the recording so they can complete them. Ask Ss to compare answers, then go through them as a class. Ask Ss if they have had similar conversations and which of the two is more familiar.

Answers:
1 a stop playing tennis.
  b she booked the court.
  c the court was free and the hotel receptionist said he could play.
  d try to book the court between four and five.
2 a was checking her phone/emails rather than listening to him.
  b she's got an important meeting the next day.
  c no digital devices at dinner, but time to work after dinner.
  d how long she is going to work after dinner.

Audioscript 5.11

Conversation 1
A: Excuse me! ... Hello.
B: Hi.
A: Hello. Um, I've actually booked this tennis court.
B: Oh, right.
A: Yeah. So, would you mind stopping your game?
B: Well, the court was free when we arrived, so the hotel receptionist said we could play.
A: Yes, but I booked it and I'm here now.
B: What time did you book it for?
A: Between three and four and it's quarter past three right now.
B: Yeah, that's the problem. If you're more than ten minutes late, then they give the court to someone else.
A: Well, they didn't tell me that when I booked. I don't think it's fair.
B: Yeah, and I don't think it's fair for us to have to stop our game.
A: But I booked the court!
B: But *you* were late.
A: That wasn't my fault. There was a queue at reception and ...
B: Look! Let's try to find a solution, shall we?
A: Hmmm.
B: From your point of view, you've booked this court and from mine we're allowed to play now.
A: That's pretty much it, yes.

B: Why don't we see if we can book the court between four o'clock and five o'clock. If it's free then, we can decide who plays now and who plays later.
A: I don't think that's fair. I booked the court!
B: Yes, I understand that. Unfortunately, the rules say that you were too late.
A: Yes, but I didn't know that …
B: I know you didn't know, and I don't think you've done anything wrong, but neither have we! So, let's see if we can book the court for the next hour. If we do that, then we'll all be able to play tennis.
A: Well, OK. I guess that sounds reasonable.
B: Good. I'll call the receptionist. Hang on a minute …

Conversation 2
C: So anyway, I talked to Mike and Mike told me that it was all a misunder…. Are you listening to me?
D: What? Um, oh, yes, of course. Your bike. You were talking about your bike.
C: My bike? I was talking about Mike!
D: Oh, sorry.
C: Are you checking your phone?
D: Yeah. Sorry. Look, it's just that I've got a big meeting tomorrow and there are some emails that I need to … sorry.
C: But it's dinner time and you're working!
D: I know but this meeting is important!
C: Am I not important, too?
D: That's not fair! Of course you're important, but you know my job is really demanding.
C: So is mine, but I still find time for you!
D: Look. Let's put this to one side and think of a solution.
C: Well, we definitely need a solution. This can't go on.
D: You're annoyed because I'm looking at my phone and I'm stressed because I've got a big meeting tomorrow.
C: OK.
D: What about if we make a rule: no digital devices at dinner.
C: Uh-huh.
D: But then I get some time after dinner to do some work.
C: After dinner?
D: Yeah. It makes sense because you get what you want and I get what I want.
C: I don't think that's going to work. We need to set a time limit.
D: A time limit?
C: Yep, you need a limit on how long you're going to work, otherwise you might work all evening.
D: You're right. Any suggestions?
C: Let's say an hour.
D: OK. So, no digital devices at dinner, but I get an hour after dinner to do some work?
C: Yep.
D: All right. That's OK with me.
C: Good.
D: OK, I'm putting my phone away. Now tell me what the problem was with your bike.
C: My bike?!
D: Only joking …

7 Refer Ss to the phrases and ask them to listen again and mark them M for the man or W for the woman. **Stronger classes** may be able to do this without listening again. Go through the answers as a class.

Answers:
1 a M b W c W
2 a W b W c W

8 Refer Ss to the Useful phrases box, asking them to complete it with phrases from Ex 7. Do the first example together, then ask Ss to continue in pairs. When they finish, go through the answers as a class and deal with any questions. Drill phrases to help Ss feel comfortable saying them.

Answers:
1 Let's put this to one side and think of a solution.
2 From your point of view … and from mine …
3 It makes sense because …
4 I guess that sounds reasonable.
5 I don't think that's fair.
6 You're right. Any suggestions?

9a Ask a **stronger student** to read the situation aloud to the class or read it yourself. Ask Ss to complete the conversation using the prompts in brackets and the phrases they have studied. Monitor, supporting and correcting. Go through the answers together, accepting any reasonable suggestions.

b Ask Ss to practise the conversation in pairs. Ask fast finishing or more confident Ss to try again without looking at their books. Monitor and listen to see how they are doing.

Optional alternative activity

If you think your Ss are unlikely to relate to the flatmates' situation due to their age or circumstances, brainstorm various other people Ss might disagree with (friend, parent, colleague, etc.) and various things they might disagree about (money, timekeeping, office politics, etc). Build up two columns on the board. Ask Ss in pairs to choose a person and topic they find relatable and then proceed with the conversation, either by writing a conversation (**weaker classes**) or improvising a spoken conversation (**stronger classes**).

Speaking

10a Name Ss A or B in their pairs and ask them to turn to the relevant pages and read their roles. Ask Ss to start the roleplay. Monitor, listen and help as needed.

b When Ss complete their roleplay, tell them to switch roles. **Weaker pairs** may only complete the roleplay once. When they finish, have a brief feedback stage, adding errors and good examples to the board for Ss to evaluate and correct.

Reflection on learning

Write the following questions on the board:
What did you practise in this lesson?
In what other situations do you think you can use this language in the future?
Put Ss in pairs to discuss the questions. When they have finished, ask a few Ss to share their ideas with the class, but don't force them to if they'd rather not.

Homework ideas

Reflection on learning: Write your answers.
Workbook: Ex 1–5, p39
App: grammar, vocabulary and pronunciation practice

Roadmap video

Go online for the Roadmap video and worksheet.

5A Develop your readng

Introduction

The goal of this lesson is for students to understand academic texts. To help them achieve this, they will focus on understanding references to numerical data

Warm-up

Ask Ss what kinds of texts there are (novel, newspaper, blog post, letter, etc.) and build a list on the board. Elicit academic text as one of the genres. Ask Ss to tick those that they only read in their own language and those they might also read in English. Tell them this lesson is about helping them understand academic texts.

Culture notes

If Ss are working, they may feel that academic texts are not a relevant genre. You could point out that a very similar genre is used in certain business-oriented magazines, such as *The Economist*, where numerical data is frequently used. Ss wanting to study or work in the UK may know about the academic strand of the IELTS exam, which often involves reading and understanding academic texts.

1a Ask Ss to discuss the questions in pairs and tick those they can answer. To distinguish between knowledge and language, refine this by asking Ss to confirm which they could answer in English and which they could answer in their first language. After a few minutes, conduct brief feedback.

b Ask Ss to give an answer to a question of their choice. If Ss are interested, they can share this with others in the group.

2 Tell Ss to read texts 1–5 and match each with a question from Ex 1a. Tell them they have a few minutes and they should write the letter of the question beside the relevant text. Point out that there are more questions than texts so two will not be used. Allow Ss to compare in pairs, then elicit answers and ask for reasons.

Answers: 1 d   2 c   3 f   4 e   5 a

3 Ask Ss to read the texts again more carefully to answer the questions. Check they know what a *shovel* is (draw a picture on the board). Go through the answers.

Answers:
1   a banks   b by lending money
2   a one Swiss franc   b only in Lewes
3   a to repay its debts   b in 1923
4   a shovels (and other supplies for miners looking for gold)
    b to encourage people to come and buy shovels, etc. from his shop
5   a when people have goods of different value
    b when givers and recipients are from different communities, or when you can't trust the recipient to repay the gift

Optional alternative activity

Divide the texts among different Ss to read and find the answers. When they have done so, regroup Ss so they can ask the questions and tell each other. This makes the lesson a little less reading-heavy. It will probably take the same amount of time to do the activity – or even more – but the emphasis is different as there is additional speaking practice.

4a Ask Ss to look at the Focus box and take turns to read it out. As you go through, check understanding of *vertical*, *horizontal*, *column* and *row*. Ask Ss to match the visuals with the items in bold in Ex 2. Elicit which is the table to start them off.

b Ask Ss to compare in pairs, describing what is shown in each visual. Go through the answers as a class.

Answers: A = Fig. 3 (Text 3)   B = Fig. 2 (Text 2)
C = Table 4 (Text 4)   D = Fig. 1 (Text 1)

Optional extra activity

Some Ss may feel uncomfortable with maths. Point out that we can use maths-related visuals for all kinds of everyday information. Conduct a quick survey in the room, such as how many male/female Ss there are or how many have long/short hair. Work together as a class to express this in the form of a pie chart or table with columns. If Ss enjoy this, get them to devise a short survey (about any topic), conduct it and then create visuals to accompany their report.

5 Ask Ss to talk about the questions in pairs. When they finish, ask if any Ss want to share a few interesting answers with the class.

Optional extra activity

If any of your Ss use academic texts in other subjects or languages, ask them to choose and bring in a text and describe it to others, using the language of the lesson. Ideally they will choose one which contains some visuals/figures.

Homework ideas

Workbook: Ex 1–6, p40

5B Develop your writing

Introduction

The goal of this lesson is for Ss to write a detailed description of a person. To help them achieve this, they will focus on using similes.

Warm-up

Ask Ss if they have a good memory for faces or details. Tell them to turn away from their partner or neighbour and write a few brief notes about their appearance, clothes and any distinguishing features. They should then share their descriptions and see how accurate they are. Tell them that describing people is the lesson focus.

1 Put Ss in pairs to look at the photos and describe the people. This is just an introductory activity so monitor to see how their vocabulary is and help where needed.

2 Ask Ss to read the texts and answer the questions M, W, B or N. Give them a few minutes, then conduct whole-class feedback.

Answers: 1 N   2 M   3 B   4 B   5 W   6 B   7 N   8 M

3 Refer Ss to the box. Ask them to circle the correct descriptions, using one colour for the man and a different one for the woman. After a few minutes, elicit answers and deal with any questions. If possible, project the box on the board and annotate it there. **Weaker classes** may find it easier to complete the answers for just one of the people.

> **Answers:**
> **Man:** 60s, short, slim build, receding, grey, moustache, stubble, light complexion, prominent nose, birthmark
> **Woman:** middle-aged, tall, elegant, short, wavy, smooth complexion, pointed chin, blue eyes, scar

4 Ask Ss to read the texts again and answer the questions. They can discuss in pairs before checking as a class.

> **Answers:** a paragraph 3 b paragraph 2 c paragraph 1

5a Give Ss a few minutes to read again more carefully and mark each feature A or B. With **weaker classes**, point out that the features are set out in pairs, one for each text, so they may find it easier to look at two at a time. When they finish, go through the answers.

> **Answers:** 1 A 2 B 3 B 4 A 5 A 6 B 7 A 8 B

b Discuss as a class, telling Ss to circle the numbers of the positive text features.

> **Answers:** 1, 4, 5, 7

6a Ask Ss to look at the Focus box and read the explanation of a simile. To check, ask which words are generally used (*as*, *like*). Then ask them to find two more similes in text A. Check as a class.

> **Answers:** … as bold as brass … Cool as a cucumber …

Optional extra activity

The common similes in the Focus box are fixed expressions recognisable to native speakers. Ss can translate them into their own language (they are often very similar). Ss can also try to create their own fun new similes using *as* (+ adjective) and *as a* (+ noun). Point out that *as* is pronounced /əz/ in these expressions because it is weak.

b Ask Ss to complete the sentences from the Focus box. If they don't know all of the similes, they can try and guess the answers. Check as a class.

> **Answers:** 1 as dull as ditchwater 2 as light as a feather
> 3 as hard as nails 4 as bright as a button
> 5 as proud as a peacock

Prepare

7a Refer Ss to the headings and ask them to make notes on someone of their choice. Point out it could be someone they know quite well or someone they met briefly but who had a big impact on them. Monitor and support with ideas and vocabulary as needed.
b Ask Ss to work alone to create two similes, comparing ideas in pairs. Monitor and check that they are accurately formed.
c Refer to the paragraph descriptions in Ex 4. Ask Ss to recall which element of the description comes first (how they met). Tell them to organise their notes in this sequence.

Write

8a Ask Ss to write their descriptions. Monitor and be available to help with spelling, simile formation and corrections.
b When they finish, ask Ss to exchange descriptions with a partner and give feedback. Monitor and ensure the points being made are valid.

Teaching tip

Introduce Ss to the idea of a correction code. This is where the reader identifies the types of problems in written work but does not actually correct them. Instead, they mark the text with relevant codes and the writer corrects the text themselves when it is returned, using the codes as clues. This makes both writer and reader engage more with the correction and editing process. Common codes include: GR (grammar), T (tense), SP (spelling), P (punctuation), WW (wrong word) and WO (word order). This can also be used in your own correction of Ss' work and encourages student independence.

Optional extra activity

Ss write their description alone, then read it to another student in the class. They look at the criteria in Ex 7a–c and discuss if any improvements can be made. They then work together on a second draft.
Alternatively, put the following focus instructions on the board:
Read your partner's work and discuss these questions:
- *Is the description clear?*
- *Is there anything which is unclear for the reader?*
- *Does it include at least two similes?*
- *Is it organised into clear paragraphs?*

Homework ideas

Workbook: Ex 1–8, pp.42–43

5c Develop your listening

Introduction

The goal of this lesson is for Ss to understand presentations. To help them achieve this, they will focus on matching information with visuals.

Warm-up

Ask Ss to discuss whether they have to give or attend presentations in their work or studies and what they feel about them. Ask them what tools are used, such as projectors and presentation software, and what they find interesting, boring or stressful about presentations.

1 Ask Ss to read and discuss the questions in pairs. After a few minutes, conduct brief, whole-class feedback.

Culture notes

A **restaurant chain** is a group of restaurants with the same name that is either operated as a single business or as a franchise, where the brand is bought by an individual who runs the restaurant according to the rules of the brand and buys their food products, packaging, etc. Chains are well placed to monitor trends and employ mystery shoppers to ensure the food/experience is consistent across the different branches.

2 ⏵ **5.7** Tell Ss they will hear the introduction to a presentation. Ask them to read the questions, then listen and make notes. Ss compare answers in pairs before going through as a class.

Answers:
1 to give the results of research that Melanie Rose-Mason has been carrying out into customer satisfaction at their chain of restaurants
2 because people are eating out and ordering food in more
3 Customer satisfaction is falling.
4 She compared video of the restaurants from 2004 to now.

Audioscript 5.7

I'd like to begin by thanking you for coming to my presentation today. My name is Melanie Rose-Mason and I work for a small chain of restaurants here in the city. What I'd like to do is to give you the results of some research we've been conducting into customer satisfaction at our restaurant chain.

Now, you may or may not be aware that in recent years the restaurant industry has been doing very well. Eating habits have been changing and more and more people are now eating out, or ordering in food, rather than cooking for themselves at home. This has led to many new restaurants. At the same time, however, customer satisfaction has been falling. This is a trend that has been seen throughout the restaurant industry. We wanted to know why this is, so we compared video of our restaurants in 2004 with video of our restaurants now and tried to understand what was happening. The results might surprise you.

3 ⏵ **5.8** Tell Ss they'll now listen to the rest of the presentation and should make notes on the reasons for the changes listed. Play the recording, then ask Ss to compare in pairs before going through the answers as a class.

Answers:
1 Customers check their phones, ask for the wifi code or ask for a group photo before they've even looked at the menu.
2 They are less likely to settle for second best.
3 The food goes cold because people continue to look at their phones or take photos of their food to post online.
4 Customers are busy with their mobile phones.

Audioscript 5.8

What we found is that the problem is not our restaurants. The problem, to be completely honest, is our customers! Let me explain why.

Firstly, let's look at that fall in customer satisfaction. As you can see from my first slide, it's been a slow but steady fall. Customers nowadays are more likely to complain, more likely to post a negative review and more likely to give a restaurant a lower satisfaction rating. Now, you could argue that this is because customers expect more, however our research showed that something else was going on.

Our first discovery was that diners are taking longer to eat their meal. As this visual shows, in 2004 a typical meal took one hour and five minutes while today it takes almost two hours. That's a rise of 75 percent.

Why is this, do you think? Well, the first reason is that it takes a lot longer for customers to order their food. As you can see, back in 2004 customers took on average eight minutes to order their meal while now customers take on average 21 minutes. That's two and a half times as long. The reason for this is that the first thing customers do when they sit down is look at their mobile phones. Then they ask for the wifi code or sometimes, as more than half of our diners did, they ask the waiter or waitress to take a group photo of them. All of this takes a long time and as a result, when the waiter comes to take their order, they often haven't even looked at the menu yet.

It's also interesting to note that the number of people who ask for a different table has risen slightly. This visual illustrates that point. Back in 2004, it was around six percent of diners, whereas now it's closer to nine percent. The reason seems to be that people nowadays are less likely to accept second best. If they see a better table with a better view, they want it!

We've also seen a sharp rise in the number of people who send their food back. As this chart illustrates, in the past only around one in 25 diners sent their food back, while now that figure is closer to one in five. That's a huge increase and it's expensive for restaurants and again, the reason for the increase is the mobile phone. Diners now tend to either continue looking at their phones when their food arrives or they spend up to three minutes taking pictures of their food to post on social media. As a result, the food goes cold and the customer sends it back.

Now, take a look at this next slide. It shows that the time between finishing the meal and leaving the restaurant has risen dramatically. Customers now take three times as long as they did in 2004. Again, this seems to be because they are busy with their mobile phones.

Obviously, it's extremely difficult to say to a customer, 'Can you stop looking at your phone?', but at the same time our research points to one conclusion. Customer satisfaction is falling because customers are making themselves unhappy, and it's highly likely that they're making themselves unhappy because they're spending time on their mobile phone rather than enjoying the experience of being in a restaurant. In fact, a few restaurants have even started asking customers to hand in their phones when they enter the restaurant.

So, let me tell you about how we have tried to tackle this problem and improve customer satisfaction …

4 Read through the Focus box as a class, with Ss taking turns to read sections aloud. Tell Ss they will listen again more carefully and should match each point (1–6) with the correct slide, A or B. Give Ss a few minutes to look over the slides, then play the recording. With **weaker classes**, you may want to stop after each section to allow Ss to compare answers. Go through the answers as a class.

Answers: 1 A 2 B 3 A 4 B 5 B 6 A

Optional extra activity

Ss use the language in the Focus box to describe the remaining slides. They can prepare this in pairs, then present to another pair.

5 Ask Ss to discuss the questions in pairs. Conduct a brief whole-class discussion to find out if the presentation reflects the class's habits or not.

Optional extra activity

Ss work in pairs to develop a questionnaire about mobile phone use, or another related area such as takeaway deliveries or fast-food consumption. They conduct their questionnaire in the group, collecting data and then preparing slides to illustrate the results. Pairs then use these slides to give peer presentations, using the language of the lesson. Alternatively, they could write a report using the data.

Homework ideas

Workbook: Ex 1–3, p42

6 OVERVIEW

6A Love it or loathe it?
Goal | talk about things you love and loathe
Grammar | verb + -ing and infinitive with to
Vocabulary | common idioms
GSE learning objective
Can use a range of language to express degrees of enthusiasm

6B We can work it out
Goal | summarise a negotiation
Grammar | reported speech
Vocabulary | negotiating
GSE learning objective
Can summarise the position at the end of a negotiation in some detail

6C Tricky conversations
Goal | paraphrase what someone has said
Language focus | verb patterns after reporting verbs
Vocabulary | reporting verbs
GSE learning objective
Can paraphrase in simpler terms what someone else has said

Check and reflect
Review exercises and communicative activities to practise the grammar, vocabulary and functional language from Units 5 and 6.

Roadmap video
Go online for the Roadmap video and worksheet.

VOCABULARY BANK

6A Common idioms
6B Reporting verbs

DEVELOP YOUR SKILLS

6A Develop your listening
Goal | understand informal discussions
Focus | recognising signpost expressions
GSE learning objective
Can distinguish between fact and opinion in informal discussion at natural speed

6B Develop your reading
Goal | understand a website
Focus | recognising irony
GSE learning objective
Can recognise the author's use of irony in a simple text, if guided by questions

6C Develop your writing
Goal | write an email of complaint requesting action
Focus | using comment adverbs
GSE learning objective
Can write a forceful but polite letter of complaint, including supporting details and a statement of the desired outcome

---

6A Love it or loathe it?

Introduction
The goal of this lesson is for students to talk about things they love and loathe. To help them achieve this, they will revise verbs + -ing and infinitives with *to* and vocabulary of common idioms.

Warm-up
Write the title of the lesson on the board and underline the words *love* and *loathe*. Explain that *loathe* means to hate. Pronounce the two words and focus on the different vowel sounds /ʌ/ and /əʊ/. Write a random jumble of words containing the two sounds on the board and ask Ss to categorise them according to the correct vowel sound. In feedback, say each word in turn before checking answers to give an extra opportunity to hear the pronunciation. Example words:
/ʌ/ *run, fun, must, sun, under, juggle*
/əʊ/ *coat, know, phone, most, roam, ghost*

> **Teaching tip**
> Activities such as this warm Ss up in a general sense, getting them into English and ready for the lesson. If your Ss like focusing on contrasting sounds, build such stages into your regular warm-ups and use them for revising vocabulary. Look for spelling patterns and point out instances where there is no sound and spelling correspondence.

Listening and vocabulary

Common idioms

1 Put Ss in pairs and ask them to discuss the question. After a few minutes, ask pairs for their answers and get Ss to share their opinions about what they love and loathe.

2a 6.1 Tell Ss they will listen to eight conversations. They should first write numbers 1–8 in their notebook, then write the topic of each conversation as they listen. Ss should tick (✓) each topic if the speaker loves it and cross it (✗) if they loathe it. Play the recording, then check the answers as a class.

> **Answers:**
> 1 a date that one speaker went on ✗
> 2 techno music from the neighbour ✗
> 3 parking near the hospital ✗
> 4 new high-definition TVs ✓ (but too expensive)
> 5 shooting stars in the night sky ✓
> 6 a neighbour who is moving away ✓
> 7 giving speeches ✓
> 8 a dessert (cheesecake) in a restaurant ✓

Audioscript 6.1

Conversation 1
A: So how was your date, then?
B: He didn't stop talking about himself the whole evening.
A: I hate it when people do that.
B: Me, too. First, he told me about his job, then his car, then his motorbike, then his plans for the future …
A: Self-obsessed. I bet he didn't ask you a single question.
B: Not a single one! And he looked so kind and clever.
A: Just goes to show, doesn't it? You can't judge a book by its cover.
B: Very true.

Conversation 2
A: Can you hear that?
B: What?
A: That music. It's coming from next door, I think.
B: Oh, yeah. Sounds like techno. Just ignore it.
A: I can't. It's driving me up the wall.
B: Why don't you ask him to turn it down?
A: I can't do that, either. We don't talk to each other any more.
B: Oh, is he the one you had a row with?
A: Yeah, that's him.

Conversation 3
A: … so, after I left work on Friday I went to visit Audrey in hospital.
B: Audrey?
A: My neighbour. She's just had an operation, so I thought I'd go and see her. I tried to park but it was impossible. Couldn't find a space.
B: Parking is terrible round there.
A: Awful. It's such a pain. Anyhow, I found a space eventually and went to see her. She was looking so much better.
B: Oh, that's good to hear.

Conversation 4
A: Hey, you seen those new TVs?
B: What, the fancy high-definition ones?
A: Super high-definition, eight-k screen with built in surround-sound audio.
B: Sounds amazing.
A: Yeah.
B: You thinking of getting one?
A: Are you joking? They cost an arm and a leg. No, I thought you might want to buy one.
B: Me? What makes you think I can afford one?
A: Well, you're always into the latest gadgets and tech, so …
B: No way! They're too expensive.

Conversation 5
A: Extraordinary, isn't it.
B: Beautiful … See that?
A: What?
B: It was a shooting star … There's another one.
A: Wow! It takes your breath away, doesn't it?
B: Totally.

Conversation 6
A: I see he's got a 'for sale' board up.
B: Who?
A: Your neighbour. Mr Jenkins.
B: What, old Mr Nosey Parker. I didn't know he was moving!
A: Yeah, the sign says, 'for sale'. Are you sad he's going?
B: Are you serious? I'm over the moon.
A: So you're not going to miss him.
B: Not for a second. He's always poking his nose into my business. Hopefully somebody nice will move in and I'll have a neighbour I like for a change.

Conversation 7
A: So, are you ready?
B: Yep, all set.
A: Have you learnt your speech?
B: Yep, got it word perfect.
A: You're not at all nervous, are you?
B: Why should I be?
A: Well, you're about to give a speech in front of several hundred people. That would make most people nervous.
B: Nah! It's a piece of cake. I love giving speeches. I can listen to the sound of my own voice!
A: OK, well, good luck!
B: Thanks, but I don't really need it. I've got it all up here.

Conversation 8
A: Oh, this is good. This is really good.
B: The cheesecake?
A: You have to try it. It's amazing.
B: Oh, yes, that's really good!
A: Isn't it!
B: It's out of this world. The best cheesecake I've ever tasted. Mmmm. Just one more bite.
A: Hey! It's also *my* cheesecake, so if you want more, get your own!
B: Oh! That's so mean.

b Ask Ss to listen again and complete the idioms. Ask Ss to compare in pairs and help as they do this. When they finish, elicit answers. Write the answers on the board to ensure Ss have them correctly. Point out that *take your breath away* can also have a negative meaning.

Answers:
1 judge a book by its cover
2 driving me up the wall
3 such a pain
4 cost an arm and a leg
5 takes your breath away
6 over the moon
7 a piece of cake
8 out of this world

Vocabulary checkpoint
An **idiom** is a group of words in a fixed order. Its meaning is usually different from the meanings of the individual words on their own. Idioms are easy to use for native speakers but particularly challenging for learners as they rarely correspond when translated into other languages. The origin of some idioms can be explained: *over the moon* may be related to a 16th century nursery rhyme, for example. Others are inexplicable. For some idioms, the words are fully fixed – *You can't judge a book by its cover* – while others have a little more flexibility with tense and number – *He's driving me up the wall, They drove me up the wall,* etc.

c This exercise acts as a check on understanding of the idioms. Ask Ss to match the idioms and meanings, then check in pairs before going through the answers as a class. Drill the phrases as needed.

Answers: 1 g 2 b 3 c 4 h 5 d 6 f 7 a 8 e

3 Ask Ss to change the underlined sections to create their own sentences. Do an example together on the board first, then ask Ss to continue alone. Monitor, helping with vocabulary and accuracy. When they finish, ask a few Ss for examples.

Optional extra activity
Ask Ss to work together and write a conversation that ends with one of the idioms. When they finish, pairs should join up into groups of four and read out their conversations – but only up to the idiom. The listening pair should guess the idiom, using the context to help them. This will check if Ss have understood the appropriacy of the idioms in context.

VOCABULARY BANK 6A p161
Common idioms
This is an optional extension to the vocabulary section, extending the lexical set and providing further practice. If you're short of time, this can be done for homework.

1 Refer Ss to the idioms in bold and ask them to match them to the meanings. Ask Ss to complete this exercise by using their existing knowledge, guessing or using their devices. In feedback, point out the stress and drill.

Answers: 1 d 2 g 3 a 4 e 5 h 6 b 7 c 8 f

2 Refer Ss to pictures A–D and ask them to match them with four idioms from Ex 1. Go through the answers.

Answers: **A** be under the weather **B** have a heart of gold **C** get the wrong end of the stick **D** be on cloud nine

3 Ask Ss to discuss the questions in pairs, then go through the answers.

Answers:
1 be on cloud nine, have a heart of gold
2 be down in the dumps, be under the weather, get on someone's nerves, pay over the odds
3 get on someone's nerves
4 similar: be on cloud nine
  opposite: be down in the dumps
5 pay over the odds

Further practice
Photocopiable activities: 6A Vocabulary, p214
App: 6A Vocabulary practice 1 and 2

Grammar
Verb + -ing and infinitive with to
4 Focus attention on the text. Ask Ss where they may see a text like this (a book review or blurb), then ask them to read and discuss the question. Tell Ss they have two minutes to encourage them to read quickly, then allow them to compare in pairs before eliciting ideas.

5 Ask Ss to read the answers to the six questions in Ex 4 and match them by writing question numbers 1–6 beside letters a–i. Point out that there are more than six answers, so some questions are used more than once. Complete the first example as a group, then ask Ss to continue alone before comparing in pairs. Go through the answers.

Answers: a 6 b 4 c 1 d 1 e 2 f 1 g 5 h 1 i 3

6 Tell Ss you will now use the answers in Ex 5 to study some grammar. Ask Ss to read the grammar box carefully and match each phrase in bold in Ex 5 with its use. Ask them to work alone first, then in pairs, then elicit answers and deal with questions as a class.

Answers: a 2 b 2 c 1 d 6 e 3 f 5 g 4 h 1 i 5

Grammar checkpoint
Ss may want to use *for* + *-ing* to express purpose. Point out that this structure may be used when we describe the function of an object: *What's it for? It's for drying your hair.* To express the answer to the question *Why*, the infinitive is used: *Why are you studying English? To get a better job.* (not ~~For getting a better job.~~)

7a 6.2 Ask Ss to listen to the sentences and underline the stressed parts. If you think it's useful, explain the information in the Pronunciation checkpoint below, using the examples given.

Answers:
1 a Did you re<u>mem</u>ber to <u>lock</u> the <u>door</u>?
   b Do you re<u>mem</u>ber <u>lock</u>ing the <u>door</u>?
2 a I <u>tried</u> to <u>eat</u> <u>less</u> <u>sugar</u>.
   b I <u>tried</u> <u>eat</u>ing <u>less</u> <u>sugar</u>.
3 a I <u>stopped</u> <u>talk</u>ing to her.
   b I <u>stopped</u> to <u>talk</u> to her.

Pronunciation checkpoint
When we speak at normal speed, certain words (and the syllables within those words) are stressed. The stressed syllable is longer and louder. Stress generally falls on the main (lexical) verb and nouns. This is because these words carry meaning. Auxiliary verbs, articles and prepositions are usually weak and are often pronounced with a weak schwa sound /ə/. Point out that stress usually falls on a vowel.

b Point out *to* in the sentences that use the infinitive in Ex 7a. Ask Ss to discuss the difference in meaning between the sentences in each pair. When they finish, elicit ideas. A timeline showing the sequence of the two actions could be helpful (see Optional alternative activity below).

Answers:
1 a = Are you sure you didn't forget? The speaker thinks it was the other person's duty.
   b = Do you have a memory of doing it? The speaker doesn't think it was the other person's duty.
2 a = At one particular moment in the past I tried to do this.
   b = Over a period of time in the past I attempted to do this (and it was difficult).
3 a = I refused to talk to her again.
   b = I stopped what I was doing in order to talk to her.

Optional alternative activity
It can be helpful to show some of these contrasting sentences on a timeline:

1a *Remember and lock the door are two actions that are in sequence. First I remember, then I lock.*
1b *Here a memory of a past action is retrieved. Earlier I locked the door, then later I remember doing it.*
3a *In the past, I talked to her on several occasions. After that, I stopped talking to her (maybe because we had a disagreement).*
3b *I stopped what I was doing in order to talk to her. So, first I stopped, then I talked.*

c Play the recording again, asking Ss to chorally repeat the sentences after they hear them. You may want to pause the recording after each sentence and ask individuals to repeat, paying attention to stressed words/syllables and weak forms.

8a Look at the first gapped sentence as a class and elicit the answer. Ss then work alone to write the verbs in the correct form in the gaps, referring to the grammar box, then check in pairs. Check answers with the whole class. Drill chorally and individually as needed in feedback.

Answers:
1 a Watching b drinking   2 a to hold b talking
3 a to cross b to remember   4 a eating b worrying
5 a to help b to speak   6 a Calling b explaining

b Ask Ss to think about their own answers to the questions in Ex 8a. Then put Ss in pairs to ask and answer. Monitor and help with vocabulary and ideas.

> **Optional alternative activity**
>
> Ss may struggle to think of ideas. If this is the case, ask pairs to repeat the answers provided or ask Ss to invent suitable answers.

> **LANGUAGE BANK 6A**   pp.146–147
>
> *Stronger classes* could read the notes at home. Otherwise, go over the notes with Ss. In each exercise, elicit the first answer as an example. Ss work alone to complete the exercises, then check their answers in pairs. In feedback, check answers with the whole class. Ss can refer to the notes to help them.
>
> Answers:
> 1 1 eating 2 doing 3 to feel 4 both 5 feeling
>   6 to improve 7 to note 8 to take
> 2 1 Spending 2 promised to visit 3 no point (in) arguing
>   4 remember locking 5 stop to have

> **Further practice**
>
> **Photocopiable activities:** 6A Grammar 1, p212; 6A Grammar 2, p213
> **App:** 6A Grammar practice 1 and 2

Speaking

Prepare

9a 🔊 6.3 Tell Ss they are going to hear two people talking about things they love and loathe. Ask Ss to listen and note the three things they discuss and if they agree or disagree. When they finish, ask Ss to compare in pairs before eliciting answers. Ask Ss what they think of the three things talked about.

> Answers:
> people eating with their mouth open – agree
> sandy beaches on a hot summer's day – disagree
> waiting for buses – disagree

> **Audioscript 6.3**
>
> **A:** Do you want to go first?
> **B:** No, you go first.
> **A:** All right. What do you think about people eating with their mouth open?
> **B:** Oh, I loathe that.
> **A:** Me too. It drives me up the wall if I'm in a restaurant and I have to watch someone doing that.
> **B:** Absolutely. I keep wanting to say, 'Where are your manners?' like my mum used to say to me.
> **A:** Yeah! OK, your go.
> **B:** All right. What do you think about sandy beaches on a hot summer's day?
> **A:** Oh, I'm not a big fan, really.
> **B:** No?
> **A:** No. All that sand getting in your clothes and your towel. It's a bit of a pain.
> **B:** Oh, I love it. Warm sand under your feet, the cool sea. It's heavenly.
> **A:** Well, I guess we'll just have to agree to disagree on that one.
> **B:** Yeah, but come on! What's not to like about a day at the beach?
> **A:** I like swimming in the sea and I like the beach, just not sandy beaches. Give me a nice pebbly beach any day.
> **B:** All right. As you say, we have to agree to disagree. Your go.
> **A:** What do you think about waiting for buses?
> **B:** Well … I don't love it but I don't loathe it, either.
> **A:** No? I can't stand it. It drives me up the wall, just standing around, wasting time, waiting for a bus to appear …

b Ask Ss to work alone and make a list of three things they love and three they loathe. Allow plenty of thinking time for this.

Speak

10a When they are ready, put Ss in pairs to discuss the things they chose. Refer them to the Useful phrases to guide their discussion. Monitor and help if necessary.

b When pairs finish, ask them to move around and talk to different partners to try and find someone who they agree with about everything on their lists.

> **Teaching tip**
>
> 'Pair and share' is a good technique for getting Ss to talk to new people. It means repeating the activity with a new partner and it refreshes the classroom dynamic. If you have plenty of space, have Ss do this as a whole-class mingle. If space is limited, Ss can simply turn their chair and talk to those on adjoining tables. Shy Ss may need help in finding new partners, so move around the group and help as needed, as well as ensuring Ss are completing the activity correctly.

> **Reflection on learning**
>
> Write the following questions on the board:
> *What do you like and loathe about English?*
> *How might the language of today's lesson help you in situations outside the classroom?*
> Put Ss in pairs to discuss the questions. When they have finished, ask if anyone wants to share their ideas with the class, but don't force them if they'd rather not.

> **Homework ideas**
>
> **Ex 9b:** Ss write a paragraph describing something they like and something they loathe.
> **Language bank:** 6A Ex 1–2, pp.146–147
> **Workbook:** Ex 1–6, p44
> **App:** grammar, vocabulary and pronunciation practice

Fast route: continue to Lesson 6B
Extended route: go to p91 for Develop your listening

6B We can work it out

Introduction

The goal of this lesson is for students to summarise a negotiation. To help them achieve this, they will study reported speech and vocabulary related to negotiating.

Warm-up

Begin the lesson with a game of 'Beat the clock'. Write a space on the board for each letter of the target word, in this case *negotiate*, which has nine letters: _ _ _ _ _ _ _ _ _. Draw a circle on the board to represent a clock. Ss must call out letters that might appear in the word. If they are right, you add the letter in its place. If they are wrong, you write the letter on the board and advance the clock 5 minutes, starting from 12.00. If Ss can complete the word before you advance the clock all the way round, they beat the clock. This is a fun game for revising random vocabulary. Once you have the word *negotiate* on the board, ask Ss to define it and tell them this is today's topic.

Vocabulary

Negotiating

Culture notes

You might get an upgrade when staying in a hotel or taking a flight. It means that you are given something better than what you paid for, so a first-class flight instead of an economy flight or a room with a better view. Upgrades are sometimes given as a business perk. A phone upgrade means getting a newer model at the end of your contract.

Regarding asking for discounts, there may be cultural differences for Ss about when and where it's appropriate to negotiate. Some may have experienced more of a fixed-price culture, while for others it may be standard practice to discuss the cost of things.

1 Ask Ss in what situations they might negotiate, such as for products or services. Put Ss in pairs to discuss the questions for a few minutes, then conduct brief feedback.

2a Ask Ss to read the texts, then use the words in the boxes to replace the underlined phrases. When going through the answers, ask individual Ss to read the text aloud with the substitutions in place. Drill new words and phrases as needed.

Answers: 1 bond 2 conflict 3 build trust 4 praise
5 criticise 6 tension 7 fall out 8 stay calm 9 interrupts
10 cooperate

b This is an opportunity for Ss to practise the new vocabulary. Ask Ss to work alone and complete the sentences. Monitor and help with vocabulary and ideas, ensuring Ss are forming accurate sentences.

3 Refer Ss to the example and ask them to compare sentences from Ex 2b in pairs, using the question and answer format shown. After a few minutes, ask a few individual Ss to read their ideas aloud and invite others to agree or disagree with them.

Teaching tip

When Ss speak in front of the group, make sure that others have a listening focus to encourage them to listen to each other and not talk. To keep the response stage from becoming too time-consuming or repetitive, only ask a few random Ss dotted around the class to respond. This keeps everybody alert and is more flexible than going around all Ss in a predictable order.

4a Refer to the list of words. Ask Ss to say them aloud, then decide which sound they use. See the Pronunciation checkpoint below.

b 6.6 Play the recording and ask Ss to confirm their answers. List the words on the board under the three sounds. Play the recording again for Ss to listen and repeat.

Answers: 1 /sh/ 2 /sh/ 3 /z/ 4 /z/ 5 /s/ 6 /sh/
7 /sh/ 8 /z/ 9 /s/ 10 /sh/

Pronunciation checkpoint

Spend some time looking at the articulation of the sounds focused on. /s/ and /z/ are formed using the same parts of the mouth and tongue position, but /s/ is unvoiced and /z/ is voiced. Get Ss to place their hand on their throat to feel this difference in vibration. /ʃ/ (marked /sh/ in SB) has the tongue in a more central position. Encourage Ss to feel their way around the different sounds and draw diagrams on the board to show them. Keep this playful and focus primarily on Ss hearing the difference if they struggle with this.

VOCABULARY BANK 6B p161
Reporting verbs

This is an optional extension to the vocabulary section, extending the lexical set and providing further practice. If you're short of time, this can be done for homework. Exercises can also be set as extension work for fast finishers during the lesson.

1 Ask Ss to match the verbs in the box with the speech in A–J alone, then check in pairs before going through the answers as a class.

Answers: A congratulate B forbid C justify D beg
E urge F guarantee G claim H propose I decline
J request

2a Ask Ss to match sentences 1–10 with the speech in A–J from Ex 1. Go through the answers.

Answers: 1 H 2 F 3 G 4 C 5 I 6 J 7 D 8 B
9 A 10 E

b Ask Ss to complete the sentences with the past simple of the verbs in Ex 1. Go through the answers as a class.

Answers: 1 proposed 2 guaranteed 3 claimed
4 justified 5 declined 6 requested 7 begged 8 forbade
9 congratulated 10 urged

3 Ask Ss to discuss in pairs. When they finish, ask a few pairs to share ideas with the class. There are no fixed answers.

Further practice

Photocopiable activities: 6B Vocabulary, p217
App: 6B Vocabulary practice 1 and 2

Listening

5a Discuss with **weaker classes** what a *crisis* is (= a time of intense difficulty or danger). Give examples such as a hostage, economic or personal crisis. Ask Ss to guess what a crisis negotiator does, then read the text and answer the questions in pairs. When they finish, have a show of hands to see who thinks they might be a good crisis negotiator and ask them to say why.

b Refer Ss to the list of qualities. Discuss as a class and tick the qualities on the board or write the numbers there.

6a 6.7 Tell Ss they'll now listen to a crisis negotiator and should check their answers to Ex 5b. Ask Ss to compare in pairs, then confirm the correct answers as a class. Discuss as a class how well they predicted or what surprised them.

Answers: 1, 2, 5, 6

Audioscript 6.7

Clive: … So, Robin, the two bank robbers are still holed up inside Westermare Bank and they're still refusing to come out. Back to you in the studio.

Robin: Thank you, Clive. As the situation at the Westermare Bank enters its second day, we ask, 'What is the best way to negotiate in a crisis?' To answer that question, here in the studio we have professional crisis negotiator, Claudia Whitman. Claudia, tell me, what does your job involve?

Claudia: Well, as you say, I'm a professional crisis negotiator, which basically means that I negotiate with people who are in a crisis situation.

Robin: Like the armed robbers who are refusing to come out of the bank?

Claudia: Exactly.

Robin: And what do you say to people in that situation? At the end of the day, it must be extremely difficult to get them to do what you want.

Claudia: It is difficult, but you have to approach it from the right angle. The key is to build trust with the person you are talking to. That way, they're more likely to cooperate.

Robin: How do you do that? How do you talk to them?

Claudia: Well, first off, I wouldn't use the word *talk*. We all know the phrase *talk is cheap*. It's better to use the word *speak*. It's more direct. I'd say, *Can I speak to you?* That helps to build trust.

Robin: OK, so, how else do you build trust? What would you say to the men in Westermare Bank?

Claudia: Basically, what's most important is that you actively listen.

Robin: Actively listen?

Claudia: That's right. When someone talks, don't interrupt them. Never say *Yes, but*, because that shows you want to argue rather than listen. That creates conflict and tension. Instead, if someone says *I'm not coming out*, you repeat that back to them as a question. *So, you're saying you don't want to come out?*

Robin: … and that shows you're listening.

Claudia: Exactly. And if they tell you about their problems, or share something else that's personal, make sure you recognise what they're doing. Don't say *Everyone has problems*. Say *Wow! You've had some really difficult problems*.

Robin: OK, I've got that. Now imagine they're really angry or emotional. What do you do then?

Claudia: Then you stay calm, recognise how they're feeling and accept it. One of the worst things you can say is *Calm down!* That's so annoying! Instead, you should say *I can see you're angry and I understand why*.

Robin: Do you ever talk about your own problems?

Claudia: Yes, I do. It's one way to build trust. Sometimes I say *I'll let you into a secret. I've also done some really stupid things in my life*. It's important that you are honest and don't tell lies.

Robin: So, you've really got to be open with them?

Claudia: Absolutely. At the same time, you've got to be a bit smart. For example, crisis negotiators know that the word 'willing' is very useful?

Robin: Really? Why is that?

Claudia: When you say *Would you be willing to do something for me?* you're much more likely to get a positive response than if you say *Would you do something for me? Willing* is one of the most powerful words we have in a negotiation situation.

Robin: Fascinating stuff. OK, that's all we've got time for. Thank you, Claudia Whitman.

b Ask Ss to work in pairs and tick the phrase they think was better and discuss why. Then tell them they'll listen again to check their answers. Play the recording, ask Ss to compare in pairs, then confirm the correct answers.

Answers:
1a *Speak* is more direct.
2b It shows you are listening.
3a It shows you are acknowledging that they have told you something personal.
4b It shows you accept/understand how they feel.
5b It helps to build trust.
6b You are much more likely to get a positive response with *willing*.

Grammar

Reported speech

7 Ask Ss to read Zuzanna's words and underline the reported speech. Go through the answers as a class. If you are able to, project the text and underline the examples on the board.

Answers: Yesterday I <u>asked my daughter to put</u> her phone down and have a conversation with me. She <u>told me that I wasn't</u> the boss and that she <u>could</u> make her own decisions. I usually get angry when she says things like that, but yesterday I tried a different tactic. I <u>said that I could understand</u> how she felt, but I just wanted to have a chat. I <u>asked her if she would be willing</u> just to talk for a few minutes. We ended up talking for an hour. It felt like a big success!

8 Ask Ss to use the examples to help them complete the rules in the grammar box. Allow plenty of time for this. Monitor and help. Go through the answers and be prepared to give further explanations as needed.

Answers: **1** back **2** past **3** statements **4** infinitive with 'to'

Grammar checkpoint

Most of the issues around the reporting structures relate to form rather than meaning. *Say* and *tell* are not that different, it's just that *tell* is followed immediately by a direct object and *say* isn't. This confusion leads to common errors such as *He said me I am wrong* or *He told I was wrong*. Point this out and monitor for errors in form.

9a This is a controlled practice exercise that focuses Ss on choosing the correct form. Report the first one together, then ask Ss to continue alone. When they finish, ask Ss to compare answers and then go though them as a class.

Answers:
1 Lena asked her why she was always telling her what to do.
2 Zuzanna asked her if/whether she had tidied her room.
3 Lena asked her to help her with her homework.
4 Lena told her (that) she was going to sleep over at a friend's house the next/following day.
5 Zuzana said (that) she couldn't do that because she had school the next/following day.
6 Lena told her (that) school was really stressing her out.
7 Zuzanna told her (that) she would understand when she was older.
8 Lena asked her why she hadn't washed her jeans.

b 🔊 **6.8** Look at the example as a class. Explain that Ss should listen and then report what they hear. Play each conversation and ask Ss to report it in pairs. When Ss finish, check answers with the whole class. Drill chorally and individually if you think it's useful.

> **Answers:**
> 1 She asked him if/whether he had tidied his room that week.
>   He said he had done that the previous week.
> 2 He asked him if/whether he could stay over at a friend's house the following night.
>   He said (that) it was a school night, so he couldn't.
> 3 She asked her how school had been that day.
>   She asked her why she always asked that question.
> 4 He asked her to put her dirty clothes in the wash.
>   She asked him if/whether she had to.
> 5 She asked him what he was going to do that weekend.
>   He said (that) he didn't know but he would probably go into town with some friends.

Audioscript 6.8

Conversation 1
Mother: Have you tidied your room this week?
Male teen: I did that last week!

Conversation 2
Male teen: Can I stay over at a friend's house tomorrow night?
Father: It's a school night, so you can't.

Conversation 3
Mother: How was school today?
Female teen: Why do you always ask that question?

Conversation 4
Father: Could you put your dirty clothes in the wash?
Female teen: Do I have to?

Conversation 5
Mother: What are you going to do this weekend?
Male teen: Don't know. I'll probably go into town with some friends.

LANGUAGE BANK 6B pp.146–147

Stronger classes could read the notes at home. Otherwise, go over the notes with Ss. In each exercise, elicit the first answer as an example. Ss work alone to complete the exercises, then check their answers in pairs. In feedback, check answers with the whole class. Ss can refer to the notes to help them.

Answers:
1 1 that 2 she 3 to 4 had 5 am/was 6 if/whether
  7 me 8 would 9 when/if 10 the
2 1 Our boss told us he was leaving the company.
  2 Pietro asked me whether I had been there that evening.
  3 I said to the class that I would be late the next day.
  4 I told him that she didn't want to see me.
  5 Maria wanted to know when the parcel would arrive.

Further practice

Photocopiable activities: 6B Language focus 1, p215; 6B Language focus 2, p216
App: 6B Language focus practice 1 and 2

Speaking

Prepare

10a Tell Ss they are going to do a roleplay. Put Ss in pairs. Name alternate Ss A or B and ask them to turn to the relevant pages to select and read their role cards. Ss A and B must agree on the same topic.

b Ask Ss to make a few notes alone about what they want to say. Monitor and help with vocabulary. Give them a few minutes to make notes and deal with any queries. With ***weaker classes***, organise AA and BB pairs so they can help each other prepare.

Speak

11a Put Ss in AB pairs to carry out their roleplay negotiation and try and reach a solution.

b Put Ss in new pairs to report back on their roleplay. Point out that they should use reporting structures to describe what they said to their previous partner. Monitor for this. With ***weaker classes***, ask Ss to write a few sentences summarising their roleplay before telling their new partner. Ask a few pairs to share the result of their roleplay and discuss who had the best outcome. Give some feedback on their use of reported speech.

Optional extra activity

If the roleplays are unsuitable or Ss need further practice, you can use these additional role cards about flatmates and housework.
Student A
You live with a flatmate. Your flatmate doesn't do much housework, so you have to do most of it. This is starting to annoy you. Every day you tidy and clean the kitchen. Your flatmate just leaves their dishes in the sink. Every week you clean the bathroom. Your flatmate never does this. Your flatmate has suggested getting a cleaner, but you don't think this is a good idea because it is expensive.
Student B
You live with a flatmate. Your flatmate is always cleaning or complaining about cleaning. You have a very busy job and you don't have time to clean the house as much as they do. After you cook your dinner, you leave your dishes in the sink because you want to eat before you wash them. When you finish your dinner, your flatmate has usually washed the dishes already. You want to pay a cleaner to clean the house because this will solve the problem.

> #### Reflection on learning
> Write the following questions on the board:
> *How could this lesson be useful in the future?*
> *What would you recommend for someone who needs to negotiate in English? Why?*
> Put Ss in pairs to discuss the questions. When they have finished, ask if anyone wants to share their ideas with the class, but don't force them if they'd rather not.

Homework ideas

Ex 11a: Ss write a report on a successful or unsuccessful negotiation they have experienced.
Language bank: 6B Ex 1–2, pp.146–147
Workbook: Ex 1–4, p45
App: grammar, vocabulary and pronunciation practice

Fast route: continue to Lesson 6C
Extended route: go to p106 for Develop your reading

6c Tricky conversations

Introduction
The goal of this lesson is for students to paraphrase what someone has said. To help them achieve this, they will revise verb patterns after reporting verbs, as well as related vocabulary.

Warm-up
Write the title of the lesson on the board and elicit that *tricky* = difficult. Ask Ss to discuss what tricky conversations might be about a) at work b) with a partner or c) with a family member. When they finish, ask for ideas and discuss which kind of tricky conversation is the worst/hardest!

Vocabulary
Reporting verbs
1a Ask Ss to look at the pictures, then work in pairs and discuss the questions. Give them a few minutes, then compare ideas as a class. Ask a few pairs to share their story with the class.

Optional extra activity
Ask Ss to roleplay a conversation to go with one of the pictures. You can allocate different pictures to different pairs, or they can choose one themselves.

b Ask Ss to discuss the questions. Have a show of hands to see which of the situations Ss would find most awkward and why.

c Refer Ss to the example. Ask pairs to think of and discuss a difficult conversation they or a friend has had. When they finish, invite a few pairs to share the situations they discussed.

2a 6.9 Tell Ss they will listen to six conversations. They should read through the summaries first and check they understand the verbs, then listen and choose the correct alternatives as they do so. Go through the answers.

> Answers: 1 accused, apologised   2 reminded, agreed
> 3 blamed, admitted   4 refused, convinced
> 5 advised, threatened   6 insisted, denied

Audioscript 6.9
Conversation 1
Father: Hey! Where's my piece of apple cake?
Daughter: Stephen ate it, didn't you, Stephen?
Father: Stephen?
Stephen: Sorry. It was just too tempting!

Conversation 2
Daughter: OK, I'm off. Bye!
Father: Don't forget to call me when you get there!
Daughter: Call you?
Father: Yeah. I just want to know that you've arrived safely.
Daughter: OK, I'll call you when I get there. Bye.
Father: Bye, love.

Conversation 3
Man 1: Shall I ring the bell?
Woman: Yeah, do it. We're half an hour late, you know.
Man 1: Yeah, because of the traffic.
Woman: It wasn't the traffic. We're late because you took two hours to get ready!
Man: Yeah, I suppose you're right. It was my fault.
Man 2: Hi! Really good you could make it.
Woman: Sorry we're late.
Man 2: Don't worry! Come in, come in.

Conversation 4
Woman: I have a question for you.
Man: OK.
Woman: Err, will you marry me?
Man: Marry you? No.
Woman: No?
Man: No.
Woman: But … but … I've got a good job and a nice apartment and a luxury car!
Man: A luxury car?
Woman: Yeah.
Man: Hmm … OK then. I'll marry you.

Conversation 5
Man: What are you doing?
Woman: What does it look like? I'm changing the wheel.
Man: Don't do it like that. Use the other spanner and turn it towards you …
Woman: If you don't go away, I'm going to throw this spanner at you!
Man: OK, OK, I'm going!

Conversation 6
Father: Sally, can you unlock the door and come out here, please?
Sally: No.
Father: Sally, come on, unlock the door.
Sally: I'm not coming out.
Father: Sally, I really want you to unlock the door and come outside!
Sally: What?
Father: Sally, did you hit your brother?
Sally: No! He's lying.
Father: Well, someone hit him. He's crying now.
Sally: It wasn't me!
Father: OK, Sally, let's go downstairs and talk about it.

Vocabulary checkpoint
Point out the distinction between *blame* and *accuse*. Both mean that you think somebody did something wrong. *Accuse* is the action of speaking about the person who has supposedly done something wrong. *Blame* doesn't have to be spoken. *Threaten* is to say that you will act, usually if somebody doesn't do what you want. You may want to give further examples in context to help Ss with the meanings of the verbs.

b Ask Ss to look at their answers to Ex 2a and the surrounding grammar and choose which group each verb belongs to, marking them 1–3. Point out that some verbs can go in more than one group. Go through the answers as a class, using the examples to confirm.

> Answers:
> 1 can take *it* as an object: admit, deny
> 2 can take a pronoun as an object: accuse, threaten, blame, convince, remind, advise
> 3 doesn't need an object: agree, refuse, insist, apologise

c This exercise involves choosing the correct verbs and applying the correct patterns. Allow plenty of time for this. With **weaker classes**, go through the exercise first, discussing which verb to use for each sentence, then ask Ss to write the summarising sentences. **Stronger classes** can work on verb selection and summarising at the same time. Monitor the class to support and correct. Go through the answers as a class.

> Answers: 1 He denied it.   2 She convinced me.
> 3 He refused.   4 He blamed the weather.
> 5 He threatened me.   6 He advised me.   7 She reminded me.
> 8 He apologised.   9 She agreed.   10 He insisted.
> 11 She accused me.   12 He admitted it.

3 This is an opportunity to see the verbs in context. Ask pairs to read through and discuss which quotes they agree with and explain why. With **weaker classes**, go through as a class and discuss the meanings first. When they finish, ask a few pairs to choose one quote they feel strongly about and tell the class about it. There are no fixed answers.

4a 🔊 **6.10** Ask Ss to listen and mark the stress with a dot or small box over the syllable that is stressed. Go through the answers. Share the information in the Pronunciation checkpoint below if you think Ss will find it useful.

Answers: offer, threaten

> **Pronunciation checkpoint**
> Ss at this level should know that any word of more than one syllable has a primary stress. This means one syllable is pronounced longer and louder than the others. Two-syllable nouns, adjectives, and adverbs are usually stressed on the first syllable. Two-syllable verbs are usually stressed on the second syllable. The unstressed syllable is weak and often represented by the schwa sound /ə/.

b Ask Ss to listen again and repeat chorally.

> **Further practice**
> Photocopiable activities: 6C Vocabulary, p220
> App: 6C Vocabulary practice 1 and 2

Reading

> **Culture notes**
> A **blind date** brings together two people who have not met before for a date. It is often arranged by friends who know them both and think they may get on well.
> A **drivethrough** restaurant is a type of fast food outlet that originated in the US, where you order and receive the food without leaving your car.

5 Tell Ss they are going to read some social media comments (1–6) and they should match each to one of the summaries (a–g). Give them a few minutes, then conduct brief feedback by asking individual Ss for answers. Deal with any vocabulary queries.

Answers: 1 f 2 e 3 a 4 d 5 c 6 b

6 Put Ss in pairs to discuss the questions. When they finish, go through the answers as a class. There are no fixed answers, but see if Ss agree on the most awkward with a show of hands.

> **Teaching tip**
> An aspect of developing reading skills is responding to what we have read and relating it to our own lives. Encourage Ss to make personal responses to texts and not only view reading as a 'comprehension' task. Ss can respond personally by drawing on their own real-life experiences when appropriate. Alternatively, they can make hypothetical responses to situations they have less experience of. To aid hypothetical responses, you could provide a few sentence starters such as: *I doubt I'd ever …; There's no way I'd …; I can't imagine ever …*, etc.

Language focus
Reporting verbs

7 Tell Ss that they are going to use examples from Ex 5 to study a language point. Refer Ss to the verbs in bold in Ex 5 and ask them to write them in the correct sections of the Language focus box. Ask pairs to compare, then elicit answers from individual Ss.

Answers: 1 agree 2 convince 3 advise 4 admit 5 insist 6 accuse

> **Teaching tip**
> Encourage Ss to look at surrounding words (or co-text) when looking at new verbs in order to notice their patterns of use. Point out the importance of recording these patterns in their notebooks rather than just the individual verbs or their translations, for example: *admit (doing sth); advise (so to do sth); insist (on doing sth); convince (so to do sth); accuse (so of doing sth)*. Ss can use *sth* and *so* to represent *something* and *someone* when recording verb patterns, as in the examples above. Spend some time discussing how Ss record language in their notebooks or devices if you feel it's useful. Ss could also compare their notes and discuss how they make them.

8a Refer Ss to the Language focus box. Ask Ss to write the sentences using the words in brackets. Ss can compare answers in pairs before you go through them as a class.

Answers:
1 He admitted getting a few things wrong in his report.
2 He insisted on paying me back.
3 She agreed to change the date of the meeting.
4 He blamed me for losing the match.
5 She accused me of playing really badly.
6 She convinced me to try that new shampoo.
7 He denied breaking it.
8 She apologised for getting angry.

> **Grammar checkpoint**
> Using an example, note how the speech marks are removed when we report speech and remind Ss of the tense change. Draw attention to the changes in the subject and direct object by using the example provided. This approach should support **weaker classes**.

b 🔊 **6.11** Ask Ss to listen and write reported statements using the prompts provided. Pause the recording after each conversation to allow Ss to construct their reported statement and compare in pairs. Then go through the answers one by one.

Answers:
1 He admitted eating some of her biscuits.
2 He convinced her to eat out at the Korean restaurant.
3 He insisted on getting a refund.
4 He reminded her to return the book by Carlos Quesada.
5 He agreed to give her a hand.

Audioscript 6.11

Conversation 1
W: Did you eat some of my biscuits?
M: Yes, I did. Sorry. I'll get you some more.
W: Don't worry. Just wondering why I didn't have many left.

Conversation 2
M: Shall we eat out this evening?
W: Hmm, not sure. We haven't got much money at the moment.
M: Oh, go on. The Korean restaurant on Finch Street is really cheap …
W: Yes, but …
M: And totally delicious. The kimchi is amazing.
W: Oh, OK then.

Conversation 3
M: … so, I really think that, under the circumstances, I deserve a refund.
W: Well, we don't normally give refunds in these situations. We prefer to repair …
M: Yes, but I'm not interested in a repair. If the product is faulty, I'm entitled to a refund.
W: As I say, we don't normally …
M: I'm sorry to interrupt you, but perhaps I could speak to your supervisor and they could organise a refund for me?
W: Er … that won't be necessary, Mr Jones. I'll arrange a refund for you.
M: Thank you.

Conversation 4
M: You know that book you borrowed?
W: Book? No.
M: The one by Carlos Quesada. It was a novel.
W: Oh, with red letters on the cover?
M: That's the one. Could I have it back at some point soon? I want to lend it to my father.
W: Sure, sorry, I forgot I had it.

Conversation 5
W: Could you give me a hand?
M: Sure.
W: Just hold this while I wash it.
M: No problem.

LANGUAGE BANK 6C pp.146–147

Stronger classes could read the notes at home. Otherwise, check the notes with Ss. In each exercise, elicit the first answer as an example. Ss work alone to complete the exercises, then check their answers in pairs. In feedback, check answers with the whole class. Ss can refer to the notes to help them.

Answers:
1 1 accused … stealing/taking 2 denied knowing
3 refused to admit 4 blame … wanting
5 admitted taking/stealing 6 apologised … causing
7 insisted … paying 8 agreed to stop

Further practice

Photocopiable activities: 6C Language focus 1, p218; 6C Language focus 2, p219
App: 6C Language focus practice 1 and 2

Speaking

Prepare

9 Explain that Ss are going to write a short conversation and then perform it. Put them in pairs and ask them to read the situation and the opening lines of the conversation. Give them a few minutes to write the rest of the conversation. As they write, monitor and help with ideas and accuracy.

Speak

10a Ask pairs to take turns performing their conversations while others listen and make notes.

b Ask Ss to report all the conversations they heard in pairs, using the verbs in the box. Look at the example as a class to show what you expect. Monitor and note down examples of good language use and errors to go over during feedback.

Optional alternative activity

Instead of performing to the whole class, pairs can perform their conversations in groups of four to eight Ss. The choice depends on the size of the class, how confident your Ss are about performing and the time available. The first option will take longer and be more demanding but it will provide a lot more conversations for Ss to report on afterwards. The second option will be quicker and Ss will have to do less reporting afterwards, so it might be better suited to *weaker classes*.

Reflection on learning

Write the following questions on the board:
How do you think you'll use the language you studied in today's lesson?
What would you advise a student of English to do to help them remember their lessons?

Put Ss in pairs to discuss the questions. When they have finished, ask if anyone wants to share their ideas with the class, but don't force them to if they'd rather not.

Homework ideas

Language bank: 6C Ex 1, pp.146–147
Workbook: Ex 1–4, p46
App: grammar, vocabulary and pronunciation practice

Fast route: continue to Check and reflect
Extended route: go to p126 for Develop your writing

6 Check and reflect: Units 5–6

Introduction

Ss revise and practise the language of Units 5 and 6. The notes below provide some ideas for exploiting the activities in class, but you may want to set the exercises for homework or use them as a diagnostic or progress test.

1 Ss match the sentence halves alone, then check in pairs. Go through the answers as a class.

Answers: 1 e 2 g 3 b 4 h 5 a 6 d 7 c 8 i 9 f

2 Ss complete the sentences using the correct form of the verbs in the box. Go through the answers as a class.

Answers: 1 have taken 2 to be 3 have found 4 had invested 5 have paid 6 have known 7 driven / been driving

3 Ss work alone to choose the correct alternatives. Go through the answers.

Answers: 1 find them 2 must go to court 3 admit 4 a judge or jury 5 serious 6 burglar 7 are given 8 doesn't get caught

4a Ss work alone to choose the correct words for the gaps. Go through the answers.

Answers: 1 several 2 each/every 3 lots 4 none 5 few 6 all 7 no 8 every/each

b Ss cover the story and try to retell it to a partner.

5 Ss work alone to complete the sentences with a word starting with the letter provided. Ask Ss to compare in pairs, then go through the answers.

Answers: 1 investment 2 recession 3 donation 4 bargain 5 Inflation 6 pension

6 Ss choose an adverb from box A and an adjective from box B to complete each sentence. Go through the answers.

Answers: 1 perfectly safe 2 totally lost 3 widely available 4 highly unlikely 5 bitterly cold

7a Ss use the words in the box to complete the questions. Go through the answers.

Answers: 1 leg 2 moon 3 cake, pain 4 wall 5 breath 6 world

b Ss ask each other three of the questions. **Fast finishers** can ask and answer more questions.

8 Ss use the verbs provided to complete the conversations. Go through the answers, paying attention to correct verb forms.

Answers: 1 going back, To sort out, to turn on 2 smoking, feeling / to feel 3 to ask, to avoid 4 taking, feeling 5 visiting, sitting 6 being, to listen, talking

9a Ss use the words in the box to complete the questions. They don't need to change the form of the words. Go through the answers.

Answers: 1 bond 2 fall out 3 praise 4 criticise 5 stay calm 6 interrupt 7 tension/conflict 8 conflict/tension

b Ss choose and discuss three of the questions in pairs. **Fast finishers** can discuss more. When they finish, elicit a few popular answers.

10 Ss work alone to complete the reported statements. Ask them to compare in pairs, then go through the answers.

Answers:
1 … (that) her teacher was giving her too much homework
2 … Tim (that) she didn't believe (that) he was really 35
3 … (that) he would be late home from college that evening
4 … her if/whether she had done her homework yet
5 … her mum why she couldn't give her a lift to the party
6 … Chloe if she wanted to go/come to the party

11 Ss complete the second sentence using one of the verbs provided plus two or three other words. Go through the answers.

Answers: 1 convinced us to buy 2 apologised for being 3 accusing Greg of stealing 4 refused to take 5 insisted on paying/that he paid 6 reminds me to

12a Ask Ss to complete the second and third responses so that they have a similar meaning to the first response.

Answers: 1 entirely, own 2 fault, nothing 3 deal, sort 4 OK, sense

b Ask Ss to practise the conversations in pairs, first with books open, then again with books closed.

Reflect

Ask Ss to rate each statement alone, then compare in pairs. Encourage them to ask any questions they still have about any of the areas covered in Units 5 and 6.

Roadmap video

Go online for the Roadmap video and worksheet.

6A Develop your listening

Introduction
The goal of this lesson is for students to understand informal discussions. To help them achieve this, they will focus on recognising signpost expressions.

Warm-up
Ask Ss to discuss what they find easier to understand in English, a news broadcast or a conversation between people. After a brief discussion, ask them to identify what distinguishes the two. (The first is formal and scripted; there is often just one speaker. The second is informal and unscripted; it's likely to contain idiomatic language as well as overlap where both speak at the same time.) Most Ss probably find it easier to understand a scripted monologue, even on a complex subject.

1 Ask Ss to discuss the questions in pairs. Give your own example of annoying expressions if you can (they could be in the Ss' language or English). After a few minutes, elicit ideas and see if there are any expressions that are common.

2a 🔊 6.4 Tell Ss they are going to hear people talking about expressions they hate. Play the recording for Ss to write the missing words. Go through the answers as a class and write them on the board to ensure Ss spell them correctly. Ask Ss if there are equivalent phrases in their first language and whether they find them annoying.

Answers: 1 So 2 Basically 3 Literally 4 moment, time 5 reality 6 face 7 end, day 8 is, is 9 honest 10 personally

Audioscript 6.4

1
Umm … I really object to people using 'So' at the start of every sentence. 'So, how are you?' 'So, I went out last night …'. 'So, nice socks you're wearing!' It's just not necessary. Please, stop it everyone, please!

2
Expressions I love to hate? Oh, yeah, 'basically'. It drives me crazy. 'Basically, I'm not sure what to do.' 'Basically, I've eaten all the doughnuts.' 'Basically, I think you're crazy.' It doesn't mean anything, that's the problem.

3
Well, I don't really have any phrases I hate … Oh, hang on! I hate 'literally'. Why do people say that when they don't mean it? Like, people say, 'I literally nearly died', when 'literally' means, 'I'm not exaggerating'. But of course, they are exaggerating. All they mean is that they were a bit surprised. They didn't nearly die at all, so why say 'literally'? It's completely misusing the word.

4
A: Which … which one is it again, that you hate?
B: Oh, 'at this moment in time'?
A: Yes, 'at this moment in time'.
B: Hate that. Everybody says it nowadays when what they mean is, 'at the moment'. So, why don't they say, 'at the moment'?
A: Yes, you hate it!
B: When someone says, 'Oh, at this moment in time, it's not a good idea', I think, 'Why do you say that?' Just say, 'at the moment'!
A: Yes, you really hate it!

5
I hate … oh yeah, 'the reality is …'. People use it to, you know, end a conversation. Like, they're trying to say, 'This is the absolute truth and you can't argue with it'. But usually, it's not the reality or the truth at all. It's just their opinion.

6
'Let's face it' … that's the one I hate most. You know, like, 'Let's face it, it's not very good'. Or 'Let's face it, it's awful'. People always use it to say something negative. And usually I think, 'What are you talking about? I am facing it … and I don't agree!'

7
Hmm … my personal bugbear is, 'At the end of the day'. You know, when someone says something like, 'At the end of the day, it's not important', or, 'At the end of the day, it doesn't matter'. I don't know why I hate it so much. I guess it's just because people who use it say it all the time.

8
I don't like, 'It is what it is' meaning, like, 'there's nothing you can do to change it'. It just sounds really … stupid. 'Nothing you can do about it. It is what it is!'

9
Yeah, quite a lot of phrases annoy me but my pet hate is, 'To be honest', as in, 'To be honest, I don't like it'; 'To be honest, I'm over the moon'; 'To be honest, blah, blah, blah'. It's such an unnecessary phrase 'coz we always expect people to be honest and to say what they think.

10
A: Oh, what's that phrase you hate.
B: 'Speaking personally'?
A: That's it! 'Speaking personally'.
B: Yeah, I hate that. It means absolutely nothing.

b Play the recording again and ask Ss to choose the reasons given, a or b. With **weaker classes**, check that Ss understand that *mean* has two slightly different meanings in the statements: 1) = to intend (I don't mean it); and 2) = to represent (it doesn't mean anything). Ask Ss to compare in pairs, then check the answers as a class.

Answers: 1 a 2 b 3 a 4 b 5 a 6 a 7 b 8 a 9 b 10 a

3 Go through the Focus box carefully as a class, reading each section and discussing the examples. Ask Ss if they can think of more signpost expressions that appear to carry little meaning. If they come up with some, try and categorise them according to the functions in the Focus box.

4a 🔊 6.5 Tell Ss they are now going to listen to two conversations. Ask them to listen and note each topic, then go through the answers as a class.

Answers: 1 visiting Uncle Tommy
2 whether to buy an electric bike or a small car

Audioscript 6.5

Conversation 1
A: Let's talk about this coming weekend.
B: OK.
A: Basically, we need to decide what to do.
B: What do you mean?
A: Well, we promised to visit Uncle Tommy on Sunday and he's expecting us.
B: Oh, not again!
A: Yes, again.
B: To be honest, Dad, I'd rather not go.
A: I know that, but we have to go once in a while and, let's face it, we haven't seen him for six months or more.
B: You said, 'We need to decide', but actually, you've already decided, haven't you?
A: Well …
B: Visiting him is so boring. All he ever talks about is his illnesses.
A: Look, I'm not really looking forward to visiting him either, but it is what it is.
B: Come on, Dad. Do we really have to go?
A: Yes, really. The reality is he's family. One day you'll be old and you'll want your family to visit you.
B: I'm not going to talk about my illnesses when I'm old.

Conversation 2
A: Can I ask your advice?
B: About what?
A: Well, I've saved up a bit of money over the last year to buy a bike, an electric bike, but now I'm wondering whether to keep saving for another year or so and buy a small car. What do you think?

B: At the end of the day, it's your choice, but I think buying a bike is the better option. You need it right now. You're wasting money on buses at the moment.
A: True. I'm literally going to die if I have to squash onto another bus. But with a bike, I'll have to cycle in winter, too. I'll get wet!
B: You can buy some waterproofs to keep you dry.
A: But it'll be cold and …
B: Look, there's no point complaining about it. It is what it is. With a bike you get wet, but it's not the end of the world. You need transport and at this moment in time a bike is a good option for you.
A: But a car is warm and safe and …
B: … polluting and, don't forget, it's expensive to run a car, particularly if it goes wrong. Let's face it, it doesn't make sense. If you waste time saving for a car, you'll regret it.

b Tell Ss they're going to listen again and ask them to read through the questions before playing the recording. Ask Ss to listen to answer the questions, then put them in pairs to check. With **weaker classes** you may need to pause the recording between the two conversations. Go through the answers as a class.

> **Answers:**
> 1 a on Sunday
>   b (over) six months ago
>   c his illnesses
>   d talk about her illnesses
> 2 a for a year
>   b it's a squash and the cost
>   c cycling in winter and getting wet
>   d It's not polluting and it's cheaper.

c Ask Ss if they can recall the signpost expressions used. Refer them to the Focus box and ask them to tick (✓) the expressions they heard. If Ss have access to the audioscript, they may like to listen again and underline the expressions. This approach can support **weaker classes**.

> **Answers:** They hear all of the signpost expressions except *Speaking personally*.

5 Ask Ss to work in pairs to match the expressions in bold with the relevant categories in the Focus box. Go through the answers as a class.

> **Answers:** a 4 b 1 c 5 d 2 e 3

6 This is an opportunity to practise the signpost expressions. Give pairs a few minutes to choose a topic and think about which expressions they could use, including a range of signpost expressions. Then ask them to begin their discussion. Monitor and listen. In feedback, draw attention to significant errors and give feedback on their use of the new language.

Optional extra activity

Put Ss in groups and give them some cards with the signpost expressions on, in a pile face down. Ask each student to choose a card, then start the conversation. Ss should try and subtly use the expression on their card without others noticing. If they manage to do so, they take another card and keep the one they used. If another student notices that they've used a signpost expression, they challenge them and, if they are correct, the challenger takes the card. The winner has the most cards at the end.

Homework ideas

Workbook: Ex 1–6, p47

6B Develop your reading

Introduction

The goal of this lesson is for students to understand a website. To help them achieve this, they will focus on recognising irony.

Warm-up

Ask Ss what kinds of texts they read and whether they read on their phones or other digital devices. Ask Ss if they ever read printed books and newspapers. Discuss how digital and printed texts differ. For example, digital texts are often shorter and can adapt to fit different screen sizes. They also contain links to other content. Printed texts have a fixed format and are often longer. Some people say they are easier to read.

1 Ask Ss to talk about the questions in pairs. After a few minutes, conduct brief feedback. Ask pairs to compare answers in groups, then select a few Ss to share some responses with the class. Ss don't have to agree.

2 Refer Ss to the two article introductions. Ask them to read quickly and decide which is humorous and which is serious. Ask them to compare in pairs, telling each other why, then check answers. Accept any reasons they give, but there is no need for detailed feedback as they will learn about this in the Focus box.

> **Answers:** A = serious   B = humorous

3 Refer Ss to the Focus box. Ask them to read it, then find examples of irony in the introduction to article B. Give them a few minutes to do this. With **weaker classes**, work through the Focus box together, asking individuals to read sections aloud and allowing time for questions. During feedback, ask Ss to identify the type of irony in each underlined part (see information in brackets in the answers below).

> **Answers:**
> Run? Hide? Try to negotiate? (Say something ridiculous but pretend it is serious.)
> It's a question that concerns many city dwellers. (Say something ridiculous but pretend it is serious.)
> Fortunately, the internet is full of advice. (Say one thing but mean the opposite.)
> … one handy article … (Say one thing but mean the opposite.)
> You might want to print it out. (Say something ridiculous but pretend it is serious.)
> … just in case you unexpectedly meet a lion in the street. (Say something ridiculous but pretend it is serious.)

4 Tell Ss they will now read the rest of article B. Refer them to the questions and give them a few minutes. Ask Ss to compare answers in pairs. After a few minutes, elicit answers and discuss any issues.

> **Answers:**
> 1 what you shouldn't do when you meet a lion (run)
> 2 what you should do when you meet a lion
> 3 It will want to eat you.

5 Tell Ss they are going to read the article again for detail. Give Ss five minutes to answer the questions, using an online timer if you like, then ask them to discuss in pairs. Go through the answers as a class.

> **Answers:** 1 F 2 T 3 F 4 F 5 T 6 F

Teaching tip

To assist Ss in developing specific reading skills, it can be helpful to give time limits. While these don't need to be stuck to rigidly, they create a focus. This is quite useful, especially if a text may not initially be perceived as interesting. Ss respond to the challenge of reading quickly to answer a task and get more involved. Comparing in pairs after reading helps assure Ss of their answers and evens out ability in a group before whole-class feedback.

6 This task requires Ss to apply knowledge from the Focus box. Ask Ss to read and mark each sentence (a–f) with uses 1–3 from the Focus box. Allow plenty of time for this and get Ss to compare in pairs before you go through the answers as a class.

Answers: a 2   b 3   c 2   d 3   e 1   f 3

7 This is intended as a fun activity after the reading. Discuss the first picture together, then ask Ss to continue in pairs. When they finish, go through the answers as a class. Ask Ss if they can think of more examples of irony.

Answers:
1 Someone has used graffiti to complain about graffiti.
2 The sign that says the establishment is committed to excellence is spelt incorrectly.
3 The driver obviously wasn't driving safely.

Homework ideas

Workbook: Ex 1–5, pp.48–49

6c Develop your writing

Introduction

The goal of this lesson is for students to write an email of complaint which requests action. To help them achieve this, they will focus on using comment adverbs.

Warm-up

Ask Ss if they have ever complained about services or goods and, if so, what the outcome has been. Discuss what's important in complaining successfully (providing evidence; being confident; getting legal backing; asking for compensation, etc.).

1a Ask Ss to discuss the situations in pairs or small groups. Have a whole-class discussion of their ideas and write useful vocabulary on the board.
b Ask Ss to read the phrases and match them to the three situations in Ex 1a. Point out that some phrases can fit more than one situation. Ss should work alone initially, then compare in pairs. Give them a few minutes to do this. Conduct whole-class feedback and clarify any doubts. Point out that the parts in bold are formal and more likely to be written than spoken.

Answers: a 1 (or 2)   b 1 or 2 (or 3)   c 3   d 2   e 1   f 3
g 3 (or 1)   h 2   i 1

Optional extra activity

Ss work in pairs to paraphrase the parts in bold using less formal language. For example: **a** it broke; **b** get your money back; **c** it's the law; **f** it wasn't as good as we thought.
Discuss when we would use the more formal expressions (in writing) and the less formal ones (in a face-to-face discussion or on the phone).

2 Refer Ss to the three emails, explaining that they are all complaints. Ask Ss to complete them with phrases from Ex 1b, then put them in pairs to compare. After a few minutes, elicit answers and deal with any questions.

Answers: 1 f   2 c   3 g   4 i   5 a   6 e   7 h   8 d   9 b

3a Ask Ss to read the complete emails again and answer questions 1–3 about each one. When they finish, ask Ss to compare in pairs, then go through the answers as a class. Ask Ss to comment on how reasonable each email is.

Answers:
1 1 They didn't enjoy the festival.
   2 They weren't allowed to bring much water in. There were too few toilets.
   3 a 50 percent refund
2 1 Their flight was delayed.
   2 mechanical failure
   3 a €250 refund per person
3 1 The laptop has stopped working.
   2 not known
   3 a refund

b Tell Ss you'll now look at the language used in the emails. Ask Ss to find answers to questions 1–4, advising them to highlight information in the emails. When they finish, ask Ss to compare in pairs, then go through the answers as a class. If you have access to a projector, highlight the answers in the emails on the board. Point out that the highlighted phrases are mostly fixed and need little variation.

Answers:
1 I am writing to complain about …
   I am writing to you regarding …
   I am writing concerning …
2 we are requesting a 50 percent refund on …
   I am making a claim for …
   Please accept this email as my claim for a refund.
3 I look forward to hearing from you at your earliest convenience.
   I look forward to your prompt response.
   I hope to hear from you at your earliest convenience.
4 (possible answers)
   we were only allowed to …
   we were forced to …
   The only thing more difficult …
   As I'm sure you are aware …
   I attach a copy of the receipt …
   What's more …

4a Refer to the Focus box and ask Ss to take turns to read sections to the class. Ss should then underline the comment adverbs in the emails, first working alone, then discussing in pairs before checking as a class. Ask individual Ss to read the adverbs aloud to check pronunciation, then drill as needed.

> **Answers:**
> 1 Sadly, Frankly, Predictably, clearly, Hopefully
> 2 Apparently, obviously, Reluctantly, Consequently
> 3 Unfortunately, obviously, clearly

> **Vocabulary checkpoint**
> *Apparently* is used to say that you have read or been told something but you don't know if it's true, or to correct a fact that is not true. It's often used when we are gossiping about people. If you do something *reluctantly*, you do it slowly to show that you are not really happy about it. *Naturally* means of course.

b This activity checks understanding of the adverbs. Ask Ss to work alone to choose the correct alternatives, then discuss in pairs or small groups. When they finish, have whole-class feedback to check answers.

> **Answers:** 1 Unfortunately 2 Naturally 3 Apparently
> 4 Luckily 5 Reluctantly 6 frankly 7 Predictably 8 Sadly
> 9 clearly 10 Astonishingly

5 Refer to the email extracts, explaining that Ss should improve them by adding two or more comment adverbs to each one. With **weaker classes**, complete the first one together, then ask Ss to continue alone. When they finish, go through their answers as a class. There are several options, so accept anything that sounds reasonable.

> **Possible answers:**
> **Sadly**, the mobile phone has been a disappointment since I bought it. It is **astonishingly** slow to start up which **obviously** makes it difficult to use. **Unfortunately**, it often crashes in the middle of a call, which is annoying. **Apparently**, it is described as a 'top of the range' model. **Luckily**, the item is still under warranty.
> **Unfortunately**, the actual colour of the sweatshirt is much darker than the image online. I like the colour online, but **sadly** I don't like the actual colour. **Consequently**, I believe I am entitled to a refund as **clearly** the item is different from what I expected.

Prepare

6 Tell Ss they are now going to write a complaint email. Ask Ss to read the bulleted list and discuss which situation they want to write about and use questions 1–5 to decide what details to include. Monitor as they prepare and be available to help with ideas or language.

Optional alternative activity

Divide the situations among the group. Give pairs of Ss the same situation to complain about and ask them to prepare together. This enables speaking practice but is more limited and focused if time is short. When it comes to the final writing stage, pairs can refer to their own notes. When they finish, they can read and check each other's work and give feedback before exchanging emails with a pair who have made a different complaint.

Write

7 Ask Ss to use their notes to write their email. If they have been working in pairs until now, Ss should write alone, but they can continue to support each other while they write (for example, helping with spellings). Monitor and help if necessary. When they finish, refer them to the checklist and ask them to evaluate and edit their work.

8 Ask Ss to work in new pairs, exchange emails and check each other's work. They should write a comment on their partner's work to help them improve it. Point out that *Would be even better if …* is a good way to introduce a constructive comment. Ss receive their work back and then write a final draft.

Optional alternative activity

Ask Ss to write their email on computers or other devices if they have access. Ss can send their emails to you or other Ss when completed. If appropriate, Ss can answer each other's emails with positive responses (or refusals!).

Homework ideas

Workbook: Ex 1–10, pp.50–51

7 OVERVIEW

7A Possible futures
Goal | talk about possible consequences of situations
Grammar | real conditionals
Vocabulary | social issues
GSE learning objective
Can precisely express the potential consequences of actions or events

7B Business plans
Goal | describe future plans with degrees of probability
Grammar | future forms and degrees of probability
Vocabulary | collocations with *make*, *take*, *do* and *give*
GSE learning objective
Can describe future plans and intentions in detail, giving degrees of probability

7C Cultural awareness
Goal | summarise a situation and give opinions and advice
Grammar | introductory *It*
Vocabulary | personal and professional relationships
GSE learning objective
Can summarise and give opinions on issues and stories and answer questions in detail

7D English in action
Goal | lead a discussion and come to a decision
Vocabulary | meetings and discussions
GSE learning objective
Can lead a discussion so that the group is able to make a decision

VOCABULARY BANK

7A Compound nouns

7B Collocations with *make, take, do* and *give*

DEVELOP YOUR SKILLS

7A Develop your reading
Goal | understand websites and longer texts
Focus | recognising cohesive devices
GSE learning objective
Can recognise the use of cohesive devices to link ideas within and between paragraphs in a written text

7B Develop your writing
Goal | write notes during a conversation
Focus | using abbreviations in notes
GSE learning objective
Can write detailed notes from a face-to-face conversation

7C Develop your listening
Goal | understand a radio programme
Focus | recognising examples
GSE learning objective
Can recognise when examples are being given in a structured presentation on an unfamiliar topic

7A Possible futures

Introduction
The goal of this lesson is for students to talk about potential consequences of situations. To help them achieve this, they will revise real conditionals and vocabulary in the context of social issues.

Warm-up
Before the lesson starts, write the following quotes on the board and ask Ss to work in pairs to discuss their meaning:
'An optimist is a person who sees a green light everywhere, while a pessimist sees only the red stoplight. The truly wise person is colour blind.'
'Is the glass half empty or half full? It depends how you look at it.'
After a few minutes, ask Ss for their ideas.

Vocabulary

Social issues

1a Refer Ss to the photos (A–D) and ask them to discuss the question in pairs. Monitor and help with new vocabulary where necessary. After a few minutes, elicit answers and add useful words and phrases to the board.

Answers: A energy efficiency B inequality C homelessness D life expectancy

> **Teaching tip**
> Introductory tasks like this are designed to activate Ss' existing knowledge of the subject matter and to raise awareness of the vocabulary they will need in the lesson. This stage also creates interest and a desire to express opinions in English, so take the opportunity to highlight any other relevant vocabulary that arises during the feedback stage.

b Ask Ss to match the vocabulary in bold in Ex 1a with meanings a–j, writing the relevant letters beside numbers 1–10. Put Ss in pairs to compare. When they finish, have whole-class feedback.

Answers: 1 e 2 j 3 b 4 i 5 f 6 a 7 d 8 h 9 c 10 g

c This exercise checks understanding of the vocabulary. Give pairs a few minutes to decide if the statements are positive or negative, marking each one + or –. Clarify that Ss need to look at the whole of each statement, not just the parts in bold. Go through the answers.

Answers: Positive: 2, 4, 5, 6, 8, 10 Negative: 1, 3, 7, 9

> **Teaching tip**
> Checking understanding is an important stage in learning new language. It helps learners confirm their understanding and makes it memorable for them. If Ss have questions, they can ask them here, and should be encouraged to do so. Avoid simply asking, 'Do you understand?' as Ss will often just say yes, whether they do or not! Useful methods of checking understanding include: categorising (as in Ex 1c), matching with synonyms or definitions, answering simple concept-checking questions, reading more examples in context and translation into L1.

2 ◆ **7.1** Ask Ss to listen and mark the schwa /ə/ sounds. Pause after each word or phrase to allow Ss time to discuss. Play the recording again and check answers as you go.

Answers: 1 unempl**o**yment 2 inequ**a**lity 3 p**o**verty
4 s**o**cial unrest 5 life expect**a**ncy 6 int**o**lerance
7 homel**e**ssness 8 en**e**rgy effici**e**ncy 9 healthc**a**re costs
10 living st**a**ndards

Pronunciation checkpoint
As Ss will know, all English words with more than one syllable have a primary stress that is longer and louder than the other syllables. In many cases, the unstressed syllable(s) is a schwa /ə/ or weak form, as seen. This may differ from Ss' first language, where all syllables have an equal weight. Ss' pronunciation will sound more natural if they stress and observe weak forms. Importantly, understanding that they exist also aids Ss' listening skills.

3a Ask Ss to discuss in pairs, pointing out the verb *will* and explaining that they should think about life in the future. When they finish, nominate pairs to say what they think about each statement and ask for their reasons.

b Using a show of hands, find out who feels optimistic, who feels pessimistic and who feels neutral about the future. Ask a few Ss to give reasons for their feelings.

VOCABULARY BANK 7A p162
Compound nouns
This is an optional extension to the vocabulary section, extending the lexical set and providing further practice. If you're short of time, this can be done for homework.
1 Ask Ss to read the sentences and choose the correct words to make compound nouns. Ss can discuss first in pairs, then go through the answers as a class.

Answers: 1 care 2 health 3 side 4 weather 5 Global
6 civil 7 prime 8 natural 9 carbon 10 climate

2 Ask Ss to complete the table with the compounds from Ex 1. They can compare in pairs before going through the answers as a class.

Answers:
noun + noun: care home; health centre; side effects; weather forecast; carbon footprint; climate change
adjective + noun: global warming; civil rights; prime minister; natural resources

3 Ask Ss to work in pairs to write the questions. Monitor and correct as needed. Ask Ss to ask and answer with a new partner. There are no fixed answers.

Further practice
Photocopiable activities: 7A Vocabulary, p223
App: 7A Vocabulary practice 1 and 2

Reading
Culture notes
VR is an abbreviation for virtual reality: a set of 3D images and sounds produced by a computer that people seem to be able to 'enter' and take part in. They wear a VR headset to immerse themselves in the virtual experience. VR has been common in video games for years but is increasingly used in the workplace by engineers, builders, architects, etc.
AI is an abbreviation for artificial intelligence. It describes the power of computers to achieve cognitive functions that have previously been considered only human, such as decision making, learning or problem solving. For example, in the medical field AI has been shown to do better than humans at areas such as diagnosis and interpretation of scans.

4 Tell Ss they are going to quickly scan three texts and choose the best title for each. Check/Pre-teach *virtual reality* (VR) and *artificial intelligence* (AI). Ask Ss to compare, then check answers.

Answers: 1 b 2 c 3 a

Optional alternative approach
Name Ss A, B and C and allocate one text to each. Ask them to read their text only, then tell their partners about it. As the texts are short, allow two minutes for reading and five minutes for telling each other. Ss can then look at the titles together and decide which one is right for each text. This approach may suit Ss who don't like reading much and need to develop speaking skills.

5a Ask Ss to work in pairs and decide if the statements are true or false. They need to work together and refer to all three texts. Go through the answers. Where statements are false, elicit the true answers.

Answers:
1 T
2 F We will be able to choose any world we like.
3 F Only adults will get the UBI.
4 F You can top up your UBI by working.
5 F It is when AI becomes smarter than humans.
6 T

b Put Ss in small groups to discuss. When they finish, have whole-group feedback.

Grammar
Real conditionals
6a Tell Ss they are going to use the texts to focus on some grammar. Ask them to look at the opinions and decide which text in Ex 4 they are about. They should work in pairs, marking each opinion 1, 2 or 3. Go through the answers.

Answers: a 2 b 1 c 3 d 1 e 3 f 2 g 2

b Ask Ss what the grammar is (conditionals) and whether they can name the conditional forms seen (they may name them as zero and first conditionals). Ask Ss to read the grammar box, matching four sentences from Ex 6a to 1–4 and choosing the correct alternatives for 5–7. Complete the first example together, then Ss can continue in pairs. If time is short, Ss can write the sentence letters (a–g) in gaps 1–4. Go through the answers and deal with further questions.

Answers: 1 g 2 e 3 f 4 c 5 as soon as 6 unless
7 assuming

Grammar checkpoint

Provided can also be expressed as *providing* with no change in meaning. *As long as* has a slightly less formal tone than *assuming* and *provided*.

Remind Ss that the two clauses, condition and result, can be reversed with no change in meaning. When the result clause comes first, there is usually no comma between the clauses.

7a Explain that Ss must decide if one or both forms are possible to complete each sentence. Complete the first example as a class, then ask Ss to work alone to choose the correct verbs, referring to the grammar box to help them. Ask them to check in pairs, then check answers with the whole class. Ask Ss to read the whole sentence aloud so you can check pronunciation and drill as needed.

Answers: **1** a **2** both **3** a **4** both **5** a **6** a **7** a **8** b

b Ask Ss to tick the sentences they agree with and cross those they disagree with. Put them in pairs to compare and change those they disagree with to make them true. Have brief whole-class feedback to see which statements most people agree with.

Optional alternative activity

If Ss are not particularly engaged by the topic of VR, UBI and AI, get pairs to write their own general truths and predictions about their own lives, their country and the world. Encourage them to use real conditionals. They can share their statements with a new pair who may then agree/disagree with them.

LANGUAGE BANK 7A pp.148–149

Stronger classes could read the notes at home. Otherwise, check the notes with Ss. In each exercise, elicit the first answer as an example. Ss work alone to complete the exercises, then check their answers in pairs. In feedback, elicit Ss' answers and drill the questions. Ss can refer to the notes to help them.

Answers:
1 **1** a, g **2** b, e **3** d, f **4** c, h
2 **1** if you see/notice **2** when I call **3** As soon as
  4 there may/might be **5** assuming that she

Further practice

Photocopiable activities: 7A Grammar 1, p221; 7A Grammar 2, p222
App: 7A Grammar practice 1 and 2

Speaking

Prepare

8a Ask Ss to look at the situations and mark them G for *good outcome* and B for *bad outcome*. They can do this quickly without thinking too much about it as they will speak in depth about the topics later. There are no fixed answers.

Optional extra activity

Ask Ss to add two more future situations to the list. With **weaker classes**, you may prefer to brainstorm these as a class and write ideas on the board.

b Ask Ss to choose two situations and make notes on the possible outcomes. Allow a few minutes for this and monitor to support, ensuring Ss are not writing full sentences.

Speak

9a Put Ss in pairs and ask them to share their ideas and listen to each other. Point out that they should extend the discussion by questioning and explaining the reasons for their views. Move around the class and listen, helping if necessary.

b Ask Ss to move around the room to find new partners and repeat the discussion two or three more times. When they finish, ask Ss if they found someone with similar views. Give some feedback on how they managed the language point.

Teaching tip

When Ss are using language freely, monitor closely but don't interrupt the flow of their conversation. This means not making eye contact or engaging Ss directly. It's a good idea to monitor with a notebook, writing examples that you can later use to show how well Ss are using the target language. If errors arise, wait until after the speaking stage to draw attention to them. At this point, you can write or project them on the board and ask Ss to correct them themselves. This helps Ss become independent learners.

Reflection on learning

Write the following questions on the board:
If you want to remember this lesson, what will you do?
How could you use this language outside the class?

Put Ss in pairs to discuss the questions. When they have finished, ask if anyone wants to share their ideas with the class, but don't force them to if they'd rather not.

Homework ideas

Language bank: 7A Ex 1–2, pp.148–149
Workbook: Ex 1–5, p52
App: grammar, vocabulary and pronunciation practice

Fast route: continue to Lesson 7B
Extended route: go to p108 for Develop your reading

7B Business plans

Introduction

The goal of this lesson is for students to describe future plans with degrees of probability. To help them achieve this, they will revise future forms and degrees of probability and collocations with certain common verbs.

Warm-up

Ask Ss if they know the word for a person who sets up an original business, taking quite a lot of risks but also benefiting from all the rewards (= *entrepreneur*). To prompt this, you could name or show pictures of well-known entrepreneurs such as Oprah Winfrey or Jeff Bezos (see Culture notes below). Tell Ss this is today's topic and ask them to turn to Ex 1.

Culture notes

Examples of famous entrepreneurs include Jeff Bezos, who built Amazon from an online bookstore, and Oprah Winfrey, an American talk show host, actress and philanthropist. It is no surprise that many famous entrepreneurs are also multi-millionaires or billionaires. If possible, name some entrepreneurs you think Ss will have heard of – ideally including one or two from their own countries.

Listening

1 Refer Ss to the questions and ask them to discuss in pairs. Conduct brief feedback and ask Ss to share personal qualities they think are important, adding new words to the board.

2 Refer Ss to the advert and ask them to discuss in pairs. Tell Ss to ignore words they don't know as you'll be looking at them later. When they finish, conduct feedback and ask a few Ss to share their ideas.

3a 🔊 7.2 Tell Ss they will listen to Rafaela talking about the challenge. Allow them time to read through the questions, then play the recording so they can answer them. Go through the answers.

> **Answers:** 1 a concert 2 on one singer
> 3 with £5 for each ticket sold 4 on social media

Audioscript 7.2

I've always fancied myself as a music promoter. I organise a big barbeque for my friends every summer on the beach and usually some friends play instruments and sing and it's a lot of fun. And sometimes I think – perhaps I could organise a concert! So, I'm going to take this opportunity to try. I'm organising a concert … in seven days! I've made a plan and I'm probably going to spend most of the money on one headline act, a singer I know called Gilda Alves. It sounds a bit risky but it makes sense to me. She's quite a big name, at least around here, and that will attract people. She'll hopefully say, 'Yes', because she's a friend of mine but, if she doesn't, I'm not sure what I'll do. It's unlikely that I'll find someone to take her place at such short notice.

In terms of the venue, I'll definitely try to make a deal with the theatre in town. I know that they don't have a play on at the moment. I don't think I'll pay them a fee. Instead, I'm probably going to offer them £5 for every ticket I sell, but I haven't quite worked it all out yet.

I'm planning to sell tickets for £15 each and I reckon I should easily sell a couple of hundred. I doubt that I'll set up a website, there's not really enough time, but I'm definitely going to spend a bit of money on marketing to tell people about the event.

You can't do without social media, so I'm giving priority to that. I may well pay my brother to give me a hand. He's quite good at that sort of thing and he'll do a good job in terms of getting the word out, although he can be a bit bossy, so I have to make sure he doesn't try to take control of the whole project. In fact, rather than pay him, I might ask him to help in exchange for a free ticket to the concert. I hope I'll make a profit. Fingers crossed!

b Ask Ss to discuss Rafaela's plan in pairs, then have a whole-class discussion of its potential weaknesses. There are no fixed answers.

4 Ask Ss to read through the sentences, then play the recording again for them to choose the correct alternatives. Clarify that sometimes both options are grammatically possible, but they should select the words they hear. Ask pairs to compare, then go through the answers as a class.

> **Answers:** 1 organising 2 probably going to 3 I'll
> 4 It's unlikely 5 definitely try 6 don't think I'll 7 planning to
> 8 doubt 9 may well 10 might ask

Optional extra activity

If Ss have access to the audioscript, ask them to listen and read at the same time, underlining the future verb forms in the script.

Grammar

Future forms and degrees of probability

5 Explain that you will now use the sentences from the listening to study some grammar. Ask Ss to read through the grammar box, then look at the sentences in Ex 4 to decide where both options are grammatically possible. Go through the answers, referring to the grammar box as needed.

> **Answers:** 1, 3, 6 (but second alternative more natural), 7

6a 🔊 7.3 Ask Ss to read the sentences, then mark the sentence stress as they listen to the recording. They can do this by underlining or highlighting the stressed parts. Share the information in the Pronunciation checkpoint below if you think it's useful.

> **Answers:**
> 1 I'm **pro**bably going to **try** to **make** a **deal**.
> 2 I'm **def**initely going to **spend** a **bit** of **mo**ney.
> 3 It's **like**ly that they're going to **say yes**.
> 4 It's un**like**ly that we're going to **make** a **loss**.
> 5 I **don't think** we're going to **sell all** the **tick**ets.
> 6 I **doubt** he's going to **help** us.

b Ask Ss to listen again and repeat, focusing on the rhythm of the sentences.

Pronunciation checkpoint

Ss may need reminding that sentence stress causes some words to be louder and longer, and others to be softer. To help them reproduce this rhythm, show the pattern of stress by raising your hand or arm to match the stresses, orchestrating as Ss repeat. Backchaining can also help to emphasise where sentence stress lies. This involves Ss repeating the sentence in sections, starting from the end: *deal / make a deal / try to make a deal / I'm probably going to try to make a deal*.

7a Write the first sentence on the board and ask Ss to correct it. Ss then work alone to correct the other sentences. Check answers with the whole class.

Answers:
1 I'll **definitely sell** more than 200 tickets.
2 It's **possible** I'll ask some friends for help.
3 I'm wondering whether **to** send out emails.
4 I'm probably **going to** / I'll probably spend a lot of money on marketing.
5 **It's** unlikely that I'll get much sleep next week.
6 **I don't think I'll** organise catering.
7 I **may well** promote the event online.
8 We're planning **to** offer some tickets for free.

Optional alternative approach

Give pairs of Ss mini whiteboards to write the corrections on one by one, and then hold them up to show you. If they are not correct, let them have another try. If you have an interactive whiteboard, get learners up to the board to do the corrections there. Both these methods are good for more outgoing classes that like to compete with each other.

b Refer Ss to the example and give another with *planning* yourself, so that Ss are aware there are several options. Then ask Ss to continue with the other words in the box. **Weaker classes** should write first and then tell a partner. Ss can check in pairs before whole-class feedback.

LANGUAGE BANK 7B pp.148–149
Stronger classes could read the notes at home. Otherwise, check the notes with Ss. In each exercise, elicit the first answer as an example. Ss work alone to complete the exercises, then check their answers in pairs. In feedback, elicit Ss' answers and drill the questions. Ss can refer to the notes to help them.

Answers:
1   1 d   2 c   3 a
2   1 k   2 a   3 c   4 f   5 h   6 j   7 b   8 i

Further practice

Photocopiable activities: 7B Grammar 1, p224; 7B Grammar 2, p225
App: 7B Grammar practice 1 and 2

Vocabulary

Collocations with *make, take, do* and *give*

8 Ask Ss to write the words in the box beside the correct verbs. They can do this from their existing knowledge and by instinct and guesswork. As you go through the answers, discuss the meanings of the collocations.

Answers:
1 make: a deal; a profit; sense
2 take: someone's place; a risk; charge
3 do: research; a good job; without
4 give: it your best shot; priority to; someone a hand

Vocabulary checkpoint
Ss may benefit from further clarification on some of the vocabulary.
Give it your best shot is a fixed expression meaning to try your best on one occasion, often when it seems you don't have much chance of success. For example: *He had an interview for that job. He gave it his best shot, but he didn't get it.*
Give someone a hand is to help someone. For example: *I'm struggling with this bag, can you give me a hand?*
Both expressions are quite informal. Ask Ss to write contextualised examples like this in their notebooks.

9 This exercise checks understanding of the collocations. Ask Ss to replace the underlined words with a collocation from Ex 8. They may need to change some parts of some expressions, for example pronouns. Ask Ss to work alone initially, then discuss ideas in pairs. Go through the answers and further clarify as needed.

Answers: 1 take charge of   2 give priority to   3 do research
4 taking a risk   5 give us a hand   6 make a deal
7 take our place   8 give it your best shot   9 make a profit
10 do without   11 make sense   12 do a good job

VOCABULARY BANK 7B   p162
Collocations with *make, take, do* and *give*
This is an optional extension to the vocabulary section, extending the lexical set and providing further practice. If you're short of time, this can be done for homework.
1 Ask Ss to complete sentences 1–12 with the phrases in the boxes. Ss can discuss first in pairs, then go through the answers as a class.

Answers: 1 my day   2 the most of   3 a difference
4 them for granted   5 advantage of   6 him seriously
7 a favour   8 you good   9 the job   10 them a hard time
11 way   12 the game away

2 Ask Ss to rewrite the sentences using phrases from Ex 1. Complete the first one together, then ask Ss to continue alone before checking in pairs. Check answers as a class.

Answers: 1 take for granted   2 does you good
3 given someone a hard time   4 done you a favour
5 give way   6 made your day

3a Ask Ss to work alone and write answers to three of the questions in Ex 2.
b Put Ss in pairs to discuss. When they finish, ask a few pairs to share interesting points or points they agreed on.

Further practice

Photocopiable activities: 7B Vocabulary, p226
App: 7B Vocabulary practice 1 and 2

Speaking

Prepare

10 🔊 **7.4** Tell Ss they are going to listen to how Rafaela's concert went. Introduce the phrase *a mixed bag* (= some positive and some negative things). Refer to the list and ask Ss to listen and make notes. Ask them to discuss in pairs after listening, then go through the answers.

> **Answers:**
> She sold about 60 tickets, which is not as many as she hoped.
> She made no profit.
> She should have paid staff to help her.
> She was happy with the social media campaign that her brother organised.
> She didn't send out emails to family and friends, which she should have done.
> She didn't get any photos of the event because she didn't hire a photographer.

Audioscript 7.4

OK, so, you wanna know how it all went, right? Well, it was a mixed bag, to be honest. In the end, I sold about 60 tickets and that was a bit disappointing. It certainly wasn't the 200 I was hoping for and it meant that I made about £900, but then of course, I had to repay the initial £500 so I was only left with £400, which is what I agreed to pay Gilda, the singer. So basically, zero profit. Like I said, a bit disappointing really after a week of work.

Basically, I got a few things wrong, which is not surprising given how much time I had to prepare.

The biggest mistake I made is that I forgot about staff. I thought I could do it all myself but, on the actual night of the concert, I had to take tickets at the front door and help the musicians backstage and be in 20 other places at once and it was all a bit chaotic, so … yeah, that didn't go so well. I'm pretty sure that quite a few people got in without paying, but there was nothing I could do about that. So, lesson one is, don't try to do everything yourself. You're going to need to pay for help.

The second thing is that I just forgot about the power of email. I was really happy with the social media campaign that my brother organised and that's how most people heard about the concert, but what I should have done is just emailed all my friends and family and told them what was happening and asked them if they'd like to come along and bring a friend or two. That way I would probably have reached 200 people easily, but I was so focussed on attracting the general public that I forgot about friends and family.

And lastly, and this really hurts, I don't have any photos of the event. The concert itself was amazing and Gilda gave such a great performance, but I don't have any photos or video because I was so busy doing other things. So next time, I'm going to hire a professional photographer.

And yes, there is going to be a next time. It was really hard work, but I loved every minute of it, so I'm going to do it again next year!

11a Ask Ss to work in pairs to choose an idea from the list, then discuss its pros and cons. With **weaker classes**, do this for one of the ideas as a class and build up two lists, pros and cons, on the board. Move around the class, monitor and help with vocabulary or ideas as needed.

Culture notes

A **pop-up** shop or café is a short-term use of a space for retail. The advantage is that the space does not have all the costs associated with permanent shops or cafés, such as furniture, staff and taxes. Some businesses start off as a pop-up to test a product or concept, then become more permanent if the idea works. A market stall is similar, in that it can be rented on a short-term basis to sell goods in a public market place.

b Refer to the example business plan and ask pairs to write similar ones. With **weaker classes**, you may want to go over the example and discuss other options for each section. While pairs complete their plans, monitor and help as needed.

12a When they finish writing their business plans, tell pairs to ask and answer questions about their plans to try and refine them. They should use the questions in Ex 9.

b Remind Ss about the problems with Rafaela's plan. Ask them to consider if there are any weaknesses in their own plans.

Speak

13a Put Ss in new pairs to explain their plans and ask each other questions.

b Join pairs up into small groups. Tell groups to discuss all the plans they have made or heard about. Groups then decide which plans they think are most likely to succeed.

c Groups vote on which plan is most likely to be profitable, then share their choice with the class.

> **Optional alternative idea**
>
> Allocate the ideas in Ex 11a to pairs, so that all the ideas are used equally. After the planning stage, arrange Ss in groups of four, with each member talking about a different entrepreneur plan. Group members then take turns to present their plans before deciding on the best one. This is good for **stronger classes** who like to talk and is a good way of making sure that everybody participates.

> **Reflection on learning**
>
> Write the following questions on the board:
> *What was the most enjoyable part of this lesson for you? Why?*
> *How are you going to remember what we studied today?*
> Put Ss in pairs to discuss the questions. When they have finished, ask if anyone wants to share their ideas with the class, but don't force them to if they'd rather not.

> **Homework ideas**
>
> **Ex 11–13:** Ss design a promotional poster for one of the plans discussed.
> **Language bank:** 7B Ex 1–2, pp.148–149
> **Workbook:** Ex 1–5, p53
> **App:** grammar, vocabulary and pronunciation practice

Fast route: continue to Lesson 7C
Extended route: go to p128 for Develop your writing

7C Cultural awareness

Introduction
The goal of this lesson is for students to summarise a situation and give opinions and advice. To help them achieve this, they will study introductory *It* and vocabulary in the context of personal and professional relationships.

Warm-up
Tell an anecdote about a cultural misunderstanding that has happened to you or a friend. For example, a friend visiting Thailand patted a child on the head in a friendly way, but people told him afterwards he shouldn't have done that. Ask Ss why the friend was confused (because in Thailand the head is considered a sacred part of the body so touching a stranger on the head is inappropriate). Elicit what this kind of misunderstanding is called (= cross-cultural misunderstanding).

Vocabulary
Personal and professional relationships
1 Ask Ss to look at the photos and discuss the questions in pairs. After a few minutes, invite feedback.

Answers: **A** Turkey **B** Japan **C** Sweden

Culture notes
A **stereotype** is a commonly held but oversimplified belief about a group of people. Stereotypes of British people include that they drink tea every day at 3.00 p.m. or that they are very polite and always saying sorry. While there is often an element of truth, stereotypes can be negative. Ask Ss what the stereotype for their nationality is, if you think they'll be happy to talk about it.

Optional alternative activity
If you have a multilingual class, get them to first discuss in same nationality groups and then regroup into mixed nationalities. If all your Ss come from the same place, they could be allocated different aspects of behaviour to consider and then report on, for example eating, workplace, drinking, visiting people's homes and gift-giving.

Optional extra activity
If the topic is interesting to your Ss, ask the following quiz questions and tell Ss to discuss them:
1 What should you do when you arrive for work at an office in Spain? (Greet all your co-workers individually before you sit down and start work.)
2 What should you do if you disagree with your boss in the Netherlands? (Say what you think calmly and clearly.)
3 What should you not do in a restaurant in South Korea? (Leave a tip – it's considered rude.)
4 What should you do on entering a house in Turkey? (Take your shoes off. Many houses have extra pairs of slippers for guests.)

Reveal the answers, then ask Ss if they know of other countries (including theirs) where the behaviour is similar or quite different.

2a Ask Ss to match the relationships with the words in the box. Go through the answers and drill pronunciation as needed.

Answers: **1** flatmate **2** co-worker **3** senior colleague **4** acquaintance **5** ex-partner **6** client **7** sister-in-law **8** distant relative **9** classmate **10** brother-in-law

b This is an opportunity to share ideas and practise the vocabulary. Put Ss in pairs to discuss. With **weaker classes**, go over key greetings vocabulary before Ss start: *hug, kiss (on the cheek), shake hands, bow, wave, nod*.

c Discuss as a class, feeding in your own knowledge if Ss struggle to come up with ideas.

Further practice
Photocopiable activities: 7C Vocabulary, p229
App: 7C Vocabulary practice 1 and 2

Language focus
Introductory *It*
3 Put Ss in pairs to read the situations and discuss the questions. Check ideas as a class. There are no fixed answers. If Ss struggle to come up with ideas for question 2, you could ask these prompt questions:
a *Does the classmate believe that, one day, he might need to borrow some money?*
b *Why doesn't the boss want to give him the job?*
c *Has the person moved to a new country?*
d *Is the person well off and can he afford it?*

Teaching tip
Some Ss can be insensitive when commenting on cultures that are different from their own and cause offence without realising it. Make it clear that people do things differently in different places and whilst we can comment on this, we should not criticise it. If Ss are insensitive, point this out gently by asking them to consider how aspects of their own culture might appear to others.

4a 🔊 7.8 Ask Ss to listen and decide which two of the situations in Ex 3 are being discussed. Go through the answers.

Answers:
Conversation 1: situation 2
Conversation 2: situation 3

b Ask Ss to listen again more carefully and complete the sentences. Ask them to compare in pairs and play the audio a third time if necessary. Go through the answers.

Answers:
1 **a** me that
 b me to hear
 c that
 d just that
2 **a** like
 b as though
 c her to answer
 d that

Audioscript 7.8

1
A: Now, this one from Maria is very interesting.
B: Yes, it strikes me that she's in a very difficult situation.
A: Yep, it's a lose-lose situation.
B: I mean, it amazes me to hear he's applied for the job in the first place.
A: Yeah, that's unusual.
B: It's not that he's done something very wrong ...
A: No ...
B: It's just that it's not very ... diplomatic.
A: Would you want your sister-in-law as your boss?
B: No way!
A: Me neither!
B: So, I wonder if they're from different cultures and have different expectations.
A: It sounds like they might be.
B: It would be interesting to know.

2
B: Um-hum, another difficult situation, for Lisa this time.
A: Yes. It looks like she wants to make friends with her colleagues ...
B: Yes ...
A: But she doesn't like their questions. It sounds as though she finds them too ...
B: Personal?
A: Yes, too personal.
B: It bothers her to answer these kinds of questions.
A: I totally understand her feelings.
B: Yes, me too. I mean people have different ways of being friends in different cultures ...
A: Sure.
B: So, it follows that they might not be comfortable with another way of being friends.
A: Absolutely.
B: So again, I wonder if Lisa has just moved to a new country and if she's finding things difficult.
A: Yes, I think you're right.

5 Ask Ss to read through the Language focus box, then match sentences from Ex 4b with sections 1–4, according to their pattern. With **weaker classes**, complete this as a class and discuss any questions.

Answers:
1 a 2 b 4 c 1 d 1
2 a 3 b 3 c 4 d 1

6a 🔊 7.9 Ask Ss to listen and underline the stressed words. **Stronger classes** can underline the words first, then listen to check.

Answers:
1 It's <u>not</u> that I really dis<u>like</u> him or anything. It's <u>just</u> that he's a little bit <u>strange</u>.
2 It's <u>not</u> that I don't want to <u>go</u> or anything. It's <u>just</u> that I'm really <u>busy</u>.
3 It's <u>not</u> that I don't under<u>stand</u> or anything. It's <u>just</u> that I <u>need</u> you to re<u>peat</u> it.
4 It's <u>not</u> that I've <u>fallen</u> in <u>love</u> or anything. It's <u>just</u> that I <u>really</u>, <u>really</u> like him.

b Ss listen again and repeat the examples chorally and individually.

7a Refer back to situation 4 in Ex 3. Ask Ss to complete the sentences about the situation, using the words in brackets. **Weaker classes** can write out the whole sentences in their notebooks. Monitor and help as necessary. When they finish, put Ss in pairs to check, then go through the answers as a class.

Answers: 1 It sounds as though 2 It's not that
3 It strikes me that 4 It feels to me that 5 It looks like
6 It seems to me that 7 It amazes me to hear that
8 It bothers me that

b Put Ss in pairs to discuss which sentences they agree or disagree with. Have a brief whole-class discussion to see which ideas are shared.

LANGUAGE BANK 7C pp.148–149
Stronger classes could read the notes at home. Otherwise, check the notes with Ss. In each exercise, elicit the first answer as an example. Ss work alone to complete the exercise, then check their answers in pairs. In feedback, elicit Ss' answers. Ss can refer to the notes to help them.

Answers:
1 1 it's 2 amazes 3 seems 4 if 5 It's 6 worries 7 it
   8 like 9 upsets 10 follow

Further practice

Photocopiable activities: 7C Language focus 1, p227; 7C Language focus 2, p228
App: 7C Language focus practice 1 and 2

Speaking

Prepare

8 Put Ss in AA and BB pairs. Ask them to read their information. Pairs should discuss their situation and describe their reactions to it.

Speak

9a Organise Ss into AB pairs. Ask pairs to summarise and discuss the situations they read about on their role cards, explaining any cultural aspects and reacting to each other's information. Refer Ss to the Useful phrases. If you have a multilingual class, there may be interesting cultural differences in their responses.

b Ask pairs to try and agree on the advice to give each person. Ask a few pairs for their ideas. There are no fixed answers.

Reflection on learning

Write the following questions on the board:
How do you think today's lesson will help you in the future?
How could you use some of the language of today's lesson outside the class?
Put Ss in pairs to discuss the questions. When they have finished, ask if anyone wants to share their ideas with the class, but don't force them to if they'd rather not.

Homework ideas

Language bank: 7C Ex 1, pp.148–149
Workbook: Ex 1–5, p54
App: grammar and vocabulary practice

Fast route: continue to Lesson 7D
Extended route: go to p92 for Develop your listening

7D English in action

Introduction
The goal of this lesson is for students to lead a discussion and come to a decision. To help them achieve this, they will revise vocabulary connected to meetings and discussions.

Warm-up
Ask Ss if they have to attend or lead meetings at work or school and how they feel about that. After a few minutes, lead a discussion on Ss' meeting experiences. Tell them that today's lesson is going to help them understand how to manage discussions in English. Discuss how confident they feel about this.

> **Teaching tip**
> Some Ss may need English for work, others may simply be learning English at school, others for travel or perhaps to read academic textbooks and journals. They may not be planning on using it for work or even visiting an English-speaking country. If you know how and when Ss are likely to use English, it can help you plan relevant lessons.

Vocabulary

1 Ask Ss to discuss the questions in pairs. After a few minutes, ask a few pairs for their ideas and write useful vocabulary on the board for each question.

2a Ask Ss to match the words or phrases in bold with the meanings, using the context to help them. Ask Ss to check answers in pairs, then go through them as a class.

> **Answers:** 1 c 2 f 3 h, e 4 a 5 d, b 6 g, j 7 i

b Ask pairs to say whether they agree or disagree with the sentences, then have brief whole-class feedback to see which points most people agree on. This may link back to cultural issues as discussed in the previous lesson.

Listening 1

3a 🔊 7.12 Tell Ss they will listen to the start of three meetings. They should note the purpose of each meeting. Go through the answers.

> **Answers:**
> 1 to start planning this year's swimming club party
> 2 to agree on the winners of this year's hospitality awards
> 3 to look at visitor numbers for the website (and see if any updates or changes need to be made)

Audioscript 7.12

Meeting 1
A: OK … has everyone got coffee?
B/C/D: Yes. / Yep. / Uh-huh.
A: Great. Help yourself to biscuits, of course.
B/C/D: OK. / Yep.
A: All right, let's get started, shall we?
B/C/D: OK. / Yep. / Sure.
A: Welcome, everyone. I think you all know Beatrice.
C/D: Hi Beatrice.
B: Hi!
A: Beatrice helped with the swimming club party last year.
D: It was a great party.
B: Thanks.
A: Certainly was. And I'd like to welcome Caspar.
B/D: Nice to meet you, Caspar.
C: Hello. Nice to meet you all, too.
A: Caspar has offered to help out with the swimming club – he's a keen swimmer.
B/D: Nice. / The more the merrier.
A: So, our goal today is to start planning this year's swimming club party. As you know, this year is the tenth anniversary of our swimming club …
B/C/D: Yay! Woo-hoo!
A: … so, the first thing we have to sort out is …

Meeting 2
E: Now … have you all got a copy of the agenda?
F/G/H: Yes. / Yep. / Think so.
E: Good. Let's get down to business.
F/G/H: OK. / Sure.
E: It's good to see you all here. I know some of you had an early start to get here …
F/G: Yeah! / You can say that again!
E: Has everyone met Francesco?
G/H: Hello. / Hi.
E: Francesco, this is Gina and this is Harriet.
F: Gina, Harriet.
E: As you all know, Francesco is the owner of The Meridian, the nightclub in the centre of town and he's kindly agreed to help us this year. Thank you, Francesco!
F: My pleasure!
E: Now, the purpose of the meeting today is to agree on the winners of this year's hospitality awards. We've got lots of awards to decide: best new café of the year; best new restaurant; best new hotel, and many more, so we need to get on and make some decisions. However, the first item on the agenda is finding a presenter for the award ceremony, which is in two weeks' time. I have a few suggestions but I want to get your ideas first, so, …

Meeting 3
I: … yeah, so that's what he told me anyway.
J: Yeah, strange, isn't it?
I: Very strange. Anyway, water anyone?
K,L: No. / Fine thanks.
I: Let's make a start, shall we?
K: Good idea. I've got to be back around 11.
I: OK. Anyone else got to be back early?
J,L: No. / Not really.
I: Well, thanks for coming everyone. I think we all know each other by now! How long have we been having these meetings? A couple of years at least.
L: Bit more, I think.
I: Anyway, our goal today is to look at visitor numbers for the website and see if we need to make any updates or changes. So, numbers were up a bit last month, weren't they, Jessica?
J: Yep, they were. We had over 5,000 visitors to the website last month which is ten percent up on this time last year.
I,K,L: That's good news. / Good to hear.

b Refer Ss to the gapped sentences to listen again and complete. Ask them to compare in pairs, then go through the answers.

> **Answers:** 1 a coffee b welcome   2 a met b agenda
> 3 a start b goal

c Refer to the Useful phrases box, asking Ss to complete the gaps with phrases from Ex 3b. Ask Ss to compare in pairs, then go through the answers as a class. Point out that *However* in item 6 is not part of the expression.

> **Answers:**
> 1 Has everyone got coffee?
> 2 Let's make a start, shall we?
> 3 I'd like to welcome Caspar.
> 4 Has everyone met Francesco?
> 5 Our goal today is to look at visitor numbers …
> 6 The first item on the agenda is …

4a 🔊 **7.13** Tell Ss they will now listen to the pronunciation of some key phrases. Play the audio and point out the linking sounds. Share the information in the Pronunciation checkpoint below if you think Ss will find it useful.

b Ask Ss to practise saying the phrases together in pairs, then listen to individuals as a class. Play the audio again if necessary for them to repeat. Elicit the extra sound in each case (1 'w' 2 'y' 3 'w' 4 'y') and point out that in sentence 4, the sound is not added but comes from the end of the word *today*.

Pronunciation checkpoint

When a noun begins with a vowel, we change *a* to *an*, for example *an egg*. Ask Ss why we do this (to make it easier to pronounce). To ease pronunciation between two vowel sounds in adjacent words, an extra consonant sound is introduced for the same reason. This is called intrusion and is a common feature of connected speech. Depending on the surrounding vowels sounds, the introduced sound will be 'w', 'y' or 'r'. For example:

The media 'r' are to blame.   I 'y' agree.   I want to 'w' eat.

5a Ask Ss to first locate two adjacent vowels, then say them together to decide if the intruded sound is 'w' or 'y' and mark it in. Point out that one sentence has two pairs of adjacent vowels.

b 🔊 **7.14** Ask Ss to listen and check. Drill as needed to reinforce pronunciation.

Answers:
1 Let's meet again the day 'y' after tomorrow.
2 It's good to see 'y' all of you could come.
3 I'd like to 'w' ask you 'w' a question.
4 Let's go 'w' over the main points again.

6 Ask Ss to complete the conversations with three words in each gap. Ss can work in pairs to do this, referring to the previous exercises to help them. Give them plenty of time, then go through the answers as a class, asking pairs to read out the conversations.

Answers: 1 purpose of the 2 good to see 3 got a copy
4 make a start 5 first item on 6 Has everyone met

Listening 2

7a 🔊 **7.15** Ask Ss to read through the statements, then tell them they will hear three more extracts from the meetings they heard before. Play the audio and ask Ss to mark the statements true (T) or false (F). Ask Ss to check together, then go through the answers.

Answers: 1 a F b T   2 a T b F   3 a T b F

Audioscript 7.15

Meeting 1
B: … so anyway, that's my view.
A: Thanks, Beatrice. So, in short, you think that hiring a hotel for the party is going to be too expensive?
B: Yeah, I think so. The prices can be quite high, particularly in the centre of town.
A: Yep, that's a good point. Um, Caspar, what are your thoughts?
C: Well, I did have one idea …
B: But of course there are hotels on the outskirts of town which are more reasonably priced and …
A: Let me interrupt you there, Beatrice. I want to give everyone a chance to speak and we haven't heard from Caspar yet.
B: Sorry.
C: Yeah, I was just saying that I had one idea which is to hold the party on a riverboat.
A/C: That's an interesting idea! / Nice idea!
C: There are a few to choose from and they hold about 50 people, which is enough for the party and the good thing is they aren't too expensive.
A: Nice idea. Caspar, do you think you could research some prices for us and email that information to everyone?
C: Sure.
A: And Beatrice, maybe you could see if there are any hotels that are within our budget?
B: Do you mean on the outskirts of town?
A: Preferably not. The town centre would be better.
B: Well, as I said, I don't think there are any in the centre of town that are within our budget. You see, the rent that hotels have to pay is really high and they've got the cost of all their staff, too. My aunt and uncle used to run a hotel and …
A: Um, I think we're getting off topic, Beatrice. It's interesting stuff but we've only got 15 minutes left and there are still a couple of items on the agenda.
B: Oh, sorry.
A: No problem. Now, I'd like to move on to the next item on the agenda. That's the cost of …

Meeting 2
F: … what I loved about this restaurant was the fish. It was so firm and tasty. Delicious! Yeah.
E: So, basically, Francesco, that restaurant gets your vote.
F: Yes, definitely.
E: Great. So, I think we have a winner for best restaurant, but we'll come back to a vote later on. OK, moving on, let's talk about the best café. Gina, any thoughts?
G: Well, I think that Lizzie's Café is outstanding. It makes the best coffee in town and it does some really interesting lunch dishes as well. There's nowhere else like it, actually.
E: Interesting! What does everyone else think about Lizzie's Café?
G: And of course, the decoration is wonderful! It reminds me of the cafés that I used to go to with my father when I was a girl. There was one particular café I remember which had the most delicious cakes …
E: Let's stay on topic, Gina. We've still got a lot to get through!
G: Oh, yes, sorry.
E: Let's get someone else's input. Harriet, I'd like to hear your views on this. What do you think is the best café in town?
H: Well, I have to agree with Gina, really, Lizzie's Café gets my vote. It's definitely the best café in town.
E: Francesco?
F: Great café, great food … apart from the pasta. They just don't cook it quite right! I could definitely give them a few tips on how to cook pasta.
E: Well, let's save that for another meeting! Apart from the pasta, is Lizzie's Café still your favourite café?
F: Well … yes, I guess it is. I like The Bakery Café too, but I think Lizzie's Café is better.
E: Well, that looks like a winner, but we'll take a vote at the end of the meeting. OK, let's move on to the next category. The best hotel in town. There are several we need to discuss …

Meeting 3
J: … so, we're losing a lot of people because they can't find what they want on the home page.
I: So, just to summarise, you're suggesting that we change the home page?
J: That's right.
I: All right. Do you think you could talk to the website designer, Jessica, and see how much that'll cost?
J: OK.
I: Then we can discuss it again at the next meeting. Now, moving on, you've got some ideas for social media, haven't you, Frank?
F: Well, not really social media. It's more that I wanted to talk about the blog. I wanted to propose a series of blogs about the effect of the new …
I: I'll have to stop you there, Frank. We decided not to talk about the blog today. Let's save that for another meeting.
F: But it's all part of the website.
I: You're right, but we just don't have time. Keith needs to go at 10.30.
K: Yeah, sorry.
F: Oh, yeah, OK.
I: Thanks. Has anyone else got any quick thoughts about how to improve the social media?
J: Actually, yes, I do. What I was thinking was that we should …

b Ask Ss to listen again and complete the sentences, then go through the answers.

Answers:
1 **a** interrupt you   **b** move on to
2 **a** else think   **b** save that
3 **a** to summarise   **b** you could

c Ask Ss to check their answers with the Useful phrases box.

8 Tell Ss there is one mistake in each conversation related to the language of the lesson. It could be grammatical or lexical. Complete the first one together, then ask Ss to continue alone, then in pairs. Go through the answers. If you have access to a projector, project the text and highlight the changes on the board.

Answers:
1 B: I think we're getting **off** topic, Leo.
2 B: … so, just **to** summarise, you want to get the mayor's opinion?
3 A: OK, thanks Sandro. Let's get someone else's input. Eva, what are your **thoughts**?
4 A: Any more thoughts? No? OK, moving **on**, let's talk about the date of the next meeting.
5 B: **Let** me interrupt you there, Sofia. I'd like to move on to the next item on the agenda.
6 B: Thanks Elise. Alma, I'd like to hear your views **on** this.

Speaking

9a Tell Ss they are going to roleplay a meeting. Put Ss in groups of three and name them A, B and C. Ask Ss to turn to the relevant pages and read their role cards carefully, making a few notes on which phrases they could use. When they finish planning, ask groups a few general questions to check that they know their roles: *Which of you is Fran? Who is Lex? What's the meeting about? Who is leading it?*

> **Teaching tip**
> Information-gap activities, where Ss in pairs or groups have slightly different but related information, are very good for developing Ss' communication skills. The element of the unknown makes the classroom conversation more like a real-life conversation. To maintain the information gap, it's important for Ss not to show each other their role cards. Checking that everyone knows their role and clarifying who speaks first are helpful classroom management ideas that enable the activity to begin smoothly.

b Ask Ss to start the roleplay. Monitor and listen to how they are using the phrases.

10 Give some feedback on the language used, then ask Ss to swap roles and repeat the roleplay. They will need a little time to read their new role first.

> **Reflection on learning**
> Write the following questions on the board:
> *In what situations do you think you could use this language in the future?*
> *Do you feel your listening and speaking skills are getting better? Why (not)?*
> Put Ss in pairs to discuss the questions. When they have finished, ask a few Ss to share their ideas with the class, but don't force them to if they'd rather not.

Homework ideas
Workbook: Ex 1–5, p55

Roadmap video
Go online for the Roadmap video and worksheet.

7A Develop your reading

Introduction
The goal of this lesson is for students to understand websites and longer texts. To help them achieve this, they will focus on recognising cohesive devices.

Warm-up
Ask Ss if they consider themselves to be organised and good at preparing or if they are more of a 'last minute' person. Ask them to discuss whether they make lists before shopping, prepare a bag the night before travelling or plan meals in advance. Tell Ss this lesson is about *preppers* and ask if they know what they are (see Culture notes below).

Culture notes
Survivalism is primarily a North American concept. Individuals who actively prepare for emergencies such as natural disasters call themselves **preppers**. They stockpile goods, learn survival skills and prepare to become self-sufficient in the event of a catastrophe.

1 Ask Ss to discuss the questions in pairs. When they finish, have whole-class feedback and write useful vocabulary on the board.

2a Tell Ss they're going to read a website article about preppers. Refer Ss to the three options and ask them to read and tick the thing(s) that preppers believe. Tell **weaker classes** there is only one thing. Give them just a few minutes for this to encourage fast reading, then ask pairs to share ideas before you elicit the answer.

Answer: 1

b Tell Ss they will now read the text again more carefully to answer the questions. Give them a few minutes. Tell them there will be vocabulary they don't know and you will look at this later, so they shouldn't use dictionaries or devices. In feedback, ask Ss to compare answers, then go through them as a class.

> **Teaching tip**
> To help Ss focus on specific information tasks, tell them to first underline any question words which appear in the questions and think about what kind of answer will be expected. For example: *How many* – the answer will be a number; *Who* – the answer will be a person or group of people; *Why* – the answer will be a reason. If you think your class will benefit, try this technique with this reading task.

Answers:
1 to help people learn how and why to prepare for a disaster
2 They should prepare for them in order to survive. They can happen anywhere and at any moment. There are many different kinds to prepare for and they are becoming more common.
3 people who live in urban areas
4 assess the risks in their area ('take stock of your situation')
5 water
6 enough for at least a month; food with a long shelf life
7 so that you can leave very quickly, with no notice ('at the drop of a hat')
8 between one and three (at home, in the car, at work or school) per person

3 Ask Ss to find phrases 1–8 in the article, then use the context to match them with meanings a–h. Elicit the answers. In feedback, discuss which phrases are fixed and which can be substituted. (1, 2, 6 and 7 are fixed but 3, 4, 5 and 8 can be substituted: *take stock of your life*, *you won't last five minutes*, *a day's worth of food*, *take a detailed look at*.)

Answers: 1c 2g 3d 4b 5e 6h 7a 8f

Vocabulary checkpoint
Point out the register (formality or informality) of new vocabulary: *mod cons* and *get real* are both more likely to be spoken English. However, *take stock of a situation* and *take an in-depth look* are more formal. Ss could go through their notebooks and mark F or I where they recognise vocabulary to be formal or informal.

4 This task checks understanding of some phrases in the article. Ask Ss to work alone and choose the correct purposes, using the context to help them. They should choose the correct letter, then check in pairs. Don't go through the answers yet as Ss will use the Focus box for this.

5a Ask Ss to read the Focus box, find the phrases from Ex 4 and check their answers. With **weaker classes**, go through the Focus box as a class, reading sections aloud and allowing time for questions.

Answers: 1a 2c 3c 4b 5b 6c 7a

b Refer Ss back to the article and ask them to find and underline any other phrases from the Focus box. When they finish, check answers. If you have access to a projector, project the text and underline the phrases there.

Answers: Not just … but … too (paragraph 2)
in other words (paragraph 6)   namely (paragraph 6)

6 Ask Ss to complete the summary by adding cohesive devices from the Focus box. Move around the class to prompt and support. Clarify that more than one option is often possible for each gap. Have whole-class feedback and let Ss know when other options are possible.

Answers:
1 such as/for instance/for example
2 To put it another way/In other words/The point is that
3 instead of/rather than
4 These days
5 especially/in particular/namely
6 as I mentioned/as stated
7 in particular

7 This is an opportunity for Ss to comment on what they have read. Put Ss in small groups to discuss the questions. When they finish, have whole-class feedback and encourage open discussion. Use a show of hands to find out whether more people think preppers are sensible or overcautious.

Homework ideas
Workbook: Ex 1–5, p56

7B Develop your writing

Introduction
The goal of this lesson is for students to write notes during a conversation. To help them achieve this, they will focus on using abbreviations in notes.

Warm-up
Tell Ss you're going to give them some information and they should listen carefully and make notes. Include some facts and figures in your information and say it quite rapidly, for example: *20 people are needed for a health survey. They need to visit the hospital twice a week, on Mondays and Wednesdays, for a month. They should be between 40 and 60 years old.* When you finish, ask pairs to discuss and compare notes. Ask for feedback. Discuss what can help when making notes (using abbreviations, symbols, etc.) and tell them this is the focus of today's lesson.

1 Put Ss in pairs to discuss the questions for a few minutes. When they finish, ask a few pairs for their ideas. Ask for a show of hands to see who thinks they have a good memory. Discuss why they think that.

2 🔊 7.5 Ask Ss to look at the three sets of notes. Explain that the notes are about a surprise party and that they should listen and decide which notes are best, A, B or C. Give them a few minutes to read them over, then play the recording. Pairs should compare answers and discuss what might be wrong with the other notes. Conduct whole-class feedback, discussing reasons for Ss' choices.

Answers:
B is the best.
A is too short to be useful. There is not enough detail to remember what, for example, 'neighbours' means.
C has too much detail. The notes are in complete sentences and it is not usually possible to write complete sentences while you are taking part in a conversation.

Audioscript 7.5
A: Hey! How's it going?
B: Yeah, not bad, thanks. Actually, I was thinking about organising a surprise party for our teacher next Friday. What do you think?
A: A surprise party? Is it her birthday?
B: Yeah. It's an important one as well. It would be really nice to do something special for her.
A: Yeah, sounds like a good idea. Do you want me to give you a hand?
B: Yeah, that would be great. There's too much for one person to do. Do you think you could take on some of the jobs on my to-do list?
A: Sure. Hang on, let me get a pen and paper … OK. What do you want me to do?
B: Well, the first thing is to find a venue for the party. I was thinking either in the park over the road, but that's not ideal because it'll probably rain on Friday, or …

A: Or?
B: Or ... your apartment?
A: My apartment?
B: Yeah. It's big enough and it's quite close and ...
A: OK, I'll check with my neighbours, especially the downstairs family. It's quite a big favour to ask but I'll see what they say. How many guests will there be?
B: Good question. There are 20 people on the course but, if some people can't come and others bring a friend, I reckon it'll be about 25 people.
A: OK. I'll talk to my neighbours.
B: I think we should have a bit of food. Nachos, dips, sausage rolls, that kind of thing.
A: Not sausage rolls. The teacher is vegetarian and so are half the class.
B: Good point.
A: Is there a budget?
B: I was thinking of asking for a contribution from people who come – about £2 each.
A: So, let's say a budget of approximately £50 but probably a bit less because some people always forget to pay.
B: Yeah, that makes sense. Can you organise the snacks, then?
A: Yeah, OK. Are we going to send out invitations?
B: Yes! Could you put together something on the computer?
A: Well, I'm not very good at that kind of thing, but I'll give it my best shot. What needs to be on the invitation?
B: Well the date, the time, the venue and your phone number in case people need to call. That's all, I think.
A: OK, I'll make a quick digital invitation and we can send it to people on the class chat app.
B: Great. Maybe you could make a birthday card at the same time?
A: A birthday card?
B: Yeah, something simple, you know, just a photo of the teacher and *Happy Birthday* and ...
A: OK, OK. Have you thought about a present?
B: I was thinking about a voucher. What do you think?
A: Sounds like a good idea. We could buy a voucher for about £20 and then there'd still be money for food and drinks.
B: Great. Could you organise that voucher?
A: Me again?
B: Yeah? Why?
A: OK.
B: Now, we can't have a party without decorations. Have you got anything we could use?
A: I've got some lights and some balloons and stuff. I'll find those.
B: I was hoping you'd say that.
A: So, let me summarise. I'll ask my neighbours if we can have the party at my apartment, I'll organise the food, I'll send the invitations, I'll make a birthday card, I'll buy a voucher and I'll find the decorations. Does there seem to be anything wrong with that list?
B: Er ... I see what you mean.
A: Yeah?
B: We've forgotten the music! Maybe you could take charge of that. Are you any good at DJ-ing?
A: ... I'll think about it.

3a Refer Ss to the list and ask Ss to tick those types of words that are used in B in Ex 2. Elicit answers and deal with any questions. Point out that words like articles and auxiliary verbs are not needed because they don't carry meaning. Key words are likely to be information-carrying words like nouns and main verbs.

Answers: ✓ nouns, verbs, abbreviations

b Tell Ss to read the notes in B again and tick the techniques they find. When they finish, go through the answers as a class. If you have a projector, underline relevant parts of the notes as you go through feedback.

Answers:
✓ use bullet points to separate notes
✓ write the important facts or action points only
✓ use headings
✓ use full stops to show which words are abbreviations

4 Ss now practise the techniques seen. Look at the example together, then ask Ss to continue alone. With **weaker classes**, complete one or more further examples. Clarify that several answers may be possible. When you go through the answers, project the exercise onto the board if you are able to and add the notes there.

Possible answers:
1 ask everyone to sign card
2 invite other teachers
3 take photo of teacher for card
4 approx. 10 extra guests at party
5 ask teacher favourite shop for voucher
6 teacher free Friday evening?
7 ask Renate to sing at party
8 ask Fred about party at his apartment

Optional alternative activity

Divide the exercise up, with some pairs doing 1–4 and others doing 5–8. They should check together before going through the answers. This is suitable for **weaker classes** or if time is short.

5 Ask Ss to read the Focus box and highlight any abbreviations in B in Ex 2. They should compare in pairs, then check as a class.

Answers: esp., approx., <, etc., NB, b/c, info., no., approx.

6 Ask Ss to discuss which techniques they use. Refer them back to the warm-up activity to see.

Optional extra activity

Ss take turns to give each other instructions and make notes. For example, they could give some directions or instructions involving numbers, times, etc.

7 Refer Ss to the notes, asking them to rewrite them using the techniques seen so far. Allow plenty of time for this, then go through the answers, accepting variations where they seem correct.

Suggested answers:
1 water garden esp. if no rain
2 NB water houseplants
3 turn on 1 light in living room at approx. 9 p.m.
4 turn on TV → people think house occupied
5 feed cat 2 x per day
6 give < 1 cup cat food
7 v. important: give cat water
8 not nec. keep junk mail
9 send Mr J photo of bills i.e. gas, electricity, etc.

Prepare

8a 🔊 7.6 Tell Ss they'll now listen and complete some partially written notes. Ss should read through the existing notes first, then listen and complete them.

b Ask Ss to compare notes in pairs. Go through the answers, writing them on the board. Answers are likely to vary.

Suggested answers:
1 dead mouse 2 x per week
2 2nd drawer in freezer
3 no other food!
4 water every day, esp. if dirty
5 hold by head/tail/after food
6 temp. every day, >24 degrees
7 1 x per week
8 at no. 32

Audioscript 7.6

A: Thanks so much for looking after my flat while I'm away. I feel so much better knowing that someone will be here to look after everything.
B: Yeah, no problem.
A: And look after my little snake, of course.
B: Wait a minute – did you say, 'snake'?
A: Uh-huh.
B: I didn't know you had a snake.
A: He's really friendly and very easy to look after.
B: Oh, OK. Well, you'd better tell me what I need to do, then.
A: OK, well, first of all: food. You need to feed him one dead mouse twice a week.
B: A dead mouse? How do I catch and kill a mouse?
A: You don't need to do that, silly. You can buy them from the pet shop. I've got a pack of 12 in the freezer, second drawer, so that will be enough while I'm away.
B: OK, a dead mouse twice a week. Just drop it into his tank?
A: That's right, once it's defrosted. And don't give him chocolate.
B: Chocolate?
A: Or any other kind of food. Just the mice.
B: No – other – food.
A: And please change the water in his tank every day.
B: Every day.
A: Yep.
B: All right, water – change – every day …
A: And just keep an eye on his water. Sometimes he makes the water dirty and then you have to change it anyway. Now, a word on handling. He loves it when you spend a bit of quality time with him. You know, pick him up, talk to him …
B: Pick him up?
A: You'll get used to it. But remember, don't hold him by the head or by the tail. Hold him by the middle section of his body.
B: What?!
A: You'll be fine! And don't pick him up if he's just eaten. That can be uncomfortable for him.
B: OK …
A: And check the temperature of the tank every day. Bertie is …
B: Bertie?
A: Yes, Bertie. Bertie is a cold-blooded animal, so he can't generate his own heat. If the tank goes below 24 degrees centigrade, it can be dangerous for him.
B: OK, check temperature every day. Must be more than 24 degrees.
A: Now one last thing. Please could you clean the tank once a week.
B: How?
A: Just pick up Bertie and put him in this box. Then you can clean the tank with a cloth. If you have any problems, you can talk to Maggie at number 32.
B: Is she a vet?
A: No, but she knows a lot about snakes.
B: Right then. Is that it?
A: That's it. And don't look so worried! You and Bertie might become friends …

Write

9a 🔊 7.7 Now Ss will make notes themselves. Read the instruction together and ask Ss to make notes as they listen. Play the recording.

b Ask Ss to compare notes in pairs and discuss how they could be improved. Go through the answers as a class.

> **Possible answers:**
> Test = 60 percent, NB only just pass
> **Advice**
> 1 tenses = important, esp. past simp. & pres. perf., NB when sth happened → past simp.
> 2 prepositions = ✓
> 3 reporting verbs = ↓, e.g. accuse, admit, etc., NB recommend + verb + -ing
> 4 listening = ↑
> 5 speaking & writing = not so good, NB 1 x essay per week

Audioscript 7.7

A: OK, take a seat. So, how did you feel you did in the test?
B: Well, not so well really. I think I failed.
A: Well, I have your test results here. As you can see, you got 60 percent which is a pass. So, well done!
B: Oh! Thanks!
A: Having said that, it's only just a pass.
B: Yes, I understand.
A: I think you're capable of much more. So, I think you have some work to do before the next test in two months.
B: I think so, too.
A: So, are you ready for some advice?
B: Yes.
A: First, I think you need to work on tenses because you made a lot of mistakes here. You're still making some errors with the past simple and present perfect. Sometimes you use the wrong one. Remember, if you say when something happened, you use the past simple.
B: Er, OK.
A: In terms of prepositions – very good. Excellent knowledge of prepositions and phrasal verbs, not so good in terms of reporting verbs.
B: Reporting verbs?
A: Yes, *accuse, admit, deny, insist,* that kind of thing.
B: OK.
A: You got less than 50 percent correct, which is disappointing, especially compared with your last test where you got more than 70 percent correct.
B: What sort of mistakes am I making?
A: You're confusing the *-ing* form and infinitives. For example, after *recommend* we use the *-ing* form, but you used an infinitive.
B: OK, OK. So I should say, 'She recommended seeing the film', not 'She recommended to see the film'.
A: Exactly. Now, your receptive skills are good, especially listening. Your score is much higher than last time. But …
B: My productive skills are not good?
A: That's right, your speaking and writing scores were not so good, especially your writing, actually. Lots of room for improvement there. I think you need to write me an essay every week from now on.
B: An essay every week?!
A: Yes. I'll give you a list of topics, but I'd like to see an essay from you every week. That should help improve your writing. Now let's look at the essay you wrote in the exam …

Homework ideas

Workbook: Ex 1–7, pp.58–59

7c Develop your listening

Introduction

The goal of this lesson is for students to understand a radio programme. To help them achieve this, they will focus on recognising examples.

Warm up

Ask Ss if they ever tell lies and what reasons there could be for doing that. Give a few examples to focus their thoughts: a friend asks if she looks good in a new dress, a child asks about something that is hard to explain for their age, etc. Explain that a lie which is told to protect someone's feelings is called a *white lie*. Ask Ss to share more examples of white lies in pairs, then have brief whole-class feedback on their examples and experiences.

1 Ask Ss to look at the cartoon and discuss the question in pairs. After a few minutes, ask for feedback.

2 Ask Ss to read the quotes and answer the question. Discuss as a class. There are no fixed answers. When they finish, check which quote most people agree with using a show of hands.

3 🔊 **7.10** Tell Ss they are going to listen to the introduction to a radio programme. Ask them to read through the questions, then listen and make notes. Go through the answers as a class.

> Answers:
> 1 what the British say and what they actually mean
> 2 She is from São Paolo but now lives in the UK.
> 3 half past eleven or later

Audioscript 7.10

Here in São Paolo, one of the biggest cities on Earth, and where I come from, there are many things to get used to, including the sheer size of the place, the cosmopolitan vibe, the prices and of course the traffic. And if you're not Brazilian, you also need to get used to the difference between the time people say a party will start, and the time it actually starts. For instance, if a Brazilian person says, 'The party is starting at ten', what he or she really means is, 'Don't arrive before half eleven'. And even that might be a bit early!

However, every country has a habit of saying one thing but meaning another, as I found out when I moved to the UK four years ago. Take the phrase 'It's not bad', for example. Did you know that to a Brit that can mean anything from 'It's great' to 'It's awful'? I certainly didn't know that, and it caused me a lot of problems, as I'll explain.

4 Refer Ss to the Focus box and read it through, then play the recording again for them to complete the sentences. When they finish, put them in pairs to compare. Go through the answers as a class.

> Answers:
> 1 ... is starting at ten, Don't arrive before half eleven.
> 2 ... bad, great, It's awful

5a 🔊 **7.11** Tell Ss they'll now hear the rest of the radio programme. Give them time to read through the questions first and deal with any queries before playing the recording. They should listen and tick the correct option(s). Check the answers as a class.

> Answers: 1 b 2 a 3 c 4 a 5 a, c 6 c

Audioscript 7.11

I'm a graphic designer and when I first arrived in London I applied for several jobs. Each time I went for an interview, I came out feeling like a genius. The interviewers would look at my portfolio and say things like, 'We really like your work!', but ... I never got the job and I didn't know why. It was as though everyone was speaking a language that I didn't understand. It made me feel stupid.

It bothered me that I couldn't trust what people said. In the end, a British friend helped me to understand what was happening. It turned out that I was simply misinterpreting what people said. Politeness, he explained, is very much a part of the culture in Britain. This means that the British don't like to offend others or make them feel bad. So, when a person says, for instance, 'We really like your work', you don't know if they really like your work or if they hate it and they are just being polite.

So how do you know what someone actually means? Well, without knowing the person or being able to see their facial expression, it's often hard to tell, but there are some general rules you can follow. Take the phrase 'I'll call you', for example. What that really means is 'I'm ending the conversation'. As in most big cities, people in London are always in a rush and they often don't have time to call, but they like to think they do!

Another thing to understand is that understatement and overstatement are a big part of how the British express themselves. They tend to talk about big problems as though they're small and small problems as though they're big. For example, if someone looks at your work and says 'I just have a few minor comments', then you can be pretty sure that they have a lot of comments and what they really mean is something like 'Rip it up and start again'. Or another favourite of mine is when people say, 'There's been a slight change of plan!' A rough translation of this is 'Get ready, because the whole plan has changed'.

In other situations, politeness means that someone might seem to take responsibility for a problem, when really they think that you have made the mistake. To give an example, they might say, 'It's probably my fault', when what they really mean is 'It's definitely your fault'. In this situation the very worst thing you can say is 'Yes', because it shows that you think it's their fault, too!

And there are a few phrases you will hear quite a lot if you get into discussions with the British. For instance, when someone says, 'I hear what you're saying,' what they mean is that they disagree. A better translation might be, for instance, 'You're wrong, but I don't want to talk about it anymore'. The same meaning applies when someone says, 'I'll bear that in mind'. Both of these phrases are a convenient way of stopping a discussion before it becomes too heated.

Of course, not everyone is like this. In certain places it struck me that people were very direct. Each region in the UK has a different culture and each person has a particular relationship to that culture. However, over time, I've found that this British trait of saying one thing and meaning another is important enough to explain to visitors when they arrive from abroad, so that they avoid misunderstandings like mine.

So, every six months or so I go back to Brazil to see my friends and family and to feel 'normal' again. Sometimes I take a British friend with me and we go out into town together. 'Come round about ten', I say, but then I have to remember to add: 'Actually, I mean "Don't come round before half eleven and, even then, I might still be in the shower!"'.

b Ask Ss to listen again and complete the table. Play the recording, then tell Ss to compare answers in pairs before whole-class feedback. If Ss are in the UK (or have visited), ask them if they agree with the speaker.

> Answers:
> 1 I'm ending the conversation.
> 2 Rip it up and start again.
> 3 Get ready, because the whole plan has changed.
> 4 It's definitely your fault.
> 5 You're wrong, but I don't want to talk about it anymore.
> 6 You're wrong, but I don't want to talk about it anymore.

6 Ask Ss to work in pairs to discuss. Monitor and help with ideas and language as necessary. If you have a multilingual class, pair Ss with different nationalities to maximise discussion. When they finish, discuss as a class.

Optional extra activity

Ss prepare a guide to their country, with information for visitors on some of the points covered in this lesson. They can extend this to include advice on what to wear, what gifts to bring when visiting people's homes, etc. With multilingual classes, Ss can go on to make presentations to each other. With monolingual classes, they can prepare a wall display or write an article for a publication such as a student magazine.

Homework ideas

Workbook: Ex 1–3, p58

8 OVERVIEW

8A It's so predictable ...
Goal | talk about your favourite film/TV series
Grammar | second conditional
Vocabulary | events in films
GSE learning objective
Can give a detailed summary of a film including information about the plot, characters and setting

8B On the run
Goal | talk about other options and outcomes in the past
Grammar | conditionals in the past
Vocabulary | searching and hiding
GSE learning objective
Can talk about possibilities in the past with precision

8C Great art?
Goal | develop an argument for a class debate
Grammar | linkers of concession
Vocabulary | visual art
GSE learning objective
Can develop an argument well enough to be followed without difficulty most of the time

Check and reflect
Review exercises and communicative activities to practise the grammar, vocabulary and functional language from Units 7 and 8.

Roadmap video
Go online for the Roadmap video and worksheet.

VOCABULARY BANK
8A Film
8C Word building: the arts

DEVELOP YOUR SKILLS

8A Develop your listening
Goal | understand fast, unscripted speech
Focus | recognising when words are missed out
GSE learning objective
Can understand unscripted speech delivered quickly, if the accent is familiar

8B Develop your reading
Goal | understand the plot of a narrative
Focus | distinguishing background detail from main events
GSE learning objective
Can understand the plot of extended narratives written in standard, non-literary language

8C Develop your writing
Goal | write a review of a film or book
Focus | including relevant information
GSE learning objective
Can write a structured review of a film, book or play with some references and examples

8A It's so predictable ...

Introduction
The goal of this lesson is for students to be able to discuss their favourite films and TV series. To help them achieve this, they will revise second conditional and vocabulary relating to events in films.

Warm-up
Ask Ss if they watch films and where (home/cinema/phones). Ask pairs to write down as many words as they can connected with making films. Give them a two-minute time limit, then get a few pairs to read out their lists. Build a list of useful vocabulary on the board. Examples might include: *scene, location, script, cast, costumes, soundtrack, special effects, sequel*. Introduce the word *plot* (= the story of a film). Ask Ss if they can identify the films in the pictures on pp.62–63 and name the film genres and the basic plot. Discuss as a class.

Reading and vocabulary
Events in films

Culture notes

The films / film series shown are:
Slumdog Millionaire: Based on the 2005 novel *Q & A*, this is a British drama film starring Dev Patel and directed by Danny Boyle.
Mission Impossible: This is a series of American spy films, starring Tom Cruise.
James Bond: This series of British films, starting with *Dr No* in 1962, is based on the novels by Ian Fleming about a fictional spy called James Bond. The character has been played by many actors over the years, including Sean Connery and Daniel Craig.
Romeo and Juliet: Based on the Shakespeare play, this 1996 film transports the action to the modern day, starring Leonardo di Caprio.
Lord of the Rings: Based on the Tolkien novels, *Lord of the Rings* was adapted to a series of three fantasy films directed by Peter Jackson and filmed in New Zealand.

1 Make sure that Ss understand *predictable* (= you know what's going to happen). Ask Ss to discuss the questions in pairs. Monitor and help with new vocabulary where necessary. After a few minutes, elicit ideas and add any further useful vocabulary to the board.
2 Tell Ss they will read an article about plot types. Ask Ss to read the headings and check understanding of key words, then work alone to match the headings with the plot types. Tell Ss to check answers in pairs, then go through them as a class.

Answers: 1 d 2 b 3 a 4 c

Optional extra activity

Ask Ss to work in pairs to think of a film for each of the four plot types. When they finish, put two pairs together to take turns saying the film names. The listening pair identifies the plot types.

3a Focus attention on the words in bold in Ex 2. Ask Ss to replace them with the words in the box, changing the words as needed. Complete the first example as a class, then ask Ss to continue alone. When they finish, ask Ss to compare in pairs, then go through the answers as a class. Elicit and mark stress on any new words.

Answers: 1 confront 2 abandoned 3 overcome
4 trapped 5 tricked 6 betrayed 7 goes on a mission
8 captured 9 survive 10 face 11 rescued 12 murdered

> **Teaching tip**
> Vocabulary can be grouped together thematically in lexical sets, for example: furniture, sports, feelings, events in films (as in this lesson). Research shows that we find it easier to retrieve specific vocabulary items when they were first seen alongside other members in the same set. Encourage Ss to help associate vocabulary items by grouping them into positive or negative, or writing their own examples combining several items from the set: *The villains captured the victim and threatened to murder her, but luckily she was rescued and survived. After years of being betrayed and tricked, the hero finally faced her fears and confronted her enemy.*

b Ask Ss to ask and answer the questions using vocabulary from Ex 3a. **Weaker classes** can write the questions and answer them themselves, then work in pairs to discuss. Give an example of your own if you can. Monitor, correcting where needed.

c Ask Ss to take turns to talk about their favourite film or TV series, using the vocabulary from Exercise 3a. Monitor and help with expressions where necessary. When they finish, have a whole-class comparison and give feedback on any errors in the vocabulary by writing them on the board and asking Ss to correct them.

> **Optional extra activity**
> Show a montage of suitable film/TV images or provide a list of titles to help Ss with this stage. **Stronger classes** can do Ex 3c with the items in the box covered; **weaker classes** can refer to the vocabulary to help them.
> To focus further on the target vocabulary, ask listening Ss to tick the words in Ex 3a each time they hear them. The winner in each pair is the one who has used most of the target vocabulary.

VOCABULARY BANK 8A   p163
Film

This is an optional extension to the vocabulary section, extending the lexical set and providing further practice. If you're short of time, this can be done for homework.

1a Ask Ss to find six types of film in the box, using their instinct or devices/dictionaries. Then elicit answers as a class.

Answers: classic, documentary, fantasy, musical, science fiction, thriller

b Ask Ss to circle five other words in the box that are both nouns and verbs. Go through the answers and further clarify meaning as needed.

Answers: cast, plot, release, set, shoot

2 Ask Ss to choose the correct alternatives, then go through the answers as a class.

Answers: 1 release   2 musical   3 plot   4 documentary   5 soundtrack   6 costumes   7 cast

3a Ask Ss to discuss the film stills in pairs, using words from Ex 1, before whole-class feedback. There are no fixed answers. The film stills are from *The Favourite* and *The Third Man*.

b Ss work in pairs using the vocabulary from Ex 1 to describe a film they know. Encourage them to ask follow-up questions. When they finish, ask a few pairs to report back.

> **Further practice**
> **Photocopiable activities:** 8A Vocabulary, p232
> **App:** 8A Vocabulary practice 1 and 2

Grammar
Second conditional

4a 🔊 8.1 Tell Ss they're going to listen to three people talking about their favourite film. Ss should listen for the plot type each speaker mentions. Go through the answers. Ask Ss if they agree with each speaker about the type of plot.

> **Answers:**
> **Speaker 1** – Defeat the Monster
> **Speaker 2** – The Quest
> **Speaker 3** – Defeat the Monster

> **Audioscript 8.1**
>
> **Speaker 1**
> My all-time favourite film is *Castaway*. It stars Tom Hanks as Chuck, a guy who's trapped on a desert island after his plane crashes. He has no hope of being rescued and he feels abandoned by everyone. He has to overcome his fears in order to escape. It's a classic Defeat the Monster plot, where the monster is how to escape the island. If I was in his situation, I might stay on the island and wait to be rescued. I wouldn't be brave enough to try to escape!
>
> **Speaker 2**
> My favourite film is *The Hunger Games*. It stars Jennifer Lawrence as Katniss, a young woman who is forced to fight others in a violent contest in order to survive. She has to face various enemies who want to destroy her, but her biggest enemies are the ones who organised the contest. It's a classic Quest plot type because she is fighting so that she can keep her sister safe. If I were Katniss, I would fight for my life, too. Everyone wants to survive. Unfortunately, I don't think I would last very long.
>
> **Speaker 3**
> My favourite film is *The Shawshank Redemption*. It stars Tim Robbins as Andy, a man who is accused of a crime he didn't commit and locked up in prison for life. Still he tries to do good by starting a library. At one point he has the chance to prove his innocence, but he is betrayed by one of the guards. Near the end, Andy tricks the guards and escapes. It's a Defeat the Monster plot type. Were I to find myself in this situation, I don't know what I would do. I imagine I would try my hardest to escape.

b Ask Ss to listen again more closely to complete the sentences. Play the recording, twice if needed, pausing between speakers to allow time to write. Ask Ss to compare in pairs, then go through the answers, writing them on the board to ensure they are correct.

> **Answers:**   1 If I was   2 might stay   3 wouldn't   4 If I were   5 would fight   6 would   7 Were I   8 would do   9 would

5 Tell Ss you are going to use sentences from the listening to study some grammar. Ask them what the grammar point is (second conditional) and elicit what they can remember about the form and use. Then refer to the grammar box, asking Ss to read it through and complete it with sentences from Ex 4b. Ss can discuss in pairs before checking as a class. With **weaker classes**, project the exercise and complete it as a class.

> **Answers:**
> 1 If I were Katniss, I would fight for my life, too.
> 2 I imagine I would try my hardest to escape.
> 3 Were I to find myself in this situation, I don't know what I would do.

Grammar checkpoint

Ss will have studied conditionals before. They may want to discuss the difference between *If I were* and *If I was* and may have been told that one of these forms is wrong. Point out that *If I were* has traditionally been the preferred option, but that *If I was* has lately become an equally accepted form. Point out that *If you were* is correct, while *If you was* is a non-standard form. With inversion, *Were I* is the only option possible. When discussing the order of clauses, remind Ss that we don't need a comma when the result clause comes first. We only use a comma when the condition clause (*If* clause) comes first.

6a 🔊 **8.2** Ask Ss to listen to the sentences to notice the inclusion of the extra sound /w/ between *do/go* and *if*. If you think it's useful, explain the information in the Pronunciation checkpoint below, using the examples given.

Pronunciation checkpoint

This exercise looks at how we sometimes join a vowel sound at the end of one word to a vowel sound at the beginning of the next word with a /w/ sound. This feature of pronunciation is called intrusion. If Ss are interested, spend some time pronouncing the sentences both with and without the intruding /w/ sound – they should find it more difficult without the extra consonant.

b Ask Ss to chorally repeat the sentences after they hear them. You may want to mark the stress with your hand to help Ss repeat. As the sentences are quite long, Ss could also repeat in clauses.

7a This exercise practises the form. Look at the example together and complete the second one as a further example. Then ask Ss to continue alone, referring to the grammar box. Clarify that sometimes more than one answer may be possible. Ask Ss to check in pairs, then check answers with the whole class.

Answers:
1 a could choose, would choose   b to get bored, might choose
   c would, choose
2 a was/were able to steal, may find out   b would look
   c could find out
3 a would go, happened   b was watching, would need
   c would, do, found out

b Put Ss in pairs to ask and answer the questions in Ex 6a and 7a. When they finish, ask a few pairs to share one of their partner's interesting responses.

LANGUAGE BANK 8A   pp.150–151

Stronger classes could read the notes at home. Otherwise, check the notes with Ss. In each exercise, elicit the first answer as an example. Ss work alone to complete the exercises, then check their answers in pairs. In feedback, elicit Ss' answers and drill the questions. Ss can refer to the notes to help them.

Answers:
1 1 a   2 b   3 b   4 b   5 a   6 b
2 1 would   2 were   3 both   4 start   5 wouldn't   6 would
   7 did   8 both   9 offered   10 wouldn't

Further practice

Photocopiable activities: 8A Grammar 1, p230; 8A Grammar 2, p231
App: 8A Grammar practice 1 and 2

Speaking

Prepare

8a Tell Ss they are going to talk about a favourite film or TV series. Refer them to the bulleted list and ask them to make notes, using language from today's lesson. Move around the class and help with vocabulary as needed.

b Ask Ss to complete the sentence about their chosen film. Point out that *hero* is now often used for both male and female characters as *heroine* has traditionally been associated with a weaker character that is rescued.

Speak

9 Put Ss in pairs to tell each other about their films or TV series. Refer them to the Useful phrases. When they finish, ask each pair if they have heard about a new film or series they might like to see. Take a class vote on the one most Ss would like to see.

Optional extra activity

Choose a film as a class that Ss think they would enjoy, or perhaps one that they have seen in their language but not in English. Show the class the film poster or other film stills and promotional images. Ss in pairs write a description of the film, using the vocabulary of the lesson. Watch the film, or sections of it, as a class. Finally, Ss can write a review.

Reflection on learning

Write the following questions on the board:
How could watching films in English help you?
How was today's class different for you?
Put Ss in pairs to discuss the questions. When they have finished, ask if anyone wants to share their ideas with the class, but don't force them to if they don't want to.

Homework ideas

Language bank: 8A Ex 1–2, pp.150–151
Workbook: Ex 1–5, p60
App: grammar, vocabulary and pronunciation practice

Fast route: continue to Lesson 8B
Extended route: go to p93 for Develop your listening

8B On the run

Introduction
The goal of this lesson is for students to talk about other options and outcomes in the past. To help them achieve this, they will revise conditionals in the past and vocabulary about searching and hiding.

Warm-up
Write these sentence starters on the board and ask Ss to complete them:
*If I could live anywhere … If I was on a desert island …
If I had plenty of money …*
Put Ss in pairs to compare. In feedback, point out that these are imaginary situations, so Ss should be using second conditional forms.

Reading and vocabulary
Searching and hiding
1 Ask Ss to think about their answer, then discuss in pairs. When they finish, elicit ideas and ask Ss to justify them. There are no fixed answers.

2a Tell Ss they will read two stories about people trying to disappear and answer some questions. Give them five minutes to encourage focused reading, telling them to ignore the words in bold for the moment, then put them in pairs to compare and discuss. Elicit answers.

Answers:
1 that he had died in a plane crash at sea
2 Two navy jets spotted his plane. At the crash site, investigators found a book with missing pages, on which campsites were listed. They found Marcus at one of the campsites.
3 He set up a website with information about Patrick's case.
4 He traced Patrick through his IP address and asked someone else to make contact with him.

Optional alternative approach
Arrange Ss into AB pairs. As read text 1 and Bs read text 2. Pairs then take turns telling each other about what they read and answer the questions together. This may suit classes who would benefit from more speaking practice.

b Ask Ss to work in pairs and discuss the mistakes each person made. Elicit answers and ask Ss which person made the most or silliest mistakes.

Suggested answers:
Marcus didn't disguise himself. He left the book with missing pages in the plane. He didn't break the windscreen.
Patrick stayed in touch with friends. He logged on to the website a lot of times from the same place.

3 Refer to the words in bold in the stories. Ask Ss to discuss the meanings and match them with the definitions, using the context and their prior knowledge to help them. **Weaker classes** may need to use dictionaries. Go through the answers as a class and further clarify as needed.

Answers: 1 spotted 2 disguised 3 traced 4 headed for
5 pursue 6 keep an eye on 7 hunt for 8 deceive
9 identify 10 tracked

Vocabulary checkpoint
Ss may struggle with this task, as there are several similar words. Provide more information and examples to help Ss differentiate. Point out that *trace* means to go back and find someone or something that was lost, whereas *track* means to follow someone or something so that you always know where it is – sometimes secretly and/or with electronic equipment. People *track* parcels when they are being delivered, following their progress. They are not *pursuing* them. A police car might *pursue* criminals. People *hunt* animals in order to kill them, though we can also use *hunt* in a more general sense, meaning to look for something that is hard to find. Ss can record some examples to help them remember the distinctions. Point out that all the verbs in Ex 2 take regular past tense endings, apart from *keep (an eye on)*.

4a This activity enables Ss to personalise and practise the words in Ex 2. Ask Ss to work alone to complete the sentences. Monitor to help and correct. There is no need for whole-class feedback as Ss will all have different ideas, but if you see a lot of Ss are struggling to think of completions, go through ideas as a class to provide options for **weaker students** to copy.

b Put Ss in pairs to compare answers.

Further practice
Photocopiable activities: 8B Vocabulary, p235
App: 8B Vocabulary practice 1 and 2

Grammar
Conditionals in the past
5a Tell Ss you will use information from the stories in Ex 2 to study some grammar. Ask Ss to read the sentences, choose their answers, then discuss in pairs. Go through the answers as a class. This clarifies the concept of third conditional (imagining different outcomes in the past) so allow plenty of time to explore it if there is any uncertainty.

Answers: 1 a yes   b yes   2 a yes   b yes

b Ask Ss to read the grammar box carefully, then choose the correct alternatives. With **weaker classes**, ask individuals to read sections of the box aloud and complete the exercise together. Ask Ss to identify the conditional types in pairs, then check with the whole class.

Answers: 1 had (third conditional)
2 might have (third conditional)   3 wouldn't (mixed conditional)

Grammar checkpoint
Ss may not have come across mixed conditionals before. Point out that only second and third conditionals can be mixed, where either the cause or the result is in a different time frame. Look at the examples in the grammar box together and discuss some more linked examples like the ones below, so that Ss can see the distinction:

If he'd arrived on time, we'd have caught the train. =
he didn't arrive (past); we didn't catch the train (past) =
third conditional

If he'd arrived on time, we'd be in London now. =
he didn't arrive (past); we are not in London (present) =
mixed conditional

If he was a more punctual person, we'd have caught the train =
he is not punctual (present); we didn't catch the train (past) =
mixed conditional.

6 🔊 **8.6** Ask Ss to listen for the pronunciation of *would have* and *wouldn't have*. If you think it is useful, share the information in the Pronunciation checkpoint below.

Pronunciation checkpoint
Point out that as the auxiliary verb *have* is unstressed, /æ/ is reduced to a weak schwa sound /ə/. Additionally, /h/ is reduced or removed by the preceding consonant /d/ or /t/, as the words run together: /wʊdəv/ /wʊdəntəv/. Encourage Ss to pronounce these words as a single chunk, rather than two or three separate words.

7a Look at the description of the TV show and discuss as a class whether any Ss have seen a similar programme. Ss then work alone to complete the sentences, referring to the grammar box, then check in pairs. Check answers with the whole class.

Culture notes
On the Run is a mix between a reality TV show and a game show. The format of this type of show is that a team of two act as fugitives trying to run from highly skilled investigators. Each pair attempts to evade capture for a period from 48 hours to 28 days in a specific geographical region in order to win a cash prize. The programme is transmitted so members of the public can even get involved. Ss may know of other similar programmes such as *Hunted*.

Answers:
1 a ... taken her smartphone with her, the hunters wouldn't have caught her.
   b ... have caught her if she hadn't taken her smartphone with her.
2 a ... used his bank card in a shop, the hunters wouldn't have been able to track his location.
   b ... have been able to track his location if Evan hadn't used his bank card in a shop.
3 a ... survived for 21 days, she wouldn't be rich now.
   b ... be rich now if she hadn't survived for 21 days.
4 a ... seen the CCTV camera in the shop, he wouldn't have gone in.
   b ... have gone in if he had seen the CCTV camera in the shop.
5 a ... become the viewers' favourite, he wouldn't be working as a model now.
   b ... be working as a model now if he hadn't become the viewers' favourite.

b Look at the first sentence starter with the class and discuss possible completions using both mixed and third conditionals. Then ask Ss to write the three sentences for themselves. When they finish, have whole-class feedback to see if Ss have similar answers.

Teaching tip
This short activity enables Ss to make their own connections with the target language. Personalisation and creating memories in language is part of effective learning. Include personalisation stages to help Ss feel that they are expressing their real selves in English. While sometimes Ss may prefer to copy, writing their own meaningful examples has more impact on their retention of new language. Sharing the ideas aids the social dynamic of the classroom.

LANGUAGE BANK 8B pp.150–151
Stronger classes could read the notes at home. Otherwise, check the notes with Ss. In each exercise, elicit the first answer as an example. Ss work alone to complete the exercises, then check their answers in pairs. In feedback, elicit Ss' answers and drill if needed. Ss can refer to the notes to help them.

Answers:
1 1 e, h 2 a, f 3 c, g 4 b, d
2 1 hadn't robbed, wouldn't have arrested
   2 hadn't released, might not have emailed
   3 might not have been caught, hadn't emailed
   4 wouldn't have used, weren't/wasn't
   5 hadn't committed, wouldn't have

Further practice
Photocopiable activities: 8B Grammar 1, p233; 8B Grammar 2, p234
App: 8B Grammar practice 1 and 2

Speaking
Prepare
8 Tell Ss they are going to be contestants in the show *On the Run* that they read about in Ex 7a. Put Ss in pairs, name alternate Ss A and B, then tell Ss to turn to the relevant pages, read their information and do the quiz together.

Speak
9 When they finish the quiz, have whole-class feedback to see who made the most good decisions. Discuss whether Ss would like to participate in this kind of show and why (not).

Reflection on learning
Write the following questions on the board:
What would you do if you hadn't studied English?
How have you overcome any weaknesses? What strategies can you share?
Put Ss in pairs to discuss the questions. When they have finished, ask if anyone wants to share their ideas with the class, but don't force them to if they don't want to.

Homework ideas
Ex 4: Ss write an article about someone who tried to disappear. It can be a real news story or an invented one.
Language bank: 8B Ex 1–2, pp.150–151
Workbook: Ex 1–4, p61
App: grammar, vocabulary and pronunciation practice

Fast route: continue to Lesson 8C
Extended route: go to p110 for Develop your reading

8C Great art?

Introduction
The goal of this lesson is for students to develop an argument for a class debate. To help them achieve this, they will revise linkers of concession and vocabulary related to visual art.

Warm-up
Put Ss in pairs or small groups to name at least two types of art (sculpture, painting, ceramics, photography, drawing, filmmaking, etc.) and two places where you can see art (at a gallery, in the street, in people's homes, etc.). When they finish, elicit ideas and add useful vocabulary to the board. Tell Ss that this is today's topic.

Reading and vocabulary
Visual art
1 Ask Ss to discuss the questions in pairs. Give them a few minutes, then go through their answers as a class. There are no fixed answers.

2 Refer to the box and ask Ss to use the words to answer the questions. With **weaker classes**, you may want to look at the pictures together and pre-teach/check some of the vocabulary shown.

> **Suggested answers:**
> 1 **A** an installation **B** a sculpture, a statue
>   **C** a watercolour, a still life **D** a portrait, an oil painting
>   **E** a landscape, a sketch **F** a landscape, an oil painting
>   All: an original artwork
> 2 an abstract artwork, an original artwork, a portrait, a landscape, a still life, a watercolour, an oil painting
> 3 an abstract artwork, a sculpture, an installation, an original artwork, a statue

Optional extra activity
Make a set of cards or self-adhesive notes containing vocabulary from Ex 2. Give each student (or pair) a card. Ask them to check the meaning of their word, then write a definition for it. They can use their devices if necessary. Tell Ss/pairs to take turns reading out their definitions. Listening Ss try to guess which word is being defined.

3a Ask Ss to read the texts and find the five pieces of information in each one. Ask them to work alone and make notes.

b Put Ss in pairs to compare, then go through the answers.

Answers:

Artist	Name of artwork	Type of artwork	Surprising fact	Other details
Dove Bradshaw	Fire Extinguisher, 1976	original artwork/ installation	Dove didn't make it, only labelled it.	Dove became well-known.
Sara Goldschmied and Eleonora Chiari	Where shall we go dancing tonight?	installation	It was thrown away by the cleaners.	It increased the artists' fame.
Damien Hirst	Spot paintings	abstract painting	Hirst's assistants have painted almost all of them.	There are more than 1,400 of them. Some have sold for millions of dollars.

4 This is an opportunity to personalise the topic and practise the vocabulary. Refer Ss to the questions and ask them to discuss. When they finish, compare answers as a class. There are no fixed answers.

VOCABULARY BANK 8C p163
Word building: the arts
This is an optional extension to the vocabulary section, extending the lexical set and providing further practice. If you're short of time, this can be done for homework.

1 Ask Ss to complete the table in the appropriate categories, using their instinct or devices/dictionaries. Then elicit answers as a class.

Answers: 1 art 2 artistic 3 composition 4 composer
5 edit 6 editor 7 entertainment 8 entertainer
9 entertaining 10 illustration 11 illustrator 12 painting
13 painter 14 photograph 15 photograph
16 photographer 17 produce 18 producer
19 productive 20 publish 21 publisher 22 sculpture

2 Ask Ss to choose correct forms of words from Ex 1 to complete the texts. Ss can work alone, compare in pairs, then go through the answers as a class.

Answers:
1 paintings, artistic, sculpture, sculptors
2 photographers, photographic, illustrative
3 entertainment, entertaining, composers
4 published, editor, illustrators

3 Ask Ss to discuss in pairs using vocabulary from Ex 1. Encourage them to ask follow-up questions. When they finish, ask a few pairs to report back.

Further practice
Photocopiable activities: 8C Vocabulary, p238
App: 8C Vocabulary practice 1 and 2

Language focus
Linkers of concession
5a Refer Ss to the two pairs of ideas. Ask them to look at Text 1 and locate the linkers that connect each pair of ideas. Confirm the answers and ask Ss to identify the function of the words (linking two ideas that contrast).

Answers: 1 Even though 2 although

b Ask Ss to look for more linkers of concession in Texts 2 and 3, then check their answers in the Language focus box.

Answers:
Text 2: However, Despite
Text 3: in spite of, Nevertheless

Grammar checkpoint

Ss may not have studied conjunctions of concession in detail before. Point out that *in spite of* and *despite* need to be followed by *the fact (that)* when preceding a clause (subject + verb): *although it was raining = despite the fact (that) it was raining*. Alternatively, *in spite of* and *despite* can be followed by a simple noun or *-ing* form: *despite the rain, in spite of having enough money*. Ss should also note that *of* is only used with *in spite* but not *despite*: *in spite of the rain = despite the rain*.

Though is less formal than *although* and *even though* and is the only one that can come at the end of a sentence. *Even though* is somewhat more emphatic. *Although* is the most neutral.

6 🔊 **8.7** Ask Ss to listen and underline the words they hear. Check their answers. With **stronger classes**, Ss can try and write the whole sentence.

Answers: 1 in spite of 2 although 3 despite 4 though

Audioscript 8.7

1 His name is on each painting in spite of the fact that he didn't paint any of them.
2 She became very famous, although only after she died.
3 She became well-known for the work despite not making it.
4 He bought it though he knew it was a fake.

7 Ask Ss if they have heard of Banksy (see Culture notes below). Read the instruction as a class and look at the first example. Ss work alone to complete the other sentences, using the linker in brackets and referring to the Language focus box. Ask Ss to check in pairs before going through the answers with the whole class.

Culture notes

Banksy is an anonymous British street artist who has used street graffiti to make powerful social and political commentary in the UK and around the world. As a consequence, his work has become very popular in the art world and has sometimes sold for large prices after being removed from its original street location. The infamous 2018 shredding of one of his artworks was probably a social comment by Banksy on the commercialisation of his work, but sadly it had the opposite effect as the value of the work went up and not down! See Optional extra activity below for more information on the shredded artwork.

Answers:
1 Banksy painted it onto a wall in London despite the fact that it is illegal to do this.
2 Gradually the image became well-known. Nevertheless, Banksy's identity remained a secret.
3 In 2014 it was removed and sold in spite of the fact that it was graffiti, not a painting. / In spite of the fact that it was graffiti, not a painting, in 2014 it was removed and sold.
4 It was then sold for £500,000, even though Banksy painted it for free. / Even though Banksy painted it for free, it was then sold for £500,000.
5 *Girl with Balloon* came top, although it's a relatively modern artwork. / Although *Girl with Balloon* came top, it's a relatively modern artwork.

Optional extra activity

Ask Ss what they think of *Girl with Balloon* and graffiti art in general. Ask Ss if graffiti is a growing art form in their country or if they know of other countries where it has social or artistic importance.

Describe the rest of the story of *Girl with Balloon*: In 2018 a framed copy of the image was sold at auction for over £1,000,000. As soon as it was sold, the picture self-destructed by shredding itself. Banksy had installed a shredder in the frame when he created it in 2006. The image was renamed *Love is in the Bin* and is the first artwork in history to be created live during an auction.

LANGUAGE BANK 8C pp.150–151

Stronger classes could read the notes at home. Otherwise, check the notes with Ss. In each exercise, elicit the first answer as an example. Ss work alone to complete the exercises, then check their answers in pairs. In feedback, elicit Ss' answers. Ss can refer to the notes to help them.

Answers:
1 1 I've never understood abstract art, **even though** I studied art at college.
   2 ✓
   3 The new installation was quite **popular. However,** it was removed after only three weeks.
   4 **Despite the brilliant colours/Despite the fact that the colours are brilliant**, we find this landscape quite depressing.
   5 Van Gogh's paintings are really vibrant in spite of **the fact that he was** such an unhappy person.

Further practice

Photocopiable activities: 8C Language focus 1, p236; 8C Language focus 2, p237
App: 8C Language focus practice 1 and 2

Listening

8a 🔊 **8.8** Tell Ss they are going to hear part of a debate on contemporary art. Ask Ss to listen and note the three main arguments, then check as a class.

Answers:
1 Real art involves a lot of craft or skill, contemporary art doesn't.
2 Real art makes us feel real emotions, contemporary art doesn't.
3 Real art is not about money, contemporary art is.

b Tell Ss to listen again and note the examples given to support each argument. Point out that they are listening for names of artists and artworks.

Answers:
1 Rembrandt's *The Night Watch*, da Vinci's *Mona Lisa*, van Gogh's *Sunflowers*
2 a sculpture that looks like a block of concrete
3 van Gogh

Audioscript 8.8

Ladies and gentlemen, I'm going to be honest with you. I don't like contemporary art. I don't get it and I certainly don't want to go to an art gallery to look at it. Why pay money to go and look at something my five-year-old niece could have done? In my view, almost all contemporary art is not real art.

What are the qualities of real art? Even though it is hard to define art, we know that real art has a high level of craft or skill that an ordinary person cannot achieve. Ask yourself this: could you have painted Rembrandt's *The Night Watch*? Could you have painted da Vinci's *Mona Lisa*? Could you have painted van Gogh's *Sunflowers*? The answer is certainly no and the reason is that those artists had skill. That is why they were great artists. They used that skill to create their work and they worked on paintings for long periods of time. They were masters of their craft.

What else does real art do? Well, for one thing it makes us feel certain emotions and, although we can't explain them, they are very real. It expresses ideas that we can't quite put into words. It contains a whole world of information in one image. In spite of sometimes being beautiful, contemporary art does not do this. When you see a sculpture that looks like a block of concrete, what do you think of? Personally, I think of nothing apart from 'Why did the artist make that?'

Thirdly, it goes without saying that real art is not about money. When van Gogh was alive, he didn't paint for money. In fact, he only sold one painting in his lifetime. He painted because he was an artist and he had to express himself. Contemporary artists, however, have one eye on their art and the other on their bank balance. Why else would you put a squiggle on a piece of paper and then try to sell it?

In summary, ladies and gentlemen, we strongly believe that contemporary art is not impressive or thought-provoking or moving or any of those things. To put it simply, despite being shown in famous galleries, contemporary art is not real art.

Speaking

Prepare

9a Tell Ss they are going to have a class debate. Discuss what debates involve (see Culture notes below). Put Ss in groups and ask each group to think of a statement or use the one provided. Each group must then divide into two teams and decide which team will argue for and which will argue against the chosen statement.

Culture notes

A **debate** is a formal discussion on a statement or **motion**, with one side arguing for and the other arguing against the motion. The two sides take turns to make and dismiss each other's points in an organised structure which is much less fluid than an ordinary conversation. A debate is usually managed by a chairperson. Parliamentary debates take place before important votes, to help ministers decide how to vote.

b Working in their teams, tell Ss to prepare some arguments and examples for their side of the debate. If they are debating the statement provided about Hollywood films, help them as needed with the ideas below. Move around the class and help the teams.

Optional extra activity

Feed in these ideas for the statement 'Hollywood films are the greatest form of art.':

For
1 Most Hollywood films take years and millions of dollars to make.
2 They are far more popular than any other kind of art.
3 They tell stories that we can all understand and relate to.
4 They require a lot of skill and hundreds of people to make.
5 Great films are still popular after decades.

Against
1 Hollywood films are entertainment, not art.
2 Most of them don't make us think deeply.
3 Films tell us what to think and feel. Real art doesn't do that.
4 The only aim of films is to make money.
5 Hollywood films won't be popular in 200 years, unlike Shakespeare or Picasso.

c Refer teams to the Useful phrases. Ask them to decide on an opening statement and a conclusion for their side of the debate.

Speak

Optional extra activity

Elicit some rules and procedures for organising a debate:

General rules
1 Everyone on your team must speak.
2 Listen to the other team as they speak, but don't interrupt.

Procedure
1 The first team gives its introduction.
2 The other team gives its introduction.
3 The first team gives its main arguments.
4 The other team gives its main arguments.
5 The first team gives its conclusion.
6 The other team gives its conclusion.
7 Members of the audience say which arguments they found the most persuasive.

10 Ask teams to decide what each team member will say and when. They can also use this time to review and amend their notes. Move around and help them with this stage.

11 Ask groups to take turns to debate in front of the class. The rest of the class decide which team/argument was most convincing.

Optional alternative activity

It could be quite time-consuming and potentially stressful for all groups to debate in front of the class. If your class is very large, you may prefer to have all the groups debating at the same time. If so, keep time by telling all the groups that they have two minutes to make their first point, two minutes to take the first round of questions, and so on. Groups should all finish at the same time and then reflect on how they did. If one or two groups want to, they can repeat the debate for the whole class.

Reflection on learning

Write the following questions on the board:
How will this lesson be relevant to you in the future?
What area of language would you like to spend more time on?
Why is it important for you?

Put Ss in pairs to discuss the questions. When they have finished, ask if anyone wants to share their ideas with the class, but don't force them to if they don't want to.

Homework ideas

Ex 4: Ss write a description of an artwork.
Language bank: 8C Ex 1, pp.150–151
Workbook: Ex 1–6, p62
App: grammar, vocabulary and pronunciation practice

Fast route: continue to Check and reflect
Extended route: go to p130 for Develop your writing

8 Check and reflect: Units 7–8

Introduction

Ss revise and practise the language of Units 7 and 8. The notes below provide some ideas for exploiting the activities in class, but you may want to set some exercises as homework or use them as a diagnostic or progress test.

1 Ss match the words and examples alone, then check in pairs. In feedback, ask Ss to read the words and phrases out so that you can check pronunciation.

Answers: 1 e 2 i 3 b 4 j 5 f 6 a 7 d 8 h 9 c 10 g

2 Ss find and correct the mistakes alone, then check in pairs. Check answers with the whole class.

Answers:
1 As soon as this problem *is solved*, another one will emerge.
2 ✓
3 As soon as computers *are able to/can* think, they'll take over our lives.
4 ✓
5 There will always be conflict *unless* humans radically change.
6 You'll understand this grammar *if* you study hard. / You won't understand this grammar unless you study hard.

3a Ss use the jumbled words in bold to write the sentences in the correct order. Go through the answers as a class.

Answers:
1 I will definitely go ...
2 It is possible that I will be ...
3 I am wondering whether to travel ...
4 I will probably live ...
5 It is unlikely that I will earn ...
6 I may well move home ...
7 I am planning to change ...

b Ss discuss the sentences in pairs, saying which are true for them. Encourage them to ask follow-up questions to find out more information.

4 Look at the instructions as a class. With **weaker classes**, do the first one together as an example. Ss choose the correct verbs, then decide on the form. Check answers with the whole class.

Answers: 1 make, taking 2 give 3 took, did 4 giving 5 did, give 6 done, make 7 take

5 Ss complete the text alone using the words provided, then check in pairs. Check answers with the whole class.

Answers: 1 brother-in-law 2 distant 3 classmates 4 flatmates 5 co-workers 6 senior colleagues 7 acquaintance 8 client

6a Ss choose the correct alternatives in a–e alone, then match responses a–e with the sentences 1–5. Tell Ss to compare answers, then check with the whole class.

Answers: 1 d, strikes 2 a, that 3 e, occurs to 4 b, though 5 c, amazes

b Ss practise the conversations in pairs. **Stronger classes** can do this first with their books open and then with their books closed.

7 Ss match the sentence halves to make correct sentences. Check the answers as a class.

Answers: 1 b 2 g 3 a 4 c 5 d 6 h 7 f 8 e

8a Ss use an appropriate form of the words in the box to complete the conditional sentences. They can check in pairs before checking answers as a class.

Answers: 1 could be 2 Would ... walk, weren't enjoying 3 found, would ... keep 4 to win, would give 5 saw 6 didn't have/couldn't have

b Ask Ss to choose three of the questions to ask a partner. **Fast finishers** can ask more. When they finish, ask a few pairs to share interesting answers.

9 Ss choose the correct alternatives alone, compare in pairs, then check the answers as a class.

Answers: 1 keep an eye on 2 spotted 3 tracked 4 disguise, deceive 5 traced 6 hunting

10 Ss should read the sentences carefully to find the mistakes. Point out that only two sentences are fine. Go through the answers as a class.

Answers:
1 If Fred hadn't invested all his money in the wrong shares, he *wouldn't have* lost it.
2 If he had known the price of the shares would crash, he *could have invested in* something else.
3 ✓
4 His wife might not have left him if he *hadn't lost* everything.
5 ✓
6 He would never *have* got into this mess if he had listened to his father's advice.
7 He *would* probably still be with his family if he hadn't been so greedy.

11 Ask Ss to match the descriptions with the words. Ss can try alone, then help each other before going through the answers as a class.

Answers: 1 g 2 a 3 d 4 h 5 c 6 b 7 e 8 f

12 Ss should underline the linker and replace it with a correct one. Clarify that there may sometimes be more than one option. Go through the answers.

Answers:
1 Though/Although/Even though he was in his sixties ...
2 However/Nevertheless/Despite this/In spite of this, he produced ...
3 Despite/In spite of the high price ...
4 ... despite the fact that she can't paint.
5 Although/even though Beethoven ...
6 Despite/In spite of being famous ...

13 Ss match the sentence halves to make correct sentences. Go through the answers as a class.

Answers: 1 e 2 j 3 g 4 c 5 h 6 b 7 a 8 i 9 d 10 f

Reflect

Ask Ss to rate each statement alone, then compare in pairs. Encourage them to ask any questions they still have about any of the areas covered in Units 7 and 8.

Roadmap video

Go online for the Roadmap video and worksheet.

8A Develop your listening

Introduction

The goal of this lesson is for students to understand fast, unscripted speech. To help them achieve this, they will focus on recognising when words are missed out.

Warm-up

Ask Ss in pairs to make a list of what they do when meeting up with a group of friends (visit the cinema, go to the park, have coffee, etc.). After a few minutes, elicit their ideas. Introduce the term *book club*. Ask Ss if they know what one is and whether they'd like to join one. Explain that today's lesson will feature a book club.

Culture notes

A **book club** (or book group) is a group of people who meet regularly to talk about a book that they have all read. There is no fixed format, but most groups meet in each other's homes and have a drink or meal, as well as discussing the book they have chosen for that meeting. Groups range in size but the average is probably six to eight people. Often book clubs are not very serious – they tend to be much more about socialising than literature!

1 Ask Ss to discuss in pairs. After a few minutes, conduct brief feedback and see if there are any books or TV series which are particularly popular.

2a Tell Ss they are going to read some book club conversations and decide if the comments are positive or negative. Ask Ss to look at the conversations and mark them P or N. Assure them they don't need to fully understand the underlined expressions as you'll look at them later. Go through the answers.

Answers: 1 negative 2 negative 3 positive 4 positive

b Ask Ss to match the underlined phrases in Ex 2a with the meanings. Point out that one meaning matches two phrases. Ask Ss to compare in pairs, then go through the answers as a class. Point out which phrases are used only for books (*a real page-turner, can't put it down*).

Answers: 1 far-fetched 2 can't put it down
3 relate to/identify with 4 can't get into it 5 left me cold
6 struck a chord (with me) 7 a real page-turner

3 8.3 Ask Ss to listen to the conversations from Ex 2a and cross out any words that are not said. Ask them to compare in pairs, then go through the answers. If you have access to a projector, project the conversations and cross out the missing words there. Ask Ss why they think the words are missed out.

Answers:
1 A: Hey, ~~have~~ you read *Tricked and Betrayed*? What did you think of it?
   B: ~~I'm~~ not sure really. ~~I~~ just can't get into it for some reason. ~~I~~ can't relate to the main character.
2 A: So, ~~did~~ you like that book I lent you?
   B: ~~Do~~ you mean *Abandoned*? ~~It~~ left me cold, actually. ~~It was~~ a bit far-fetched, I thought.
3 A: ~~Are~~ you reading this book? What do you think of it?
   B: ~~It's~~ a real page-turner, isn't it? ~~I~~ can't put it down.
4 A: ~~Have~~ you read this?
   B: ~~I'm~~ reading it at the moment, actually. The main character – wow! ~~She's~~ really struck a chord with me. ~~I~~ can identify with her a lot.

4 Refer to the Focus box. Ask Ss to read it through carefully and answer the question. Go through the answer as a class, discussing what kinds of words are missed out and whether meaning is affected (it isn't).

Answer: auxiliary verb in questions, verb *be* in questions, verb *be* and subject in answers, *it* + verb in statements with *'s* or *was*.

Vocabulary checkpoint

Ss may notice how we use *a bit* to soften criticism before a negative comment, as in the example *It was a bit far-fetched*. Ask Ss to write some more examples.

5a 8.4 Tell Ss they will hear three more conversations and they should listen and complete them, writing down exactly what the speakers say. Ss can compare in pairs to help each other after they listen.

b Play the recording again before you go through the answers as a class.

Answers: 1 great book 2 Like it? 3 Not sure 4 's a bit
5 You seen 6 What series 7 's called 8 Amazing
9 What're you 10 Read it 11 's not my

Audioscript 8.4

1
A: Oh, *Love's Winter* – great book. Like it?
B: Not sure, really. 's a bit romantic for me.

2
B: You seen that new series on Netflix?
A: No. What series?
B: 's called *Lost in London*. Amazing!

3
A: What're you reading?
B: *Red Lines*. Read it?
A: No. 's not my cup of tea.

6 8.5 Ask Ss to listen to another book discussion and choose the correct alternatives. Explain that they should underline the correct answers, then discuss their ideas in pairs. Go through the answers as a class.

Answers: 1 *Lotta's Luck* 2 Richardson 3 future
4 spy thriller 5 positive 6 positive 7 negative

Unit 8

Audioscript 8.5

F: So, Rhona, what did you think of it?
R: The book? *Lotta's Love*?
F: *Lotta's Luck*.
R: Sorry, *Luck*...
F: Yeah...
R: To be honest, I was a bit sceptical before I read it...
F: Oh, why?
R: Don't know really, Felix. I'd read a book by the author before...
F: Richardson?
R: Yep, Richardson, and I just couldn't get into that one.
F: OK...
R: And maybe also because I read a review beforehand and it just didn't sound like my kind of book. Sounded a bit far-fetched...
F: You thought it was far-fetched?
R: Before I read it, yeah. It just sounded ... unbelievable and I didn't think I could relate to a book about someone who's kidnapped and held hostage at some unspecified point in the future. But anyway, it turned out I was wrong.
K: You liked it?
R: Loved it! A real page-turner. I just had to know what happened next...
F: Me too! So glad you liked it.
R: I really couldn't put it down.
F: Yeah, I've been a fan of Richardson's work for a long time...
R: Really?
F: Yeah, totally, so I was a bit taken aback, too, by the description, you know, before it came out. You a fan of Richardson, Khalil?
K: She usually writes family dramas, doesn't she?
F: Yeah, quiet, thoughtful family pieces...
K: Yeah, thought so ...
F: ... this sort of 'spy thriller' type thing, set in the future was, like, completely out of the blue. But, just like Rhona, I totally loved it. Like she says, a real page-turner.
K: Sounds like I'm going to be the only voice of doubt here. Didn't like it, I'm afraid. Just couldn't get into it, you know ... left me cold!
R: Left you cold?
K: Yes ... sorry!
R: I don't care, of course, I mean you're perfectly entitled to your opinion but, yeah, just wondering what you thought of Lotta, really.
K: Lotta?
R: Yeah, I mean, amazing character, don't you think? I just identified with her so much ...
K: You felt you had something in common with her?
R: Yeah, I mean, never been kidnapped, never held hostage but as a person I really identified with her. Such a believable character.
K: No, didn't feel that at all ...
F: I did, totally – she really struck a chord with me. I mean, likewise, never been kidnapped, but there was something about Lotta which was so universal, so believable. I had to find out what happened to her because somehow it really mattered to me.
K: Good character, for sure. You know there's something very interesting about her but ... she annoyed me a lot!
R/F: Oh no!
K: ... and p'raps that's why the book left me cold. She kept making these stupid decisions that got her into trouble and each time I thought: well, duh! What do you expect when you make a decision like that?
R: Oh, no, no, no, too harsh on her.

7 Remind Ss of their discussion in Ex 1. Ask pairs to think of a book, film or TV series they both know and discuss it, using the language from today's lesson. Model an example conversation with a **stronger student** first.

Optional extra activity

Ss work in pairs to write reviews or blurbs for a book, film or TV series they have both seen or read, using the language from today's lesson. These can be used to create a wall display or class magazine.

Homework ideas

Workbook: Ex 1–5, p63

8B Develop your reading

Introduction

The goal of this lesson is for students to understand the plot of a narrative. To help them achieve this, they will focus on distinguishing background detail from main events.

Warm-up

Ask Ss to make a list of book and film genres and talk about the ones they enjoy most. Discuss their ideas as a class. Introduce core vocabulary for **weaker classes**, such as detective story, novel, romance, thriller, etc.

Culture notes

A **hacker** is a person who is highly skilled in the use of computer systems, sometimes one who illegally obtains access to private communication systems. Hackers hack into someone's computer or phone or hack into a company's or government's computer system – perhaps for profit, political statement or to compromise a security system.

1 Ask Ss to discuss the questions in pairs. After a few minutes, conduct brief feedback.

2 Ask Ss to suggest what 'white hat' and 'black hat' hackers could be, adding their ideas to the board. Then give them one minute to read the text and check their ideas. Go through the answers together and tick off any ideas mentioned on the board.

Answers:
White-hat hackers are legal, black hat hackers are illegal.

3 Ask Ss to read the novel extract and mark the statements T or F for true and false, then compare in pairs. Go through the answers as a class.

Answers: 1 T 2 F 3 T 4 F 5 T 6 F

4 Ask Ss to find and underline the phrases in the text, then use the context to match them to the meanings. They can write the letters beside the numbers, then compare answers in pairs. Go through the answers as a class and deal with any queries. Point out that *menacing* is an adjective.

Answers: 1 e 2 d 3 f 4 a 5 c 6 b

5a Refer to the Focus box and read it through as a class, with individual Ss reading sections aloud. If possible, draw a timeline on the board to show how the tenses interact, using examples from the story. Ask Ss to work alone to order the events of the story.

b Tell Ss to compare answers in pairs, then check as a class.

Answers: 1 g 2 j 3 h 4 d 5 c 6 e 7 b 8 i 9 a 10 f

Optional alternative activity

Enlarge and photocopy the events of the story and cut them into strips. Provide each group of four Ss with a set of sentences. Ask them to discuss and put them in order. This kinaesthetic task can promote discussion and it's easier for Ss to make changes to the order as they go. When they have finished and you check the answers, Ss can take a photo of the correct order and try and arrange the sentences on a timeline.

6a Put Ss in pairs to discuss what will happen next. Give them a few minutes, then elicit ideas as a class. Write suggestions on the board.

b Tell Ss they will now read the next part of the story to check their predictions. Ask Ss to turn to p172 and read. When they finish, refer back to the board and tick off any predictions that were correct.

c Ask Ss to work in pairs to write a brief summary of the story. When they finish, they can read these out to another pair who decide if any important details have been missed out.

7a Ask Ss to work in pairs and discuss the scenarios. **Weaker classes** may benefit from writing their responses first, then telling a partner.

b Ss discuss in pairs. When they finish, have a whole-class discussion of their ideas.

Optional extra activity

Ss work in pairs or groups and write the next section of the story. They pass their story to another group who evaluate it, including the accuracy in use of tenses.

Homework ideas

Workbook: Ex 1–5, pp.64–65

8c Develop your writing

Introduction

The goal of this lesson is for students to write a review of a film or book. To help them achieve this, they will focus on including relevant information.

Warm-up

Put Ss in pairs and ask them to discuss how they choose these things: a film to watch, a night out, a book to read, a place to take a holiday. When they finish, take feedback on their ideas. If the word does not come up in feedback, introduce the idea of *reviews*.

1 Put Ss in pairs to discuss the question. After a few minutes, conduct brief feedback and write useful vocabulary on the board.

2a Ask Ss to read the two reviews and answer the questions. Give them a few minutes, then ask them to discuss in pairs. Conduct whole-class feedback.

Answers:
1. the story
2. Auggie Pullman
3. a boy who looks very different and is starting school after years of being taught at home
4. We sympathise with and understand him.
5. Each frame of the film is an oil painting.
6. Armand
7. Van Gogh's final months as revealed through the conversations Armand has with the people who knew Van Gogh.
8. The reviewer thinks the plot is less important than the visual impact of the film. He also thinks it is, in some respects, clever.

Optional alternative activity

Half the Ss read the review of *Wonder* and the other half read the review of *Loving Vincent*. They then pair up to tell each other about the text they have read and work on the questions together. This does not take less time, but involves more speaking so is a good approach for Ss who enjoy talking and need to develop speaking skills. **Fast finishers** can also read their partner's text.

b Ask Ss to discuss the questions, checking that they are aware of the idea of star ratings (see Culture notes below). Allow a few minutes for this, then check ideas as a class. Have a show of hands to find out which of the two most Ss would prefer to see/read. There are no fixed answers.

Culture notes

Online reviews by members of the public are common for all products and services. The star rating system is usual, with five stars being the best and one star the worst. Public reviews are similar in format to professional ones but tend to be less formal in tone. Sometimes online reviews are manipulated, i.e. people are paid to post several reviews or even false ones. Sometimes a book can 'go viral' due to online reviews.

3 Ask Ss to read the Focus box, then decide whether each review is successful. Put them in pairs to discuss, underlining relevant sections of the reviews, then take whole-class feedback. If you have access to a projector, project the texts so that you can underline and annotate them. Point out how the present simple passive is used in the reviews.

Answers: Answers may vary, although Ss should note that both reviews meet the requirements of the Focus box so are broadly successful.

Optional extra activity

Ask Ss to underline the adjectives in the two reviews they read (*simple, striking, extraordinary, stunning, genuine, mesmerising*, etc). Spend time working on appropriate adjectives that Ss could use in the reviews they will write later, for example: *melodramatic, one-dimensional, stereotypical, thrilling, confusing, tense, unconvincing, action-packed, compelling, unoriginal*.

You can also provide useful review phrases such as: *You feel as though…; It is told from the perspective of…; the plot centres on…; the story unfolds in…; gives an exceptional performance…; not to be missed…; an impressive debut…; a moving portrayal*

4 Ask Ss to look at the reviews again and match each paragraph with its purpose. Point out that there are only four paragraphs in each review, so one purpose is not needed. Ss can compare answers before you go through as a class.

Answers: 1 d 2 e 3 a 4 c

Prepare

5 Ask Ss to choose a book or film that they know and would like to review. Look at the notes as a class, then give Ss a few minutes to complete them. Point out that *author* is for books and *director* is for films. Move around the class and offer help with language and ideas.

6a Ask Ss to write sentences about their book/film by completing the appropriate additional notes. Monitor and help, then ask pairs to compare and support each other.

b Ask Ss to write the first line of their review. Refer them back to the two example reviews and discuss how they have an impact on the reader.

Optional extra activity

Watch a film as a class before completing reviews of it. Pre-teach essential vocabulary that Ss might need which is relevant to the chosen film. Use the cover and opening credits to find out key facts such as the length, age rating, director, cast, etc.

Write

7a Ask Ss to work alone and write the first draft of their review. Monitor and help with ideas and vocabulary if necessary. When they finish, ask pairs to exchange drafts and make comments, using the Focus box as a guide.

b Ask Ss to write a second draft, incorporating their partner's suggestions for improvement.

Homework ideas

Workbook: Ex 1–9, pp.66–67

9 OVERVIEW

9A   Mysteries
Goal | speculate about unsolved mysteries
Grammar | past modals of deduction
Vocabulary | mystery
GSE learning objective
Can speculate about causes, consequences or hypothetical situations

9B   Strange theories
Goal | plan and give a convincing argument
Grammar | verb patterns
Vocabulary | knowledge
GSE learning objective
Can plan what is to be said and the means to say it, considering the effect on the recipient

9C   Celebrity
Goal | describe a personal experience
Grammar | phrasal verbs
Vocabulary | common phrasal verbs
GSE learning objective
Can bring relevant personal experiences into a conversation to illustrate a point

9D   English in action
Goal | explain a problem and ask for action
Vocabulary | describing problems with products and services
GSE learning objective
Can explain a problem and demand what action should be taken in an appropriate way

VOCABULARY BANK
9B   Confusing pairs of words
9C   Nouns formed from phrasal verbs

DEVELOP YOUR SKILLS

9A   Develop your listening
Goal | understand fast, scripted speech
Focus | understanding pauses in speech
GSE learning objective
Can understand scripted speech delivered quickly, if the accent is familiar

9B   Develop your writing
Goal | write a simple discursive essay
Focus | structuring a simple discursive essay
GSE learning objective
Can write a simple discursive essay

9C   Develop your reading
Goal | predict content from headlines
Focus | understanding newspaper headlines
GSE learning objective
Can make inferences or predictions about the content of newspaper and magazine articles from headings, titles or headlines

9A   Mysteries

Introduction
The goal of this lesson is for students to speculate about unsolved mysteries. To help them achieve this, they will revise past modals of deduction and vocabulary in the context of mystery.

Warm-up
Before the class starts, bring a bag containing several small objects and say that you found it in the hall and you don't know who it belongs to. It's a mystery. You could include a lipstick, a bus pass, car keys, an empty water bottle, etc. Ask Ss to take the things out one by one and discuss what they tell you about the person's identity and actions. This is a chance to preview the grammar to be taught, as well as the topic. If they use past modals, observe errors but don't correct them yet. Tell Ss today's class is about mysteries.

Reading and vocabulary

Mystery
1 Ask Ss to make a list in pairs. When they finish, ask for their ideas and write useful vocabulary on the board.

> **Possible answers:**   national identity document, passport, birth/marriage certificate, utility bills, biometric data (iris/face/fingerprint recognition, DNA)

2 Refer Ss to the pictures and ask them to discuss in pairs how they could relate to the story of the Somerton Man. Go through ideas as a class, writing useful vocabulary on the board. Then ask Ss to read and check their ideas.

> **Answers:**
> A Police found a suitcase belonging to the Somerton Man at the railway station. It contained neatly folded clothes.
> B He had a bus ticket in his pocket showing that he had travelled from Adelaide railway station to the beach.
> C The Somerton Man had strong calf muscles characteristic of a sports person or dancer.
> D The Somerton Man's face appeared in the newspapers, but no one came forward to identify him.

Culture notes
Somerton is a suburb of Melbourne, Australia. The Somerton Man really existed. He was discovered in 1948 and the story of his identity has challenged people ever since. If Ss are interested, there is a cartoon which tells the story here:
https://thenib.com/who-was-somerton-man
and more information here:
https://en.wikipedia.org/wiki/Tamam_Shud_case
Other more recent identity mysteries include Piano Man, who was found on a UK beach in 2005, but alive and appearing to have lost his memory. Ss may know other stories, too.

3a With **weaker classes**, you may want to pre-teach/check *red herring* (see Culture notes below). Put Ss in pairs and give them a few minutes to talk about the words in the box. **Weaker classes** can look words up on their devices. Monitor and help with new vocabulary. When they finish, ask Ss to match the words in the box with the phrases in bold. Go through the answers as a class, asking Ss to read out each sentence with its substitution.

Answers: 1 clues 2 evidence 3 identify him 4 turned out 5 motive 6 account for 7 victim 8 remains a mystery 9 a hoax 10 red herring

Culture notes

A **red herring** is distracting information that takes attention away from the main problem or issue: *The candidate used the minor issue as a red herring to distract voters from the corruption accusations against him.* Mystery writers and detective stories often introduce red herrings to arouse readers' suspicion of innocent characters. The literal meaning of a red herring is a type of smoked fish with a strong smell, which historically was used to divert hunting dogs and put them on the wrong path.

b Ask Ss to read the article again and decide if the sentences in Ex 3a are true, false or not enough information is given. They should mark each one T, F or NI. With **weaker classes**, tell Ss that in four cases not enough information is given. Get Ss to compare in pairs, then go through the answers as a class.

Answers: 1 T 2 T 3 F 4 NI 5 T 6 T 7 F 8 NI 9 NI 10 NI

c Ask Ss to suggest ideas for the unusual detail. Discuss as a class. There are no fixed answers, but Ss will find out what the detail is in the Listening section (a scrap of paper in his pocket).

Optional extra activity

Ss write the next paragraph of the article in pairs, with an imagined continuation of the story. They read their continuations aloud to the class and decide which are the best or most likely.

Further practice

Photocopiable activities: 9A Vocabulary, p241
App: 9A Vocabulary practice 1 and 2

Listening

4a 9.1 Tell Ss they are going to hear some more information about the Somerton Man. Ask them to read through the sentences and then listen and correct them, as in the example.

Teaching tip

When Ss are listening, stay still as moving around can distract them. You can observe from your seat instead. Once the recording stops, ask Ss to compare answers and, while they are doing this, monitor and observe how they have done. This will help you decide whether another listen is needed or not.

b Ask pairs to compare after they listen and agree on the corrections. While they do so, monitor and check how well they have done and play the recording again if needed. Go through the answers as a class.

Answers:
1 The Somerton Man's secret pocket contained a scrap of paper.
2 The words were from a book of eleventh-century/very old poetry.
3 Someone had found the book in his car.
4 No one has been able to work out what the 50 letters mean.
5 Jessica Thompson was a nurse.
6 Jessica refused to talk about the Somerton Man.
7 In 1945, someone else died with a book of old poetry next to them.
8 Jessica's son, Robin, was born before the Somerton Man died (in 1947).

Audioscript 9.1

The Somerton Man, as he came to be called, would probably have been forgotten were it not for one unusual detail. When the dead man's clothes were searched again a few weeks later, the coroner found a secret pocket in his trousers. In the secret pocket was a scrap of paper. It was from a page that had been ripped out of a book. There were two words on the scrap of paper and those two words were *Tamám Shud*.

Tamám Shud! What could it mean? Well, it turned out that those were the last two words from a very old poem that had been written by an eleventh-century poet called Omar Khayyám. The page had come from a book of Omar Khayyám's poetry and the words meant *It's finished* or *The end*.

Soon after, something even stranger happened. A man walked into a police station and told police that he had found a copy of Omar Khayyám's poetry in his car. Someone had thrown it through the window of his car around the time the Somerton Man died. The last page had been ripped out.

The man gave the book to the police and indeed, the scrap of paper that had been found in the Somerton Man's secret pocket was from the page ripped out of that book. At last it seemed that the police had a clue to the identity of the Somerton Man.

Inside the back cover of the book someone had written some letters and a phone number. The letters, 50 in total, were in five groups and they seemed to have no meaning. To this day, no one has been able to crack the code, if indeed it is a code. Perhaps the letters are just a secret shopping list or a red herring.

However, the phone number led police to a young woman called Jessica Thompson. Jessica was a nurse. Police asked Jessica if she knew Omar Khayyám's poetry. She did. It turned out she had given a book of his poetry to a friend but, as police later confirmed, the friend was still alive.

However, the police then showed Jessica a model of the Somerton Man's head. When Jessica saw it, she nearly fainted. Then she refused to talk about it anymore.

The death of the Somerton Man remains a mystery to this day, but more strange facts have since come to light. For example, it turns out that three years earlier, in 1945, an Australian man called George Marshall died with a copy of Omar Khayyám's poetry next to him. The victim had apparently been poisoned, although there was no clear motive for his murder, if indeed it was murder.

Another strange fact is that the nurse, Jessica, had a son, Robin, who was born in 1947. Robin turned out to be a talented dancer and he also had unusual teeth.

5 Ask Ss to discuss what they think happened. When they finish, have a whole-class discussion of their ideas.

Optional extra activity

Add Ss' suggestions for what happened to the board, using the base forms of the verbs, for example: *be murdered, kill himself, get lost, have a heart attack, be poisoned, run away*. These ideas can then be revisited after they have had the grammar focus, using the correct modal verbs for deduction. Depending on your class, Ss can either write sentences (**weaker classes**) or go straight to saying the sentences using past modal verbs.

Grammar

Past modals of deduction

6 9.2 Tell Ss they are going to listen to some people giving their opinion about what happened to the Somerton Man. Ask them to read the incomplete sentences, then listen and complete them. Ask Ss to check in pairs, then go through the answers as a class. Write them on the board so that Ss can check their spelling is correct (see Grammar checkpoint below).

Answers: 1 must have been 2 could have visited 3 may have been 4 must have been 5 can't have been 6 might not have been

Grammar checkpoint
Ss may think that *have is* in fact *of*, because it sounds that way. For this reason, it's important to write the answers to tasks around this grammar on the board. It's fine for Ss to pronounce *have* as *of* if they find it easier, as long as they are aware of the correct written form.

7 Ask Ss to read through the grammar box, selecting the correct alternatives. With **weaker classes**, do this as a class. Go through the answers and deal with any queries.

Answers: 1 is 2 isn't 3 possibly 4 -ing

8a 9.3 Ask Ss to listen and mark the stressed words in each sentence. Ask Ss how *have* is pronounced. Point out that the main stress falls on the modal and the main verb, so the auxiliary verb *have* is weak.

Answers:
A: Do you <u>think</u> he <u>might</u>'ve <u>been</u> a <u>dancer</u>?
B: Yeah, I <u>think</u> he <u>must</u>'ve <u>been</u> a <u>dancer</u>.
A: But do you <u>think</u> he <u>could</u>'ve <u>been</u> a <u>spy</u>?
B: Well, yeah, he <u>could</u>'ve <u>been</u> a <u>spy</u> as <u>well</u>.
have is pronounced /əv/

b Ask Ss to listen again and repeat chorally.

9 Write the first sentence on the board and ask Ss to choose the correct alternative using the context to help them. Then ask Ss to work alone to choose the remaining alternatives. When Ss finish, they can compare answers in pairs before going through them as a class. Ask individual Ss to read each answer aloud in a sentence and drill where needed, focusing on the weak form of *have*.

Answers: 1 could have 2 couldn't have 3 might not have
4 can't have 5 must have 6 may have

10 Ask Ss to discuss in groups. **Weaker classes** may benefit from writing a few sentences with modals of deduction first. Close the activity by asking each group for any similar or shared ideas they had. (If Ss want to know more about the Somerton Man mystery, refer them to the links provided in the Culture notes for Ex 2 above.)

Optional extra activity
Ask groups of Ss to write and then say their sentences describing what might have happened to the Somerton Man to the class. Tell them to include one that is not grammatically correct. Classmates indicate whether each sentence is correct or not with a show of hands. This encourages Ss to listen to each other as well as analyse the grammar.

Teaching tip
Ss benefit from listening to each other, not just to the teacher. When you ask Ss to share their ideas with the class, give a listening task to help them focus their attention. This also builds a positive classroom dynamic. For the same reason, when calling on Ss for answers, avoid going round the class in a predictable order. This ensures Ss are listening as they don't know when they will be called on!

LANGUAGE BANK 9A pp.152–153
Stronger classes could read the notes at home. Otherwise, check the notes with Ss. In each exercise, elicit the first answer as an example. Ss work alone to complete the exercises, then check their answers in pairs. Ss can refer to the notes to help them.

Answers:
1 1 can't/couldn't have
   2 might/could/may have
   3 must have
   4 could/might/may have
   5 could/might/may have
   6 can't/couldn't have
2 1 must have come (in) through the ceiling
   2 could/might/may have been children
   3 can't have taken (any) big items
   4 can't have used the wrong details
   5 could/might/may have got lost
   6 could/might/may have stolen the money

Further practice
Photocopiable activities: 9A Grammar 1, p239; 9A Grammar 2, p240
App: 9A Grammar practice 1 and 2

Speaking
Prepare
11 Tell Ss they are going to find out about another unsolved mystery. Put Ss in pairs, tell them to choose one of the three mysteries and then turn to the relevant page to read about it. Monitor and help with any unknown vocabulary.

Speak
12a When they are ready, ask pairs to speculate about what they think happened in their chosen mystery. Refer them to the Useful phrases and tell them to ask questions during their discussion to check their theory. Remind them that this activity is to practise past modals of deduction. Monitor and help if necessary.

Optional alternative activity
Divide the class into three groups, A, B and C. Allocate a different mystery text to each group. When all Ss finish reading, regroup them into ABC groups. Ss then take turns telling each other about what they read and explaining their theory. Finally, each ABC group decides on the most intriguing mystery and best theory. This allows more speaking time but requires less reading.

b When they finish, ask pairs to present their theories to the class. Ss vote on the most convincing theory.

Reflection on learning
Write the following questions on the board:
What could you have done better in this lesson?
What do you want to spend more time on? Why is it important for you?
Put Ss in pairs to discuss the questions. When they have finished, ask if anyone wants to share their ideas with the class, but don't force them to if they'd rather not.

Homework ideas

Ex 11: Ss write a paragraph about one of the mysteries from today's lesson.
Language bank: 9A Ex 1–2, pp.152–153
Workbook: Ex 1–5, p68
App: grammar, vocabulary and pronunciation practice

Fast route: continue to Lesson 9B
Extended route: go to p94 for Develop your listening

9B Strange theories

Introduction
The goal of this lesson is for students to plan and give a convincing argument. To help them achieve this, they will revise verb patterns and vocabulary about knowledge.

Warm-up
Before the class starts, ask Ss to work in pairs and write the names of the planets. When they finish, elicit as many planet names as you can and ask Ss what they know about the solar system, focusing on Earth (it's the third planet from the sun; it has one moon; it rotates once every 24 hours; it orbits the sun once every 365 days, etc.). Ask Ss how we know these things (science) and if knowledge has changed throughout history. Elicit that some people used to think Earth was flat, and that today's lesson is about strange theories.

Reading

1a Ask Ss to discuss the questions in pairs. This will probably be a very brief discussion with no fixed answers. Discuss as a class.

Culture notes
Early Greek philosophers mentioned a spherical Earth. According to Diogenes, Pythagoras was the first to call Earth round in around 500 BC. Circumnavigation by Magellan and Columbus in the 16th century enabled further understanding of the shape of the planet.

b Ask Ss to read about flat earthers and then work together as a class to create some questions to ask a flat earther. Write these on the board.

2a Ask Ss to read the article and find answers to their questions from Ex 1b. Ask Ss to work alone to read the text, then allow Ss a brief check in pairs before feedback. Tick off any questions answered on the board.

Culture notes
NASA (National Aeronautics and Space Administration) is a United States agency responsible for the country's space programme. As well as enabling space exploration, including sending astronauts to the moon and the International Space Station, NASA is more widely concerned with education and developments in science.

b Ask Ss to read the article again more carefully to find the answers to the statements and mark them T or F. When they finish, ask Ss to compare in pairs, then go through the answers as a class.

Answers: 1 T 2 F 3 T 4 T 5 T

c Tell Ss to discuss the questions, first in pairs and then as a class.

Vocabulary

Knowledge

3a Focus attention on the words in the box and ask how they might be linked (they are about knowledge/science) and what kind of words they are (verbs). Ask Ss to match each verb to its definition, explaining that there is one extra verb. Go through the answers.

Answers: 1 observe 2 suspect 3 research
4 misunderstand 5 prove 6 conclude 7 theorise 8 fake
9 assume

Vocabulary checkpoint
Remind Ss that sometimes a word can be both a noun and a verb. Ask Ss to find three words like this in Ex 3a (*suspect*, *research*, *fake*). A *suspect* = a person who is suspected in a crime context. With words like this, often the noun is stressed on the first syllable, but the verb is stressed on the second. Ask Ss if they can think of more words which are both nouns and verbs (*import*, *export*, *record*, *intern*, *convert*, etc.).

b Ask Ss to go back to the article and find noun forms of the verbs in Ex 3a. Go through the answers as a class. Build up a list on the board and elicit the stressed syllables.

Answers:

Verb	Noun
assume	assumption
conclude	conclusion
fake	fake
know	knowledge
misunderstand	misunderstanding
observe	observation
prove	proof
research	research
suspect	suspicion
theorise	theory

4a Refer to the list and the underlined vowels. Ask Ss to work in pairs, say each word and decide on the vowel sounds. They should mark each word pair S for same or D for different.

b 🔊 9.7 Play the recording for Ss to check, then go through the answers. Play the recording again for Ss to repeat. Make sure Ss respect the syllable stress and don't overemphasise the sound being focused on, which may not be the stressed syllable.

Answers: 1 different 2 same 3 different 4 different
5 different 6 different 7 same 8 same

5a Ask Ss to go through the sentences and choose the correct alternatives. Check this as a class, then ask Ss to complete the sentences with their own ideas. Allow plenty of time for this and monitor to help.

Answers: 1 proof 2 assumed 3 conclusion 4 observe
5 knowledge 6 suspect 7 theory

b Put Ss in pairs to read out their sentences and continue the conversation by asking follow-up questions. When they finish, ask a few pairs to choose the best completion to share with the class.

VOCABULARY BANK 9B p164
Confusing pairs of words
This is an optional extension to the vocabulary section, extending the lexical set and providing further practice. If you're short of time, this can be done for homework.
1 Ask Ss to match the pairs of words in bold with meanings a and b. Discuss the distinctions in meaning as you go through the answers.

Answers:
1 a remember   b remind
2 a amusing   b enjoyable
3 a raises   b has risen
4 a lives   b 's staying
5 a sympathetic b likeable
6 a expensive b valuable
7 a lay   b lie
8 a damaged   b injured

2 Ask Ss to work alone to complete the sentences with the correct option. Discuss the different meanings as you go through the answers.

Answers:
1 amusing 2 injured 3 remind 4 stay 5 rising
6 likeable 7 lie 8 valuable

Further practice
Photocopiable activities: 9B Vocabulary, p244
App: 9B Vocabulary practice 1 and 2

Grammar
Verb patterns
6 Ask Ss to complete the paragraph with the words and phrases in the box. Ask them to compare in pairs.

7 Refer Ss to the grammar box to check their answers, then deal with any queries as a class. Point out that in many cases *that* may be left out after the verb with no change in meaning.

Answers: 1 people laughing   2 laughing   3 people to look
4 to think   5 that   6 me accept   7 you that

8a Ask Ss to rewrite the sentences using the verbs provided. They should work alone, using the grammar box to help them, then check in pairs. Go through the answers as a class and write each verb pattern on the board to ensure Ss have it correctly.

Answers:
1 I guarantee that the Earth is round.
2 I expect you to doubt it.
3 I suggest (that) you research it for yourself.
4 Some people dislike listening to scientists.
5 The evidence persuaded me (to believe) (that) it's true.
6 The research made me question my beliefs.

b This is an opportunity to practise more freely. Tell Ss they should write their recommendations and questions using the verbs in the grammar box. Give them a few minutes to think and write. Ask Ss to compare in pairs before whole-class feedback. There are no fixed answers, but you can focus on correct/incorrect usage of verb patterns.

Optional alternative activity
Ss who struggle with ideas can refer to their devices to get information which can inform their recommendations. The context can be extended to facts about other planets.

LANGUAGE BANK 9B pp.152–153
Stronger classes could read the notes at home. Otherwise, check the notes with Ss. In each exercise, elicit the first answer as an example. Ss work alone to complete the exercises, then check their answers in pairs. In feedback, elicit Ss' answers and drill where needed. Ss can refer to the notes to help them.

Answers:
1 1 both 2 tell me 3 her that 4 believing 5 to think
   6 that I throw away 7 both 8 function
2 1 At our school, they didn't let us ~~to~~ have mobile phones in the classroom.
   2 I promise ~~to~~ you that it was just a misunderstanding.
   3 ✓
   4 My boss doesn't mind me ~~take~~ *taking* a longer lunch break as long as I work late.
   5 We recommend ~~to try~~ *(that) you try/ trying* the new Italian restaurant.
   6 The talk sounded strange but our neighbours encouraged ~~to go us~~ *us to go*.

Further practice
Photocopiable activities: 9B Grammar 1, p242; 9B Grammar 2, p243
App: 9B Grammar practice 1 and 2

Speaking
Prepare
9 Put Ss in pairs and name alternate Ss A and B. Tell Ss to read their information, asking Student Bs to turn to the relevant page. Ask Ss to prepare to present and discuss their ideas about the Moon landings. Monitor and help, reminding Ss about verb patterns.

Speak
10a When they are ready, ask AB pairs to roleplay their discussion. Refer them to the Useful phrases and monitor and listen. When they finish, give feedback on language used.

> **Teaching tip**
> To encourage Ss to use language freely, move around the class or place yourself centrally and listen but try not to engage once Ss have started. Note both good examples of language use and errors. When Ss have finished, focus on positive points first and then add errors with the target language (in this case, verb patterns) to the board. Ss can decide how to correct these in their pairs. Elicit and add the corrections to the board using a different colour and get Ss to copy the corrections into their notebooks.

b Ask Ss to swap roles and repeat the roleplay. When they finish, give feedback again and ask them which role they preferred and who spoke most convincingly.

Reflection on learning

Write the following questions on the board:
How could this language be useful in your daily life?
What would you recommend to someone who wanted to improve their English?

Put Ss in pairs to discuss the questions. When they have finished, ask if anyone wants to share their ideas with the class, but don't force them to if they'd rather not.

Homework ideas

Language bank: 9B Ex 1–2, pp.152–153
Workbook: Ex 1–5, p69
App: grammar, vocabulary and pronunciation practice

Fast route: continue to Lesson 9C
Extended route: go to p132 for Develop your writing

9C Celebrity

Introduction

The goal of this lesson is for students to describe a personal experience. To help them achieve this, they will revise common phrasal verbs in this context.

Warm-up

Write the word *celebrity* on the board and ask Ss to define it (= a famous person, especially in the field of sport or entertainment). Ask Ss if they can name some celebrities or show some images of famous people for them to identify. Put Ss in small groups to compare ideas. When they finish, ask Ss for names and write them on the board. Tell them today's lesson is about celebrities.

Culture notes

A **celebrity** is sometimes defined as a person who is 'famous for being famous'. Members of the public can become celebrities by participating in reality TV shows or by building up their followers on social media. Celebrity endorsement, which involves well-known people claiming to use products on their social media platforms, is big business.

Listening and vocabulary

Common phrasal verbs

1a Discuss the questions as a class. If Ss don't have much to say, use the Culture notes above to help them and discuss as a class.

b Ask Ss to read through and tick the sentences they agree with, then compare with a partner. Encourage them to justify their ideas. There are no fixed answers. When Ss finish, ask for a show of hands to see which statements are the most popular.

2a 9.8 Tell Ss they are going to listen to three stories about celebrities. Ask Ss to read through the questions quickly, then play the recording, pausing after each story to allow Ss to make notes and compare answers. Elicit the answers.

Answers:
1 a They had fake press badges and were going to say that they were from a magazine.
  b They went backstage, no one stopped them and they chatted to Rui Letife.
2 a Who painted the *Mona Lisa*?
  b He went away for a few weeks.
3 a She got a place on a reality TV show.
  b She cried and then she got on with her life and her studies.

Culture notes

One of the speakers refers to '15 minutes of fame'. This is related to a comment attributed to Andy Warhol, a 1960s American conceptual artist, who stated that one day everybody would be world-famous for 15 minutes.

Audioscript 9.8

1
Celebrities are just ordinary people. My friend and I decided to try and get backstage at a Rui Letife concert. Actually, my friend came up with the plan. I thought it was a stupid idea but I didn't want to let her down. Anyway, we printed fake press badges and we made up a story that we were from a magazine and were doing a review of the concert. After the concert, we walked backstage. We just pretended that we owned the place and it turned out that we didn't need press badges. There was no one to stop us, and the first person we saw was Rui Letife, just sitting there, chilling out, drinking water after the show. We chatted to him for a while and we told him what we'd done and he thought it was totally hilarious. He even signed our T-shirts for us! Really nice guy, like I say, just an ordinary person really.

2
Not every celebrity wants to be famous, you know. A friend of mine was on a TV quiz show, like the one where you win a lot of money if you answer all the questions correctly. Anyway, he's basically quite a shy guy, you know, he doesn't like to stand out but he's very smart. So, the presenter asked him the first question which was, 'Who painted the *Mona Lisa*?'. You know, the first question is always an easy one, it's Leonardo da Vinci, but for some reason my friend said 'Leonardo di Caprio'. I think he was just stressed or he had a brain freeze or something and everyone started laughing but he just didn't know why, he couldn't figure it out. Then the presenter said, 'Is that your final answer?' and he said, 'Yes' and, you know, he was out of the show on the first question. After that his life changed completely. The video went viral and he became a figure of fun – he was in all the newspapers and everything and they made out that he was the stupidest man in the country and they camped outside his house waiting for an interview. He stuck it out for a couple of days and then he just left in the middle of the night and went away for a few weeks. He lost his job and everything. Now, when he goes for a job interview or meets a new person, they always ask, 'Are you that guy who, you know, dot, dot, dot?' I think he'll always be remembered for that one mistake.

3
In today's world, anyone can be a celebrity. I should know, I've had my 15 minutes of fame. I'll tell you how it happened. I came across an advert one day for a TV show, you know, a reality show where you start with ten people in a house and the audience votes one out every week. I didn't think it through, I just applied and got a place on the show. I was really shocked, you know, like, I never expected that to happen, and then apparently I came across quite well on TV because the audience kept voting to keep me in and, in the end, I was one of the last three people left on the show. The next month or so was the most extraordinary of my life – chat shows, radio interviews, news shows – and I just loved it. I was a celebrity and I went partying with other celebrities and I kept seeing my name in the newspapers. And then, all of a sudden, it stopped. No one wanted an interview. No one wrote about me. When I realised it was all over, I just burst into tears. I had no plan B. I couldn't get over how quickly it all stopped.

It took a while but, in the end, I realised I had to get on with my life. I decided to finish my studies and got a job and that's where I am now. But if I said I never missed the celebrity lifestyle, I'd be lying!

b Explain that Ss should choose phrasal verbs in the box that have the same meaning as the underlined phrases. Do a few examples together, clarifying that the form may need to be changed, then ask Ss to work alone to complete the exercise. Give them a few minutes. Ss can check ideas in pairs, but don't go through the answers yet as they will listen for these.

c Play the recording again so Ss can check their answers. Pause where necessary to allow time for writing and correction. Go through the answers as a class.

Answers:
1 a came up with   b let her down   c made up   d turned out
2 a stand out   b figure it out   c made out that   d stuck it out
3 a came across   b think it through   c get over   d get on with

Optional alternative activity
If Ss have access to the audioscript, they can listen and read at the same time. They should underline the phrasal verbs in context. This may help them further with the meanings.

Optional extra activity
Ss work in pairs. One student says the sentences in Ex 2b. Their partner reformulates the sentences using phrasal verbs. **Weaker classes** can do this with their books open, **stronger classes** can try with books closed.

3a This task helps consolidate the meaning of the verbs and their natural collocations. Look at the example as a class and discuss why it's wrong (we can't let down objects, only people). Then ask Ss to continue alone. Ask them to check in pairs, then go through the answers and further clarify as needed.

Answers:
Cross out: 1 car   2 people   3 an apology   4 by chance
5 life   6 a secret   7 my time   8 the emotions

b Ask Ss to change the sentences in Ex 3a so they are true for them. They can use the collocations provided or come up with new ones. They should tell each other their sentences in pairs.

VOCABULARY BANK 9C   p164
Nouns formed from phrasal verbs
This is an optional extension to the vocabulary section, extending the lexical set and providing further practice. If you're short of time, this can be done for homework.

1 Ask Ss to complete the nouns using the words in the box. Discuss the meaning as you go through the answers. Point out the stress pattern (the nouns are stressed on the first syllable but the phrasal verbs they derive from are stressed on the second part: BREAKdown; break DOWN).

Answers:
1 down   2 break   3 back(s)   4 look   5 out   6 put
7 down   8 fall   9 through   10 over

2 Ask Ss to work alone to complete the sentences with the correct words. Go through the answers.

Answers:
1 cutbacks   2 outbreak   3 takeover   4 breakthrough
5 workout   6 letdown   7 outlook   8 downfall   9 input
10 breakdown

Further practice
Photocopiable activities: 9C Vocabulary, p247
App: 9C Vocabulary practice 1 and 2

Language focus
Phrasal verbs
4 Ask Ss to read through the Language focus box, then complete it with phrasal verbs from Ex 2b. Check as a class, then spend time discussing and eliciting further examples of separable/inseparable and transitive/intransitive phrasal verbs.

Answers: 1 turn out (that)   2 make out (that)
3 let someone down   4 figure something out   5 stick it out
6 think it through   7 get over something
8 get on with something

Vocabulary checkpoint
It can be difficult to guess the meaning of many phrasal verbs. They usually have more formal synonyms (*let down* = *disappoint*, *think through* = *consider*, *make out* = *pretend*, *turn out* = *transpire*, etc.). It's fine for Ss to use the synonyms rather than the phrasal verbs if they find them simpler to manage. However, Ss should recognise that the phrasal verb equivalents are much more common in native English speech.

Grammar checkpoint
Ss may not have come across the term 'particle' before. In a phrasal verb, the particle is usually stressed but in verb + preposition, the preposition is not stressed, for example: I **got on** with my **life**. I **got** on the **bus**.
In phrasal verbs, the verb + particle has a different meaning from the literal meaning, which is not obvious from the parts, for example: *John went up the stairs.* = verb + preposition; *Prices went up.* = phrasal verb.

5a 9.9 Ask Ss to listen and complete the conversation with phrasal verbs. Play the recording a second time if needed. Ss can check in pairs before going through the answers.

Answers: 1 get over it   2 stands out   3 figured it out
4 make out   5 get on with it   6 let me down

Audioscript 9.9
A: Look! It's her, that actress!
B: I can't get over it!
A: She really stands out. I have to talk to her.
B: What shall we do?
A: Let's think it through.
B: I've figured it out!
A: Have you come up with a plan?
B: Let's make out we're film directors.
A: And we want her in our film!
B: Let's get on with it!
A: Don't let me down.
B: Hey! Where's she gone?
A: We've missed our chance.

b Ask Ss to read the information in the box, then practise the conversation together. Monitor, listen and give feedback. A confident pair may like to read the conversation for the class.

Pronunciation checkpoint
Ss may need reminding that consonant to vowel linking is a common feature of normal English speech. It is not sloppy or poor pronunciation. Point out that running words together helps their own speech sound more natural and recognising this feature will aid their listening skills.

6 Ask Ss to read the texts and decide if the underlined parts are correct. Point out that the meaning is correct but the word order might be wrong, or there might be an extra word. Ss work alone to check and correct the sentences, then compare in pairs. Monitor and help as needed, then check answers.

> **Answers:** 1 come up with something 2 figure it out 3 ✓
> 4 stood out 5 get over it 6 ✓ 7 ✓ 8 made out
> 9 making it up 10 ✓ 11 stick it out 12 got on with

Optional extra activity

After checking answers, ask pairs to practise reading the four texts aloud to each other, focusing on their pronunciation. Remind them to link sounds when appropriate, referring back to Ex 5b if necessary.

7 Put Ss in pairs to ask and answer the questions. When they finish, ask a few pairs to report back on something interesting their partner told them.

Optional alternative activities

1 Ss write their own questions using the lesson's phrasal verbs and ask their partner.
2 Ss choose or are allocated one of the questions, which they use to survey the class. They then report back on their findings.

LANGUAGE BANK 9C pp.152–153

Stronger classes could read the notes at home. Otherwise, check the notes with Ss. In each exercise, elicit the first answer as an example. Ss work alone to complete the exercises, then check their answers in pairs. In feedback, elicit Ss' answers. Ss can refer to the notes to help them.

Answers:
1 1 He was shy and didn't want to stand out.
   2 The children made up a great story. / The children made a great story up.
   3 I have always looked up to my father.
   4 I have always got on with the people I work with.
   5 You really shouldn't have let us down.
2 1 came across a leaflet
   2 handed it in
   3 looking forward to the day
   4 figure them out / think them through / think things through / figure things out
   5 think things through / figure things out / figure them out / think them through

Further practice

Photocopiable activities: 9C Language focus 1, p245; 9C Language focus 2, p246

Speaking

Prepare

8a Explain that Ss are going to talk about meeting a celebrity. If you have ever met a celebrity, tell them about it. If not, tell them who you might like to meet, then ask them to discuss the questions in pairs. Go through the answers as a class and discuss their reasons.

b Ask Ss to make notes about a real or imagined experience of meeting a celebrity. Monitor and help with vocabulary and ideas. As this is likely to be an invented experience, encourage Ss to use the full range of their imagination! (See Teaching tip below.)

> **Teaching tip**
> It can be liberating for Ss to use their imagination during language practice. It introduces an element of fun and creativity for speakers/writers and can be entertaining for listeners/readers. Research shows that humour can make new language more memorable as it's linked to amusing or ridiculous contexts. Build up possible answers to each question in Ex 8b on the board, encouraging Ss to come up with unusual situations and activities by giving an example yourself. For example:
> *I bumped into the Queen of England once – it turned out we were staying in the same hotel in Barbados. She was water skiing in a bright pink wetsuit, which really stood out!*

Speak

9a Put Ss in pairs to tell each other about their celebrity encounter. Point out that they should try to include some phrasal verbs from this lesson. Monitor and listen for how well they are using the verbs, as well as narrative tenses.

b Ask Ss for brief feedback, then ask them to find a new partner and tell their celebrity anecdotes again.

> **Reflection on learning**
> Write the following questions on the board:
> *How useful was the topic of today's lesson?*
> *How will today's vocabulary be helpful outside the class?*
> Put Ss in pairs to discuss the questions. When they have finished, ask if anyone wants to share their ideas with the class, but don't force them to if they'd rather not.

Homework ideas

Language bank: 9C Ex 1–2, pp.152–153
Workbook: Ex 1–5, p70
App: grammar, vocabulary and pronunciation practice

Fast route: continue to Lesson 9D
Extended route: go to p112 for Develop your reading

9D English in action

Introduction

The goal of this lesson is for students to explain a problem and ask for action. To help them achieve this, they will revise vocabulary for describing problems with products and services.

Warm-up

Tell Ss that you have bought something and it's not as you expected. For example, you ordered a shirt online and when it arrived the colour was different from how it looked on the website. Ask Ss if they have been in similar situations and what they would do in this case. Discuss the various options and difficulties (return it, call the company, email a complaint, put up with it, etc.), adding useful vocabulary to the board. Tell Ss this is the focus of today's lesson.

Listening 1

1 Ask Ss to discuss the questions in pairs. After a few minutes, ask a few pairs for ideas. Add any useful vocabulary to the board.

2a 9.10 Explain that Ss are going to hear the start of six phone conversations. They should write the numbers 1–6 in their notebook, then listen and tick each caller who is able to speak to the person they want to. Ask Ss to check their answers in pairs before conducting feedback.

Answers: 1, 2, 5

Audioscript 9.10

1
A: Good morning, Lifestyle Publications.
B: Hi. I'm calling about my magazine subscription.
A: OK.
B: Is there someone there who could help me?
A: Is it a billing enquiry?
B: No. It's about the delivery of my magazine.
A: I'll put you through to someone who can help.
B: Thanks.
C: Hello, Aisha Betts, logistics department.

2
A: Hello, Hatton Plumbers.
B: Hi. Can you put me through to Bernardo Silva?
A: Who shall I say is calling?
B: It's Melissa McAlistair.
A: I'll just put you on hold while I check if he's available. Bear with me.
B: Sure.
C: Bernardo Silva.
B: Hello, Mr Silva. It's Melissa McAlistair here. I'm calling about …

3
A: Hello, Felix's phone.
B: Oh, hi. I was trying to get through to Felix. Is he there? It's Jamie.
A: Hello, Jamie. Felix is in the shower. Could you call back in a few minutes?
B: Sure. No problem.
A: Thanks. Bye, Jamie.

4
A: Hello, Daydream Services.
B: Hello, I have an enquiry. I hope someone can help me.
A: What is it concerning?
B: I wanted to ask about the advert for a new assistant. Has the position been filled?
A: I'll put you through to recruitment. They'll be able to answer your questions.
B: Thank you.
C: You're through to the recruitment department. Please leave a message and we'll get back to you as soon as …

5
A: Tenet Mobile. How can I help you?
B: Hi. I'm calling about the last bill I received. Could I speak to someone in the billing department?
A: I'll put you through.
C: Hello, billing department. How can I help you?
B: Hi. I'm calling about the last bill I received …

6
A: Hi. Hannah speaking.
B: Hey, Hannah. It's Nozomi. Is Alex there with you? He's not picking up and I need to talk to him.
A: Hey, Nozomi. No, Alex has just popped out.
B: Oh, no!
A: Shall I get him to call you when he gets back?
B: Sure. Do that. Thanks.
A: No problem. Catch you later.
B: Yep, bye.

b Tell Ss they will listen again for more detail. Give them a few minutes to read through the sentences, then ask them to write the missing words as they listen. You may need to pause to allow **weaker classes** time to write.

c Refer Ss to the Useful phrases box to check their answers, then conduct feedback.

Answers: 1 who could help 2 you on hold 3 call back in 4 answer your questions 5 speak to someone 6 get him to

3 9.11 Explain that Ss will hear the start of five conversations and they should decide on the best response, a or b. Give them a minute or two to read through the responses, pointing out that *pop out* means go out for a short time, then play the recording. Pause after each one for Ss to discuss, then go through the answers.

Answers: 1 a 2 b 3 b 4 b 5 a

Audioscript 9.11

1
A: Hello, GMH.
B: Hello. Can you put me through to Ms Ruiz?

2
A: Hello, Cranston Media.
B: Hi. Can you put me through to someone in the billing department?

3
A: Hi.
B: Hi, Camila. It's Jian. Is Usman there?

4
A: Good morning, Hayes Furniture.
B: Good morning. I'm calling about a recent order. I want to ask about delivery dates and times. Is there someone there who could help me?

5
A: Redstone Fashion. How can I help you?
B: It's Zahra. I'm trying to get through to Roger. Is he there?

4 Refer to the situations and the Useful phrases box, then ask Ss to start their mini roleplays in pairs. Remind them that the objective is to practise the Useful phrases and be appropriately formal or informal. Monitor to see how they manage. When they finish, give feedback on good use of language or ask confident pairs to perform their roleplays for the class.

Optional extra activity

If Ss enjoy the roleplays, pair them with different partners and repeat. To make phone roleplays more realistic, ask Ss to sit back to back so that they can't see each other. Discuss how speaking on the phone can be more difficult because we can't help each other with facial expressions or gestures.

Vocabulary

5a Tell Ss they are going to extend their vocabulary around things going wrong. Ask them to match the phrases in bold (1–10) with the meanings (a–j). Ss can work alone, then go through the answers as a class.

> Answers: 1 c 2 i 3 g 4 e 5 a 6 h 7 j 8 d 9 f 10 b

b This is an opportunity to practise the vocabulary. Put Ss in pairs to discuss the questions. When they finish, ask a few pairs to report back on an interesting experience.

Listening 2

6 🔊 9.12 Remind Ss about the six phone conversations in Ex 2a. Tell them they are going to listen to the rest of three of them. Play the recording so Ss can answer the questions. Ask pairs to compare, then go through the answers as a class.

Culture notes

A **subscription** is a way of accessing a service or product regularly. A magazine subscription means that an issue of the magazine is delivered to you each week/month at home. You usually pay for it online in advance. Point out the verb form is *subscribe (to)*.

> **Answers:**
> **Conversation 1**
> 1 The first issue of her magazine didn't arrive.
> 2 Her card was refused.
> 3 the missing issue to be sent out straight away and a refund
> 4 She says she will talk to her manager about it.
>
> **Conversation 2**
> 1 Her boiler is not working.
> 2 It sounds like an electrical problem.
> 3 She wants the plumber to come back and fix it today.
> 4 He will try and come that evening.
>
> **Conversation 3**
> 1 The phone bill was higher than usual.
> 2 The customer made several international calls.
> 3 the money to be refunded immediately
> 4 No. He will research it further and call the customer back.

Audioscript 9.12

Conversation 1
C: Hello, Aisha Betts, logistics department.
B: Hi. I'm calling about my new magazine subscription.
C: OK. How can I help?
B: The problem is that the first issue didn't arrive.
C: Oh, I'm sorry to hear that. Let me check to see what happened.
B: Thanks.
C: Could you just confirm your full name and postcode for me.
B: Yes, it's Amira Khan and the postcode is RG17 2PP.
C: Thanks. And your date of birth?
B: 21, 7, 94.
C: Thank you. Bear with me while I check the system for you. … OK. I can see that your card was refused.
B: Refused? Why?
C: I'm afraid it doesn't give that information. Let me just try to take the payment again … OK, … well that payment's been processed now. I'm sorry about that. I don't know what the problem was.
B: Good! Well … I'd like you to send out the first issue of the magazine that I missed as quickly as possible.
C: Yes, I understand. I'll sort that out for you right away.
B: And given the inconvenience, I think I deserve a refund.
C: OK. I'll have a word with my manager.
B: OK, thanks.
C: And I'm really sorry for the inconvenience this has caused.
B: Yep, OK.
C: Is there anything else I can do for you today?
B: No, that's it.
C: OK, have a great day.
B: Yep, you too. Bye.

Conversation 2
C: Bernardo Silva.
B: Hello, Mr Silva. It's Melissa McAlistair here. I'm calling about the work you did for me last week.
C: Oh, OK. I do a lot of work. Just remind me where you live.
B: 12 Strafton Street.
C: Oh, yes. What can I do for you, Mrs McAlistair?
B: Well, it's about the boiler. It's not working … again.
C: Oh, that's not good.
B: No.
C: Can you tell me what it's doing?
B: Well, when I turn on the hot water it doesn't do anything. The water's cold.
C: OK. And is the red light on?
B: No, there are no lights on.
C: Right. Well, it sounds like an electrical problem.
B: Would it be possible to come and fix it today? We all had to have cold showers this morning!
C: We're completely booked up at the moment, I'm afraid. I can make it over to you … let's see … next Wednesday.
B: Next Wednesday! You're not serious!
C: Yep, 'fraid so. It's a busy time of year.
B: But we have no hot water.
C: Yeah, that's difficult, I know. Have you got a neighbour whose shower you can use till next week or something like …
B: Sorry, but that's not the point. Last week we paid you to fix the boiler but it's not fixed.
C: Well, this sounds like a new problem to me.
B: Look, I'd really like you to come over sooner. We have a young child and we need hot water.
C: Look, I'll see what I can do.
B: Thank you.
C: I can't promise anything but I'll try and come this evening.
B: Thank you very much. I appreciate it.
C: All right. Hopefully see you then.
B: Yep. Bye!

Conversation 3
C: Hello, billing department. How can I help you?
B: Hi. I'm calling about the last bill I received. I've got a problem with it.
C: OK. Do you have your account number?
B: Yes, it's 3-3-5-9-G-N.
C: OK. And can you confirm your date of birth?
B: 21, 7, 96.
C: Mr Mueller?
B: That's right.
C: How can I help you, Mr Mueller?
B: Well, my last bill was much higher than usual and I want to know why that is.
C: Let's take a look. Well, I see that you made several international calls last month and …
B: International calls?
C: Yes.
B: Where to?
C: Australia.
B: Australia? But I don't know anyone in Australia! There must be a mistake.
C: So you didn't make those calls?
B: No, I didn't.
C: They were all made at 1.30 in the morning.
B: Well, then I was asleep, so it can't have been me.
C: Well, bear with me a moment, I'm just going to put you on hold.
B: OK.
C: Mr Mueller?
B: Yes.
C: Apologies for keeping you waiting. I'm sorry, but my manager says there's nothing we can do. If the calls are on your bill then …
B: Sorry to interrupt you, but maybe it's better if I talk to your manager. Could you put me through?
C: Well, OK. Hold on a minute.
D: Hello, Mr Mueller?

B: Hello.
D: Mr Mueller, my colleague has explained the situation and I'm afraid there's really nothing …
B: Can I just interrupt you there. I didn't make those calls, so I am not going to pay for them. It's really that simple.
D: I understand, Mr Mueller, but …
B: Look, when I go to bed I turn my phone off. Every night, without fail. Do you believe me?
D: Of course I believe you, Mr Mueller, but …
B: Then could you refund the money that was taken from my account, immediately? Otherwise, I will have to take my complaint further.
D: Look, Mr Mueller … I'll tell you what I'll do. I'll look into this further and try to find out what happened. I'll make sure that you get a call back in the next two days.
B: OK, but I expect a refund and some kind of compensation for the time I've lost on this.
D: I understand, Mr Mueller. As I say, I'll make sure you get a call back within two days.
B: OK.
D: Is there anything else I can do for you today?
B: No, that's all. Thank you.
D: Not at all. Have a nice day now.

7 Tell Ss they are going to listen again more carefully. Tell them to read the extracts, then play the recording so they can complete them with two words each time. Pause after each conversation to allow Ss time to write. Ask pairs to compare, then go through the answers as a class.

> Answers:
> 1 a calling about   b I deserve
> 2 a possible to   b promise anything
> 3 a problem with   b make sure

8 Refer Ss to the Useful phrases and ask them to complete the numbered gaps with sentences from Ex 7. Go through the answers, discussing the meaning of any phrases they are unsure of.

> Answers:
> 1 I'm calling about my new magazine subscription.
> 2 I've got a problem with it.
> 3 Given the inconvenience, I think I deserve a refund.
> 4 Would it be possible to come and fix it today?
> 5 I can't promise anything but I'll try and come this evening.
> 6 I'll make sure that you get a call back in the next two days.

9a 9.13 Ask Ss to read and listen to the sentences, paying attention to the underlined sounds. Put Ss in pairs to discuss what happens to the pronunciation of the sounds, then read the information box as a class.

> Answer: The underlined sounds are not pronounced clearly and some of them disappear completely.

b Play the recording again or say the sentences yourself. Ask Ss to listen and repeat.

10 Ask Ss to write the conversations in the correct order. With **weaker classes**, do the first one together, then ask students to continue in pairs. Go through the answers as a class.

> Answers:
> Conversation 1: 1 e   2 d   3 a   4 b   5 c
> Conversation 2: 1 c   2 b   3 e   4 f   5 a   6 d
> Conversation 3: 1 d   2 c   3 a   4 g   5 f   6 e   7 b

Speaking

11a Explain that Ss will now do a roleplay. Put them in groups of three and name them A, B and C. Ask Ss to turn to the relevant pages and read their roles.

b When they are ready, ask the groups to start their roleplays. Student A speaks first.

c When the groups finish, ask them to swap roles and repeat. If they are enjoying themselves, have a third swap so each student tries all three roles. Listen for the language of today's lesson and give feedback on how well Ss used it.

> **Reflection on learning**
> Write the following questions on the board:
> *In what situations do you think you will use this language in the future?*
> *How did your roleplay conversations improve during the lesson?*
> Put Ss in pairs to discuss the questions. When they have finished, ask a few Ss to share their ideas with the class, but don't force them if they'd rather not.

Homework ideas

Reflection on learning: Write your answers.
Workbook: Ex 1–5, p71
App: grammar, vocabulary and pronunciation practice

Roadmap video

Go online for the Roadmap video and worksheet.

9A Develop your listening

Introduction

The goal of this lesson is for students to understand fast, scripted speech. To help them achieve this, they will focus on understanding pauses in speech.

Warm-up

Display pictures of a pipe, a deerstalker hat and a violin or show images of Sherlock Holmes films and books. Ask Ss to discuss how they are connected. Some may come up with Sherlock Holmes. Explain that today you will be learning more about this famous fictional character.

Culture notes

Sherlock Holmes is a fictional detective who features in stories by Sir Arthur Conan Doyle, the first of which was published in 1887. His companion and assistant is Doctor Watson. Holmes is famous for his logical approach to solving crimes. He always wore a deerstalker hat, played the violin and smoked a pipe. The fictional character of Holmes lived at 221b Baker Street, a central London location which is now The Sherlock Holmes Museum. There have been many films and TV series of the stories.

1 Ask Ss to discuss the question in pairs. After a few minutes, elicit answers and write useful vocabulary on the board.

Optional extra activity

Play a short clip from a Sherlock Holmes film or TV series and get Ss to identify Holmes and Watson. They can also shout out if they spot Holmes's deerstalker hat, pipe or violin.

2 Refer Ss to the pictures and ask them to discuss who the people are and what is happening. As you elicit ideas, take the opportunity to pre-teach *mud* and *slippers* and talk about the meaning of *deduce* (= to work something out from the available information).

3 🔊 **9.4** Tell Ss they are going to listen to three extracts from Sherlock Holmes stories that accompany the pictures in Ex 2. They should listen and choose the correct options. With **weaker classes**, complete the first one together to show what to do and be ready to pause the recording as needed. Go through the answers as a class.

> **Answers:** 1 a 2 b 3 a

Audioscript 9.4

Extract 1
Narrator: From the Sherlock Holmes mystery *The Adventure of the Stockbroker's Clerk*.
Sherlock Holmes has just arrived at the house of his friend, Doctor Watson. He notices that Doctor Watson has been ill recently.
Holmes: I see that you've been unwell lately. Summer colds are always a little annoying.
Watson: I couldn't leave the house for three days last week due to a severe cold. I thought, however, that I had recovered completely.
Holmes: So you have. You look remarkably healthy.
Watson: How, then, did you know about it?
Holmes: My dear fellow, you know my methods.
Watson: You deduced it, then?
Holmes: Certainly.
Watson: And from what?
Holmes: From your slippers.
Narrator: Watson glanced down at the new slippers which he was wearing.
Waton: How on earth … ?
Narrator: … Watson began, but Holmes answered his question before it was asked.
Holmes: Your slippers are new. You could not have had them more than a few weeks. The soles of your slippers, which are at the moment facing me, are slightly burnt. For a moment, I thought they might have got wet and been burnt when you dried them. But there is a small piece of paper on the sole with the price on it. Water would, of course, have removed this. It is obvious, then, that you have been sitting with your feet stretched out to the fire, which you would only do at this time of year, in June, if you were feeling ill.
Narrator: Like all of Holmes's reasoning, it was simplicity itself once it was explained.

Extract 2
Narrator: From the Sherlock Holmes mystery, *The Adventure of the Speckled Band*. Sherlock Holmes is talking to a woman who has arrived at his apartment to ask for help.
Holmes: You must not fear. We shall soon sort everything out, I have no doubt. You have come in by train this morning, I see.
Woman: You know me, then?
Holmes: No, but I can see a return ticket in your left glove. You must have started early, and you had to travel in a horse and cart, along heavy roads, before you reached the station.
Narrator: The woman was clearly surprised, and stared at Holmes.
Holmes: There is no mystery, my dear madam. There is mud on the left arm of your jacket in seven places. The mud is perfectly fresh. There is no vehicle, apart from a horse and cart, which throws up mud in that way.
Woman: Whatever your reasons might be, you are perfectly correct.

Extract 3
Narrator: From the Sherlock Holmes mystery, *A Study in Scarlet*. Doctor Watson has just found out that Sherlock Holmes doesn't know that the Earth goes round the Sun. Watson is very surprised!
Watson: Holmes's ignorance was as remarkable as his knowledge. He seemed to know almost nothing about literature, philosophy and politics. My surprise was greatest, however, when I found that he didn't know anything about Copernicus, the planets in the Solar System and the fact that the Earth goes around the Sun. It seemed extraordinary to me that anyone in the nineteenth century did not know that the Earth travelled round the Sun. I could hardly believe it.
Holmes: You appear to be astonished. Now that I do know it, I shall do my best to forget it.
Watson: To forget it!
Holmes: You see, I think that a brain is like a little empty room, and you have to stock it with the furniture that you choose. It is a mistake to think that the empty room has elastic walls and can stretch to any extent. Believe me, there comes a time when for every new piece of knowledge, you forget something that you knew before. It is very important, therefore, not to have useless facts pushing out the useful ones.
Watson: But the Solar System!
Holmes: It doesn't matter to me! You say that we go round the Sun. If we went round the Moon it would not make the slightest bit of difference to me or to my work.

4a Ask Ss to listen again more carefully and answer the questions. Play the recording, pausing between extracts to allow Ss time to write.

b Ask Ss to discuss their answers in pairs, then go through them as a class. Discuss which of the three extracts Ss found the most entertaining or clever.

> **Answers:**
> 1 a If they had got wet, the paper price sticker would have come off.
>   b Watson sat with his legs outstretched to the fire when he was ill.
> 2 a There is a return ticket in her left glove.
>   b There is fresh mud on her left sleeve, which could only have come from a horse and cart.
> 3 a He is very surprised.
>   b You forget something that you already knew.

5a Refer Ss to the Focus box. Read it through as a class, with individuals reading sections aloud, then ask Ss to mark the pauses on the three extracts. Have a whole-class discussion on where the pauses should come but do not confirm yet. If you can, project the text and mark the pauses there.

b 🔊 **9.5** Tell Ss to now listen to the extracts and check where the pauses come. Tell **weaker classes** how many pauses there are in each extract. When they finish, ask Ss to check in pairs. Go through the answers as a class.

> **Answers:**
> 1 But there is a small piece of paper | on the sole | with the price on it
> 2 Water would | of course | have removed this
> 3 It is obvious | then | that you have been sitting | with your feet stretched out to the fire | which you would only do at this time of year | in June | if you were feeling ill

6 🔊 **9.6** Ask Ss to listen and mark the pauses. Go through the answers as a class. Ss can also add in punctuation, as in the answers below.

Answers: There is no mystery, | my dear madam. | There is mud on the left arm of your jacket | in seven places. | The mud is perfectly fresh. | There is no vehicle, | apart from a horse and cart, | which throws up mud in that way.

Optional extra activity

Ss work in pairs and take turns to read the extracts in Ex 5a and 6, pausing at the right places. Ss can also record themselves and listen.

7 Ss discuss in pairs. To prompt them, you could display pictures of famous TV or film detectives that they may know. When they finish, have a show of hands to see which fictional detectives are the most popular and discuss why.

Homework ideas

Workbook: Ex 1–2, p74

9B Develop your writing

Introduction

The goal of this lesson is for students to write a simple discursive essay. To help them achieve this, they will focus on structuring a simple discursive essay.

Warm-up

Ask Ss to discuss what they know about space exploration. If you can, display an image from a space-themed film like *Gravity*, or one of a real moonwalk. Tell them this is today's topic.

1 Put Ss in pairs to discuss the photos and the questions. Conduct brief feedback by asking pairs about each question in turn. Add useful ideas and vocabulary to the board. Leave the ideas on the board as Ss will return to them in Ex 3.

2a Ask Ss to complete the quiz alone. Give them a few minutes, emphasising that you don't expect them to know all the answers. Then ask Ss to compare answers in pairs, but don't conduct whole-class feedback yet as Ss will self-check their answers.

b Ask Ss to turn the page upside down and check answers. Then go through the answers as a class.

Culture notes

The American astronaut Neil Armstrong was the first man to walk on the moon, in 1969, followed a few minutes later by his fellow astronaut, Buzz Aldrin. They spent a total of 21 hours on the moon. The Soviet cosmonaut Yuri Gagarin was the first human to go into outer space, completing an orbit of the Earth in 1961.

3 Ask Ss to read the essay on space exploration and compare it with their ideas in Ex 1. When they finish, tick off any ideas on the board that are the same.

4a Ask Ss to read the essay more carefully, matching ideas a–f with paragraphs 2–4. Clarify that Ss should match two ideas to each of the three paragraphs, then check with a partner. Go through the answers as a class.

Answers: Paragraph 2: c, e Paragraph 3: a, f Paragraph 4: b, d

b Ask Ss to identify the main idea and supporting idea in paragraphs 2–4, choosing from the ideas in Ex 4a. Complete the first one as a class, then ask Ss to work in pairs to identify the other ideas. Go through the answers, pointing out that the main idea usually appears first in the paragraph.

Answers:
Paragraph 2: main idea = c, supporting idea = e
Paragraph 3: main idea = a, supporting idea = f
Paragraph 4: main idea = d, supporting idea = b

c Ask Ss to look back at the essay and tick the features they can see. Go through the answers as a class, clarifying any doubts. Ask Ss if the writing is formal or informal, on the basis of what they have ticked (formal).

Answers: complete sentences, the writer's opinion, explanations of unknown acronyms (e.g. *NASA*)

5 Refer to the Focus box and ask Ss to read it to themselves. Then put them in pairs to discuss the question. Elicit and check answers. Be prepared to answer questions about the meaning of the phrases.

Answers:
It is easy to see why many people believe that …
but I am convinced that …
First and foremost, …
Furthermore, it is a fact that …
There is no doubt that …
In summary, …

Prepare

6a This exercise helps Ss develop their ideas. Ask pairs to talk about all three topics. With **weaker classes**, go through the topics together and build up ideas on the board (for and against) for each one.

b Ask Ss to choose a topic, decide their position (for or against) and make notes. **Weaker classes** may like to do this in pairs or small groups so they can share ideas.

7 Ask Ss to organise their notes following the structure provided, deciding which ideas are stronger (main ideas) and which are secondary (supporting ideas).

Optional extra activity

Ask Ss to work in small groups and write each idea on a separate sticky note. When it comes to organising ideas, they can physically move them around into paragraphs rather than rewrite them. This is a useful planning idea for discursive essays on any topic.

Write

8a Ask Ss to write their first draft. Monitor and be available to help with ideas and vocabulary. Remind Ss to check their draft against the advice in the Focus box. There is no need for whole-class feedback because all Ss will be working on different ideas.

b Ask pairs of Ss to exchange essays and use the checklist to suggest improvements to each other's first drafts. Monitor and be available as an advisor if they are not sure.

c When Ss receive their essay back, they should redraft it, incorporating their partner's feedback.

Unit 9

Optional alternative activity

Divide Ss into two groups and give both groups the same essay topic. Each group works together to list arguments for opposing viewpoints, one for and one against. Each group then presents their ideas to the class. When they finish listening to all ideas, Ss decide on their preferred viewpoint and write their essay accordingly.

Optional extra activities

1 Pin the finished essays up on the walls in your classroom and let the Ss walk around and read each other's work.
2 Ss write an essay on one of the other topics in Ex 6a.

Homework ideas

Workbook: Ex 1–8, pp.74–75

9c Develop your reading

Introduction

The goal of this lesson is for students to predict content from headlines. To help them achieve this, they will focus on understanding newspaper headlines.

Warm-up

Ask Ss what ways we can find out what is happening in the world (news reports online or in print, conversation with friends/colleagues, TV, social media, etc.). Discuss the advantages and disadvantages of the different ways. Tell Ss that this is today's topic.

1a Ask Ss to look at the questions and discuss in small groups. When they finish, invite feedback from a few groups.

b Ask Ss to look at the photos and headlines, then answer the question. They can discuss in pairs, then check as a class.

Answers:
A more sensational (language in the headline: first name given only, colloquial language *axed*, exclamation mark, alliteration)
B more serious (language in the headline: fired, full name given)

Optional extra activity

Bring in some examples of sensationalist and serious newspapers for Ss to look through. They don't necessarily have to be in English. Ask Ss to each choose an article that interests them and write a three-line summary of it. Ss can then work in groups to present a mini news show. They should decide what order to present their chosen stories in, then read out their headlines and summaries. If you have access to recording or videoing facilities, it can be fun to record this and watch it back.

Culture notes

Serious newspapers focus on reporting facts. More sensationalist news articles are intended to be shocking and exciting rather than serious. When read online, sensational headlines are sometimes referred to as **clickbait** – they are designed to persuade as many people as possible to click on them in order to generate advertising revenue. Sensationalist reporting tends to be more difficult for learners to understand because it uses a lot of play on words and idiomatic informal language, which is accessible primarily to proficient speakers.

2 Ask Ss to read both articles, then choose the correct answers to the questions. Give a short time frame of no more than five minutes to encourage reading for main ideas. Go through the answers as a class.

Answers: 1 b 2 a 3 c 4 a 5 c 6 a

3 Ask Ss to read the articles again carefully and answer the questions. Clarify that all the questions apart from one require two answers – one from each article. With **weaker classes**, tell them that question 3 only needs one answer. Ss can highlight where they find the answers in the texts. Allow plenty of time for this as it requires careful reading. Ask Ss to compare, then go through the answers as a class.

Answers:
1 A He turned up late many times and argued with the director.
  B He had a disagreement with the director.
2 A He's very upset and recovering at home.
  B He's thinking about his future. Article doesn't say how he feels.
3 A/B He said Ashley is 'very well respected in the entertainment business and a fine young actor'.
4 A They said he was a flop and a clown and he wasn't a good actor.
  B They said he was continually late and difficult to work with.
5 A His first solo album had very few sales. He was booed after he forgot the words to his only hit song.
  B He was criticised for his live performances.

Optional extra activity

Ask Ss if they can find any information which is in one of the articles but not the other.

Answers:
The sensationalist article notes how much money Ashley Rice-Stubbs won in the reality TV show, that his first album flopped and that his agent blamed the director.
The serious article notes that Ashley Rice-Stubbs was disrespectful on the reality TV show.

4 Ask Ss to decide whether each feature belongs to sensationalist or serious reporting. Go through the answers.

Answers: 1 sensationalist 2 serious 3 sensationalist 4 sensationalist 5 sensationalist 6 serious 7 sensationalist 8 sensationalist

5a Read the first part of the Focus box as a class and elicit examples of headline grammar in the two article headlines (no auxiliary verbs or articles). Then read the rest of the Focus box and ask Ss to underline the dramatic nouns and verbs from the Focus box in the two articles. Elicit answers and discuss the meaning of unknown words.

Answers:
verbs: axe, row, vow, slam, flop
nouns: row, flop
(all in Article A)

150

Pronunciation checkpoint

Ss may be interested in how words with the same spelling have different pronunciations. In this exercise we have *vow* and *row*, both with the same vowel sound /aʊ/. Ask Ss if they can suggest more examples with this sound-spelling combination (*now, cow, how*). Then look at the other pronunciation of *row* /rəʊ/ (= to move a boat or a line, such as in a table or cinema) and elicit further examples of this sound-spelling combination (*show, flow, low*). Discuss with Ss if they find phonemes useful for their vocabulary records and point out how these are used in dictionaries.

b Look at the example as a class and discuss the changes needed to rewrite the headline in a grammatically normal way (tense changes, less dramatic vocabulary, adding articles). Ss should work alone on the other headlines, then compare in pairs. Go through the answers as a class and write them on the board, allowing some variation in responses.

Suggested answers:
1 The government has promised that it will take action over the emergency.
2 Gail Lee has criticised her manager after an argument.
3 The leader is trying to start emergency negotiations.
4 There has been bad news for the mayor.
5 The Fab Five album has failed (to be popular/to sell).
6 The government is going to prohibit smoking in parks.
7 Three people have been injured after/in an explosion.
8 (The) GGV (company) is going to get rid of/end plans to build a new headquarters.

6 Ask Ss to discuss in pairs. When they finish, have a whole-class discussion to see which points Ss broadly agree on. Add useful vocabulary to the board.

Teaching tip

Remind Ss that reading news articles in English is good practice as they will probably already have some knowledge of the story and they can use this to help them guess the meaning of new words. Suggest Ss access free online news if they are interested in this.

Homework ideas

Workbook: Ex 1–5, pp.72–73

10 OVERVIEW

10A Will I be happy?
Goal | talk about future events
Grammar | future perfect and future continuous
Vocabulary | personal fulfilment
GSE learning objective
Can speculate about a future event using a range of linguistic devices

10B Believe it or not!
Goal | maintain a discussion on interesting facts
Grammar | articles
Vocabulary | fame
GSE learning objective
Can pass on a detailed piece of information reliably

10C New solutions
Goal | give detailed opinions
Grammar | compound adjectives
Vocabulary | persuasion and enforcement
GSE learning objective
Can justify a viewpoint on a topical issue by discussing pros and cons of various options

Check and reflect
Review exercises and communicative activities to practise the grammar, vocabulary and functional language from Units 9 and 10.

Roadmap video
Go online for the Roadmap video and worksheet.

VOCABULARY BANK
10A Phrases with *life*
10B Verb prefixes

DEVELOP YOUR SKILLS

10A Develop your writing
Goal | write a magazine article
Focus | attracting and keeping the reader's attention
GSE learning objectives
Can use fact and opinion effectively in writing

10B Develop your listening
Goal | extract the main points from a news programme
Focus | distinguishing fact from opinion
GSE learning objective
Can extract the main points from news items, etc. with opinions, arguments and discussion

10C Develop your reading
Goal | understand an article
Focus | inferring the meaning of words from context
GSE learning objectives
Can guess the meaning of an unfamiliar word from context

10A Will I be happy?

Introduction
The goal of this lesson is for students to talk about future events. To help them achieve this, they will revise future perfect and future continuous and vocabulary connected with personal fulfilment.

Warm-up
Before the class starts, write on the board: *next year, five years' time, ten years' time*. Ask Ss to describe in pairs how they think their lives might have changed at those different future points. Monitor and listen to how Ss are using future forms but don't correct yet. Elicit feedback and find out if Ss have similar hopes for the future. Introduce the adjective *fulfilled* (= satisfied because you are using your abilities) and its noun, *fulfilment*. Elicit a few aspects of life which are connected with being fulfilled (work, friendships, etc.).

> **Teaching tip**
> By asking Ss to talk about the future before they have formally studied it, you will be able to assess how much work they need in this area. You'll also be able to activate Ss' existing knowledge of the topic and raise interest in the lesson content. There is no need to tell Ss that is what you are doing.

Reading and vocabulary
Personal fulfilment

1 Ask Ss to talk about the question in pairs. Ask a few pairs for their feedback and have a whole-class discussion to see if Ss agree on what's most important.

> **Optional extra activity**
> Ask Ss to rank the elements of a fulfilling life in order of importance (work, friendships, relationships, family, health/exercise, spirituality, financial security, home, etc.).

2a Put Ss in pairs and focus attention on the article. Ask Ss to read and answer the question, then give them a few minutes to discuss their answers. Go through the answers as a class. There are no fixed answers.

b Tell Ss they should match the underlined phrases in the article with the ones in the box. Ask them to add numbers to the phrases in the box, then compare in pairs. Go through the answers and help with meaning as needed.

Answers: 1 like-minded friends 2 a soul mate
3 a sense of adventure 4 a place of my own
5 my true vocation 6 purpose in life 7 a sense of belonging
8 core principles 9 my great passion 10 artistic ability
11 a unique talent 12 a place I can call home

Vocabulary checkpoint
Point out that the expressions in the box are mostly semi-fixed phrases, with some limited variation possible. For example, we can say *like-minded people*, not just *like-minded friends*. We can have a *sense of fun, humour* or *adventure*. We can say *core values* as well as *core principles*. Fixed phrases with no variation possible include *a place of my own* and *soul mate*.

3 Ask Ss to work in pairs to ask and answer questions using the phrases in the box. With **weaker classes**, elicit useful sentence starters, such as *Do you think everyone has …* or *Would you say you have …* , and complete a further example as a class to provide a clear model. When they finish, ask a few pairs to report back on something they learnt from their partner.

Optional alternative activity

With **weaker classes**, ask Ss to write sentences using the phrases in Ex 2b. They can then say their sentences to a partner who should agree or disagree, then ask further questions. This is a more supported approach which allows extra thinking time and focuses on statements rather than questions.

VOCABULARY BANK 10A p165
Phrases with *life*

This is an optional extension to the vocabulary section, extending the lexical set and providing further practice. If you're short of time, this can be done for homework.

1 Explain that all the phrases a–j contain the word *life* and spend some time discussing the meanings. Ask Ss to complete the sentences with the phrases, then go through the answers as a class.

Answers:
1 e   2 b   3 i   4 a   5 g   6 f   7 c   8 h   9 j   10 d

2a Ask Ss to work alone and write answers to four questions. **Fast finishers** and **stronger students** can write more.
b Put Ss together to ask and answer their questions. Encourage further discussion.

Further practice

Photocopiable activities: 10A Vocabulary, p250
App: 10A Vocabulary practice 1 and 2

Grammar

Future perfect and future continuous

4a 🔊 10.1 Focus attention on the text and tell Ss they are going to hear five responses. Ss should decide if each speaker is a student, middle-aged or retired as they listen and note key words or details that make them think this. Ask Ss to compare answers, then go through the answers as a class. Encourage Ss to justify their answers as responses may vary.

Suggested answers:
1 Kevin is probably a student.
2 Martha is probably a middle-aged person.
3 Tess is probably a student.
4 Pavel is probably retired.
5 Ayesha: impossible to say

Audioscript 10.1

Presenter:
Now, let's pick up on the issue of questions for your future self. What we wanted to know was: what three questions would you ask?
We've been flooded with responses from all over the country, for example this one from Kevin in Leicester. Kevin had these three questions for his future self:
'Will I still be sharing a flat?'
'Will I still be working as hard as I am now?'
'Will I have written that book I'm always planning to write?'

All good questions, Kevin, and I certainly hope that you find time to write that book! In fact, the theme of finding more time to do things that we want to do was a very common one among our listeners. For example, Martha from Stockport asked:
'Will my son still be living at home with me?'
'Will he finally have found a job?'
'And will I be living the quieter, more relaxed life that I've always wanted?'
Well Martha, no idea about your son, but I can certainly empathise with that need for a quieter life.
Of course, other people had entirely different preoccupations. For example, Tess from London asked:
'In ten years' time will I have found my true vocation?'
'Who will I be hanging out with?'
'And will I have found my soul mate?'
And Pavel from Swansea asks:
'Will I have suffered any major health problems?'
'Will I still be living near my son and daughter-in-law?'
'And will I have worked out how to use a smartphone?'
It's never too late to learn, Pavel!
Finally, Ayesha has this to say: she says, 'I wouldn't ask anything. I'd just smile and wait for my future self to disappear back to the future. You see, if I knew the future, I could change it, and that seems a bit scary to me!'
Very good point, Ayesha. More of your emails tomorrow. Time for the weather …

b Ask Ss to listen again and complete the questions. When they finish, ask them to compare answers and identify the tenses. Go through the answers as a class.

Answers:
1 Will, be working: future continuous
2 Will, have found: future perfect
3 will, be hanging: future continuous
4 Will, have suffered: future perfect

Teaching tip

Write the answers to listening activities on the board as you go through them, especially when focusing on grammar, to make sure that what Ss have written is spelt correctly. When you have done this, work as a class to identify the two tenses. Have a brief discussion on the differences in the two forms and their meanings before looking at the grammar box.

Optional extra activity

Ss discuss which of the speakers' concerns they most closely identify with.

5 Refer to the grammar box. Ask Ss to read it through and choose the correct options, then check answers. Point out that the expressions *in one year's time* and *in ten years' time* refer to the future and note the different positions of the apostrophes. Remind Ss that the present participle is the verb form ending in *-ing*.

Answers: 1 before   2 often   3 in progress
4 present participle   5 after   6 before   7 start

6 🔊 10.2 Ask Ss to listen to the questions to hear how *Will you have* and *Will you be* are pronounced. Go through the answers. Drill Ss in the question forms if you think they will benefit.

Answers:
have is pronounced with a weak form /həv/.
Sometimes /h/ is dropped: /əv/
be is also pronounced with a weak form /bi/.

7a Look at the first set of prompts and the example answer. Point out that Ss need to look at the context, then choose the best tense to complete the questions, future perfect or continuous. Ss then work alone to write the questions, referring to the grammar box, then check in pairs. Check answers with the whole class.

Answers:
1 One year from now, will you still be studying English?
2 One year from now, will you have taken any trips abroad?
3 One year from now, will you be living with your soul mate?
4 One year from now, will you be hanging out with the same friends?
5 Five years from now, will you be living in the same place?
6 Five years from now, will you have found your soul mate?
7 Five years from now, will you have learnt a new language? OR will you be learning a new language?
8 Five years from now, will you have found your true vocation?
9 When you retire, will you be living in a different place?
10 When you retire, will you be exercising every day?
11 When you retire, will you have found true happiness?
12 When you retire, will you have found your/a purpose in life?

b Ask Ss to ask and answer the questions in pairs. Monitor and help if necessary. When they finish, ask a few pairs to share their answers with the class.

LANGUAGE BANK 10A pp.154–155

Stronger classes could read the notes at home. Otherwise, check the notes with Ss. In each exercise, elicit the first answer as an example. Ss work alone to complete the exercises, then check their answers in pairs. In feedback, elicit Ss' answers and drill if needed. Ss can refer to the notes to help them.

Answers:
1 1 have 2 by 3 will 4 be 5 before 6 more 7 won't 8 still
2 1 'll be living
   2 'll have found
   3 might still be trying
   4 probable (that) I'll have retired
   5 doubt (that) I'll still be saving
   6 probably won't be working
   7 certain (that) I won't have seen
   8 won't have lost

Further practice

Photocopiable activities: 10A Grammar 1, p248; 10A Grammar 2, p249
App: 10A Grammar practice 1 and 2

Speaking

Prepare

8a Tell Ss they are going to write some questions they might ask a future self. Ask them to choose from the topics or think of their own.

b Ss should work alone and write questions using the future perfect and continuous, starting with 'Will I …'. Monitor and ensure they are doing this correctly. There is no need for whole-class feedback as Ss will write about different topics, but you could elicit a few examples if some Ss are struggling.

Speak

9a Put Ss in pairs to ask and answer their questions. Point out that Ss need to predict their partner's future when giving answers. They should use their imagination to think of interesting and positive answers but they don't necessarily have to be realistic! When they finish, give feedback on how they managed the tenses.

b Ask Ss to repeat the activity with a new partner. When they finish, ask them if there was a lot of difference between the answers given by their two partners.

Teaching tip

During a speaking activity with personal information (especially ones where Ss comment on each other's lives, as in Ex 9a), encourage Ss to be kind to each other. Explain clearly what they will be doing while you set up the activity and give an example. Clarify that you expect Ss to respect each other and be sensitive when discussing personal information. In feedback, keep the tone upbeat and look out for any Ss who may find the lesson content upsetting due to their personal circumstances.

Reflection on learning

Write the following questions on the board:
How useful was the topic of today's lesson?
How will today's vocabulary be helpful outside the class?
Put Ss in pairs to discuss the questions. When they have finished, ask if anyone wants to share their ideas with the class, but don't force them to if they'd rather not.

Homework ideas

Ex 7a: Ss write a paragraph about their life one year, five years and ten years in the future.
Language bank: 10A Ex 1–2, pp.154–155
Workbook: Ex 1–5, p76
App: grammar, vocabulary and pronunciation practice

Fast route: continue to Lesson 10B
Extended route: go to p134 for Develop your writing

10B Believe it not!

Introduction

The goal of this lesson is for students to maintain a discussion on interesting facts. To help them achieve this, they will revise articles and vocabulary in the context of fame.

Warm-up

Write three unrelated surprising statements about yourself on the board, two of which are true and one false. For example: *I've been to Antarctica. I used to be in an ice hockey team. I know three coding languages.* Invite Ss to ask questions to discover which statement is false. Explain that you will invent answers to try and hide your untrue statement. When they finish questioning you, elicit which statement most Ss think is untrue and confirm the answer. If time allows, Ss can repeat the activity in pairs, with their own three statements. Tell Ss that the topic of today's lesson is surprising facts.

Reading and vocabulary

Fame

1 Refer to the photos and ask Ss to identify what they show, then ask if they can suggest any surprising facts about each. Do this as a whole-class activity, then ask Ss to turn to p174 to check their ideas. When they finish, discuss which they predicted correctly or which facts are the most surprising.

Culture notes

LeRoy Robert Ripley (1890–1949) was an American sports cartoonist. He became famous for creating the *Believe It or Not!* newspaper cartoons and, later, his own radio and television shows, which featured odd facts from around the world.

2a Tell Ss they are going to read an article about a man called Robert Ripley. Give them a few minutes to read and find out why he was famous. Elicit the answer.

Answers: He was famous for his newspaper column called *Believe It or Not!* that was full of strange facts. He later wrote books and had radio and TV shows.

b Ask Ss to read the article more carefully and decide if the statements are true or false, underlining where they find the answers in the text. Allow a few minutes but don't let Ss check new words on their devices. When they finish, tell Ss to compare answers, then go through them as a class.

Answers:
1 T
2 T
3 F He was a newspaper sports cartoonist.
4 T
5 F They started as newspaper cartoons.
6 F He travelled the world searching for new facts and became the focus of public attention.

Optional extra activity

Ss discuss if there are books or TV shows about odd or surprising facts in their country. Ss discuss what they think about such books/programmes and why people like them.

3 Ss will have noticed the words and phrases in bold when reading. Point out that they were able to complete Ex 2b without needing to check the meaning of all the phrases. Ask them to now use the context to match the phrases with their meanings. Look at the first answer together, then ask Ss to continue and compare in pairs before going through the answers. Be prepared to answer questions as needed.

Answers: 1 high-profile 2 gone unnoticed 3 an instant hit 4 shot to fame 5 big break 6 unknown 7 started out 8 in the public eye 9 legacy 10 had taken the US by storm

4a This is an opportunity to personalise and practise some of the vocabulary. Ask Ss to read the questions first and clarify any problems with meaning. Set a timer for three minutes and tell pairs to ask and answer as many of the questions as they can in the time given.

Teaching tip

Sometimes it's a good idea to set specific time limits for tasks, particularly when developing exam skills where Ss need to work fast and under some pressure. Additionally, some Ss also enjoy working against the clock as it's fun and introduces an element of competition, especially when they work in teams. Timed activities also encourage a focus on fluency rather than accuracy and can change the classroom dynamic by adding energy to the lesson. Ss who get anxious about speaking can also benefit from the distraction of a time limit.

b When they finish, find out which pair answered the most questions. Elicit some interesting answers from a few pairs.

Optional alternative activity

Put Ss in teams of four to answer the questions. In this case, allow more time so that everyone gets a chance to speak. This might be suitable for classes who need more speaking practice or those who have mixed interest in the topic of fame. If you are teaching a multilingual class, you may want to group Ss with the same nationalities together so they can talk about people from their own country.

VOCABULARY BANK 10B p165
Verb prefixes

This is an optional extension to the vocabulary section, extending the lexical set and providing further practice. If you're short of time, this can be done for homework.

1 Ask Ss to use guesswork or their device/dictionary to complete the sentences with the correct prefixes. As you go through the answers, ask Ss to talk about the meaning the prefixes added.

Answers:
1 misbehaving, enforce   2 disappeared, endanger
3 misunderstand, disagree   4 regain, enable
5 mislead, misinformed   6 rewriting, rearrange

2a Ask Ss to discuss the question in pairs. When they have finished, lead a general feedback. And confirm the answers. Ask Ss to think of more examples.

Answers:
1 re- 2 en- 3 mis- 4 dis-

Further practice

Photocopiable activities: 10B Vocabulary, p253
App: 10B Vocabulary practice 1 and 2

Grammar
Articles

5a Ss may not have studied articles in detail before. This approach exposes them to the language in context and then analyses it, so there is no need to mention articles at this point. Ask Ss if they can complete the facts with the correct alternatives. Emphasise that they are not expected to know and encourage discussion but don't confirm answers yet as they will listen to them.

b 🔊 10.3 Play the recording and tell Ss to listen and check the answers to Ex 5a. Pause the recording as needed. Ask Ss to discuss in pairs, then check with the whole class. Ask Ss how many they guessed correctly.

> **Answers:** 1 102 2 nuts 3 dynamite 4 rodents 5 the US 6 0.005

6a Ask Ss to read the sentences in Ex 5a again and underline or highlight *a*, *an* and *the*.

b Refer to the grammar box and ask Ss to use the underlined examples in Ex 5a to help them choose the correct alternatives. Go through as a class and ask further concept-checking questions as needed. Remind Ss that this is a complex grammar area that consists of a lot of categories and examples rather than just a few rules.

> **Answers:** 1 a or an 2 the 3 the 4 Don't use 5 a or an 6 the 7 Don't use 8 the 9 the

7 🔊 10.4 Ask Ss to listen to the text and underline *the* as they do so. When they finish, ask Ss to discuss the two pronunciations of *the*. Go through the answers as a class and give further examples as checks.

> **Answers:** *The* is pronounced /ðə/ when it appears before a word which begins with a consonant sound. However, it is pronounced /ðiː/ before a word which begins with a vowel sound.

Grammar and pronunciation checkpoint
Ss will know that we use *a* before consonants and *an* before vowels. They may wonder why we say *a university*, not *an university*. Explain that it is due to the sound, not the letter, that starts the word. The starting sound of *university* is /j/, which is a consonant sound. Another example of this rule is *an hour*, where *h* is silent. Compare with *a house*, where *h* is pronounced. Similarly, the pronunciation of *the* depends on the sound which follows, not the spelling. So *the hour* is pronounced /ðiːjaʊə/ but *the house* is pronounced /ðəhaʊs/.

8a Tell Ss they are now going to practise using articles. Ask them to complete the sentences using *a*, *an*, *the* or no article. When they finish, put Ss in pairs to check together, referring to the grammar box to confirm the rules. Go through the answers and discuss which rule is being applied.

> **Answers:** 1 an 2 – 3 A 4 the 5 a 6 the 7 – 8 the 9 – 10 a 11 the 12 the 13 the 14 – 15 a 16 –

b Ask Ss to discuss which text is not true, then turn to p170 to check their answers.

> **Answers:** In fact, the Atacama Desert is not the driest place on Earth. There are parts of Antarctica which are drier.

LANGUAGE BANK 10B pp.154–155

Stronger classes could read the notes at home. Otherwise, check the notes with Ss. In each exercise, elicit the first answer as an example. Ss work alone to complete the exercises, then check their answers in pairs. In feedback, elicit Ss' answers and deal with any questions. Ss can refer to the notes to help them.

Answers:
1 1b 2a 3b 4a 5a 6b
2 If you ever go to the west coast of **the** United States, make sure you visit the Hollywood Walk of Fame. This is a stretch of pavement which starts at ~~the~~ Hollywood Boulevard, covers **a** total distance of over 1.3 miles, and which contains the names of over 2,500 famous actors in pink stars. Whether **an** actor has shot to ~~the~~ fame overnight or has worked for ~~the~~ years to become famous, it is an honour to be included here, but it also costs **the** actor about $30,000! The Walk of Fame is one of **the** busiest attractions in Hollywood with millions of visitors **a** year, and you never know, while you're there you may also run into one of **the** stars whose name appears there.

Further practice
Photocopiable activities: 10B Grammar 1, p251; 10B Grammar 2, p252
App: 10B Grammar practice 1 and 2

Speaking
Prepare
9 Name alternate Ss A or B, then ask them to turn to the relevant pages and read their information. Explain that Ss need to choose two facts from their lists and then think of and write down another false fact of their own. Monitor and help with vocabulary as needed.

Speak
10a Put Ss in AB pairs to tell each other their three interesting facts (two from their lists and one false one of their own). Point out the Useful phrases and encourage Ss to use them to introduce each fact. Monitor and make notes for correction. When they finish, ask Ss to try and identify their partner's false 'fact'.

b Ask Ss to repeat the activity with more facts from the lists or a new partner. Conduct whole-class feedback, including correction.

Reflection on learning
Write the following questions on the board:
What is the most challenging aspect of studying English for you? How could you use the speaking practice we did today outside the class?
Put Ss in pairs to discuss the questions. When they have finished, ask if anyone wants to share their ideas with the class, but don't force them to if they'd rather not.

Homework ideas
Ss write an interesting facts story for a wall display.
Language bank: 10B Ex 1–2, pp.154–155
Workbook: Ex 1–5, p77
App: grammar, vocabulary and pronunciation practice

Fast route: continue to Lesson 10C
Extended route: go to p95 for Develop your listening

10c New solutions

Introduction
The goal of this lesson is for students to give detailed opinions. To help them achieve this, they will revise compound adjectives and vocabulary relating to persuasion and enforcement.

Warm-up
Ask Ss to make a list of typical rules/laws in public places and why those things are important. Give an example yourself, such as: *No littering – someone could fall over and it looks messy*. Put Ss in pairs to tell each other. If your class is very large or time is short, do this as a class. Ask pairs to report back and write useful vocabulary on the board.

Reading

1 Refer to the questions and photos, then put Ss in pairs to discuss. During feedback, have a show of hands to see if Ss do these things and what they think about them. There are no fixed answers.

2 Focus attention on the text. Ask Ss to read and answer the question. Give them just 1–2 minutes to encourage skimming. When they have finished, ask them to compare in pairs, then go through the answers as a class.

> **Answers:** the problem of walking and texting then crossing the road; a possible solution is LED 'traffic' lights in the pavement

Optional alternative activity
Discuss in detail what the photos show before Ss read, gathering ideas about what is shown and writing them on the board. Use the photos to pre-teach useful vocabulary from the reading text, including *pedestrian, electronic device, cross the road*. This approach is suited to **weaker classes** who may struggle with some of the vocabulary.

3 Tell Ss they will read the article again more carefully and answer the questions. Give them a few minutes, then ask them to compare in pairs before going through the answers.

> **Answers:**
> 1 what's going on around you
> 2 It suggests that pedestrians who do this are putting themselves and others in danger.
> 3 pedestrians who are looking at their phones while they cross the road
> 4 if they will change the way people behave

4 Ask Ss to discuss the questions in pairs, then have a whole-class discussion. Have a show of hands to see which solution is preferred.

Optional extra activity
If Ss feel strongly about the topic, ask them to work in groups to create posters or leaflets for a publicity campaign about walking and texting. They can extend this to include other modern anti-social behaviours that they would like to stop, for example: using your phone when being served in a shop or having dinner; wearing headphones when you're with other people; taking selfies in inappropriate places; checking your phone during meetings.

Language focus
Compound adjectives

5 Ask Ss to read the Language focus box silently, then underline the compound adjectives in the article. Alternatively, ask Ss to take turns to read sections aloud, discussing and dealing with questions as they do so. Ss can then underline the compound adjectives. Go through the answers and discuss the meanings.

> **Answers:** built-up, high-tech, internet-connected, absent-minded, densely-populated, narrow-minded, hard up, well-off, state-of-the-art, so-called, long-term

Vocabulary checkpoint
Point out that while compound adjectives are usually joined by a hyphen, there are no clear rules. The hyphen tells us that the words are connected; compare *the man-eating crocodile* with *the man eating crocodile*. Hyphens are most commonly used when the compound adjective comes before the noun; when after the noun they are not usually applied, for example: *the well-known author*, but *the author is well known*. As compounds become more frequently used, they sometimes achieve single-word status, for example: *daytime TV, childlike personality, worldwide problem*.

6 🔊 10.8 Ask Ss to listen to the adjectives and underline the main stress. Ask Ss to compare before eliciting answers and drilling the adjectives.

> **Answers:**
> All the adjectives are stressed on the (first part of the) second word:
> self-**con**fident, well-**ed**ucated, absent-**min**ded, high-**tech**, well-**off**, long-**term**, densely-**pop**ulated, narrow-**mind**ed, hard-**wor**king, long-**dis**tance

7a Ask Ss to rewrite the sentences using the compound adjectives from Ex 6. Look at the first example as a class, then ask Ss to continue alone. Monitor and help as necessary. Go through the answers as a class.

> **Answers:**
> 1 Are you well-educated?
> 2 Are you absent-minded?
> 3 Have you got a high-tech watch?
> 4 Are you self-confident?
> 5 Are some of your friends well-off?
> 6 Are you hard-working?
> 7 Do you live in a densely-populated area?
> 8 Are you narrow-minded?

b Ask Ss to work in pairs to ask and answer the rewritten questions. When they finish, ask a few Ss to report back on their partner using a compound adjective.

LANGUAGE BANK 10c pp.154–155
Stronger classes could read the notes at home. Otherwise, check the notes with Ss. In each exercise, elicit the first answer as an example. Ss work alone to complete the exercise, then check their answers in pairs. In feedback, elicit Ss' answers and drill as needed. Ss can refer to the notes to help them.

> **Answers:**
> 1 1 built-up 2 narrow-minded 3 high-tech 4 user-friendly
>   5 six-year-old 6 part-time 7 well-educated 8 so-called

Further practice

Photocopiable activities: 10C Language focus 1, p254;
10C Language focus 2, p255
App: 10C Language focus practice 1 and 2

Listening and vocabulary
Persuasion and enforcement

8 Tell Ss they are going to read about selfies and ask them to predict what the problem is. Discuss briefly, then ask them to read the text. Discuss as a class if anyone has seen or heard of this happening and ask for suggestions to prevent it.

9a 🔊 10.9 Explain that Ss are going to listen to four people suggesting solutions for the selfie problem. Tell them to listen and make notes. Ss can compare in pairs, then check the answers as a class.

> **Answers:**
> 1 Educate people with posters and warnings.
> 2 Reduce the number of cars in the city centre.
> 3 Put up signs and create no-selfie zones in dangerous places.
> 4 Introduce a law banning people from taking selfies

> **Audioscript 10.9**
>
> **Speaker 1**
> I don't think it helps to fine people for taking selfies – it just makes people angry when they have to pay money. It's better to educate them not to do it. Posters and warnings and that kind of thing is enough. I don't believe in punishing people for taking photos.
>
> **Speaker 2**
> The best way to prevent these kinds of accidents with pedestrians is to reduce the number of cars entering city centres. The city should charge motorists for using busy roads. That always works. The best way to catch everyone is to install cameras that read your number plate. London has a scheme like this and it works well, so I hear.
>
> **Speaker 3**
> In my opinion, you just need to put up a few signs in places where it might be dangerous, you know, create no-selfie zones and … that's all really. It's better to discourage people from doing something than ban it completely. You treat people like children when you ban something.
>
> **Speaker 4**
> You need to introduce a law to stop people from taking selfies and then you need to enforce that law. Simple! Arrest people if you have to. No one is above the law. These days we're far too tolerant of bad behaviour.

b Ask Ss to complete the sentences with words in the box. Play the recording again so Ss can check. Go through the answers as a class and deal with questions on vocabulary as needed. Encourage Ss to note down the verb patterns, for example: fine someone for doing something, educate people (not) to do something, discourage people from doing something.

> **Answers:**
> 1 a fine   b educate
> 2 a charge b install
> 3 a put up b discourage
> 4 introduce, enforce

10a Ask Ss to discuss the opinions in Ex 9b in pairs, ticking those they agree with and saying why. They can agree with more than one opinion. When they finish, have a show of hands to see which is the most popular opinion and discuss why as a class.

b Look at the example as a class. Clarify that Ss only need to work on the sentences in Ex 9b that they disagreed with, changing them so they are true for them. Ss compare their new sentences when they finish.

Further practice

Photocopiable activities: 10C Vocabulary, p256
App: 10C Vocabulary practice 1 and 2

Speaking
Prepare

11 Focus attention on the text. Ask Ss to read and make a list of possible solutions and prepare pros and cons for each. Come up with one possible solution together as an example, then ask Ss to continue in pairs. Monitor and support with vocabulary as needed. There are no fixed answers.

Speak

12a Put Ss in groups of three or four to talk about their possible solutions. Ask group members to take turns speaking and refer them to the Useful phrases. Remind Ss to listen to each other and try to agree on the two best solutions. Monitor and listen to how Ss are using the language from today's lesson.

b At the end, ask each group to present their two chosen solutions to the class. When they finish, decide as a class on the two best solutions. Give feedback on the language used in the presentations.

> **Reflection on learning**
>
> Write the following questions on the board:
> *What was most enjoyable about today's lesson?*
> *How could you use this language outside the class?*
> Put Ss in pairs to discuss the questions. When they have finished, ask if anyone wants to share their ideas with the class, but don't force them to if they'd rather not.

Homework ideas

Language bank: 10C Ex 1, pp.154–155
Workbook: Ex 1–5, p78
App: grammar, vocabulary and pronunciation practice

Fast route: continue to Check and reflect
Extended route: go to p114 for Develop your reading

10 Check and reflect: Units 9–10

Introduction

Ss revise and practise the language of Units 9 and 10. The notes below provide some ideas for exploiting the activities in class, but you may want to set the exercises for homework or use them as a diagnostic or progress test.

1 Ask Ss to work alone to complete the sentences with the correct words in the box, then check in pairs. Check answers with the whole class.

> **Answers:** 1 hoax 2 mystery 3 victim 4 clue 5 evidence 6 motive 7 identify 8 red herring

2 Ask Ss to complete the sentences so that they express the same information, using a modal verb. Complete one as a class, then ask Ss to work alone. Ask Ss to check in pairs before going through the answers as a class.

> **Answers:** 1 may/might/could have taken 2 must have been driving 3 may/might not have said 4 can't/couldn't have seen 5 can't/couldn't have been speaking

3 Ask Ss to match the sentence halves. They can work alone, then check in pairs before going through the answers as a class.

> **Answers:** 1 f 2 d 3 g 4 a 5 b 6 e 7 c

4a Ss work alone to complete the sentences. Remind them to look at the verbs before the gaps to help them with this. Go through the answers as a class. Ask Ss to read out the whole sentence and drill as needed.

> **Answers:** 1 interrupting 2 laugh 3 to change 4 know 5 criticising

b Ss tick the sentences that are true for them, then work in pairs to compare answers.

5 Ss use a verb from box A and a particle from box B to complete each sentence with the correct phrasal verb. They may need to change the form of the verb. They can work in pairs, then check answers as a class.

> **Answers:** 1 figure, out 2 let, down 3 stick, out 4 stands out 5 turned out 6 made, up

6 Ss work alone to decide on the correct word order, then check in pairs. Go through the answers as a class.

> **Answers:**
> 1 thought it through
> 2 will come up with a clever solution
> 3 make out the accident was all my fault
> 4 came across these old photos
> 5 Just get on with it.
> 6 never figure it out

7a Ss match the sentence starters and endings to make complete sentences. They can work in pairs to compare, then check the answers as a class.

> **Answers:** 1 d 2 f 3 a 4 e 5 g 6 b 7 h 8 c

b Ask Ss to work alone to tick the sentences they agree with, then compare with a partner. When they finish, discuss as a class to see which sentences are most popular.

8 Ask Ss to complete the sentences with the correct future form of the verb in brackets. When they have finished, go through the answers as a class and deal with any questions.

> **Answers:** 1 'll have finished 2 will, be catching 3 'll be travelling 4 Will, have had 5 'll, be working 6 'll have made

9 Tell Ss the underlined phrases are not quite right and they should change them to make them correct. Complete an example as a class, then ask Ss to continue alone. They can compare in pairs, then go through the answers as a class.

> **Answers:** 1 high-profile 2 legacy 3 started out 4 an unknown 5 unknown 6 big break 7 public eye 8 instant hit

10 Ask Ss to complete the text with the correct articles (or no article). Complete the first example as a class, then ask Ss to continue alone. They can compare in pairs, then go through the answers as a class.

> **Answers:** 1 the 2 – 3 – 4 a 5 the 6 the 7 the 8 an 9 – 10 the 11 – 12 –

11 Ask Ss to complete the definitions with the correct compound adjectives. Complete the first example as a class, then ask Ss to continue alone. They can compare in pairs, then go through the answers as a class.

> **Answers:** 1 well-known 2 20-year-old 3 good-looking 4 densely-populated 5 self-confident 6 high-tech 7 part-time 8 two-page

12a Ask Ss to complete the sentences with the correct verbs in the box. Complete the first example as a class, then ask Ss to continue alone. Ss can compare in pairs, then go through the answers as a class.

> **Answers:** 1 fine 2 discourage 3 educate 4 introduce 5 enforce 6 install 7 put up

b Ask Ss to tick and discuss the solutions they agree with. Have a whole-class show of hands to see which ideas are the most popular.

13a Ask Ss to use the words in the box to complete the conversations. Complete the first example as a class, then ask Ss to continue alone. Clarify that Ss may need to change the form of some words. Ss should compare in pairs, then go through the answers as a class.

> **Answers:** 1 refused, mistake 2 down, check 3 get, put 4 working, turned 5 booked, sort 6 arrived, stock

b Ss work together in pairs to practise the conversations.

Reflect

Ask Ss to rate each statement alone, then compare in pairs. Encourage them to ask any questions they still have about any of the areas covered in Units 9 and 10.

Roadmap video

Go online for the Roadmap video and worksheet.

10A Develop your writing

Introduction

The goal of this lesson is for students to write a magazine article. To help them achieve this, they will focus on attracting and keeping the reader's attention.

Warm-up

Ask Ss to discuss in pairs whether they ever read magazine articles (online or in print) and what they find interesting or not so interesting about them. Discuss their ideas as a class. Elicit typical magazine topics (fashion, politics, sport, computing, celebrity gossip, etc.) and bring in a range of magazines to show the class if possible.

1a Put Ss in pairs to discuss the questions. After a few minutes, conduct brief feedback and compare ideas as a class.
b Ask Ss to read the competition question. Give them a few minutes to discuss with a partner, then conduct whole-class feedback and add useful vocabulary to the board.
2a Ask Ss if they make notes before writing an essay. Refer Ss to the two sets of notes, clarifying that they were written by the same person. Ask Ss which set they think was written first. Then put them in pairs to discuss the questions. Elicit answers and deal with any questions.

> **Answers:**
> 1 set A first, set B second
> 2 Set A shows ideas. Set B organises those ideas.

b Tell Ss to look at how the second set of notes is organised. Ask Ss whether they follow similar steps when writing and if so, why.
3 Tell Ss they will now read the article. Ask them to read it quickly and see what information the writer added. As they read, they should tick the points on the plan that are mentioned and highlight new information in the article. Ask Ss to check in pairs, then go through the answers. If possible, project the text and annotate the answers and where they are found.

> **Answers:**
> more details about how high-tech shops work
> how it feels to shop in those places
> examples of how shops will use their detailed knowledge of customers

Culture notes

Ss may not be familiar with some of the shopping methods mentioned in the article. *Scanners* are handheld devices used by shoppers in some supermarkets to save time and avoid using the till. Customers pick out their shopping, scan the barcode and then pack the shopping themselves. *Online shopping* is ordered on your computer or phone and then delivered to your home at a time that you choose. A supermarket employee goes around and picks what you ordered. If something you chose is not available, the supermarket chooses a substitute for you. Some services even put the food in the fridge for you when they deliver it to your home.

4a Ask Ss to read the article again and answer the questions. Give them up to five minutes. They can underline sections of the text and make notes, then compare answers before you go through as a class.

> **Answers:**
> 1 liked
> 2 They have got rid of the cashier.
> 3 so that people can see and touch goods before buying online
> 4 less queuing, waiting and travelling to the shop itself
> 5 You might be able to summon a mobile shop with an app on your phone.
> 6 It may be harder for ordinary people to start their own shop. It might be harder to explore and discover new things.

b Ask Ss to find and underline words or phrases in the text that match the meanings. Point out the paragraph references to help Ss. When they finish, give them a few minutes to discuss in pairs, then ask for answers and discuss as a class.

> **Answers:** 1 there's no denying that …
> 2 our urban environment   3 done away with   4 stuffed with
> 5 yet more   6 summon   7 only time will tell

5 Ask Ss what the difference between an article and an essay is, then refer them to the Focus box. Ask Ss to read it through and check their ideas. Monitor and help as necessary. Go through the answers as a class.

> **Answers:** An article is less formal than an essay and the writing has to be more interesting and grab people's attention more.

Prepare

6a Tell Ss they are going to write a magazine article. Read the instruction as a class and ask Ss to choose a topic or think of their own. With **weaker classes**, choose one topic and brainstorm ideas and useful vocabulary as a class on the board.
b Ask Ss to work alone or in pairs to make notes. Monitor and help as necessary.

Optional alternative activity

Give each student or pair some self-adhesive notes. Ask them to write each idea on a separate note. When it comes to organising their ideas, they can unpeel and move the notes around on a page. This is a great planning tool as it's very flexible.

c Ask Ss to organise their notes. Point out that they don't need to use all their ideas but should choose the best ones. If Ss are struggling, put pairs with the same topic together to support each other.

Write

7a Refer Ss to the checklist before they write. Ask them to write their article. Move around the class and help with ideas and expressions.
b Ask Ss to swap with a partner and use the checklist to give each other feedback.

Teaching tip

Ss may sometimes struggle to correct each other's work, or 'correct' something that is grammatically fine! Point out that the checklist does not require them to correct the grammar but to have a more holistic view of the success of the piece of writing. However, if you do want Ss to correct each other's language as well, you could provide a correction code and tell Ss to identify no more than five errors. Example correction code: SP = spelling, T = tense, P = punctuation, GR = grammar, WO = word order.

Homework ideas

Ss write a magazine article on the cultural influence of the English-speaking world on other cultures.
Workbook: Ex 1–7, pp.82–83

10B Develop your listening

Introduction

The goal of this lesson is for students to extract the main points from a news programme. To help them achieve this, they will focus on distinguishing fact from opinion.

Warm-up

Ask Ss if they listen to the news, watch it on TV or read it (on their phone or in print). Ask them to discuss what medium they prefer and why. Tell them today's class is about understanding a news programme and point out that this skill will also be useful for listening to presentations at work.

Culture notes

A **meteorite** is a solid piece of debris from an object, such as a comet or asteroid, that originates in outer space and reaches the surface of the Earth. A **meteor** is similar, but when the piece of debris enters the Earth's atmosphere, pressure and chemical reactions cause it to heat up and form a fireball, also known as a **shooting star**.

1a Ask Ss if they know much about meteors or meteorites, reassuring them that you don't expect them to know much! Then ask Ss to guess the answers to the questions in pairs. After a few minutes, conduct brief feedback but don't confirm answers yet as Ss will hear them.

b 🔊 10.5 Tell Ss they are going to listen to check their answers. Go through the answers as a class. If appropriate, Ss could discuss whether they have seen any films about meteorites striking Earth or if they think we should worry about this possibility.

Answers: 1 a 2 b 3 a 4 a

Audioscript 10.5

We hear about meteors and meteorites quite a lot, but do you know the difference between the two? Well, a meteor is actually a rock from space that has entered the Earth's atmosphere, but which burns up before it hits the surface of the Earth. It burns up because it reaches temperatures of up to 1,650 degrees Celsius when it enters the atmosphere. If the rock, or at least a bit of it, actually survives this temperature and hits the surface of the Earth, it is called a meteorite. One of the biggest meteorites ever is probably the one that hit Earth 66 million years ago and wiped out the dinosaurs.

The hole that a meteorite leaves on the surface of the Earth is called a crater. The largest known meteorite crater is called Vredefort Dome in South Africa. It is 300 kilometres wide.

2a 🔊 10.6 Tell Ss they are going to listen to the first part of a news report about a meteor strike. They should answer the questions while they listen.

Audioscript 10.6

Reporter: … back to Gabby in the studio.
Gabby: Now, a flash of light, a loud bang and confirmation from the government that it was, indeed, a meteor that flashed across the sky on Thursday evening in Southern Ontario. Hundreds of eyewitnesses reported the strange sight and several car dashboard cameras captured it.
Researchers have confirmed that the meteor entered the Earth's atmosphere and fell towards the ground at about 6.19 p.m. All available evidence suggests the meteor was about one metre in diameter and weighed a few metric tonnes. The flying rock blazed a path across the sky and residents saw a bright yellow light and wide smoke trails as they looked up at the sky. It is not known where the rock hit the Earth, if indeed any of it survived that long.
Scientists have speculated that the meteor was part of a larger one that mostly burnt up as it entered the Earth's atmosphere.
Here to discuss this event with me in the studio is our most high-profile astronomer, Professor Ana Santos …

b Play the recording again and ask Ss to compare notes in pairs. Go through the answers as a class.

Answers:
1 Thursday evening, Southern Ontario
2 one metre in diameter, several metric tonnes
3 no one knows (it might not have hit the Earth)

3 🔊 10.7 Ask Ss to read the statements, listen to the second part of the news report and decide whether each statement is true or false. When the answer is false, Ss should correct it. Ask Ss to check answers in pairs before whole-class feedback.

Answers:
1 F Only Hugo Martin has written a book.
2 F It doesn't hit the Earth's surface, it mostly burns up in the atmosphere.
3 F about once every 500,000 years
4 T
5 T
6 F It was a meteor. It didn't hit the Earth, but exploded 30 km above the Earth.

Audioscript 10.7

Gabby: Here to discuss this event with me in the studio is our most high-profile astronomer, Professor Ana Santos … along with Professor Hugo Martin, who has written a book about meteor strikes. Welcome both of you. Now, Professor Santos, is it true to say that meteor strikes are far from a rare occurrence?

Ana Santos:	Yes, absolutely. In fact, our planet is bombarded with 60 tonnes of space material every day but almost …
Gabby:	Every day?
Ana Santos:	Yes, every day, but almost all of it simply vaporises in our atmosphere and never reaches the Earth's surface.
Gabby:	So it just burns up.
Ana Santos:	That's right. Most of this space material comes from asteroids and it's very small, it's effectively space dust – we refer to it as micrometeoroids – and the friction caused by the speed it's travelling at makes it burn up – literally nothing reaches the ground.
Gabby:	But sometimes something does reach the ground, doesn't it?
Ana Santos:	That's right. If a piece of rock from space reaches the ground, then it's referred to as a meteorite – the word that most people know.
Gabby:	And should we be concerned about these meteorites? Do they pose a danger to us?
Ana Santos:	Well, if a large meteor is coming our way then there's not much we can do about it, but to be honest, it's really not worth worrying about because …
Hugo Martin:	Umm … If I could just come in here.
Gabby:	Yes, Professor Martin.
Hugo Martin:	Hmm, I think that actually we should, in fact, be concerned about meteor strikes and we should, I believe, do much more to find and track those … those possible meteorites.
Gabby:	Professor Santos?
Ana Santos:	Well, I would argue that large meteor strikes are very rare, you get one every half a million years on average, so it's highly unlikely that we'll experience a big one in our lifetime. So basically, no reason to worry.
Gabby:	Professor Martin, you've written a book about meteor strikes, haven't you?
Hugo Martin:	Yes, indeed, and I would, umm, I would argue, as I say, that we should be, umm, concerned about meteor strikes. They are, actually, quite common.
Ana Santos:	… yes but only small ones.
Hugo Martin:	Only small ones, that's true, but even a small, umm, small meteorite can be quite dangerous.
Ana Santos:	I'm not convinced that they can be very dangerous, not to a large number of people.
Gabby:	Let's come on to the most famous meteor strike of all, the one that wiped out the dinosaurs.
Hugo Martin:	Yes, absolutely, well, to the best of our knowledge, a meteor strike killed the dinosaurs and actually 70 percent of life on Earth.
Ana Santos:	Could I just say something? In fact the dinosaurs were probably killed by climate change, but many scientists believe that the climate change itself was caused by a meteor strike.
Hugo Martin:	Yes, quite right, indeed.
Gabby:	So, what other significant meteor strikes has the Earth experienced in more recent history?
Hugo Martin:	Well, most, of course, go unnoticed, but for example, just recently, in 2018 a meteorite crashed into the mountains, the umm, the Ural mountains in Russia and injured about 1,000 people.
Gabby:	How did it injure them? Were they hit by it?
Hugo Martin:	No, not at all, In fact, you see, the meteorite caused a yellow fireball in the sky, much like the one in Canada in your, umm, news report, and everyone, you see, everyone rushed to the window to look at it and when the meteorite hit the ground, hit the Earth, the impact, it umm, shattered windows over a large area and it was that which caused the injuries: broken glass.
Gabby:	I see, so no one was actually hit?
Hugo Martin:	No, although it does happen. There was a meteorite which, umm, which crashed through someone's roof in Alabama, I think.
Ana Santos:	Yes, Alabama.
Hugo Martin:	… and it bounced off the radio, and hit the owner of the house, would you believe!
Ana Santos:	This was an incredibly small meteorite though.
Hugo Martin:	Indeed, indeed, it was, but within the last 100 years we have seen other famous meteor strikes which have been much more destructive …
Gabby:	Go on.
Hugo Martin:	Well, a few years ago, a meteor exploded over Chelyabinsk in Russia and that was about 20 metres in diameter and weighed more than the Eiffel Tower.
Ana Santos:	But it didn't actually hit Earth.
Hugo Martin:	No, it actually exploded about 30 kilometres above the Earth, but it had the potential to do a great deal of damage.
Gabby:	OK, well, I'm afraid that's all we've got time for. I'd like to thank my guests, Professor Ana Santos and Professor Hugo Martin, for coming in today … .

4 Refer Ss to the Focus box to read through alone, then ask them to discuss the sentences in pairs, deciding if they are facts (F) or opinions (O). Ask Ss for their answers. Find out whether this distinction is the same in their first language.

Answers: 1 F   2 F   3 O   4 O   5 F

5 Ask Ss to listen to the second part of the news report again, focusing on things the two speakers disagreed on. Discuss as a class. If Ss have access to the audioscript, they may benefit from reading it as they listen.

Answers: 1, 2

6 Tell Ss they are going to practise distinguishing between fact and opinion. Look at the first example as a class, clarifying that the underlined section shows it's an opinion (superlative form), then ask Ss to continue alone, using the Focus box to help them. Ask them to check in pairs, then go through the answers as a class.

Answers:
1 O – superlative form (most impressive),
2 F – passive (was detected)
3 F – statistic (99.9 percent)
4 O – introductory phrase (It's obvious to me that)
5 O – probably
6 O – should
7 F – statistic (70 percent)

Optional extra activity

Ask Ss to research another area of interest and present a mixture of facts and opinions about it to the class. You could provide a variety of topics related to health, where there is a mix of fact and opinion easily available online and in various publications, for example: the Mediterranean diet and long life; intermittent fasting; High Intensity Interval Training (HIIT); veganism.

7 Ask Ss to discuss the questions. If Ss are not so interested in the topic, keep it brief and discuss as a class.

Homework ideas

Workbook: Ex 1–5, p79

10c Develop your reading

Introduction

The goal of this lesson is for students to understand an article. To help them achieve this, they will focus on inferring the meaning of words from context.

Warm-up

Ask Ss what kind of qualities people who become leaders or socially popular have. Ask individuals to make a list of four adjectives that tend to describe such people and then compare in pairs before whole-class feedback. Introduce the word *charisma* and explain its meaning (see Culture notes below). Decide as a class a few names of well-known charismatic people.

Culture notes

Charisma /kəˈrɪzmə/ is a special presence or power that some people have naturally that makes them able to influence other people and attract their attention and admiration. **Charismatic** /ˌkærɪzˈmætɪk/ people are sometimes described as charming, enchanting or attractive and are usually self-confident. They are often good storytellers and good listeners. Frequently, they become leaders or public figures.

1a Ask Ss to look at the photos and discuss the questions. After a few minutes, conduct brief feedback.

b Ask Ss to discuss the questions in pairs. You may need to prompt Ss with ideas from the Culture notes below. Ask a few pairs to share ideas with the class.

Culture notes

Editing photos to make yourself more attractive has become common. It is possible to crop shots so that background is changed and to use filters or overlays to alter your appearance.

Other ways to enhance your professional profile might be to add recommendations and testimonials. If you have a website, you can optimise it to enhance your public profile, so that people find you quickly when searching online.

2 Tell Ss to read the first part of the article and answer the questions. Tell them they have a few minutes to do this and should not use their devices to check words they don't know. Check the answers as a class. Point out that *could do with* = find useful. Ask Ss what kind of article the text is (general interest, not very serious).

Answers:
1 He believes he can help everyone to be more charismatic.
2 everyone (in order to stand out)
3 **Strong:** good at building rapport
   Weak: nervous when doing public speaking; doesn't take herself seriously

3a Ask Ss to read again quickly and underline any words they don't understand. Emphasise that they should NOT look them up or discuss them yet.

b Refer to the Focus box and call on individual Ss to read sections aloud to the class. Discuss as a class whether any Ss underlined the phrases in bold from Ex 4a.

4a Ask Ss to read the article again more carefully to choose the correct meanings, using the strategies from the Focus box. They should work alone.

b Ask Ss to compare in pairs. Go through the answers as a class, discussing which strategies helped them.

Answers: 1a 2b 3c 4c 5a 6c 7a

5 Ask Ss to read the second half of the article and decide if the statements are true or false – again without using any devices or dictionaries. Give them a time limit of three minutes, then ask for answers. Highlight where these appear in the article if you can, projecting the text on the board.

Answers: 1T 2F 3F 4T 5F 6T

6a Ask Ss to underline phrases in the article that they are not sure of. Tell them to guess the meaning, using the strategies from the Focus box.

b Ask Ss to compare in pairs, then check their answers using their device or a dictionary. Go through the answers as a class and deal with any questions.

7 Ask Ss to discuss the questions in pairs, then conduct brief feedback to see if they agree and what their reasons are.

Optional extra activity

Discuss with Ss why we might be better off not using dictionaries (to prepare for exams, to build skills in guesswork, sometimes the meaning provided is wrong or they choose the wrong meaning from several, it's time consuming, etc.). If Ss are heavy translation/dictionary users, find out if they will consider changing their approach after this lesson.

Homework ideas

Workbook: Ex 1–7, p81

RESOURCE BANK

Photocopiable activities index

LESSON	LANGUAGE POINT	PAGE
1A	**Grammar 1:** Question forms **Grammar 2:** Question forms **Vocabulary:** Verbs with dependent prepositions	167 168 169
1B	**Grammar 1:** Past simple, past continuous, *used to, would, keep* + *-ing* **Grammar 2:** Past simple, past continuous, *used to, would, keep* + *-ing* **Vocabulary:** Phrases to describe emotions	170 171 172
1C	**Language focus 1:** Verb + noun collocations **Language focus 2:** Verb + noun collocations **Vocabulary:** Adjectives of character	173 174 175
2A	**Grammar 1:** Present perfect simple and continuous **Grammar 2:** Present perfect simple and continuous **Vocabulary:** Phrases with *get*	176 177 178
2B	**Grammar 1:** The passive **Grammar 2:** The passive **Vocabulary:** Social action	179 180 181
2C	**Language focus 1:** *-ed* and *-ing* adjectives **Language focus 2:** *-ed* and *-ing* adjectives **Vocabulary:** Common complaints	182 183 184
3A	**Grammar 1:** Past perfect simple and continuous **Grammar 2:** Past perfect simple and continuous **Vocabulary:** Memory	185 186 187
3B	**Grammar 1:** Comparatives and superlatives **Grammar 2:** Comparatives and superlatives **Vocabulary:** Character adjectives	188 189 190
3C	**Language focus 1:** Forming adjectives **Language focus 2:** Forming adjectives **Vocabulary:** Arguments	191 192 193
4A	**Grammar 1:** Relative clauses **Grammar 2:** Relative clauses **Vocabulary:** Adjectives to describe things	194 195 196
4B	**Grammar 1:** Obligation and prohibition **Grammar 2:** Obligation and prohibition **Vocabulary:** Job requirements	197 198 199
4C	**Language focus 1:** Forming verbs with *en* **Language focus 2:** Forming verbs with *en* **Vocabulary:** 21st century words	200 201 202
5A	**Grammar 1:** Mistakes in the past **Grammar 2:** Mistakes in the past **Vocabulary:** Money phrasal verbs	203 204 205
5B	**Grammar 1:** Quantifiers **Grammar 2:** Quantifiers **Vocabulary:** Crime (robbery)	206 207 208
5C	**Language focus 1:** Adverb + adjective collocations **Language focus 2:** Adverb + adjective collocations **Vocabulary:** Money	209 210 211

LESSON	LANGUAGE POINT	PAGE
6A	**Grammar 1:** Verb + -*ing* and infinitive with *to* **Grammar 2:** Verb + -*ing* and infinitive with *to* **Vocabulary:** Common idioms	212 213 214
6B	**Grammar 1:** Reported speech **Grammar 2:** Reported speech **Vocabulary:** Negotiating	215 216 217
6C	**Language focus 1:** Verb patterns after reporting verbs **Language focus 2:** Verb patterns after reporting verbs **Vocabulary:** Reporting verbs	218 219 220
7A	**Grammar 1:** Real conditionals **Grammar 2:** Real conditionals **Vocabulary:** Social issues	221 222 223
7B	**Grammar 1:** Future forms and degrees of probability **Grammar 2:** Future forms and degrees of probability **Vocabulary:** Collocations with *make*, *take*, *do* and *give*	224 225 226
7C	**Language focus 1:** Introductory *it* **Language focus 2:** Introductory *it* **Vocabulary:** Personal and professional relationships	227 228 229
8A	**Grammar 1:** Second conditional **Grammar 2:** Second conditional **Vocabulary:** Events in films	230 231 232
8B	**Grammar 1:** Conditionals in the past **Grammar 2:** Conditionals in the past **Vocabulary:** Searching and hiding	233 234 235
8C	**Language focus 1:** Linkers of concession **Language focus 2:** Linkers of concession **Vocabulary:** Visual art	236 237 238
9A	**Grammar 1:** Past modals of deduction **Grammar 2:** Past modals of deduction **Vocabulary:** Mystery	239 240 241
9B	**Grammar 1:** Verb patterns **Grammar 2:** Verb patterns **Vocabulary:** Knowledge	242 243 244
9C	**Language focus 1:** Phrasal verbs **Language focus 2:** Phrasal verbs **Vocabulary:** Common phrasal verbs	245 246 247
10A	**Grammar 1:** Future perfect and future continuous **Grammar 2:** Future perfect and future continuous **Vocabulary:** Personal fulfilment	248 249 250
10B	**Grammar 1:** Articles **Grammar 2:** Articles **Vocabulary:** Fame	251 252 253
10C	**Language focus 1:** Compound adjectives **Language focus 2:** Compound adjectives **Vocabulary:** Persuasion and enforcement	254 255 256
Photocopiable notes and answer key		257–279

1A Grammar 1 Question forms

Welcome to all our new and returning students

1 Put the words in the correct order to make direct or indirect questions, then tick the appropriate box.

1 you / could / tell / if / I'm / me / right place / in / the
_____ for the English class?   ☐ direct ☐ indirect

2 have / you / English / studied / where
_____ previously?   ☐ direct ☐ indirect

3 did / you / out / how / about / find
_____ this class?   ☐ direct ☐ indirect

4 ask / can / you / I / whether / studied / have / abroad
_____ before?   ☐ direct ☐ indirect

5 most / what / you / improve / hoping / to / are
_____ in this class?   ☐ direct ☐ indirect

6 teacher / was / who / your
_____ last year?   ☐ direct ☐ indirect

7 did / you / to / when / decide / take
_____ this course?   ☐ direct ☐ indirect

8 where / I / you / ask / may / got / coursebook / your
_____ from?   ☐ direct ☐ indirect

9 we / will / finish / time / what
_____ here today?   ☐ direct ☐ indirect

10 who / pen / does / this / belong
_____ to?   ☐ direct ☐ indirect

11 where / library / the / you / know / do
_____ is?   ☐ direct ☐ indirect

12 I / what / wonder / we'll / to / do / have
_____ for homework.   ☐ direct ☐ indirect

2 Work in pairs. Take turns to ask and answer the questions. If the question is direct, phrase it as an indirect question.

1A Grammar 2 Question forms

1 Find out if your partner knows where a supermarket is.

2 Find out when your partner checked in to the hostel.

3 Find out where your partner has been today.

4 Find out who your partner is travelling with.

5 You've heard that there is a free walking tour that leaves from the hostel. Find out what time it starts.

6 Find out where your partner is from.

7 Find out if your partner knows the weather forecast for tomorrow.

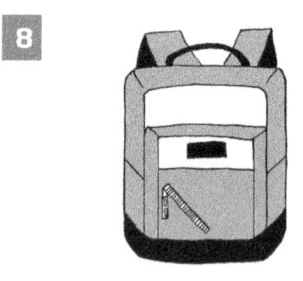

8 Find out where your partner got their backpack from.

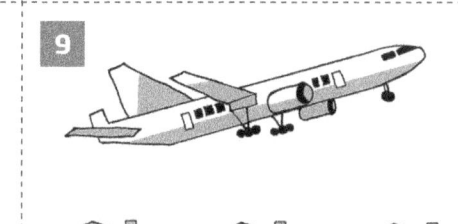

9 Find out how your partner travelled to London and how long it took them.

10 Find out whether your partner is reading anything at the moment.

11 Find out what the wifi password for the hostel is.

12 Find out if your partner is enjoying their travels so far.

13 Find out who owns the (invisible) guitar in the corner.

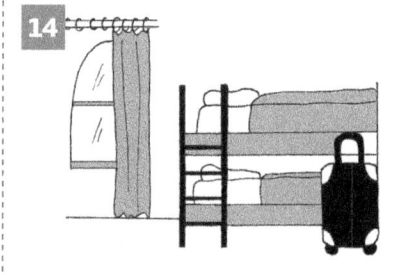

14 Find out how long your partner is staying in London for.

15 Find out what your partner is doing tomorrow.

1A Vocabulary — Verbs with dependent prepositions

1 Complete the sentences with the correct preposition.

	Me	Classmate
1 I don't need to work _____ one thing at a time. I'm used to multi-tasking.		
2 I believe _____ the power of a strong last-minute effort for meeting deadlines.		
3 I think more _____ my plans for next year than next week.		
4 I know what FOMO stands _____ .		
5 I sometimes suffer _____ FOMO!		
6 I concentrate _____ work or study better when I take notes by hand rather than typing.		
7 It would really surprise my friends if I belonged _____ a white-water rafting club.		
8 I generally try to deal _____ messages as soon as I receive them.		
9 I don't use a calendar, I just rely _____ my memory.		
10 I usually smile _____ strangers I pass on the street.		

2 Tick the statements that are true for you. For each one, think about why you chose your answer.

3 Work in pairs and compare your answers.

4 Change partners. Compare the most interesting information from your first discussion.

1B Grammar 1 Past simple, past continuous, used to, would, keep + -ing

1 **Complete the texts with the correct past form of the words in brackets. Use the past simple, past continuous, *used to*, *would* or *keep* + *-ing*. Use each form at least once. Sometimes more than one form is possible.**

Small change, big impact

a I ¹_____ (drive) my flatmate crazy because I ²_____ (lose) my keys around the house so often. I ³_____ (put) them down in a special spot and then ⁴_____ (forget) where that special spot was. I ⁵_____ (spend) ages looking for them. Finally, my flatmate ⁶_____ (put up) a key holder by our front door and ⁷_____ (insist) that I hung my keys there. It ⁸_____ (be) simple, but life-changing. I haven't lost my keys since!

b I ⁹_____ (look) for ways to simplify my life when I ¹⁰_____ (read) that many successful people ¹¹_____ (wear) the same thing every day, like a uniform. Apparently, these people ¹²_____ (save) a lot of time and mental energy by doing this. I ¹³_____ (not have) a lot of money to spend on new clothes, so I ¹⁴_____ (build) my uniform over time. I ¹⁵_____ (decide) to buy clothes that were navy, white or brown. I ¹⁶_____ (think) it might be boring, but it has definitely made my life easier.

c I ¹⁷_____ (find) writing in English difficult. I ¹⁸_____ (can) think of ideas, but I ¹⁹_____ (make) a lot of mistakes. I ²⁰_____ (complain) in class one day when my teacher ²¹_____ (suggest) that I read my work aloud to check it. I ²²_____ (be) surprised to find that it actually ²³_____ (help). I ²⁴_____ (do) it and my writing has become a lot more accurate.

2 **Read the texts and answer the questions.**
- What life changes have the people made and why?
- Have you ever tried anything similar?

3 **Work in pairs and discuss the questions.**
- Think of a change you've made in your life (it could be big or small). What was it?
- Did it have a big impact?

1B Grammar 2 — Past simple, past continuous, *used to*, *would*, *keep* + *-ing*

Student A

Complete the statements about yourself. Make three of the statements false.

1 I used to hate _____ but now I quite like it!

2 When I was a child, I would often _____ after school.

3 I didn't use to care about _____ as much as I do now.

4 One time, I _____.

5 I kept _____ until I was _____
_____.

6 A few years ago, I wouldn't often _____.

7 Every morning last week, I _____.

8 Where I grew up, there was a _____
and we would _____.

Student B

Complete the statements about yourself. Make three of the statements false.

1 I used to enjoy _____ but now I don't!

2 When I was a child, I would never _____.

3 I didn't use to think about _____.

4 A few years ago, I would often _____.

5 Something I kept talking about for years afterward was _____
_____.

6 Every day when I was at primary school, I _____.

7 Once, I _____.

8 When I was little, I lived near a _____
and would often _____.

1B Vocabulary — Phrases to describe emotions

1 Work in pairs and discuss the questions.
- Are you a fan of watching or playing sports? Why/Why not?
- Do you think there are any life lessons to be learned from sports?

2 Complete the text with the words in the box.

| ashamed | believe | completely | eyes | impact | inspired | mind | numb | shock | total |

Volleyball has had a big, big **1**_____ on my life so I couldn't **2**_____ my luck when my family managed to get tickets to the national finals. I was going to cheer for players who **3**_____ me so much and this was going to be our year!

When we lost, it was **4**_____ devastating. Some of the players were bawling their **5**_____ out, and the fans were in **6**_____. I felt so **7**_____.

My sister, the only family member who isn't a volleyball fan, thinks we're **8**_____ fools to take a sport so seriously. She says it blows her **9**_____ that losing a game could cause people to cry and talk about it for weeks. I think she's a bit **10**_____ of our obsession!

3 Work in groups and discuss the questions.
- Would you ever be devastated by a sports result? Why/Why not?
- Do you think fans are total fools if they take sports too seriously? Why/Why not?
- What kind of people inspire you most?

1C Language focus 1 Verb + noun collocations

1 Work in groups and discuss the questions.

- When do people make promises to themselves?
- What kinds of promises are common?
- What do you think makes people more likely to keep them?

2 Choose the correct alternatives to complete the promises.

Promises to myself

1. I'm going to review the notes I *keep/take* in class so that I remember more.
2. I'm going to make *time/hours* for exercise every day.
3. I'm going to *make/do* my bed each morning.
4. I'm going to *take/make* more of an interest in world affairs.
5. I'm going to be more organised so I can *meet/keep* my deadlines.
6. I'm going to *speak/voice* my opinion at work more.
7. I'm not going to *break/lose* the rules any more.
8. I'm going to *take/make* charge of my future more confidently.
9. I'm going to *resolve/remain* a dispute with my neighbour.
10. I'm going to *remain/resolve* calm even when I'm nervous.
11. If something doesn't *make/take* sense to me, I'm going to ask about it.
12. I'm going to be more open to talking to people when waiting in *line/queue*.
13. I'm not going to lose my *anger/temper* at the little things.
14. I'm going to *keep/remain* all my promises!

3 Work in groups and discuss the questions.

- Which of the promises would be the hardest to keep?
- How could you help a friend keep each promise on the list?

1C Language focus 2 — Verb + noun collocations

1	Managers should resolve	a	make their own beds.
2	The best way to meet	b	time for yourself every day.
3	It's important to make	c	charge in an emergency situation.
4	It's impolite to use your phone while waiting	d	calm at the sight of blood.
5	If you think you're going to lose	e	a favour when someone's done something nice for you.
6	From four years old, children should	f	opinions online than in face-to-face discussions.
7	People won't break	g	your temper, try counting to ten in your head.
8	It's easier to voice	h	sense to me initially, but I understand them now.
9	I know how to take	i	interest in similar hobbies to their families.
10	The most effective way to take	j	their minds.
11	I don't remain	k	keep than people expect.
12	People usually take an	l	deadlines is to start early.
13	Some things about English didn't make	m	in line at a shop.
14	It's nice to be able to return	n	disputes between their employees.
15	Young people these days are taught to speak	o	the rules if they understand the reasons behind them.
16	Promises are harder to	p	notes in English class is by hand.

1C Vocabulary — Adjectives of character

1 Work in pairs. Read the clues and complete the puzzle. The letters in the shaded column form a mystery word.

Personality puzzle

1. Always thinking that people are going to do bad things.
2. Friendly and socially confident.
3. Wanting to try new things even if they are a bit dangerous.
4. Always believing that other people are honest.
5. Not giving enough attention to things in order to avoid harm or damage.
6. Being very careful and not taking risks.
7. Not showing opinions or emotions.
8. Not hiding opinions or emotions. Honest and easy to speak with.
9. Often loud and the centre of attention.
10. Trusting your own ability and not worrying about what other people think.
11. Anxious and a little frightened.
12. Over-anxious about everything.
13. Planning well and knowing where everything is.

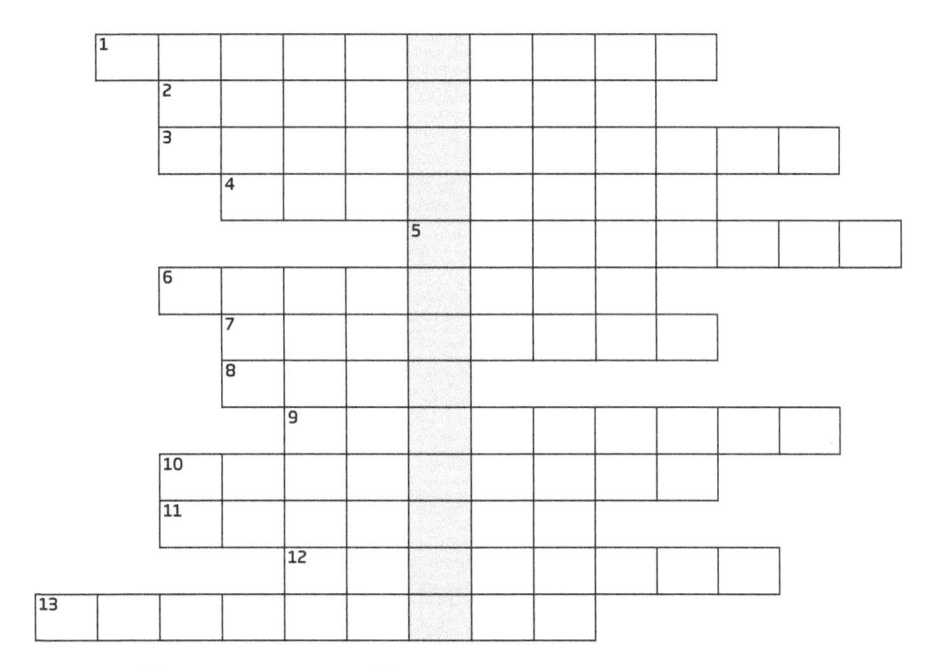

The mystery word is _____ .

2 Choose three different professions, e.g. reporter, pharmacist, coach. Work in pairs and discuss the question. Use the words from the puzzle and your own ideas.

- What do you think would be valuable personality qualities for each one? Use words from the puzzle and your own ideas.

2A Grammar 1 Present perfect simple and continuous

1 Choose the correct alternatives to complete the situations.

1

I ¹'ve meant/'ve been meaning to reply to your invitation all week but I ²'ve been/'ve been being busy with a work project, sorry! Anyway, my cousins ³have just called/have just been calling to say they're coming to stay this weekend. I ⁴'ve hoped/'ve been hoping to introduce you for a while. Is it OK to bring them along to the barbecue?

2

I ⁵'ve entered/'ve been entering an online photo competition and the prize is a trip to New York City. I ⁶'ve watched/'ve been watching people vote online and my picture ⁷has received/has been receiving over a thousand votes so far. I've got such a good chance of winning that I ⁸'ve read/'ve been reading about attractions in the city.

3

Every summer my friends and I take a trip together, but this year no one ⁹has made/has been making a decision about where to go, and it's getting on my nerves! Laura ¹⁰has suggested/has been suggesting renting a house but Hannah thinks it will be too expensive. Hannah and Ed ¹¹have argued/have been arguing about the dates all week. I just don't understand what ¹²has got/has been getting into everyone. Holidays are supposed to be fun!

2 Read the situations again. Match situations 1–3 with the proverbs a–c.

a *Don't count your chickens before they're hatched.* ___

b **Too many cooks spoil the broth.** ___

c THE MORE THE MERRIER. ___

3 Choose one of the proverbs above or another one you know. Write a paragraph giving an example of it, using the present perfect simple and continuous.

4 Work in groups. Compare your examples from Exercise 3. Can the other members guess which proverb you chose?

2A Grammar 2 Present perfect simple and continuous

1 Complete the questions. Use the present perfect simple or present perfect continuous form of the words in brackets. Sometimes both forms are possible.

DIGITAL TECHNOLOGY SURVEY

1. How long _____ (you / use) digital technology?
2. How much time _____ (you / spend) in front of a screen recently?
3. _____ (you / think about) reducing the time you ever spend on technology?
4. When it comes to the internet, _____ (anything / get) on your nerves lately?
5. What's the best thing _____ (you / ever / see) on the internet?
6. _____ (you / ever / take) an online course?
7. _____ (you / use) any digital tools over the last few months to help you learn English?
8. How many online communities _____ (you / ever / belong to)?
9. _____ (you / follow) any celebrities over the past year on social media?
10. Think about your friends. How many _____ (you / never / meet) face-to-face?
11. _____ (you / already / taken) any photos today? How many?
12. Do you think attitudes towards technology _____ (gradually / change) in recent years? In what ways?

2 Work in groups and discuss the questions in Exercise 1.

2A Vocabulary Phrases with *get*

1 Complete the phrases in the questions with *get* to match the meaning in brackets.

1. What sound _____ your _____ the most? (annoy)
   Name _____ Answer _____

2. Do you prefer people _____? (speak very directly)
   Name _____ Answer _____

3. Where do you tend to _____ with friends? (meet up)
   Name _____ Answer _____

4. What is the most interesting thing you _____ at secondary school? (have the opportunity to do something)
   Name _____ Answer _____

5. How do you prefer companies you buy things from to _____ with you? (contact)
   Name _____ Answer _____

6. Are you going to _____ this weekend? (relax)
   Name _____ Answer _____

7. What sorts of projects or hobbies might you _____ with? (become very focused on or emotional about)
   Name _____ Answer _____

8. Has anything in the news _____ recently? (made someone notice something)
   Name _____ Answer _____

9. Do you often _____ that you've forgotten something, but you don't remember what it is? (think or sense that something is probably true)
   Name _____ Answer _____

10. Tell your classmate a joke. Do they _____? (understand)
    Name _____ Answer _____

2 Ask each question to a different classmate. Write their answer on your sheet.

3 Work in pairs and compare your answers.

2B Grammar 1 The passive

1 Follow the maze from start to finish. Only move through squares where the sentence is grammatically correct.

	1	2	3	4
START	The law was changed recently.	More research will be needed.	Teenagers are not allowed to be on the streets after midnight.	A lot of property got badly damaged.
5 More money will spent to tackle the problem.	**6** Has any research carried out on this topic?	**7** The mayor is working very hard to be get re-elected.	**8** Oh no, our flight has cancelled!	**9** They will get told off if they're caught.
10 The law isn't be enforced adequately.	**11** The skate park is used by many people – from toddlers to teens.	**12** Research is being carried out to measure the progress which has been made.	**13** Will teens be warned about the dangers of lack of sleep?	**14** I hope we're notified about the upcoming changes.
15 Mobile phones shouldn't be blame for everything!	**16** The problems need to be tackled one at a time.	**17** By 2050, I think all fizzy drinks will ban.	**18** People are being ask to turn off their mobiles.	**19** When you arrived, had the door been left unlock?
20 Iceland has been applauded for the significant progress that has been made.	**21** More funding was requested, but it was declined.	**22** The monorail hadn't be built when we last visited.	**23** More ought to done to encourage teens to get a good night's sleep.	**24** People haven't be warned about the dangers of sugar.
25 A safe space should be set up where teens can share their ideas for change.	**26** We were be told to leave without any explanation whatsoever.	**27** The price of public transport has been reduced.	**28** New facilities will need to be built in the near future.	**29** When you saw the lamp, had the damage been repaired?
30 Illegal behaviour mustn't be accepted as normal.	**31** Parents must be encouraged to spend time with their teenagers.	**32** You'll get sent a letter which has all the details.	**33** Did you get show the plans before building was start?	**FINISH**

2 Work in pairs. Correct the incorrect sentences.

2B Grammar 2 The passive

Student A

1 The school has been given a lot of money, and I think it _____ on a new swimming pool.

2 Please ignore the smell in the living room. It _____ just _____ last week.

3 Have you heard the news? A new sports centre _____ by the river next year.

4 When we got to the airport, we discovered that our flight _____ .

5 The head teacher can't see you right now. She's actually _____ by someone from the local paper.

6 Every day, about 1.9 billion fizzy drinks _____ around the world.

7 I don't know how the book _____ , but please accept my apologies.

8 Watch out! Always look both ways before crossing the road! You _____ !

Your partner's missing verbs:

| get told off   had been caught   haven't been told   isn't being used   'm going to be picked up
| were instructed   will be closed   will get promoted |

Student B

1 As soon as the fire broke out, we _____ to leave the building immediately.

2 By the time we saw the news about the break-in, the robbers _____ already _____ .

3 I'm not sure what our English assignment topic is, we still _____ .

4 If you need somewhere to work quietly, you can use room 15. It _____ at the moment.

5 We'll have to find another way to drive into the city. The main road _____ from next week for repairs.

6 I won't need to get a taxi from the airport because I _____ by my uncle.

7 If you use your phone in a cinema, you might _____ .

8 I've been in the same position at work for a few years now, so I hope I _____ very soon.

Your partner's missing verbs:

| are sold   being interviewed   could have been killed   got damaged   had been cancelled
| should be spent   was painted   will be built |

2B Vocabulary — Social action

take	action
tackle	the problem
increase	funding
carry	out research
ban	the use of
do	more to
warn about	the dangers
crack down	on
offer	alternatives
enforce	a law

2C Language focus 1 -ed and -ing adjectives

1 Match the word stems in the box with the sentence pairs 1–8 in Exercise 2.

| ~~alarm~~ confuse delight encourage frustrate satisfy scare tempt |

2 Complete the sentences with the correct form of the adjective.

1 _____ alarm _____
   A It's _____ how often luggage seems to go missing at airports.
   B I'm _____ to hear how many customer complaints there have been this year.

2 _____
   A The message was so rude, I'm _____ to delete her from my contacts.
   B That beautiful pool looks very _____. Fancy a swim?

3 _____
   A I know the work I'm doing makes a difference, it's very _____.
   B It was a hard decision, but I'm _____ that I made the right choice.

4 _____
   A I'm feeling really _____ after our chat, thank you.
   B The atmosphere in the class was positive and _____.

5 _____
   A The internet is down – again! It's so _____!
   B I'm _____ by the poor customer service.

6 _____
   A I'm really _____ about the situation, I don't know how I feel!
   B These instructions are really _____. I think I need some help.

7 _____
   A She told him off for _____ his grandmother while she was asleep.
   B I want to ask you something, but I'm _____ you're going to say 'no'.

8 _____
   A Thank you for your kind invitation. I'd be _____ to attend your party.
   B He was _____ in a luxurious bath when the doorbell rang.

3 Choose a word stem from Exercise 1 and write your own pair of sentences.

(_____)

1 _____

2 _____

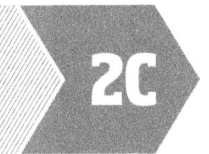

2C Language focus 2 — *-ed* and *-ing* adjectives

List A

1. Fancy a slice of my grandmother's prize-winning chocolate cake?
2. It was once a gorgeous beach, but it has been ruined by pollution.
3. So I'm lying in my bed in the dark and I hear a 'tap tap tap' on the window.
4. He put on a blindfold, hopped on a unicycle and then began to juggle bananas.
5. I finally got to the front of the queue and the rude staff refused to serve me.
6. Did you know that the eyes of reindeer change colour from gold to blue depending on the season?
7. The storm meant we were stuck in the departure lounge for seven hours.
8. I arrived at the exam room, but realised I'd got the time wrong!
9. What false advertising! The tickets were 40 euros each, but with extra charges they cost me 52 euros.
10. My teacher promised all the students that we'd make good progress if we came to all the classes.

List B

1. All the late-night studying paid off, I got an A+!
2. My coach said I have a good chance of getting on the team if I continue to train hard.
3. The nerve of that cold caller! I told her I wasn't interested, but she rang back three times.
4. He's been in hospital for a week and the doctors still don't know what's wrong.
5. We have to move house next week, and I also have a huge assignment due a few days later.
6. Did you hear Ava and Jan's happy news? They're engaged!
7. My business is in trouble – customer numbers have dropped by 80% since last year.
8. My neighbours were burgled last night while they were watching TV.
9. My nose won't stop running, I must be allergic to one of the plants.
10. Let's get a puppy! It will be a reason to go for walks and get more exercise, and they're so cute!

Instructions

Take turns to read a comment to your partner. Your partner responds to each comment using an appropriate phrase with an *-ed* or *-ing* adjective.

Useful phrases:

How … That's … Sounds … + ing.
That makes me … You sound … You must be so … You must have been … + ed
I get … when …

alarm	astonish	convince	delight	depress	encourage
entertain	exhaust	frustrate	infuriate	insult	overwhelm
satisfy	scare	stress	tempt	upset	worry

2C Vocabulary — Common complaints

A: Grrr, that was a **cold caller**, trying to get me to change broadband companies.

B: Oh no, **aggressive salespeople** are the worst!

A: Yeah, the guy kept pushing me to answer questions. I can't stand being pressured by **rude staff**, but I still felt bad hanging up!

B: That reminds me of your laptop that wouldn't charge. I remember you felt sorry for the salesperson, even though he was the one who had sold you a **faulty product**!

A: I did, until I became absolutely infuriated by all his **broken promises** to credit my account with the refund!

B: Oh yeah, that **billing dispute** went on for ages. Did you ever resolve it?

A: Sadly, I couldn't. The company ads saying 'customers are our number one' really annoy me. It's completely **false advertising**! By the way, have your new trainers arrived?

B: They have, thanks. I eventually got them last week, but two months after I placed my order. Talk about **slow delivery**! And there was no apology or anything!

A: There never is! It's the **lack of communication** from these companies that I find most irritating.

B: I wonder if everyone has as many **poor customer service** experiences as we do!

3A Grammar 1 Past perfect simple and continuous

1 Read the blog post and answer the questions.

- What had the writer forgotten to do? _____
- What happened next? _____

| HOME | BLOGS | FORUMS | ABOUT | CONTACTS |

In my English class we **¹**'d prepared/'d been preparing for final presentations for a whole month, and my group was scheduled to present on Monday at 9.00 a.m. These presentations were very important. The teacher **²**had told/had been telling us they were worth half our final grade. Imagine my horror when I woke up that day at 8.45 a.m. I **³**'d forgotten/'d been forgetting to set my alarm!

I messaged my group to say I was going to be late. They **⁴**'d been getting/'d got quite worried because we **⁵**'d arranged/'d been arranging to meet early for a final practice of our presentation and I **⁶**hadn't arrived/hadn't been arriving or **⁷**hadn't called/called. I quickly got ready and ran out of the house.

The pavement was wet because it **⁸**had rained/had been raining all night. Suddenly, I slipped over on the path and fell heavily. Even though I **⁹**'d never broken/'d never been breaking a bone before, I knew from the pain that it was what I **¹⁰**'d done/'d been doing.

By the time I checked my phone at the hospital later that morning, I **¹¹**'d received/'d been receiving twelve increasingly frustrated messages from my group members. They **¹²**'d wondered/'d been wondering what on earth **¹³**had happened/had been happening to me.

In the end, they **¹⁴**'d continued/'d been continuing with the presentation as planned, but the teacher said I wouldn't get any marks unless I had a very good excuse for my absence. Even though oversleeping was the real reason I **¹⁵**'d missed/'d been missing the presentation, my broken wrist provided a very good excuse indeed!

2 Complete the blog post with the correct alternatives. More than one option may be possible.

3 Write your own story about something that went wrong, but worked out OK in the end. Use the past perfect simple and continuous.

3A Grammar 2 — Past perfect simple and continuous

I co-ordinated the cleaning up of rubbish that had been left on a river bank after a huge storm. I organised more than 500 volunteers, who left the river bank cleaner than it had been before the storm.

I found a colleague on the floor where he had collapsed. I knew that he'd been suffering from an illness and found some medicine in his bag, which saved his life.

I'd just finished lunch at a café when I saw a woman steal an elderly man's bag. I chased after her and managed to grab the bag. I later learnt that the man had been keeping his life savings in that bag.

I'm a physiotherapist. Although I'd been saving for years to buy a house, after my sister suffered a back injury, I decided to use the money to start a low-cost treatment centre. Over 200 people have stayed at my centre so far.

I ran seven marathons in seven days and raised over £1,000,000 for a local hospital that had treated my nephew. I managed to finish the final race, even though I'd been suffering from flu for 24 hours.

I spent twenty years cycling round the world, visiting areas where natural disasters had occurred. I wrote a book about my experiences and donated the profits to several international charities.

I rescued a family from a fire in their home, even though I hadn't met them before. The family, who'd been sleeping at the time, are all safe and well.

I climbed a mountain to save the life of a friend who'd broken a leg and had been lying there injured for over four days. Despite the danger, I managed to reach my friend and bring her down the mountain safely.

One day I had been surfing when I noticed a whale had got stuck on the sand further up the beach. I kept the whale alive then helped it swim away when the sea came in.

You are an imposter. Tell no one. You have come to the heroes' dinner to meet the star! You must make up a story about a heroic act you did to convince everyone you are one of the real heroes.

Find someone who ...	Name(s)
1 ... organised 500 volunteers to clean up a river bank after a huge storm _____ (leave) it covered in rubbish.	
2 ... helped an elderly man who _____ (keep) his life savings in a bag.	
3 ... ran seven marathons to raise money for the hospital which _____ (treat) his/her nephew.	
4 ... rescued a family, who _____ (sleep), from a burning building.	
5 ... saved a whale, that _____ (get) stuck on a beach.	
6 ... saved the life of a colleague who _____ (collapse) from an illness.	
7 ... used all the money that he/she _____ (save) to open a rehabilitation centre.	
8 ... wrote a book about his/her twenty years cycling to areas where natural disasters _____ (occur).	
9 ... climbed a mountain to save a friend who _____ (lie) there for several days with a broken leg.	
10 ... is an imposter who has pretended to be a hero because he/she _____ (heard) his/her favourite star would be here!	

3A Vocabulary — Memory

A good memory for names

For most people, faces are more memorable than names.

Bear in mind that many people have no memory of a name because they weren't concentrating when they were told it.

To memorise names, listen carefully and repeat it.

Then think of something the name reminds you of.

I'll never forget the first time I used this tip. I met a Harry and he had red hair like Prince Harry. Very easy for me to recall!

3B Grammar 1 Comparatives and superlatives

1 Work in pairs and discuss the questions.

- Do you have brothers or sisters?
- Are they older or younger than you?
- How do you think having siblings affects a person?

2 Complete the magazine article with the words and phrases in the box.

| a much | as (x2) | bit | by far | close as | far more | less | more of a | much more |
| slightly | than | the | the more | the most | | | | |

The most fierce rivalry in the world

For many people, ¹_____ the greatest rival they will ever face is their own brother or sister. Studies have shown that while growing up, siblings spend ²_____ time with each other than with anyone else. Often, this isn't all smooth sailing. One study found that siblings aged three to seven fought on average 3.5 times per hour. The closer siblings were in age, ³_____ frequent the disagreement. Rivalry still exists, but is ⁴_____ less obvious among siblings of different genders. Interestingly, some studies indicate that where one sibling shows ⁵_____ skill at a certain activity, the other sibling may avoid that activity altogether. Experts say parents can reduce sibling rivalry by treating children ⁶_____ equally as possible.

YOUR STORIES

Julie
My sister is just a little ⁷_____ younger than me, eleven months. Whatever hobbies I took up, she wanted to copy them. When I was taking tennis lessons, she also decided to start, and before long became ⁸_____ better player. The same thing happened with dance, violin and swimming. It really was ⁹_____ frustrating thing ever.

Asim
My twin brother is ¹⁰_____ clown than me – I'm quite shy and reserved. The more people laugh, ¹¹_____ more jokes he makes. I've never really tried to be funny because I'll never be as entertaining ¹²_____ he is.

Marcos
I'm the sixth of seven siblings and we've always got on well, probably more easily ¹³_____ in some other families because my parents were very strict about being fair and kind. We're as ¹⁴_____ ever these days, in fact, we all live ¹⁵_____ than ten minutes walk from each other!

3 Work in pairs and discuss the questions.

- Do you agree that sibling rivalry is the most fierce in the world? Why/Why not?
- Are the stories in the article similar to your own experiences? Why/Why not?

3B Grammar 2 Comparatives and superlatives

1 Circle the appropriate number to show how much you agree or disagree with each statement (1=strongly disagree, 5=strongly agree).

2 Rewrite the statements so that they are true for you. Use comparatives, superlatives and modifiers.

Luck plays more of a role in success than most people think.	1	2	3	4	5
I'm far more interested in competing against myself than against other people.	1	2	3	4	5
People tend to become much more stubborn with age.	1	2	3	4	5
The more confident someone is, the more successful they'll be.	1	2	3	4	5
In sport, genetics are as important as hard work.	1	2	3	4	5
I'm by far the most competitive person in my family.	1	2	3	4	5
As fantastic as it is to represent a country in an elite sport, I wouldn't want to.	1	2	3	4	5
The closer countries are situated geographically, the greater their rivalry.	1	2	3	4	5
Older siblings are far less likely to be outrageous than their younger siblings.	1	2	3	4	5
I'm more of a dreamer than a doer.	1	2	3	4	5

3 Work in groups and compare your answers.

3B Vocabulary Character adjectives

1 Complete the words to form adjectives of character. The first letters have been given to help you.

1 How **com**_____ would you say you are? Do you always have to win?

2 Are you a **tho**_____ person? Do you do things to help others?

3 Why do you think some people are more **de**_____ than others and can stay focused on success?

4 Where is the line between being **con**_____ and being **ar**_____ ?

5 Would you be more insulted if you were called **ine**_____ at your job or **unpr**_____ ?

6 What do you think is the best way to convince a **st**_____ person to change their mind?

7 When could being **bo**___ be a positive trait? When could it be a negative trait?

8 What do you think it means to be mentally **to**_____ ?

9 Who is the most **rea**_____ person you know?

10 Who is someone you consider to be truly **rem**_____ ? Why?

2 Work in groups and discuss the questions in Exercise 1.

3C Language focus 1 — Forming adjectives

1 Complete the gaps in each row by making adjectives from the words in the first column.

colour / history / poison	_colourful_ costume festival parrot	_poisonous_ gas snake substance	_historic_ moment place voyage
danger / economy / success	1 _____ growth policy problem	2 _____ animal driving situation	3 _____ campaign project speech
allergy / class / do	4 _____ be ... to something rash reaction	5 _____ plan recipe timeframe	6 _____ car case example
logic / nightmare / tradition	7 _____ folk song values way of life	8 _____ road journey situation	9 _____ argument explanation solution
accept / scare / trick	10 _____ problem situation bit	11 _____ behaviour standard substitute	12 _____ dream monster movie
child / history / use	13 _____ argument behaviour game	14 _____ event novel period	15 _____ advice information tip
class / fool / meat	16 _____ casserole gravy stew	17 _____ behaviour decision thing to say	18 _____ architecture composer music

2 Write five sentences about your life or opinions. Use five of the collocations from Exercise 1.

_____
_____
_____
_____

3 Work in pairs. Take turns reading your sentences aloud without saying the adjective. Can your partner guess the adjective?

3C Language focus 2 — Forming adjectives

-ous	poison	-ous	fool
-ish	meat	-y	trick
-y	success	-ful	danger
-ous	use	-less	hope
-ful	child	-ish	comfort
-able	scar(e)	-y	logic
-al	disrespect	-ful	histor(y)
-ical	tradition	-al	do
-able	nightmar(e)	-ish	accident
-al	accept	-able	econom(y)
-ic	colour	-ful	point
-less	allerg(y)	-ic	outrag(e)

3C Vocabulary Arguments

Team A

| clashing | compromise | contradict | down | have | intervene | issue | pick | see | up |

Your team will argue for these statements.

1 If you witness bullying, it's your duty to _____ .
2 Even if you don't _____ eye-to-eye with someone, you can usually ignore your differences.
3 Never, ever _____ your teacher.
4 If you _____ an issue with someone, it's best to sort it out in private.
5 Never _____ a fight with someone who's bigger than you!

Your team will argue against these statements.

6 If you want to avoid _____ with others, find a job you can do alone.
7 The underlying _____ in every fight is power.
8 Ganging _____ on someone is sometimes a necessary evil.
9 Avoid backing _____ in any situation. It's a sign of weakness.
10 There's always a _____ if you're open to it.

Team B

| clashing | compromise | contradict | down | have | intervene | issue | pick | see | up |

Your team will argue against these statements.

1 If you witness bullying, it's your duty to _____ .
2 Even if you don't _____ eye-to-eye with someone, you can usually ignore your differences.
3 Never, ever _____ your teacher.
4 If you _____ an issue with someone, it's best to sort it out in private.
5 Never _____ a fight with someone who's bigger than you!

Your team will argue for these statements.

6 If you want to avoid _____ with others, find a job you can do alone.
7 The underlying _____ in every fight is power.
8 Ganging _____ on someone is sometimes a necessary evil.
9 Avoid backing _____ in any situation. It's a sign of weakness.
10 There's always a _____ if you're open to it.

4A Grammar 1 Relative clauses

1 Read the articles about three art exhibitions. Complete the article with relative pronouns. Sometimes more than one answer is possible.

A Indoor rain

Look and touch: Artworks visitors can experience
In the Rain Room, [1]_____ was designed by Hannes Koch and Florian Ortkrass, over 1,000 litres of water fall from the ceiling every minute. What's even more astonishing is that people [2]_____ move through the room remain dry. This experience is possible thanks to special camera software [3]_____ senses exactly where each visitor is, [4]_____ is quite amazing! The unique artwork has found a home in Sharjah, UAE, [5]_____ it is a popular attraction both tourists and locals enjoy.

B Jump in

Can you remember the last time [6]_____ you did something just for fun? In the centre of London there's a gallery [7]_____ an exhibition room was turned into a pool of balls for adults. There were 81,000 white balls, [8]_____ gave the room a very elegant look that impressed everyone [9]_____ they first walked in. Those [10]_____ visited were invited to jump in and play. Many adults enjoyed the opportunity the artwork provided to feel like a child again.

C Room of spots

Yayoi Kusama is a famous Japanese artist, [11]_____ work is known for its vivid colours. She has worked with a number of galleries to create places [12]_____ visitors create art together. It starts with a white room, [13]_____ contains white furniture. Visitors are given brightly-coloured spots [14]_____ they enter the space which they can place on the walls, furniture, ceiling and floor. Over time, the spots [15]_____ people add change the room from plain to colourful. The works of art they create are colourful and completely original – no two are alike!

2 Write the pronoun that has been omitted from a relative clause in the last sentence of each paragraph.

A _____   B _____   C _____

3 Work in pairs and discuss the question.

- Which art experience appeals to you the most? Why?

4A Grammar 2 — Relative clauses

An artist	whose work I admire	is Frida Kahlo.
Something	that I'd love to own	would be a pair of designer sunglasses.
The time	when I am most creative	is late at night.
The colour	which I wear most often	is vivid-pink!
The best gallery in the world	, where many famous artworks are housed,	is the National Gallery in London.
My favourite possession	, which is decorative rather than useful,	is a poster of Van Gogh's sunflowers.
I don't like artwork	that	I don't understand.
A city I'd like to visit	, where there is plenty of elegant architecture,	is St Petersburg, Russia.
I like the work of artists	who	push the boundaries of art.
My family	, when I think about it,	were always my hugest supporters.

4A Vocabulary — Adjectives to describe things

Cheap
Words you CANNOT use:
- Expensive
- Cost
- Money

Chunky
Words you CANNOT use:
- Thick
- Fat
- Thin

Decorative
Words you CANNOT use:
- Useful
- Practical
- Beautiful

Designer
Words you CANNOT use:
- Label
- Name
- Fashion

Elegant
Words you CANNOT use:
- Beautiful
- Lovely
- Stylish

Flimsy
Words you CANNOT use:
- Strong
- Weak
- Thin

Identical
Words you CANNOT use:
- Same
- Twins
- Look

Rectangular
Words you CANNOT use:
- Shape
- Square
- Long

Oval
Words you CANNOT use:
- Shape
- Egg
- Round

Priceless
Words you CANNOT use:
- Value
- Price
- Cost

Sparkly
Words you CANNOT use:
- Shining
- Star
- Diamonds

Vivid
Words you CANNOT use:
- Clear
- Bright
- Colourful

4B Grammar 1 Obligation and prohibition

1 Leon is about to start a new job at a cinema. His colleague, Maya, is explaining more about his role before he begins.

Complete the parts of the conversation with the words in the box.

| aren't   don't have to   had to   mustn't   was allowed |

Maya: OK, Leon. Firstly, people can take drinks into the theatre, but you ¹_____ let them take in any glasses.

Leon: I think I ²_____ to take in a glass of lemonade once. Has the rule changed?

Maya: Yes, just last month after someone dropped a glass and we ³_____ clean up all the smashed pieces.

Leon: Oh dear. So, how about food?

Maya: You may need to give people a reminder that they ⁴_____ allowed to bring in their own. You ⁵_____ to say that to everyone, only if you suspect they've got a bag full of snacks!

| got to   must   need   needed   had to |

Leon: Is there anything else I ⁶_____ to know?

Maya: Well, there's a strict policy that people ⁷_____ turn off their mobile phones during the film. If they use them, we've ⁸_____ politely ask them to leave the cinema.

Leon: Have you ever ⁹_____ to ask someone to leave?

Maya: There was one time when I almost ¹⁰_____ , but as soon as I marched towards the woman, she turned her phone off!

| didn't need   don't   got to   have to   required |

Leon: Sounds like a relief that you ¹¹_____ to actually say anything.

Maya: Yeah, it was! The other thing I've ¹²_____ mention is about the first aid certificate.

Leon: Go on.

Maya: We're all ¹³_____ to have one, just in case there's an emergency.

Leon: OK, I'll ¹⁴_____ do a course then.

Maya: You will, but you ¹⁵_____ need to organise it yourself. There's one for all new staff next Tuesday, if you're available.

Leon: Great, where do I put my name down?

2 Work in pairs. What things are allowed and not allowed in cinemas where you live?

4B Grammar 2 — Obligation and prohibition

present obligation	past obligation
present no obligation	past no obligation
present prohibition	past prohibition
We have to …	We needed to …
We don't have to …	We weren't allowed to …
We had to …	We were required to …
We don't need to …	We've got to …
We're not required to …	We didn't need to …
We haven't got to …	We're required to …
We can't …	We couldn't …
We're not allowed to …	We need to …
We didn't have to …	We mustn't …
We weren't required to …	We must …

4B Vocabulary — Job requirements

1. **Work in pairs and discuss the questions.**
   - What would be your dream job? Why?

2. **Read the cover letter and answer the questions.**
   - What job is Nick applying for
   - What relevant experience does he have?

3. **Find and correct seven mistakes in the cover letter.**

Dear Ms Daniels,

I am writing to apply for the position of ice cream flavour designer at Creamery Products.

As you will see from my attached CV, I have food science degree from the University of Devon and five years' experience working in an ice cream shop. I have a passion in creative desserts and won a local recipe award for the development of a white chocolate and pear cake recipe.

Regarding the marketing requirements of the position, I have been told that I have a natural fluent for sales. I have strong communication skills and in addition to English, I am also flair in Spanish. I am able to bother with complex instructions and multiple projects.

I believe my background on food science and my enthusiasm make me a great candidate for this role on the Creamery Products team. Please note that I would have willing to move cities for this position, were my application successful.

Thank you for considering my application.

Yours sincerely,

Nick Mason

---

4. **Write a cover letter for your dream job. Use some of the phrases from the lesson.**

4C Language focus 1 Forming verbs with *en*

1 Add the affix *en* to each word to form a verb. Include any spelling changes.

1	hard*en*	short*en*	sad*den*	*en*rage
2	length	weak	danger	tight
3	rich	bright	sweet	soft
4	joy	able	sure	broad
5	short	wide	large	less
6	loose	force	strength	straight

2 Underline the word in each row in Exercise 1 which is the odd one out in form.

3 Complete the questions with the correct verb form of the words in the box.

bright   broad   length   rich   short   strength   sweet   weak

1 What different things might people use to _____ their food?
2 It is often said that if you want to _____ your mind, then you should go travelling.
3 What kinds of simple things _____ your day?
4 I need someone to _____ my new jeans; they're too long.
5 They need to _____ that old bridge, so that it doesn't collapse.
6 Which would _____ your life the most: saying yes more or saying no more?
7 If they vote against him, it will _____ his position of power.
8 Doctors need to _____ the amount of time they spend with each patient; it's not enough.

4 Work in pairs and discuss the questions in Exercise 3.

4C Language focus 2 — Forming verbs with *en*

Student A

1. **Work with another Student A. Complete the sentences with the correct verb form of the word in brackets. Discuss what the context might be for each sentence.**

   1. Could we _____ it even more? (large)
   2. I like it just as it is, I don't think it really needs to be _____. (sweet)
   3. The more you wear them, the more they'll _____! (soft)
   4. Apparently, they're _____ the road. (wide)
   5. I'll put it on my calendar right now to _____ I don't forget. (sure)
   6. It's brilliant! – it has _____ me to get my work done faster! (able)

2. **Work with Student B. Listen to Student B's sentences a–f and respond with one of the sentences 1–6 from Exercise 1.**

   a. I put together this chair myself from a kit. What a shame it's wobbly.
   b. Can you see the screen OK or would you like me to adjust it for you?
   c. The bus this morning was speeding and kept creeping onto the wrong side of the road!
   d. Is it true that you can't sit on the grass? I'd love to have my lunch under that tree.
   e. I love these trousers, but they're a bit long for me.
   f. You're certainly looking full of energy this morning!

Student B

1. **Work with another Student B. Complete the sentences with the correct verb form of the word in brackets. Discuss what the context might be for each sentence.**

   1. Could you _____ it slightly, please? (bright)
   2. I've been eating a new cereal, which is _____ with extra vitamins. (rich)
   3. That's the official rule, but they don't usually _____ it. (force)
   4. I know a good place if you want to get them _____. (short)
   5. How terrifying – sounds like it _____ your safety. (danger)
   6. You've just got to _____ the screws a bit more. (tight)

2. **Work with Student A. Listen to Student A's sentences a–f and respond with one of the sentences 1–6 from Exercise 1.**

   a. What do you think of this photo? Is it a good size?
   b. The traffic was terrible this morning. We were waiting for ages on Lime Street.
   c. The college open day is on the last Sunday of this month. Hope you can make it!
   d. Try a cup of this tea I found at the market. It's meant to be nice with honey.
   e. How are you finding your new computer?
   f. I bought a pair of shoes last week, but they're still really difficult to get on.

4C Vocabulary — 21st century words

Student A

Across:
- 2. hashtag
- 5. virtual
- 7. emoji
- 8. google
- 9. selfie
- 13. crowdsource
- 14. tech-savvy

Student B

- 1 down: contactless
- 2 across
- 3 down: time-poor
- 4 down: animated
- 5 across
- 6 down: binge-watch
- 7 across: m_ _
- 8 across
- 9 across: e-_ _
- 10 down: unfriend
- 11 down: paywall
- 12 down: meme
- 13 across: r w _ _
- 14 across: e h _ _

5A Grammar 1 Mistakes in the past

1 Read the regrets and discuss which you think are the most common.

Ten money regrets

a Starting a business that failed.
b Splashing out on an expensive wedding.
c Buying a car on finance.
d Losing money to a person who wasn't honest.
e Not starting to save earlier for when you retire.
f Getting a credit card.
g Spending too much on non-essentials.
h Lending to friends.
i Making a bad investment.
j Not having a financial plan.

2 Complete the statements with the correct form of the words in brackets. Some verbs will need to be changed to negative.

1 I trusted an online friend, but I _____*shouldn't have sent*_____ (should / sent) her any money. I never heard from her again. __d__

2 My friend _____ (supposed / pay) me back what he borrowed, but he keeps making excuses. ____

3 I wish we _____ (sign up) for the car loan. Over a two-year period, we ended up paying almost double what it was worth. ____

4 I would be in a better position now if I _____ (float) through my 20s ignoring my finances. ____

5 I _____ (ought / realise) that I would be tempted to use it for things I didn't need. I just can't seem to pay it off. ____

6 It _____ (could / be) just as lovely somewhere simpler, surrounded by our very closest family and friends. ____

7 I wish I _____ (begin) putting aside money earlier. I'd love to be able to stop working soon. ____

8 I _____ (should / spent) less on clothes and games. ____

9 The fund _____ (supposed / lose) money. We were told it was low risk. ____

10 If only I _____ (know) that the market for our product would be so competitive. ____

3 Match statements 1–10 with regrets a–j in Exercise 1.

4 Work in pairs. Take turns saying one of the statements from Exercise 2 and responding with a sentence from the box or your own ideas.

> I guess everyone has things that they would do differently.
> I'm sorry to hear that it didn't work out the way you hoped.
> Perhaps it's not too late to make a change.
> That sounds like a really difficult situation.

5A Grammar 2 — Mistakes in the past

Noughts and crosses battle

Round 1

Your cousin is furious because you contradicted her, while she was telling a story to friends.	You bought some shoes, which didn't fit you, online.	You bumped into your old head teacher at a concert, but you couldn't recall her name.
You left your designer umbrella on the bus yesterday.	A real regret you have.	You stayed up late last night to binge-watch a whole series. Now you're exhausted!
You wanted to go to a concert last night, but all the tickets had sold out.	You unfriended someone on social media by accident and now he's not talking to you.	You put up a poster on a school/office noticeboard without realising you needed to ask first.

Round 2

You got rid of an old book and now you've realised it belonged to your mother.	You ordered some food that's too spicy for you, despite the waiter's warning.	You thought the show was starting at 8 o'clock but it had started at 7.
You tripped over someone's laptop cable.	A real regret you have.	You wasted ten minutes speaking to an aggressive salesperson about a vacuum cleaner!
You let your friend copy your assignment and you both got in big trouble.	Your colleague said something offensive in a meeting. You regret not standing up to her.	You regret being so stubborn in an argument you were having with a friend.

Round 3

You promised to message your grandmother yesterday but you didn't.	You forgot to set your alarm and overslept.	You got carried away in a project and missed the deadline.
You wanted to learn to play a musical instrument but never have.	A real regret you have.	You left a pot on the stove and it caught fire.
You lost some money in a business deal with someone you thought was a friend.	You lost touch with an old friend, who you really miss.	Your flat was in a huge mess, when your parents came to visit unexpectedly.

5A Vocabulary — Money phrasal verbs

Top money tips for students

Make sure you only **live**

on what you have.

Track your spending to see what your money is really **going**

on each week.

Then identify possible areas where you could **cut**

back on expenses.

Be sure to **set**

aside savings each month for emergencies.

Avoid **splashing**

out on luxuries, but do allow yourself a little fun.

Some people limit themselves by **taking**

out the same amount of cash every week. When it's gone, it's gone!

It probably goes without saying, but don't **stock**

up on items you don't need!

Don't **get**

into any unnecessary debt.

If you find yourself in difficulty, then **pay**

back the loan with the highest interest rate first.

Manage your money or it will manage you!

5B Grammar 1 Quantifiers

1 Complete the blog posts with the words in the boxes.

| a few   a little   a lot of   any   either   every   many   most   much   several |

HOME | ABOUT US | BLOGS | CONTACT

THE RUNAWAY MILLIONAIRES
PART ONE

I'm going to tell you **1**_____ bit about an unusual theft that happened in New Zealand just **2**_____ years ago.

A guy owned a petrol station in a small town. Like **3**_____ business owners, he asked his bank for an overdraft and they agreed. When he next checked how **4**_____ money he had in his account, he was shocked to discover that the bank had given him ten million dollars!

Without asking for **5**_____ explanation, the guy transferred **6**_____ of the money to accounts abroad. **7**_____ days later, he and his girlfriend fled to Asia, where they spent **8**_____ money on five-star hotels and other luxuries. Almost **9**_____ New Zealander followed the case, wondering whether **10**_____ of the runaways would ever be caught.

| all   both   couple   few   little   loads of   neither   no   plenty   some |

HOME | ABOUT US | BLOGS | CONTACT

THE RUNAWAY MILLIONAIRES
PART TWO

Fast forward a **11**_____ of years, and the woman was arrested when she entered New Zealand to renew her passport. She insisted that her partner had told her that he'd won **12**_____ the money and she had absolutely **13**_____ clue about the fund's true origin. **14**_____ months later, the guy too was caught crossing a border.

In separate trials, **15**_____ of them were found guilty, despite the court agreeing that **16**_____ of them had planned to steal anything before the bank error. The guy was sentenced to four years and seven months in prison and the woman had to stay at her home for nine months.

What would you do if you found ten million dollars in your bank account?

COMMENTS

I have very **17**_____ sympathy for them. **18**_____ people would actually spend millions of dollars that didn't really belong to them. – *Ifan*

I'm pretty sure **19**_____ of people would have done the same thing! Who doesn't dream of having **20**_____ money arrive in their account? – *Amber*

2 Work in pairs. Retell the story in your own words and discuss the question.

- Do you agree with either of the comments?

5B Grammar 2 Quantifiers

How _____ books have you read this year?	Do you drink _____ coffee or tea?
many	either / any / much

How _____ time do you spend outdoors?	What's something you have _____ patience for? (clue = not much)
much	little

What do you think _____ people are afraid of?	What is something _____ people like, but you do? (clue = not many)
most / man / some / a few / few	few

How _____ meals do you know how to cook without a recipe?	Where are a _____ places that you like to spend time? (clue = two)
many	couple of

Do you own _____ objects that are over fifty years old?	Do you have _____ cousins?
many / any	any / many

In a film, do you prefer _____ of humour or lots of suspense? (clue = starts with *p*)	How _____ sleep do you like to get each night?
plenty	much

5B Vocabulary — Crime (robbery)

Team A

`arrest   charged   found   in   sentenced`

Case #1

Jen Gowers was cleaning the floor of a supermarket at 4.00 a.m., when Robber #1 broke **1**_____ to the building. Jen grabbed the closest thing, a banana, and threw it at the robber's head, as hard as she could. He ran away, but Jen was sure he wouldn't evade **2**_____ for long. The next day, the robber went to police and complained about the bruises on his face. Jen was **3**_____ with assault. She couldn't afford to pay for a good lawyer and was **4**_____ guilty by a jury. She was **5**_____ to three months in jail.

Our sentence:
_____

Team B

`left   pleaded   researched   to   trial`

Case #2

At her **1**_____ Robber #2 said she just wanted money to buy lunch, and hadn't **2**_____ or planned her crime. She had entered a bookshop and screamed she would shoot if she wasn't given money. Sales staff refused because the gun in her bag was obviously just a banana. After she **3**_____ the scene of the crime, she was caught eating her weapon 100 metres down the road. She **4**_____ guilty to robbery and was sentenced **5**_____ one year in jail.

Our sentence:
_____

Team C

`broke   caught   evade   in   scene`

Case #3

Robber #3, who stole a £20,000 ring from a jeweller's, was seen leaving the **1**_____ of the crime on security cameras. However, he managed to **2**_____ arrest by hiding inside a zoo, where he survived for ten days by eating bananas meant for the elephants. One night, he **3**_____ into the zoo café, an alarm went off, and he was finally **4**_____ . At his trial, Robber #3 was sentenced to one year **5**_____ jail for the robbery and two years for hiding in the zoo. He is only 16.

Our sentence:
_____

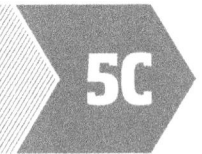

5C Language focus 1 — Adverb + adjective collocations

1. Look at the left-hand column. Tick the combinations that collocate and cross out the one that doesn't.

2. Look at the right-hand column. Complete the statements with the appropriate adverb + adjective collocation from the same row. More than one combination may be possible in some cases.

3. Circle the appropriate number to show how much you agree or disagree with each statement (1 = strongly disagree, 10 = strongly agree).

1	deeply concerned deeply normal deeply personal deeply religious	Learning is a _____ journey, and students should be given plenty of freedom to choose what and how they learn. Disagree 1 2 3 4 5 6 7 8 9 10 Agree
2	relatively essential relatively new relatively simple relatively small relatively warm	For me, recalling what I've learned in previous lessons is _____ . Disagree 1 2 3 4 5 6 7 8 9 10 Agree
3	totally difficult totally lost totally unacceptable totally wrong	I feel _____ if I study on my own without friends or classmates. Disagree 1 2 3 4 5 6 7 8 9 10 Agree
4	perfectly good perfectly known perfectly legal perfectly normal perfectly safe	Pen and paper are _____ tools for learning, and I prefer them to new technology. Disagree 1 2 3 4 5 6 7 8 9 10 Agree
5	extremely dangerous extremely difficult extremely important extremely rare extremely right	I find it _____ to concentrate if there is music on in the background. Disagree 1 2 3 4 5 6 7 8 9 10 Agree
6	entirely different entirely new entirely possible entirely small	It's _____ that you might find me working on an assignment the night before it is due! Disagree 1 2 3 4 5 6 7 8 9 10 Agree
7	absolutely cold absolutely essential absolutely ridiculous absolutely right absolutely true	Breakfast is _____ for me to have a productive day. Disagree 1 2 3 4 5 6 7 8 9 10 Agree
8	bitterly cold bitterly concerned bitterly disappointed bitterly divided bitterly opposed	I get _____ if I get a poor mark. Disagree 1 2 3 4 5 6 7 8 9 10 Agree
9	completely different completely difficult completely honest completely new completely wrong	I like classmates to give _____ feedback and correct me if I make an error. Disagree 1 2 3 4 5 6 7 8 9 10 Agree
10	highly effective highly new highly qualified highly successful highly unlikely	It's _____ that I'll ever become a teacher myself. Disagree 1 2 3 4 5 6 7 8 9 10 Agree

4. Work in pairs and discuss your ideas.

5C Language focus 2 Adverb + adjective collocations

1 Complete the adverbs.

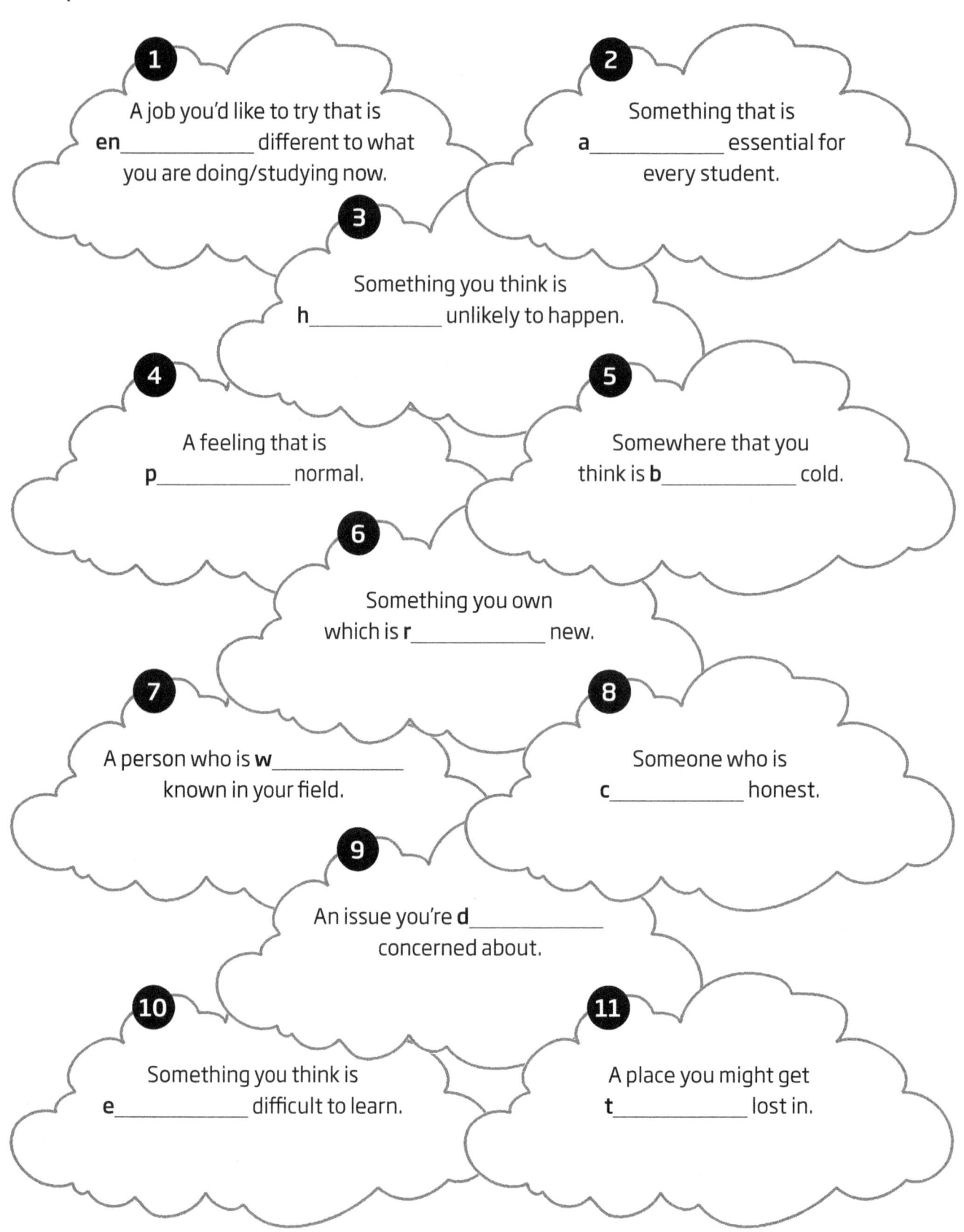

1. A job you'd like to try that is en_____ different to what you are doing/studying now.

2. Something that is a_____ essential for every student.

3. Something you think is h_____ unlikely to happen.

4. A feeling that is p_____ normal.

5. Somewhere that you think is b_____ cold.

6. Something you own which is r_____ new.

7. A person who is w_____ known in your field.

8. Someone who is c_____ honest.

9. An issue you're d_____ concerned about.

10. Something you think is e_____ difficult to learn.

11. A place you might get t_____ lost in.

2 Write a response in the clouds for eight of the sentences in Exercise 1. Make sure your responses are not in order.

5C Vocabulary — Money

Worksheet A

1 If you want to save more money, you need to either cut back on your expenses or increase your BEEP!   (income)

2 I'm planning an amazing trip around the world with my best friend, so I'm putting aside money each month into my BEEP account.   (savings)

3 People around the country are deeply concerned about the chance of another BEEP.   (recession)

4 _____

(interest = BEEP)

5 _____

(donation = BEEP)

Worksheet B

1 My grandparents have retired, but they receive a BEEP from the government.   (pension)

2 There was a sale and I found a shirt I wanted which had 70% off. What a BEEP!   (bargain)

3 Twenty years ago milk was a third of the price it is now. Most supermarket items have tripled in cost because of BEEP!   (inflation)

4 _____

(investments = BEEP)

5 _____

(budget = BEEP)

6A Grammar 1 — Verb + -ing and infinitive with to

1 Work in pairs and discuss the question.

- What do you think are the most common hopes and dreams people have? Think about the following areas:

  adventure   animals   career   self-improvement   travel

2 Complete the text with the -ing or infinitive form of the verb in brackets.

Hopes and dreams

A survey of over two thousand people revealed goals they wanted to achieve or experiences they wanted to have during their lifetime. Here are some of the things they mentioned.

Career
1. Some people said they intended _____ (work) abroad.
2. Others said it was important _____ (get) to the top of their field.
3. Plenty of people think it would be worth _____ (change) career completely.

Travel
4. Many people imagined _____ (take) a year off to travel the world.
5. Others dream of _____ (relax) on an island.
6. A lot of people said it would be wonderful _____ (visit) a friend or relative abroad.

Animals
7. It was popular _____ (want) to hold a koala.
8. Some people would choose _____ (see) elephants in the wild.
9. Others said they would enjoy _____ (ride) a camel!

Adventure
10. _____ (drive) a motorcycle was a popular wish.
11. It was common to think about _____ (enter) a big running race.
12. A few people couldn't help _____ (dream) about entering a reality TV show.

Self-improvement
13. One third of people said they want to learn _____ (speak) another language.
14. _____ (play) an instrument was on many people's lists.
15. Many people would like to volunteer their time _____ (help) other people.

3 Complete the sentences with ideas from the text or your own ideas.

I'd hate _____
I dream of _____
I intend _____
I'd enjoy _____
It'd be wonderful _____
_____ would be amazing!

4 Work in groups and compare your ideas.

6A Grammar 2 Verb + -ing and infinitive with to

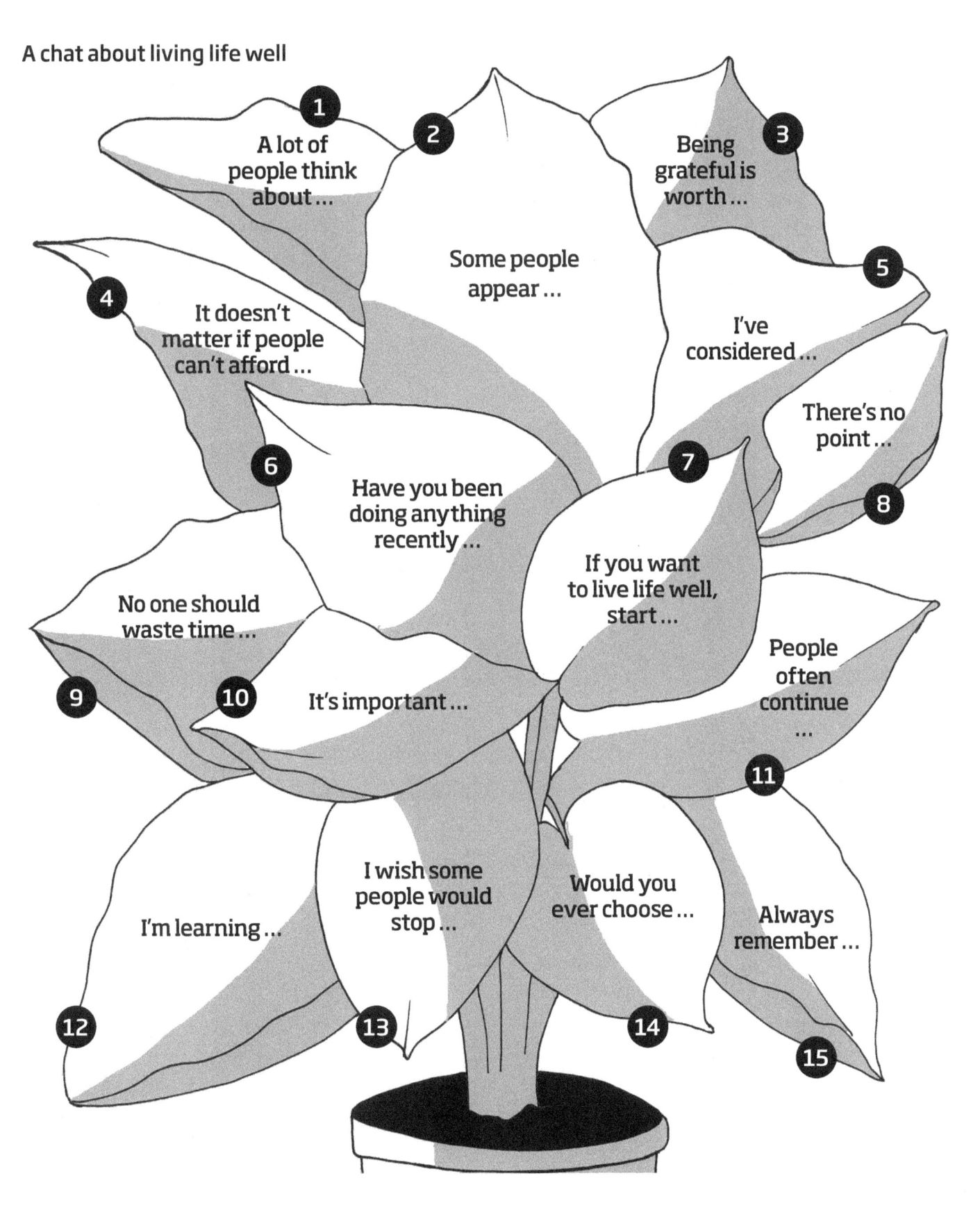

A chat about living life well

1. A lot of people think about …
2. Some people appear …
3. Being grateful is worth …
4. It doesn't matter if people can't afford …
5. I've considered …
6. Have you been doing anything recently …
7. If you want to live life well, start …
8. There's no point …
9. No one should waste time …
10. It's important …
11. People often continue …
12. I'm learning …
13. I wish some people would stop …
14. Would you ever choose …
15. Always remember …

Verb bank

| be | change | come | do | give | have | help | improve | like | live | reduce | rest | spend | take | think |
| try | waste | watch | work on | worry | | | | | | | | | | |

6A Vocabulary — Common idioms

BIG NIGHT OUT

Read the things that people loved or loathed about their night at a concert.
Correct the common idioms in each sentence. Two of the sentences are correct.

1 The tickets may have cost a leg and an arm, but it was worth it.
___

2 That last song really took the breath away. What an amazing voice!
___

3 I was astonished to see Elina there. I guess you can't judge a book by its cover.
___

4 It drives me on the wall when people leave their seats in the middle of a song.
___

5 I was over the stars to get tickets for my birthday and it didn't disappoint me.
___

6 It was such a pain when other fans kept screaming. It wasn't them I paid to hear!
___

7 The dancers were excellent. They made their routines look like a piece of bread!
___

8 The whole concert was out of the world. It was absolutely fantastic!
___

6B Grammar 1 Reported speech

1. Read the conversation in the left-hand column between Tom and a stallholder, and answer the question.
   - Would you have negotiated more or less than Tom did?

2. Complete the reported speech in the right-hand column using two words in each gap.

3. Work in pairs. Read the seller's reported speech again and answer the question.
   - What negotiation strategies does the seller use?

Tom:	I'm interested in the bags, could you get one down for me to look at please?	I said **1**_____ _____ interested in the bags and asked the seller **2**_____ _____ one down for me to look at.
Stallholder:	Certainly. All the bags were made by people in my family.	She **3**_____ _____ that all the bags **4**_____ _____ made by people in her family.
Tom:	How much are they?	I **5**_____ _____ much **6**_____ _____ .
Stallholder:	Do you like the orange or the green?	She **7**_____ _____ I liked the orange or the green.
Tom:	I prefer the green one.	I told her **8**_____ _____ the green one.
Stallholder:	You have excellent taste because the green one is my best bag. It costs 200 pesos and the orange bag costs 100.	**9**_____ _____ I had excellent taste and that the green one was her best bag. It cost 200 pesos and the orange bag cost 100.
Tom:	Oh. Would you accept 150 pesos for the green bag?	**10**_____ _____ whether she **11**_____ _____ 150 pesos for the green bag.
Stallholder:	I can't, but I can give you a very special price for the two bags of 250 pesos.	She told me **12**_____ _____ , but she **13**_____ _____ me a very special price for the two bags of 250 pesos.
Tom:	OK, I'll take them both.	I said I **14**_____ _____ them both.

PHOTOCOPIABLE © Pearson Education Limited 2020

6B Grammar 2 — Reported speech

Student A

Tell me ...	Name	Notes
1 about a time when you won something.		
2 about your dream job.		
3 about something you will definitely do this weekend.		
4 about somewhere you've visited recently.		
5 about the best present you've ever received.		
6 about what you're going to do during the next holidays.		
7 about something you're enjoying doing at the moment.		
8 whether you have a lucky number, and what it is.		

Student B

Tell me ...	Name	Notes
1 about a time you had a nice surprise.		
2 about your dream home.		
3 about the best day you've had in your life so far.		
4 whether you're thinking about doing something fun soon and, if so, what.		
5 about something you really want to do in in the future.		
6 about something you're spending a lot of time doing at the moment.		
7 about the most interesting place you've ever visited.		
8 if you've got a favourite book and, if so, what it is.		

6B Vocabulary — Negotiating

1 Choose the correct alternatives to complete the sentences.

Negotiating strategies	Helpful	Unhelpful	It depends
1 Ask the other person questions to *build/grow* trust.			
2 *Criticise/Conflict* the other person to weaken their position.			
3 Build a *bond/cooperation* by talking about shared interests or goals.			
4 Mention a previous *conflict/praise*.			
5 *Build/Stay* calm no matter what.			
6 *Bond/Interrupt* the other person.			
7 Threaten to leave if the other person doesn't *cooperate/interrupt* with what you want.			
8 Increase *calm/tension* by waiting a few seconds before responding.			
9 *Praise/Cooperate* the other person for being a bold negotiator.			
10 Agree with whatever the other person wants to avoid *falling out/falling in*.			

2 Choose one of the following situations.

- [ ] A parent negotiating with their teenager/parent about what time to come home.
- [ ] A business owner negotiating a sales contract.
- [ ] Flatmates negotiating who will do different jobs around the house.
- [ ] Other _____

3 Work in pairs. Think about the situation chosen in Exercise 2 and decide whether strategies 1–10 in Exercise 1 would be helpful, unhelpful or whether it would depend on the particular situation.

4 Work in groups and compare your ideas. Then answer the question.
- Which strategies would be helpful in your negotiations?

6C Language focus 1 — Verb patterns after reporting verbs

1 Complete the sentences with the correct form of the word in brackets. Add a person/pronoun and preposition if necessary.

WHAT WOULD YOU SAY?

1 It's your flatmate's responsibility to pay the electricity bill, but she keeps forgetting. When the payment is late, you have to pay a fine.
  A You threaten ____to leave____ (leave) the flat if she doesn't organise herself better.
  B You decide to remind _____ (pay) every month.
  C You advise _____ (let) you organise the electricity bill from now on.
  D Other _____

2 Your boss is looking for some papers, which you accidentally threw out yesterday.
  A You deny _____ (know) anything about where they have gone.
  B You accuse a colleague _____ (take) them.
  C You admit _____ (get) rid of them and say you're very sorry.
  D Other _____

3 Your university lecturer decides to move the due date on your project worth 50% to a week earlier.
  A You refuse _____ (hand in) your project early and organise a class protest.
  B You immediately agree _____ (complete) the project earlier.
  C You insist _____ (hear) the reason for the change before you agree.
  D Other _____

4 You're having lunch with your cousin and suddenly remember it's his birthday.
  A You apologise at least three times _____ (forget).
  B You somehow convince _____ (believe) that you knew all along.
  C You blame him _____ (not / mention) it to you!
  D Other _____

5 A friend asks your opinion of his new hairstyle. You don't like it.
  A You admit _____ (not / like) it as much as his old one.
  B You decide _____ (pretend) it's fantastic.
  C You politely refuse _____ (give) an opinion by asking where he had it done.
  D Other _____

2 Choose your answers to the quiz. Then work in pairs and compare your ideas.

6C Language focus 2 — Verb patterns after reporting verbs

If someone denies	doing something, how could you tell if they're lying?
Do you appreciate it when people remind	you to do tasks or is it annoying?
What does it mean if people agree	to disagree about an issue?
Are there any foods you would refuse	to try?
How would you feel if your date insisted	on paying for your meal?
Have you ever blamed	technology for a mistake you made?
How might shop assistants convince	a customer to buy their products?
Do you ever apologise	for things that weren't your fault?
Have you ever been accused	of being too nice?
How would you advise	a person to prepare for their first job interview?
If you heard someone threatening	to hurt someone else, what could you do?
Why is it hard for some people to admit	to being wrong?

6C Vocabulary — Reporting verbs

Pair A

1 Complete the argument between friends with the correct form of the verbs in the box. Then practise reading the conversation aloud.

| accuse   admit   agree   apologise   deny   refuse |

- **A:** I'm not going to ¹_____ with you just because you're being difficult.
- **B:** Are you ²_____ me of being difficult?
- **A:** ³_____ it – you are!
- **B:** I am not. I think you should ⁴_____.
- **A:** You can't ⁵_____ that you're not making this conversation easy!
- **B:** I ⁶_____ to get into an argument about it. It's a waste of time.
- **A:** Fine, let's change the subject!

2 Now perform your argument from Exercise 1 for Pair B. Then listen and complete Pair B's argument below.

- **A:** I must ⁷_____ that you stop interrupting me while I'm talking.
- **B:** I'm not ⁸_____ you would ever finish!
- **A:** May I ⁹_____ you that you asked me for the full story of what went wrong!
- **B:** And from what you've said, you have only yourself to ¹⁰_____.
- **A:** I'd ¹¹_____ you to think very carefully about what you say next.
- **B:** Are you ¹²_____ me?
- **A:** Let's just say that if you interrupt again, you won't be having any of this chocolate.

Pair B

1 Complete the argument between friends with the correct form of the verbs in the box. Then practise reading the conversation aloud.

| advise   blame   convince   insist   remind   threaten |

- **A:** I must ⁷_____ that you stop interrupting me while I'm talking.
- **B:** I'm not ⁸_____ you would ever finish!
- **A:** May I ⁹_____ you that you asked me for the full story of what went wrong!
- **B:** And from what you've said, you have only yourself to ¹⁰_____.
- **A:** I'd ¹¹_____ you to think very carefully about what you say next.
- **B:** Are you ¹²_____ me?
- **A:** Let's just say that if you interrupt again, you won't be having any of this chocolate.

2 Listen to Pair A's argument and complete the gaps below. Then perform your argument from Exercise 1 while they listen.

- **A:** I'm not going to ¹_____ with you just because you're being difficult.
- **B:** Are you ²_____ me of being difficult?
- **A:** ³_____ it – you are!
- **B:** I am not. I think you should ⁴_____.
- **A:** You can't ⁵_____ that you're not making this conversation easy!
- **B:** I ⁶_____ to get into an argument about it. It's a waste of time.
- **A:** Fine, let's change the subject!

7A Grammar 1 Real conditionals

1 Read the posts on a forum. Match the infuences in the box with the posts a–e.

> childhood   friends   information   society attitudes   what you read

2 Choose the correct alternatives to complete the posts.

You tell us: What makes someone care about an issue?

a _____

If you ¹*grow/will grow* up in a family who think something is important, it's a huge influence. For example, ²*when/unless* children spend a lot of time in nature with their parents, they're more likely to care about environmental issues as adults.
— AKIO

b _____

³*Assuming/Unless* you choose stories with a range of views, reading fiction can have a real impact on what you care about. If I see a homeless person in future, I ⁴*am/will be* kinder to them because of a novel I read about people who live on the streets. That book had a big impact on me.
— FINN

c _____

Learning about a problem might help, ⁵*as soon as/unless* you think about it too often. If I ⁶*hear/will hear* too often about an issue like climate change, I just feel overwhelmed.
— JACK

d _____

If your friends ⁷*care/will care* deeply about a certain issue, they'll likely influence you to care about it too. It's a social thing. I ⁸*go/'ll be going* to a gender equality march this weekend, provided that my friends come with me!
— PETRA

e _____

⁹*As soon as/As long as* enough people in society care about something, many other people will immediately make changes to belong to the majority. For instance, if I ¹⁰*carry/will carry* a plastic bag now, I feel embarrassed because they're not acceptable here anymore.
— HELENE

7A Grammar 2 Real conditionals

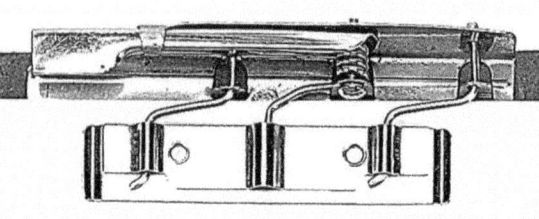

Are these situations acceptable and, if so, under what conditions?

1. Someone downloads a film for free.
   ☐ Acceptable   ☐ Not acceptable
   Provided that / When _____

2. A student encourages classmates to participate in social unrest.
   ☐ Acceptable   ☐ Not acceptable
   Unless / If _____

3. Celebrities advertise a product they have never used.
   ☐ Acceptable   ☐ Not acceptable
   When / Provided that _____

4. A city council bans homeless people from sleeping on the streets.
   ☐ Acceptable   ☐ Not acceptable
   If / As long as _____

5. Someone lies about their experiences at a job interview.
   ☐ Acceptable   ☐ Not acceptable
   As long as / Assuming _____

6. A company advertises unhealthy food directly to children.
   ☐ Acceptable   ☐ Not acceptable
   If / As long as _____

7. Someone puts a photo of someone else online without their permission.
   ☐ Acceptable   ☐ Not acceptable
   If / Assuming _____

8. A company employs children living in poverty to make goods.
   ☐ Acceptable   ☐ Not acceptable
   Assuming / Unless _____

7A Vocabulary — Social issues

CONNECTIONS

- poverty
- inequality (adjective form) _____
- homelessness (adjective form) _____
- healthcare costs
- social unrest
- intolerance (adjective form) _____
- energy efficiency (adjective form) _____
- living standards
- life expectancy
- unemployment (adjective form) _____

7B Grammar 1 Future forms and degrees of probability

1 Choose the correct alternative to complete the responses to questions 1–4.

Future possibilities

1 What are you planning to do this weekend?

A few friends and I are ¹*planning/thinking* enter a competition – we've got to make a short film in 24 hours. Two of my friends are twins so we ²*may/are* possibly going to make a comedy about that.
I ³*doubt/think* we'll win anything, but we ⁴*are/will* definitely try to produce something entertaining.

Nassim

2 Is it likely you'll ever move from this area?

My whole family lives here and ⁵*are/it's* unlikely that they'll let me go far! So I'm ⁶*unlikely/probably* just going to live in Bogotá. I may ⁷*well/think* travel though. In fact, I'm thinking ⁸*to/about* visiting my friend in Costa Rica this June.

Maria-Paula

3 What will you be doing at this time next year?

It's hard to say! I'm ⁹*wondering/thinking* whether to change jobs because I ¹⁰*may/don't* think there'll be many opportunities for promotion where I am now. It's also possible ¹¹*that/to* I'll start my own business. But I probably ¹²*don't/won't* be brave enough to do that.

Coby

4 Might you try any adventurous activities in the future?

I ¹³*probably/may* well try diving, although I don't think I ¹⁴*'m going to/'ll* definitely do it with sharks or anything scary like that. I ¹⁵*probably won't/doubt* I'll ever do anything extreme involving heights as I hate them and I hate flying! So, I'll ¹⁶*definitely/possibly* never go skydiving!

Lidiya

2 Work in pairs. Ask and answer the questions in Exercise 1.

7B Grammar 2 Future forms and degrees of probability

1 Complete the statements so that they are true for you. Use the phrases in the box.

> It's likely/unlikely/possible that I'll …
> I may well …
> I'm planning to …
> I'll probably/possibly/definitely …
> I'm probably/possibly/definitely going to …
> I probably/possibly/definitely won't …
> I think/don't think/doubt I'll …
> I'm wondering whether to …

		Classmate(s) with similar answer
1	_____ take public transport this week.	
2	_____ go somewhere new this year.	
3	_____ become an entrepreneur.	
4	_____ be on stage soon.	
5	_____ eat out this weekend.	
6	_____ play a video game today.	
7	_____ sell something this month.	
8	_____ receive more than fifty messages today.	
9	_____ give someone a hand today.	
10	_____ ride in a helicopter.	
11	_____ forget to do something this week.	
12	_____ be at our next English class.	

2 Interview other classmates and see if you can find someone who has a similar probability of doing each item. It doesn't matter if different phrases are used as long as the meaning is similar.

7B Vocabulary — Collocations with *make*, *take*, *do* and *give*

Phrase box

a _____ a deal
b _____ a profit
c _____ charge
d _____ a risk
e _____ without
f _____ sense
g _____ priority
h _____ a good job
i _____ it your best shot
j _____ someone's place
k _____ someone a hand
l _____ research

1. START
2. I'm so nervous about the big exam today!
3. We had a quiz night to raise funds for the local hospital.
4. The catering company has cancelled! Do you know anyone else?
5. Why on earth is there ice cream in the microwave?
6. Did you speak to your colleagues about who is going to work the late shift?
7. Does the project plan seem logical to you?
8. I don't think I can carry all these shopping bags myself.
9. We came last out of the twenty teams in the new business challenge.
10. Would the venue managers give us a discount because our concert is for charity?
11. Could you find out if any similar projects have been done before?
12. The hotel is located in a country area, and it doesn't have wifi.
13. This crossword puzzle is quite tricky.
14. I have some tickets to a concert, but I'm not feeling well.
15. Shall I quit my job to travel the world?
16. I had a job interview, but I didn't get the position.
17. We've had over fifty job applications for the position. How will we choose?
18. Oh no, I've left my phone at home today.
19. Could you read my essay to check what I'm saying is clear?
20. Everyone in the group is fighting about what to do next.
21. The concert will be the first time I'll be singing in front of an audience.
22. Have you decided which universities to apply for?
23. Do you like to give directions to others in team activities?
24. Look at this kitchen! What a mess!
25. I hope we didn't make a loss at the market stall today.
26. I couldn't buy eggs, because the shop had completely sold out!
27. You're going to paint the café walls black? That's a very unusual choice.
28. There are five people waiting for the doctor. Who will be seen first?
29. Where can I get some good ideas for the new business challenge?
30. FINISH

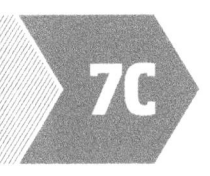

7C Language focus 1 Introductory *It*

1 Complete the texts with the words in the box.

LIFE IN A NEW COUNTRY:
What feels different to you?

| as if | it sounds | me | me to | seems to | turns out |

After three weeks here for work, I've noticed a few differences. It feels **1**_____ most people here are quite polite when you first meet them. It amazes **2**_____ see people waiting in queues so neatly. It also strikes **3**_____ that people say sorry, even if someone else bumps into them in the street.

Sometimes **4**_____ as if people are being very serious and then it **5**_____ that they're actually making a joke. It **6**_____ me that even locals can't always tell either!

| alarms me | appears | as though | feels like |
| just that | not that |

I'm studying for a year in a small town where it **7**_____ everyone knows each other. So far, it **8**_____ that the culture is quite casual compared to what I'm used to.

It seems **9**_____ there are nature reserves and fun new places to explore everywhere. It **10**_____ that we have to watch out for poisonous snakes and spiders though. It's **11**_____ I'm scared of them exactly, it's **12**_____ I'd rather see them from a distance.

7C Language focus 2 Introductory *It*

Student A

Put the words in the correct order to complete the sentences. Tick the sentences which are true for you. Check and compare your answers with Student B.

		Me	B
1	_____ knows what they're doing! (appears / it / everybody else / that)		
2	_____ I don't have time. (not / reading, / that / like / I / just / that / it's / don't / it's)		
3	_____ is increasing. (concerns / inequality / me / it / that)		
4	_____ about the ideal age right now. (it / as / feels / I'm / though)		
5	_____ would disagree with their bosses. (surprises / it / to / me / think / people / that)		
6	_____ have finished this activity. (sounds / some / classmates / it / if / as)		

Student B answers
1 It looks as though I'm
2 It bothers me that people
3 It occurs to me that it's
4 It's not that I can't cook, it's just that
5 It alarms me to think that there
6 It seems that we

Student B

Put the words in the correct order to complete the sentences. Tick the sentences which are true for you. Check and compare your answers with Student A.

		Me	B
1	_____ going to be extremely busy next week. (I'm / it / looks / though / as)		
2	_____ are so quick to judge other people's behaviour. (bothers / me / people / that / it)		
3	_____ easier than ever to travel. (occurs / me / it / to / that / it's)		
4	_____ I don't enjoy it. (that / I / just / it's / can't / cook, / not / it's / that)		
5	_____ is so much online data about me. (it / me / there / that / to / alarms / think)		
6	_____ should be taught about cultural differences at school. (seems / it / we / that)		

Student A answers
1 It appears that everybody else
2 It's not that I don't like reading, it's just that
3 It concerns me that inequality
4 It feels as though I'm
5 It surprises me to think that people
6 It sounds as if some classmates

7C Vocabulary — Personal and professional relationships

Is it true?
Some people in the class have an **acquaintance** who is famous.

Is it true?
Almost nobody in the class would ever invite a **client** to their home.

Is it true?
A lot of people in the class think you shouldn't spend time with **co-workers** outside of work.

Is it true?
Most people in the class believe you could be good friends with an **ex-partner**.

Is it true?
Almost everyone in the class thinks it would be foolish to ask a **senior colleague's** age.

Is it true?
Most classmates who have a **sister-in-law** get on really well with her.

Is it true?
Everyone knew at least one **classmate** in the group before starting this class.

Is it true?
At least three people have been in contact with a **distant relative** this month.

Is it true?
No one in the class has a **flatmate**.

Is it true?
Most people wouldn't tell a **superior** if they had food in their teeth.

8A Grammar 1 Second conditional

1 Put the words in the correct order to form second conditional sentences.

1 If I was attending a film awards ceremony, _____ .
   (wear / I / outrageous / would / clothes / really)

2 _____ , I'd choose world peace, a sports car and a world trip.
   (I / to / were / three wishes / if / have)

3 If I could do it well without practising, _____ .
   (I / guitar / play / would / to / love / the)

4 _____ , I'd be relaxing on a beautiful beach.
   (I / if / be / right / could / anywhere / now)

5 If I wrote a film, _____ .
   (would / happy / it / definitely / a / ending / have)

6 _____ , if I had more time.
   (could / more / I / get / done)

7 I might become famous _____ . Who knows?
   (I / Hollywood / if / lived / in)

8 _____ , I'd try to look on the bright side of life.
   (were / if / you / I)

9 If I wasn't studying English, _____ .
   (be / I'd / Portuguese / learning)

10 _____ , I wouldn't have understood the plot in this one.
    (I / hadn't / earlier / films / if / seen / the)

11 If I had to have the same dinner every day for a year, _____ .
    (choose / definitely / sushi / I'd)

12 I wouldn't have enjoyed this evening as much _____ .
    (if / here / hadn't / been / you)

2 Write second conditional sentences.

8A Grammar 2 Second conditional

Student A

1 My partner's extremely rich family doesn't accept me. Help!

If I were you, ...

2 I've got a very sore throat.

If I were you, ...

3 I'm going to a costume party tonight but don't have time to go shopping. What could I go as?

If I were you, ...

4 My boss of three months still pronounces my name incorrectly. Shall I say anything?

If I were you, ...

Student B

1 My workmates have invited me on a boat trip, but I get sea sick.

If I were you, ...

2 I've noticed my colleague is taking pens from the office home. Shall I say anything?

If I were you, ...

3 I think I waste too much time on the internet.

If I were you, ...

4 I've been invited to dinner by my friend's parents. What shall I take?

If I were you, ...

8A Vocabulary — Events in films

| abandoned | betrays | capture | confronts | faces | go on a mission | murder |
| overcome | rescues | survive | trapped | tricks |

A teenager wins a trip to ¹_____ to Mars, a twenty-year journey on a new spaceship.

A couple celebrating their wedding on a beautiful island receive a death note from someone threatening to ²_____ the guests unless a huge amount of money is paid.

A rare white tiger escapes from the zoo and a new police officer has to help ³_____ it before it hurts someone.

A jealous person ⁴_____ his famous friend by selling one of his secrets to the media.

After skiing off a trail, two adventurers get lost in the mountains. They have to fight to ⁵_____.

A young adult ⁶_____ the difficult choice of whether to follow their parents' wishes and become a dentist, or their own dream of becoming a performer.

A bank employee is ⁷_____ in a dull job until he is invited to spy on his boss by the CIA.

A grandmother has to ⁸_____ her fear of flying in order to visit her grandchild, who lives abroad.

A lonely person ⁹_____ and cares for a baby penguin with a broken leg.

A criminal ¹⁰_____ someone into buying a car which was used in a crime. Now the police are chasing the buyer.

Two injured soldiers are ¹¹_____ by their group in enemy territory and must escape.

A group of science students suspects their professor is from another planet and ¹²_____ her about it.

8B Grammar 1 Conditionals in the past

1 Read the stories and answer the question.

- What do the three stories all have in common?

2 Read the sentences about the stories. Choose the correct alternatives to complete them.

A After a morning of last-minute sightseeing on holiday, my partner and I jumped into a taxi. We asked the driver to stop by our hostel on the way to the airport and both ran in to grab our suitcases. A big mistake! When we came out, the taxi had disappeared, along with our small rucksacks, which contained cash and some souvenirs. Luckily, I'd insisted we keep our passports in a money belt. It was impossible to find the driver, as we couldn't even remember what company the taxi was from.

1 If one of us had stayed in the taxi, we _____ our things.
   a wouldn't have lost   b would have lost
2 It _____ worse if we had kept our passports in our rucksacks.
   a had been   b would have been
3 If we _____ the taxi number, we might have been able to trace the driver.
   a had noted   b noted
4 If we hadn't been leaving that day, we _____ the incident to the police.
   a had reported   b could have reported

B I was taking my first exam at university and I couldn't believe how many pages there were. I flipped to the back: ten questions! I knew the material, but I only managed to answer seven questions. After the exam, my friend told me that it said on the front that we only had to answer three of the questions. Oops! From then on, I was very careful to always read exam instructions!

1 If I _____ the instructions carefully, I wouldn't have written so many answers.
   a would read   b had read
2 If I hadn't tried to write so many answers, I _____ more time on each question.
   a couldn't have spent   b could have spent
3 If my friend hadn't pointed it out, I _____ my mistake!
   a might not have realised   b might realised
4 I _____ so careful with instructions now if I hadn't had this experience.
   a wouldn't have been   b wouldn't be

C I was watching a film at my friend's house. After it finished, I realised that I had knocked over my black coffee on their new cream carpet. Despite our best efforts to clean it, we couldn't remove the mark. My friend said it didn't matter, but I could tell she was really annoyed. Now I can't drink black coffee anymore because it reminds me too much of that incident!

1 If I wasn't so careless, I _____ over my drink.
   a wouldn't have knocked   b would have knocked
2 If I _____ the spill straight away, we might have been able to remove the mark.
   a would notice   b had noticed
3 If their carpet hadn't been a light colour, the mark _____ so obvious.
   a couldn't have been   b wouldn't have been
4 I might still drink black coffee if I _____ so guilty about ruining the carpet.
   a didn't feel   b felt

3 Think of a story about a mistake which could have been avoided. Write conditional sentences about how the situation could have been different.

I lost my keys at the beach once. If I had closed my bag properly, they wouldn't have fallen out.

_____
_____
_____

4 Work in groups and compare your stories and conditional sentences.

8B Grammar 2 — Conditionals in the past

1 If you hadn't come to class today, what would you be doing now?

2 What might your name have been if you had chosen it yourself?

3 If you had found some money on the way to class, what would you have done with it?

4 If you hadn't studied what you did, what other subject might you have chosen?

5 If you hadn't decided to take this class, what would you have done instead?

6 If the weather had been different on the weekend, would it have changed your plans?

7 How would your life be different if you had been born fifty years earlier?

8 If you could have got up at any time today, what time would you have chosen?

9 If you could have gone anywhere on holiday last year, where would you have chosen?

10 How might your life have been different if you had had more siblings?

11 If you hadn't been able to get to class the usual way today, how else could you have got here?

12 If you had been invited to star on a TV show as a child, would you have done it?

8B Vocabulary Searching and hiding

1 Find ten words or phrases related to searching and hiding in the word search.

h	d	r	h	n	u	h	x	l	r	q
d	e	c	e	i	v	e	s	g	o	h
i	p	o	a	h	d	i	f	j	i	e
t	u	i	d	e	n	t	i	f	y	s
r	r	f	f	e	c	r	p	c	k	i
a	s	u	o	a	h	a	a	r	o	h
c	u	g	r	d	u	c	e	t	t	u
k	e	e	p	a	n	e	y	e	o	n
e	d	a	y	c	t	b	s	p	o	t
s	d	i	s	g	u	i	s	e	n	e

1 _____ 6 _____
2 _____ 7 _____
3 _____ 8 _____
4 _____ 9 _____
5 _____ 10 _____

2 Complete the sentences with the correct form of the words and phrases in Exercise 1.

1 I need to _____ the time. I've got another appointment straight after this.
2 I know it's only 9.00 p.m., but I'm _____ bed. I've got to be up early in the morning!
3 I like _____ myself on a running app so I can see my route and calculate the distance I've travelled.
4 I'm useless at lying. I doubt I could _____ anyone even if I tried.
5 I've _____ five ways I'm going to improve my English in the next month.
6 I didn't want anyone to recognise me so I wore a cap and some dark glasses to _____ myself.
7 I'm thinking about _____ a career with the police.
8 Great blog post, but I'm afraid I've _____ a couple of spelling mistakes.
9 I spent Friday night _____ my distant relatives online. I love family history!
10 I've spent ages shopping but I'm still _____ for the perfect gift for my sister!

3 Work in pairs and discuss the questions.
- Which sentences are most like something you would say?
- Which sentences would you never say?

8C Language focus 1 Linkers of concession

1 Match the questions and answers.

2 Choose the alternatives to complete the replies.

1 How was the film?

2 How was the exhibition?

3 How was the job interview?

4 How was the first class?

5 How was the trip to the mountains?

6 How was the traffic on your way here?

7 How's your brother?

8 How are you feeling?

a *However/In spite of the fact* that my legs were shaking under the table, I think it went OK!

b To be honest, I'd love to see more of him. *Even though/Nevertheless*, I hear he's healthy and happy!

c We had a great time skiing, *although/despite* I've still got bruises from falling over!

d The sculptures are definitely worth seeing, *despite/however* the long queues.

e It was really fun *in spite of the fact/in spite* my being the only student who didn't know anyone else.

f *Despite/Even though* it didn't have great reviews, I found it hilarious! You'll love it!

g *Although/Despite* having no coffee this morning, I'm actually feeling great!

h I thought it would be terrible at this time of day. *Although/However*, once we got off the main roads, it was fine.

3 Work in pairs. Ask and answer the questions.

8C Language focus 2 — Linkers of concession

Student A

Situation 1

You recently went on a class trip to visit an art exhibition. You had an awful time. You are going to complain to Student B about the things you didn't like including:
- The tickets were expensive.
- You had to walk for 30 minutes in the rain to get there.
- There was a long queue.
- You thought the paintings were strange.

Complain about your experience to Student B. Try to respond to whatever Student B says using linkers of concession.
B: *The paintings really made me think.*
A: *Although you say the paintings made you think, I just thought they were strange.*

Situation 2

Imagine there is a new sculpture in a nearby park. You really like it because:
- It's elegant.
- It won a national sculpture competition.
- It was donated to the park by a rich individual.
- It is bringing new visitors to the park.

Listen to the comments Student B makes and respond using sentences that have a linker of concession.
B: *The design of the sculpture is very simple.*
A: *You're right, it is simple. Nevertheless, I like it.*

Student B

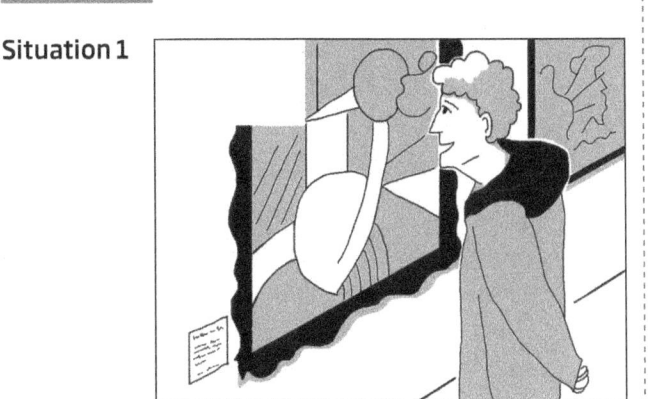

Situation 1

You recently went on a class trip to visit an art exhibition. You had a wonderful time. Your reasons include:
- You felt lucky that you got to see the work by a famous artist.
- You passed an amazing bakery on the way there, which had delicious snacks.
- There was a lot of time to chat with classmates.
- The paintings made you think.

Listen to the comments Student A makes and respond using sentences that have a linker of concession.
A: *The tickets were so expensive.*
B: *In spite of the cost, I thought it was worthwhile.*

Situation 2

Imagine there is a new sculpture in a nearby park. You aren't a fan because:
- The design of the sculpture is very simple.
- It wasn't made by a local artist.
- You heard it was very expensive.
- You've spoken to several people who think it's ugly.

Complain about your experience to Student A. Try to respond to whatever Student A says using linkers of concession.
A: *I actually really like the sculpture.*
B: *Even though you like it, I've spoken to several people who think it's ugly.*

8C Vocabulary — Visual art

Abstract artwork	Sketch	Sculpture	Still life
Statue	Print	Collage	Landscape
Oil painting	Watercolour	Installation	Portrait

9A Grammar 1 — Past modals of deduction

1 Read the puzzle. What do you think the answer is? Read the conversation in Exercise 2 to check your ideas.

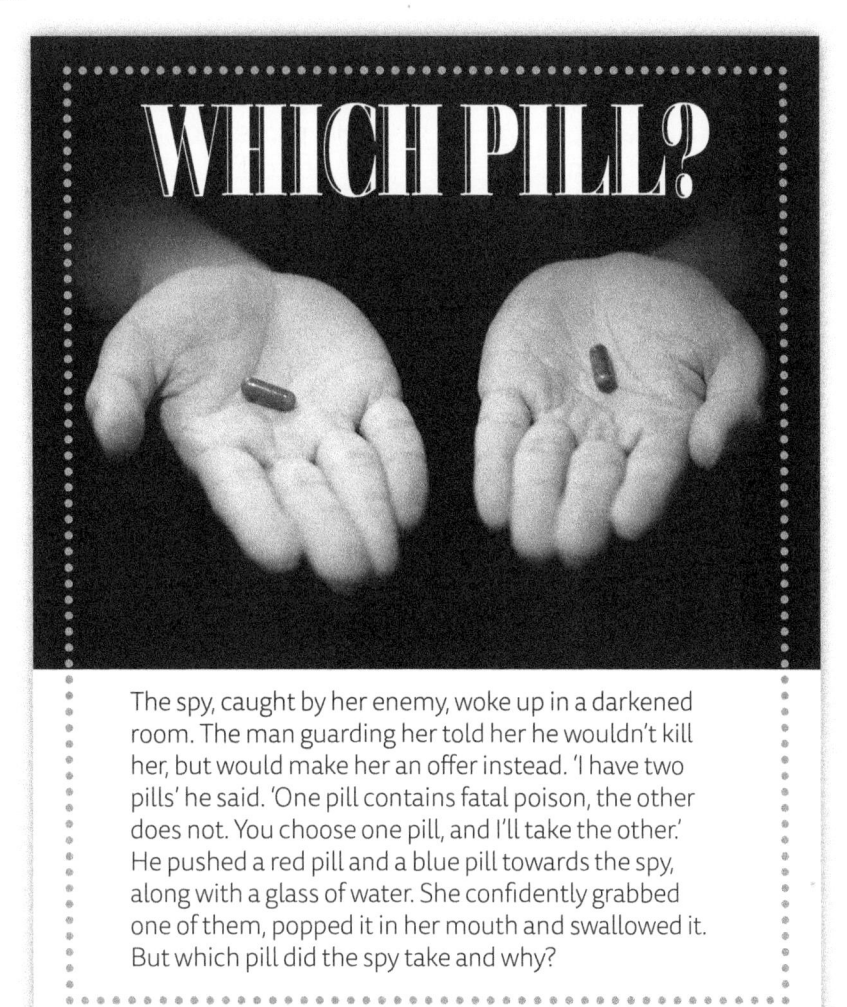

WHICH PILL?

The spy, caught by her enemy, woke up in a darkened room. The man guarding her told her he wouldn't kill her, but would make her an offer instead. 'I have two pills' he said. 'One pill contains fatal poison, the other does not. You choose one pill, and I'll take the other.' He pushed a red pill and a blue pill towards the spy, along with a glass of water. She confidently grabbed one of them, popped it in her mouth and swallowed it. But which pill did the spy take and why?

2 Complete the conversation with the past modal form of the verbs in brackets.

A: OK, so which pill do you think the spy ¹ _might have chosen_ (might / choose)?
B: I think she ² _____ (may / grab) the blue one. Red seems a dangerous colour to me.
A: I think that's too obvious. The colour ³ _____ (could / be) a red herring.
B: The spy ⁴ _____ (might / realise) the situation was hopeless and not even cared if she was poisoned.
A: It still doesn't make sense. The guard ⁵ _____ (couldn't / know) which pill the spy was going to choose, so why would he take the risk of having to eat the other one?
B: The guard ⁶ _____ (may / plan) to secretly swap whichever pill the spy chose for a poisoned one.
A: But the spy grabbed the pill so quickly, surely he ⁷ _____ (couldn't / swap) them.
B: Still, we don't know whether the guard is telling the truth about the poison. The pills ⁸ _____ (may not / contain) any poison at all.
A: That's it! The poison ⁹ _____ (must / be) in the glass of water instead!
B: Yeah, so the spy ¹⁰ _____ (could / take) either pill. What's important is that she didn't drink any of the water.

3 Work in pairs and practise reading the conversation.

9A Grammar 2 Past modals of deduction

1
Wren had only had her driving licence for a day when she found herself going the wrong-way on a one-way street. A police officer saw her but didn't stop her. Why might the police officer not have done anything?
_____

2
Steve was the last man on earth. His phone rang. Who could have been on the other end?
_____

3
Nina's father had five children. The names of the first four were April, May, June and July. What was the name of his fifth child?
_____

4
Three people were in a boat in a storm. The boat sank, but rescuers noticed that only one of the people got their hair wet. How could this have been possible?
_____

5
Zoey and Zeb were both born on 3rd January 2009. Despite being born to the same parents, they aren't twins. How could this have been possible?
_____

6
Selma throws a ball as hard as she can. Although she is alone, the ball travels 15 metres then returns to her. How could she have got the ball to come back?
_____

7
Everyone in Alvaro's class handed in an assignment except for Alvaro. Nevertheless the head teacher told Alvaro he had done excellent work. Why might the head teacher have said that?
_____

8
A person is lying dead in the middle of a field of corn. There is nothing around except corn and an unopened package. What must have happened?
_____

9A Vocabulary Mystery

1. **Work in pairs and discuss the questions.**
   - Why do you think so many people enjoy mysteries?
   - Do you like to know a lot about films or series you watch, or do you like to be surprised?

2. **Complete the opinion piece with the words in the box.**

   > accounted for   clues   evidence   hoax   identifies   motives   red herring   remain a mystery   turns out   victim

   ### Don't give me any ¹_____ !

   Personally, I like what happens in a film or series to ²_____ until I watch it for myself.
   Here's a list of things I can't stand:

   ① Advertisements for a film or series
   There's usually far too much ³_____ about what's going to happen. For example, the advertisement shows the best dramatic action scene, or ⁴_____ which characters will fall in love.

   ② The friend who tells you everything
   They don't have bad ⁵_____ , but they talk through all the details of a film or series you want to watch before you can stop them.

   ③ Someone says there's a surprise
   They haven't ⁶_____ the fact that knowing to expect the unexpected completely changes the way you experience the plot.

   ④ Reviews which falsely promise not to give details
   Often, they still indicate how everything ⁷_____ in the end with phrases like 'a very encouraging film' or 'a depressing tale'.

   ⑤ A silly ⁸_____
   This is when someone tells you something which is a complete ⁹_____ 'Keep an eye on the cat.' or 'The real ¹⁰_____ isn't who you think.' It's so annoying because you spend the whole film looking for the fake detail instead of enjoying the story!

   Your rating

3. **Circle a number to rate how you feel about each way clues are revealed.**

4. **Work in groups. Compare your ratings and discuss the following questions.**
   - How much does knowing how a story turns out affect your enjoyment of it?
   - Do you agree that film advertisements tend to have too many clues? Why/Why not?
   - Would you ever tell your friend some sort of red herring before they watched a movie?
   - Have you heard of any interesting hoaxes? Have you ever fallen victim to one?

9B Grammar 1 Verb patterns

1 Complete the posts about hiccups with the phrases in the box.

> drinking   getting   me to feel
> me to frighten   myself sitting
> people giving me   that I will give
> that you will get   the hiccups stop
> you that   you to   you to tell

Original post

Sharat — 21 July

I can't stand ¹_____ hiccups. I'm asking
²_____ me your very best cures please!
#hiccups #goaway #advice

Replies

Kari — 21 July
I don't mind ³_____ a fright to try to make them go away.
Obviously, you can't expect ⁴_____ you online though – sorry!

Alan — 21 July
I guarantee ⁵_____ rid of your hiccups if you close your eyes, press your upper lip and count to ten. I can assure ⁶_____ it works every time!

Mara — 21 July
I would advise ⁷_____ have a glass of water. I'd recommend ⁸_____ it as quickly as you can.

Osman — 22 July
I imagine ⁹_____ by a cool blue lake. It helps ¹⁰_____ calm and the hiccups usually go.

Leta — 22 July
Being offered money can make ¹¹_____ ! Sharat, I promise ¹²_____ you a pound if you can call me and hiccup on the phone!

2 Work in groups and answer the question.
- How likely do you think it is that each hiccup cure would work?

9B Grammar 2 Verb patterns

... anyone to be in the office on a Sunday.	I told my boss that I don't mind ...	... working late as long as I know in advance.	My brother became a vet, but we always imagined ...
... he would be on the stage!	My sister has just got engaged and it makes ...	... me feel happy to see her so in love.	I went to the supermarket but I'm afraid I didn't remember ...
... to get those things you wanted. Sorry!	I'll be at work early tomorrow, so I promise ...	... to do it first thing in the morning.	We're short of money at the moment so I've realised ...
... that we can't afford to go abroad this year.	My apologies for being late. I assure ...	... you that it won't happen again.	The sales staff persuaded ...
... me that I needed to buy the shoes.	My English teacher recommended ...	... that I keep a notebook of new phrases.	I'm really scared of flying, so I can't stand ...
... going anywhere by plane.	I didn't want to say anything, but could I ask ...	... you to turn your music down please?	When I bought the tickets, they guaranteed ...
... that I would enjoy the concert or they'd give me a refund.	My grandfather repeats himself, but I don't mind ...	... him doing that. He's eighty-nine!	This puzzle is really tough. Could you help ...
... me figure it out?	He needed to learn English for his new job, so he told ...	... us he'd never give up, no matter how hard he found it.	I haven't seen you for ages and I really miss ...
... you coming around for a chat.	We wanted a pay rise but we couldn't persuade ...	... our boss to change his mind.	Could you open the curtains please? I want to let ...
... more light come into this room.	It was a huge task, and even though I wanted ...	... to do it all by myself, it was much too difficult.	I'm surprised to see you here. I didn't expect ...

9B Vocabulary Knowledge

Useful language

That's definitely …	I haven't ever ⁷o _ _ _ _ _ v _ _ that myself.
A lot of people ¹a _ _ _ m _ that's …	I'd need to do more ⁸r _ _ _ a _ _ _ .
How would you ²p _ _ v _ it is …	… ⁹f _ k _ .
I ³k _ o _ that's …	… true.
I ⁴s _ _ _ e _ _ _ that's …	… not true.
That ⁵t _ _ o _ _ _ is …	… only a theory.
I think we can ⁶c _ _ _ _ _ _ d _ that it's …	… a ¹⁰m _ _ _ _ _ _ _ _ _ t _ _ _ _ _ _ .

Useful language

That's definitely …	I haven't ever ⁷o _ _ _ _ _ v _ _ that myself.
A lot of people ¹a _ _ _ m _ that's …	I'd need to do more ⁸r _ _ _ a _ _ _ .
How would you ²p _ _ v _ it is …	… ⁹f _ k _ .
I ³k _ o _ that's …	… true.
I ⁴s _ _ _ e _ _ _ that's …	… not true.
That ⁵t _ _ o _ _ _ is …	… only a theory.
I think we can ⁶c _ _ _ _ _ _ d _ that it's …	… a ¹⁰m _ _ _ _ _ _ _ _ _ t _ _ _ _ _ _ .

Theory	Our conclusion
1 The number thirteen is unlucky.	
2 At least one of the English teachers at this school is a spy.	
3 If there's pink sky in the morning, it's more likely to rain during the day.	
4 Birds fly away before earthquakes.	
5 People are either good at languages or maths.	
6 The moon is getting closer to the earth each year.	
7 Washing hands prevents the spread of diseases.	
8 Dark chocolate is good for you.	
9 You're more likely to get hurt by a shark than a falling fridge.	
10 It's impossible to kiss your own elbow.	

9C Language focus 1 — Phrasal verbs

Choose the correct alternatives to complete the rules.

Rules for fans

1. If you _____ , the number one rule is to show respect.
   a come across a celebrity **b** come a celebrity across

2. _____ that many celebrities don't mind a quick chat, as long as fans are polite!
   a Turns it out **b** Turns out

3. _____ before you post a celebrity's current location on social media, they might not appreciate it.
   a Think through it **b** Think it through

4. Try to _____ whether it's appropriate to approach them. Perhaps smile and try and make eye contact.
   a figure out **b** figure it out

5. If the celebrity is trying to _____ , be prepared that they may not want a photo.
   a get on with life **b** get on life with

6. Don't take it personally if the celebrity isn't willing to talk. They have to _____ sometimes or they wouldn't have any privacy.
   a let down people **b** let people down

7. If you're going to a 'meet and greet' event, there may be a long queue. Be ready to _____ for some time.
   a stick it out **b** stick out it

8. Don't talk about the celebrity like they can't hear you! _____ as really rude!
   a It comes across **b** Comes it across

9. _____ ahead of time. For example, ask about their work or what inspires them.
   a Come up a few things to say with **b** Come up with a few things to say

10. Avoid asking about personal details. For example, if you've read the celebrity is _____ – don't ask about it!
    a getting over a break up **b** getting a break up over

9C Language focus 2 — Phrasal verbs

1 Make sure you _____ carefully before you take action.
through / think / things

2 Trust yourself to _____ forward independently.
way / out / a / figure

3 Stop dreaming and just _____!
with / get / on / it

4 Try to _____.
from / out / the / stand / crowd

5 Sometimes it's better to _____ to avoid hurting someone's feelings.
up / make / something

6 Even though _____ is hard, don't give up!
it / sticking / out

7 Make sure you don't _____.
across / as / too / come / outrageous

8 If you have to _____, be honest about your reasons.
down / someone / let

9 If you're in a tricky situation, the sooner you can get out of it, the sooner you will _____!
it / over / get

10 _____ when you're not afraid to admit that you don't know everything.
turn / better / things / out

11 Work together with someone else and you're more likely to _____.
up / come / good / with / a / solution

12 The secret to success is to _____ what you're doing, even if you don't.
make / you / out / that / know

246 PHOTOCOPIABLE © Pearson Education Limited 2020

9C Vocabulary — Common phrasal verbs

JOB OF THE WEEK: Celebrity PR Manager
Interview with Jules Broadway

☆ *Jules, you're a Celebrity Public Relations Manager. What does that mean?*

I work with celebrity clients to help them ¹_____ positively to the public. Celebrities want to ²_____ but also need to make sure it's for the right reasons.

☆ *What skills are important in your job?*

I need to communicate well and be able to ³_____ ideas quickly.

☆ *What do you do when a celebrity ⁴_____ ?*

I try to take a minute to ⁵_____ plan. Sometimes, there's something active to do, like making an apology, and other times, the celebrity just has to ⁶_____ and hope another story comes up soon so that the public will ⁷_____ .

☆ *Have you ever come across a celebrity who was really difficult to work with?*

You do hear stories of celebrities who will only sit on red chairs and drink nothing but organic carrot juice, but often people just ⁸_____ . Nevertheless, I have worked with a few people who have ⁹_____ that they're the only people in the world that matter.

☆ *Do you wish you were a celebrity?*

Not really! It ¹⁰_____ that being a star is like living in a goldfish bowl. You and I might not always ¹¹_____ , but our errors aren't being watched in the same way that celebrities' mistakes are.

☆ *What's the best piece of advice you give your clients?*

Once you have made a decision, just ¹²_____ .

come across	come up with	figure out a
get on with it	get over their bad behaviour	lets their fans down
made out	make that kind of thing up	stand out
stick it out	think our actions through	turns out

10A Grammar 1 Future perfect and future continuous

1 **Choose the correct sentences to make conversations.**

Conversation 1

1. **A:** Do you think you will have finished with the laptop by 8.30 p.m.?
   B: Do you think you will be finishing with the laptop by 8.30 p.m.?
2. **A:** Sorry, I suspect I'll still have written this cover letter.
   B: Sorry, I suspect I'll still be writing this cover letter.
3. **A:** I hope you won't have worked on it all night!
   B: I hope you won't be working on it all night!
4. **A:** I'll definitely have it done by midnight. That's when the applications close!
   B: I'll definitely be having it done by midnight. That's when the applications close!

Conversation 2

1. **A:** Will you have come to hockey training this afternoon?
   B: Will you be coming to hockey training this afternoon?
2. **A:** I've pulled a muscle in my leg, so I doubt I'll have joined in.
   B: I've pulled a muscle in my leg, so I doubt I'll be joining in.
3. **A:** I hope it'll have healed before the big game on Saturday.
   B: I hope it'll be healing before the big game on Saturday.
4. **A:** A week will have passed since the injury, so I'm fairly certain it'll be better by then.
   B: A week will have been passing since the injury, so I'm fairly certain it'll be better by then.

Conversation 3

1. **A:** Will you have done anything on Saturday morning?
   B: Will you be doing anything on Saturday morning?
2. **A:** I'll probably just have relaxed at home. Why do you ask?
   B: I'll probably just be relaxing at home. Why do you ask?
3. **A:** My friend will have arrived from Berlin and I'll be showing him around the city. Care to join us?
   B: My friend will be arriving from Berlin and so I'll have shown him around the city. Care to join us?
4. **A:** Sounds good. Hopefully, the rain will have stopped by then.
   B: Sounds good. Hopefully, the rain will be stopping by then.

2 **Work in pairs. Practise reading the conversations.**

10A Grammar 2 Future perfect and future continuous

1 Circle a number from 1 (unlikely) to 5 (very likely) to show how likely you think the following things are to happen in the future.

Twenty years from now …	Unlikely				Likely
1 fewer people will be buying a place of their own.	1	2	3	4	5
2 fashion will have changed a lot.	1	2	3	4	5
3 almost all public libraries will have closed.	1	2	3	4	5
4 most people won't be driving petrol cars anymore.	1	2	3	4	5
5 smartphones will have become a thing of the past.	1	2	3	4	5
6 people will be living with the consequences of climate change.	1	2	3	4	5
7 scientists will have found new cures for some diseases.	1	2	3	4	5
8 people will be feeling happier overall.	1	2	3	4	5

2 Work in groups and discuss your answers to Exercise 1 using the phrases below.

probably	I would think
more than likely …	I'm fairly certain …
almost certainly	I'm not very confident
definitely	It's probable that …
It's more than likely …	I doubt …
I suspect …	I guess …

3 Write sentences about other things that will have changed in the future.

_____
_____
_____
_____

10A Vocabulary — Personal fulfilment

purpose	in life
artistic	ability
true	vocation
unique	talent
soul	mate
great	passion
place of	my own
a sense	of belonging
like-minded	friend
a place I can	call home
sense of	adventure
core	principles

10B Grammar 1 Articles

1 Read the sentences and correct any errors the students have made with articles.

Five things about me – Kemala

1. I grew up in Jakarta, capital of Indonesia.
2. I saw the snow for first time this year.
3. I have played the basketball since I was nine.
4. I can't imagine the life without mobile phone.
5. I recently started a small business. I've been spending a lot of time building a business lately.

Five things about me – Zoltan

1. Even though I'm architect, my favourite subject at the school was the music.
2. I went to USA last year and stayed with the host family near the Lake Tahoe.
3. I think the young people should learn to play the instrument.
4. On Saturdays I play in a band at a restaurant.
5. The most important things in my life are family, work and band.

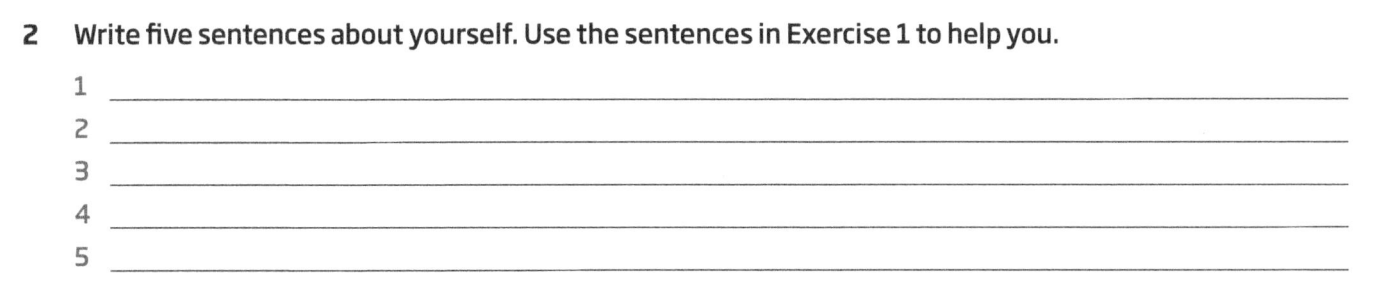

2 Write five sentences about yourself. Use the sentences in Exercise 1 to help you.

1. _____
2. _____
3. _____
4. _____
5. _____

3 Work in pairs and compare your sentences. Check each other's use of articles.

4 Work in pairs and discuss the question.
- Are there any similarities in what you and your partner wrote?

10B Grammar 2 Articles

1 Choose the correct alternatives to complete the quiz questions. Then answer the questions.

HAVE YOU EVER ... ?

... known someone with [1]*a/the* same birthday as you?	
... watched [2]*the/no article* sun rise from the top of a hill?	
... had [3]*a/the* conversation with [4]*a/no article* person from [5]*the/no article* Czech Republic, [6]*the/no article* Vietnam or [7]*the/no article* Kingdom of Saudi Arabia?	
... met someone with [8]*a/the* very similar name to yours?	
... seen [9]*a/no article* leaves changing colour in [10]*an/no article* autumn?	
... been on [11]*a/the* bus or train and suddenly realised that it was [12]*a/the* wrong one?	
... tried [13]*an/the* online workout for [14]*the/no article* yoga or another form of [15]*the/no article* exercise?	
... felt [16]*an/no article* earthquake?	
... spoken [17]*the/no article* English to someone who wasn't [18]*no article/a* student or teacher?	
... read [19]*a/no article* book translated from [20]*a/the* different language?	
... visited [21]*a/the* most famous tourist site in [22]*the/no article* country where you were born?	
... ever learned [23]*the/a* new word, then kept coming across [24]*the/a* word afterwards?	

2 Work in groups and compare your answers. Then answer the question.
- Did any of the group's answers surprise you?

10B Vocabulary Fame

1 Read the beginning of a story about fame.

> Her mother always joked that Kinsley had started singing before she could talk. She had the voice of an angel.

2 Work in pairs and choose one of the endings below or your own ending.

- [ ] Everyone said Kinsley had used her fame to change the country for the better.
- [ ] Kinsley decided to retire from the entertainment industry for a quieter life.
- [ ] To celebrate, Kinsley threw a huge party on her private island for her family and friends.
- [ ] Other _____

3 Work in pairs and make notes about what will happen in the middle of the story. Use as many of the words and phrases in the box as you can.

big break   go unnoticed   high-profile   instant hit   in the public eye   legacy shot to fame   started out   take the … by storm   unknown

_____
_____
_____
_____
_____
_____
_____
_____
_____
_____
_____
_____
_____
_____

4 Work in pairs. Take turns sharing your stories.

10C Language focus 1   Compound adjectives

Complete the blog posts with the correct form of the words in the box.

How are you different from what people expect?

age   art   fashion   tech   term

Some people think I'll be a bit old-¹_____ just because I'm middle-²_____ . Actually, I really like state-of-the-³_____ technology. I'm a big fan of high-⁴_____ devices and even met my long-⁵_____ partner on a dating app.

distance   kilometre   mind   old   will

People look surprised when they find out I'm into long-⁶_____ running. Apparently, I don't look like someone who is fit enough to run a twenty-⁷_____ race. They should be a bit more open-⁸_____ ! I train four times a week and am very strong-⁹_____ too. I'm trying to be a good example for my fifteen-year-¹⁰_____ brother.

centre   know   mind   profile   social

As a high-¹¹_____ blogger, some people imagine I'm really self-¹²_____ and send awful anti-¹³_____ messages. It's not easy being well-¹⁴_____ . I'm thankful for my lovely like-¹⁵_____ friends who tell me not to care!

10C Language focus 2 Compound adjectives

absent-minded	brightly-lit	broken-down
densely-populated	hard-working	high-tech
internet-connected	like-minded	long-term
middle-aged	narrow-minded	old-fashioned
part-time	run-down	self-confident
short-term	state-of-the-art	strong-willed
ten-page	twenty-five-year-old	well-behaved
well-educated	well-known	well-off

10C Vocabulary — Persuasion and enforcement

1 Complete the sentences with the words in th ebox.

| charged   discourage   educate   enforce   fined   installed   introduce   put up |

2 Put the sentences in the correct order to continue the story.

I share a house with three friends. One is quite absent-minded and keeps leaving the stove on, which is obviously very dangerous. Friends turn out to be the most difficult people to _____ .

The first time it happened, we heard beeping and rescued the pan. It's lucky that the landlord had _____ smoke alarms.

We all thought it was a one-time thing, but just in case, I _____ a sign reminding us all to turn off the stove.

However, the sign wasn't enough to _____ my friend because only a few days later, the stove was accidentally left on again.

This time, a pan of rice had boiled dry and the wall (and my excellent sign!) was damaged. The landlord _____ us for repainting the wall.

We decided it was time to _____ a tougher punishment.

From now on, we've all agreed that anyone who leaves the stove on will be _____ the cost of a take-out pizza for everyone.

Of course, it's really hard to _____ any rule when you're dealing with friends!

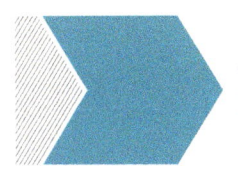

Photocopiable notes and answer key

1A

Grammar 1 Question forms

Materials: One worksheet per student

Instructions:

Distribute the worksheets. For Ex 1, check Ss understand that they need to re-order the words to form direct or indirect questions. Demonstrate with the first question if necessary. When Ss have finished, encourage them to compare their answers in pairs, then check answers as a class.

For Ex 2, ask Ss to identify which questions are direct and indirect. Put Ss in pairs to practise asking and answering the questions, but make it clear that any direct questions need to be asked as indirect ones, as if it is the first class and they are being as polite as possible to unknown classmates. Model question 2 indirectly as an example. Monitor, listen to the indirect questions, and check for the correct word order. Encourage Ss to self/peer correct their question forms.

Answer key:

1
1. Could you tell me if I'm in the right place   *indirect*
2. Where have you studied English   *direct*
3. How did you find out about   *direct*
4. Can I ask whether you have studied abroad   *indirect*
5. What are you hoping to improve most   *direct*
6. Who was your teacher   *direct*
7. When did you decide to take   *direct*
8. May I ask where you got your coursebook   *indirect*
9. What time will we finish   *direct*
10. Who does this pen belong   *direct*
11. Do you know where the library   *indirect*
12. I wonder what we'll have to do   *indirect*

Indirect questions: 1, 4, 8, 11, 12
Direct questions: 2, 3, 5, 6, 7, 9, 10

2
Suggested answers:
2. May I ask where you have studied English previously?
3. Can I ask how you found out about this class?
5. Could you tell me what you're hoping to improve most in this class?
6. Could I ask who your teacher was last year?
7. May I ask when you decided to take this course?
9. Do you know what time we'll finish here today?
10. I wonder who this pen belongs to.

Grammar 2 Question forms

Materials: One card per student

Instructions:

Tell Ss that they are going to practise forming questions that they might ask when meeting strangers in a travel situation. Elicit what a hostel is then tell Ss to imagine they are staying in a hostel in London. Read the following questions and get Ss to think about an imaginary answer. *Where are you from? Why did you travel to London? When did you arrive? How did you get there? What have you been doing today?*

Give each student in your class a card. If you have more than 15 Ss in your class, you can use some cards more than once. If you have fewer than 15 Ss, use the number of cards for the number of Ss you have.

Ask Ss to think of an appropriate question using the prompt on the card. To assist, you could write some phrases to start indirect questions on the board: *Do you know …; May / Can / Could I ask …; I wonder …*. Give Ss a few minutes to check their question form with the person next to them. Monitor and help if necessary.

Have a class mingle. Ss take turns to ask and answer their questions with another student, then swap cards. Encourage Ss to use indirect questions as appropriate and to ask follow-up questions to extend each conversation. Ss then find a new partner and ask the new question. If a student gets a card they have already seen, they could ask the question using a different starter. When they have finished, elicit answers from the class and correct if necessary.

Answer key:
Suggested answers:
1. Do you know where there's a supermarket?
2. May I ask when you checked in to the hostel?
3. Can you tell me where you've been today?
4. May I ask who you're travelling with?
5. I've heard that there is a free walking tour that leaves from the hostel. Do you know what time it starts?
6. Can I ask where you're from?
7. Do you have any idea what the forecast is for tomorrow?
8. Could I ask where you got your backpack from?
9. Could you tell me how you travelled to London? May I ask how long it took?
10. Can I ask if you are reading anything at the moment?
11. Do you know what the wifi password for the hostel is?
12. How are you enjoying your travels so far?
13. I wonder who owns that guitar in the corner.
14. Can I ask how long you're staying in London for?
15. May I ask what you are doing to do tomorrow?

Vocabulary Verbs with dependent prepositions

Materials: One worksheet per student

Instructions:

Distribute the worksheets. For Ex 1, Ss complete sentences 1–10 with the correct preposition. Check answers as a class and elicit the meaning of *FOMO*. Explain that FOMO stands for *Fear of missing out*. It means a feeling of anxiety, or unhappiness, you have because you think that other people are doing more exciting things than you are.

For Ex 2, Ss decide whether each statement is true for them or not. Ss tick the sentences that are true for them in the *Me* column and think about reasons for their answers in preparation for the discussion phase.

For Ex 3, put Ss in pairs. Tell Ss to discuss their answers for each sentence and to make notes in the *Classmate* column. Encourage Ss to use the verb + preposition in their discussion rather than *sentence 1*, etc.

For Ex 4, put Ss in new pairs. Ss compare the information from their first discussion. Ask a few Ss to share with the class.

If time allows, Ss could discuss all the statements with their new partner.

Answer key:
1
1 on 2 in 3 about 4 for 5 from 6 on 7 to 8 with
9 on 10 at

1B

Grammar 1 Past simple, past continuous, used to, would, keep + -ing

Materials: One worksheet per student

Instructions:
Distribute the worksheets. Read through the instructions to Ex 1 and emphasise that there may be more than one answer in some cases. Where this is possible, Ss should consider the variety within the text as a whole and make sure each form is used at least once. Ss complete the texts individually, then compare in pairs. Check the answers as a class.

Once you have checked the answers with the class, ask Ss to answer the questions in Ex 2, either in pairs or on their own.

Give Ss a few minutes to think about Ex 3, then put Ss in pairs or small groups to discuss their ideas.

Alternatively, ask Ss to write the story of the change they made, using each tense at least once. Tell Ss to share their stories in pairs and check each other's tenses.

Answer key:
1
1. used to drive / would drive
2. kept losing / used to lose / would lose
3. used to put / would put
4. forget / would forget / used to forget
5. used to spend / would spend
6. put up
7. insisted
8. was
9. was looking
10. read
11. were wearing / wore / kept wearing / would wear
12. saved / were saving / would save
13. didn't have
14. built
15. decided
16. thought
17. used to find / found
18. could
19. used to make / would make / made / kept making
20. was complaining
21. suggested
22. was
23. helped
24. kept doing

2
a The person used to lose their keys a lot so started to hang them on a key holder by the door.
b The person wanted to make life simpler, so began to wear a personal uniform.
c The person used to make a lot of mistakes in their written work in English. He/She started reading it aloud to check it, which helped.

Grammar 2 Past simple, past continuous, used to, would, keep + -ing

Materials: One copy of worksheet A and worksheet B per pair of Ss

Instructions:
Tell Ss a (real or imagined) statement about yourself using at least three forms from the lesson, e.g. *I **used to live** in China and people **would always look surprised** when they **heard** me speaking Mandarin.* Repeat the statement a couple of times if necessary.

Get Ss to decide whether the statement is true or false and tell the person next to them. Reveal whether it is true or false (or what parts of the statement are true or false).

Put Ss in pairs and distribute one A and B worksheet per pair of Ss.

Ask Ss to complete the statements individually. Explain that the statements should be about themselves and that five of the statements should be true and three of the statements should be false. Encourage **fast finishers** to add more detail to their statements (either written or just think of verbal details they will share).

Ss take turns to discuss one of their statements. Their partner must then guess if it is true or false.

This activity can also be run as a class mingle. Ss move around the classroom, sharing and guessing answers to each statement with a different partner.

Vocabulary Phrases to describe emotions

Materials: One worksheet per student

Instructions:
Put Ss in pairs to discuss the questions in Ex 1 and elicit some ideas as feedback. Ask Ss to work individually to complete Ex 2, then compare their answers in pairs before checking as a class.

Put Ss in groups of three or four to discuss the questions in Ex 3. Conduct whole class feedback.

Answer key:
2
1 impact 2 believe 3 inspired 4 completely 5 eyes
6 shock 7 numb 8 total 9 mind 10 ashamed

1C

Language focus 1 Verb + noun collocations

Materials: One worksheet per student

Instructions:
Distribute the worksheets and discuss the questions in Ex 1 in groups or as a class. Ss then select the correct answer for each sentence in Ex 2 and compare their answers in pairs. Check answers as a class.

Look at the first promise with the class (*I'm going to review the notes I keep/take in class so that I remember more*). Elicit some possible actions that someone who wants to keep that promise could take, e.g. *decide what kind of notes you are going to take, read some information about note-taking strategies online, listen carefully in class and write down the main points, rather than everything the teacher says.*

Put Ss in pairs or small groups to discuss the questions in Ex 3. If time is short, allocate each group one or two promises to think of actions for, which they then report back to the class. If time allows, groups could think of actions for all the promises.

Answer key:

2
1 take 2 time 3 make 4 take 5 meet 6 voice
7 break 8 take 9 resolve 10 remain 11 make 12 line
13 temper 14 keep

Language focus 2   Verb + noun collocations

Materials: One worksheet per group of Ss, cut into cards

Instructions:
Put Ss in groups and give each group a set of cards to spread out face up on the table. Ss take turns to match two cards to form a statement. When all the statements have been completed, groups discuss whether or not they agree with each statement and why. When all groups have finished, conduct whole class feedback.

Answer key:
1 n 2 l 3 b 4 m 5 g 6 a 7 o 8 f 9 c 10 p 11 d
12 i 13 h 14 e 15 j 16 k

Vocabulary   Adjectives of character

Materials: One worksheet per pair of Ss

Instructions:
Read the first clue on the worksheet to the class and elicit what personality trait is being described (*suspicious*). Put Ss in pairs and distribute the worksheets. Ss work in pairs to read the clues and complete the puzzle.

After Ss have finished, they can check the puzzle is correct by checking the vertical word (*conscientious*) in the grey squares.

Ask Ss to do the task in Ex 2 in their pairs, then compare their ideas with another group.

Alternatively, this worksheet can be set as an individual exercise for homework.

Answer key:

1	s	u	s	p	i	c	i	o	u	s	
	2	o	u	t	g	o	i	n	g		
	3	a	d	v	e	n	t	u	r	o	u	s
		4	t	r	u	s	t	i	n	g	
				5	c	a	r	e	l	e	s	s
	6	c	a	u	t	i	o	u	s		
		7	r	e	s	e	r	v	e	d	
		8	o	p	e	n					
			9	e	x	t	r	o	v	e	r	t
	10	c	o	n	f	i	d	e	n	t	
	11	n	e	r	v	o	u	s			
			12	n	e	u	r	o	t	i	c
13	o	r	g	a	n	i	s	e	d		

The mystery word is *conscientious*.

2A

Grammar 1   Present perfect simple and continuous

Materials: One worksheet per student

Instructions:
Elicit what the word *proverb* means (*a short, well-known statement that gives advice or expresses something that is generally true*). Write a proverb on the board, e.g. *Practice makes perfect*. Ask Ss to discuss in pairs what the phrase means and whether they have a similar proverb in their own language.

Distribute the worksheets. In Ex 1, Ss work individually to select the most appropriate verb form. Put Ss in pairs to compare their answers before checking as a class. Explain that each of the situations in Ex 1 relates to a proverb. Put Ss in pairs to read the proverbs (a–d) in Ex 2 and match them to the situations in Ex 1 (1–3).

For Ex 3, Ss work individually, or in pairs, to select one of the proverbs (or another one they know) and write a paragraph giving an example of the proverb. Remind Ss to use the present perfect simple and continuous.

For Ex 4, put Ss in small groups to compare their examples from Ex 3 and see if the other members of their group can guess the proverb they chose. Alternatively, this could be done as a whole class activity.

Answer key:

1
1 've been meaning 2 've been 3 have just called
4 've been hoping 5 've entered 6 've been watching
7 has received 8 've been reading 9 has made
10 has suggested 11 have been arguing 12 has got

2
1 c Used to indicate that the more people there are, the better a situation will be. In this situation, the host might reply with this proverb to indicate that the cousins are welcome to come to the barbecue.

2 a (Note that many people simply say *Don't count your chickens ….*) Used to say that you should not make plans that depend on something good happening, because it might not. In this situation, the writer is planning a trip to New York before winning the competition to go there.

3 b (Note that many people simply say *Too many cooks ….*) Used when you think there are too many people trying to do the same job at the same time, so that the job is not done well. In this situation, too many people are trying to organise the holiday, which is making it difficult.

Grammar 2   Present perfect simple and continuous

Materials: One worksheet per student

Instructions:
Distribute the worksheets and, in Ex 1, direct Ss to the first question as an example. Put Ss in pairs to decide how to complete the question using the prompts in brackets (answer = *have you been using*). Elicit why the present perfect continuous is used here, rather than the present perfect simple (the question is asking about something that continues into the present). Ask Ss to work in their pairs to complete the remaining questions. Check answers as a class.

For Ex 2, put Ss in groups of three or four to discuss the questions. Conduct whole class feedback.

As an optional follow-up activity, put Ss in pairs to design a similar survey about a hobby or topic of interest, using the questions from the digital technology survey as a model. Ask Ss to write at least three questions using the present perfect simple and at least three using the present perfect continuous. Put Ss in new pairs to ask and answer the questions in their surveys. Ss then report back to their original partner.

> **Answer key:**
> **1**
> 1 have you been using
> 2 have you spent/have you been spending
> 3 Have you thought about/Have you been thinking about
> 4 has anything been getting/has anything got
> 5 you have ever seen
> 6 Have you ever taken
> 7 Have you been using/Have you used
> 8 have you ever belonged to
> 9 Have you been following/Have you followed
> 10 have you never met
> 11 Have you already taken
> 12 have been gradually changing/have gradually changed

Vocabulary   Phrases with *get*

Materials: One worksheet per student

Instructions:

Distribute the worksheets. For Ex 1, look at the first sentence with the class and elicit the *get* phrase which could complete the question (*gets on* your *nerves*). Ss work individually to complete the remaining questions and then check as a class. Note that Ss will need to tell an (appropriate) joke for Question 10. If they don't know one, give them the opportunity to find a suitable joke online.

For Ex 2, Ss move around the classroom to discuss each question with a new partner. Encourage Ss to ask a follow-up question to extend each conversation.

For Ex 3, when Ss have completed their sheet, put Ss in pairs to share what they found out (they only hear one each).

> **Answer key:**
> **1**
> 1 gets on (your) nerves   2 to get straight to the point
> 3 get together   4 got/get to do   5 get in touch
> 6 get some rest   7 get carried away   8 got your attention
> 9 get the feeling   10 get it

2B

Grammar 1   The passive

Materials: One worksheet per student

Instructions:

Distribute the worksheets. Explain, for Ex 1, that Ss need to make their way through the maze by following a path through sentences which are grammatically correct. Ask Ss to complete the activity individually and then compare their answers with a partner. Check the correct path through the maze as a class.

For Ex 2, put Ss in pairs to correct the incorrect sentences in Ex 1. Check answers as a class.

> **Answer key:**
> **1**
> Path through the maze = 1, 2, 3, 4, 9, 14, 13, 12, 11, 16, 21, 20, 25, 30, 31, 32, 27, 28, 29
> **2**
> **Corrected sentences:**
> 5 More money will **be** spent to tackle the problem.
> 6 Has any research **been** carried out on this topic?
> 7 The mayor is working very hard to be (/to **get**) re-elected.
> 8 Oh no! Our flight has **been** cancelled.
> 10 The law isn't **being** enforced adequately.
> 15 Mobile phones shouldn't be **blamed** for everything!
> 17 By 2050, I think all fizzy drinks will be **banned**.
> 18 People are being **asked** to turn off their mobiles.
> 19 When you arrived, had the door been left **unlocked**?
> 22 The monorail hadn't **been** built when we last visited.
> 23 More ought to **be** done to encourage teens to get a good night's sleep.
> 24 People haven't **been** warned about the dangers of sugar.
> 26 We were (/**be**) told to leave without any explanation whatsoever.
> 33 Did you get **shown** the plans before building was started?

Grammar 2   The passive

Materials: One A and B worksheet per pair of Ss, cut in half

Instructions:

Distribute the worksheet halves. Put Ss in A/B pairs, working with someone who has the same worksheet half. Tell Ss to read the gapped sentences together and discuss which words could go in the gaps (without writing anything down yet.)

Put Ss in A/B pairs and tell them not to look at each other's worksheets. Student A reads aloud one of their partner's missing verbs (more than once if necessary), and Student B works out which sentence on worksheet B it goes in and reads back the completed sentence. Ss take turns until all their sentence are completed. Check answers as a class.

As an optional follow-up, encourage Ss to write their own sentences using their partner's missing verbs.

> **Answer key:**
> **A**
> 1 should be spent   2 was (just) painted   3 will be built
> 4 had been cancelled   5 being interviewed   6 are sold
> 7 got damaged   8 could have been killed
> **B**
> 1 were instructed   2 had (already) been caught
> 3 haven't been told   4 isn't being used   5 will be closed
> 6 'm going to be picked up   7 get told off   8 will get promoted

Vocabulary   Social action

Materials: One worksheet per group of Ss, cut into cards

Instructions:

Put Ss in groups of three or four and give each group a set of cut up cards. Ask Ss to spread the cards out on the desk face down and take turns to turn over two cards. If the cards match and make a collocation, the student must say a sentence using the cards/ collocation. If Ss have correctly matched the cards and made a sentence, they can keep them. Otherwise, Ss place the cards back down on the table in the same position. The winner is the student with the most cards after all the collocations have been matched.

As an optional follow-up, tell groups to choose an issue and write sentences about it using some of the collocations from the activity which relate to that topic. Write some example topics on the board for Ss to choose from (e.g. *discrimination, climate change, people feeling lonely, robots taking jobs*). Ask each group to share some of their sentences with the class.

Answer key:
Answers on original worksheet: take action, tackle the problem, increase funding, carry out research, ban the use of, do more to, warn about the dangers, crack down on, offer alternatives, enforce a law.

Suggested sentences on the topic of discrimination:
*We think everyone needs to **do more to** tackle the problem of discrimination.*
*We could **increase funding** for education programmes.*
*We should also **crack down on** companies who do not offer equal opportunities for everyone.*

2C

Language focus 1 *-ed* and *-ing* adjectives

Materials: One worksheet per student

Instructions:
Distribute the worksheets and go through the instructions. Tell Ss to complete Ex 1 and Ex 2 individually. Put Ss in pairs to compare their answers, then check as a class.

For Ex 3, ask Ss to write their own pair of sentences, using Ex 2 as a model. Put Ss in pairs or groups to test each other.

Answer key:
1
1 alarm **2** tempt **3** satisfy **4** encourage **5** frustrate
6 confuse **7** scare **8** delight
2
1 A alarming   B alarmed
2 A tempted   B tempting
3 A satisfying   B satisfied
4 A encouraged   B encouraging
5 A frustrating   B frustrated
6 A confused   B confusing
7 A scaring   B scared
8 A delighted   B delighting

Language focus 2 *-ed* and *-ing* adjectives

Materials: One worksheet per pair of Ss, cut into three

Instructions:
Put Ss in A/B pairs. Give each student a List A or a List B, and give an instruction sheet to each pair. Tell Ss not to show each other their lists. Go through the instruction sheet with the class. Elicit the meaning of the words *blindfold*, *juggle* and *reindeer* (you could use pictures to do this). Demonstrate the activity. Read one of the comments to the class (e.g. *Fancy a slice of my grandmother's prize-winning chocolate cake?*) and elicit an appropriate response from one of the Ss (e.g. *I'm tempted!*). Emphasise that there is more than one appropriate way to respond to each comment (e.g. *I'm tempted!, Sounds tempting!*). Tell Ss to complete the exercise in their pairs.

With a **weaker class**, you could suggest a slower practice round, then a repeat for a quickfire round, where Ss have to respond to each comment quickly (as in a typical conversation). **Stronger Ss** could go straight to the quickfire response practice. While Ss do the activity, monitor, and listen for appropriate adjective forms and word choices.

For extra practice, Ss swap lists and repeat.

Answer key:
Suggested answers:
A
1 I'm tempted!   **2** How depressing!
3 You must have been scared!   **4** How entertaining!
5 How insulting!   **6** That's astonishing!
7 You must have been exhausted.
8 You must have been stressed!
9 I get infuriated when that happens.   **10** Sounds encouraging!
B
1 You must be satisfied.   **2** How encouraging!
3 That's infuriating!   **4** You must be so worried.
5 You sound overwhelmed!   **6** They must be delighted!
7 Sounds upsetting!   **8** That's alarming!   **9** Sounds frustrating!
10 I'm convinced!

Vocabulary Common complaints

Materials: One worksheet per pair of Ss, cut into cards

Instructions:
Put Ss in pairs and give each pair a set of cards. Ask Ss to work together to order the conversation. To make it easier, tell Ss what the first card is. Check the answer as a class. Then tell Ss to practise reading the conversation aloud in pairs.

An alternative option (if you are short of time) is to give each pair a copy of the complete worksheet, so they can read the conversation aloud together, without the ordering stage.

Answer key:
The conversation is in the correct order on the original worksheet.

A: Grrr, that was a cold caller, trying to get me to change broadband companies.
B: Oh no, aggressive salespeople are the worst!
A: Yeah, the guy kept pushing me to answer questions. I can't stand being pressured by rude staff , but I still felt bad hanging up!
B: That reminds me of your laptop that wouldn't charge. I remember you felt sorry for the salesperson, even though he was the one who had sold you a faulty product!
A: I did, until I became absolutely infuriated by all his broken promises to credit my account with the refund!
B: Oh yeah, that billing dispute went on for ages. Did you ever resolve it?
A: Sadly, I couldn't. The company ads saying 'customers are our number one' really annoy me. It's completely false advertising! By the way, have your new trainers arrived?
B: They have, thanks. I eventually got them last week, but two months after I placed my order. Talk about slow delivery! And there was no apology or anything!
A: There never is! It's the lack of communication from these companies that I find most irritating.
B: I wonder if everyone has as many poor customer service experiences as we do!

3A

Grammar 1 Past perfect simple and continuous

Materials: One worksheet per student

Instructions:

For Ex 1, ask Ss to quickly read the blog post to find the answers to the questions without focusing on the verb forms yet. Elicit the answers.

For Ex 2, ask Ss to re-read the blog carefully and select the appropriate verb forms. Put Ss in pairs to compare their answers, then check as a class. Point out that the main events in the story are still told in the past simple. As an optional extension, ask Ss to work in pairs to retell the story in their own words.

For Ex 3, ask Ss, working individually, to write real, or imaginary, stories about something that went wrong. Ask Ss to include some background using the past perfect simple and continuous. Ss then share their stories with another student and check their partner has used appropriate verb forms.

Answer key:

1
The writer had forgotten to set an alarm so they were going to be late for a presentation. However, he/she had an accident on the way to class so they missed the presentation anyway.

2
1 'd been preparing **2** had told **3** 'd forgotten
4 'd been getting **5** 'd arranged **6** hadn't arrived
7 called (Although *hadn't called* is possible, it is common to leave out the *had/hadn't* in the second verb in the sentence.)
8 both forms are possible **9** 'd never broken **10** 'd done
11 'd received **12** 'd been wondering **13** had happened
14 'd continued **15** 'd missed

Grammar 2 Past perfect simple and continuous

Materials: One worksheet per student

Instructions:

Tell Ss that they are going to play a mystery roleplay game called *A dinner for heroes* to practise the past perfect simple and continuous. Elicit the meanings of *hero* (someone who is admired for doing something extremely brave or good) and *imposter* (someone who pretends to be someone else in order to trick people).

Set the scene: You are at a special exclusive dinner for ordinary people who are heroes. Invitations have been sent to people who have done something very brave or good. There is a special celebrity guest speaker (here you could give the name of a major celebrity who you think will resonate with your class, e.g. a pop star or sports star). However, someone attending the dinner is an imposter, who is only pretending to be a hero to meet the celebrity.

Give each student one of the role cards. They must not reveal what their card says to anyone else. With larger classes, you can allocate Ss sitting together the same card, so they can discuss the scenario together. Tell Ss to read the card. Monitor and help with vocabulary if necessary. Allocate the imposter role to a confident student, or take on the role yourself.

Give each student a copy of the *Find someone who...* worksheet. Tell Ss to complete the items on the worksheet with the correct form of the verb. Elicit the answers. Then, give Ss about ten minutes to mingle and ask each other questions about their heroic deeds to work out who did what, and who the imposter is (add Ss name to the 'name' column). Elicit the answers.

As an optional follow-up, have a discussion and class vote on who the greatest hero is.

Answer key:
1 had left **2** had been keeping **3** had treated
4 had been sleeping **5** had got **6** had collapsed
7 had been saving **8** had occurred **9** had been lying
10 had heard

Vocabulary Memory

Materials: One worksheet for the class, or several copies if you have a large class

Instructions:

Before the activity, pin the worksheet(s) to the board, or tape them to a table at the front of the room. Ss should not be able to read the worksheet(s) from where they are sitting.

Put Ss in groups of three (A/B/C) and explain that they are going to do a running dictation. Student A is the first writer and needs a pen and paper. Ss B and C start as the runners. They run to the worksheet, read as much as they can remember then return and repeat it to A, who must write it down. The runners are not allowed to write anything down.

Every few minutes (or after a few sentences have been dictated), call out 'change' and the groups must rotate who is writing. This continues until Ss have written down the whole text. The first group to finish gets 10 points, the second 9 points and so on. Ss get an additional point for every sentence which is completely correct. The group with the most points wins.

As a final challenge, with books closed, ask Ss to try to remember which words and phrases are target vocabulary from the lesson activity, and underline them in their copy of the text. Check answers as a class.

As an optional follow-up, put Ss in pairs to discuss any tips they use to remember people's names or other information, then ask them to share some of their ideas.

Answer key:

Answers for final challenge:
a good memory for, memorable, bear in mind, no memory of, memorise, reminds you of, 'll never forget, recall

3B

Grammar 1 Comparatives and superlatives

Materials: One worksheet per student

Instructions:

Distribute the worksheets. Put Ss in pairs to discuss the questions in Ex 1 and then ask them to share some of their ideas with the class.

For Ex 2, ask Ss to read the title and the first sentence of the article, then elicit the answer to item 1 as an example. Tell Ss to complete the remaining gaps individually, referring to the grammar box in the Students' Book as required. Put Ss in pairs to compare their answers, then check the answers as a class.

Put Ss in pairs or groups of three. Tell Ss to discuss the questions in Ex 3. Elicit some ideas.

Answer key:

2
1 by far **2** much more **3** the more **4** slightly **5** far more
6 as **7** bit **8** a much **9** the most **10** more of a **11** the
12 as **13** than **14** close as **15** less

Grammar 2 Comparatives and superlatives

Materials: One worksheet per student
Instructions:
Distribute the worksheets. For Ex 1, ask Ss to read the statements and circle the appropriate number next to each one to show how much they agree or disagree with the statement. Then, for Ex 2, tell Ss to amend or rewrite the statements in line with their opinions, modifying the comparatives or content appropriately. Monitor and help where necessary.

When Ss have finished, put them in groups of three or four and, for Ex 3, ask them to discuss each statement, giving their opinion and using as many modified comparatives and superlatives as possible. Elicit feedback from Ss in open class and correct any errors you heard while monitoring.

Vocabulary Character adjectives

Materials: One worksheet per student
Instructions:
Distribute the worksheets. For Ex 1, explain that Ss need to write the missing letters to form the adjectives of character from the lesson. This could be done in pairs, individually or for homework.

For Ex 2, put Ss in groups to check their answers, then check answers with the class. Then ask Ss to discuss the questions in Ex 1. Encourage Ss to use the adjectives of character as much as possible in their discussion. To finish, ask each group to choose one of the questions and share their ideas with the class.

Answer key:
1
1 competitive   2 thoughtful   3 determined
4 confident, arrogant   5 inexperienced, unpredictable
6 stubborn   7 bold   8 tough   9 reasonable   10 remarkable

3C

Language focus 1 Forming adjectives

Materials: One worksheet per student
Instructions:
Explain that Ss are going to do an exercise where they practise forming adjectives and matching them to nouns that they are often used with. Write the words *costume, festival, parrot* on the board, and elicit one of the adjectives from the lesson that might be used with all of these items (*colourful*).

Distribute the worksheets. For Ex 1, explain that the three missing adjectives in each row can be formed from the root words in the left-hand column of the row. Ss work in pairs, or individually, to complete the exercise. Check answers as a class. Demonstrate the pronunciation and syllabic stress of words as required.

For Ex 2, ask Ss to write five sentences about their life or opinions using some of the collocations from Ex 1, although **stronger Ss** can write more. This exercise could be set for homework.

Put Ss in pairs for Ex 3. Monitor and check Ss are using correct adjective forms.

Answer key:
1
1 economic   2 dangerous   3 successful   4 allergic   5 doable
6 classic   7 traditional   8 nightmarish   9 logical   10 tricky
11 acceptable   12 scary   13 childish   14 historical
15 useful   16 meaty   17 foolish   18 classical

Language focus 2 Forming adjectives

Materials: One worksheet per group of Ss, cut into domino cards
Instructions:
Put Ss in groups of three or four and give each group a set of dominoes, which they should shuffle. Each student gets five dominoes and extras are placed face down in a pool on the table. One domino is taken from the pool and placed face up. The first student then places a matching domino at one end to create a complete adjective and says a sentence using it. If a student is unable to place a domino, they must draw an extra one from the pool. Ss take turns until the first student to place his/her final domino on the table wins.

Answer key:
The domino cards are: outrage**ous**, fool**ish**, trick**y**, danger**ous**, hope**ful**, comforta**ble**, log**ical**, histor**ical**, do**able**, accident**al**, econom**ic**, point**less**, poison**ous**, meat**y**, success**ful**, use**less**, child**ish**, scar**y**, disrespect**ful**, tradition**al**, nightmar**ish**, accept**able**, colour**ful**, allerg**ic**

Vocabulary Arguments

Materials: One A and B worksheet per pair of Ss, cut in half
Instructions:
Put Ss in A/B pairs. Give half the pairs a Team A worksheet and the other half a Team B worksheet. Ask pairs to work together to read the statements and complete them with the words in the box. Check answers as a class.

Explain that pairs of Ss are going to have mini-debates against each other about each statement. However, rather than using their real opinion, they need to argue for, or against, the statement according to what is on their sheet.

Give pairs about ten minutes to read through the statements that they need to argue for or against, and think of how they might support their arguments.

Put Ss in groups of four, made up of Team A and Team B pairs. Teams debate each statement on the worksheet. To finish, choose some of the statements to discuss as a class.

Answer key:
1 intervene   2 see   3 contradict   4 have   5 pick   6 clashing
7 issue   8 up   9 down   10 compromise

4A

Grammar 1 Relative clauses

Materials: One worksheet per student
Instructions:
Ask Ss whether anyone has heard of, or been to, any artwork experiences where the visitor can interact with the art.

Distribute the worksheets. Go through the instructions for Ex 1 with the class. Read through the first sentence with the class and complete it as an example.

Tell Ss to complete the article in Ex 1 with relative pronouns (for some items more than one relative pronoun may be possible). Put Ss in pairs to compare their answers, then check as a class.

Read through the instructions for Ex 2. Look at the last sentence of text A with the class and help them to identify the relative clause with the pronoun omitted (*a popular attraction (which/that) both tourists and locals enjoy*). Put Ss in pairs to look for the relative clause in the last sentence of the other texts. Check answers as a class.

Ask Ss to discuss Ex 3 with their partner, then ask a few Ss to share their ideas.

As an optional follow-up, have a relative clause web quest. Ask Ss to briefly research one of the art experiences in the article or another art experience online. Ask Ss to notice and note the use of relative clauses in the webpages/texts they find. Are they defining or non-defining? Ss then share at least one example of each type in small groups.

Answer key:

1
1 which (non-defining) 2 who/that (defining)
3 which/that (defining) 4 which (non-defining)
5 where (non-defining) 6 when/that (defining)
7 where (defining) 8 which (non-defining) 9 when (defining)
10 who/that (defining) 11 whose (non-defining)
12 where (defining) 13 which (non-defining)
14 when (defining) 15 which/that (defining)

2
A a popular attraction (that/which) both tourists and locals enjoy
B the opportunity (that/which) the artwork provided
C the works of art (that/which) they create

Grammar 2 Relative clauses

Materials: One worksheet per group of three Ss, cut into cards

Instructions:

Put Ss in groups of three. Give each group a set of cards, which they spread out face up on the desk in groups by shaded background colour. Student A picks up a dark grey card to start the sentence. Student B must pick up the appropriate light-grey relative clause to follow, then Student C finds the appropriate white-coloured card to finish the sentence. For the next sentence, Student B picks first, and so on. The activity continues until all the sentences are complete. Ss may need to rearrange some sentences to ensure all cards are used.

To follow-up, remove the final cards in each sentence. Ask Ss to take turns to complete each sentence so that it is true for them.

Answer key:
See order on worksheet for answers:
An artist whose work I admire is Frida Kahlo.
Something that I'd love to own would be a pair of designer sunglasses.
The time when I am most creative is late at night.
The colour which I wear most often is vivid-pink!
The best gallery in the world, where many famous artworks are housed, is the National Gallery in London.
My favourite possession, which is decorative rather than useful, is a poster of Van Gogh's sunflowers.
I don't like artwork that I don't understand.
A city I'd like to visit, where there is plenty of elegant architecture is St Petersburg, Russia.
I like the work of artists who push the boundaries of art.
My family, when I think about it, were always my hugest supporters.

Vocabulary Adjectives to describe things

Materials: One set of cards per group of four

Instructions:

Put students in groups of four. Two Ss belong to Team A and the other two Ss belong to Team B. Teams can give themselves their own name if they want. Each group of four has a set of cards face down. A student from Team A picks up a card and looks at the word. That student then has one minute to elicit that word from the other student in Team A, but without using any of the words that are not allowed. Whilst this is happening, one of the Team B members is timing the proceedings and the other is checking that none of the forbidden words are used. When they have finished, Team B have a go at trying to elicit a word on another card, whilst Team A members time them and check that the forbidden words aren't used. Teams, and team members, keep alternating until there are no more cards left.

When a team guesses correctly, it keeps the card. The team with the most cards at the end, wins the game.

When the game is over, ask the Ss which words were the hardest to describe.

4B

Grammar 1 Obligation and prohibition

Materials: One worksheet per student

Instructions:

Brainstorm some actions that are prohibited at the cinema with the class. Read the introduction to Ex 1 on the worksheet to the class, then distribute the worksheets.

Elicit the answer to item 1 as an example. Tell Ss to complete the remaining gaps individually, referring to the grammar box in the Students' Book as required. Put Ss in pairs to compare their answers before checking as a class.

For Ex 2, put Ss in pairs. Ask Ss to discuss the question *What things are allowed or not allowed in cinemas where you live?*. Elicit a few ideas.

Answer key:

1
1 mustn't 2 was allowed 3 had to 4 aren't 5 don't have
6 need 7 must 8 got to 9 needed 10 had to
11 didn't need 12 got to 13 required 14 have to 15 don't

Grammar 2 Obligation and prohibition

Materials: One worksheet per group of three, cut into cards

Instructions:

Put Ss in groups of three. Give each group a set of cards. Ask Ss in each group to work together to put all the cards into the six categories of obligation and prohibition (dark grey cards). Check answers as a class.

When Ss have put the cards into groups, ask them to think about, and discuss obligation, and prohibition, as it relates to their experiences of being a student in their past and present. Tell Ss to take turns to say a phrase starting with one of the sentence starters on a white card and then to turn the card over, e.g. *We have to bring our coursebooks to each lesson*. The activity finishes when all the cards have been turned face down.

Answer key:

Present obligation: We have to … We've got to …
We must … We need to … We're required to …
Past obligation: We had to … We were required to … We needed to …
Present no obligation: We don't have to …
We don't need to … We're not required to …
We haven't got to …
Past no obligation: We didn't have to … We didn't need to …
We weren't required to …
Present prohibition: We mustn't … We can't …
We're not allowed to …
Past prohibition: We weren't allowed to … We couldn't …

Vocabulary   Job requirements

Materials: One worksheet per student
Instructions:
Brainstorm some ideas of dream jobs with the class and then distribute the worksheets. Put Ss in pairs to discuss the questions in Ex 1 and Ex 2.
In Ex 3, ask Ss to correct the (seven) mistakes. This can be done in pairs or individually.
When Ss have compared their answers in pairs (or with another pair), check answers as a class. Write the correct forms on the board, so that Ss have an accurate model to replicate when writing their own cover letter.
For Ex 4, ask Ss to write a cover letter for their dream job. Emphasise that it should include at least six of the phrases from the lesson and should use correct forms. This could be set for homework. Ss swap and correct each other's letter if they find any mistakes.
Alternatively, after correcting the letter, Ss could roleplay helping each other to practise for a job interview. Put Ss in pairs to write some questions based on the lesson phrases. Ss take turns to be the interviewer.

Answer key:
2
The position is for ice cream flavour designer and marketing assistant. Nick has a degree in food science, experience working in an ice cream shop and has won a prize for a cake recipe.
3
Dear Ms Daniels,
I am writing to apply for the position of ice cream flavour designer at Creamery Products.
As you will see from my attached CV, I have a food science degree from the University of Devon and five years' experience working in an ice cream shop. I have a passion ~~in~~ for creative desserts and won a local recipe award for the development of a white chocolate and pear cake recipe.
Regarding the marketing requirements of the position, I have been told that I have a natural ~~fluent~~ flair for sales. I have strong communication skills and in addition to English, I am also ~~flair~~ fluent in Spanish. I am able to ~~bother~~ cope with complex instructions and multiple projects.
I believe my background ~~on~~ in food science and my enthusiasm make me a great candidate for this role on the Creamery Products team. Please note that I would ~~have~~ be willing to move cities for this position, were my application successful.
Thank you for considering my application.
Yours sincerely,
Nick Mason

Answer key:
4
Suggested answer:
Dear Mr Rogers,
I am writing to apply for the position of security analyst at Bytepip Tech.
I have a degree in computer science from the University of Hamilton and ten years' coding experience. I have a passion for identifying and preventing security issues before they happen. I have strong communication skills and, in addition to English, I am also fluent in Spanish. I am able to cope with complex instructions and multiple projects.
I believe I have the background and enthusiasm to make a great contribution to the Bytepip Tech team. Please note that I would be willing to relocate for this position, were my application successful.
Thank you for considering my application.
Yours sincerely,
Kate Smith

4C

Language focus 1   Forming verbs with *en*

Materials: One worksheet per student
Instructions:
Distribute the worksheets. Explain that Ss need to add a prefix or suffix to each of the words in Ex 1, then, in Ex 2, underline the words that do not have the same form as the others. Decide which word is the odd one out in the first row together as an example. Ask Ss to complete the exercise individually then compare in pairs before checking as a class.
In Ex 3, Ss complete the questions individually using the words in the box. In Ex 4, put Ss in pairs to discuss the questions and elicit a few ideas for each with the class.

Answer key:
1 and 2
1 harden   shorten   sadden   <u>enrage</u>
2 lengthen   weaken   <u>endanger</u>   tighten
3 <u>enrich</u>   brighten   sweeten   soften
4 enjoy   enable   ensure   <u>broaden</u>
5 shorten   widen   <u>enlarge</u>   lessen
6 loosen   <u>enforce</u>   strengthen   straighten
3
1 sweeten   **2** broaden (broaden someone's mind is a collocation)
3 brighten (brighten someone's day is a collocation)   **4** shorten
5 strengthen   **6** enrich (enrich someone's life is a collocation)
7 weaken   **8** lengthen

Language focus 2   Forming verbs with *en*

Materials: One A and B worksheet per student
Instructions:
Distribute the worksheets. Put Ss in A/A and B/B pairs to complete Ex 1. Ss complete the sentences with the correct verb form of the word in brackets, then check their answers with another pair with the same sheet. Then Ss discuss possible contexts for each sentence. Emphasise that the sentences correspond to contexts a–f in Ex 2 on the other worksheet, not their own worksheet.
Put Ss in A/B pairs to do Ex 2. Ss should not show each other their worksheets. Ss take turns to read one of their contexts a–f, and the other student responds with an appropriate sentence 1–6

from their worksheet. Check as a class. For extra practice, Ss could swap A/B worksheets and repeat Ex 2.

Answer key:

1
A
1 enlarge 2 sweetened 3 soften 4 widening 5 ensure 6 enabled
B
1 brighten 2 enriched 3 enforce 4 shortened 5 endangered 6 tighten

2
A
a 6 b 1 c 5 d 3 e 4 f 2
B
a 1 b 4 c 5 d 2 e 6 f 3

Vocabulary 21st-century words

Materials: One worksheet per pair of Ss, cut in half

Instructions:

Divide the class into two groups. Give a Student A worksheet to half the Ss in the class and a Student B worksheet to the other half. Ask Ss to work with someone with the same worksheet half as them, check they understand all of the words written in their crossword and think of clues for each word, e.g. definitions or descriptions of the target language. Monitor and help if necessary.

Put Ss in A/B pairs and tell them not to look at each other's worksheets. Make sure that Ss know how to ask for clues e.g.: *What's 5 across?* and *What's 1 down?* Write these questions on the board as prompts if necessary. Ss work together and give each other clues so they can complete their crosswords.

Finish with a class round up, reading the sample clues below (out of order), and asking Ss to call out the word that each one refers to.

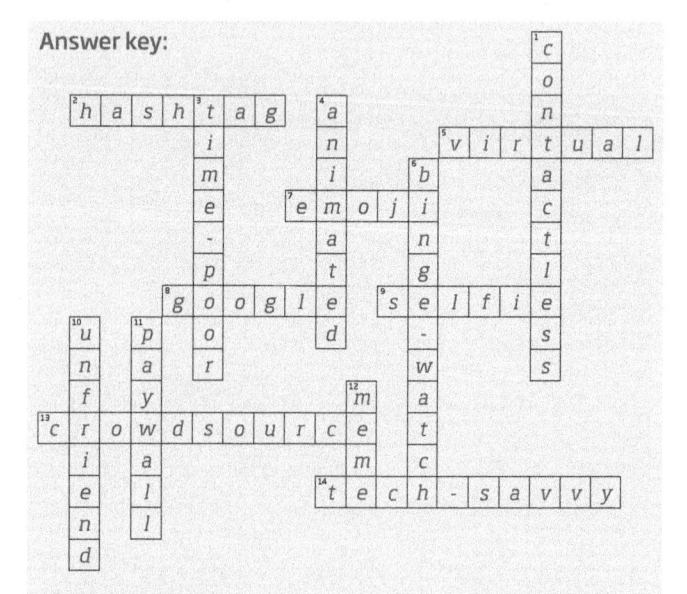

Answer key:

Across/down: 2 hashtag, 5 virtual, 7 emoji, 8 google, 9 selfie, 13 crowdsource, 14 tech-savvy; 1 contactless, 3 time-poor, 4 animated, 6 binge-watch, 10 unfriend, 11 paywall, 12 meme

Suggested clues:

1. If this service is available on your debit card or credit card, you can use it to pay for things by waving it over or putting it on a card machine without using a pin number. (*contactless*)
2. This is a word in a social media message with a symbol in front of it which indicates what the message is about. (*hashtag*)
3. Someone who is very busy could be described as this. (*time-poor*)
4. When digital pictures, cartoons or gifs move, they can be described as this. (*animated*)
5. If someone is shown around a place or a website online rather than in person, the tour can be described as this. (*virtual*)
6. This is a verb which means to watch a lot of episodes of a series in a short space of time. (*binge-watch*)
7. This is a tiny picture which is used on social media or in text messages, often to show different feelings. (*emoji*)
8. This is a verb which is often used to talk about searching for information on the internet. (*google*)
9. If someone takes a picture of themselves using their mobile, it's called this. (*selfie*)
10. If someone removes a friend from their list of contacts on social media, they do this. (*unfriend*)
11. If the content on a website is not available for free, that means the site has this. (*paywall*)
12. Pictures with a funny quote that circulate on the internet are called this. (*meme*)
13. This is a verb which means to get members of the public to do work or think of ideas for you, usually for little or no money. (*crowdsource*)
14. Someone who knows a lot about using technology could be described as this. (*tech-savvy*)

5A

Grammar 1 Mistakes in the past

Materials: One worksheet per student

Instructions:

Distribute the worksheets. Put Ss in pairs to read the list of regrets in Ex 1 and discuss which are most common. Elicit a few ideas. Read through the instructions for Ex 2 and do the first item with the class as an example. Point out that Ss will need to decide whether to use a positive or negative verbs depending on the context. Ask Ss to complete Ex 2 and Ex 3 individually, then compare their answers in pairs before checking as a class.

For Ex 4, go through the sample sentences in the word box that could be used to respond to someone sharing a regret. Put Ss in pairs to practise saying the regrets from Ex 2 and responding kindly. For more of a challenge, ask Ss to use other made-up regrets or other responses.

Answer key:

2
1 shouldn't have sent 2 was supposed to pay 3 hadn't signed up 4 hadn't floated 5 ought to have realised 6 could have been 7 had begun 8 should have spent 9 wasn't supposed to lose 10 had known

3
1 d 2 h 3 c 4 j 5 f 6 b 7 e 8 g 9 i 10 a

Grammar 2 Mistakes in the past

Materials: One worksheet per pair (have a few extra copies for fast finishers)

Instructions:

Put Ss in pairs and distribute the worksheets. Check Ss are familiar with noughts and crosses, and, if necessary, demonstrate it on the board. (Ss play in pairs and take turns to draw a nought or a cross in one square of a nine-square grid. The first player to get three symbols in a row, vertically, horizontally or diagonally, wins.)

Explain that this version works the same way except, before drawing their symbol in a given square, Ss need to use one of the phrases from the grammar box in the Students' Book to express the regret in the square. For example, in round 1 on the worksheet, the first regret is, *Your cousin is furious because you contradicted her while she was telling a story to friends*. Answers to this could be: *I shouldn't have said anything. / She wasn't supposed to get angry. / I could have talked to her about it afterwards*. Encourage Ss to use a wide range of phrases if possible, and to help each other if necessary.

Ss play three rounds of the game with their partner. **Fast finishers** could play additional rounds on extra sheets or could take turns to speak on the topics in squares left unused in their games.

When Ss have finished, ask each student to share one of the sentences they made during the game.

Vocabulary   Money phrasal verbs

Materials: One worksheet per group of three Ss, cut into cards

Instructions:

Put Ss in groups of three. Give each group a set of cards, which they spread face up on the table. Ss work together to order the tips in the list so that they make sense.

When Ss have completed the matching activity, check the answers with the class. Tell Ss to discuss which would be the most and least helpful piece of advice for a student who lives in their area. Conduct whole class feedback.

Alternatively, photocopy an additional worksheet for each group so that Ss can check their own answers. When they have finished matching, give them the sheet to check. Ss can then move on to the discussion at their own pace.

Answer key:
The pieces of advice are:
Make sure you only live on what you have.
Track your spending to see what your money is really going on each week.
Then identify possible areas where you could cut back on expenses.
Be sure to set aside savings each month for emergencies.
Avoid splashing out on luxuries, but do allow yourself a little fun.
Some people limit themselves by taking out the same amount of cash every week. When it's gone, it's gone!
It probably goes without saying, but don't stock up on items you don't need!
Don't get into any unnecessary debt.
If you find yourself in difficulty, then pay back the loan with the highest interest rate first.
Manage your money or it will manage you!

5B

Grammar 1   Quantifiers

Materials: One worksheet per student

Instructions:

As an optional warmer to arouse interest in the story, write on the board a few words from the text: *theft, New Zealand, petrol station, bank account, overdraft, ten million, luxurious*. Tell Ss that they are going to read some blog posts about a true story, which includes these words. Put Ss in pairs to speculate about what might have happened.

Distribute the worksheets. Encourage Ss to skim the story and then to complete the blog posts with the words in the boxes. When Ss have finished, put them in pairs to compare their answers before checking as a class.

For Ex 2, put Ss in pairs to discuss the question, then elicit a few opinions.

Answer key:

1
1 a little   2 a few   3 many   4 much   5 any   6 most
7 Several   8 a lot of   9 every   10 either   11 couple   12 all
13 no   14 Some   15 both   16 neither   17 little   18 Few
19 plenty   20 loads of

Grammar 2   Quantifiers

Materials: One card per student, folded along the dotted line

Instructions:

Give out one pre-folded card per student with the question facing upwards. Place the rest of the cards question side up on a central desk. This is the question pool. If you have more than twelve Ss, place some duplicate cards in the pool.

Ask Ss to decide what quantifier will go in the gap to complete the question. Point out that some cards have an extra clue to help them fill the gap. Once the student has worked out which quantifier they think goes in the gap, they can check on the back of their folded card.

Explain that Ss are going to mingle, asking the question on their card. The other student will then have to make up a response on the spot trying to use quantifiers. Encourage Ss to notice that some questions have more than one quantifier in them. Tell Ss that they should try to use a range of quantifiers in the answers (not just the one on the card). After working with one partner, they place their question back in the question pool and take a new one.

To assist **weaker Ss**, and to encourage the use of a wider range of quantifiers whilst they are mingling, write the quantifiers from the grammar box in the Students' Book on the board as prompts.

Monitor, listen to quantifier use in the discussion, and encourage Ss to self-/peer correct. Finally, choose one or two of the card topics and elicit some answers using quantifiers from the class.

Answer key:

Suggested answers:
How <u>many</u> books have you read this year? I've only read a <u>few</u> books, I don't have <u>much</u> time for reading.
Do you drink <u>either</u> coffee or tea? Yes, I drink <u>both</u>. I like to have a <u>couple of</u> cups of coffee <u>every</u> morning.
How <u>much</u> time do you spend outdoors? To be honest, I don't spend <u>much</u> time outdoors during the week. I spend a <u>few</u> minutes in between classes. I do try to spend <u>some</u> time in nature on the weekends if I can.
What's something you have <u>little</u> patience for? I have <u>little</u> patience for people who think they're better than everyone else. Luckily, <u>most</u> people aren't like that.
What do you think <u>few</u> people are afraid of? I doubt <u>many</u> people would be scared of something like a pencil. But, I guess there might be <u>a few</u>!
What is something <u>few</u> people like, but you do? Well, I like chocolate, but <u>plenty of</u> people like that. I can't think of <u>many</u> things that I like that others wouldn't.
How <u>many</u> meals do you know how to cook without a recipe? I have <u>loads of</u> meals I can cook off by heart.

Where are a <u>couple of</u> places that you like to spend time? There are <u>plenty of</u> places I like to spend time, including the beach and the countryside.

Do you own <u>any</u> objects that are over fifty years old? I don't think I have <u>many</u> old things. I suppose I've got a <u>couple of</u> old photographs somewhere.

Do you have <u>many</u> cousins? Yes, I have <u>a lot of</u> cousins, twenty-four of them. I see <u>most</u> of them quite often although <u>a few of</u> them live abroad.

In a film, do you prefer <u>plenty of</u> humour or <u>lots of</u> suspense? I like <u>both</u> those things!

How <u>much</u> sleep do you like to get each night? I like to get <u>plenty of</u> sleep. I can't function well on <u>little</u> sleep.

Vocabulary   Crime (robbery)

Materials: One worksheet per group of three Ss, cut into thirds

Instructions:

Tell Ss that they are going to read about three different robberies that involve bananas, all inspired by true stories. Elicit from them how they think a robbery could involve a banana. Put Ss in groups of three (Teams A, B and C) and give each of them one of the cases. Ask them to read their case and complete it with the words in the box.

In their groups, Ss discuss each case and whether they think the sentence was fair. If not, Ss can decide on their own sentence for each person, which may include jail time or some other consequence, e.g. a fine or working in the community. Conduct whole class feedback.

As an optional follow-up, ask Ss to make up their own banana robbery story, perhaps using one of the ideas they brainstormed during the warmer, and as many of the target words and phrases as possible.

Answer key:

A
1 in 2 arrest 3 charged 4 found 5 sentenced
B
1 trial 2 researched 3 left 4 pleaded 5 to
C
1 scene 2 evade 3 broke 4 caught 5 in

5C

Language focus 1   Adverb + adjective collocations

Materials: One worksheet per student

Instructions:

Distribute the worksheets. For Ex 1, focus Ss on the left column of row 1. Elicit the correct collocations. For Ex 2, read statement 1 with the class and elicit which of the remaining combinations with the adverb *deeply* best fits in the gap (*deeply personal*). Ask Ss to complete the statements individually, then check answers as a class.

For Ex 3, tell Ss to circle a number to show the degree to which they agree or disagree with the statements. Then, for Ex 4, put Ss in pairs or small groups to discuss their answers.

Answer key:

1
The combinations that do not collocate are listed below. All other items are correct.
1 deeply normal   2 relatively essential   3 totally difficult
4 perfectly known   5 extremely right   6 entirely small
7 absolutely cold   8 bitterly concerned   9 completely difficult
10 highly new

2
1 deeply personal   2 relatively simple   3 totally lost/wrong
4 perfectly good   5 extremely difficult   6 entirely possible
7 absolutely essential   8 bitterly disappointed
9 completely honest   10 highly unlikely

Language focus 2   Adverb + adjective collocations

Materials: One worksheet per student

Instructions:

Distribute the worksheets. For Ex 1, ask Ss to complete the adverbs in each sentence individually. Check the answers with the class and take the opportunity to model the correct syllabic stress of each adverb + adjective combination. For Ex 2, ask Ss to write down something in each cloud that is a response to eight of the sentences in Ex 1. Explain that Ss should only write items that they don't mind sharing with a classmate. Emphasise that Ss should only use between one and four words, and that they should write the items out of order.

Put Ss in pairs. Ss swap worksheets to guess their partner's response, e.g.

A: *Did you write 'Venice' because it's somewhere you might get totally lost in?*
B: *No, I wrote it because I went in winter and it was bitterly cold there!*

When Ss have finished, elicit a few different ideas for each item from the class.

Answer key:

1
1 entirely   2 absolutely   3 highly   4 perfectly   5 bitterly
6 relatively   7 widely   8 completely   9 deeply   10 extremely
11 totally

Vocabulary   Money

Materials: One A and B worksheet per pair of Ss, cut in half

Instructions:

Give each student a worksheet (A or B) and ask them not to show anyone else. Put Ss in pairs so that they work with someone with the same A or B worksheet. Explain that the clues are sentences which use the word in brackets, but the word has been replaced with BEEP. All the BEEP words are related to the lesson vocabulary. In their pairs, Ss read the sentences they have been given and write their own sentences for the last two words.

Put Ss in A/B pairs. Ss take turns to read the clues. The other student must guess the word that BEEP stands for. If the student can't guess, the other student must try to give other clues or definitions to assist, until all the words have been guessed.

Alternatively, ask Ss to write their sentences individually before pairing up for the guessing stage.

> **Answer key:**
> **Worksheet A**
> 1 income 2 savings 3 recession 4 Students' own sentence
> 5 Students' own sentence
> **Worksheet B**
> 1 pension 2 bargain 3 inflation 4 Students' own sentence
> 5 Students' own sentence

6A

Grammar 1   Verb + -ing and infinitive with *to*

Materials: One worksheet per student

Instructions:

Tell Ss that a survey was done of over two thousand people's hopes and dreams in the following areas: career, travel, animals, adventure and self-improvement. For Ex 1, put Ss in pairs to talk for two minutes about the kinds of things people might have said in response to the survey.

Distribute the worksheets. Ask Ss to complete the sentences in Ex 2 individually. Emphasise that the form of each verb depends on the words or phrases that precede the gap (or follow it if it is a subject). Put Ss in pairs to compare their answers before checking as a class.

As a follow-up, ask Ss to complete the sentences in Ex 3 with their own ideas. Put Ss in small groups to share their ideas and see if Ss have any dreams in common.

Alternatively, Ss could re-read the statements from the text and discuss whether or not they would like to do each item. Groups could report back to the class using some of the verbs and phrases from the text, e.g. *We would all like to try working abroad.*

> **Answer key:**
> **2**
> 1 to work (following the verb *intend*)
> 2 to get (following *it + be + adjective*)
> 3 changing (after the phrase *be worth*)
> 4 taking (following the verb *imagine*)
> 5 relaxing (following a preposition)
> 6 to visit (following *it + be + adjective*)
> 7 to want (following *it + be + adjective*)
> 8 to see (following the verb *choose*)
> 9 riding (following the verb *enjoy*)
> 10 Driving (subject)
> 11 entering (following a preposition)
> 12 dreaming (following the phrase *couldn't help*)
> 13 to speak (following the verb *learn*)
> 14 Playing (subject)
> 15 to help (infinitive of purpose)

Grammar 2   Verb + -ing and infinitive with *to*

Materials: One worksheet per pair of Ss

Instructions:

Put Ss in pairs and distribute the worksheets. Explain that they are going to practise selecting -ing/infinitive forms, while having a chat about living life well. Ask Ss to take turns to make a sentence using one of the prompts, e.g. *1 A lot of people think about reducing their technology use, but it's extremely difficult!* or *2 Some people appear to be happy, but are actually quite lonely.* Tell Ss to use a verb from the verb bank or their own ideas. Other Ss in the group should respond to the statement or give an answer if the Ss has formed a question. The next student in the group then chooses a different prompt. Monitor and listen for appropriate verb form choices.

When Ss have finished, ask each student to share one of the statements they made, going around the room in quick succession.

> **Answer key:**
> 1 -ing
> 2 infinitive
> 3 -ing
> 4 infinitive
> 5 -ing
> 6 infinitive
> 7 both forms can be used without a change in meaning
> 8 -ing
> 9 -ing
> 10 infinitive
> 11 both forms can be used without a change in meaning
> 12 infinitive
> 13 both forms can be used (with a change in meaning)
> 14 infinitive
> 15 both forms can be used with *remember*, but in this sentence, it is likely to be followed by an infinitive, meaning that people shouldn't forget to do something

Vocabulary   Common idioms

Materials: One worksheet per pair

Instructions:

Put Ss in pairs. Distribute the worksheets. Go through the instructions. Explain that idioms are said word for word, so it is important to learn them. Tell Ss to read through each statement, decide whether there is an error, then correct it if necessary. **Fast finishers** could practise saying the statements and have their partner respond. Check answers with the class.

As an optional follow-up, put Ss in small groups. Tell Ss to re-read the idioms on the sheet and discuss whether there are any similar or equivalent idioms to each one in other languages they know. Elicit a few ideas.

> **Answer key:**
> 1 cost <u>an</u> arm and a leg   2 took <u>my</u> breath away   3 correct
> 4 drives me <u>up</u> the wall   5 over the <u>moon</u>   6 correct
> 7 a piece of <u>cake</u>   8 out of <u>this</u> world

6B

Grammar 1   Reported speech

Materials: One worksheet per student

Instructions:

Distribute the worksheets. For Ex 1, ask Ss to read the conversation in the left-hand column and decide whether they would have negotiated more or less than Tom did in the situation. Elicit some ideas.

For Ex 2, focus Ss on the first sentence in the right-hand column and elicit how Tom's direct speech (in the left column) can be changed into reported speech. Point out that each gap has two words in it. When Ss have completed the exercise individually, put them in pairs to compare their answers, then check as a class.

For Ex 3, put Ss in pairs to identify negotiation strategies in the seller's reported speech. Elicit some ideas.

As an optional follow-up, ask Ss to work in pairs, or small groups, to brainstorm tips that a buyer like Tom could use in a market negotiation. Then, put Ss in pairs from different groups to discuss what was said in their group discussion (using reported speech), e.g. *My group said that you could pretend that you weren't very interested (in the bags).*

Answer key:
2
1 I was **2** to get **3** told me **4** had been **5** asked how
6 they were **7** asked if/whether **8** I preferred **9** She said
10 I asked **11** would accept **12** she couldn't **13** could give
14 would take

3
Suggested answers:
The seller said that the bags were made by people in her family.
The seller asked Tom which bag he liked before giving prices.
The seller told Tom a higher price for the colour he liked.
The seller offered a special deal for buying two bags.

Grammar 2 Reported speech

Materials: One worksheet per pair of Ss, cut in half
Instructions:
Distribute the worksheet halves. Tell Ss to mingle and interview different classmates for each question and make notes of their answers. Allow Ss 10–15 minutes for this.

Put Ss in A/B pairs. Ask Ss to take turns to report back to each other on what they learnt about their classmates using a range of phrases using *say* and *tell*, e.g. *Liana said her dream job was to be a travel writer. Martin told me that he had been to London.* Monitor and listen for appropriate reported speech forms.

When Ss have finished, get feedback (using reported speech) from different members of the class about any interesting information they found out.

Vocabulary Negotiating

Materials: One worksheet per student
Instructions:
Distribute the worksheets. For Ex 1, ask Ss to choose the correct alternatives to complete each sentence, by considering prepositions, collocations and word class. Ss select the correct words individually. Then put Ss in pairs to compare their answers before checking as a class.

Go through the instructions for Ex 2 with the class. In their pairs, ask Ss to choose a situation or write one of their own, making sure a range of situations are chosen in the class.

For Ex 3, tell Ss to discuss the items on the sheet in relation to the situation they chose in Ex 2 and tick the column in the table they agree with (helpful/unhelpful/it depends).

For Ex 4, put Ss in groups to compare their ideas, elicit a few ideas from the class, then answer the question *Which strategies would be helpful in your negotiations?*.

As an optional follow-up, ask Ss to discuss the following questions in groups.
- Can you think of ways to build trust in a negotiation?
- What are the best ways to stay calm in a negotiation?
- What actions might increase or decrease tension in a negotiation?

Answer key:
1
1 build **2** Criticise **3** bond **4** conflict **5** Stay **6** Interrupt
7 cooperate **8** tension **9** Praise **10** falling out

3
Suggested answers:
The answers will depend on the context of the negotiation. However, 2, 4, 6 are likely to be unhelpful in most negotiations, and 5 is likely to be helpful in most negotiations.

6C

Language focus 1 Verb patterns after reporting verbs

Materials: One worksheet per student
Instructions:
Distribute the worksheets. Go through the instructions for Ex 1 and emphasise that Ss will need to add a pronoun and/or a preposition to some of the items. Tell Ss to complete the sentences individually, then compare their answers in pairs before checking as a class.

For Ex 2, ask Ss to answer the quiz questions for themselves. Point out that they can choose to add their own answer (D), but need to use a reporting verb. Put Ss in pairs to discuss their answers and give reasons for their choices.

Answer key:
1
1 A to leave **B** her to pay **C** her to let
2 A knowing **B** of taking **C** getting
3 A to hand in **B** to complete **C** on hearing
4 A for forgetting **B** him to believe **C** for not mentioning
5 A not liking **B** to pretend **C** to give

Language focus 2 Verb patterns after reporting verbs

Materials: One worksheet per small group of Ss, cut into cards
Instructions:
Put Ss in groups of three or four and give each group a set of cards. Ask Ss to work together to match the question halves. Encourage them to notice the patterns following the reporting verbs as they do the activity. Check the answers as a class. Tell Ss to take turns to choose a question to discuss in the group. When Ss have finished, choose one or more of the questions and elicit some answers from the Ss.

Answers:
If someone denies doing something, how could you tell if they're lying?
Do you appreciate it when people remind you to do tasks or is it annoying?
What does it mean if people agree to disagree about an issue?
Are there any foods you would refuse to try?
How would you feel if your date insisted on paying for your meal?
Have you ever blamed technology for a mistake you made?
How might shop assistants convince a customer to buy their products?
Do you ever apologise for things that weren't your fault?
Have you ever been accused of being too nice?
How would you advise a person to prepare for their first job interview?
If you heard someone threatening to hurt someone else, what could you do?
Why is it hard for some people to admit to being wrong?

Vocabulary   Reporting verbs

Materials: Two worksheet halves per pair of Ss

Instructions:

Put Ss in A/B pairs and give each pair two copies of the same worksheet half. Tell Ss to work with their partner to complete the gaps in the argument in Ex 1 using the words in the box. Monitor and check verb forms are correct.

For Ex 2, tell Ss to prepare to perform the argument in Ex 1 for another pair. Ask Ss to work in their pairs to practise their arguments. Organise pairs into groups of four to take turns to perform their arguments. Ss should perform it twice, once for the other pair to listen, and once for the other pair to write down the missing words.

Answer key:

1 and 2
A
1 agree   2 accusing   3 Admit   4 apologise   5 deny   6 refuse
B
7 insist   8 convinced   9 remind   10 blame   11 advise   12 threatening

7A

Grammar 1   Real conditionals

Materials: One worksheet per student

Instructions:

Put Ss in pairs. Ask them to think about social issues that are important to them and to discuss the question *What makes someone care about a social issue?*

Distribute the worksheets. For Ex 1, Ss individually read the posts a–e and match them with the issues in the box. Check answers as a class. Ask Ss to complete Ex 2 individually, then compare their answers in pairs before checking as a class.

As an optional follow-up, tell Ss to discuss their own ideas about each post, using real conditionals where possible, e.g. *Assuming someone spends a lot of time with their friends, I think that they would probably be the biggest influence on their attitudes. I don't think reading would make much of a difference, unless someone chooses books with strong social messages.*

Answer key:

1
a childhood   b what you read   c information   d friends
e society attitudes

2
1 grow   2 when   3 Assuming   4 will be   5 unless   6 hear
7 care   8 'll be going   9 As soon as   10 carry

Grammar 2   Real conditionals

Materials: One worksheet per student

Instructions:

Distribute the worksheets. Ask Ss to read situation 1 and tick whether they think it's acceptable or unacceptable. Then tell Ss to write a sentence under each situation using one of the conjunctions given. This sentence should reflect their view as to whether the situation is acceptable or not, e.g. *When people download films for free, it isn't fair for the people who made it* or *Provided that the film is old, then it's OK to download it.* Alternatively, the writing stage could be done in pairs. While Ss are ticking the boxes and writing their sentences, monitor and help where necessary.

When Ss have finished, put Ss in groups of three or four and ask them to discuss each of the situations in turn. Monitor and note down any errors related to real conditional structures that you hear. When Ss have finished discussing the situations, elicit feedback from one or two groups on their opinions and deal with any errors on the board.

Answer key:

Suggested answers:
1 Provided that the film is copyright-free, this is acceptable.
2 If it's for a worthy cause, then I think it's acceptable.
3 Provided that the company is aware the celebrity doesn't use its product, I think it's OK. / When a celebrity doesn't want to use a particular product, then they shouldn't really advertise it.
4 As long as the council has good accommodation and support for homeless people, I think this is acceptable.
5 Assuming it's not a really big lie, I think employers expect this.
6 If a food is really unhealthy, I don't think it's acceptable to advertise it to children.
7 Assuming this photo was embarrassing and everyone could see it, it could damage your reputation, so I think this is unacceptable.
8 Unless the company helps to educate the children and gives them a fair salary, this is unacceptable to me.

Vocabulary   Social issues

Materials: One worksheet per pair of Ss

Instructions:

Put Ss in pairs and distribute the worksheets. Tell Ss that some of the nouns on the worksheet have an adjective form. Give Ss a minute to write down the adjective forms in the gaps on the sheet, using a dictionary if necessary, then elicit the answers from the class.

Explain that finding connections between vocabulary or concepts can help Ss to remember them. In their pairs, Ss take turns to state a possible connection between two nouns on the sheet, drawing a line between the two. Write some useful phrases on the board for Ss to use, e.g. *X relates to Y because ..., The connection between X and Y is that ..., X affects Y when ...* . More than one connection between the same pair of nouns is allowed. Give Ss ten minutes to find as many connections as they can between the words. Put pairs together in groups of four to compare and discuss their diagrams.

Write the following discussion questions on the board. Tell groups to discuss the questions, then elicit some responses from the class.
- *Which words did you connect most to the other nouns?*
- *Did you notice any pairs, or groups of nouns, that had lots of connections between them?*
- *Which nouns were the most difficult to connect to others? Can you think of other nouns that you could add to the diagram that they might they connect to?*

Answer key:

Adjective forms (clockwise): homeless, energy efficient, unemployed/unemployable, intolerant, unequal

Suggested answers:
Homelessness relates to poverty because homeless people live in poverty.
A connection between intolerance and inequality is that the more unequal a society is, the more intolerant people might be.
Living standards affect life expectancy because high living standards would probably lead to a higher life expectancy.

It is likely that *energy efficiency* will be the most difficult to connect to other nouns in the diagram. Nouns it might connect with could include: *climate change, electricity, heating, transport*.

7B

Grammar 1 — Future forms and degrees of probability

Materials: One worksheet per student

Instructions:

Distribute the worksheets and go through the instructions for Ex 1 with the class. Tell Ss to complete the responses in Ex 1 individually, then compare their answers in pairs before checking as a class. For Ex 2, put Ss in pairs to ask and answer questions 1–4, encouraging them to use a range of phrases from the grammar box from the Students' Book. Alternatively, Ss could write responses to each of the questions. If you have a private class online space with discussion forums, these questions could be posted there. Ss could choose to respond to two of the questions and write two replies to other Ss.

Answer key:

1
1 planning   2 are   3 doubt   4 will   5 it's   6 probably
7 well   8 about   9 wondering   10 don't   11 that
12 won't   13 may   14 I'm going to   15 doubt   16 definitely

Grammar 2 — Future forms and degrees of probability

Materials: One worksheet per student

Instructions:

Distribute the worksheets. In Ex 1, tell Ss to complete the statements so that they are true for them, using a range of different phrases from the word pool box. When Ss have finished writing their sentences, for Ex 2, ask them to mingle to try to find someone with a similar probability for each item. Emphasise that it is the probability that is important rather than the exact phrase, e.g. *I doubt I'll ride in a helicopter = I probably won't ride in a helicopter = It's unlikely I'll ride in a helicopter*. When Ss find someone with a similar answer, they write the classmate's name on the sheet. When they have finished, ask Ss to compare their findings with a partner or conduct whole class feedback.

Answer key:
Students' own answers

Vocabulary — Collocations with *make, take, do* and *give*

Materials: One worksheet, a dice and three counters per group of three Ss

Instructions:

Put Ss in groups of three. Give each group a copy of the worksheet, a dice and three counters. Tell Ss to work together to complete the phrases in the box with the correct verb (*make, take, do* or *give*). Ss then place their counters on the 'Start' square. Student A rolls the die and moves the counter the number of spaces indicated. Ss must think of a reply to the sentence they land on using one of the phrases in the box. Ss take turns to roll, move and respond. The first student in each group to reach the 'Finish' square is the winner. Ss can play more than once if time allows, as they are likely to land on different squares.

Answer key:
Phrase box
a make   b make   c take   d take   e do   f make   g give
h do   i give   j take   k give   l do

Suggested answers:
2 **Give** it your best shot!
3 I hope you **made** a good profit.
4 I hope we can find someone to **take** their place.
5 No idea! It doesn't **make** sense!
6 We **made** a deal that we'll take turns.
7 Yes, you've done a good job. It all **makes** sense.
8 I'll **give** you a hand.
9 Oh well, you **gave** it your best shot.
10 We might be able to **make** a deal if we ask nicely.
11 Sure, I'll **do** some research and get back to you.
12 That's fine. We can **do** without it.
13 Would you like me to **give** you a hand?
14 I'd be happy to **take** your place.
15 It would be **taking** a risk, but it's up to you!
16 You **gave** it your best shot. Better luck next time.
17 **Give** priority to people who have experience and a well-written cover letter.
18 You'll have to **do** without it.
19 Most of it's fine, but the third paragraph didn't **make** sense to me.
20 Someone needs to **take** charge!
21 I'm sure you'll **do** a really good job!
22 I'm still **doing** research, but I have to decide soon.
23 Yes, I love to **take** charge.
24 I know! Could you g**ive** me a hand to clean it?
25 It would definitely be better if we made a profit.
26 Oh well, we'll just have to **do** without.
27 Yes, I thought **do** something different.
28 They'll **give** priority to anyone who's got something serious.
29 Why don't you start by **doing** some research on the internet?

7C

Language focus 1 — Introductory *it*

Materials: One worksheet per student

Instructions:

Distribute the worksheets. Ask Ss to read the texts and complete them with the words in the boxes before comparing answers in pairs and checking as a class.

Answer key:

1
1 as if   2 me to   3 me   4 it sounds   5 turns out   6 seems to
7 feels like   8 appears   9 as though   10 alarms me
11 not that   12 just that

Language focus 2 Introductory *it*

Materials: One A and B worksheet per pair of Ss

Instructions:

Give each student one half of the worksheet. Ask Ss to work individually to complete the sentences, then tick the sentences that are true for them. Put Ss in A/B pairs to check each other's answers verbally (the answers to the other part of the worksheet are at the bottom of each worksheet half) and to ask each other whether the statements are true for them. Ss should give reasons for their answers.

To extend **stronger Ss**, ask Ss to respond to each of their partner's statements with another phrase beginning with introductory *it*. e.g.

A: *It's not that I don't like reading, it's just that I don't have time.*
B: *It sounds like you're busy.*

When Ss have finished, read a few of the statements aloud and elicit possible responses using introductory *it*.

As an optional follow-up, ask Ss to work in pairs to make up their own sentences using the sentence prompts in the answers sections of the worksheet.

Answer key:

A
1 It appears that everybody else
2 It's not that I don't like reading, it's just that
3 It concerns me that inequality
4 It feels as though I'm
5 It surprises me to think that people
6 It sounds as if some classmates

B
1 It looks as though I'm
2 It bothers me that people
3 It occurs to me that it's
4 It's not that I can't cook, it's just that
5 It alarms me to think that there
6 It seems that we

Vocabulary Personal and professional relationships

Materials: One card per student

Instructions:

Give one of the cut-up cards to each student and allow them time to read it. If there are more than ten Ss in the class, use some of the cards twice. Ask Ss to work with a partner and discuss whether they think their statements are true or false for the class. Ss mingle and survey the class to find out whether their statement is true or false. Remind Ss to turn their statement into a question in the second person, e.g. *Do you have an acquaintance who is famous?* When Ss have spoken to everyone, ask them to feed back the results to their original partner. Finally, elicit feedback from each student about whether their statement was true or false and whether they had predicted the answer correctly.

Answer key:
Students' own answers

8A

Grammar 1 Second conditional

Materials: One worksheet per student

Instructions:

Distribute the worksheets. For Ex 1, explain that Ss should put the words in the correct order to form second conditional sentences. Go through the first item together as an example. Ask Ss to put the words in the correct order to complete the rest of the remaining sentences. Put Ss in pairs and tell them to compare their answers before checking as a class.

For Ex 2, ask Ss to write two or three of their own similar sentences using the second conditional. Then tell Ss to share in pairs or small groups.

Answer key:

1
1 I would wear really outrageous clothes
2 If I were I to have three wishes
3 I would love to play the guitar
4 If I could be anywhere right now
5 it would definitely have a happy ending
6 I could get more done
7 if I lived in Hollywood
8 If I were you
9 I'd be learning Portuguese
10 If I hadn't seen the earlier films
11 I'd definitely choose sushi
12 if you hadn't been here

Grammar 2 Second conditional

Materials: One worksheet per pair, cut in half

Instructions:

Remind Ss that the second conditional is often used when giving advice, particularly with the phrase *If I were you …* . Tell Ss that they are going to give advice to each other about different situations. Put Ss in A/B pairs and give each student one half of the worksheet. Ask Ss to take turns to read the questions and discuss possible responses. Tell Ss to write down their best answer. Then put Ss in new A/A and B/B pairs to compare and check their answers. When Ss have finished, elicit some advice for each problem and check the use of the second conditional is correct.

Answer key:
Students' own answers

Vocabulary Events in films

Materials: One worksheet per group of Ss, cut into cards

Instructions:

Put Ss in groups of three. Give each group a set of the cut-up cards face down, except for the word pool card. Tell Ss to imagine that they are working for a film studio. The producer has asked them to choose the three best concepts for a film from a short description. Ss need to take turns to turn over one of the description cards and read it out to the group, who decide which word completes it. Tell Ss to write the answer in the gap. When all the cards are complete, ask Ss to discuss and decide on the three best ideas. Have a class vote.

Alternatively, give each student a copy of the worksheet to complete (this could be done for homework). Tell Ss to decide individually on the three best film ideas. Put Ss in groups of three to compare their lists and choose the top three between them.

As an optional extension, tell Ss to choose their favourite idea to develop into a one-minute presentation to the class about what the film would be about. Ask Ss to listen to the presentations and vote on whose movie should get made.

Answer key:
1 go on a mission   2 murder   3 capture   4 betrays
5 survive   6 faces   7 trapped   8 overcome   9 rescues
10 tricks   11 abandoned   12 confronts

8B

Grammar 1   Conditionals in the past

Materials: One worksheet per student
Instructions:
Distribute the worksheets. For Ex 1, give Ss a few minutes to read the three stories and decide what they have in common. Elicit the answer. Then, for Ex 2, ask Ss to choose the correct alternatives to complete the sentences. Get Ss to compare their answers in pairs before checking as a class. As an optional extension, ask Ss to identify which of the conditionals are mixed (B4, C1).

If you can, tell Ss an anecdote about a time you lost or found something and how it could have been different using past conditionals. Give Ss a few minutes to think about a situation that happened to them, or someone they know which could have been avoided. Ask Ss to write conditional sentences about it. Monitor and help as required. Put Ss in small groups to share their stories and check each other's conditional sentences are correct.

Answer key:
1
All the stories are about mistakes which could have been avoided by being more careful.
2
A 1a   2b   3a   4b
B 1b   2b   3a   4b
C 1a   2b   3b   4a

Grammar 2   Conditionals in the past

Materials: One worksheet per group, cut into cards
Instructions:
Put Ss in groups of three or four. Give each group a set of cards face down. Ss take turns to pick up a card and pose the question to the other members of the group, who must answer using a past conditional structure. Monitor and listen for the correct use of conditional forms.

When Ss have finished, read out one or two of the questions to the class and elicit responses. Provide feedback on errors you heard during the discussion (without identifying Ss). Write sample errors on the board and ask Ss to correct them.

Alternatively, tell Ss to have a class mingle. Give each student one card. Put Ss in pairs to ask and answer their questions. When they have finished, Ss swap questions and find a new partner to talk to. Set a time limit, e.g. ten minutes, for this activity.

Answer key:
Students' own answers

Vocabulary   Searching and hiding

Materials: One worksheet per student
Instructions:
Explain that the words and phrases related to searching and hiding from the lesson can be used in a range of situations in everyday situations. Distribute the worksheets. For Ex 1, ask Ss to find ten words or phrases related to searching and hiding in the word search. Ss complete the wordsearch individually.

For Ex 2, explain that the gaps in the sentences are all words and phrases found in the wordsearch from Ex 1, although some words will change tense. Ss complete the sentences individually.

Go through the instructions for Ex 3. Make it clear that the discussion about the likelihood of saying a sentence is around the idea of the sentence rather than the exact words. Put Ss in pairs to discuss the questions. Ask Ss to report back some of the things which they were the most or least likely to say.

Answer key:
1

h	d	r	h	n	u	h	x	l	r	q
d	e	c	e	i	v	e	s	g	o	h
i	p	o	a	h	d	i	f	j	i	e
t	u	i	d	e	n	t	i	f	y	s
r	r	f	f	e	c	r	p	c	k	i
a	s	u	o	a	h	a	a	r	o	h
c	u	g	r	d	u	c	e	t	t	u
k	e	e	p	a	n	e	y	e	o	n
e	d	a	y	c	t	b	s	p	o	t
s	d	i	s	g	u	i	s	e	n	e

2
1 keep an eye on   2 heading for   3 tracking   4 deceive
5 identified   6 disguise   7 pursuing   8 spotted   9 tracing
10 hunting

8C

Language focus 1   Linkers of concession

Materials: One worksheet per student
Instructions:
Distribute the worksheets. Go through the instructions with the class. Tell Ss to complete Ex 1 and Ex 2 individually. Put Ss in pairs to take turns to read a question and reply to check their answers. Check as a class.

As an optional follow-up, ask Ss to work in pairs to adapt the questions to be relevant to them and think of their own replies using linkers of concession, e.g.
A: *How was your weekend?*
B: *It was great despite the rain.*

Answer key:
1
1 f   2 d   3 a   4 e   5 c   6 h   7 b   8 g
2
a In spite of the fact   b Nevertheless   c although   d despite
e in spite of   f Even though   g Despite   h However

Language focus 2 Linkers of concession

Materials: One worksheet per pair, cut in half
Instructions:
Tell Ss that they are going to do a roleplay where two people disagree about works of art to practise using linkers of concession. Put Ss in A/B pairs and give each student one half of the worksheet. Give Ss time to read the first situation and ask any questions before they roleplay the situation. Tell Ss to use their own ideas in addition to those on the sheet. Monitor, listen and note any incorrect uses of linkers of concession. As feedback, write any examples of incorrect use (without identifying the speaker) on the board for the group to correct. Repeat with the second situation.

If you don't have much time, cut the worksheet in half horizontally and use only one situation. You could use the other in a future class for revision.

If you think your Ss will struggle to use linkers of concession spontaneously, you could give them a full copy of the worksheet to scaffold the activity, so that they can see what their partner is going to say and prepare sentences in advance. This could be done in A/A and B/B pairs.

Vocabulary Visual art

Materials: One worksheet per pair/group of Ss, cut-up into cards
Instructions:
Put Ss in pairs, or groups of three, and give each group a set of cards. Tell Ss to use the cards to play pelmanism by spreading them out on the desk face down and taking turns to turn over two cards. If the cards match, the student keeps the cards and then has a short discussion with the other(s) about why they do, or don't like, that kind of art. If the cards are not a correct match, the student places them back down on the table in the same place he/she took them from. The winner is the student with the most cards after they have all been matched.

Answer key:
1 Abstract artwork 2 Collage 3 Installation 4 Landscape
5 Oil painting 6 Portrait 7 Print 8 Sculpture 9 Sketch
10 Statue 11 Still life 12 Watercolour

9A

Grammar 1 Past modals of deduction

Materials: One worksheet per student
Instructions:
To start the activity, read out the puzzle on the worksheet and ask Ss to briefly think about what the answer might be. Distribute the worksheets. For Ex 1, ask Ss to read the puzzle and come up with an answer. Ss read the uncompleted conversation to see if their answer is correct.

For Ex 2, Ss re-read the puzzle again to complete the conversation with the past modal form of the verbs in brackets. Tell Ss to complete the exercise individually. Then, for Ex 3, put Ss in pairs to compare their answers before checking as a class.

In Ex 3, Ss practise reading the conversation aloud in pairs.

Answer key:
2
1 might have chosen 2 may have grabbed 3 could have been
4 might have realised 5 couldn't have known
6 may have been planning 7 couldn't have swapped
8 may not have contained 9 must have been
10 could have taken

Grammar 2 Past modals of deduction

Materials: One worksheet per group of three Ss, cut into cards
Instructions:
Put Ss in groups of three and give each group a set of puzzle cards face down. Ask Ss to take turns to pick a card and read the puzzle to the group. They must discuss the possible problem using past modals of deduction. If they can agree on an answer, they write it on the card. If they can't think of an answer, they can put the card to one side and move on to the next one. Ask Ss to continue the activity for fifteen minutes, or until all cards have been discussed. Conduct whole class feedback. Ask Ss to give their guesses using modals of deduction before revealing the answers.

Alternatively, set a time limit of ten minutes. Groups compete to see who can solve the most puzzle cards during that time.

Another alternative is to use the puzzle cards one-by-one as warmers or a way to fill the last five minutes of the class. It is a good way to revise modals of deductions over the next few classes.

Answer key:
1 Wren can't have been driving, she must have been walking.
2 It must have been one of the four billion people in the world who aren't men.
3 The last child must have been called Nina.
4 The two people who didn't get their hair wet must have been bald.
5 Zoey and Zeb might have been part of a set of triplets, or there could have been even more siblings in a multiple birth.
6 Selma might have thrown the ball straight up in the air or she could have thrown it straight at a wall.
7 Alvaro must have been the teacher.
8 The person must have been skydiving and his parachute can't have opened.

Vocabulary Mystery

Materials: One worksheet per student
Instructions:
Put Ss in pairs. Distribute the worksheets and ask Ss to discuss the questions in Ex 1. Ask a few Ss to share their ideas. Distribute the worksheets. For Ex 2, give Ss time to complete the opinion piece in Ex 2 individually with the words in the box. Then put Ss in pairs to compare their answers and check as a class. When Ss have done their rating for Ex 3, put them in small groups to discuss their ratings and the questions in Ex 4. When Ss have finished, elicit any interesting hoaxes that Ss have fallen for or heard about.

Answer key:
2
1 clues 2 remain a mystery 3 evidence 4 identifies
5 motives 6 accounted for 7 turns out 8 red herring
9 hoax 10 victim

9B

Grammar 1 — Verb patterns

Materials: One worksheet per student

Instructions:

To introduce the topic of the worksheet, consider sharing a personal anecdote, e.g. tell Ss about a time you got the hiccups and some of the cures you tried, or how you recently heard about someone who had the hiccups for a year and how annoying that would be. Elicit any different cures for hiccups Ss have heard of or tried.

Distribute the worksheets. Ask Ss to read the conversation and complete the gaps in Ex 1 using the phrases in the box. Remind Ss that they need to look at the preceding verb, not the verb in the phrase. Monitor and help as required. Put Ss in pairs to compare their answers, then check as a class. For Ex 2, give Ss a few minutes to discuss the cures in small groups. Elicit a few responses.

Answer key:

1
1 getting **2** you to tell **3** people giving me **4** me to frighten
5 that you will get **6** you that **7** you to **8** drinking
9 myself sitting **10** me to feel **11** the hiccups stop
12 that I will give

Grammar 2 — Verb patterns

Materials: One set of cards per group of Ss

Instructions:

Put Ss in groups of three or four and give each group a set of domino cards, which they should shuffle and place face down on the table. Tell Ss to take four cards each to start. One student puts a domino card on the table. The next student tries to place a matching card at either end. If Ss are unable to place a card, they take a new one from the pile (or miss a go if there are no cards left). When a student matches the two halves of a domino card, they read the full sentence aloud. The other Ss must say if they think it is correct or not. Ask Ss to continue to do this in turns until the first student to place his/her final domino on the table wins.

Alternatively, ask Ss to work collaboratively to match the sentences on the dominoes. This could be done before or instead of the game above.

Answer key:
The dominoes are:
I'm surprised to see you here. / I didn't expect … / … anyone to be in the office on a Sunday.
I told my boss that I don't mind … / … working late as long as I know in advance.
My brother became a vet, but we always imagined … / … he would be on the stage!
My sister has just got engaged and it makes … / … me feel happy to see her so in love.
I went to the supermarket but I'm afraid I didn't remember … / … to get those things you wanted. Sorry!
I'll be at work early tomorrow, so I promise … / … to do it first thing in the morning.
We're short of money at the moment so I've realised … / … that we can't afford to go abroad this year.
My apologies for being late. I assure … / … you that it won't happen again.
The sales staff persuaded … / … me that I needed to buy the shoes.
My English teacher recommended … / … that I keep a notebook of new phrases.
I'm really scared of flying, so I can't stand … / … going anywhere by plane.
I didn't want to say anything, but could I ask … / … you to turn your music down please?
When I bought the tickets, they guaranteed … / … that I would enjoy the concert or they'd give me a refund.
My grandfather repeats himself, but I don't mind … / … him doing that. He's eighty-nine!
This puzzle is really tough. Could you help … / … me figure it out?
He needed to learn English for his new job, so he told … / … us he'd never give up, no matter how hard he found it.
I haven't seen you for ages and I really miss … / … you coming around for a chat.
We wanted a pay rise but we couldn't persuade … / … our boss to change his mind.
Could you open the curtains please? I want to let … / … more light come into this room.
It was a huge task, and even though I wanted … / … to do it all by myself, it was much too difficult.

Vocabulary — Knowledge

Materials: One worksheet per pair of Ss, cut into three sections

Instructions:

Tell Ss that they're going to discuss a list of theories to practise using the vocabulary related to the lesson. Give each student one copy of the *Useful language* card (there are two copies on the worksheet to save on photocopying). Ask Ss to write one letter in each space to complete the phrases individually. Explain that the phrases can be combined in different ways to form different sentences. Check answers as a class.

Put Ss in pairs and give them the list of theories. Ask Ss to discuss each theory and write their opinion about it in the *Our conclusion* column. Encourage Ss to use the phrases in the *Useful language* box and their own ideas. Conduct whole class feedback.

As an optional follow-up, allocate each student, or pair, one of the theories to research briefly for homework and report back to the class (or post to a class online forum) what they found out, using the words from the lesson as appropriate.

Answer key:
1 assume **2** prove **3** know **4** suspect **5** theory
6 conclude **7** observed **8** research **9** fake
10 misunderstanding

Suggested conclusions:
1 **A lot of people assume** that's true, but we think we can conclude it's **not true**.
2 We **haven't ever** observed that ourselves, but how would you **prove** it isn't true?
3 **That's definitely true**.
4 We'd need to do **more research** on that **theory**.
5 We **suspect** that's **a misunderstanding**.
6 We **suspect** that's **true**, but we'd need to do **more research**.
7 We **know** that's **true**.
8 A lot of people **assume** that's **true** and we hope they're right.
9 We're pretty sure that's **not true**, but how would you **prove** it?
10 We haven't ever observed anyone do it, but we **suspect** it's **only a theory**.

9C

Language focus 1 Multi-word verbs

Materials: One worksheet per student

Instructions:
Ask the class: *How would you act if you came across a celebrity? Is there anything you shouldn't do?* Elicit some ideas. Distribute the worksheets and focus Ss on the first item as an example. Read alternatives **a** and **b** within the sentence and elicit which is the best fit and why (**a** because *come across* is inseparable). Tell Ss to complete the rules individually. Then put Ss in pairs to compare their answers before checking as a class.

Answer key:
1 **a** (*come across* is inseparable)
2 **b** (*turn out*, with this meaning, is inseparable)
3 **b** (*think through* is separable and the pronoun *it* must come before the particle)
4 **a** (no pronoun is necessary here because the object is the phrase *whether it's appropriate to approach them*.)
5 **a** (*get on with* is a phrasal verb with two particles and the object comes after the second particle)
6 both (*let down* is separable so both answers are possible. However, b is more common.)
7 **a** (*stick out* is separable and the pronoun *it* must come before the particle)
8 **a** (*come across* is inseparable)
9 **b** (*come up with*, meaning *think of*, is a phrasal verb with two particles and the object comes after the second particle)
10 **a** (*get over*, with this meaning, is inseparable)

Language focus 2 Multi-word verbs

Materials: One worksheet per group of Ss, cut into cards

Instructions:
Put Ss in pairs or groups of three. Give each group a set of cards. Tell Ss to divide the cards among themselves and to re-order the words on each of their cards to complete the sentence. Ss then take turns to read their advice to the group for the others to check. Ask Ss to check their answers with you if they're not sure.
Then explain that each piece of advice contradicts another piece. Ask Ss to work together to match each piece of advice with the one that contradicts it. When Ss have finished, ask them to discuss which is the better piece of advice from each pair. Elicit some ideas.

Answer key:
1 think things through
2 figure out a way
3 get on with it
4 stand out from the crowd
5 make something up
6 sticking it out
7 come across as too outrageous
8 let someone down
9 get over it
10 Things turn out better
11 come up with a good solution
12 make out that you know

Conflicting advice:
1 and 3   2 and 11   4 and 7   5 and 8   6 and 9   10 and 12

Vocabulary Common multi-word verbs

Materials: One top half of the worksheet per pair, one or two sets of phrases per class, tape or adhesive

Instructions:
This activity is a running dictation. In preparation, stick the phrases on a wall in the classroom. Ss should not be able to read the phrases from where they are sitting. Put Ss in pairs and explain that they will have five minutes to read an interview and predict the missing phrases, which all include multi-word verbs from the lesson. Tell them not to write them down at this stage. After the five minutes are up, allow one student from each pair to run up and read a phrase, then run back and dictate it to their partner who writes it down in the correct place. They continue to do this until you call *change*, and the writer and runner must swap roles. The first pair to finish (with the correct answers) are the winners. Check answers as a class.

Alternatively, if running is not suitable for your Ss or classroom, give each pair a copy of the phrase sheet and ask Ss to complete the text as a regular dictation.

Answer key:
1 come across   2 stand out   3 come up with
4 lets their fans down   5 figure out a   6 stick it out
7 get over their bad behaviour   8 make that kind of thing up
9 made out   10 turns out   11 think our actions through
12 get on with it

10A

Grammar 1 Future perfect and future continuous

Materials: One worksheet per student

Instructions:
Distribute the worksheets. Tell Ss that in this exercise they will practise when to use the future perfect and future continuous in conversations. For Ex 1, read the sentences 1A and 1B in conversation 1 aloud and elicit which is the correct sentence (*1A*). Ask Ss to read the remaining sentences and circle the correct ones. For Ex 2, put Ss in pairs to compare their answers before checking as a class. Ask Ss to practise reading the conversations aloud in pairs.

Answer key:
1
1 1A 2B 3B 4A
2 1B 2B 3A 4A
3 1B 2B 3A 4A

Grammar 2 Future perfect and future continuous

Materials: One worksheet per student

Instructions:
For Ex 1, ask Ss to read the statements 1–8 and circle a number from 1 (unlikely) to 5 (very likely) according to how likely they think the things listed are to happen in twenty years' time.

For Ex 2, put Ss in small groups to discuss their responses. They should use adverbs, or phrases, to describe their level of certainty where possible, e.g. *I'm fairly certain fewer people will be buying a place of their own*. They may also need to change *will* and *won't* to express some ideas, e.g. *Smartphones almost certainly won't have become a thing of the past*. Useful phrases and adverbs are listed in the table on the sheet to act as a prompt. Encourage Ss to tick the phrases as they use them to try to avoid repetition. Tell groups to try to decide which of the statements they think are the most and least likely. Get feedback from the class.

Then for Ex 3, tell Ss to discuss and write some of their own ideas of what will have changed in the future. Elicit a few ideas.

Vocabulary   Personal fulfilment

Materials: One worksheet per group of Ss, cut into cards

Instructions:

Put Ss in groups of three or four and give each group a set of cut-up cards. Tell Ss to start by matching the cards to form the collocations from the Students' Book lesson. Then ask Ss to use the cards to play pelmanism by spreading them out on the desk face down and taking turns to turn over two cards. If the cards match and make a collocation, the student must make a sentence with them. If they correctly match the cards and make a sentence, they can keep them. Otherwise, the student places them back down on the table in the same place he/she took them from. The winner is the student with the most cards after all the collocations have been matched.

> **Answer key:**
> The cards are: purpose in life; artistic ability; true vocation; unique talent; soul mate; great passion; place of my own; a sense of belonging; like-minded friend; a place I can call home; sense of adventure; core principles.

10B

Grammar 1   Articles

Materials: One worksheet per student

Instructions:

Distribute the worksheets. Explain that Ss may need to add, change or remove articles and that in some instances the articles are correct. Tell Ss to complete Ex 1 individually. Then put Ss in pairs to compare their answers before checking as a class. For Ex 2, give Ss time to write their own sentences.

For Ex 3, put Ss in pairs to compare their sentences and check that their partner's articles are correct (checking with you if necessary). Ask each student to share one of their sentences with the class as group feedback. For Ex 4, ask Ss to discuss the question. Elicit a few ideas.

> **Answer key:**
> 1
> **Kemala**
> 1 I grew up in Jakarta, **the** capital of Indonesia.
> 2 I saw ~~the~~ snow for **the** first time this year.
> 3 I have played ~~the~~ basketball since I was nine.
> 4 I can't imagine ~~the~~ life without **a** mobile phone.
> 5 I recently started a small business. I've been spending a lot of time building ~~a~~ **the** business lately.
> **Zoltan**
> 1 Even though I'm **an** architect, my favourite subject at ~~the~~ school was ~~the~~ music.
> 2 I went to **the** USA last year and stayed with ~~the~~ **a** host family near ~~the~~ Lake Tahoe.
> 3 I think ~~the~~ young people should learn to play ~~the~~ **an** instrument.
> 4 On Saturdays I play in a band at a restaurant.
> 5 The most important things in my life are family, work and **the** band.

Grammar 2   Articles

Materials: One copy of the worksheet per student

Instructions:

Distribute the worksheets. Ask Ss to choose the correct alternatives to complete the quiz questions then answer them by putting ticks and crosses in the right-hand column. For Ex 2, put Ss in small groups to compare their answers (both to the exercise and the quiz) and to discuss whether any answers were a surprise. Check as a class.

> **Answer key:**
> 1
> 1 the   2 the   3 a   4 a   5 the   6 no article   7 the   8 a
> 9 no article   10 no article   11 a   12 the   13 an
> 14 no article   15 no article   16 an   17 no article   18 a   19 a
> 20 a   21 the   22 the   23 a   24 the

Vocabulary   Fame

Materials: One worksheet per student

Instructions:

Read the beginning of the story to Ss, then tell them that they are going to decide what happens next. Put Ss in pairs. Give each student a worksheet so they can both make notes later in the activity.

Ask Ss to read the possible endings in Ex 2 and decide on one (or their own). Then, in Ex 3, ask Ss to make up a story about what happens in the middle of the story using the words in the box. Suggest to Ss that they may like to work out the order in which the words will be included in the story first and then add some extra details. They shouldn't write out the full story, but they do need to have enough notes to retell it using the target words. Encourage Ss to practise retelling the story.

Finally, in Ex 4, put Ss in new pairs or groups to share their stories and compare them. As an optional follow-up, Ss could write up the full story for homework.

Alternatively, make the writing stage a competition to see which pair can use the most target words in their story.

10C

Language focus 1   Compound adjectives

Materials: One worksheet per student

Instructions:

Distribute the worksheets. Look at the first item with the class as an example. Elicit which word goes in the gap and how it needs to be changed. Tell Ss to complete the blog posts, then put Ss in pairs to compare their answers before checking as a class.

> **Answer key:**
> 1
> 1 fashioned   2 aged   3 art   4 tech   5 term   6 distance
> 7 kilometre   8 minded   9 willed   10 old   11 profile
> 12 centred   13 social   14 known   15 minded

Language focus 2 Compound adjectives

Materials: One worksheet per group of Ss, cut into cards

Instructions:

Put Ss in groups of four or five. Give each group a set of cards. Tell Ss to divide the adjectives into sets according to whether they would normally describe a person, a thing or both. To do this, Ss divide the cards among themselves, then take turns to read a card aloud and add it to the appropriate set, with assistance from the group if necessary. If the word describes a thing, they should think of a noun it could describe, e.g. *a brightly-lit room*. Once all the cards have been divided into groups, check answers as a class.

Next, tell Ss to shuffle the cards and put them in a pile face down. They take turns to pick a card and try to describe it to the group without saying the second word in the item, e.g. *This adjective means something that's very modern, like a computer or a device, it's high-…* (*tech*). / *The old building was very run-…* (*down*). The student who completes the compound adjective correctly first gets to keep the card. As soon as a word is guessed, the next student can take a word.

Alternatively, to assist Ss with finding nouns to collocate with the adjectives, write some of the nouns from the answer box on the board. Otherwise, tell Ss to look up words in a suitable dictionary, e.g. the Longman Dictionary of Contemporary English https://www.ldoceonline.com/.

Answer key:

Suggested answers:

person:
absent-minded, hard-working, like-minded, middle-aged, self-confident, strong-willed, well-behaved, well-educated, well-off

thing:
brightly-lit (room)
broken-down (car)
densely-populated (area / city)
high-tech (device)
internet-connected (classroom / accommodation)
short-term (arrangement / plan / forecast)
state-of-the-art (solution / hospital / technology)
ten-page (document / brochure)

both:
long-term (partnerer / relationship / contract)
narrow-minded (person / attitude / view)
old-fashioned (person / clothing / attitude)
part-time (worker / job)
run-down (area / person – note that if a person feels run-down, it means they are tired or unwell – it cannot go before a noun)
twenty-five-year-old (person / house)
well-known (author / family / film / saying)

Vocabulary Persuasion and enforcement

Materials: One worksheet per group of three Ss, cut into cards

Instructions:

Put Ss in groups of three. Start by reading the first two sentences of the story from the instruction card aloud. Ask Ss to discuss some possible solutions to the problem. Elicit some ideas. Then give each group a set of cards including the instruction card. Give Ss time to complete Ex 1, to add words to the sentences and Ex 2, to put the sentences in order. Then check answers as a class.

As a follow-up, ask Ss to discuss the following question: *Do you agree that it's hard to enforce rules when you're dealing with friends? Why/ Why not?*

Answer key:

1

1 educate **2** installed **3** put up **4** discourage **5** charged **6** introduce **7** fined **8** enforce

2

The correct order is:

I share a house with three friends. One is quite absent-minded and keeps leaving the stove on, which is obviously very dangerous. Friends turn out to be the most difficult people to educate.

The first time it happened, we heard beeping and rescued the pan. It's lucky that the landlord had installed smoke alarms.

We all thought it was a one-time thing, but just in case, I put up a sign reminding us all to turn off the stove.

However, the sign wasn't enough to discourage my friend because only a few days later, the stove was accidentally left on again.

This time, a pan of rice had boiled dry and the wall (and my excellent sign!) was damaged. The landlord charged us for repainting the wall.

We decided it was time to introduce a tougher punishment. From now on, we've all agreed that anyone who leaves the stove on will be fined the cost of a take-out pizza for everyone.

Of course, it's really hard to enforce any rule when you're dealing with friends!

NOTES

NOTES

NOTES

NOTES

NOTES

NOTES

NOTES

NOTES

Pearson Education Limited
KAO TWO
KAO Park
Hockham Way
Harlow, Essex
CM17 9SR
England
and Associated Companies throughout the world.

english.com/roadmap

© Pearson Education Limited 2020

All rights reserved; no part of this publication may be reproduced, stored in a retrieval system, or transmitted in any form or by any means, electronic, mechanical, photocopying, recording, or otherwise without the prior written permission of the Publishers.

Photocopying The Publisher grants permission for the photocopying of those pages marked 'photocopiable' according to the following conditions. Individual purchasers may make copies for their own use or for use by the classes they each. Institutional purchasers may make copies for use by their staff and students, but this permission does not extend to additional institutions or branches. Under no circumstances may any part of this book be photocopied for resale.

First published 2020

Eighth impression 2022

ISBN: 978-1-292-22842-6

Set in Soho Gothic Pro

Printed and bound in Great Britain

Illustration acknowledgements
Illustrations by Morokoth Fournier des Corats

Photo acknowledgements
The publisher would like to thank the following for their kind permission to reproduce their photographs:

123RF.com: Dmitrii Shironosov 254, Pierangelo Roberto 238, Soloway 254;
Alamy Stock Photo: Ellen Isaacs 215, Tithi Luadthong 238; **Getty Images:** Chang, Min-Chieh 239, Eugenesergeev 238, JW LTD 227, Kali9 188, Leon Neal / Staff 194, Lupashchenkoiryna 238, Lupashchenkoiryna / Kathy Collins 238, RamonBerk 194, Searsie 214, Stuart Miller 227, Vicki Jauron, Babylon and Beyond Photography 238, Yaroslav Kushta 238; **Pearson Education Ltd:** Coleman Yuen 238;
Shutterstock.com: alaver 238, Clivewa 238, Guteksk7 238, Marketlan 170, Raysthink 194, Syda Productions 254, Xtuv Photography 238.

Every effort has been made to trace the copyright holders and we apologise in advance for any unintentional omissions. We would be pleased to insert the appropriate acknowledgement in any subsequent edition of this publication.